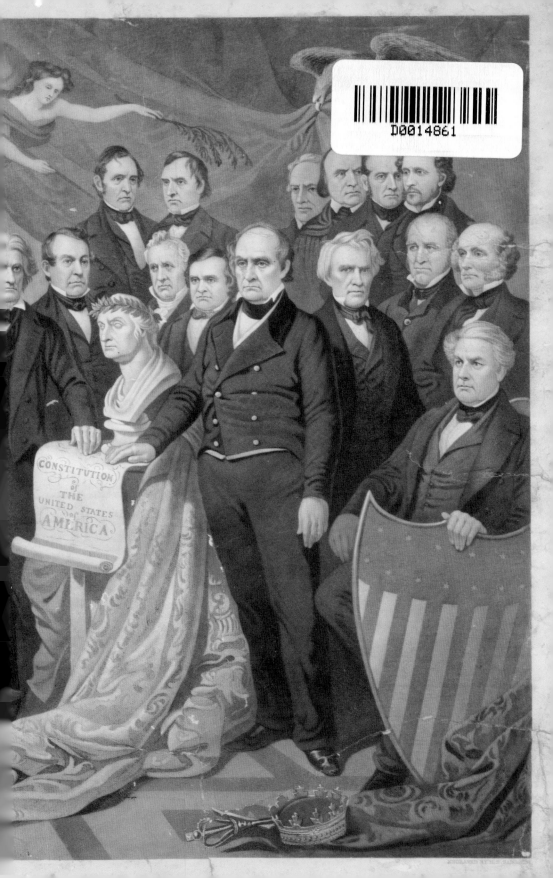

CONSTITUTION
OF
THE
UNITED STATES
of
AMERICA

ALSO BY SIDNEY BLUMENTHAL

A Self-Made Man: The Political Life of Abraham Lincoln, 1809–1849

The Strange Death of Republican America

How Bush Rules

The Clinton Wars

This Town (play)

Pledging Allegiance: The Last Campaign of the Cold War

The Reagan Legacy (Editor with Thomas Byrne Edsall)

Our Long National Daydream: A Pageant of the Reagan Years

*The Rise of the Counter-Establishment: From Conservative Ideology
to Political Power*

The Permanent Campaign

WRESTLING WITH HIS ANGEL

The
Political Life
of
Abraham Lincoln,
Volume II, 1849–1856

SIDNEY BLUMENTHAL

Simon & Schuster
New York   London   Toronto   Sydney   New Delhi

Simon & Schuster
1230 Avenue of the Americas
New York, NY 10020

First Simon & Schuster hardcover edition May 2017

SIMON & SCHUSTER and colophon are registered trademarks of Simon & Schuster, Inc.

For information about special discounts for bulk purchases, please contact Simon & Schuster Special Sales at 1-866-506-1949 or business@simonandschuster.com.

The Simon & Schuster Speakers Bureau can bring authors to your live event. For more information or to book an event contact the Simon & Schuster Speakers Bureau at 1-866-248-3049 or visit our website at www.simonspeakers.com.

Interior design by Joy O'Meara

Manufactured in the United States of America

10   9   8   7   6   5   4   3   2   1

Library of Congress Cataloging-in-Publication Data

Names: Blumenthal, Sidney, 1948–
Title: Wrestling with his angel : the political life of Abraham Lincoln, 1849–1856 / Sidney Blumenthal.
Description: First Simon & Schuster hardcover edition. | New York : Simon & Schuster, 2017. | Includes bibliographical references and index.
Identifiers: ISBN 9781501153785 (hardback) | ISBN 9781501153792 (trade paper) | ISBN 9781501153808 (ebook)
Subjects: LCSH: Lincoln, Abraham, 1809–1865—Political career before 1861. | Lincoln, Abraham, 1809–1865—Political and social views. | Lincoln, Abraham, 1809–1865—Childhood and youth. | Lincoln, Abraham, 1809–1865—Marriage. | Politicians—Illinois—Biography. | Lawyers—Illinois—Springfield—Biography. | Illinois—Politics and government—To 1865. | United States—Politics and government—1815–1861. | Presidents—United States—Biography. | BISAC: BIOGRAPHY & AUTOBIOGRAPHY / Presidents & Heads of State. | HISTORY / United States / Civil War Period (1850–1877). | BIOGRAPHY & AUTOBIOGRAPHY / Historical.
Classification: LCC E457.35 .B55 2016 | DDC 973.7092—dc23 LC record available at http://lccn.loc.gov/2015027339

ISBN 978-1-5011-5378-5
ISBN 978-1-5011-5380-8 (ebook)

For Paul and Alison

CONTENTS

	Timeline of Major Events	*xi*
	Cast of Major Characters	*xv*
PROLOGUE	Wrestling with His Angel	*1*
ONE	White Negroes	*9*
TWO	The Civil War of Old Rough and Ready	*41*
THREE	The Art of the Deal	*83*
FOUR	The Consequences of the Peace	*105*
FIVE	What Is to Be Done?	*129*
SIX	A Hero's Welcome	*151*
SEVEN	The Making of the Dark Horse	*167*
EIGHT	The Victory March of Old Fuss and Feathers	*187*
NINE	The Death of Henry Clay	*199*
TEN	The Waterloo of the Whigs	*211*
ELEVEN	The Acting President of the United States	*225*
TWELVE	I, Thomas Hart Benton	*253*
THIRTEEN	The Triumph of the F Street Mess	*263*
FOURTEEN	A Self-Evident Lie	*293*
FIFTEEN	Citizen Know Nothing	*321*
SIXTEEN	The Conquest of Kansas	*333*
SEVENTEEN	Imperialism, the Highest Stage of Slavery	*347*
EIGHTEEN	Armed Liberty	*355*
NINETEEN	The Failure of Free Society	*367*
TWENTY	The Blood of the Revolution	*383*
TWENTY-ONE	Senator Lincoln	*431*

TWENTY-TWO   The Republican   443
TWENTY-THREE   Destiny and Power   473

               Acknowledgments   481
               Notes   485
               Bibliography   535
               Illustration Credits   549
               Index   551

TIMELINE OF MAJOR EVENTS

March 31, 1849:   Lincoln returns to Springfield from Washington to practice law

July 16, 1849:   Robert S. Todd dies

October 28–November 7, 1849:   Lincoln in Lexington, Kentucky, to serve as co-counsel in the *Todd Heirs v. Wickliffe* case

February 1, 1850:   Edward Baker Lincoln dies

March 31, 1850:   John C. Calhoun dies

July 9, 1850:   President Zachary Taylor dies

September 7, 1850:   The Compromise of 1850 passes the Congress

September 20, 1850: The Illinois Central Railroad Tax Act passes the Congress

December 21, 1850:   William Wallace Lincoln born

January 17, 1851:   Thomas Lincoln dies

April 13, 1851:   Captured fugitive slave Thomas Sims marched in chains through the streets of Boston to a federal warship to be returned to his master in Georgia

June 1, 1851:   Harriet Beecher Stowe's *Uncle Tom's Cabin* begins serialized publication in the abolitionist Washington, D.C., newspaper, the *National Era*

October 1, 1851:   Herman Melville's *Moby-Dick, or The Whale* published

December 5, 1851:   Louis Kossuth, Hungarian revolutionary, arrives in New York City

January 8, 1852:   Lincoln writes a resolution at a Springfield meeting expressing sympathy for liberal revolutions in Europe

January 1852:   The *Democratic Review*, supporting the presidential candidacy of Stephen A. Douglas and under the editorship of his adviser George Nicholas Sanders, insults his rivals

June 5, 1852:   Franklin Pierce nominated as the Democratic Party presidential candidate

June 20, 1852:   Winfield Scott nominated as the Whig Party presidential candidate

June 29, 1852:   Henry Clay dies

July 6, 1852:   Lincoln delivers his eulogy for Henry Clay

August 11, 1852:   John P. Hale nominated as the Free Soil Party, or Free Democratic Party, presidential candidate

August 14 and 26:   Lincoln speaks in Springfield on behalf of Winfield Scott's campaign

October 24, 1852:   Daniel Webster dies

November 2, 1852:   Franklin Pierce elected president

March 4, 1853:   Franklin Pierce inaugurated as president

March 5, 1853:   President Pierce offers Jefferson Davis the cabinet position of secretary of war

April 4, 1853:   Thomas "Tad" Lincoln born

April 18, 1853:   Vice President William R. King dies; Senate president pro tempore David Rice Atchison next in line of succession to the presidency

December 30, 1853:   Gadsden Treaty negotiated with Mexico

1854:   Publication of *Sociology for the South, or The Failure of Free Society*, by George Fitzhugh

January 22, 1854:   Stephen A. Douglas and members of the F Street Mess meet at the White House with President Pierce and Jefferson Davis to negotiate the terms of the Kansas-Nebraska Act

January 24, 1854:   "The Appeal of the Independent Democrats in Congress to the People of the United States," signed by senators Salmon P. Chase and Charles Sumner, to protest the Kansas-Nebraska Act, published

February 28, 1854:   First meeting of a group calling itself the "Republican Party," Ripon, Wisconsin

April 1, 1854:   Lincoln writes a private refutation of Fitzhugh's *Sociology for the South*

April 19–26, 1854:   Lincoln appears as co-counsel in the *McCormick v. Manny* case, but chief counsel Edwin Stanton rejects his participation

May 15, 1854:   Dred Scott, a slave in Missouri, in his suit for his freedom, *Scott v. Sanford*, is denied by the U.S. Circuit Court and appeals to the U.S. Supreme Court

May 30, 1854:   Kansas-Nebraska Act passes the Congress

June 2, 1854:   Under martial law in Boston, captured fugitive slave Anthony Burns is transported back to his master in Virginia

July 10, 1854:   Cassius Clay speaks in Springfield against the threat of slavery in Kansas with Lincoln in attendance

August 1, 1854:   Twenty-four settlers under the auspices of the New England

Emigrant Aid Society establish the free state town of Lawrence in Kansas

October 4, 1854: Lincoln speaks against the Kansas-Nebraska Act for more than three hours at the Illinois House of Representatives with Douglas in the audience; after his speech a group of abolitionists invite him to join their meeting of the "Republican Party," but he declines

October 16, 1854: Lincoln delivers speech at Peoria against the Kansas-Nebraska Act

November 7, 1854: Lincoln elected to the Illinois House of Representatives

November 10, 1854: Lincoln resigns his seat in the legislature to run for the U.S. Senate

November 29, 1854: Invasion of more than 1,700 pro-slavery "Border Ruffians" from Missouri steal the election of the Kansas territorial delegate to the Congress through violence and intimidation

February 8, 1855: Lincoln, realizing that he lacks the votes to be elected to the Senate and that his continuing candidacy would elect the pro-Douglas Democrat, throws his support to anti-Nebraska Democrat Lyman Trumbull, who wins

March 30, 1855: "Border Ruffians" led by Senator David Atchison steal the election of the territorial legislature

June 16, 1855: William Walker invades Nicaragua to proclaim it a "slave republic"

August 5, 1855: Andrew Reeder, the first territorial governor of Kansas, removed by President Pierce for his objections to fraudulent elections

August 15, 1855: Lincoln writes in a letter to George Robertson, the co-counsel in the *Todd Heirs* case: "Our political problem now is 'Can we, as a nation, continue together *permanently—forever—* half slave, and half free?' "

August 24, 1855: Lincoln writes in a letter to Joshua Speed: "You enquire where I now stand. That is a disputed point. I think I am a Whig; but others say there are no Whigs, and that I am an abolitionist."

October 7, 1855: John Brown and his sons arrive in Kansas

October 23, 1855: Free state settlers meet at Topeka to adopt a constitution banning slavery in the territory, elect a governor, and designate Andrew Reeder its congressional delegate

February 22, 1856:   The Know Nothing Party, or American Party, nominates former president Millard Fillmore as its presidential candidate

February 22, 1856:   First national convention of the Republican Party takes place at Pittsburgh

February 22, 1856:   Lincoln writes the platform at a meeting of antislavery editors at Decatur as the founding document of the Illinois Republican Party and calls for its first convention

CAST OF MAJOR CHARACTERS

FAMILY

Thomas Lincoln, father, died 1851

Mary Todd Lincoln, wife

Robert Todd Lincoln, son, born 1843

Edward Baker "Eddie" Lincoln, son, born 1846, died 1850

William Wallace "Willie" Lincoln, born 1850

Thomas "Tad" Lincoln, born 1853

Robert Smith Todd, father-in-law, died 1849

Ninian W. Edwards, brother-in-law

KENTUCKY

Robert Jefferson Breckinridge, Whig politician, Mary Todd's distant cousin, Presbyterian minister

Cassius Marcellus Clay, antislavery crusader, Henry Clay's cousin

George Robertson, Lincoln's co-counsel for the Todd family in *Todd Heirs* case, former congressman, state official, and judge

Alfred Francis Russell, slave, Polly Wickliffe's grandson, Mary Todd's cousin, future president of Liberia

Joshua Speed, Lincoln's former Springfield roommate, plantation owner

James Speed, brother of Joshua Speed, antislavery state senator, Lincoln's future attorney general

Robert Wickliffe, the "Old Duke," defendant in *Todd Heirs* case, leader of pro-slavery forces

Robert Wickcliffe, Jr., the "Young Duke," pro-slavery politician

Mary "Polly" Owen Todd Russell Wickliffe, Robert S. Todd's cousin, wife of the "Old Duke"

LINCOLN'S CIRCLE IN ILLINOIS

William H. Bailhache, editor, *Illinois Daily Journal*

Edward D. Baker, congressman

Edward L. Baker, editor, *Illinois Daily Journal*

John W. Bunn, Springfield merchant, funder of Lincoln's campaigns

David Davis, Circuit Court judge, Whig politico

Jesse W. Fell, Bloomington lawyer and businessman, editor, *Bloomington Panta-graph,* Whig politico, operator of Underground Railroad station

Joseph Gillespie, Whig state senator

Anson Henry, Whig politician, Lincoln's doctor

William Henry Herndon, Lincoln's law partner

Ward Hill Lamon, Whig lawyer

Stephen T. Logan, Lincoln's former law partner, Whig politician

Richard Oglesby, Whig lawyer

John Todd Stuart, Lincoln's former law partner, Whig politician

Leonard Swett, Whig lawyer

Henry Clay Whitney, Whig lawyer

Richard Yates, Whig congressman

ILLINOIS POLITICS

William Bissell, Anti-Nebraska Democratic congressman, later governor

Sidney Breese, Democratic U.S. senator, railroad entrepreneur

John Calhoun, Democratic politician, Lincoln's former supervisor as a surveyor

Ichabod Codding, abolitionist, organizer of the Republican Party

Zebina Eastman, abolitionist, editor, *Free West*

Thomas Harris, Democratic congressman

Norman B. Judd, state senator, anti-Nebraska Democrat

Charles Henry Lanphier, editor, *Illinois State Register,* pro-Douglas newspaper

Owen Lovejoy, abolitionist, brother of martyred antislavery editor Elijah Lovejoy, organizer of the Republican Party

Joel Matteson, Democratic governor

John M. Palmer, state senator, anti-Nebraska Democrat

Charles H. Ray, editor, *Chicago Tribune*

William A. Richardson, Democratic congressman from Illinois, Douglas's ally

Paul Selby, editor, *Morgan Journal,* organizer of the Republican Party

George Schneider, editor, *Illinois Staats-Zeitung,* organizer of the Republican Party

James Sheahan, editor, *Chicago Times,* pro-Douglas newspaper

Lyman Trumbull, judge, Illinois Supreme Court, U.S. senator

Elihu B. Washburne, anti-Nebraska congressman

John Wentworth, Chicago political boss, Free Soil congressman, later Chicago mayor

THE SENATE

David Rice Atchison, Senator from Missouri, president pro tempore, F Street Mess

Robert W. Barnwell, senator from South Carolina

Thomas Hart Benton, senator from Missouri

Jesse Bright, senator from Indiana

Andrew Pickens Butler, senator from South Carolina, F Street Mess

John C. Calhoun, senator from South Carolina

Lewis Cass, senator from Michigan

Salmon P. Chase, senator from Ohio

Henry Clay, senator from Kentucky

Daniel Dickinson, senator from New York

Archibald Dixon, senator from Kentucky

Stephen A. Douglas, senator from Illinois

Hamilton Fish, senator from New York

Henry S. Foote, senator from Mississippi

John P. Hale, senator from New Hampshire

Robert M. T. Hunter, senator from Virginia, F Street Mess

James M. Mason, senator from Virginia, F Street Mess

John Pettit, senator from Indiana

Robert Barnwell Rhett, senator from South Carolina, editor, *Charleston Mercury*

William Henry Seward, senator from New York

James Shields, senator from Illinois

Charles Sumner, senator from Massachusetts

Benjamin Wade, senator from Ohio

Daniel Webster, senator from Massachusetts, President Fillmore's secretary of state

Henry Wilson, senator from Massachusetts

THE HOUSE OF REPRESENTATIVES

John C. Breckinridge, congressman from Kentucky

Joshua Giddings, congressman from Ohio, Lincoln's former boardinghouse mate

Horace Mann, congressman from Massachusetts

Philip Phillips, congressman from Alabama, F Street Mess

Alexander Stephens, congressman from Georgia

Robert Toombs, congressman from Georgia

NEW YORK POLITICS

John Van Buren, son of former President Martin Van Buren, Free Soil Party leader

John A. Dix, former U.S. senator, Free Soil Party leader

Horace Greeley, editor, *New York Tribune*

Henry J. Raymond, editor, *New York Times*, lieutenant governor

Horatio Seymour, Democratic governor

James Watson Webb, editor, *New York Courier and Inquirer*

Thurlow Weed, editor, *Albany Evening Journal*, Whig Party leader

MASSACHUSETTS POLITICS

Charles Francis Adams, son of President John Quincy Adams, Conscience Whig

Rufus Choate, former senator and congressman, political adviser to Daniel Webster

George Ticknor Curtis, Daniel Webster's lawyer and biographer, enforcer of the Fugitive Slave Act

Abbott Lawrence, Massachusetts Whig leader, minister to Britain

Amos Adams Lawrence, industrialist, funder of the New England Emigrant Aid Society

John G. Palfrey, Conscience Whig, Free Soil congressman

Robert Rantoul, prominent attorney, Daniel Webster's business partner, antislavery advocate, appointed U.S. senator

Lemuel Shaw, Chief Justice of the Massachusetts Supreme Judicial Court, father-in-law of Herman Melville

Eli Thayer, founder, the New England Emigrant Aid Society

NATIONAL POLITICS

Francis Preston Blair, member of President Andrew Jackson's Kitchen Cabinet, politico

John Minor Botts, former Whig congressman from Virginia, convention king-maker

Howell Cobb, governor of Georgia, former speaker of the house, congressman

William W. Corcoran, leading banker in Washington, D.C.

George W. Crawford, President Taylor's secretary of war

John J. Crittenden, President Fillmore's attorney general, U.S. senator

George Fitzhugh, pro-slavery ideologue, author of Sociology for the South, or *The Failure of Free Society*

John W. Forney, clerk of the House of Representatives, Democratic operative, editor, *Washington Union*

Louis Kossuth, Hungarian revolutionary leader

Thomas Parker, sculptor of statue atop the Capitol

John A. Quitman, Governor of Mississippi, leader of the States Rights Party

Winfield Scott, former general, Whig presidential candidate in 1852

George Nicholas Sanders, Douglas's political adviser, editor, *Democratic Review*

Beverley Tucker, editor, *Washington Sentinel*

William Walker, pro-slavery soldier of fortune, or "filibuster"

Levi Woodbury, justice of the Supreme Court, former governor and senator from New Hampshire

THE PIERCE ADMINISTRATION

James Buchanan, minister to England, former secretary of state, and senator from Pennsylvania

Virginia Clay, wife of Senator Clement Clay of Alabama, Jefferson Davis's mistress

Caleb Cushing, attorney general, former congressman from Massachusetts

Jefferson Davis, former senator from Mississippi, secretary of war

Varina Davis, wife of Jefferson Davis

James Gadsden, minister to Mexico

Nathaniel Hawthorne, novelist, friend of Franklin Pierce

William R. King, vice president, former senator from Alabama, intimate friend of James Buchanan

William L. Marcy, secretary of state, former governor and senator from New York

John Y. Mason, minister to France

Jane Appleton Pierce, wife of Franklin Pierce

Pierre Soule, minister to Spain, former senator from Louisiana

ABOLITIONISTS

Leonard W. Bacon, Connecticut Congregationalist minister, author of *Slavery Discussed*

Gamaliel Bailey, editor, *National Era*, publisher of *Uncle Tom's Cabin*

Henry Beecher, pastor, Brooklyn Plymouth Church

Ralph Waldo Emerson, Transcendentalist philosopher

William Lloyd Garrison, editor, *The Liberator*

Theodore Parker, Unitarian minister, head of Boston Vigilance Committee

Wendell Phillips, Boston crusader

Gerrit Smith, funder of radical abolitionists, congressman from New York

Harriet Beecher Stowe, author, *Uncle Tom's Cabin*

Henry David Thoreau, writer

KANSAS

John Brown, free state settler

William Phillips, free state settler, lawyer

Andrew Reeder, first territorial governor

Wilson Shannon, second territorial governor

Benjamin F. Stringfellow, pro-slavery crusader

John H. Stringfellow, pro-slavery crusader, editor, *Squatter Sovereign*

SLAVES

Anthony Burns, escaped from Virginia, captured and returned to his master, purchased by abolitionists

William and Ellen Craft, escaped from Georgia, authors, *Running One Thousand Miles for Freedom*

Frederick Douglass, born Frederick Bailey, escaped from Maryland, abolitionist leader, author, *Narrative of the Life of Frederick Douglass, an American Slave*

Frederick "Shadrach" Minkins, escaped from Virginia

Solomon Northup, escaped from Louisiana, author, *Twelve Years a Slave*

William Parker, escaped from Maryland, murdered his master in the "Christiana Riot," led to Canada by Frederick Douglass

Dred Scott, sued for his freedom in Missouri

Thomas Sims, escaped from Georgia, caught and returned to his master

Garland H. White, Congressman Robert Toombs's house servant, escaped and captured, later a Union Army soldier and chaplain

PRESIDENTS OF THE UNITED STATES

Zachary Taylor, 12th President

Millard Fillmore, 13th President

Franklin Pierce, 14th President

James Buchanan, 15th President

"And Jacob was left alone; and there wrestled a man with him until the breaking of the day."

—GENESIS 32:24

WRESTLING WITH HIS ANGEL

Abraham Lincoln, October 27, 1854, Chicago, Illinois

WRESTLING WITH HIS ANGEL

———— •◦•◦• ————

After Abraham Lincoln's one term in the Congress and his return to his spare law office in the Tinsley Building in Springfield, he stared into the distance for long periods of time. His partner, William Henry Herndon, recalled him breaking one of his melancholy silences with a cry of anguish. "He said gloomily, despairingly, sadly, 'How hard, oh! how hard it is to die and leave one's country no better than if one had never lived for it! The world is dead to hope, deaf to its own death-struggle, made known by a universal cry, What is to be done? Is anything to be done? Who can do anything? and how is it to be done? Did you ever think of these things?' "

A great revolution was required to bring Lincoln out of the wilderness. In order to understand his presence in the transforming events that would eventually carry him to the presidency and their profound influence upon him, the events must be chronicled. To do Lincoln justice, the history must be done justice. Lincoln would be diminished, simplified and flattened into a one-dimensional character without the complexity he had to work through. Unlike smaller politicians, he had a long historical view but applied it in fine detail as he went along. He took no shortcut, not that there ever could be one. To understand Lincoln more fully, the historian needs to attempt understanding his times nearly as closely as he did.

Premonitions of civil war, shattering deaths, fatal compromises, crushing defeats, corrupt bargains, brazen betrayals, and reckless ambition joined in a pandemonium of political bedlam. Presidents rose and fell. The party of

Lincoln, the Whig Party, flew apart. Passionate movements raged across the landscape. On the Western plains, a pristine battlefield was cleared, democracy trampled in the name of popular sovereignty, and ruffians and pilgrims armed for a struggle to the death over slavery.

The old party distinctions were erased, but there were no new and more compelling distinctions on the shelf. The nascent Republican Party, originally a sectarian radical outlying group, was not recognized as a credible alternative. An anti-immigrant movement, the Know Nothings, overnight attracted many more adherents. An older generation of political titans departed, the imposing triumvirate of Henry Clay, Daniel Webster, and John C. Calhoun, none having reached the presidency each desperately sought, all ultimately victims of their own curdled hopes. With their passing, the conflicts of political ages faded like yellowing newspapers. A new generation arose who knew not Jefferson and Jackson as living breathing souls; but as these new men climbed the ladder grappling for position and power, trying to reach the top, they stepped on broken rungs.

No one could have foreseen the surprising spiral of events that began when Zachary Taylor, the victorious general of the Mexican War ("Give them a little more grape, Captain Bragg!"), was elected president as the Whig Party candidate. He was a military hero above politics, a Southern slaveholder from Louisiana, with no decipherable record on any issue, standing on no platform whatsoever. "Old Rough and Ready" was assumed to be the ideal wooden figurehead for the ship of state, as intellectually opaque as an inanimate object, and articulate in making what were perceived to be only creaking noises. He was utterly lacking in experience with the cunning men of the Congress, who expected to run the show. It was a revelation that Taylor turned out to have clear and emphatic views, and a shock that he was strongly against the extension of slavery in the territory he had seized as the prize of the Mexican War. President Taylor was even more forceful than the abolitionist orators and pamphleteers, or the antislavery congressmen (like Lincoln) who had voted time and again in vain for the Wilmot Proviso, which would have prohibited slavery in the Mexican Cession. Taylor threatened a declaration of war against the Southern Rights movement if it treasonously opposed him, and stated he would personally draw his sword as commander-in-chief to lead the army to crush resistance. Then, as abruptly as Taylor stunned the South, he was struck down, probably by the cholera epidemic that was sweeping the country.

The civil war that seemed imminent terminated into an armistice. Taylor's successor, Millard Fillmore, a lifelong Whig Party placeman, elevated to the vice presidency from his rightful station as the New York State comptroller, had an unusual temperament melding bland complacency and overheated resentment. Determined to discard the well-defined intentions of Taylor, who had banished him as a nonentity from his councils, Fillmore conciliated the South in the Compromise of 1850, which he pronounced the "permanent settlement." Its political effect was to stifle slavery as a national controversy, deliver a mortal blow to the Whigs, splitting them into Northern and Southern wings, and empower the Democrats again as the natural governing party.

The landslide election of Franklin Pierce in 1852 appeared to settle the political question far to the horizon, but this was an illusion. Beneath the serene surface on which Pierce skated to the presidency was a roiling sea. A well-mannered Northern man of Southern sympathies, he was pliant under pressure. The grandiose ambitions and petty hatreds of others easily overwhelmed him as he turned to brandy for solace and Jefferson Davis for guidance.

The once and future rivals of Lincoln combined to blow to smithereens the cornerstone of civil and political peace. Senator Stephen A. Douglas, of Illinois, yet another self-made man, and Secretary of War Jefferson Davis, of Mississippi, highhanded heir to slaveholding wealth and the acting president of the United States, each had visions of an American imperium, prophecies that converged in their collaboration on the Kansas-Nebraska Act, which repealed the Missouri Compromise, forbidding slavery north of a fateful line of latitude. The parallel lives of these two men would define Lincoln's.

Pandora's box, as Secretary of State William L. Marcy, an old Jacksonian, warned, had been foolishly unlatched: "This Pandora's box—the Nebraska question." Though the rupture was sudden, it was not unforeseen. During the debate over the Compromise of 1850, Henry Clay had held aloft a piece of wood from Washington's coffin. "It was a warning voice coming from the grave to the Congress now in session," he said, "to beware, to pause, to reflect before they lend themselves to any purposes which shall destroy that Union which was cemented by his exertions and example." In another speech, Clay warned of "the yawning abyss below, which will inevitably lead to certain and irretrievable destruction." Daniel Webster spoke in horror of Southern "secession," which would produce "a crash of the universe." Jefferson Davis had described the country "blind" on "a volcanic mountain" that would explode if Southern rights of slavery were not respected. He forecast the creation of "a Southern Confederacy." On his deathbed, John C. Calhoun, the "cast-iron man" of the master class, Davis's mentor, predicted, "The Union is doomed to dissolution, there is no mistaking the signs.

Within days of the passage of the Kansas-Nebraska Act on May 30, 1854, Lincoln and his friends joined the battle. The lead editorial in the *Illinois State Journal* on June 6, written possibly by Herndon, as always with Lincoln's approval, express or tacit, appeared under a mocking headline—"The Question Settled!" "If there is the least evidence that the people of the free States are disposed to sit down quietly under the accumulated insults and wrongs sought to be inflicted upon them by this slavery-extension administration, and its servile supporters, we do not see evidence of it. On the contrary almost everywhere we see a general uprising and condemnation by the people of the wanton, un-called-for and grievous wrong sought to be inflicted upon this country by Pierce, Douglas & Co."

Douglas's newspaper, the *Illinois State Register,* returned the fire, editorializing that the *Illinois State Journal* "opens its batteries upon Senator Douglas' Nebraska bill, following in the wake of the New York Tribune, and renewing the 'agitation' of the 'nigger' question, by humorously ! charging Douglas with opening that question. . . . Niggerdom is preparing for a new onslaught." As Lincoln began to draw together the anti-Nebraska coalition, the *Register* warned, "The people of this district will want pledges" against "all alliances with niggerism," and it praised Old Whigs who resisted "the fusion with niggerism."

In a stroke, the old order cracked apart. All that had been proclaimed to be permanent shattered into pieces; everything settled came undone. The Kansas-Nebraska Act made possible the extension of slavery to the West as only one element in a strategy to create a "slave empire" in the hemisphere, as Lincoln would later put it. Now Lincoln, the former surveyor, precisely measured the fissures of the conflict. Lincoln, the lawyer, carefully constructed his arguments political and constitutional. Lincoln, the politician, coolly calculated the force of his opponents and the potential coalition of his allies. Lincoln, the defender of the Declaration of Independence, invoked "the blood of the revolution." Lincoln, the Shakespearean, invoked "blood" and "blood." Stepping onto the stage of history to speak at the Illinois House of Representatives on October 4, 1854, he never left it.

In two brief autobiographies Lincoln depicted himself in this interregnum

period as strangely contented in a kind of imperturbable internal exile, becoming nearly indifferent to politics, immersed in his legal practice. "Always
a whig in politics, and generally on the whig electoral tickets, making active
canvasses—I was losing interest in politics, when the repeal of the Missouri
Compromise aroused me again. What I have done since then is pretty well
known," he wrote on December 20, 1859, to his friend Jesse Fell, as he was
contemplating his race for the presidency. In another short account, he told
the journalist John L. Scripps of the *Chicago Tribune*: "In 1854, his profession
had almost superseded the thought of politics in his mind, when the repeal of
the Missouri compromise aroused him as he had never been before."

But the legend of Cincinnatus, the Roman aristocrat summoned from his
farm by alarm to rescue the endangered republic—the story that had draped
Washington with classical prestige—did not properly fit Lincoln. He was
not a hero above the fray who reluctantly felt duty-bound to descend into the
political arena. While the Whigs had a tradition of drawing upon a variation of the Cincinnatus theme in nominating gallant generals for president—
William Henry Harrison, Zachary Taylor, and Winfield Scott—pretenders
to the Washington mantle—the professional politician who was in truth
consumed with anxiety about his own and the country's future was hardly
part of that line. (His "beau ideal," Henry Clay, was the only politician, the
only man who was not a general, ever to receive the presidential nomination
of the Whig Party. The first Republican candidate, John C. Frémont, in 1856,
was also a daring military figure. In the line of continuity of Old Whig politicians, Lincoln was the second since Clay to gain a presidential nomination.)

It was about this decisive juncture in Lincoln's career in 1854, when he
revealed himself as recognizably Lincoln, that Herndon wrote the most famous description of his ambition. "That man who thinks Lincoln calmly sat
down and gathered his robes about him, waiting for the people to call him,
has a very erroneous knowledge of Lincoln. He was always calculating, and
always planning ahead. His ambition was a little engine that knew no rest."

Time was not standing still waiting for Lincoln to make his emergence.
It was accelerating all along. Time was indifferent to him, but he was not
indifferent to the time. Lincoln could not have entered as a cogent and capable political actor unless he maintained a grasp of the nuances unfolding
for years. During that interregnum between when he left the Congress and
spoke against the Kansas-Nebraska Act there was little he could do to advance the Whig Party, which collapsed under the strains of both false peace
and harsh conflict. Lincoln only seemed to be offstage. He did not disappear,

even if his name did not prominently appear. Even while ambling on his horse Old Bob from county courthouse to courthouse in the Eighth Judicial Circuit of Illinois, he was constantly attending to what was happening beyond it. His fixation on his perpetual rival Douglas never wavered. His attention on the larger events was neither inadvertent nor casual; nor was he present merely by implication or allusion. He was out of the limelight, but the rapidly spinning world was under his gaze.

He and Herndon maintained the best private library in town, subscribed to newspapers and journals from across the country and from London, and both regularly wrote anonymous editorials for the *Illinois State Journal,* the Whig paper of which Lincoln was virtually the coeditor. His legal circuit was also his political network. It would spring to life when his political career did, too. He never ceased his travels around a changing Illinois, where the spectacular growth of Chicago and the mass influx of German immigrants were radically reconfiguring the political calculus.

The honing of his legal skills simultaneously sharpened his political ones. His nocturnal study of Euclid's *Elements* enabled him to master the geometry of both law and politics. He was also capable of cold realism about his own limitations. He quickly if unhappily came to accept the formidable corporate attorney Edwin Stanton's ruthless dismissal of his talents as the co-counsel in the *Manny* case of 1854. Lincoln knew then he would never rise to Stanton's level in the profession, and that his true ability and opportunity, his square root, still lay in politics.

While Lincoln's party disintegrated beneath him the necessity of political parties never escaped him. He clung to the hull of the sinking Whig Party longer than some, but knew at once that a new coalition against the extension of slavery must be organized. In this period of party chaos, Lincoln cast himself into the whirlwind. As his party splintered, he began building the framework of another, even when he did not yet know it. Many movements, often overlapping, swirled across the landscape, against slavery, immigrants, and drink. But the nativist and temperance movements confounded the development of the antislavery one. Antislavery Democrats and antislavery Whigs with long grudges still regarded each other with mutual suspicion. The old partisan lines, however, were not hard and fast, and becoming looser as the Whigs dissolved. Third party abolitionist politics suffused with sectarianism, meanwhile, asserted itself as the core of a new alignment, though it could not itself attract or manage a varying and volatile coalition. Yet what had been marginal and peripheral could be brought into a new center. Some farseeing people in the abolitionist movement in Illinois understood that more proficient and gifted political leaders were required to draw the elements together, which brought them to Lincoln's doorstep. At first he dodged them; but then he led them.

Sequestering himself in the library of the state capitol as he drafted his speech against the Kansas-Nebraska Act, he constructed a coherent intellectual argument matching the elements of the political coalition that would become the Republican Party. He drew on the doctrines of the antislavery movement, of the defunct Liberty Party and its chief theorist, Senator Salmon P. Chase of Ohio, incorporating the idea of the Declaration of Independence as integral to the Constitution, which he argued was an antislavery document despite its provisions for fugitive slaves and counting slaves for representation as three-fifths of a person. He co-opted the ambiguous figure of Thomas Jefferson, slaveholding father of the Democratic Party, as author not only of the Declaration but also the inspiration for the Northwest Ordinance of 1787, which prohibited slavery in the territories. "All honor to Jefferson," proclaimed Lincoln.

The growth of Lincoln's politics and his thought was also shaped by events that were closer to home than those occurring in Washington. His experience serving as co-counsel in the *Todd Heirs* case of 1849 had been searing in his understanding of slavery as a political, economic, and social system. Failing in his attempt to recover his wife's family's fortune from the leader of the pro-slavery movement in Kentucky, Lincoln encountered its mounting power and virulence firsthand. For years afterward he turned over in his mind the menace of slavery to democracy until, in 1855, he began to envision the prospect of civil war. "I think, that there is no peaceful extinction of slavery in prospect for us," he wrote. "The signal failure of Henry Clay, and other good and great men, in 1849, to effect any thing in favor of gradual emancipation in Kentucky, together with a thousand other signs, extinguishes that hope utterly." And he would conclude, "Our political problem now is 'Can we, as a nation, continue together *permanently—forever*—half slave, and half free?' "

Making sense of the crisis from the background, Lincoln moved in accord with his own timing to the foreground. He absorbed the drama, ruminated on it, a political mind continually at work, wondering how he might move forward, how he would break through. For years he wrestled. The decline and fall of the Whigs did not inevitably mean that there would be a new party of Lincoln. There was no imperative except that which was within Lincoln himself.

CHAPTER ONE

WHITE NEGROES

————◆————

T he cholera bacteria that invades the intestines from feces-contaminated water racks the body with symptoms of severe diarrhea and vomiting, producing rapid dehydration, as well as circulatory failure, and usually swift and sudden death. A British medical researcher, John Snow, discovered the origin of the disease in 1854 and prescribed preventive hand washing, water boiling, and linen cleaning, but his work failed to receive notice. Only in 1884, when a German microbe hunter, Robert Koch, traced the bacillus to the Ganges River in India, was the cure finally realized. But its source and cure were unknown in 1849 when an epidemic swept the country and its shadow fell that summer on Lexington, Kentucky, before moving on to claim the life of President Zachary Taylor. After forty people in the town died in a single day, at the suggestion of scientists at nearby Transylvania

Cassius Marcellus Clay

University cannons were fired at regular intervals to rattle the atmosphere and somehow drive the disease away. Smoky oil lamps were lit on the streets night and day. The mayor issued a proclamation for a day of fasting "to fervently implore the Almighty for the arrest of the step of the Angel of Death." Most of the affluent of the town fled to the countryside. But bacteria were indifferent to prestige. The most influential Kentuckian, Senator Henry Clay, and his wife, Lucretia, caught the disease, but survived. His lifelong political ally and business partner, Robert S. Todd, shuttling back and forth from his summer estate, Buena Vista, kept up campaign appearances in his race for the State Senate, but after one speech was overcome with exhaustion and chills, suffered the horrible telltale signs of cholera, and died on July 16.

Todd managed to write his last will and testament, but it was signed by only one witness, therefore invalid, forcing his widow to sell and divide all his property. He also left unresolved a major lawsuit against Robert Wickliffe, his old antagonist and one of the most powerful men in Kentucky. The Todd heirs, who included Mary Todd Lincoln, designated Abraham Lincoln as an attorney to help sort out the tangled affair. Forty years old, he had just completed his one term in the House of Representatives. Despite his lobbying he had failed to secure a federal patronage post as commissioner of the Land Office and returned to Springfield to resume his law practice. He had run continuously for political office since his first campaign for the Illinois state legislature in 1832, but his political prospects now seemed dim. If he won the suit, however, he and Mary would receive a sizable share of the fortune and overnight become wealthy. Lincoln would handle hundreds of law cases over the next decade, but *Todd Heirs v. Wickliffe* was undoubtedly the most important in the development of his thought on the fundamental question of slavery and its political power. The suit, ostensibly about an inheritance, was the latest wrinkle in a power struggle over slavery in Kentucky that lasted more than two decades.

In 1833, after three years of debate, the Kentucky General Assembly enacted the Non-Importation Act, heavily fining those who brought slaves into the state for sale. The bill's sponsors intended to create conditions that would lead to gradual emancipation. Kentucky's limitation on slavery, effectively freezing the expansion of its black population and depriving slave owners of a significant profit through an unregulated slave trade, made it the most advanced of the slaveholding states. Henry Clay and Robert S. Todd supported the act. Robert Wickliffe, the largest slave owner and a state senator, was the vociferous leader of the pro-slavery movement, arguing in speeches and pam-

phlets that the act would destroy "the wealth and capital of the state." Wickliffe came from a family of early settlers, studied law with George Nicholas,
the state's first attorney general, was appointed U.S. attorney in 1805, married
a wealthy heiress who owned the largest plantation in central Kentucky, and
after she died married another wealthy heiress, a Todd cousin. His brother
Charles was a pro-slavery Whig, pas-
sionately hostile to Clay, and served as
a congressman, governor, and postmaster general under President John
Tyler. Perhaps because Robert Wickliffe's origins were humble, accused of
marrying into money, and had made
his own fortune as a land speculator,
giving him the patina of a parvenu,
he cultivated a self-consciously courtly
manner and did not discourage people from referring to him as the "Old
Duke."

Robert Wickliffe

One of the chief supporters of the
Non-Importation Act was Robert Jefferson Breckinridge, member of the
legislature and son of John Breckinridge, who as the U.S. senator from
Kentucky had been President Thomas Jefferson's floor leader and then his
attorney general. John Breckinridge had shepherded passage through the
state legislature of the Kentucky Resolutions of 1798 against the Alien and
Sedition Acts. Written by Jefferson, along with the Virginia Resolutions,
they became foundational documents of the Democratic Party. Despite John
Breckinridge's unease, the Kentucky Resolutions included an article that advocated a state's right to nullify federal policy. John Breckinridge's son was
given the middle name of "Jefferson" at Jefferson's suggestion. As heir to one
of the Democratic Party's founders, Robert Jefferson Breckinridge's party
politics developed into a family heresy, beginning with his election as a state
legislator aligned with Clay and those who became Whigs. When Calhoun
seized upon nullification, citing the Kentucky and Virginia Resolutions as
justification, Breckinridge rejected the doctrine root and branch.

Wickliffe had been his father's lawyer. But when John Breckinridge
died, young Breckinridge dismissed Wickliffe from handling the family

estate, accusing him of fraud. Wickliffe hurled the charge back. In 1830, Breckinridge published a pamphlet, *Hints on Slavery*, a seminal document in the Kentucky antislavery movement, a point-by-point rebuttal of Wickliffe's pro-slavery position. "Domestic slavery cannot exist forever," he wrote, despite being a slaveholder. "It cannot exist long quiet and unbroken, in any condition of society, or under any form of government. It may terminate in various ways; but terminate it must." At a meeting of the Female Colonization Society in Lexington, Wickliffe declared that he favored colonization to Africa only as a means to strengthen the relationship between master and slave by exporting "free persons of color." Breckinridge heatedly replied that the true purpose of colonization was to further the cause of emancipation, benefiting the white race by freeing it of the sin and burden of slavery. Wickliffe retaliated by tarnishing Breckinridge's reputation as an "abolitionist" and wrecking his political career. Breckinridge withdrew from running again for office, declaring he would not "submit" to those who had "excited prejudices." He became one of the country's leading Presbyterian ministers, waging a holy war against slavery and Wickliffe. They were just beginning their duel.

With the passage of the Non-Importation Act, it appeared that the antislavery movement was gaining traction, prompting James G. Birney before founding the Liberty Party to suggest that Kentucky was "the best site in our whole country for taking a stand against slavery." Momentum grew for a new constitutional convention that would enact a plan for gradual emancipation. Wickliffe was relentless in his efforts to block the convention and overturn the Non-Importation Act, or "the Negro Law," as he preferred to call it. It represented, he said, "the surrender of the country to the negroes." After the emergence of the militant abolitionist William Lloyd Garrison in the mid-1830s, opinion sharply shifted against the antislavery movement. Henry Clay, once an advocate of a constitutional convention, carefully calculated the political winds as he charted his presidential ambition, opposing a constitutional convention, not because he loved slavery but because he loathed abolitionists. In 1838, in a referendum, Kentuckians voted overwhelmingly against a convention. "The effect," said Clay, "has been to dissipate all prospects whatever, for the present, of any scheme of gradual or other emancipation." And he cast the blame on abolitionists.

Breckinridge joined in denouncing abolitionists, as "the most despicable and odious men on the face of the earth" and "public enemies" who advocated the "heresy" of racial "amalgamation"—"a base, spurious, degraded mixture, hardly less revolting than revolution." He consistently spoke of his hatred of slavery as a way to protect the white race. In 1836, he traveled to Glasgow to debate the English abolitionist George Thompson. Insisting on his antislavery credentials and agreeing that blacks possessed "natural rights," Breckinridge professed that "God had kept several races of men distinct" and depicted Africans as "sitting in darkness and drinking blood." The Manifest Destiny of American slaves, he revealed, was to be Westernized and colonized back to their native continent. But Thompson censured "a nation of slaveholders" ruled by "the aristocracy of skin."

Into the vacuum on the antislavery side stepped the strapping Cassius Marcellus Clay, Henry Clay's younger cousin, who had been converted to the cause as a student at Yale after hearing one of Garrison's orations. "Cash" Clay, son of one of the richest men in Kentucky, glittering in his lineage, was as born to rule as any pro-slavery planter. Raised in a mansion on one of the largest plantations in the state, he felt no need to defer to anybody. After his own family, he was most closely attached to the Todds. He was Mary's childhood playmate, lived in the Todd house when his dormitory at Transylvania University burned, and married one of the best friends of the Todd sisters, Mary Jane Warfield. In his closeness to the family, he was like a Todd brother.

Cash's arguments were as imposing as his burly physical presence. He was as vehement in his opinions and turbulent in their defense as any of his fervent opponents. He believed that slavery shackled free labor by driving down wages, making mechanics and farmers virtual slaves, and crippling commerce and manufacturing. In 1840, he ran for the state legislature against "Old Duke" Wickliffe's son, Robert Wickliffe, Jr., known as the "Young Duke." "I declare, then, in the face of all men," Cash announced, "that I believe slavery to be an evil—an evil morally, economically, physically, intellectually, socially, religiously, politically . . . an unmixed evil." The Old Duke fired back that Cash was trying to "get up a war between the slaveholders and the non-slaveholders," and was an "orator of inquisitors, the enemy of Lexington, a secret personal foe, an agitator without spirit, a liar systematically, and an abolitionist at heart." But Cash won the election handily.

He ran again the next year, ignoring the friendly counsel of Henry Clay that he would lose and should stand down. Cash's followers, "the boys" he called them, paraded through Lexington in a torchlight parade, "and the slave-party imitated our example." On April 24, he debated the Young Duke. Cash assailed his opponent's father while young Wickliffe called Cash an "abolitionist" for advocating a Northern style economy—and mentioned his wife, grounds for a challenge to a duel.

Sheer acts of violence and duels of honor were a tragic Wickliffe tradition. In 1829, when the liberal editor of the *Kentucky Gazette*, Thomas Benning, heaped abuse on the Old Duke for his pro-slavery conservatism, Wickliffe's eldest son, Charles, went to the newspaper office and shot him in the back. Charles Wickliffe hired Henry Clay as his counsel and he was acquitted for acting in self-defense. When the *Gazette* published an editorial criticizing the judgment as the result of a "packed and perjured jury," Charles challenged the new editor, James George Trotter, once a childhood friend, to a duel. After both men missed, Charles insisted on a second round, and was shot dead. Harassed for years by the Old Duke and his allies, paranoid that he would be murdered, Trotter wound up in the Lexington Lunatic Asylum.

When Cassius Clay and the Young Duke met across the Ohio River in Indiana for their duel, they stood ten paces apart and fired three times, each shot missing. (Wickliffe's second was Albert Sidney Johnston, a relative by marriage and Transylvania classmate of Jefferson Davis, who would become a leading Confederate general, killed at Shiloh.) "No apology was made on either side, and no reconciliation was proposed," wrote Cash, "and we left the ground enemies, as we came." One observer remarked that no blood was shed, though bad blood remained. Cash lost the election and accused Wickliffe and his allies of stealing it. "The upshot was, that I was victor in the legal votes, but beaten by unfair judges and corrupt methods." He proclaimed he had lost because he had "turned traitor to slavery!" Though he would never win another race, he had gained a devoted following that acted as his "compact body of personal friends," "laboring men mostly," men like Thomas Lincoln, Lincoln's Kentuckian father who fled the slave state, and others who were roused by Cash Clay's statements against their oppression: "Every slave imported drives out a free and independent Kentuckian," and, "The day is come, or coming, when every white must work for the wages of the slave." Despite his militant rhetoric he opposed immediate emancipation, denounced abolitionists like Garrison as "fanatics," equating them with "fanatic" slave owners, believed the Constitution protected slavery in the states, thought blacks were naturally an inferior race that should not be granted equal rights, and favored gradual measures. Even so, he was perched on the far edge of opinion in Kentucky. Nobody, except perhaps Robert J. Breckinridge, was more hated by the Wickliffes and the pro-slavery forces than Cassius Clay. They hated him because he was a traitor to his class incapable of being intimidated, for his insurrectionary appeals to white non-slave-owners, his utterly Southern claim to honor and open contempt for their dishonor, and willingness to meet violence with violence.

In the next contest for the congressional seat in the district, in 1843, Robert Wickliffe, Jr., the Young Duke, stood against Garrett Davis, the Whig candidate, a thoroughgoing regular, not an antislavery man, who had been endorsed by Henry Clay and Robert Todd. Wickliffe's campaign consisted of a stunt. He read a letter purporting to prove that his Whig opponent had gerrymandered the district in his favor, but carefully did not share the reply of the supposed letter writer emphatically protesting that the original document was "a damned lie." Cassius Clay took it upon himself to stalk Wickliffe accompanied by his working-class entourage. On August 1, when the Young Duke spoke in a town square without Davis being present, Clay interrupted his reading of the letter. "Mr. Wickliffe," he shouted, "justice to Mr. Davis compels me to say . . . that it was a damned lie." That same day he tracked after Wickliffe to the next town. This time Wickliffe was ready. His cousin, Samuel M. Brown, and "a crowd of desperate bullies," prepared to silence Cash for good, to "blow his damned brains out." When Clay spoke up against Wickliffe, Brown called him a "liar" and his thugs rushed him, one thumping him on the head with a club. "Clear the way and let me kill the damn rascal," yelled Brown, aiming a pistol. He fired a shot that bounced off the scabbard of Clay's knife at his chest. Clay pulled out his bowie knife, sliced off Brown's ear, gouged an eye, and slashed his head to the skull. Incredibly, Brown survived. Cash was indicted for mayhem. Henry Clay and John Speed Smith (uncle of Joshua Speed, Lincoln's close friend) defended him in a sensational trial at which they argued that Wickliffe had plotted Clay's assassination and Robert Todd appeared as a key defense witness. Cash had acted in self-defense, declared his counsel. "And, if he had not, he would not have been worthy of the name he bears!" With Henry Clay's greatest courtroom performance, the jury acquitted Cassius Clay. And Davis defeated the Young Duke.

But the pro-slavery party was gaining ground. In 1843, Wickliffe and his allies succeeded in getting the Non-Importation Act overturned in the lower house, and though it was stopped in the Senate they had momentum. During the debate, Wickliffe argued that the hidden antislavery agenda was to reduce non-slave-owning whites into slaves. They would be menial workers, like in the North and England, submissive to their masters, who by controlling their wages would control their votes. "Gentlemen wanted to drive out the black population, that they may obtain white negroes in their places," he said. "White negroes have this advantage over black negroes, they can be converted into voters; and the men who live upon the sweat of their brow, and pay them but a dependent and scanty subsistence, can, if able to keep ten thousand of them in employment, come up to the polls, and change the destiny of the country." But he aroused more than economic fear, beyond anxiety about income and wages. His case was existential. White men would no longer be white men, Kentuckians no longer Kentuckians. Through a strange alchemy performed by sorcerers, they would be turned into black men. "How improved will be our condition when we have such white negroes as perform the servile labors of Europe, of old England, and he would add now, of New England; when our body servants, and our cart drivers, and our street sweepers, are white negroes instead of black? Where will be the independence, the proud spirit, and the chivalry of the Kentuckians then?" Liberty, honor, and tradition would all be gone. Only white supremacy based on slavery could save white men from being transformed into "white negroes."

Wickliffe and his men circulated handbills written in black dialect attacking Cassius Clay as a white black man seeking to transform white men into "white negroes": "Massa Kashus M. Klay de friend ob de kullud poppy-lashum: aldough he hab a wite skin he hab also a berry brack heart." Under siege, Cash felt compelled to deny time and again that he favored emancipation because he loved black people or believed they were social equals. He was against slavery "not because the slave is black or white, not because we love the black man best, for we do not love him as well . . . but because it is just."

Cash explained his position in a letter to the *New York Tribune* that its editor, Horace Greeley, published as a pamphlet and distributed nationally. In *Slavery: The Evil—The Remedy* Cash called slavery "evil to the slave . . . evil to the master . . . source of indolence and destructive of all industry . . . mother of ignorance . . . opposed to literature . . . antagonistic to the Fine Arts . . . impoverishes the soil . . . induces national poverty . . . evil to the free laborer . . . mother and the nurse of Lynch law." Acknowledging that the Constitution protected slavery in the states, he demanded that the federal government stamp it out where it had authority—in the territories, the District of Columbia, and the seas. "The great experiment of Republican Government," he wrote, "has not been fairly tested."

On January 1, 1844, Cassius Clay emancipated his slaves. He was the ideal man for Northern Whigs to recruit for his cousin's campaign to counter the Liberty Party, the first antislavery party, which might siphon off votes. Cash defended Henry Clay in a letter to the *Tribune* from abolitionists' criticism that he was a slaveholder by assuring them that his election would generally advance the antislavery cause, adding his own view that in the future no slaveholder should be permitted to run for president. His gesture caused consternation for the candidate, who wrote that "you can have no conception . . . of the injury which your letter to the Tribune was doing" in alienating the South, and worried about the "very great delicacy of my position." While "grateful" that Cash stumped for him throughout New England and New York, "I am afraid that you are too sanguine in supposing that any considerable number of the Liberty men can be induced to support me." Henry Clay's letters trying to square the circles of Texas annexation and slavery, by announcing he was neither for nor against, damaged him in the North but failed to help him in the South. At a dinner party at Lexington, Henry Clay bitterly blamed abolitionists for his loss, provoking Cash to chide him for saying during the campaign that "abolitionists should be set apart from, and denounced by all parties," and then being upset when they "played the role you marked out for them." Again, Henry's wish for Cash's political prudence went unmet.

Henry Clay's defeat gave Cash the idea that the Whig and Liberty parties ought to merge into a new antislavery party—and that he should create a newspaper to promote it. "I look forward to the time not distant when the Whigs and Liberty Party will occupy the same ground," he wrote Salmon P. Chase, one of the leading lights of the Liberty Party who thought he could turn the small protest organization into the vanguard of a new Democratic Party that would be antislavery and which he called True Democracy. Southern newspapers had refused to republish Cash's various letters to the *Tribune* and the editor of the local paper, the *Lexington Observer*, Daniel Wickliffe, brother of the Old Duke, blackballed his writings. So Cash decided in 1845 to found his own newspaper. "They are the mouthpieces of the slaveholders, who are the property holders of the country," he wrote about the existing papers. The *Observer* editorialized, "Mr. Clay has taken the very worst time that he could to begin the agitation of that great and delicate question." The prospectus of the *True American* was reprinted in a number of antislavery papers across the country—including the *Sangamo Journal*, the Whig journal in Springfield, Illinois, for which Lincoln was the de facto coeditor and anonymously wrote many of its editorials.

Conscious of the fatal history of antislavery newspapers, Cash prepared himself for war. Before publishing an issue, he armored the paper's office with sheet metal, equipped it with muskets, shotguns, and Mexican lances, and bought two brass cannons that he filled with grapeshot and nails and aimed through the front door prepared for the onslaught of a mob. Anticipating an Armageddon, he built a trapdoor in the ceiling through which he and the staff could escape, and on the roof put a barrel of gunpowder that he planned to drop in to blow invaders to smithereens.

The *True American*'s first issue, published on June 3, under the motto "God and Liberty," called for constitutional emancipation to establish "true prosperity," the overthrow of the slave power, a "despotic and irresponsible minority," and issued a personal threat against Robert Wickliffe, Sr. "Old Man," Clay warned, "remember Russell's Cave"—where Cash nearly killed Samuel Brown—"and if you still thirst for bloodshed and violence, the same blade that repelled the assaults of assassins' sons, once more in self defense, is ready to drink of the blood of the hireling hordes of sycophants and outlaws of the assassin-sire of assassins."

The *Observer* responded to the debut of the *True American* with an editorial calling for its destruction: "It would be right to demolish by violence Mr. Clay's press." And it published "An Appeal to the Slaveholders of Fayette": "It is time, full time that slaveholders of Fayette [County] should have peace—that their rights and their security should no longer be a football to be kicked to and fro by unprincipled political jugglers and office-seekers."

Lexington was rife with rumors that the *True American* was stoking a slave insurrection. "The conduct of the slaves in Fayette is said to have changed since the publication of the True American," wrote George D. Prentice, author of an authorized biography of Henry Clay and editor of the reliably Whig *Louisville Journal*. He reported that he had "heard . . . that the slaves in the factories and the farms had refrains set to words, which they were singing to the praise of Cassius M. Clay, boasting that he was about to break the chains of their bondage, and would by the force of his character and influence elevate them to an equality with their masters."

The rising temperature over the *True American* reached a boiling point in the 1845 elections for the Congress and the Kentucky state legislature. Robert S. Todd was running as the Whig candidate for the State Senate against Charles C. Moore, a vociferous pro-slavery man in favor of overturning the Non-Importation Act, a close friend and business partner of the Old Duke, and co-director with him of the Northern Bank of Kentucky. The contest was a resumption of the feud between Todd and Wickliffe with the bad feeling heightened by the complicating and overlapping feud between Wickliffe and Breckinridge, who was Todd's friend, political ally, and distant cousin. When the Non-Importation Act was first considered, Todd had signed a petition to the legislature on a "Bill for the Emancipation of Slaves," calling slavery "a great political evil and moral wrong." Moore now charged that he was an abolitionist, "no friend of the institution." Some of Todd's nervous supporters urged him to reverse himself. He issued a statement, published in the *Observer*, not only upholding the Non-Importation Act but also acknowledging he was an early advocate. "Having been present during its discussion . . . I was in favor of its passage, and have been uniform and steadfast in its support, believing, as I sincerely do, that it is founded on principles of sound policy." But, in a concession to political practicality, he added, "I am a slaveholder. Were I an abolitionist or an emancipator in principle, I would not hold a slave."

Unable to restrain himself, Wickliffe entered the fray as though he were the candidate himself, accusing Todd of abolitionism. "Twice or thrice," he wrote, "has this Abolition Club [the Clay Club of Lexington] ordered the election of the salaried President of the Bank of Kentucky, and the majority has obeyed." To which Todd replied: "Fellow Citizens, With all the loathing that an upright man can feel towards an habitual and notorious falsifier, an unscrupulous and indiscriminate calumniator, reckless alike of fame, of honor, and of truth, I must now take my present leave of this miserable old man, and express to you my regret that to justify myself against his unprovoked assaults, unfounded charges and illiberal insinuations, I have been reluctantly compelled, in this manner and at this time, to trespass on your patience."

Intent on having the last word of invective, Wickliffe issued a manifesto, "To the Freemen of the County of Fayette," accusing Todd of making "weak and vicious" charges, of being both "craven" and radical. "Mr. Todd chooses to insinuate that I acquired my wealth by dishonesty. This insinuation is a base and infamous falsehood. This calumny was first uttered by Robert J. Breckinridge, whose slander merchant Mr. Todd is." But these were the least of his accusations. He railed repeatedly against "the abolitionist, John Q. Adams, in his war upon the institution of slavery." Of Adams's proposal to impose severe penalties on any state that would repudiate its debt, an act of nullification, the wild talk of fire-eaters in South Carolina, Wickliffe raged against him, "A more black-hearted and hellish scheme to dissolve these United States was never conceived of, much less proposed before."

Wickliffe charged that the Whigs were little more than a cover for a conspiracy against slavery. "And this club or clique, or both, first under the name of Tippecanoe, and then under that of Clay, has, through its members, opened and kept up a communication with the Abolition Societies throughout the Union from the year 1840 down to the present moment. Space does not admit of a full detail of the abominations of this Club and its mates." He claimed that Todd in his capacity of bank president kept a secret list of debtors in order to "command and control you in the exercise of your right of suffrage . . . the so-called clubites, that, spider-like, are trying to envelope [*sic*] you in their entangling web." And he pointed a finger at Cassius Clay. "Are you surprised that these clubites have established, openly and avowedly, an abolition press within your good City of Lexington, that bids defiance to you, and is scattering its sheets throughout the length and breadth of the land, proclaiming freedom to your slaves?"

The voting was spread over three days, beginning on August 4. On the last day of balloting, Todd rode through the district in an open carriage accompanied by Henry Clay, rallying the Whig faithful and narrowly carrying the victory over Wickliffe and his candidate. The next night, Henry Clay's rope factory was burned to the ground in a brazen act of arson. Then the pro-slavery men turned their wrath on the *True American*.

Cassius Clay was bedridden with typhus. But the paper continued to roll off the press. A week after the election he published an incendiary article by an anonymous slaveholder favoring full rights for blacks. "It is vain for the master," wrote the offending author, "to try to fence his dear slaves in from all intercourse with the great world, to create his little petty and tyrannical kingdom on his own plantation, and keep it for his exclusive reign." Cash contributed an editorial to accompany the piece: "For the day of retribution is at hand! The masses will be avenged!"

Four days after the rope factory burning a group of thirty men gathered to demand suppression of the "fire-brand" *True American*. Their leader was Thomas F. Marshall, nephew of the late chief justice John Marshall and a former ally and friend of Cash who had flipped from antislavery Whig to pro-slavery Democrat. He had just run for the Congress as a Democrat and been defeated. Cash had humiliated him in a public debate over Texas, turning the "white negro" charge against him, declaring that the real question was "whether we ourselves shall be slaves!" Then he flayed Marshall in the *True American* as a turncoat, an "apostate Whig," and published Marshall's previous denunciations of slavery as "a cancer . . . a withering pestilence . . . an unmitigated curse." Now Marshall announced that Cassius Clay had "assassinated" law and order, and the group delivered him an ultimatum demanding he close the paper as "dangerous to the peace of our community, and to the safety of our homes and families." Cash's defiant answer was instant: "I deny their power and I defy their action. Go tell your secret conclave of cowardly assassins that C. M. Clay knows his rights and how to defend them."

His press kept churning out extra editions. Meanwhile, he tried to calm the storm by separating himself from abolitionists. His enemies, he said, called him an "abolitionist, a name full of unknown and strange terrors and crimes, to the mass of our people," while he remained committed to gradual emancipation. "I utterly deny that I have any political association with them." As a peaceful gesture, he removed his arsenal that had turned his office into a fortress.

On the morning of August 18, more than two thousand people gathered at the Lexington courthouse to hear Thomas F. Marshall read his indictment of Cassius Clay for his crimes "for effecting the entire abolition of slavery in America," from advocating emancipation in the District of Columbia to his letters to the *New York Tribune*, which proved his intention to "finally overthrow the institution." Marshall concluded his brief with a ringing call to suppress the *True American*. "An Abolition paper in a slave state is a nuisance of the most formidable character . . . a blazing brand in the hand of an incendiary or madman, which may scatter ruin, conflagration, revolution, crime unnameable, over everything dear in domestic life." The crowd voted unanimously in approval. After the town's sheriff went to Cash's house to confiscate his office key, a Committee of Sixty, led by James B. Clay, son of Henry Clay, marched to the *True American* and removed the printing press and the type.

One Illinois newspaper that denounced the "outbreak of the mob" in Kentucky published a fanciful account of the incident. "We understand," the *Sangamo Journal* reported, "that the choice spirits consisted of about one hundred and fifty men, wearing black masks to conceal their features (this was modest at all events,) and calling themselves the black Indians that they made loud noise through the streets of Lexington, maltreated many negroes, and, besides tarring and feathering several in the public square, broke the ribs of one man, the hands of another, and so injured the eye of a third that the poor fellow will lose it. What will the people at large think of these proceedings?" The *Observer*, the Wickliffe organ, responded to the Springfield paper that the *True American* had been extirpated "without the slightest damage to property or the effusion of a drop of blood." In another editorial it jibed,

"Howl on, ye wolves! Kentucky is ready to meet and repel your whole blood thirsty piratical crew!" And yet Cash continued to publish and distribute his paper from Cincinnati, while still living in White Hall, his family's mansion on a hill overlooking Lexington.

In April 1846, an unannounced visitor knocked at his door. "Have I the pleasure of seeing Mr. Clay?" "That is my name." "Mine is Seward, from New York. I have come to see you." "Not William H. Seward?" "Yes, sir. I expected to see an older person." "And I expected to find one of more youthful aspect." Seward was forty-four years old, the former governor of New York, an antislavery champion, and one of the most influential men within the Whig Party, who had narrowly failed to elect Henry Clay president in 1844. In New York, the difference between winning and losing the critical state, which would have decided the contest for Clay, turned on the tiny margin that the Liberty Party captured.

The townspeople of Lexington had "concluded to taboo the advocate of emancipation," Seward wrote Thurlow Weed, the political mastermind and publisher of the *Albany Evening Journal*, who was his co-partner in running the New York State Whig Party. "Thus it soon became apparent that, in Lexington, there was no neutral or common ground. I must either drop Cassius M. Clay, or elevate him, in my demonstrations of respect. . . . You will readily believe that I did not hesitate. I closed gladly up to his side, rode with him, walked with him, dined with him, and made my visit to Ashland under his auspices." There they found Henry Clay. "He is evidently looking forward again to another trial for the presidency," Seward wrote Weed, "and yet, by habits of thought, action, and association, increasing the obstacles in the way of his ambition." Upon leaving the town, Seward concluded, "It was evident that I was no very welcome guest at Lexington; nor did I need anybody to explain to me that I am regarded with distrust, or a more unkindly feeling, by those who are interested in defending slavery."

When the Mexican War broke out, Cash astonished everyone by volunteering. He was elected captain of the Lexington "Old Infantry" militia and served with extraordinary bravery, facing down Mexican officers when captured with his men, saving their lives. He received a hero's return with booming cannons and a reception at which Robert S. Todd delivered the welcoming address hailing him as "my old and faithful friend." By then, the *True American* had been removed to Louisville, a safer location, and renamed the *Louisville Examiner*. But Cash had forgotten nothing and forgiven nobody. He sued James B. Clay for damages against his newspaper and received a $2,500 judgment. He also mistakenly blamed Henry Clay for the suppression of the *True American*, accusing him of purposely leaving town before the mob acted to "murder me." Cash's politics were a combustible keg of gunpowder with a lit fuse. He wanted to blow up his cousin and the Whig Party, and to create a new Emancipation Party. But he decided instead he would support Zachary Taylor, thinking of the general as above party. At the Fayette County Whig convention, Cash led an insurgency against his cousin, winning the endorsement for Taylor, and at the state convention fomented a split so that Kentucky, Clay's home state, embarrassingly sent a divided delegation to the national Whig convention. In a letter published in a pro-Taylor paper aligned with Seward and Weed, the *New York Courier and Enquirer*, Cash proclaimed that the Whig Party of Kentucky "believes that Mr. Clay cannot be elected." Chase tried to recruit him for the antislavery Free Soil Party, but although he was sympathetic he campaigned for Taylor. Much later, Cash regretted his vindictiveness toward Henry Clay, "aggravated by a misapprehension."

On February 15, 1849, the Democrats of Lexington hosted a banquet at the Phoenix Hotel on Main Street for a special guest, the newly elected U.S. senator from Illinois, James Shields, close ally of Senator Stephen A. Douglas, and "after a number of voluntary toasts were drunk, the greatest hilarity and good feeling prevailed," according to the *Observer*. Earlier in the month, the Kentucky General Assembly had issued a call for a new constitutional convention. It was the long-held dream of antislavery men in the state, but the pro-slavery forces passed it in order to write a new pro-slavery document. The Shields dinner was their happy hour. One week after the Shields fete, the legislature repealed the Non-Importation Act of 1833 and enacted an amnesty for slave traders who had violated it, an acknowledgment of the flagrant black market that had always been operating. One trader conducted his business of selling expensive young mulatto women as concubines quite openly across the street from the home of Mary Todd's grandmother. The slave traders and big slaveholders who stood to profit most were at the heart of the repeal movement.

Repeal had been successfully resisted since the act had first been enacted, but the atmosphere decisively shifted in its favor after a terror that seemed to realize the worst fears of Kentuckians since a suppressed plot for a slave insurrection in 1811, after which the General Assembly made it a crime punishable by death. On August 5, 1848, seventy-five slaves from Lexington stole weapons from their owners and escaped, likely inspired by the incident in which seventy-seven slaves from Washington attempted to escape on a ship called the *Pearl* just months earlier. Led by a white abolitionist student from Centre College, Edward J. Doyle, they fled toward the Ohio River. A posse of more than one hundred men and local militia pursued the fugitives until catching up with them, waging a pitched nighttime battle in a hemp field with one white and one black killed on each side, and ending with the capture of the slaves. After a trial, three of the black leaders were hung, the rest claimed by their owners, and Doyle sentenced to twenty years of hard labor in the state prison.

Just before the repeal, Henry Clay wrote a letter suggesting the program for a constitutional convention—gradual emancipation, colonization of all free blacks to Africa, and freedom to all born after 1855 or 1860. He was "utterly opposed to any scheme of emancipation" in Kentucky without colonization and carefully added: "If she should abolish slavery, it would be her duty, and I trust that she would be as ready as she now is, to defend the slave States in the enjoyment of all their lawful and constitutional rights." Covering this base, he argued for "the advantage of the diligence, the fidelity, and the constancy of free labor instead of the carelessness, the infidelity, and the unsteadiness of slave labor; we shall elevate the character of white labor, and elevate the social condition of the white laborer." For Kentucky, he proclaimed, "no deeds of her former glory would equal in greatness and grandeur, that of being the pioneer State in removing from her soil every trace of human slavery, and in establishing the descendants of Africa, within her jurisdiction, in the native land of their forefathers." The *Richmond Enquirer*, edited by Thomas Ritchie, trumpeted the line echoed in Southern newspapers: "Henry Clay's true character now stands revealed. The man is an abolitionist. He takes his position with [Joshua] Giddings and [John P.] Hale"—the leading abolitionists in Congress. But Clay's manifesto, moderate in intent, galvanized the antislavery forces as well.

On April 14, the Fayette County antislavery men met to select delegates for a statewide emancipation convention. The chairman was Robert S. Todd's business partner, Edward Oldham; Breckinridge, the main speaker, was elected delegate; and a resolution adopted that slavery was "contrary to the natural rights of mankind . . . opposed to the fundamental principles of free government . . . inconsistent with a state of sound morality . . . hostile to the prosperity of the Commonwealth." Just days later, Wickliffe and the pro-slavery men staged their own local meeting, condemning the antislavery resolution as "prejudicial to the best interests of the Commonwealth," emancipation as an "incalculable injury," and any candidate who supported the Non-Importation Act. The Young Duke was elected as its delegate.

The first emancipation convention in Kentucky gathered at Frankfort on April 25, with 157 delegates from counties across the state, a majority of them slaveholders and about one in every seven a minister. While they debated various plans for emancipation—Henry Clay's was probably the consensus position—they did not adopt a specific platform, unable to agree, but instead adopted the broad language of the Fayette County declaration and pledged that they would work in the constitutional convention for some version of gradual emancipation. Filled with faith in their righteous cause, they marched as Christian soldiers to evangelize for the election of delegates to the constitutional convention in the most extensive debate on slavery in Kentucky's history.

"Thank God!" exclaimed Cassius Clay on hearing of the repeal of the Non-Importation Act. "The touch of that heel has broken our slumber." At the Frankfort meeting he had announced himself in favor of "agitating" and he began canvassing the state. On June 15, he attended a speech of the pro-slavery candidate for delegate, Squire Turner, a lawyer, state legislator, and slave owner, interrupting him several times and demanding that the crowd be allowed to hear a speaker for the antislavery candidate. People shouted back and forth, someone raised the extraneous issue of state bonds, and Turner's son Cyrus called Cash "a damned liar," smashing him in the face. Cash's and Turner's men rushed into a melee. Cash was stabbed deeply in his side. Cyrus Turner held a gun to his head, pulled the trigger three times, but it failed to fire. Cash slashed him in the stomach with his bowie knife. Cyrus Turner died, mourned as the martyr of the pro-slavery cause, murdered by the "damned nigger agitator." Cash slowly recovered from his wound. Already on the defensive, having lost the Non-Importation Act, the antislavery forces retreated.

The campaign to elect delegates to the constitutional convention dominated the campaign for the General Assembly. State senator Robert S. Todd, a Henry Clay man from the beginning and friend of Cash, was challenged for reelection by a former Whig, Oliver Anderson, one of the state's biggest planters and slaveholders, a Wickliffe ally, who described himself as "a thorough pro-slavery man," and who defended slavery as "recognized and countenanced by both Scriptures of the Old and New Testament." When Anderson assailed Todd as an "emancipationist," Todd felt compelled to explain that he would not "interfere with slavery as a vested right in any manner whatever," even if he believed in the Non-Importation Act. Then he promised that if a majority voted in the constitutional convention to discard the act "I should feel myself bound, (as the question is only one of expediency) to represent their views instead of my own—that being the duty of a representative." But even conceding principle to "expediency" did not appear to improve his prospects. Momentum was on the other side.

Within a month, Todd was dead of cholera. He did not live to be swept away by the landslide. His replacement, J. R. Dunlap, trying to insulate himself by promising he was against "any interference between master and slave without the consent of the master" after Anderson attacked him for being a member of the legislature in 1833 that passed the Non-Importation Act, lost every precinct in the county.

On Election Day, a gun battle raged through the streets of Louisville between pro-slavery men and "emancipationists," including staff members of the *Examiner*. Tensions ran high, turnout was low. People dreaded they would get cholera if they gathered in public. The pro-slavery candidates won every contest for delegates but two. In a few cities, like Louisville, the anti-slavery candidates captured about 45 percent of the vote. But statewide they received only about 10 percent, about what the Free Soil Party had won. Henry Clay's endorsement and the blessing of men of the cloth like Breckinridge had counted for little.

The constitutional convention began on slavery and ended on slavery— "the institution that we have come here to protect and that we are seeking to perpetuate to posterity," as John L. Ballenger, the delegate from Lincoln County, put it. The convention started on October 1 and went to nearly Christmas Eve. It debated slavery from every angle in its favor. The scriptural case was offered at length by Albert Gallatin Talbott, a large planter and delegate from Bourbon County, later a congressman, who argued that "God did ordain and establish slavery" and to question Jesus' belief in slavery was "blasphemy." William Chenault, a delegate from Madison County (along with Squire Turner), condemned the Non-Importation Act as a device "to deprive slavery men of their rights," and claimed the authority of the ultimate founding father. "I think, sir, that the portrait of Washington, which is hanging over your head, should admonish not only Kentucky, but every slaveholding state in the Union to stand up and firmly maintain its rights over this property."

But the fullest case was made by William D. Mitchell, the delegate from Oldham County, who attacked free labor existing without slavery as a threat to all white men, elaborating on Wickliffe's doctrine of "white negroes." "Now look at the state of things in the slave state. There the menial offices—those services that attach to themselves degradation, are all performed by slaves. No matter how humble his condition, the freeman of the south feels with Cooper's scout that he is a white man, without a cross—that liberty is not only a political right but a personal distinction." After invoking James Fenimore Cooper's fictional frontier scout, Natty Bumppo, as the ideal white man, he claimed the Non-Importation Act "will be to Kentucky a Chinese shoe. Crippled in her progress, marred in her fair proportions, she will stumble forward to premature decay, with the sin of undeveloped greatness stamped upon her withered lineaments." Slavery and free labor could not be mixed—"they cannot co-exist; the presence of one banishes the other." A state must be wholly one or the other; it could not be a house divided. And the case was clear: slavery was the superior system for white men everywhere, not just the South. "Where slavery exists, the white operative, as a class, is unknown. Such, sire, I venture to affirm, is the elevating influence of slavery, that it lifts the white man above that description of labor; it converts him from a mere machine into a man. And hence it is the consequence of this incompatibility, no reliance can be placed on free labor, when slave labor is inadequate to the purpose."

Finally, Garrett Davis, the Whig congressman, friend of Clay and Todd, and enemy of Wickliffe, put his finger to the wind, and emerged as the ultimate pro-slavery advocate. In the past he had put party above slavery, but now he reversed the order. He proposed an amendment to the Kentucky Bill of Rights that would enshrine slavery as the most sacrosanct right of all: "The right of property is before and higher than any constitutional sanction; and the right of the owner of a slave to his property is the same, and as inviolable as the right of the owner of any property whatever." His amendment exalting slavery was the defining moment of the convention, the culmination of the debate—and it passed as the purest expression of the new constitution. The Non-Importation Act was voided as though it never existed and the secret ballot in voting rejected, forcing every citizen to openly declare his preference, fostering an atmosphere of intimidation. When the delegates ratified the document, James Guthrie, the convention's president, and later President Buchanan's secretary of the treasury and U.S. senator, sent them home with a valedictory. "I do not believe that the emancipationists, as a body, will rise up and battle against the will of the people of Kentucky, expressed by this convention in relation to that particular matter. . . . I do not believe they will be willing to agitate the country again on that subject, and attempt to create discord and dissatisfaction in the community."

The self-styled Emancipation Party had conducted the antislavery campaign for the constitution, stemming from the Frankfort meeting in April. On its executive committee was a state senator from Louisville, James Speed, the younger brother of Lincoln's friend Joshua Speed with whom Lincoln had once shared a room in Springfield before Speed returned home to Kentucky to run the family plantation. In a series of editorials in the *Louisville Courier*, James Speed attacked the premise of the pro-slavery proponents who denigrated free labor and the concept of the "white negro."

> It is right, it is necessary that labor should be respected and encouraged. Touch and affect it injuriously, and you injure the working man, the employer, and society in all their ramifications. Let us first glance at the effect produced by slave labor on the working man, I mean, all who from choice or necessity do that which is, or may be done by slaves. It is said and sometimes gravely written that our slaves are only kept to do menial offices. These words *menial offices* seem to constitute a clap-trap, undefinable phrase. Those who use it show more clearly than any argument I can adduce that the institution of slavery has produced its worst effects upon their minds. Labor, honorable effort, and honest industry are degraded in their eyes. . . . They are only so because of their combination or connection with slavery. Slavery thus robs labor of its dignity and true worth.

Like an elegy, he extolled the already defunct Non-Importation Act. "The law of 1833 operated as a kind of protection to free labor. The white man was secure against the further competition and consequent degradation from an increase of the number of slaves in Kentucky." But the act was wiped away and so was the vision of Kentucky headed toward a future that would lead the South to gradual emancipation and true union with the rest of the nation.

When the constitutional convention submitted its document to a statewide referendum in May 1850 it passed overwhelmingly, receiving more than two thirds of the vote, just as its framers expected. The Emancipation Party disintegrated, the *Louisville Examiner* suspended publication, and James Speed did not run for reelection; nor did his brother, who was a member of the lower house. Many demoralized Whigs simply did not bother to turn out for the referendum; others, pro-slavery but attached to Henry Clay and the Whig Party as the natural order, broke away through the fissure, defecting to the Democrats, convincing themselves they were protecting their property, their slaves.

"Others fell by the wayside; I went on to the end," wrote Cassius Clay. Public approval of the new constitution was a foregone conclusion. Rather than stump the state against it, Cash wrote five open letters in March 1850 to Daniel Webster, published in the *National Era*, tearing apart Webster's Senate floor speech in favor of the Compromise of 1850 that would create a federal Fugitive Slave Act. "I cannot but regret that you did not feel it your duty, as a Northern Senator, as Daniel Webster, as a MAN, to say a word in favor of freedom." He picked out of Webster's speech one of Webster's favorite words to eviscerate. "The Southern man who reaps all the benefits of slavery can afford to be 'moderate.' The Northern man who deems himself a millionaire only in consequence of slave-grown and slave-growing cotton can afford to be 'moderate' . . . but upon this subject of slavery the word does not convey the idea. I do not desire to be offensive; I forbear a substitute. But what are the three millions of 'peeled Africans' to think of the complacent 'moderation' of these magnanimous 'compromisers' of principle! What are we, the five millions of non-slaveholders of the South, to think of these 'moderate' gentlemen whose 'courtly complaisance' subjects us to an almost equal servitude!"

Cash drew a scene of Daniel Webster and John C. Calhoun on a sinking ship, his own version of a *Moby-Dick*–like plot as a duel (a year before the novel was published), drawing from Webster's speech the metaphor of a "wreck." "I imagine you and Mr. Calhoun amid 'the storm'; and you have both laid hands upon that 'fragment of a wreck' which is only large enough to save one from death." They hack at each other with knives, cutting each other's limbs off, "an arm—then a leg—and, at last, the death struggle! Such is the game of slavery and freedom. One or the other must die!"

Cassius Clay was not inclined to scriptural fundamentalism of any kind. Just as he invoked a higher law against Christian apologetics for slavery fortified with biblical verses, he marched straight into the sanctum of the holy of holies and flung off the purple coverlet of original intent from the Constitution, not to worship its parchment but to reveal it as a political document. "The war began with the Constitution; or, rather, the war began before the Constitution—which is, at best, as interpreted now, but a truce, not a treaty, of peace. . . . Those who had just made solemn avowals to the world of the right of all men to life, liberty, and the pursuit of happiness, were ashamed to put the word slavery in the Constitution. Washington and others looked forward to an early extinction of slavery as a fixed fact." But that original benign and complacent intention had dimmed. "The main cause of the abandonment by the South of the faith of our fathers is, as you state it, the increase of the cotton crop. But this cause has passed north of Mason and Dixon's line, and produced a change of tone in both free and slave States." He cast Webster's defense of the Compromise as the most contemptible form of rhetoric, the brilliant orator as a sophist.

> The cause is one thing; the justification is another. Your defense of the South is characteristic of the legal profession. What are truth and right in the face of one hundred millions of dollars? That which was a curse, a wrong, and a sin, in 1787, by one hundred millions of dollars, in 1850, is converted into a blessing, a right, and a religious charity. . . . As much as I abhor slavery, I abhor the defense more. One strikes down the liberty of the African; the other, mine. . . . This "political necessity" is the father of murder, of robbery, and all religious and governmental tyranny. This is the damnable doctrine upon which was built the inquisition, the star-chamber, and the guillotine. No, sir; that which is a fault in individuals, is a crime in governments. We can guard against the danger of a single assassin, but a government is irresistible and immortal in its criminal inflictions.

After the new state constitution and the Compromise, Cash gathered up the remnants of the Emancipation Party to run for governor in 1851, an act of vengeance against the Whigs, who had lost both head and heart, defaulting to either pro-slavery or milquetoast positions. He envisioned himself establishing a new organization. "I think I see the elements of a truly national liberty party brewing," he wrote Seward. "The True Democracy must be the name, since the Whigs have become the guardians of slavery." His idea of somehow realigning the Democratic Party was more in tune with Chase's political theme than Seward's, which still reflected Seward's belief that the Whigs, at least their Northern wing, must be the basis of antislavery politics. But Cash's conception of a national party was shaped by being on the losing side of the politics of Kentucky, border state and borderline, not New York.

Breckinridge had been at the forefront of the crusade for an antislavery constitution, author of the Emancipation Party's statement at its convention and of a pamphlet that appealed to "the great non-slaveholding interest . . . with the hope of substituting the race of negro slaves with the race of free whites," but he was defeated for delegate. Despairing, he declined to lend himself to Cash's latest venture. "Having proved myself faithful to my convictions," he said, "I shall now prove myself faithful to the Commonwealth." He decided instead to devote himself as the state superintendent of public instruction and became the father of Kentucky's public school system.

Whigs mostly derided Cash's campaign for governor as eccentric radicalism, "perfectly harmless," but they underestimated his capacity for mischief while overestimating their own appeal. Whig turnout fell off the cliff, so that while Cash attracted only 3,621 votes, fewer than had voted for antislavery delegates in Louisville alone two years earlier, it was sufficient to tip the election to the Democrat, who won by a margin of 850. "Thus, and forever, fell the Whig Party in Kentucky," wrote Cassius Clay. No Whig was ever again elected governor. Kentucky, which Henry Clay had projected as the vanguard of gradual emancipation, instead became the forerunner of the collapse of the Southern Whig Party and consolidation of pro-slavery forces throughout the South.

Cassius Clay gave up on the fate of Kentucky and threw himself into abolitionist politics in the North. On his travels, encountering educated and articulate free blacks, his views on race became more muddled. He had believed, like all but a very few abolitionists, that blacks were inferior. "God has made them for the sun and the banana!" he once wrote. But he came to reject his earlier views as "the force of habit and prejudice." At his mansion White Hall he sometimes dined with his former slaves, while his white employees, who refused to be seated, did "not object to wait upon them civilly." And he recalled being toasted at "a dinner party of the aristocratic blacks": "Ladies and gentlemen, please fill up your glasses; let us drink to the health of Cassius M. Clay—Liberator. Though he has a white skin, he has a very black heart."

Abraham Lincoln arrived in Lexington in late October 1849 amid the constitutional convention's proceedings to pursue the interests of the Todd family in their late father's lawsuit against Wickliffe. He had visited Kentucky, where he had spent the first seven years of his life, twice before, once as the guest of his friend Joshua Speed and again to meet his new wife's family. Now he found himself thrust into the vortex of his native state's politics, turned into mortal combat between antislavery and pro-slavery forces over Kentucky's constitution.

The plague was over. It had run its lethal course through the hot summer and taken its last victim. Grass had grown on Main Street, the windows of closed stores were caked in grime, and black mourning crepe hung from many houses. Mary came with Lincoln, undoubtedly to see her sisters and relatives, and to mourn and reminisce. She left no record of her visit, but she was unusually well-informed and politically engaged, emotionally volatile, and likely had the strongest feelings about the circumstances surrounding the death of her beloved father whose affection she had spent her life seeking. He had been a commanding figure, a prosperous and respected pillar of the community, friend of Henry Clay, the man who would be president, and if Todd was somewhat neglectful of his daughter he was kind, lending her and her husband financial support, even throwing Lincoln some of his business. In politics and philanthropy Todd had stood on the high ground of benevolence, for restricting slavery, gradual emancipation, and a member of the American Colonization Society. But his defenses faltered at last against the unceasing onslaught of Wickliffe. Demonized as an "abolitionist," he became exhausted, succumbing to cholera.

At first glance, the convoluted case of *Todd Heirs v. Wickliffe* seemed like *Jarndyce v. Jarndyce* from Dickens's *Bleak House*. A year before, Robert Todd had filed a suit against Robert Wickliffe, the Old Duke, claiming that he had illegally taken the property of Todd's cousin, Mary "Polly" Owen Todd Russell, after she had become Wickliffe's second wife. When her father, John Todd, died in 1783, she had become the sole inheritor of his estate and the wealthiest woman in Kentucky. Her first marriage, to James Russell, lasted only three years before he died in 1802, leaving her with a son, John, who died as a young man. Wickliffe and Polly married in 1826, but produced no offspring. Robert S. Todd had managed her estate before her marriage. After her death, he claimed that she had inherited her fortune on the basis of her father's will that stipulated that if she had no living heirs the estate would be divided among the descendants of John Todd's brothers. But that will was missing, perhaps lost in a courthouse fire, or, Breckinridge suggested, destroyed by Wickliffe.

In his brief Wickliffe pretended he did not know Mary. "Defendant states," he declared about John Todd's children, "that he does not know them so as to admit or deny their names or relationship," conceding that Todd "did have a daughter he thinks they called Mary who he understands married a member of Congress, his name not recollected." Mary, in fact, was like another daughter in his household, best friend of his daughter, Margaret. They had been roommates at Madame Mentelle's Boarding School and remained close. As recently as a year earlier, when Mary stayed with her father while Lincoln served in the Congress, Lincoln wrote her, warning against their friendship. "I wish you to enjoy yourself in every possible way; but is there no danger of wounding the distant feelings of your good father, by being so openly intimate with the Wickliffe family?"

Breckinridge was Todd's long-standing ally in his war with Wickliffe in which the personal and the political merged. Todd helped pay for publication of Breckinridge's polemical pamphlets against Wickliffe and distributed them at his store. In them, Breckinridge composed baroque insults to accuse Wickliffe of stealing Polly's inheritance—"that horrible degradation incurred by having betrayed the interests of a friend's family, slandered the characters of a friend's children, labored to produce dissention amongst a friend's descendants, traduced the good name of a friend's family, blackened a departed friend's character, and to crown all, sported with the feelings and name of the wife of that friend's bosom after having done your uttermost to break her heart. Have you, sir, a friend: Has your selfishness, your avarice, your violence, your insolence, your faithlessness, left to you one person, who cherishes towards you a firm, disinterested, enduring love?" Breckinridge wrote that "Robert S. Todd, Esq. of Lexington," held "the original letters, and exhibits" to prove it. Wickliffe replied at length and in kind with his own vituperative pamphlets. "Black and unmanly is the heart, who, to reach the husband, basely involves the innocent wife," he blasted.

Robert Jefferson Breckinridge

Exactly what Lincoln knew about the sordid background of the case before he arrived to secure his wife's family's honor and fortune was unclear, but as he sifted through the evidence he would have certainly discovered a dark secret rooted in the gothic realities of race, sex, and caste. He likely would have learned it from Todd's lawyer, George "Old Buster" Robertson, former congressman and former chief justice of the Kentucky Supreme Court, or Breckinridge, or both. The essence of Todd's claim was that Wickliffe had coerced his wife to hand over her properties to him once she married. Polly was a kindly believer in individual emancipation and colonization, and wished to free two slaves inherited from her grandmother for whom she had special regard, and to pay for their colonization to Liberia. But, according to Todd, Wickliffe blocked his wife's desire until she had relinquished control to him of her wealth, which encompassed the Todd ancestral home. If this was the extent of Todd's complaint it would have amounted to an accusation of greed, blackmail, and dishonor. But that was merely the surface of the charge.

There was, in fact, a living heir. He was not, however, considered a person under the law. In 1816, Polly's only child, her sixteen-year-old son, John Todd Russell, spent the summer with his grandmother, Jane Hawkins Todd Irvine, whose house servant, fifteen-year-old Milly, an octoroon she had educated, was described as "a young woman of refined manners, who bore little evidence of her Ethiopian blood." The young man conducted an affair with the young slave. In the fall, he left to attend Princeton; in the spring, she gave birth to a boy who appeared white. The child was named Alfred Francis Russell. When John Todd Russell died at the age of twenty-two, his mother sought to purchase Milly and Alfred, who were formally owned by her uncle. He would not part with them until he "extorted" the exorbitant sum of $1,200. Polly helped raise Alfred within her own home, presented to others not as a slave child but that of a friend. Upon marrying Wickliffe in 1826, her property became his, but she emancipated Milly, Alfred, and five other slaves, and paid their way to Liberia.

Breckinridge had exposed the scandal of Alfred's existence, though not his name, in 1843 in a polemic against Wickliffe. This secret was at the heart of the charge against Wickliffe because he supposedly bullied Polly to deliver her estate to him through marriage in exchange for the freedom of her grandson and his mother. "Moreover sir," wrote Breckinridge, "if amongst those slaves there was a fine lad who though held in nominal bondage, was in reality nearly white, and who had always been treated as the child of a friend rather than as a slave; if it is true that this boy, was, though the illegitimate yet the acknowledged son of the unquestioned heir-male of these great estates, and that his father in his last sickness did what he considered necessary to insure the future freedom and respectability of the child; if this last descendant of the original proprietor became by your marriage, your slave; then indeed, it is less difficult to read the mystery of these remarkable deeds, and to comprehend how the fee of a vast estate and the dower of one still greater, might be paid as the price of the liberty of a handful of bondmen." The "mystery" was nothing more than extortion. "The last reputed descendant of John Todd, if he still lives, is in poverty on the barbarous shores of Africa," wrote Breckinridge, "while the immense inheritance . . . is in the process of going by 'a descent through your blood,' 'into stranger hands.' "

The source of Breckinridge's disclosure inevitably could only have been the man sponsoring and circulating his pamphlets, cited as his attorney in this matter, identified as the safe-keeper of all the evidence, acknowledged as his friend, the manager of Polly's estate, her close relative who would have had intimate knowledge, and had motive for Breckinridge to reveal it—Robert S. Todd. He would not have given the information to Breckinridge if he did not believe it himself. Breckinridge's pamphlet was the product of collaboration. And Wickliffe publicly pointed to Todd as the scandalmonger.

In his first pamphlet attacking Breckinridge, Wickliffe had said he was "instigated by the devil," covered with "the stench of slander," and "a baron of brothels." But these were niceties compared to his new publication entitled "A Further Reply of Robert Wickliffe, to the Billingsgate Abuse of Robert Judas Breckinridge, Otherwise Called Robert Jefferson Breckinridge," painting a picture of the worst figure he could draw—the Jewish betrayer of Jesus. Breckinridge's agitation for emancipation made him nothing less than the man who gave up Jesus for crucifixion, "a downcast, sly, doggish countenance, with a pair of huge whiskers, treating with the Jews for thirty pieces of silver to betray the Saviour." While Wickliffe wrote he had "no drawing" of Breckinridge "negotiating with the universal emancipation society," the face of Judas "kissing the Saviour, and slyly handing him over to a Roman soldier," resembled that of Breckinridge "when he salutes a former companion at faro and poker."

The true father of Alfred Francis Russell and Milly's lover, Wickliffe claimed, was not John Todd Russell, but Breckinridge. "I do not pretend to say that Judas is a stranger to Miss Milly," who had fixed his bed "while he was in it." Wickliffe also accused the "Libertine" and "brothel debater" of having "sired" two "almost white" children of another "beautiful mulatto" named Louisa, with "a heaving bosom, and lips, a little thick to be sure, but panting most amorously." Though Wickliffe admitted that Milly had not named Breckinridge, he insisted that should not distract from Breckinridge's "fame as a bocanegra"—literally "black mouth" in Spanish, an expression meaning a lascivious evil speaker.

When Todd filed his lawsuit five years later in 1848, Wickliffe answered that "the said Robert S. Todd cherished undying hatred against this defendant, believing that but for him the estate sued for would have been secured to him," and that Todd was responsible for spreading the story that Polly made "her own grandchild his slave" and "extorted from her a deed of all her property to rescue the boy Alfred, the child of her deceased son, from defendant's ownership." Tellingly, Wickliffe seemed to admit that the scurrilous tale was true, refusing to categorically deny it, stating "that the story of the boy Alfred, whether true or false, was promulgated to ruin the peace and happiness of his wife," and blamed Todd for her death, that "with this malignant shaft in the bruised heart of the victim, his wife sunk into an untimely grave."

Lincoln sat with Judge Robertson in his Lexington law office taking depositions. It went badly, especially the damaging testimony of Charlotte Mentelle, Mary's old teacher and Polly's closest friend, who declared that rather than Wickliffe being coercive "he made her happy." In her memoir of Polly, Madame Mentelle explained, "As to a mixture of the two races, it never could enter her unsullied mind. Yellow people she considered the offspring of vice." According to Mentelle, Polly was shocked when she read Breckinridge's pamphlet "in which a paragraph alluded to her son, and coupled his name with a vice for which she had no indulgence, however lightly some people may think of it. . . . It cannot be understood how and in what manner the blow struck her. That son whose name had not been pronounced for years, without her leading to it; whose image was entombed in her heart as in a holy temple, and that temple desecrated!" According to Mentelle, she lost the will to live. As it happened, Madame Mentelle lived in a large house deeded to her for her lifetime by her dear friend and patron Polly, a bequest maintained by Wickliffe.

Margaret Wickliffe, Mary Todd's best friend, also testified in support of her father, confirming Mentelle's version. "My mother seemed cheerful and happy until the publication in regard to her son—she was deeply affected by it, and her health declined. She told me, that she never had a suspicion that Alfred was the son, of her son, John Todd Russell. I asked her one day, 'Why it was that she took less interest in her flowers than she had done?' She told me she had lost interest in everything since the assault Mr. Breckinridge had made upon the reputation of her dead son." Margaret rejected the naive sentimental views of emancipation of her mother and embraced the harsh politics of her stepfather. By then she had married William Preston, scion of a First Family of Kentucky, a large landowner and lawyer from Louisville, and elected a pro-slavery delegate to the constitutional convention. The Prestons, originally from Virginia, were a far-flung politically connected clan, including congressmen, senators, governors, cabinet members, and distantly Francis Preston Blair, a Democratic power broker since he was part of Andrew Jackson's Kitchen Cabinet.

Their case floundering, Lincoln and Robertson tried to change the subject to the missing will. Mary's grandmother, Elizabeth Parker, and the Reverend John Stuart, the father of Lincoln's first law partner, John Todd Stuart, and a Todd relation, testified that they had indeed seen the fabled will before it had probably gone up in smoke in a courthouse fire—in 1803.

Lincoln worked with his co-counsel to wrap up their filing before he left town in November. The court issued its judgment in May 1850, ruling in favor of Wickliffe. Mary's siblings refused to accept the decision and appealed. The case dragged on for nearly a decade, until the Kentucky Court of Appeals ruled in 1858 that Polly was quite competent in making her own decisions and had not been defrauded. Wickliffe bequeathed the Todd ancestral home to his daughter.

Wickliffe died in 1859 on the eve of the Civil War in which his allegiance would have been plain. His daughter and son-in-law were ardently pro-secession. When William Preston returned from serving as ambassador to Spain, he attempted to lead Kentucky out of the Union, but failing at that became a Confederate general, cradling his brother-in-law Albert Sidney Johnston as he bled to death from his wound inflicted while commanding the Confederate army at the Battle of Shiloh.

Cassius Clay gave up on transforming Kentucky into a modern industrial "American Switzerland," his "Kentucky System," instead touring the North to speak against slavery, and would meet Lincoln in Springfield, who had come to hear him deliver an antislavery speech. Cash would help found the Republican Party, seeking its nomination for president in 1856. After he unsuccessfully lobbied to become Lincoln's secretary of war Lincoln appointed him minister to Russia, a man of war sent far off as a diplomat. His idiosyncrasy made impossible his political advancement. Cash uniquely combined his radicalism with a Southern aristocratic temper, quick to violence, both rhetorical and physical, to compel opponents to submit to his superior position, ideological and social. The duelist could not become a politician. His vision was of the future, but his virtues of the past. But it was precisely those flaws that enabled him to hold his instinctive insight into the Southern mind and to understand that once secession had occurred war would be inevitable. Of those who campaigned for Lincoln in 1860, he wrote, "I was the only speaker, so far as I am informed, who always predicted war in case of Democratic defeat; and accepted the issue."

After his defeat running for delegate to the constitutional convention Robert J. Breckinridge wrote lengthy theological tracts between issuing statements about black inferiority to persuade whites to oppose slavery—a "feeble parasite" on "the far higher and more important interests of the white race." In the mid-1850s he turned to anti-Catholic crusading with the Know Nothing Party, blaming immigrants for undermining white native workers. "Americans must rule America," he railed. But when that cause disintegrated, faced in 1860 with a choice between his pro-slavery nephew Vice President John C. Breckinridge, presidential candidate of the Southern Democratic Party, and Abraham Lincoln, he chose Lincoln. With the war's advent his sons divided in joining sides. Breckinridge was thunderstruck by Lincoln's issuance of the Emancipation Proclamation, which he had strongly opposed, but as the war within Kentucky became especially vicious he advised the Union military commander in the state to impose martial law and was anathematized as part of Lincoln's "Secret Inquisition." At the 1864 Republican convention, he delivered the opening address as its temporary chairman. "I myself am here, who have been all my life in a party to myself," Breckinridge proclaimed. "As a Union party I will follow you to the ends of the earth, and to the gates of death!"

James Speed had contempt for the Know Nothing Party, calling it "a secret junto, or clique" that posed "more danger than in slavery." At the war's start he served as the chief mustering officer of volunteers in Kentucky for the Union army. He was elected to the State Senate in 1861, where he was the sole member to vote for a resolution for federal compensation for emancipated slaves. Even that Old Whig position was rejected. The rest, all of them Unionists, opposed emancipation under any terms. After Lincoln's reelection, he appointed Speed the attorney general.

Lincoln was broodingly silent but smoldering for years after his experience as co-counsel in the case of *Todd Heirs*. The tragic death of his father-in-law as he was attempting to preserve the old Kentucky, the aggressive triumphalism of the pro-slavery forces in destroying it, and the definitive loss of the Todd family estate to the leader of that movement, fused in Lincoln's mind. He did not express his intense feelings until the eve of his emergence as the creator of the Illinois Republican Party.

The true heir to Mary "Polly" Owen Todd Russell Wickliffe's estate was the invisible man in *Todd Heirs v. Wickliffe*. Alfred Francis Russell, his mother, Milly, three brothers, and a sister had sailed away from New Orleans to Liberia on the ship *Ajax* in 1833, settling in a district called Clay Ashland, named after Henry Clay and his estate Ashland, and established by the Colonization Society. Alfred, who became an Episcopal minister, wrote a letter to Wickliffe dated April 3, 1855, catching him up on what had transpired since he landed in Africa. "We have suffered in Africa, and suffered greatly," he wrote. "It was so long before we could find Africa out, how to live in it, and what to do to live, that it all most cost us death seeking life." Only one brother survived; Milly died in 1845. The country Alfred encountered bore a curious resemblance to the South he had left. "Coming to Liberia 22 years ago as I did, and becoming we all once thought a crippled youth. With no rich brothers, no recources. Seeing all around me, large families, influential and united & reunited by marriage, holding all the offices in the country & the avanues to every immolument, working everything aparently from hand to hand and into & for each other, and looking upon all else as a third rate thing. Made aney sky dark. This kissing the 'big toe' and this very 'big negro' business. Has to me been the greatest 'night mair' that ever crippled the energies of Liberia, and to this day the roots and limbs of those combined and self-seeking influences, sway a heavy scepter." He felt that despite the promise of a new beginning "the battle of Liberty is still to be won." Alfred had only one request of Wickliffe. He asked, since Wickliffe was retired as a lawyer and none of his sons had followed in his footsteps, whether he could send his law books. "By such a gift as may now be in your power I may remember you in future, and Liberia too may be greatly benefited & blessed." He noted that there would soon be an election in Liberia, but "whither law or unjust force and old office holders is to prevail, I will write you a long letter." He promised also to send Wickliffe some coffee beans from his first crop.

Alfred Francis Russell

In 1878, Alfred Francis Russell was elected the vice president of Liberia, and in 1883 he became the president—Mary Todd's second relation to become a president and the third native of Kentucky to become one after Jefferson Davis and Abraham Lincoln.

CHAPTER TWO

THE CIVIL WAR OF OLD
ROUGH AND READY

The inauguration of Zachary Taylor as the twelfth president on March 5, 1849, was about to transform the Washington that Lincoln had left behind when he concluded his one term in the House of Representatives. At the beginning of his administration the new Whig president, who had been elected on no platform but solely his military laurels, and had no political record or stated opinions, seemed passive and inscrutable. Nobody expected the astonishing turn of events about to happen. New antislavery champions striding onto the scene did not predict it. Even as conflict continued to stir over the Mexican Cession, whether the vast territory gained through the war, and other Western territories as well, would be opened to slav-

Zachary Taylor

ery, no one factored in what the new president might do. Then, startlingly, Old Rough and Ready revealed his determination to halt slavery's expansion by any means necessary, including military force, pledging to lead the army himself to suppress a Southern rebellion. Within months of his taking office, the country appeared to be on the knife's edge of a civil war.

None of the politics unfolding before Taylor disclosed his intentions anticipated them. As antislavery men battled their way through the political thicket they did not suppose that the gruff slave owner from Louisiana, whom they assumed would preside as a pro-slavery figurehead, might harbor ideas of his own, much less radical ones.

"Many causes conspired to diminish our vote," Salmon P. Chase complained about the Free Soil Party turnout in a letter to Charles Sumner immediately after the 1848 election. Chase of Ohio and Sumner of Massachusetts, both leaders of the antislavery cause in their states, had joined forces through the new third party. While Sumner engaged in flights of fancy about the future of the Free Soil Party after its disappointing showing, Chase was more circumspect and forward looking. He was also already immersed in another political campaign—his own for the U.S. Senate seat from Ohio. His tone was characteristically that of a high-minded idealist above the petty intrigues of politics. "I do not *seek* any office:—much less do I *claim* any. I do not even *desire* any," he wrote one of his supporters, Eli Nichols, a lawyer and Underground Railroad conductor, whom he had recruited into his effort, adding piously about the Senate seat that "the reproach of 'sinister motives'—the cheap missile of malignant detraction— would have as little influence in deterring me from accepting it, as similar attacks have had on my past action against slavery." If he were elected, he insisted, it would be only as the result of his dedication to "the cause of Free Democracy." Chase remained attached to the illusion that the Democratic Party would be the instrument to achieve the end of slavery, and he pledged fealty to old Jacksonian economic nostrums in his letter to Nichols, who had close contacts with the Democratic governor and other influential Ohio Democrats. "I am much obliged to Governor [Wilson] Shannon for his kind opinion of me," Chase flattered. His characteristic profession of humility and demurral of ambition belied his plunge into the murky waters of deal making in pursuit of political office.

Chase had begun plotting to capture the Senate seat before Election Day, and had recruited a tight team mostly of journalists to act as his agents. He understood the mechanics of modern publicity. Newspapers were at the center of the antislavery movement. Edward S. Hamlin, a former Whig congressman from the Western Reserve, was close to the most prominent antislavery member of the House of Representatives and Lincoln's boardinghouse mate, Congressman Joshua Giddings. Hamlin had moved from Cleveland, where he edited the Free Soil paper, the *True Democrat* (later to become the Cleveland *Plain Dealer*), to Columbus, the state capital, to edit a newly established newspaper, the *Daily Standard*, which was financed by Chase. He brought along another journalist and politician, John C. Vaughn, who was enlisted to promote Chase. Chase was also secretly funding the *Cincinnati Globe* out of his own bank account. A junior member of his law firm, Stanley Matthews, was working at the same time as editor of the *Herald Philanthropist* in Cincinnati, succeeding abolitionist editor Gamaliel Bailey, and he used the paper to tout Chase while lobbying for him among Democrats. Donn Piatt, from a prominent Cincinnati family, a lawyer and writer for the *Cincinnati Gazette*, joined the Chase effort as a political jack-of-all-trades. A day did not pass without a chorus of newspapers singing Chase's virtues.

More than the Senate seat was at stake. The legislature would also fill two Ohio Supreme Court seats, the chief judgeship for Hamilton County (Cincinnati), dozens of judgeships for other counties, and a host of state jobs. But party control was challenged. The Whigs, without calling a quorum, had gerrymandered House districts in Hamilton County, carving out two Whig districts from the five that were previously all Democratic. The balance of power in the newly constituted House depended on those two seats. Two Whigs and two Democrats from the contested districts appeared in Columbus, sworn in by their respective party officials. In the House, there were thirty-five Democrats, twenty-nine Whigs, and six Free Soil Whigs, who had run on combined tickets and caucused with the Whigs—a deadlock. But there were also two Free Soilers: John Morse, a Conscience Whig partial to Giddings for Senate, and Dr. Norton S. Townshend, attached to Chase. Eli Nichols negotiated with Morse an agreement that he would vote first for Giddings, but that if his bid failed he would support Chase in exchange for getting the Democrats to rescind the state's onerous Black Laws that severely restricted the movement and rights of free blacks. This deal made his vote for Chase a foregone conclusion. By campaigning for the Free Soil Party, Giddings had alienated most of the Whigs, who were hopelessly divided between him, former secretary of the treasury Thomas Ewing, and others. John C. Vaughn, a Whig, but a member of Chase's inner circle, ran as well while writing pro-Chase editorials, drawing a couple of votes, a false-flag candidate who succeeded in further splitting the Whigs and helping Chase. With Giddings unable to gain more than eleven votes at his high-water mark, Morse aligned behind Chase.

Stanley Matthews worked out a plan for the distribution of state offices, Chase wrote the bill to abolish the Black Laws and Edward S. Hamlin presented the secret deal to the most powerful Democrat in Ohio, Samuel Medary. Owner and editor of the *Ohio Statesman* in Columbus, the chief party organ, Medary was known as the "Old Wheelhorse of Democracy," and had been the chairman of the state's delegation to the 1844 Democratic convention, where he delivered it to secure the nomination of James K. Polk. Medary supported the Black Laws, but he wanted control of the state legislature more. With the Democrats in charge, he would continue to hold the lucrative state-printing contract. So the deal was made. (Medary would become one of the most notorious pro-Confederate, Copperhead editors during the war, publishing vicious columns about Lincoln—"for thine is the Power, the niggers and the soldiers.")

Chase's operatives delivered the two Free Soilers to vote to accept the two Democrats from Hamilton County, giving the Democrats in the House parity with the Whigs. When Morse wavered, Chase's men whipped him into line. Then the Free Soilers voted straight with the Democrats, giving them a majority. The Black Laws were repealed; the Democrats got all the jobs they wanted; and Chase, on the fourth ballot, was elected senator. Whigs in Ohio were enraged at the politics that had elevated Chase, anger that lingered for decades. The means of his rise always remained a drag on his higher ambition within a Republican Party that was substantially Whig in origin. Hamlin, for his part, was rewarded with the presidency of the Board of Public Works, and Matthews was made clerk of the Ohio House. (It was the beginning of Matthews's notable career. He would become a U.S. senator and eventually a justice on the U.S. Supreme Court, not least for his services as counsel to Rutherford B. Hayes before the Electoral Commission of 1876 to resolve the disputed presidential election, negotiating the final deal that made Hayes president and effectively ending Reconstruction.)

The newly elected Senator Chase arrived in Washington the day after Taylor's inauguration and was escorted around the Senate by John P. Hale, the antislavery senator from New Hampshire. "I found myself among the most celebrated men of the country. [They] were all there," Chase wrote, adding his inimitable touch of humility: "Genuinely I felt myself insignificant." He was now the third antislavery member, for Senator William Henry Seward had already arrived.

From the beginning of political time for Seward, year one being 1830, he had bonded with Thurlow Weed, first in the Anti-Masonic Party and then in forging the Whig Party of New York. Unlike the affluent and college-educated Seward, Weed rose from a farmer's son to a printer's apprentice, from which ink-stained trade he observed the influence of newspapers. Later, as the editor of the *Albany Evening Journal*, he became a shrewd and subtle power broker referred to as "The Wizard of the Lobby" or "The Dictator." He and Seward, in the phrase of their junior partner, Horace Greeley, comprised "the firm." Since the inception of the national Whig Party, "the firm" was instrumental in nominating each of its presidential candidates: William Henry Harrison in 1840, Henry Clay in 1844, and Zachary Taylor in 1848.

William Henry Seward

In New York, Seward faced opposition to his bid for the Senate from the minions of the new vice president. Millard Fillmore, the former New York state comptroller, had been a dutiful soldier in the Whig political army under the direction of "the firm," but had suddenly emerged as a rival. His followers advanced John A. Collier, a former congressman, as their candidate against Seward. Collier was the one who had nominated Fillmore at the convention as a sop to disappointed Clay supporters and to confound Weed's plan to have Seward eventually named secretary of state, a "coup d'etat," according to Weed. The Fillmore forces attacked Seward on his perceived weak point, his antislavery position, though Fillmore had once been known as antislavery, too. *Whig or Abolition: That's the Question* was the title of an anti-Seward pamphlet published in January 1849. Weed and Seward and their newspaper allies countered with a vigorous pro-Seward campaign. Seward had a majority in the Whig caucus of the New York legislature and therefore a clear path to election, but the Fillmore faction refused to show up in order to prevent a quorum for a vote. To calm the waters, one of Seward's friends, James Watson Webb, editor of the *New York Courier and Enquirer*, suggested that he write a letter that would answer his critics. So Seward pledged his party loyalty, "to which I sustain the most lasting obligations," and declared that while he was for "circumscribing slavery within its present bounds," and that even though for its eventual "removal" he was devoted to methods that were "constitutional, lawful, and peaceful." Weed considered the letter embarrassingly self-abasing, as though produced under the influence of drink—"the last paragraph looks as if it was composed under the Astor House table"—but it did the trick. Seward was elected.

Weed then summoned Seward and Fillmore to his mansion in Albany to forge a pact that all patronage decisions involving New York would be mutually decided. In particular, Fillmore insisted that Collier would receive the plum of naval agent for New York. Arriving in Washington before the inauguration Seward met with Taylor and key members of his cabinet to review patronage appointments. "I have stipulated for time and inaction concerning Marshals, Postmasters, District Attorneys, and there I leave these matters," he wrote Weed on March 1. But during the first week of the administration, Taylor named a few people to jobs on Fillmore's recommendation, infuriating Seward. He went directly to cabinet members, claiming his supremacy in matters relating to New York, having provided the decisive support for Taylor in the decisive state, and secured a number of positions. Now Fillmore was upset. So Seward went to Taylor and won his agreement that all New York jobs must be reviewed by Governor Hamilton Fish as a supposedly neutral figure but who happened to be Seward's protégé, and would confer with him and Weed on each and every prospective jobholder. Fillmore, who was initially promised that as vice president he would participate as an ex officio member of the cabinet, was cut out. All this knife work was accomplished within a week after the inauguration. "The idea of the V.P. being a member of the Cabinet has expired noiselessly," Seward wrote Weed on March 10. "Another week may work out other conclusions, which seem to me equally inevitable." In his next letter, on March 24, Seward wrote mirthfully, "The V.P., with inimitable naivete, has inquired of me when I would leave the city, saying that he should leave when I should take my departure, so as to prevent the jealousies of our friends, respectively." Governor Fish sent a letter confirming the arrangement. Then Seward wrote on March 29 to the lieutenant governor that it "finishes everything. All was ripe for it. It was read by the Secretary of State, before the President and Cabinet, assembled in my own presence. All were satisfied and gratified. New York rose up before them, a great, unanimous, confiding Whig State." Soon a Seward man, not Fillmore's Collier, became naval agent. By May, Seward and Weed had succeeded in inserting their choice into the job of customs collector of Buffalo, the number one federal post in Fillmore's hometown, the ultimate humiliation. "We could put up a cow against a Fillmore nominee and defeat him," openly crowed the *Buffalo Express*, a Weed-controlled newspaper. The vice president, seeking a meeting with the president and secretary of state, was rebuffed; they did not have time for him.

Throughout the summer of 1849, tension over the extension of slavery steadily built across the country. Every Northern state legislature but one endorsed the Wilmot Proviso, which would prohibit slavery in the new territories and every Southern legislature but one denounced it. The Virginia resolution provided the template for the other Southern ones, proclaiming that excluding slavery presented the stark alternatives of either "abject submission to aggression and outrage" or "determined resistance at all hazards and to the last extremity." At a dinner in Charleston held in honor of Senator Andrew Pickens Butler of South Carolina all glasses were raised to toast "Slavery" and "A Southern Confederacy."

On December 3, 1849, the first day of the first session of the 31st Congress, as the curtain rose on the first scene of the House of Representatives electing its speaker, it revealed a shambles. The Whig majority of the last Congress had been lost partly because of the Free Soil schism. But it was also eroded because of the drastic losses suffered among Southern Whigs. In the fall elections of 1849, President Taylor was reported to have said in Pennsylvania that Northerners should have no fear about the spread of slavery and that none of the territory gained from the Mexican War would be carved into slave states. With that, the Southern wing of the Whig Party collapsed. The even 50-50 split between Democrats and Whigs in the South turned into a 41-to-19 preponderance for the Democrats. All seven Southern governorships up for election, moreover, flipped to the Democrats, including in the four states that had just a year earlier gone for Taylor. Southern Whigs began the 31st Congress in an understandable panic.

The new House had 113 Democrats, 108 Whigs, 9 Free Soilers, and 2 Independents (who aligned with the Free Soilers)—a Democratic plurality, but no majority party. The Democrats initially rallied around the rotund figure of Howell Cobb, from Athens, Georgia, one of the wealthiest slave owners in the country, who had distanced himself from the threats of the Southern Rights Ultras and their idol, Senator John C. Calhoun of South

Carolina. The Democrats had now become a party preponderantly of the South, 68 percent of their seats from slave states but only 39 percent from free states. Conversely, the Southern Whigs were drastically reduced in numbers and embattled.

While they were thwarting Calhoun's attempt to form a united Southern bloc around his leadership, they asserted their Southern identity among the Whigs. At the Whig caucus on the evening of December 1, 1849, Congressman Robert Toombs of Georgia proposed a resolution that the party must agree not to raise the issue of abolishing slavery in the District of Columbia, which Congressman Lincoln had done a year earlier, and that the new territories must be completely open to slavery—a reverse Wilmot Proviso, which would prohibit it. The Whig leadership, at the same time under pressure from the Free Soilers, refused to capitulate to this sudden stickup. Toombs and five other Southerners, including Alexander Stephens, who had been a friend of Lincoln's and member of their Whig group they called the Young Indians, announced that they could no longer support Robert C. Winthrop of Massachusetts, the Whig speaker of the house, in his effort to retain the post. So they split from the caucus, voting for Meredith Poindexter Gentry, a phlegmatic undistinguished backbencher and large planter from Tennessee, who held that the Proviso Whigs were pressing "unconstitutional measures," according to Stephens. "These six Whigs clung to Mr. Gentry to the last," he wrote. (Gentry would become a member of the Confederate Congress.)

The Free Soilers rejected Winthrop, too. As the Southerners castigated him as pro-Proviso, the Free Soilers excoriated him as anti-Proviso. Giddings was particularly contemptuous of Winthrop, continuing his vendetta from two years earlier when he refused to vote for him after circulating a false story that Winthrop had urged support for the Mexican War in a Whig caucus. On the early ballots for speaker, the Free Soilers backed the Democrat David Wilmot of Pennsylvania, of the famous Proviso. Northern Democrats drifted away from Howell Cobb, then Southerners divided among several candidates and he fell to a mere five votes by the twenty-eighth ballot. Winthrop steadily rose, nearing a majority. To stop him, Democrats threw themselves behind an anti-Proviso northerner, William J. Brown of Indiana. Giddings scored him as outrageously sleazy: "Neither the moral nor political character of Mr. Brown recommended him to the favor of just and honorable men." But that didn't prevent the other Free Soilers from quietly approaching him to secure a secret pledge that he would support the Proviso and give them choice committee assignments in exchange. On the fortieth ballot, he climbed to within two votes of a majority, backed by a cross-eyed alliance of emancipationists and slave owners.

The Southern Whigs, having no trouble sniffing a corrupt bargain, exposed the under-the-table deal with the Free Soilers, and the two-faced Brown ignominiously withdrew his candidacy. Toombs took the floor to deliver a hot speech, speaking the unspeakable. "I do not, then, hesitate, to avow before this House and the country, and in the presence of the living God, that if by your legislation you seek to drive us from the territories of California and New Mexico, purchased by the common blood and treasure of the whole people, and to abolish slavery in this District, thereby attempting to fix a national degradation upon half the states of this Confederacy, I am for disunion." Stephens followed him to offer his apocalyptic witness. "Before that God who rules the universe, I would rather the Southern country should perish—that all her statesmen and gallant spirits should be buried in honorable graves, than submit for one instant to degradation."

The Brown ploy confounded, his supporters returned to their usual conflict. The Free Soilers retreated to voting for the hopeless Wilmot, while the Democrats whipped their members for Cobb, who was elected speaker on the sixty-third ballot, on December 23, after more than three weeks of deadlock, the first speaker ever to hold the gavel by virtue of a plurality, not a majority. The old center had not held. Instead, the contest over the speakership accelerated the centrifugal disintegration of the Whigs. The Free Soil rump factionalists revealed themselves by turns sternly principled and transparently devious, more intent on punishing their former party than in preventing a Southern Democrat from gaining power, while the Southern Whigs in their panic over their political peril were willing to enable a Democratic victory, so long as it was a Southern victory, and to use the scare tactic of ranting about "disunion." Both the Senate and the House were now in the hands of the Democrats, ready to harass the new Whig president.

Horace Mann, who succeeded John Quincy Adams in his congressional seat, and bridged the Whigs and the Free Soilers, despaired.

> Howell Cobb is Speaker; one of the fiercest, sternest, strongest pro-slavery
> men in all the South. He loves slavery. It is his politics and his patriotism,
> his political economy and his religion. And by whom was he allowed to
> be elevated to this important post? By the Free-soilers, who, at any time
> during the last three weeks, ought have prevented it, and who permitted
> it last night when the fact stared them full in the face. Mr. Winthrop was

not unexceptionable, it is true; but what a vast difference between him and a Southern, avowed champion of slavery, with all the South at his back to force him on, and at his ear to minister counsel! How strange is that hate of an evil thing which adopts the very means that secure its triumph! How strange that love of a good thing which destroys it! Now we shall have all pro-slavery committees. All the power of patronage of the Speaker, and it is great, will be on the wrong side; and this has been permitted by those who clamor most against all forbearance toward slavery, when by a breath they might have prevented it.

The day after the Free Soilers in concert with Southern Whigs threw control of the House to the Democrats, President Taylor sent his first and what would turn out to be his last annual message to the Congress. It began with a gaffe that caused general merriment: "We are at peace with all the nations of the world and the rest of mankind." Old Rough and Ready, slight and squat, inelegant and inarticulate, was a Whig by default, and disdained party politics, unlike his avid promoters, who supported him precisely for his image above partisanship. He had carefully run on no platform whatsoever. The anti–Mexican War party had put up the victorious general solely because he could win. Southern Whigs, too, felt "secure under General Taylor," as Alexander Stephens declared, trusting him implicitly because he was a Southerner, the wealthy slave owner of large Louisiana sugar plantations. His enthusiastic backers at the Whig Central Committee saw him as an iconic statue, behind whose image they could perform the usual business of politics and government. They ignored as sheer platitude his few vague remarks made before they coaxed him to run, that he would not be "the slave of a party instead of the chief magistrate of the nation" and that "he would not be the President of a party, but the President of the whole people." They misjudged him completely. He was not, after all, a hollow man without principles, but instead, as he had promised, a president with a truly national perspective. The general saw himself as above politicians, in the mold of Washington, who would shape policy in the whole country's interest as he saw it. He was not so much a Whig as a party of one and would declare that he represented a previously unknown political formation called "Taylor Republicans."

Without public notice Taylor dispatched confidential agents to California and New Mexico to help statehood forces organize to prohibit slavery. California ratified a free state constitution and elected two senators, one of them the antislavery soldier-adventurer John C. Frémont. Now, in his message to the Congress, Taylor proposed that both states skip the territorial phase and be admitted as free. Nearly everyone on all sides was stunned. Politics instantly organized along new lines either for or against the president. Northern Whigs embraced his plan, Southern Whigs felt betrayed, and Calhoun and his followers, after spearheading a resolution through the Mississippi legislature, announced a Southern convention to be held in June in Nashville to defy Taylor, a replay of Calhoun's nullification drama against President Andrew Jackson that had ended with Calhoun's humiliation. Now he planned to outflank and defeat this president.

Seward, intent on securing patronage and influence, had ingratiated himself into Taylor's trust and virtually alone had advance word on his position. He reported to Weed on December 8, two weeks beforehand, "The President will be put on the north side of the Mason's and Dixon's line; and he will not flinch from any duty. Nothing is talked of here but this insane course of the defenders of slavery." Seward had the strategy plotted. "There will be no need of passion or of any demonstration on the part of us who, not frightened at the attempt of disorganization, mean to stand firm on the rights of California and New Mexico to be free. I want that we should show that the virtue of moderation belongs to us."

Shortly after Taylor's election, Henry Clay happened to encounter the president-elect on a steamship on the Mississippi at Baton Rouge near Taylor's plantation. At first, Clay did not recognize the man of the hour, but upon being told that indeed Taylor was onboard he sought him out to tell him he "had grown out of my recognition." Their meeting did not extend beyond a handshake, "only long enough to exchange friendly salutations, without any opportunity to converse on public affairs," Clay wrote. Immediately afterward, the Kentucky legislature elected Clay to the U.S. Senate, returning him to the chamber he had left seven years earlier. In between, he had run for and lost the presidency and tried to regain the nomination and lost. Coming back to Washington, where thirty-eight years before, in 1811, "Harry of the West" had been elected speaker of the house on his first day as congressman, he believed he was reoccupying his rightful place as first among equals. He was seventy-two years old, wracked with chronic bronchitis, a symptom of the tuberculosis that would kill him, his head wreathed with wispy white hair, but he was as astute and charming as ever—and still ambitious. At the least, he expected to be swept into the president's inner circle for counsel to resolve the sectional divisions he had twice before calmed through grand compromises in 1820 and 1833. He was surprised to discover that he was treated with coldness. He imagined that even though he had been a candidate for the nomination against Taylor, party comity ought to prevail. "These people are all civil with me, but nothing more," he wrote his wife. "I think it quite likely that you may be right in supposing that neither I nor my friends will find much favor at Court," he wrote a friend shortly after Taylor was sworn in. "As to myself, having given no just cause for its frowns, I can bear them without difficulty; but the President will be unwise if he neglects or proscribes my friends. Without them, he never could have been elected." But Taylor did not think of himself as a party man.

At the White House New Year's Day reception, Clay was the magnet of attention. "Mr. Clay was there, and his movements carried with them a mass of the visitors," recorded Benjamin Brown French, the former House clerk, in his diary. "Indeed, it seemed to me as if he was 'the observed of all observers' instead of the President. As his tall form passed along the East room, surrounded by a crowd who seemed eager to obtain some notice from him, I could not but think that, after all, he was the idol of the occasion." But Clay never got closer to this White House than formality. Though his reappearance in Washington after so many absent years caused a public sensation, Southern members of the Congress from both parties regarded him with suspicion and fear. Stephens had written John J. Crittenden, now governor of Kentucky, that Clay's election as his replacement in the Senate "ought to be averted," and "more danger to the success of General Taylor's administration is to be dreaded from that source than from all others." Senator Jefferson Davis of Mississippi also wrote Crittenden to express his "regret exceedingly" that Clay, "the evil influence," was to return.

Through January, senators filed a bramble of bills on every contentious slavery question, grinding the Congress to a virtual halt, but Taylor stood aloof from the increasingly chaotic process, adhering to his own plan. The Democratic control of the Congress rendered moot the old Whig theory of a Whig president as a quasi-constitutional monarch directed by the Whig leaders of the Congress. But to Clay this presented a vacuum of leadership in a crisis of disunion for which his legislative talents and experience were uniquely suited. The Great Compromiser, who had arranged the Compromise of 1820, also called the Missouri Compromise, which settled the conflict over slavery arising from the Louisiana Purchase by balancing the admission of Missouri as a slave state with Maine as a free one and drawing a line across the country north of the 30° 60' parallel to prohibit slavery, could once again achieve another great compromise. By offering an all-encompassing proposal he could forge a comprehensive settlement that would last at least another generation. More than his past would be vindicated by his contribution to the future. He would finally resolve the sticking point that had thwarted his deepest desire to become president. His fumbling as the Whig candidate in 1844 over the annexation of Texas and slavery in his contradictory "Alabama letters" would be forgiven or forgotten. The office of the president was closed, but savior of the nation was open. He felt the chill draft of mortality at his back.

On the evening of January 21, Clay braved a cold rain to knock unannounced on the door of Senator Daniel Webster of Massachusetts. Their relationship had been distant and stiff since they had been bitter rivals for the presidency going back to 1840, but now Webster greeted him warmly. The diminutive Taylor had shut out both titans. The administration was funneling patronage in Massachusetts through Abbott Lawrence, who would have been vice president had it not been necessary to pacify the Clay men with Fillmore and was now appointed minister to Britain. Webster had personally lobbied Clayton and other officials to appoint his son, Fletcher Webster, as the U.S. attorney for Massachusetts, but his request was denied. "No disappointment to myself could come half so near my heart," he wrote a friend. After protesting to Taylor that his choice for the post was "coarse-grained," undoubtedly received as a personal insult, Webster's son was at last given the consolation prize of surveyor of the port of Boston. Clay was bestowed only one job, for his son James, but only after he humiliatingly wrote a beseeching letter to Taylor was James named chargé d'affaires for Portugal. Did Clay's service as secretary of state in the administration of John Quincy Adams count for nothing with a Whig president? The two Whig giants of their generation, both former secretaries of state, refused to believe they were anachronisms, but still believed in the marrow of their aging bones that they were set there to rule over a figurehead Whig president.

"Mr. Clay seemed to be very feeble," according to Webster, "had a very bad cough, and became quite exhausted during the interview; that he had no doubt it was Mr. Clay's anxious desire to accomplish something for the good of the country during the little time he had left upon earth."

Clay laid out for Webster his scheme, a solution not to each problem but to the whole crisis. California would be admitted as a free state. New Mexico and Utah, where slavery did not exist, would become territories, and whether they were slave or free states would be decided under the doctrine of popular sovereignty. The federal government would assume the debt of Texas, left from its days as a republic, and in exchange its western border would be fixed so that it would not, as it insisted, annex most of New Mexico, thereby putting it under slavery. Slavery in the District of Columbia would be protected, ending the agitation of recent bills filed in the last Congress, not least by "the member from Illinois," but the slave trade there prohibited, moved across the river to Alexandria. And the federal government would assume the task of capturing fugitive slaves, given that many Northern state governments no longer would do so.

When Clay had finished, Webster was persuaded. For the first time in years they would join forces. About New Mexico, he observed "she will no more have slavery than California." (In 1859, in fact, the territorial legislature of New Mexico under Southern influence adopted slavery; it was not admitted as a state until 1912, along with its former western part, Arizona. Utah, the other territory at issue, was not admitted until 1896, when it formally at least outlawed polygamy.) Webster thought that a coalition of Democrats and Southern Whigs could be mustered to pass the bill. Despite the inevitable criticism, he remarked "he could adopt the whole of it" and "he would devote himself to this cause in the Senate, no matter what might befall himself at the North."

Clay tested his policies with a number of senators and when he rose to introduce his resolutions on January 29 they were already well known. It was also known that this would be a brief speech to be followed by a major address a week later, scheduled for February 5. Clay was visibly frail, stretching to the limits of his stamina. None of his remarks were directed to the South. The entire thrust was aimed at the Northern Whigs, his rhetoric carefully framed to convince them that they had already won the debate and to appeal to their "magnanimity." All of the new territories, he projected, would be free. "I do believe that not within one foot of the territory acquired by us from Mexico will slavery ever be planted, and I believe it could not be done even by the force and power of public authority." He had not a good word to say about slavery, not that it was a "positive good" or the "cornerstone" of civilization. "Sir, it is a great mistake at the North, if they suppose that gentlemen living in the slave States look upon one who is a regular trader in slaves with any particular favor or kindness. They are often—sometimes unjustly, perhaps—excluded from social intercourse. I have known some memorable instances of this sort." He shared the antislavery repugnance for the trader and the sense of disgrace for its presence in the capital. Slave coffles shuffling past the Capitol offended him, too. "Let the slave dealer, who chooses to collect his slaves in Virginia and Maryland, go to these places; let him not come here and establish his jails and put on his chains, and sometimes shock the sensibilities of our nature by a long train of slaves passing through that avenue leading from this Capitol to the house of the Chief Magistrate of one of the most glorious Republics that ever existed. Why should he not do it? Sir, I am sure I speak the sentiments of every Southern man, and every man coming from the slave States, when I say let it terminate, and that it is an abomination; that there is no occasion for it; it ought no longer to be tolerated." He pleaded that the North must give way to conciliate, understanding that it was losing nothing in the bargain. "On your side it is a sentiment without sacrifice, a sentiment without danger, a sentiment without hazard, without peril, without loss."

Clay held up a piece of burnished wood, a gift to him of a fragment from Washington's coffin. Those in the chamber were aware of the fragility of the speaker, now invoking an authority beyond death. "It was a warning voice coming from the grave to the Congress now in session," said Clay, "to beware, to pause, to reflect before they lend themselves to any purposes which shall destroy that Union which was cemented by his exertions and example. Sir, I hope an impression may be made on your mind such as that which was made on mine by the reception of this precious relic." It was on this ancient timber that the ship of state would sail into safe harbor.

With his solemn invocation of the father of the country Clay set the stage for his elaborate speech scheduled the following week. But rather than allow the elder statesman to make his case undisturbed, one after another of the Southern Democrats challenged him. When he spoke of his plan for the Union, he was charged with betraying slavery and being unpatriotic toward the South. Senator Henry S. Foote of Mississippi reminded Clay he had supported slavery in the District in 1836 and that his current proposal was "a violation of the principle of good faith toward all the slave states." Senator James M. Mason of Virginia, close to Calhoun, who had introduced the Fugitive Slave Act, declared it "to be my duty to enter a decided protest on the part of Virginia against such doctrines."

Senator Jefferson Davis of Mississippi turned his contemptuous gaze toward Clay as the number one enemy of Southern rights. "In an evil hour some of the most distinguished of southern statesmen admitted that slavery was an evil," he wrote his personal physician in a letter on June 10, 1849. "This as it is construed takes from us all ground of defense." Clay "not only

warrants the attempts of others for its abolition but also demands of us constant efforts to remove the obstacles to its abatement."

On the floor of the Senate, Davis posed his idol Calhoun against his devil
Clay, not in the present debate, but instead from 1838. He read aloud Calhoun's resolutions twelve years earlier about the inviolability of slavery in the
District and how Clay had agreed that they were "a just cause of alarm to the
people of the slaveholding States, and have a direct and inevitable tendency
to disturb and endanger the Union." Clay was not only at war with his past,
according to Davis, but also with the South.

"Now," Davis stated, "an honorable and distinguished Senator, to whom
the country has been induced to look for something that would heal the
existing dissensions, instead of raising new barriers against encroachment,
dashes down those heretofore erected and augments the existing danger. A
representative from one of the slaveholding States raises his voice for the first
time in disregard of this admitted right." Clay was guilty of hypocrisy and
betrayal, a Southern man who had gone back on his word and tarnished his
honor, a charge of the sort that was nearly a provocation to a duel. There
would be no duel, of course, though Clay and Davis had been involved in
them in the past. Instead, Davis meant to produce the outcome of the duel
without the firing of pistols at ten paces. He wanted to strike down the old
man. His speech was the verbal equivalent of a caning.

Clay's claim, according to Davis, "that slavery would never, under any
circumstances, be established in California" was, "though stated as a fact,"
nothing "but a mere opinion," and an "erroneous and injurious opinion" at
that. Clay's insistence on admitting California as a free state, restricting slave
owners from bringing their property anywhere they wished, was more than
an affront to the South; it was an offense against nature. "The European
races now engaged in working the mines of California sink under the burning heat and sudden changes of the climate, to which the African race are
altogether better adapted. The production of rice, sugar, and cotton is no
better adapted to slave labor than the digging, washing, and quarrying of the
gold mines."

On and on Davis went with rising vehemence, seeking to provoke Clay.
"The Senator has said that he will enter upon the argument whenever I
choose to do so." "I do not choose to give way at present," replied Clay. "Now
is the time to enter upon the argument," hectored Davis. "Not until I am
done," said Clay, feeling compelled to defend his honor as a Southern man.
"I am reminded of my coming from a slave State. I tell the Senator from Mis-

sissippi, and I tell the Senator from Virginia, that I know my duty, and that I mean to express the opinions that I entertain, fearless of all mankind. . . . I am extremely sorry that this premature, and—allow me to say—in my opinion unnecessary discussion has taken place." And he observed at a future time he would demonstrate "that there is not the slightest discrepancy in my course in 1838 and now."

Jefferson Davis's dredging up the bitter clash between Calhoun and Clay from another era intended to damage Clay's character, change the subject from his new resolutions, and vindicate Calhoun—a tactic probably suggested to Davis by Calhoun. In lashing Clay, Davis omitted the context, the facts, and the result.

In 1838, both Clay and Calhoun were contending for the presidency. After Clay had successfully opposed Calhoun's effort to prohibit abolitionist literature from circulating through the mail, Calhoun offered pro-slavery resolutions to tar him as pro-abolitionist. Clay offered his own alternatives, outflanking Calhoun while maintaining his opposition to his call for suppression, dismissing Calhoun's maneuver as "the most unprofitable discussion that ever engrossed the attention of a deliberative body." Then, in March 1838, Clay ridiculed the unbendable Calhoun for suddenly performing a pirouette to embrace the opportunistic Martin Van Buren. Calhoun literally stamped his foot. "I, who have changed no opinion, abandoned no principle, and deserted no party. . . . I stamp it with scorn in the dust." He and Clay had launched their careers together as friends and allies when as war hawks for the War of 1812 Speaker of the House Clay had named the newly elected congressman the chairman of the Foreign Relations Committee. "We concur now in nothing," Calhoun declared. "We separate forever." Days later, Calhoun belittled Clay for forging the Compromise of 1833 to end the nullification crisis Calhoun had instigated. "Events had placed him flat on his back, and he had no way to recover himself but by compromise I had the mastery over him on that occasion." "The senator says," replied Clay, "I was flat on my back, and that he was my master. Sir, I would not own him as a slave." The crowd gathered in the gallery of the Old Senate Chamber shook with peals of laughter. "He MY master!" Clay continued. "And I compelled by HIM!" The audience broke into wild cheering. Calhoun was engulfed in howls of derision. "I believe," Clay wrote afterward, "he will die a traitor or a madman."

Jefferson Davis, Calhoun's surrogate, was attempting to humiliate Clay by distorting the incident in which Clay had humiliated Calhoun. "Several times he has regretted this premature discussion; but pray, sir, who introduced it?" Davis argued for the radical position of extending the boundary line between slave and free states established by the Missouri Compromise of 1820 to the Pacific, claiming New Mexico and half of California for slavery. "Anything less would be founded in fraud." Again he pressed that "whenever" Clay "chooses to make his argument I shall be ready to meet it." It was at this point that Senator William R. King of Alabama, a former diplomat, a Southerner from the establishment center of the Democratic Party, who wanted to put an end to Davis doing the bidding of Calhoun, tried to intervene. "I regret that this discussion has sprung up," he said. "I think it has been characterized by a little more feeling than the occasion has called for." But Davis's salvo, catching Clay off-guard and putting him on the defensive, cast him as bending to the North and punishing the South, and polarized the Senate. With this assault, Jefferson Davis did not quell Clay, but he accomplished something greater for himself—he laid claim to the mantle of Calhoun.

On February 5, Clay had to be helped up the Capitol steps, stopping several times to catch his breath, and guided to the Old Senate Chamber, where he would deliver his major address, his words infusing him with the stamina to speak for hours over two days. The White House, he warned, was "in danger of conflagration." The flames of "passion, passion" were dividing the country and the Senate. "At this moment, we have in the legislative bodies of this Capitol, and in the States, twenty-odd furnaces in full blast in generating heat, and passion, and intemperance, and diffusing them throughout the whole extent of this broad land." He implored his fellow senators "to repress the ardor of these passions—to look at their country at this crisis—to listen to the voice of reason."

Clay's speech appealed to the South, as his earlier one had tilted to the North, trying to allay the alienation produced by his first effort. He would not tolerate touching slavery where it already existed. "I am ready to say that if Congress were to attack within the States the institution of slavery, with the purpose of the overthrow or the extinction of slavery, then, Mr. President, 'my voice would be for war.' " The North, after all, had already won what it wanted, in retrospect making the "excitement" of the past two years over the Wilmot Proviso completely needless. "What do you want?—what do you want?—you who reside in the free States. Do you want that there shall be no slavery introduced into the territories acquired by the war with Mexico? Have you not your desire in California? And in all human probability you will have it in New Mexico also. What more do you want? You have got what is worth more than a thousand Wilmot Provisos."

On the Fugitive Slave Act, he cited the case of a slave owner whose slave escaped to Cincinnati, where he was caught but "rescued by the violence and force of a negro mob." Clay shared in the sense of Southern outrage at the flouting of the law and the menace of an apocryphal "negro mob." "Upon this subject, I do think we have just and serious cause of complaint against the free States. I think that they failed in fulfilling a great obligation; and the failure is precisely upon one of those subjects which, in its nature, is most irritating and inflammatory to those who live in slave States."

After making every argument for his resolutions, reviewing the entire history of the Missouri Compromise, his greatest achievement, and summarizing the nation's progress down to the increase in tonnage of shipping, Clay described the terrible threat of the "dissolution of the Union and war," terms that were "identical and inseparable"—"exterminating wars would follow—not a war of two nor three years, but of interminable duration—an exterminating war would follow, until some Philip or Alexander, some Caesar or Napoleon, would rise to cut the Gordian knot, and solve the problem of the capacity of man for self government, and crush the liberties of both the dissevered portions of this Union. Can you doubt it?" The Senate, he admonished, must "pause," standing "at the edge of the precipice before the fearful and disastrous leap is taken in the yawning abyss below, which will inevitably lead to certain and irretrievable destruction."

Clay had given a bravura performance, exercising the will of his mind over his body, his voice, still mellifluous, never quavering as the hours passed. His depiction of the apocalypse that would destroy the Republic seemed heartfelt coming from the shrunken physical presence of a man obviously beyond earthly ambition. But Clay's former power to direct the Congress almost as its dictator had vanished. The tribune for the nation lacked a pivotal position of power and a

The United States Senate, AD 1850

solid constituency, his elusive middle ground resting ultimately on his desire to recapture his own evanescent past. But even now Clay did not wish to play the prophet; he desperately wanted to be the statesman again.

Yet Clay had succeeded in putting an alternative to Taylor on the table. He interposed himself between the irrational forces of radical North and radical South. Refusing to acknowledge Taylor's authority, he equated him with the fanatical forces tearing the country apart. Clay remained ingrained with the Whig idea of the presidency under the regency of the Congress (to be led by Clay), a secondary branch of government, a notion he formed decades earlier as a reaction to Jackson's assumption of executive powers. Before Taylor, there had never been a living Whig president in office for more than the month the enfeebled Harrison occupied it. The Whigs supported Taylor over Clay as they had chosen Harrison over Clay, to have a shining icon instead of a bruised politician. Clay treated the president as though he was a web-covered portrait hung on the wall, but Taylor was hardly a ghost.

Taylor was furious and combative, in no mood for Clay's Compromise. The victor of the Mexican War would admit the whole of the territories gained as free states—and nothing less. "Old Rough and Ready" had no doubts he was the commander-in-chief. He was prepared to act like another general who had become president, Andrew Jackson. Among the host of wise men of Washington eager to offer him their counsel, the Louisiana slaveholder preferred to rely upon the antislavery senator from New York. "The malcontents of the South mean to be factious; and they expect to compel compromise," Seward reported to Weed on November 30, 1849. "I think the P. as willing to try conclusions with them, as General Jackson was with the Nullifiers." Seward was better informed than Taylor's antagonists. "I saw the P. on Friday," he wrote Weed two days before Clay was scheduled to deliver his major speech. "I had a good occasion and opportunity. I told him that he would get no favor nor forbearance from Congress; that faction would run into sedition; that, having saved the Union, he would be reelected. He understands himself." Taylor would enforce the Wilmot Proviso with or without congressional passage. And he did not hesitate to call in Toombs to inform him. "My course became instantly fixed," Toombs wrote Crittenden after the meeting. "I would not hesitate to oppose the proviso, even to the extent of a dissolution of the Union. The cabinet have intense hostility to Mr. Clay."

A week after Clay spoke, on February 13, Taylor submitted the antislavery constitution of California to the Congress. Southern Whig leaders, Toombs, Stephens, and Thomas Lanier Clingman of North Carolina, marched to the White House to express their opposition unless Taylor permitted slavery in New Mexico and Utah. Senator Hannibal Hamlin of Maine, then a Democrat, passed them as they left on his way to confer with Taylor, whom he found "like an enraged lion." Taylor angrily told Hamlin that the Southerners were attempting to coerce him to concede by their threats. "If there were any such treasonable demonstrations on the part of the Southern leaders and people, he would put it down by the whole power of the government, even if he was obliged to put himself at the head of the army to do it." Taylor roared, "Disunion is treason!" Hamlin recalled, "and with an expletive . . . that if they attempted to carry out their schemes while he was President, they should be dealt with by law as they deserved, and executed."

Thurlow Weed followed Hamlin into the White House to visit Taylor a few minutes later. He found him in a rage. "Did you meet those traitors?" the president demanded, referring to the delegation of Toombs, Stephens, and Clingman that had just left. Taylor told Weed that "if they were taken in rebellion against the Union, he would hang them with less reluctance than he had hung deserters and spies in Mexico!" He added that he regarded his son-in-law, Jefferson Davis, as "the chief conspirator in the scheme." Just as Jackson had threatened to hang Calhoun over nullification, Taylor vowed to hang Davis.

On March 1, Horace Mann dined at the White House, where he had his first astonishing encounter with Taylor. "He really is a most simple-minded old man," he wrote. "He has the least show or pretension about him of any man I ever saw; talks as artlessly as a child about affairs of State, and does not seem to pretend to a knowledge of any thing of which he is ignorant. He is a remarkable man in some respects; and it is remarkable that such a man should be President of the United States." Taylor took control of the discussion, telling Mann that it was impossible for the Union to be destroyed. "I have taken an oath to support it," he said, "and do you think I am going to commit perjury?" He explained that if the South resisted him, he would impose a naval blockade. "I can save the Union without shedding a drop of blood. It is not true, as was reported at the North, that I said I would march an army and subdue them: there would be no need of any." Mann was flabbergasted at what he regarded as Taylor's combination of audacity and naïveté. "And thus he went on talking like a child about his cob-house, and how he would keep the kittens from knocking it over." But Taylor meant every word, and the old general's assessment of the capacity of the South to mount a rebellion was little different than was Jackson's during the nullification crisis.

On the day Taylor submitted the California constitution, Jefferson Davis responded with a two-day marathon speech denouncing its admission as a free state. "If, sir," he concluded on February 14, "this spirit of sectional aggrandizement, or if gentlemen prefer, this love they bear for the African race, shall cause the disruption of these states, the last chapter of our history will be a sad commentary upon the justice and the wisdom of our people."

When Clay rose to speak for California's admission within the scheme of his Compromise, Foote interrupted him to demand how a senator from a slave state could "reconcile" his stand "given all the dangers which menace the southern section of the confederacy." "It is totally unnecessary for the gentleman to remind me of my coming from a slaveholding state," Clay replied. "I know whence I came, and I know my duty; and I am ready to submit to any responsibility which belongs to me as a senator from a slaveholding state. Sir, I have heard something said on this and on a former occasion about allegiance to the South. I know no South—no North—no East—no West, to which I owe any allegiance. My allegiance is to this Union and to my state; but if gentlemen suppose they can exact from me an acknowledgment of allegiance to any ideal or future contemplated confederacy of the South, I here declare that I owe no allegiance to it; nor will I, for one, come under any such allegiance if I can avoid it." Clay's phrase—"I know no North—no South—no East—no West"—would be engraved on his tombstone.

John C. Calhoun had been confined with pneumonia for weeks in his boardinghouse room across from the Capitol. He was suffering the final stages of tuberculosis, wracked by coughing fits, feverish and emaciated. Yet he had arrived in Washington for the 31st Congress with large

John C. Calhoun

plans. He sponsored the Nashville Convention of Southern States scheduled in June to reconsider the future of the Union. He carried with him the completed manuscripts of his *Disquisition on Government* and the nearly finished *Discourse on the Constitution*, his political last will and testament. But he was too ill to attend the Congress to hear Clay's oration. In his room, he dictated his answer. Shortly after noon on March 4, he slowly climbed the Capitol steps with assistance. In the Old Senate Chamber he rose only to announce that Senator James Murray Mason of Virginia would read his speech. He sank his wraithlike frame into his chair, wrapped in a black cloak, only his monumental head visible, his nearly shoulder-length hair stark white, to hear his own words spoken to the Senate.

Calhoun's argument was stiff, abstract, and closed. In style and content it was the opposite of Clay's. Where Clay had been engaging, vivid, and sought to persuade, Calhoun cast a malediction. He offered no evidence, but only conclusions. His speech was the antithesis of a factual presentation from which could be adduced certain conclusions. Instead he massed assumptions driven to a single foretold point. His bleak insight was confirmed by his life's disappointing experience and the history of the country, which to him had become one and the same twisted timber. If the South could not rule, the Union must fall. Calhoun insisted that only the most drastic constitutional revision could save the United States—and he proposed a bizarre proposal that had no chance of ever being enacted, or if it did creating anything other than paralysis, chaos, and further conflict.

"How can the Union be preserved?" Calhoun demanded. Before answering his grave question, he traced the source of division. "It will be found in the belief of the people of the Southern States, as prevalent as the discontent itself, that they cannot remain, as things now are, consistently with honor and safety, in the Union." But the root of their feeling was located deeper, in the "agitation of the slave question on the part of the North, and the many aggressions which they have made on the rights of the South." And the even deeper cause was to be found in the imbalance of "equilibrium between the two sections in the government." Since the beginning of the Republic, the North had excluded the South from three quarters of the new territory acquired, tilting the scales of representation. If the Ordinance of 1787 and the Missouri Compromise had not cordoned slavery, the South would have equal weight with the North. Now the North was grabbing all the territory gained from Mexico for itself, depriving the South "from every foot of it."

The entire North, "every portion," was "more or less hostile" to slavery, condemning it as a "sin" or "crime," "while those who are least opposed and hostile regard it as a blot and a stain on the character of what they call the 'nation.' " It was Calhoun himself who put the word "nation" in quotation marks. "Unless something decisive is done, I again ask, What is to stop this agitation before the great and final object at which it aims—the abolition of slavery in the States—is consummated? Is it, then, not certain that if something is not done to arrest it, the South will be forced to choose between abolition and secession? Indeed, as events are now moving, it will not require the South to secede in order to dissolve the Union. Agitation will of itself effect it, of which its past history furnishes abundant proof."

Compromise, he declared, must be rejected. He had contempt for the word. The "cords" of the Union were about to be "snapped," the result of constant fraying. "It is a great mistake to suppose that disunion can be effected by a single blow. The cords which bind these States together in one common Union are far too numerous and powerful for that. Disunion must be the work of time." There was "but one way" to "save" the Union. "The South asks for justice, simple justice, and less she ought not to take. She has no compromise to offer but the Constitution, and no concession or surrender to make."

Only if a constitutional amendment were passed could the crisis be averted—an amendment that would "restore to the South, in substance, the power she possessed of protecting herself before the equilibrium between the sections was destroyed by the action of this government." But Calhoun did not explain this magic amendment, his demand for the transformation of the Constitution oblique. He was referring to his utopian proposal that no one could possibly guess was lodged in his unpublished manuscript, *Discourse on the Constitution*—a plan for a dual presidency, one representing the North, another from the South, both armed with veto power. Whether the North would adopt his fantasy of a self-negating two-headed executive was the test in his mind that would determine the future of the United States.

The immediate "test question," he stipulated, was California. If it were admitted as a free state, the North would signal "the intention of destroying irretrievably the equilibrium between the two sections. We should be blind not to perceive in that case that your real objects are power and aggrandizement, and infatuated, not to act accordingly." Calhoun's conscience was clear. "Having faithfully done my duty to the best of my ability, both to the Union and my section, throughout this agitation, I shall have the consolation, let what will come, that I am free from all responsibility." Silently listening to the conclusion of his final formal speech, after laying red lines that would inevitably be crossed, he washed his hands of any culpability for the coming civil war.

On March 7, the last of the Triumvirate, Daniel Webster, rose to speak. The Godlike Daniel was not a shadow of his former self like the others, but still the picture of Olympian magnificence draped in his dark blue coat with glistening metal buttons, the uniform of the American Revolution, the most eloquent orator of the age, already immortalized for famous addresses against Calhoun and his states' rights acolytes. Nobody knew what he would say, except Clay. His worshippers in New England believed he would naturally stand with the president, while others conjectured he would propose a bill different from Clay's. From his noble opening lines it seemed that he would reiterate his immortal "Second Reply to Hayne" of 1830, his full-throated defense of Unionism against states' rights in the aftermath of the nullification crisis. "I wish to speak today, not as a Massachusetts man, nor as a Northern man, but as an American, and a member of the Senate of the United States. . . . I speak today for the preservation of the Union. 'Hear me for my cause.' " But his cause was to make Clay's arguments in his own florid style, to pacify the South and to bask in a glow of nostalgia.

After an interminable and pointless review of the history of slavery since the time of the Romans, he reached a contemporary point: the Wilmot Proviso should not be applied to New Mexico. Slavery, he claimed, simply could not exist there. The climate there, after all, was inhospitable, and therefore, according to this atmospheric logic, the Proviso was needless. On fugitive slaves, however, "here is a ground of complaint against the North well founded." He demeaned the whole antislavery movement as "these abolition societies," declaring, "I do not think them useful. I think their operations for the last twenty years have produced nothing good or valuable." Instead, he ridiculed them as a hypocritical joke. "It is my firm opinion this day, that within the last twenty years as much money has been collected and paid to the abolition societies, abolition presses, and abolition lecturers, as would purchase the freedom of every slave man, woman, and child, in the state of Maryland, and send them all to Liberia. I have no doubt of it. But I have yet to learn that the benevolence of these abolition societies has at any time taken that particular turn." The *Congressional Globe* recorded for posterity: "[Laughter.]"

Warming to his peroration, he exclaimed, "Secession! Peaceable secession! Sir, your eyes and mine are never destined to see that miracle. The dismemberment of this vast country without convulsion!" His poetic sense took over. "Sir, he who sees these States, now revolving in harmony around a common center, can expect to see them quit their places and fly off without convulsion, may look the next hour to see the heavenly bodies rush from their spheres and jostle against each other in the realms of space without producing a crash of the universe."

When Webster finished his astronomy lesson, a faint but sharp voice pierced the Senate chamber. "I cannot agree with the Senator from Massachusetts that this Union cannot be dissolved," said Calhoun, suddenly come to life. "Am I to understand him that no degree of oppression, no outrage, no broken faith, can produce the destruction of this Union? Why, sir, if that becomes a fixed fact, it will itself become the great instrument of producing oppression, outrage, and broken faith. No, sir, the Union can be broken." But Webster begged off. "I do not wish to run into a discussion of the nature of this Government. The honorable member and myself have broken lances sufficiently often before on that subject." Nor did Calhoun wish to debate. "I have no desire to do it now." But with his mordant remark he had made his point, which lanced the balloon Webster had spent three and a half hours inflating.

Webster's preamble—"I wish to speak today, not as a Massachusetts man . . ."—would become one of his most famous phrases, but it would be remembered apart from the failure of the rest of his thousands of words to shift any significant Northern sentiment in favor of Clay's Compromise. Rather than creating a sense of unity, Webster had deepened the lines of looming confrontation with the immovable Taylor.

Praised in the South, Webster was damned in the North. "Mr. Webster spoke yesterday; and (can you believe it?) he is a fallen star!" wrote Horace Mann. "Lucifer descending from heaven! We all had the greatest confidence in him. He has disappointed us all. Within a week, I have said, many times, that he had an historic character to preserve and maintain, which must be more to him than any temporary advantage. His intellectual life has been one great epic, and now he has given a vile catastrophe to its closing pages. He has walked for years among the gods, to descend from the empyrean heights, and mingle with mimes and apes! I am overwhelmed." Webster's intellectual influence and moral stature were now ruined among those in New England who had turned to him as their most eloquent statesman, a class unto himself. They had overlooked his fondness for wine and women; they chose not to make scandals out of the lining of his pockets by the State Street banks and firms to finance his luxurious indebtedness. He had always represented their idea of patriotism. But this speech was shockingly devoid of his former principles. It was the apotheosis of the Cotton Whig. Webster had smashed himself on Plymouth Rock.

John Greenleaf Whittier, a founder of the Liberty Party and Free Soil Party, serving as an editor of the *National Era*, was the poet laureate of the antislavery movement, and composed the poem "Ichabod," after the biblical Ichabod, from whom glory had departed. "All else is gone; from those great eyes, The soul has fled; When faith is lost, when honor dies, the man is dead!"

At a packed meeting at Faneuil Hall in Boston on March 25, Theodore Parker, the Transcendentalist minister, presiding as chairman, declared, "I wish we could take a mantle big and black enough, and go backward and cover up the shame of the great man who has fallen in the midst of us, and hide him till his honor and his conscience shall return. But no, it cannot be; his deed is done in the face of the world, and nothing can hide it." Parker demolished Webster's argument that slavery could not exist in California or New Mexico. It had, he reminded his audience, existed in Massachusetts and New Hampshire, and the Ordinance of 1787 was required to prohibit it from the Northwest Territory. "Not exclude slavery from California and New Mexico, because it can never exist there! Why, it was there once, and Mexico abolished it by positive law. Abolished, did I say! We are not so sure of that; I mean, not sure that the Senate of the United States is sure of it. Not a month before Mr. Webster made this very speech, on the 13th and 14th of last February, Mr. Davis, the Senator from Mississippi, maintained that slavery is not abolished in California and New Mexico." (Parker's speech, widely published in antislavery newspapers, was likely read by William H. Herndon, who avidly consumed the writings and sermons of this antislavery source "I consider grander than all the others," and which he avidly shared with his law partner.)

William Seward took the Senate floor on March 11 to deliver the first rebuke from a prominent Northerner to the Compromise—a rebuke to Clay and Webster. It was his maiden speech, but he was not considered a freshman talking out of turn, instead as the former governor of New York and confidential adviser to the president. He was, he announced, for the admission of California—and New Mexico—and any future states—unconditionally. "But it is insisted that the admission of California shall be attended by a compromise of questions which have arisen out of slavery! I am opposed to any such compromise, in any and all the forms in which it has been proposed."

Seward lacked Webster's grandeur, Clay's seductive intimacy, or Calhoun's terrifying glare. His presence was birdlike, his voice not melodious, and his address larded with lengthy classical quotations. Yet he was not a pedant, but an accomplished lawyer who systematically tore apart his opponents' arguments. California was being held hostage under the rubric of a "compromise" based on legally hollow concepts, supposedly to preserve the Union but in fact to protect slavery—"unnecessary and incongruous, and therefore false issues." In order to gain California, "I am, then, to surrender some portion of human freedom in the District of Columbia." The "principle of law" was further traduced in the demand for a Fugitive Slave Act, "unjust, unconstitutional, and immoral."

Seward attacked the idea that slavery was protected under the Constitution. Here he invoked Webster's notion of the federal compact from the nullification debate and laid the groundwork for the future Lincoln of the Cooper Union address. "The right to have a slave implies the right in someone to make the slave; that right must be equal and mutual, and this would resolve society into a state of perpetual war. But if we grant the original equality of the States, and grant also the constitutional recognition of slaves as property, still the argument we are considering fails. Because the States are not parties to the Constitution as States; it is the Constitution of the People of the United States."

Seward penetrated even deeper, in the most brilliant part of his legal argument, cutting to the root of the states' rights premise that slavery was the pillar of legitimacy for a state and therefore must be protected. The Compromise would only validate this tainted idea.

> It assumes that slavery, if not the only institution in a slave State, is at least a ruling institution, and that this characteristic is recognized by the Constitution. But slavery is only one of many institutions there. Freedom is equally an institution there. Slavery is only a temporary, accidental, partial and incongruous one. Freedom, on the contrary, is a perpetual, organic, universal one, in harmony with the Constitution of the United States. The slaveholder himself stands under the protection of the latter, in common with all the free citizens of the State. But it is, moreover, an indispensable institution. You may separate slavery from South Carolina, and the State will still remain; but if you subvert Freedom there, the State will cease to exist. But the principle of this compromise gives complete ascendency in the slave States, and in the Constitution of the United States, to the subordinate, accidental, and incongruous, institution over its paramount antagonist.

Seward demolished the arguments of the great men of the past one after another—Webster's that slavery would not thrive in arid climates; Clay's that the Union faced a mortal threat for which the Compromise was the essential solution; and Calhoun's dogma that the United States was merely a compact of states. Slavery must not be soothed, conceded, or protected as Webster proposed. The Compromise that Clay advocated would ultimately usher in civil war. "Slavery will give way, and must give way, to the salutary instructions of economy, and to the ripening influences of humanity,—that emancipation is inevitable, and is near,—that it may be hastened or hindered, and that whether it be peaceful or violent depends upon the government, whether it be hastened or hindered,—that all measures which justify Slavery or extend it, tend to the consummation of violence,—all that check its extension and abate its strength, tend to its peaceful extirpation."

Then, near his closing, Seward made a mistake. He abandoned his devastating legal reasoning to reach for a poetic touch. It was a political misstep. "The Constitution regulates our stewardship; the Constitution devotes the domain to union, to justice, to defense, to welfare, and to liberty." So far, so prosaic, but he did not stop. "But," he went on, "there is a higher law than the Constitution, which regulates our authority over the domain, and devotes it to the same noble purposes." He sought to explain how this "higher law" applied to new territories: "The territory is a part, no inconsiderable part, of the common heritage of mankind, bestowed upon them by the Creator of the Universe. We are his stewards, and must so discharge our trust as to secure in the highest attainable degree their happiness." The exalted reference to the vague Almighty might have been forgotten in passing as a banal religious offering, but it would not be forgiven. His whole speech would be defined by that one phrase—"higher law"—and haunt his political career down to the fevered convention packed into the Wigwam in Chicago in 1860 where Republicans would decide their presidential nominee.

The reaction to Seward's speech was exactly opposite to Webster's; it was hailed in the North and excoriated in the South. Both acclaim and blame cast him as the nation's chief radical. His political support for Taylor was overshadowed by his moral tribute to a "higher law." "Governor Seward's speech," wrote Horace Greeley in the *Tribune*, "will live longer, be read with more hearty admiration, and exert a more potential and pervading influence on the national mind and character than any other speech of the session." But the attacks on Seward were harsh and pervasive. Even the *Washington Republic*, the administration's mouthpiece, editorialized, "The speech must be disclaimed at once, authoritatively and decidedly." Taylor was reportedly upset, but his relations with Seward remained as friendly as before. The unhappiest man of all was Thurlow Weed, who wrote Seward that he read the speech "with a heavy heart." He believed Seward should just have presented the case for Taylor. He did not understand why he answered Foote's question positively that he would admit California as a slave state. If Seward did not put himself above "reproach and obloquy," he should know "the whole pack will be let loose."

Seward replied to Weed that even if he had not mentioned the "higher law" his critics would have savaged him. "Remember that my dissent on the fugitive slave question alone would have produced the same denunciation, if I had gone, on all the rest, with Mr. Webster." He added prophetically, "This thing is to go on to an end, near a revolution." On that point, offered as an unconvincing excuse to cover his political errors, Seward was prescient. Yet proving him right on the inevitably of being a target, Clay, on May 13, denounced him for conflating the "higher law" and "fugitive slave question." "I allude to that opinion that asserts that there is a higher law—a divine law—a natural law—which entitles a man, under whose roof a runaway has come, to give him assistance, and succor, and hospitality. Where is the difference between receiving and harboring a known fugitive slave, and going to the plantation of his master and stealing him away? A divine law, a natural law! And who are they that venture to tell us what is divine and what is natural law? Where are their credentials of prophecy?" Clay provided the answer: "the parchment from heaven supersedes the parchment from government! Wild, reckless, and abominable theories, which strike at the foundation of all property, and threaten to crush in ruins the fabric of civilized society."

On the evening of March 30, confined in his boardinghouse room, Calhoun wondered aloud whether he might deliver another major address. "If I could have but one hour to speak in the Senate," he said, "I could do more good than on any previous occasion of my life." By the early morning of the 31st he was dead. The Capitol was draped in black. At noon, on April 2, the desks removed from the Old Senate Chamber, pallbearers including Clay, Webster, and Lewis Cass carried the metal coffin to the center of the room, where it was placed on a catafalque. On the podium sat the president, the vice president, and the speaker, while the members of the Senate and the House, the cabinet, and Supreme Court surrounded the bier, to hear Calhoun eulogized by the Senate chaplain: "One of the Princes is fallen!" Clay and Webster and the other great senators decided to forget their hostility in life and praise him in death. But when Webster beckoned Thomas Hart Benton to join the chorus of mourners, he refused. "He is not dead, sir—he is not dead," he said. "There may be no vitality in his body, but there is in his doctrines. . . . Calhoun died with treason in his heart and on his lips."

For three weeks, Calhoun's body was transported through the South, from city to city, like the cortege of a head of state, where elaborate obsequies were staged in each. In Richmond, the somber ceremony featured the governor, legislature, mayor, City Council, and state militia. Similar formal funerals were conducted at Petersburg, Virginia, and Wilmington, North Carolina, until the body finally arrived in Charleston, as church bells pealed for hours, thousands paid respect before the casket displayed at Citadel Square and crowded into City Hall for the last service. Then the body was entombed in the cemetery of St. Philip's Church in a gray stone vault marked with large engraved letters: CALHOUN. Fifteen years later, William Lloyd Garrison, sent to Charleston by Lincoln as a member of the delegation to raise the flag over Fort Sumter, would lay his hand on the gravestone. That day would be April 14, 1865.

Calhoun's funeral did not calm tempers. When his death was announced in the Senate, following the eulogies from Clay and Webster, Thomas Hart Benton turned his back on Webster. The old Jacksonian had opposed the Mexican War, decrying it as aggression to extend slavery, became a vehement opponent of Clay's Compromise, and aligned himself with the Northern Whigs. His son-in-law, John C. Frémont, had just been elected the U.S. senator from California. If any member of the Senate was as irascible and quick to violence as Benton, it was Henry S. Foote, who limped from a bullet received in a duel. He and his fellow Mississippian Jefferson Davis despised each other and had engaged in a shoving match in their boardinghouse. For months Foote had been openly insulting Benton. But he engaged in more than throwing sticks and stones. He successfully managed to get the Democrats to have Benton removed as chairman of the Foreign Relations Committee. On January 16, when he accused Benton of inciting slaves to escape, Benton stormed out of the Senate. "See, he flies as did those deluded sons of Africa," said Foote, comparing him to a "degenerate Roman senator." Foote's taunts became even more personal, violating Senate decorum, calling Benton "a regular ale-house disputant," "coarse and low," and referred to "stains" on his character. "Can I take a cudgel to him here?" bellowed Benton.

The trading of insults went back and forth, until on April 17, while Calhoun's body was making its pilgrimage to its final resting place, Benton assailed Calhoun's "Southern Address" as "agitation" for disunion, crying "wolf" when there was none. Foote had not been a partisan of Calhoun, who was mentor to his rival Jefferson Davis. On the contrary, he had sided with Clay against Calhoun. But now he proclaimed Calhoun's "Southern Address," with which he had previously not agreed, as "holy work," and contrasted the unblemished characters of the signers of Calhoun's "Southern Address" with "their calumniators," designating Benton their chief. Benton suddenly stood, threw back his chair, and advanced on Foote. Another senator grabbed his arm and he started to return to his seat. But Foote pulled out a pistol, leveling it at Benton. Benton stood his ground while Foote retreated with his revolver still pointed. "I have no pistol!" shouted Benton. "I disdain to carry arms! Let him fire! Let the assassin fire!" Benton pulled open his shirt, baring his chest. Foote backed down. Benton was considered the victor. The subsequent investigation by a Senate committee cleared Foote of an assassination attempt, but censured "the practice of carrying arms in the Senate Chamber."

Calhoun's political interment had begun before his death. At the end of the last Congress the Southern Whigs had joined his meetings to unify the South behind him only in order to break up his effort. His last grim speech, delivered with one foot in his grave, had isolated him further. By June, the Nashville Convention, which he had planned as the unveiling of his de facto Southern party, assembled as a ragtag affair. Already feeling was widespread in the South that Calhoun's talk of disunion and the threats of secession were damaging Southern leverage in the face of the unyielding president and inevitable admission of California as a free state—"nothing but a pretext for a deserting of the South and her interests in the hour of danger," editorialized the *Richmond Enquirer* shortly after Calhoun's death.

Nine Southern states sent delegates to Nashville on June 3, but only Mississippi and South Carolina took the exercise seriously. Most of the delegations were skeletal. The host state of Tennessee was distinctly hostile, embarrassingly demonstrated when the legislature voted to deny recognition of the event. The convention passed a platform calling for the line of the Missouri Compromise to be extended to the Pacific and slave property to be allowed in the new territories. What attracted attention was the prominence of "Fire-Eaters" claiming Calhoun's mantle, among them William Lowndes Yancey, an Alabama congressman who had walked out of the Democratic convention of 1848 after it rejected his "Alabama Platform" demanding the extension of slavery to all the new territories, and Robert

Barnwell Rhett of South Carolina, the fire-eating editor of the *Charleston Mercury*, who wrote the official "Address of the Convention," which ended with a bang, proclaiming that slave owners "must rule themselves or perish." The entire effect of the Nashville Convention, however, was a fizzle. Even James Hammond of South Carolina, a Calhoun protégé who attended as a delegate, privately lamented the political mistiming of Rhett's firecracker. "Such men," he wrote, "spoil all movements." "It was an abortion," concluded the abolitionist *National Era*, "and not worth a word of comment." Seward scorned the gathering as "*brutum fulmen*"—"wasted thunder." And yet Southern Rights societies sprang up throughout the Deep South.

President Taylor was in a commanding position. On all sides his opponents' weaknesses were exposed. Days after the Nashville Convention, the Senate overwhelmingly rejected Jefferson Davis's resolution for lengthening the Missouri Compromise line to the Pacific—the Nashville platform cast aside. Foote, who had initially opposed Clay's Compromise, suddenly reversed himself and proposed that a Committee of Thirteen be appointed to handle it. The idea came from Thomas Ritchie, who had recruited Foote as his agent. Ritchie had been Clay's boyhood friend and grown into one of his greatest enemies, filling the columns of the *Richmond Enquirer* with calumnies against him, especially decrying the alleged "corrupt bargain" by which Clay supported John Quincy Adams for president and became secretary of state. Now he instructed Foote to inform Clay that if he would agree to the special committee Ritchie would use his newspaper, the *Washington Union*, founded to be the mouthpiece for President James K. Polk, on his behalf. Clay agreed, desperate for a lifeline and warmly receptive to the end of hostilities with Ritchie. "No one will be surprised to learn," recalled Foote, "that, in a day or two after, Mr. Clay and Mr. Ritchie met, became cordially reconciled to each other, and consulted together often in the most fraternal manner at every stage of the great struggle which at last resulted in the adoption of the Compromise enactments of 1850."

At a private dinner, the odd couple of Clay and Ritchie cemented their new alliance bantering about old wars. "Look here, Mr. Clay," said Ritchie, "if you will really save the Union, we will all forgive you for having had Adams elected in 1825 by 'bargain, intrigue, and management.' " "Shut your mouth!" exclaimed Clay. "Shut your mouth, Tom Ritchie. You know perfectly well that there never was a word of truth in that charge." "Very well, very well," conceded Ritchie, offering a gesture of compromise, "I say to you now, in hearing of this goodly company, that if you succeed in rescuing the

Republic from ruin, and I should survive you, Tom Ritchie will plant a sprig of laurel upon your grave."

Clay cleverly suggested "for various reasons of a very peculiar and delicate character," as Foote put it, that Foote be the one to propose the committee's formation with Clay as chairman. The Committee of Thirteen contained six Southerners, all in favor except for the Ultra Mason and a dissident Whig, and six northerners, all in favor except one, plus Clay as chairman. The committee became the vehicle for the Southerners and their Northern supporters to write a new bill. Ritchie remained in the shadows as a guiding force. In the internal deliberations, the members overruled Clay that Mexican law abolishing slavery should stand in the new territories and instead inserted that territorial legislatures could not forbid it. Thus, the position of the Southern Ultras was incorporated on the absolutely crucial point of the extension of slavery. This was also a rebuke of Senator Lewis Cass of Michigan, who had been the Democratic candidate for president in 1848 and campaigned on his doctrine of "squatter sovereignty" that would leave slavery as a matter to be decided by settlers. Douglas, however, successfully struck out the clause prohibiting legislatures from either establishing or forbidding "African slavery," a little victory for what he called "popular sovereignty" and the price for Northern Democrats supporting the measure.

Introduced on May 8, Taylor ridiculed the bill as an "Omnibus" and encouraged his Senate allies to take the floor to assail it. Clay, the old master, was exhausted and frayed trying to counter amendments, count votes, and muster quorums; his stamina rapidly fading, he reacted to the sort of legislative action that used to invigorate him with displays of ill temper. "He is irritable, impatient, and occasionally overbearing; and he drives people off," Webster observed. Clay attempted to position himself as the true center of debate, fighting against the extremes of Taylor and Seward on the one hand and the Southern Ultras on the other. On May 21, Clay summoned his strength for a major floor speech to answer objections to the bill, attempting to convince the Ultras that their complaints were ill founded and trivial. On the Fugitive Slave Act, he argued that it could only aid the slaveholders—no "inconvenience" at all. "Why, sir, that the slave owner, in the pursuit of his fugitive property, has to carry with him a record! That instead of carrying with him, in pursuit of his slave, at great trouble and expense, witnesses and loose affidavits, he is fortified by an authentic record! That, I say, is an advantage and a protection to the slaveholder—a great advantage." On slavery in the District of Columbia, Clay reassured: "The report neither affirms nor denies the power of Congress to abolish slavery within the District of Columbia. It says that it ought not to be done." As for the prohibition of the slave trade in the District, the bill simply moved it across the Potomac to Alexandria. "Well, what is the inconvenience of it? A slave cannot be brought within this place for sale and be here sold, but a man who wants a slave here may go to the distance of five miles and purchase one, and bring him here, not for sale, but for his own use." He insisted that Southerners had won what they really wanted. "Is there nothing done for the South when there is a total absence of all congressional action on the delicate subject of slavery; when Congress remains passive, neither adopting the Wilmot proviso, on the one hand, nor authorizing the introduction of slavery on the other; when everything is left in status quo. What were the South complaining of all along?" The new territories were still "open . . . to be occupied by slavery, if the people, when they are forming States, shall so decide." Then Clay wheeled to savage the president's position, which he described as "bleeding and threatening the well-being, if not the existence of the body politic."

Despite his rhetorical exertion, Clay was still unable to gather more than one third of the Senate in support. "The Administration, the Abolitionists, the Ultra Southern men, and the timid Whigs of the North are all combined against it," he complained. His histrionic and vitriolic tone, venting his frustration against Taylor, while insisting he stood for peace and conciliation, only hurt his cause. That night Seward dined with three pivotal Democratic senators—Douglas and Shields of Illinois and Jackson Morton of Florida—and wrote Weed that Clay's bill would lose by ten in the Senate. "If Mr. Clay knew how to yield he would separate his bills now." On June 1, Seward wrote that "delay and procrastination are killing the hopes of his abominable bill."

Seward's disgust at Clay, Webster, and the Northern Democrats supporting the Compromise grew day by day as he observed the debate. "Oh!" he wrote on June 11, "how I do despise the Northern recreants who suffer themselves to betray and sell the holiest hopes and interests of freedom under the terror of the [Southern] gasconaders. . . . I grow more and more amazed that Mr. Clay and Mr. Webster, who have seen and heard it all their long lives, should yield to it now when it is only the rehearsal of an old worn-out burlesque of tragedy." But Clay's efforts were exhausting him. "Mr. Clay's 'Omnibus Bill' lingers and drags," Seward wrote on June 20. "He is looking very haggard, and betrays impatience and temper." By the end of the month, Seward was confident the bill would go down to defeat. "The conviction has become a general one that the 'Compromise' will fall," he wrote on June 28. "I saw the President this morning. He is in fine spirits."

Seward delivered his second major speech against the Compromise on July 2, even more pointed than his last, a portent and prophecy. He described how compromise worked as a technique for advancing slavery. "The garment of compromise, thus quilted of various fabrics with artistic skill, is ingeniously pieced out with collateral conditions in a report and two other bills concerning slavery in the District of Columbia, the recapture of fugitive slaves, and other national interests or pretensions of slavery." After detailing how the Compromise's conditions in every case were "unreasonable, injurious, and oppressive," he went far beyond what any other senator had not yet dared to utter. The Compromise was merely the first step in the creation of a vast "slave empire" and would next engulf Cuba, Nicaragua, Guatemala, the Yucatán in Mexico, the whole Caribbean. "The domestic production and commerce in slaves will supplant the African slave trade, and new slave states will surround the Gulf of Mexico and cover its islands. Those new states, combined with slave states already existing, will constitute a slave empire," an empire that will "domineer not only over the southern portion of the continent" but the United States as a whole. "This, sir, is the dream of the slaveholder, and this is the interpretation thereof." Then he pulled back the curtain to reveal the full canvas of his vision, a picture of the Compromise exploding into civil war.

> Slavery and freedom are conflicting systems, brought together by the union of the states, not neutralized, nor even harmonized. Their antagonism is radical, and therefore perpetual. Compromise continues conflict, and the conflict involves, unavoidably, all questions of national interest—questions of revenue, of internal improvement, of industry, of commerce, of political rivalry, and even all questions of peace and of war. In entering the career of conquest, you have kindled to a fiercer heat the fires you seek to extinguish, because you have thrown into them the fuel of propagandism. We have the propagandism of slavery to enlarge the slave market, and to increase slave representation in Congress and in the electoral colleges—for the bramble ever seeks power, though the olive, the fig, and the vine, refuse it; and we have the propagandism of freedom to counteract those purposes. Nor can this propagandism be arrested on either side.

While Clay labored for "calm," New Mexico emerged as the most combustible flash point. In 1849, Taylor had ordered the military commander there to organize a convention of delegates to elect a territorial representative. His intention was that New Mexico would swiftly follow California in its admission as a free state. Calhoun's fear of an inexorable shift of the "equilibrium" of power toward the North would be realized. In response the Texas legislature declared that all of New Mexico east of the Rio Grande, half the territory, including half of what would become Colorado and all of Wyoming, belonged to Texas, and would be open to slavery. In the spring of 1850, Texas attempted a coup, sending a commissioner to Santa Fe to conduct Texas state elections in New Mexico counties. All local political factions united in fury to the Texas takeover. When the Texas commissioner proclaimed a date for elections, they were boycotted, not a single person voting. On May 15, New Mexicans held a convention adopting a constitution, and a month later a governor, legislature, and U.S. senators were elected. On their own, New Mexicans were making a state. The very first section of the first article of the New Mexico constitution banned slavery: "All men being born equally free and independent . . ." Taylor expected to receive official word of New Mexico's free state constitution in early July from its newly chosen senators and to endorse its statehood. He expressed open contempt for the Texas attempt to seize New Mexico, referring in a special message to the Congress on June 17 to its representative there as "styling himself commissioner of the State of Texas," and emphasizing that New Mexico did not exist for the taking, but was part of the United States. "I think there is no reason for seriously apprehending that Texas will practically interfere with the possession of the United States." In short, Texas' would-be seizure of New Mexico would put it on a collision course with the United States.

Contemptuous of the president, Texas Governor Peter Hansborough Bell, a well-born Virginian who had served as a colonel of Texas volunteers under Taylor at the Battle of Buena Vista, proclaimed that he would call the legislature into session in August to authorize its militia to take New Mexico by force. Taylor quickly reinforced the U.S. Army garrison of about seven hundred troops, doubling its size. In late June, General Alfred Pleasanton, commander of those soldiers, received his orders directly from the president at the White House. "These southern men in Congress are trying to bring on civil war," Taylor told him. "They are now organizing a military force in Texas for the purpose of taking possession of New Mexico and annexing it to Texas, and I have ordered the troops in New Mexico to be reinforced, and directed that no armed force from Texas be permitted to go into that territory. Tell Colonel Monroe [commanding in New Mexico] he has my entire confidence, and if he has not force enough out there to support him I will be with you myself; but I will be there before those people shall go into that country or have a foot of that territory. The whole business is infamous, and must be put down." Old Rough and Ready, who had never lost a battle, was prepared to ride again.

As the crisis over New Mexico careened toward the brink, Taylor's enemies harped on a scandal implicating members of his cabinet in order to cripple him. The heirs to George Galphin, a wealthy trader and planter, claiming rightful ownership of a vast tract of Georgia land predating the Revolution, hired George W. Crawford, now Taylor's secretary of war, as attorney in 1835. Crawford took the case on the contingency basis that his fee would be half of the claim. After unsuccessfully pressing the Georgia legislature for years, he brought the matter in 1848 to the House of Representatives, which in a midnight session without scrutiny granted his claim, for which he received $43,518.97. But this was a division of the principal, not the interest. As secretary of war, at his client's behest, he pursued the interest. In April 1850, the secretary of the treasury, William M. Meredith, after consulting Attorney General Reverdy Johnson, paid the interest, of which Crawford took $94,176.44 and Meredith pocketed $3,000.

Crawford misled the president about the extent of his involvement. A congressional investigation reported that the payment was not "in conformity with law and precedent." The leader of the assault in the House on Taylor was Congressman Jacob Thompson of Mississippi, an ally of Jefferson Davis, who was Taylor's former son-in-law. The Southern Ultras planned to censure the president, though he was not involved in any way in the affair. Meanwhile, Toombs and Stephens, both from Georgia, were deeply entangled, having been Crawford's chief helpers on the claim for years, first with the Georgia legislature and then the Congress.

Crawford was not only dishonest in Taylor's eyes, but also disloyal, the ultimate offense. Instead of supporting Taylor on the most contentious issue of all, Crawford lined up with Toombs and Stephens and the Southern Ultras, having the audacity to tell the president that he backed Texas in its claim to New Mexico and would not sign the order authorizing troops to reinforce the garrison at Santa Fe. In the face of the insubordination of his secretary of war, Taylor personally signed the order himself. (Crawford would preside in 1861 as chairman of the Georgia State Secession Convention.)

Taylor decided to shake up his cabinet. Quietly, he called Thurlow Weed to the White House. "He should, he said, consult no other person," recalled Weed, "and his only purpose in conferring with me was to avail himself of such information as I possessed of the character and qualifications of the men whom he might think of for the cabinet." Taylor told him he had made an initial mistake in appointing a cabinet whose majority was from the South and would rectify it by creating one mostly drawn from the free states. He would replace all three members involved in the Galphin affair. Meredith would be sent abroad as minister to France. He would appoint Congressman Edward Stanly of North Carolina, the only Southern Whig then support- ing Taylor, secretary of war. ("Stanly is the only Southern Whig who will stand by them," Toombs had written in April.) Taylor asked Weed to request that Stanly remain in Washington in case of an early adjournment of the Congress to discuss an important matter without telling him what it was. Taylor would also replace Secretary of the Navy William Ballard Preston, a Virginian, with a Northerner, yet unnamed, and Attorney General Reverdy Johnson of Maryland with a prominent but more amenable border state fig- ure, probably John J. Crittenden of Kentucky. "He then took up the question of the secretary of the treasury, about which he expressed much solicitude, deeming it far the most important department of the government." Weed suggested Governor Hamilton Fish of New York, the protégé of the firm of Seward & Weed, and Taylor decided this was a splendid idea. He was prepared to unveil his new cabinet after the Congress adjourned, perhaps on July 6 or 7, and call the Senate into a special session to confirm his appoint- ments. His plan remained a secret.

Southern Whigs in the Congress held a closed conclave on July 1 to determine their strategy against Taylor. They sent several representatives, one after another, to deliver ultimatums to the president that if he didn't re- verse his position on the Texas claim to New Mexico they would rebel. Tay- lor would not yield. Their opposition only stiffened his resolve. He would admit California and then admit New Mexico, both as free states. He met their insolence with the startling news that he considered them superflu- ous. His political position, he insisted, was strong. He told them he saw no reason to sacrifice the eighty-four northern Whigs for the twenty-four Southern ones.

Toombs and Stephens visited Taylor on July 3, demanding that he "change his policy," which, Stephens concluded, was "Seward's game, as I believed." Afterward, they met Secretary of the Navy Preston on the street in front of the Treasury Building next to the White House. "We had a long talk," Stephens recalled. "Toombs said little, that little on my side. I told Preston that if troops were ordered to Santa Fe, the President would be impeached."

"Who will impeach him?" asked Preston. "I will if nobody else does," replied Stephens.

While Toombs and Stephens delivered their ultimatum to Taylor, Clay took to the Senate floor to denounce "the administration and its partisans" for waging "war, open, undisguised war" on his Compromise.

Toombs and Stephens enraged Taylor, who believed they were plotting treason. "General Taylor never intended to shoot Messrs. Toombs and Stephens, by his simple order," said General Pleasanton, "but in case they were caught, tried, and convicted of treason, he would order the sentence of death to be carried out, and they need not expect any mercy from him."

Taylor now viewed his antagonists as Jackson viewed Calhoun. He equated the Texas seizure of New Mexico with nullification, a rebellion against the United States and those engaged in it traitors. Like Jackson, he treated it not as an ordinary difference of politics, but as an insurrection that would require the full military force of the United States to suppress. Doctrinally, Taylor was on the same page as Jackson's Proclamation Against Nullification. His duty was "preserving the Union" against an "unconstitutional" threat by a state to "our social compact" that was an act of secession—"treason against the United States." "To say that any State may at pleasure secede from the Union," Jackson had declared, "is to say that the United States are not a nation." Temperamentally, General Taylor, like General Jackson, would not hesitate. Militarily, Taylor and Jackson had the experience of leading troops into battle and as commander-in-chief Taylor possessed the superior force of the United States against the inferior volunteer militia of one or several Southern states. Like Jackson, Taylor had every confidence he would prevail. If the crisis ever came to a clash, he had no doubt that armed with the Constitution and the army he would triumph. The Southern Rights movement would be tainted while Southern Unionists empowered. New Mexico would be brought into the Union as a free state, decisively shifting the political balance of power to the North. Slavery would be contained. Secession would be conclusively defeated.

On July 4th, the *National Intelligencer* featured a threatening article signed by Alexander Stephens addressed to the president. "I wish to say to you, lest you may be mistaken in the opinions of others, that the first Federal gun that shall be fired against the people of Texas, without the authority of law, will be the signal for the freemen from the Delaware to the Rio Grande to rally to the rescue." Stephens's declaration of war heralded the coming dissolution of the United States. "When the Rubicon is passed, the days of this Republic will be numbered," he wrote, invoking the event that led to the destruction of the ancient Roman republic. "You may consider the gallant State of Texas too weak for a contest with the army of the United States. But you should recollect that the cause of Texas, in such a conflict, will be the cause of the entire South. And whether you consider Santa Fe in danger or not, you may yet live to see that fifteen states of this Union, with seven millions of people, who, knowing their rights, dare maintain them, cannot be easily conquered!"

As Stephens's inflammatory article was being circulated, Taylor attended a July 4th celebration at the Washington Monument, then under construction. In the broiling heat, surrounded by his cabinet, several of whose corrupt members he was about to replace, he listened to an hour-long oration from the loquacious Senator Foote. When he mercifully finished, Taylor was eager to return to the White House and began his departure. But, taking advantage of the president's presence, officials of the Washington Monument Society suddenly announced that there would be an additional ceremony to deposit ashes from the remains of Tadeusz Kosciuszko, the Polish military leader in the American Revolution, inside a corner of the monument. Taylor could not refuse. The speaker was George Washington Parke Custis, step-grandson of George Washington and grandson of Martha Washington, their principal heir, and, incidentally, father-in-law of Colonel Robert E. Lee, who had served under Taylor in the Mexican War. Taylor dutifully stood unprotected under the sun for another hour. Back at the White House, famished and thirsty, he devoured raw vegetables washed down with glass after glass of ice water and milk. Within hours, he was stricken with gastrointestinal distress. The doctors diagnosed cholera. He was dying.

On July 6, Congressman Stanly took the House floor to defend Taylor from charges in the Galphin affair. Calling Crawford a "bad example" and demanding the "truth," Stanly pointed to numerous examples of similar abuses by Democrats. The scandal, he stated, was being exploited as a partisan matter. "When the truth be known," he said, "the small orators of party may cry 'Galphin!' until the hills, 'Galphin!' the woods, 'Galphin!' the rocks, resound. They may buy starlings, and teach them to cry Galphin, nothing but Galphin!"

In the House, on the morning of July 9, the "special order of the day" was consideration of a new committee report on the Galphin Claim. But before it was discussed, Congressman Winfield Featherston, a Democrat from Mississippi, one of Jefferson Davis's trusted allies, introduced a resolution to censure both Crawford and Taylor. Only one other president had been censured, Andrew Jackson, in the heat of his war with the U.S. Bank, the "Bank War," and the next Congress had erased it. Censure was one step below impeachment, but it was a dangerous escalation that might easily lead to a greater conflict. Then word arrived that the president would die within the hour and the House hurriedly adjourned. Even as Davis's colleague offered the motion to censure Taylor in a scandal in which he was completely blameless and was planning soon to remove the true wrongdoers, Jefferson Davis and his second wife, Varina, hovered at the deathbed of his first wife's father as he drew his last breath.

CHAPTER THREE

THE ART OF THE DEAL

M illard Fillmore was now president.

When the last Whig president, William Henry Harrison, had abruptly died just after his inauguration in 1841 and was succeeded by his vice president, John Tyler, Fillmore had been appalled by Tyler's betrayal of the party's principles. "We are in a bad fix," he had written Thurlow Weed. "Captain Tyler has gone soul and body to the Locos." But that should not have been a surprise, for John Tyler of Virginia had always been a states' rights Democrat. Fillmore was then a Whig liegeman, loyal to the New York state party and "the firm" of Seward and Weed, having been brought up politically under Weed's tutelage since he had joined the Anti-Masons.

Millard Fillmore's incredible rise from log cabin to White House was a personal saga of an aspiring illiterate boy marrying his teacher, but the political journey from rough-hewn hovel to executive mansion was an even more

Millard Fillmore

startling tale of the unexpected consequences of party patronage. Rising from the depths of poverty, Fillmore was a politically made man. Serving as a party regular in the Congress through the 1830s and early 1840s, he had been antislavery, voting with John Quincy Adams against the Gag Rule, which banned antislavery petitions from being accepted by the Congress. Weed and Seward slated him for governor in 1844 as "our candidate," as Weed stamped him, but he was dragged to defeat when the Whig candidate Henry Clay failed to carry New York. "The firm" installed Fillmore as state comptroller, when he was suddenly nominated as vice president at the 1848 convention, plucked from obscurity as an act of retribution against his patrons. Seward and Weed had outmaneuvered Henry Clay, who they regarded as a quadrennial loser, by elevating the hero of the Mexican War, General Zachary Taylor, as the nominee for president. The upset Clay men forced Fillmore onto the ticket as the price of party unity and a New York counterweight to Seward's influence, thwarting the deal Weed had made with Taylor to appoint Seward the secretary of state, which would have placed him in line to become president. By political tradition, men from the same state could not hold the vice presidency and the office of secretary of state. Fillmore was the available substitute man from New York, his immediate qualification to trump Seward, and as a man without qualities his paramount recommendation was that he would be a nuisance to nobody. He had neither a gift for oratory nor policy, though some for the minor arts of politics. Throughout his whole career he had been a vessel steered by others, not propelled by greater talent, skill, or intellect. He had spent his entire life serving as a party regular, placeman, and secondary character. He owed his political career to the designs of others. In whatever post he held, Fillmore always filled in.

As vice president, presiding as president of the Senate, he was a dignified and even suave but inert presence. Fillmore usually appeared preternaturally bland, reflecting his conventionality and contentment, described by one visitor as "an amiable and benevolent old gentleman." But beneath his smoothness his bile simmered. "Timid, vacillating, credulous, unjustly suspicious, when approached by his prejudices," Senator Hamilton Fish of New York reported to Weed. Fillmore's resentment was located in mental dimness that aroused his sensitive sense of inferiority as a righteous cause against perceived social slights. He had a reactive frame of mind, often responding with a kind of startle reflex in flashes of petulance to surprising events as personal offenses. Normally complacent, his thin skin was easily rubbed raw. His vanity exceeded his mediocrity.

After unexpectedly being lifted from a minor state job to the vice presidency solely in order to deny his former superior Seward his prize, Fillmore found himself powerless, frustrated, and resentful. Seward and Weed had insinuated themselves into Taylor's confidence as his most trusted advisers. They gained access to patronage, relegating Fillmore to his usual inferior status from which he plotted against "the firm" that had made him.

As vice president, Fillmore had been surreptitiously blocking those Seward's men whom Taylor had nominated to federal patronage posts. His ally was Senator Daniel J. Dickinson, the Democratic senator from New York, a Northerner close to the Southern Democrats, who represented the Wall Street financial houses enmeshed in the cotton trade, and was the chairman of the Finance Committee with control over the vast patronage of customs houses. Days before Taylor's death, Fillmore had bluntly told the president that if the bill on territories that Taylor opposed came to a tie in the Senate he would exercise his vice presidential vote as president of the Senate to pass it, but "not out of any hostility to him or his administration," as Fillmore falsely observed later.

The day after Taylor's death, Seward, filled with "apprehensions that his administration will be conducted in a spirit of war and proscription against me, and all with whom I act," urged Fillmore to retain the cabinet as it was except for corrupt Secretary of War George W. Crawford. But the next day, even before Taylor's funeral, the resignations of the entire cabinet were accepted. And the day after that, Seward lamented to Weed, "You are very wise in staying away. I wish I were as far off." He watched as Taylor's enemies enveloped Fillmore, and Fillmore embraced them. "Slavery Whigs and Democrats demand a change of the Cabinet, and a surrender to the Compromise. . . . Thus Providence has at last led the man of hesitation and double opinions, to the crisis, where decision and singleness are indispensable."

Rumors wafted through Washington until July 20, when Fillmore officially announced Webster as secretary of state, making him first among equals in the new cabinet. "The government is in the hands of Mr. Webster, and Mr. Clay is its organ in Congress," Seward wrote Weed. Webster and Clay greeted Taylor's death as the stroke of heaven. "There were circumstances attending the death of General Taylor, that were so fortunate," Webster wrote only a week afterward, "that, for his own fame and character, and for the gratification of all to whom he was most dear, he may be said to have died fortunately." Walking through the Capitol, encountering Congressman

Henry Washington Hilliard of Alabama, a Southern Whig close to Toombs, Webster remarked, "Mr. Hilliard, if General Taylor had lived we should have had civil war." (Hilliard, as a colonel in the Confederate army, would organize a battalion of Alabama volunteers known as "Hilliard's Legion.") "I think the event that has happened," Clay wrote, referring to Taylor's death, "will favor the passage of the Compromise Bill."

Webster and Clay had experienced a similar reversal of fortune before. When William Henry Harrison suddenly died, their best-laid plans were undone. Webster as Harrison's secretary of state was positioned to direct the administration from within, while Clay was poised to guide its policies in the Senate. Tyler's ascension forced both out of power. With Taylor's demise, however, the consequences for them were the opposite of what they were with Harrison's death. Fillmore would now play John Tyler, His Accidency II, but a Tyler who instead of expelling Webster and Clay would rely on them. They had been out, but now they were in.

Taking the Senate floor for another major speech on July 22, Clay believed that in only two weeks a revolution had taken place. No longer staring down the barrel of Taylor's artillery, he felt safe on the high ground as the man of reason, explaining the value of "compromise" to "restore the harmony of the country." He lectured the South that the bill gave it every advantage. "Now, what complaint can the South make if the whole scheme is carried out? The South gains a virtual abandonment of the Wilmot proviso, avoids the assumption of any power dangerous to the institution of slavery within the States, or the application of such power to slavery without the States, and secures nine hundred miles of now disputed territory . . . and she gets a fugitive slave bill, which I trust will be rendered efficient; and she also gets, as I trust I shall be able to show in the progress of my argument, the abandonment of the agitation of the abolition in the District of Columbia. What more can the South ask?"

He chided the North that in failing to support the Compromise it was irrational, stirring up by antislavery agitation, not facing facts. "One of the misfortunes of the times is the difficulty in penetrating the northern mind with truth, to make it sensible to the dangers which are ahead." If that was not pointed enough, he declared that his bill would put an end to the scourge of abolitionism once and for all. "There is not an abolitionist in this Senate chamber or out of it, anywhere, that is not opposed to the adoption of this compromise plan. And why are they opposed to it? They see their doom as certain as there is a God in heaven who sends His providential dispensations to calm the threatening storm and to tranquillize agitated man." Then he dramatically turned to Senator John P. Hale of New Hampshire, and proclaimed, "As certain as that God exists in heaven, your business, your vocation is gone."

Just as he used Hale as a symbol for disruptive abolitionism that would be quelled by his Compromise, he picked out a remark by Jefferson Davis about slave "breeding" to instruct him and other Ultras on how their vulgar language was damaging the South. Davis had maligned him as a disloyal Southerner and in return he would put him in his place as an uncouth blowhard. "This talk, sir, about the cotton power, the lords of the loom, and the breeding of slaves, will do for the bar-rooms of cross-road taverns; but I never hoped or expected to hear upon the floor of the Senate such epithets applied to the great manufactures of the North and the cotton-growers of the South." Davis had, according to Clay, presented a perverted version of the mind of the South when he had spoken of "breeding." "No such purpose ever enters, I believe, into the mind of any slaveholder. He takes care of his slaves; he fosters them, and treats them often with the tenderness of his own children." In truth, however, slave trading, including breeding, was the single greatest commerce in the country, greater than railroads and factories, and Clay had just failed to limit it in his home state of Kentucky, where he was overwhelmed by his own Ultras. His past descriptions of slavery had been filled alternatively with condemnation and tortured ambivalence, but now he adopted the condescending tone of an old lord of the manor, explaining that the true soul of the slave owner was that of a benevolent philanthropist. In order to put down Jefferson Davis, one of the largest slaveholders in Mississippi, Clay overlooked what he well knew, that Davis's comment about "breeding" was utterly realistic about the plantations of the Deep South, though it did not apply to Clay's management of his own beloved Ashland.

After cuffing Davis for his coarseness, Clay obliquely criticized the fire-eating speech of Robert Barnwell Rhett, the *Charleston Mercury* editor, promoting secession after the Nashville Convention. This prompted Senator Robert W. Barnwell of South Carolina to interrupt him for being "a little disrespectful to a friend I hold very dear." Clay conceded that he had "some respect" for Rhett. "But, if he pronounced the sentiment attributed to him of raising the standard of disunion and of resistance to the common government, whatever he has been, if he follows up that declaration by corresponding overt acts, he will be a traitor, and I hope he will meet the fate of a traitor." That spontaneous statement provoked the greatest applause in the packed galleries, the most memorable part of his speech. "The Senate is not a theater," the president pro tempore, Senator King of Alabama, admonished the audience.

In his recitation of familiar arguments, Clay added a new wrinkle. It was that New Mexico should not be admitted as a state because of the racial character of its population—Indians and "half-breeds." "There is scarcely any people so low in the stage of civilization, even the Eskimos, or the Indians on any portion of our continent, that they may not comprehend and be able to adopt laws suited to their own condition—few, simple, clear, and well understood, for, in their uncivilized state, it is not necessary for them to have a cumbrous code of laws. But it is a widely different thing whether the people of New Mexico may not be capable of passing laws adapted to their own unripe and yet half-civilized condition. I speak not of the American portion of the population there, but of the Indians, the Pueblo Indians, and some of the half-bloods. . . . For one, sir, I must say I should be utterly unwilling to receive New Mexico as a state in her present immature condition." He did not mention that "half-civilized" New Mexico had ratified a state constitution outlawing slavery and conducted elections of officials, including U.S. senators. Clay did not acknowledge or perhaps understand that he had introduced a novel and radical constitutional concept. It was that states could not be admitted if they had substantial populations of nonwhites—and nonblacks. A state with a population of a majority of blacks would be approved because they would not be counted as citizens, or three-fifths of a person. But a state with Indians and Hispanics, and virtually no blacks, posed a different challenge. Under Clay's new test, such a state would be excluded solely on the basis of its racial character.

Seward rose three days later to refute Clay's racialism and make the case for New Mexico's admission. He argued that the residents of New Mexico had been naturally invested with the rights of American citizens when its territory was acquired from Mexico under the express terms of the Treaty of Guadalupe Hidalgo. "All these are rights of which the United States can deprive no community on earth." The treaty "contains no provision whatever for bringing that Territory into provincial or territorial degradation." The framers of the Constitution never "contemplated Colonies, or Provinces, or Territories, at all," but "nothing less than states." New Mexico, Seward pointed out, already had fulfilled the requirement for statehood, creating "a republican form of government." "You have all seen and read her constitution. . . . But we are told that the people of New Mexico are unfit for self-government. Sir, this objection comes too late." New Mexicans were "a mingled people," but no less entitled to rights. New Mexico had "the same rights as coming into the Union as Texas had." New Mexico was owed "justice" and "magnanimity." "Sir, there is not in the history of the Roman Empire an ambition for aggrandizement so marked . . . a transaction so unjust to a conquered people as this. But what is the apology for it?" He urged that New Mexico be admitted immediately.

As if on cue, Seward was ambushed. The attack was led by Senator Thomas Pratt, a Democrat of Maryland, who as governor had been infuriated by the refusal of Pennsylvania to return fugitive slaves. (During the Civil War, Pratt refused to take a loyalty oath to the United States and was imprisoned.) Now he lambasted Seward for his rhetorical flourish about a "higher law," which he claimed displayed "utter disregard of the Constitution, and his oath to uphold it." Pratt was not arguing over philosophy, but insisted that Seward asserted a "higher law" above the constitutional protection of slavery in the states. "I deny it," replied Seward. Senator Roger Baldwin, Whig of Connecticut, grandson of Roger Sherman, signer of the Declaration of Independence, and opponent of the Compromise, rose to Seward's defense. "I must simply say that I did not understand the sentiment of the Senator from New York as stated by the Senator from Maryland." "Everybody else did," interjected Foote. Then Pratt moved to expel Seward from the Senate. Taylor was no longer available to threaten with censure or impeachment, but Seward was his scapegoat. It was impermissible to speak ill of the dead president, not the living senator.

Senator William L. Dayton, Whig of New Jersey, also related to a signer of the Declaration, and opposed to the Compromise, tried to diffuse the farce, suggesting that Seward withdraw his measure on New Mexico. "I object!" shouted Clay, seeking to prolong Seward's humiliation. His intervention suggested his intrigue in the expulsion gambit. "The yeas and nays are so ordered," Pratt chimed. Seward refused to withdraw his proposal. "Though I stand alone," he declared defiantly, "I shall be convinced that I stand right." He demanded that the Senate proceed with his trial of expulsion. And he read aloud the entire constitution of New Mexico into the record, including its prohibition of slavery and appeal to "the Sovereign Ruler of the Universe." Hale stood up, announcing his belief in the Almighty, too. "I ought to be expelled, because I believe it." Pratt replied that he, too, had as "high respect for that higher power that is so frequently desecrated here, as the Senator from New Hampshire." "I call the senator to order for saying I desecrated the name of the Most High." "He did not say so," Foote jumped in. At that, Salmon Chase chimed in that "the words used by the Senator from Maryland were just those words which he has now stated." Hale objected, "When did I ever say that that part of the Constitution which recognized the holding of slaves as property as contrary to the Divine Law?" Pratt backed down about Hale, but again turned his wrath on Seward. Jefferson Davis impatiently moved for adjournment. But Clay did not want the taunting and tainting of Seward to end. He moved for "yeas and nays," and the motion to adjourn failed, so the drama was drawn out. Chase defended Seward again and Foote accused him of speaking in the "language of Jesuitical mystery." "Order! Order!" shouted senators throughout the chamber. Foote explained he wasn't referring to Chase, who was, after all, raised by an Episcopal bishop. "I speak of another person." That person was "the Senator from New York," who had been "defended . . . by all the abolition presses of the North." Finally, a vote was taken on Seward's proposal. He was the sole vote recorded in favor. Hale, Baldwin, and Chase abstained. Seward stood alone in the theater of the Senate.

The war on Seward and Weed went into full swing. Every federal jobholder who owed his position or loyalty to "the firm" was purged. After dismissing the entire cabinet, Fillmore was determined to dismantle every vestige of the Taylor administration root and branch down to the smallest office, especially those associated with Seward. Lewis Benedict, the postmaster of Albany, a special friend of Weed, was fired. His replacement began holding up the distribution of Weed's *Journal*. Fillmore's allies started an Albany newspaper to undercut the *Journal*, editorializing that Weed was "Generalissimo-in-chief of the Abolition forces." "I see that the hounds are let loose upon you," Seward wrote him, "and that you stand nobly at bay."

Following Seward's "expulsion," Clay was able to move his bill toward a momentous conclusion on July 31. "Here we are in the whirl of the agony of final debate," wrote a gloomy Seward. "It is quite apparent that the slave power is to have its triumphs in the Senate, and there is little reason to hope that it will be less successful in the House of Representatives." But as Clay demanded approval of his magnificent Compromise, the towering edifice it had taken him months to construct, involving the careful adjustments of the Committee of Thirteen, swayed, creaked, and toppled, first brick by brick, then all at once. In just a few brief moments, Clay's monument was rubble covered in a cloud of dust. Texas, New Mexico, and California were stripped out, and only Utah, the desert of the Mormons, remained. The usually severe Jefferson Davis broke into a wide smile. The reserved Chase grabbed the hand of Senator Pierre Soule, the Ultra from Louisiana. And Seward was reported to have danced like a top on the floor of the Senate.

By consolidating all the elements of his bill into the "Omnibus," Clay had given those upset at one or another aspect of it reason to vote against the whole. He depended ultimately on his reputation and eloquence, as though they were power itself. Clay still thought of himself as the dictator of the Congress, but now he lacked the means of compulsion to lend material incentives to sustain his persuasion. His image as a statesman had a deep history behind it, but his influence was now hollow. Nor could the new president do much to sustain him. Fillmore had been in the White House only three weeks, and had not yet begun operating all the levers of government and patronage. Staring at the ruins, Clay wordlessly walked out of the Senate never again to propose another piece of legislation. He left Washington for Newport to buoy his sinking health in the ocean waves.

Benton, exultant and mocking, took center stage in the well of the Senate. He had survived both Foote's pistol and Clay's Compromise. "I am kindly tempered, and disposed to do pleasant things to everybody," he said. The "gentlemen of the compromising party" had developed "an opinion that I was not kindly disposed to them, and I now wish to give them a proof to the contrary. Their vehicle is gone, all but one plank, and I wish to save that plank for them, by way of doing homage to their work. The omnibus is overturned, and all the passengers spilled out but one. We have but Utah left—all gone but Utah! It alone remains, and I am for saving it as a monument of the herculean efforts of the immortal thirteen."

At this moment of Clay's humiliation, a new man, nearly two generations younger than Clay, energetic and even more ruthless, stepped forward into the vacuum to pick up the pieces. His ambition burned as brightly as that of the youthful "Harry of the West." Unlike Clay, he was not trying to set the capstone of a career marked by the crumbling of his fondest hopes, the Compromise as compensation for repeatedly losing the presidency, but to lay the foundation for a rise to the highest office Clay never reached. Henry Clay was yesterday's man, Stephen A. Douglas the coming man.

Douglas was unsurprised when the "Omnibus" crashed. He predicted it would happen months before. "By combining the measures into one bill the committee united the opponents of each measure instead of securing the friends of each," he wrote. "I have thought from the beginning that they made a mistake in this respect." He took over from Clay the day he departed from the chamber. His assumption of Clay's failure was no ordinary substitution; it marked a changing of the guard, a demarcation line between political eras.

At thirty-seven years old, only in his first term, Douglas's reputation for political and legislative skills among his new colleagues was so respected after observing him for four years in the House that he was at once granted chairmanship of the powerful Senate Committee on Territories and made one of President Polk's floor leaders. His tactical instincts were finely tuned, his stamina boundless, and his socializing round-the-clock. His consumption of whiskey morning, noon, and late night only enhanced his standing as one of the most convivial members. The "Little Giant" with the leonine mane regularly startled his fellow politicians by jumping into their laps and clapping them on the back. He was described as "magnetic" before the word "charisma" was invented. His rise was so meteoric that he seemed an unstoppable force of nature. But if there was one aspect of his character that suited him to rescue the Compromise, above all, it was that he was a speculator. His career was a series of risks and gambles. He speculated in politics; he speculated with money; he speculated on money in politics; and that speculation made him successful in politics, which in turn made him a fortune. Bringing to bear the financial forces staking him in his speculations, Douglas worked behind the scenes to grease the way through the previously impassable.

The Compromise had hit the end of the line, but now it was to move forward with the speed of a locomotive on another track—and that track was the Illinois Central Railroad. Illinois occupied the geographically strategic position between the North and West—and from North to South along the Mississippi River. And the railroad would become a man-made Mississippi. In 1836, the legislature granted a charter for a railroad running from Galena in the northwest corner to the southernmost tip of Illinois at the confluence of the Mississippi and Ohio Rivers. The company that got the charter was the partnership of Darius B. Holbrook, a Boston investor, and Sidney Breese, then a district court judge. Holbrook purchased the land that would be the southern terminus to be called Cairo, and the company was called the Cairo City and Canal Company. But when the Panic of 1837 struck and its whirlwind destroyed the London bond house financing the scheme, it collapsed. Breese was elected U.S. senator in 1842, became chairman of the Committee on Public Lands, and sought a federal charter for a land grant to a new company based on the old one, called the Great Western Railway, of which he and Holbrook remained the partners. The bill passed the Senate, but failed in the House, where it was undercut by Douglas, who thought it was a confidence game to jack up the value of the virtually worthless tract at Cairo to make a windfall profit for Breese. After Douglas's election to the Senate, he battled Breese for two years over their competing proposals. Finally, Douglas succeeded in ousting Breese from the Senate by securing the election of his ally James Shields, chief of Illinois' Irish Democrats. The Great Western Railway bid evaporated. On the first day of the Senate session, January 3, 1850, Douglas introduced his bill for the construction of the Illinois Central Railroad, which was referred to the Committee on Public Lands, where Shields now sat.

Douglas's Illinois Central would not originate at Galena, but Chicago, where Douglas had moved in 1847. He bought vast tracts of land along the Illinois and Michigan Canal, opened in 1848, a sluiceway of commerce to Chicago. These lucrative real estate opportunities were almost certainly made possible by his relationship with William B. Ogden, the wealthiest man in Chicago, its first mayor, a Democrat with whom Douglas dined in his lakefront mansion and who was also the chief investor in the canal. At that moment there was not a single train track in the city; by 1860 Chicago would be the junction of more railroads than anyplace else on earth. Ogden would become known as the Railway King of the West, involved in dozens of railroads, and crown his success in 1869 as president of the Union Pacific, the first transcontinental line. (His attorney, Samuel Tilden, based in New York, became the biggest corporate lawyer in the country, and as the Democratic presidential candidate in 1876 won the popular vote but was denied victory through a deal that ended Reconstruction.)

As Douglas laid the groundwork for the Illinois Central, he strategically purchased large tracts of real estate whose value would skyrocket with the building of the railroad. He began in 1849 with lakefront property that he expanded soon to seventy-five acres that happened to run exactly along the planned IC right-of-way. Meanwhile, he acquired thousands of acres on the west side of Chicago as well as along the Chicago River and near Lake Calumet, which would directly profit from the railroad. It is likely that his financing came from Ogden and other friendly bankers who were counting on his political leverage for their own mutually beneficial projects.

"He had an inspiration for land," wrote John W. Forney. "He justly believed that where there are large risks there should be large recompense." Forney floated effortlessly through government, politics, and journalism as a Democratic operative (until he metamorphosed into a Republican)—editor of various Pennsylvania newspapers, deputy collector at the Philadelphia customs house, and, by the early 1850s, clerk of the House of Representatives while at the same time editor of the *Washington Union*, the Democratic organ. "To him," Forney wrote in tribute to Douglas, "I am indebted for my first and only speculation—the better to be recollected because it was successful." Douglas confided to him the planning begun in 1853 for the Northern Pacific Railroad, unfolding a map of its route.

> "How would you like to buy a share in Superior City, at Fond du Lac, the head of Lake Superior?" . . . "But," I said, "old fellow, I have no money, and to buy a share in the proposed location will require much." "No," he replied, "I can secure you one for $2500, and you can divide it with" naming one of the best of the future Confederates, "and he will be greatly obliged." I knew nothing of the location, had never been there, had no money of my own, but I saw Judge Douglas was in earnest and wanted to serve me, and when he left, I borrowed the $2500, bought a share, divided it with the Southern gentleman referred to, who honorably paid his $1250; and after cutting my share into five parts, sold and gave three fifths to other friends, and with my two fifths bought the Waverley House, in Washington. The proceeds of my moiety of the one share of Superior City realized $21,000. For that I was indebted to Stephen A. Douglas—God bless him!

Douglas's grandiose plan for the Illinois Central and not so incidentally for the profitability of his real estate had been thwarted in the 30th Congress. His bill passed the Senate, but was blocked in the House. Still in the game, Holbrook had bribed a clerk of the Illinois legislature to sneak into a measure the transfer to his cabal of any land rights for the railroad the federal government intended to give to Illinois. When Douglas discovered the skullduggery, Holbrook offered him half the profits from the Cairo property. But Douglas vowed that federal land grants for the railroad would only be made directly to the state. Finally, he ended the Holbrook-Breese threat by ousting Breese from his Senate seat and installing his sidekick Shields.

Douglas, however, faced a bigger obstacle. In the Senate, his bill had been attacked as an unconstitutional violation of states' rights, the old Jacksonian hostility to internal improvements, by Foote and Davis of Mississippi and King and Clemens of Alabama—and the unified delegations of those states in the House. So, in November 1849, Douglas decided to outflank them through an excursion to his other family property—his Mississippi plantation.

Douglas, once rejected by Mary Todd as louche, had at last found his lovely Southern belle in Martha Martin, who had been educated at finishing schools and spoke French. Her father, Colonel Robert Martin, nephew of a U.S. senator and governor of North Carolina, owned an eight-hundred-acre plantation on the Dan River, just across the border from Danville, Virginia, and a large cotton plantation of 2,500 acres worked by 150 slaves on the Pearl River near Philadelphia, Mississippi. Martha was the cousin of the North Carolina congressman, David S. Reid, who sat next to Douglas when he first arrived in the House. On their wedding day in 1847, Colonel Martin presented the Mississippi plantation as a gift to the couple. Douglas persuaded Martin that he should still hold the title for political reasons. Upon Martin's death a year later he deeded the plantation to his daughter and her heirs, while Douglas served as property manager for which he received 20 percent of its annual income. (When his wife died in 1853, the plantation was inherited by the two Douglas sons while Douglas continued as manager.) It was a characteristically artful arrangement allowing Douglas to have it both ways, legally not to be a slave owner yet to profit from slavery. The Little Giant stood on the pedestal of the cotton kingdom—and above it.

Douglas never uttered an antislavery sentiment in his life. His most measured statement of this period, in 1848, was that in the North "it is not expected that we should take the position that slavery is a positive good—a positive blessing." He took no moral stand whatsoever. "Now we say to you of the South, if slavery be a blessing, it is your blessing; if it be a curse, it is your curse; enjoy it—on you rest all responsibility!" He would routinely rail against black equality, accuse his opponents of favoring it, and beat them with the word "nigger." His central hate figures were abolitionists, around whom he constructed virtually all his rhetorical arguments. His criticisms of Southern Ultras inevitably concluded that they were aiding and abetting abolitionism. "I have no sympathy for abolitionism on the one side, or that extreme course on the other which is akin to abolitionism," he said. In the House, he had consistently voted to uphold the Gag Rule and referred to slavery as "Southern rights." His embrace of Cass's "squatter sovereignty," of "non-intervention" in the extension of slavery, became the core of Douglas's political ideology, a pastiche of plebiscitary democracy and states' rights that he propounded as a constitutional principle. He played no role in originating what he trumpeted as "popular sovereignty," but became its chief standard bearer. He deployed it to seize the broad middle and stigmatize others as either abolitionists or Ultras. The muddled concept carried him far, until it led him into a swamp of no return. He could never adequately explain why popular sovereignty ruled out secession. If the states were the creators of the federal union, then they retained the authority to secede. But if the federal union was a compact that created the states, then popular sovereignty itself was trumped. These two propositions were, of course, irreconcilable. Douglas was not interested in settling this question, but finessing it. Nor could Douglas ever define just who "the people" were under popular sovereignty. That was to be decided by the circular logic that the people would determine who they were. In Kansas, the case study of popular sovereignty, his idea of democracy turned into a question of who had more men with rifles. Every argument Douglas made could to a virtually unerring degree be reduced to its self-serving political essence. Many of his gambits were ingenious, but the root of his thought was almost always expedience. Yet he presented his schemes as earthshaking ideas developed from a profound constitutional philosophy.

At the beginning of his brilliant career, when Douglas glowed with possibility, before he had made enemies of virtually everyone in the Democratic Party, he had made his statements about the moral neutrality of slavery and condemned Southern Ultraism as "akin to abolitionism" as counterpoint to the debate in which Foote threatened to hang Hale. Foote had also addressed Douglas on the slavery question and warned that ultimately he would find himself without ground to stand on. In a paragraph, Foote captured Douglas's method and predicted the whole course of his future. "I beg the senator from Illinois to recollect there is another mode of obtaining that popularity which is expressed in the adage, '*In media tutissimus ibis*,' [the middle ground is the safest] and that there is such a thing as winning golden opinions from all sorts of people; and it may be that a man of mature power, young, and aspiring as he may do to high places, may conceive that, by keeping clear of all union with the two leading factions, he will more or less strengthen himself with the great body of the American people, and thus attain the high point of elevation to which his ambition leads. But if the senator from Illinois thinks that a middle course in regard to this question is best calculated to serve his purpose, he is mistaken."

During the 1848 campaign, in New Orleans, Douglas promised that if he were ever obligated to support the Wilmot Proviso he would resign from the Senate. From the moment of its introduction, he had voted to table the Proviso and when that failed voted against it each and every time it appeared as an amendment to a bill. His record diametrically opposed Lincoln's. Cass carried Illinois, but after the election pro-Proviso Democratic legislators from Chicago and northern counties combined with Whigs and Free Soilers to pass a resolution ordering the state's U.S. senators to support the Proviso. Whigs baited Douglas to resign. But he simply presented the legislative resolution to the Senate and then filed a motion for tabling it. He labeled the resolution nothing but a "party trick" and assailed the Proviso as a "mischievous and wicked measure." But his ability to push it aside in the Senate hardly finessed the antislavery sentiment in Illinois.

Facing difficulties in his home state and in Washington, Douglas outflanked his opponents through a secret foray to the South. After inspecting the family plantation in Mississippi, he paid a visit on the president and directors of the Mobile Railroad, a project stalled from lack of funding. Douglas had proposed that the Mobile line be joined to the Illinois Central, extending it from Chicago to the Gulf of Mexico, the fabled North–South line to be made possible by federal land grants. When he explained that their own representatives were thwarting this vision, they were irate, pledging on the spot to remove the obstacle. "I told them it was necessary to keep quiet, and secret, as to my connection in the matter," Douglas recalled. Soon, the legislatures of Mississippi and Alabama sent instructions to their congressional delegates to vote for the Illinois Central Railroad. Startled, Senator King "cursed" and Senator Davis "swore." "Davis did not know what in the world was the matter, and refused to believe it." Douglas played a little game "to conceal my connection with their instructions," and told them he had the votes to pass the bill without them, allowing them to beg him to amend it to include the Mobile connection, which then passed. "All this occurred during the excited times of slavery discussion and agitation in 1850"—a little noticed deal that greased the way for the stalled Compromise.

Douglas's interest in the Illinois Central intersected with another great interest—the Texas bond lobby. The value of Texas securities was completely dependent on resolution of the Texas issues involved in the overall deal. Among the chief holders of these bonds was William W. Corcoran, the leading banker in Washington, of Corcoran and Riggs. A native of the capital, a Southern city, he was a Southern man with Southern principles. He was also a philanthropist and art collector, but he was mainly fixed on achieving indemnification of Texas bonds by financing the lobby for the Compromise, acting as "the principal sponsor, initiator, or guiding spirit in countless phases of politico-financial enterprise connected with the compromise and compromisers," according to historian Holman Hamilton. His chief agent in Washington was James Hamilton, the governor of South Carolina during the nullification crisis and a former congressman, who long ago left behind an allegiance to Calhoun's dogmas for Corcoran's fees. Miraculously, on March 7, 1850, the day Webster delivered a speech in favor of the Compromise, Corcoran canceled his $6,000 debt note.

Much of the propaganda for the Compromise was handled by a journalist with a Viennese accent, Francis J. Grund, a murky but glittering chameleon, drifting in allegiance from Van Buren to Harrison, from Democrats to Whigs, and back and forth, but now in the pay of the Texas bond lobby. Grund was the author of a scandalous book, *Aristocracy in America: From the Sketch Book of a German Nobleman*, published in 1839, a gossipy exposé of the underbelly of the upper classes, an antithesis to Tocqueville's *Democracy in America*. Grund was a man for all parties, political and social. As the Washington correspondent of both the *Philadelphia Public Ledger* and the *Baltimore Sun*, he churned out hundreds of pieces promoting the Compromise that would profit his benefactor. Grund himself had also become a large holder of Texas bonds.

When Clay's "Omnibus" failed on July 30, Texas bond prices plummeted. Then Douglas took over. After clearing the remnant of Clay's wreckage out of the way by passing the bill on Utah, Douglas put together a Texas boundary bill in which the state would be compensated $10 million for giving up its claim to New Mexico east of the Rio Grande. Astonishingly, it passed on August 9. With that, it was clear that Douglas would swiftly pass each and every bill in short order. He had created an irresistible momentum. Senator Barnwell of South Carolina attributed it to the Texas bond lobby. "The tens of millions of money to the Texas creditors carried the day," he wrote. He even believed the entire crisis and the Texas boundary dispute with New Mexico had been "gotten up" by James Hamilton and the "others interested in the Bonds of Texas. I cannot else account for the whole proceeding." It appeared that money talked.

But there was another persuasive force at work. When Webster was appointed secretary of state his most urgent task had nothing to do with foreign affairs. He took charge at once of federal patronage to secure passage of the floundering Compromise. His State Department clerks were immediately ordered to draw up lists of candidates for judgeships based on their loyalty to the Fillmore administration. Congressmen and senators could influence the selections only if they voted for the Compromise. Seventy-eight nominees for federal jobs from New England were held in suspense until the Compromise vote. Under Webster's pressure six New England Whigs switched from opponents to backers and the two New Jersey Whig senators and others abstained. When Clayton of Delaware had been Taylor's secretary of state, he had held the Delaware Whigs in place, but with Webster dangling patronage they all defected. Webster also controlled the government printing contracts for newspapers and federal advertising, a major source of revenue. He forced forty-two editors out of their positions across the country for not supporting the Compromise, about two thirds, and redirected ads to rival publications, removing them with particular vengeance from Weed's *Albany Journal* and giving them instead to the *Albany Register.*

When the Fugitive Slave Act was called up on August 26, Douglas, who had virtually camped out in the Old Senate Chamber while field-marshaling bills, was absent. He was in New York, arranging the details of a $4,000 note with bankers to pay for a parcel of his Chicago real estate. Receiving word that the vote was about to take place, he rushed back to Washington, but missed final passage. His vote, in any case, was not needed. The Fugitive Slave Act swept through the Congress with the unanimous support of every Southern and border state representative. Afterward, on September 12, Douglas made his views plain to his colleagues, explaining Illinois' strict Black Code. "We do not wish to make our state an asylum for all the old and decrepit and broken-down negroes that may emigrate or be sent to it," he said. "We desire every other state to take care of her own negroes, whether free or slave, and we will take care of ours." Almost certainly, the *Congressional Globe* had cleaned up his language, substituting "negroes" in its printed record.

In the antic last days of voting on the last piece of the Compromise, the floor of the House swarmed with lobbyists. An anxious W. W. Corcoran was present "continually," he wrote. The night the final bill passed, on September 7, a salute of one hundred guns was fired, government buildings were illuminated, and fireworks lit the sky. The Marine Band serenaded Clay beneath the window of his room at the National Hotel. And Texas bond prices skyrocketed, increasing in value almost overnight by one third.

The Wilmot Proviso to prohibit slavery in the territories gained in the Mexican War was as dead as President Taylor. (Lincoln, who called himself "a Proviso man," had voted numerous times for it in the last Congress.) In five separate pieces of legislation comprising the Compromise of 1850, Texas ceded its claim to New Mexico in exchange for federal assumption of its debt; California was admitted as a free state; New Mexico and Utah would be allowed to decide whether they would enter the Union as slave or free states;

the slave trade was removed from the District of Columbia; and a federal Fugitive Slave Act enacted.

"If any man has a right to be proud of the success of these measures," Jefferson Davis declared, "it is the senator from Illinois."

While Douglas was orchestrating passage of the Compromise bill he constantly kept his eye on his ultimate prize—the Illinois Central Railroad. As the Senate debated Douglas's bill on New Mexico on August 16, the day after his California bill passed, W. W. Corcoran, acting at Douglas's direction, placed $5,000 in Illinois state bonds and $12,000 in U.S. bonds into the account of Congressman Thomas H. Bayly of Virginia, chairman of the House Ways and Means Committee, where all spending bills originated, and from which pressure could be applied on any other member. Bayly, an old ally of Thomas Ritchie, had been present at his meeting with Clay to establish a cordial entente to push the Compromise. Now Bayly had reason to be Douglas's enduring friend. Shortly after Corcoran arranged the bonds for Bayly, Douglas put in his own order for himself. "I fix no limit to the amount," he wrote Corcoran, "for I am satisfied that it is a good investment, and consequently desire as many as you are willing to purchase and hold for me."

The day after the celebration of the Compromise, Douglas switched to the railroad. The Illinois Central bill rested at the bottom of the House calendar buried under ninety-seven bills ahead of it. But with the assistance of Bayly the ninety-seven bills with greater priority instantly melted away and Douglas's legislation miraculously rose to the number one position. When the bill had been defeated the previous year, it was heavily opposed by the Northeastern delegations. Through Congressman John Wentworth, a Democrat from Chicago, Douglas made an approach to Webster, who told Wentworth to meet with his close associate, Congressman George Ashmun of Massachusetts. "Mr. Webster thinks that you and I, by acting in concert, can do our respective people and the country at large a great deal of good," said Ashmun. "What do you say?" "You know what we Illinois men all want," Wentworth replied. "Lead off." "Now, help us upon the tariff where you can, and where you cannot, dodge." But there was another element besides trading votes for the railroad for votes in favor of the tariff. Wall Street and State Street banks were the main holders of Illinois bonds, which had been depressed since the collapse after the Panic of 1837 of the state's internal improvement program (engineered by the then Whig leader in the Illinois House of Representatives, Abraham Lincoln). Douglas rewrote the bill so that 7 percent of the railroad's income would be paid to the state, eliminating the long-standing debt and floating its bonds. By that device, he fostered the creation of the Illinois bond lobby, which sprang to life to support him. His bill also offered land directly to the railroad company in a checkerboard pattern that would enable sale of the land in order to finance construction. The amended measure passed easily through the Committee on Public Lands, where James Shields managed it. Twenty days after the passage of the Compromise, on September 17, the Illinois Central Railroad Tax Act handily passed in the House. Three days later, it easily passed in the Senate.

"It was the votes of Massachusetts and New York that passed the bill," Breese wrote Douglas, "and you and I know how they were had." "If any man passed a bill," Douglas boasted, "I did that one."

A blue-chip board for the Illinois Central was assembled from New York and Boston financiers, nearly all holders of Illinois bonds. In February 1851, lobbied by Douglas, the Illinois state legislature approved the incorporation of the Illinois Central and handed over the federal land grant to the new firm. The railroad soon purchased Douglas's lakeshore real estate at a windfall profit for its right-of-way in Chicago.

The legend of the Compromise took hold almost immediately upon its passage and has lasted in history even longer than the mythology of the Lost Cause. It is the story of Henry Clay, a latter-day Cincinnatus, returning to the capital after years of absence, suddenly alarmed by raised voices, and brilliantly crafting and shepherding the legislation that would save the Union, postponing by a decade the bloodletting of the Civil War, which only lacked a brilliant figure like Clay to avoid. His masterful legislation, reprising his role in the Missouri Compromise of 1820, was his final act of devotion, giving his life for his country. His patriotic statesmanship shone above the opposition—zealous partisans, petty factionalists, fanatical abolitionists, and Ultra sectionalists besetting him on all sides. "Had there been one such man in the Congress of the United States as Henry Clay in 1860–'61," wrote Foote, "there would, I feel sure, have been no civil war. Had Mr. Clay himself been then living, the same high toned patriotism and consummate statesmanship which had been so efficiently instrumental in 1819, in 1832, and in 1850," would once again have been applied "in preserving the Republic from the horrors of civil butchery, and from the yet greater evils sure to result from disunion."

Clay played the role of the hero above party to the hilt and after Douglas managed the passage of the Compromise he could not handle he unabashedly took full credit. Invited to address the Kentucky General Assembly, he confided that in his deliberations, "I was in conference and consultation quite as often, if not oftener, with Democrats than Whigs." Hailed by newspapers as the second coming of George Washington, the second father of his country, Clay arrived for the second session of the 31st Congress in December 1850 fatally ill, coughing spasmodically, but still possessed of his sense of theatricality. At the cultural event of the season, the concert of Jenny Lind, the "Swedish Nightingale," Clay waited for Webster and Fillmore to enter to polite applause before walking down the main aisle after the overture to a standing ovation.

In his Annual Message to the Congress, on December 2, Fillmore proclaimed that the Compromise was nothing less than "a final settlement" and that "we have been rescued from the wide and boundless agitation that surrounded us, and have a firm, distinct, and legal ground to rest upon." He considered the "adjustment," as he called it, to have created a permanent political consensus that removed slavery forever from controversy. By the time Fillmore declared the "final settlement," it had become the central assumption of politics. Less than two weeks after the Compromise was approved, during a debate on a stringent bill providing five years in prison for "enticing or assisting of slaves to escape from their owners," giving teeth to the Fugitive Slave Act, Cass dismissed antislavery objections as futile irritations. "I do not believe any party could now be built up in relation to this question of slavery," he said. "I think the question is settled in the public mind. I do not think it worthwhile to make speeches upon it."

But Clay's Compromise was not conceived as a compromise; nor did it produce a lasting armistice or truce. From the beginning it was intended to undermine Taylor's policy, which would admit California and New Mexico as free states, and grant the South no favors and exemptions for or extensions of slavery. Clay's bill conjured a quasi-party to do battle against the Whig president, promising to save the Union against the threat of secession and civil war. But if the danger Clay suggested were imminent, the commander-in-chief, Old Rough and Ready, would have handily crushed it. Clay's Compromise was at base an appeasement. Through the public relations ploy of moving the notorious slave pens in the shadow of the Capitol, a source of "agitation" for antislavery crusaders and even embarrassment to proper pro-slavery legislators, across the Potomac to Alexandria, Clay was still belatedly attempting to resolve the political contradictions that had plagued his failed presidential campaigns. When Taylor's death opened the door for Clay's success in passing his bill, he stumbled at the threshold. He was too desperately ambitious for a crowning legacy to see that he was forcing too much at once without having secured enough backing. He had been a master of the Congress since he had entered it in 1811, elected speaker of the house on his first day, but his final act collapsed from his grandiosity. His faulty strategy required a more adroit political tactician in Douglas to divide his monumental bill into pieces and to pass them one by one. Only then were the results of the election of 1848 overturned and Taylor buried politically as well as literally. But by then, Clay had departed from the stage.

In creating the Compromise Clay set in motion the destruction of his greatest legacy—the Whig Party. If he was the founding father of any American institution, besides establishing the power of the speaker of the house, it was that one. He had forged it as a national party, the party of Union, transcending sectional antagonism, neither pro-slavery nor antislavery, but of economic development, an "American system." By calming the South through the Compromise of 1850, Clay smoothed the internal conflicts of the Democratic Party and heightened the frictions among the Whigs. The Fugitive Slave Act was left as the chief organizing tool of abolitionists, tearing the Whigs apart and propelling its Northern and Southern wings to fly in opposite directions. Clay's Compromise made it politically untenable for Southern Whigs to remain Whigs. The Democrats, by contrast, now appeared the party of national unity, constitutional virtue, peace, and progress. After Fillmore hailed the "final settlement," the terms seemed set for a long period of Democratic rule. And yet the world moved.

At its core, the "final settlement" contained an unsettling flaw. Clay's Compromise of 1850 contradicted his Compromise of 1820. New Mexico, Utah, and half of California were dealt with without regard for the sacrosanct line of the Missouri Compromise that had guaranteed peace in its time. But the Compromise of 1850 did not claim to supersede the earlier one. It said nothing about it at all. Instead it applied the doctrine of popular sovereignty to the territories, but did not stipulate that it would be operable for additional ones. Jefferson Davis, who insisted on the legal relevance of the Missouri Compromise, which he felt should be expunged, in opposing the Compromise of 1850, had a point. Which remained in force? Resolving the dilemma in the next case, the Kansas and Nebraska Territory, by erasing the line of the Missouri Compromise, would trigger the armed conflict the Compromise of 1850 had supposedly made impossible.

Fillmore had approved the Compromise believing he would be venerated for his lasting achievement rather than signing his "political death warrant," as Thurlow Weed put it. Once the conflict over slavery resumed it would be on the ashes of the Whig Party. But Clay at the time of the Compromise was probably astute enough to understand that he was sacrificing his mortal party for his immortal reputation. If anyone knew it, Clay knew that the winners write the history. The irony of Henry Clay, however, remained overshadowed by his image in history. And even modern historians have printed the legend, as one of Clay's biographers, Robert V. Remini, wrote, "the Compromise of 1850 did, in a very real sense, prevent the permanent separation of the Union—thanks to Henry Clay."

In New Mexico, the Compromise provided for territorial status leading to popular sovereignty that, according to Clay and Webster, by reason of its climate, would inevitably establish a free state. The reality, however, involved empowerment of pro-slavery forces and suppression of the territory's short-lived democracy. New Mexico's constitution banning slavery and its elected representatives were immediately swept aside. Fillmore appointed James S. Calhoun, a Southern Whig from Georgia, as territorial governor, and he spent his year in office attempting to impose slavery before dying of scurvy. He did succeed in enacting a peonage system forbidding the indebted poor, the vast majority of the population, from quitting the service of their masters, slavery in all but name, though without a slave trade. Subsequent Democratic presidents appointed pro-slavery governors, who created a harsh Black Code in 1857 and "protection of property in slaves" in 1859, followed by a fugitive slave act that specifically outlawed emancipation. On the eve of the Civil War, New Mexico was for all intents and purposes a slave territory on its way to being admitted as a slave state. Politics, not climate, had everything to do with it. It was not until fifteen years after the Compromise of 1850, when Abraham Lincoln managed the passage of the Thirteenth Amendment abolishing slavery, that New Mexico's slave laws were finally overturned.

CHAPTER FOUR

THE CONSEQUENCES OF THE PEACE

In the flush of victory, President Fillmore sought to finish off "the firm." It was not sufficient that he had won the Compromise; he was intent on destroying Seward and Weed. But the last act of his revenge tragedy would leave him politically dead on the stage and the Whig Party in shambles. "The drama has its acts, and the plot is no plot without reaction," Seward wrote Weed just after the passage of the Compromise. "I look for reaction now." "Freedom's banner trails in the dust at Washington," Weed editorialized in his *Albany Journal*. "Histories were written, detailing how the great peril of disunion, imminent in 1850, was in that year, by congressional wisdom, happily ended forever," recorded Seward's memoir of the period (authored by his son Frederick Seward, accurately reflecting his father's judg-

Daniel Webster

ments). "Some of these volumes, still extant, were for years used in schools, teaching the boys lessons that they afterward unlearned at the point of the bayonet. It was not enough to say that it was 'settled.' One was expected to admit that it was 'finally settled.' Phrases about that 'finality' became a test between political orthodoxy and 'abolition' heresy."

The first political test of the Compromise came at the New York state Whig convention at Syracuse less than three weeks after its passage, on September 27. Francis Granger, who had been Harrison's postmaster general, lately a Fillmore ally, presided as chairman. The pro-Fillmore conservatives called themselves the "Silver Grays" after Granger's distinguished mane, while dubbing the pro-Seward group the "Woolly Heads," a racial epithet. Hugh Maxwell, collector of the port of New York, and his deputy, acted as whips for the Silver Grays. Granger installed the reliable Congressman William A. Duer as chairman of the platform committee, who issued a report in favor of the Compromise and left Seward unmentioned. Seward's men proposed a resolution against the Compromise that praised Seward for his stand in the Senate. Weed sensed an opening and successfully maneuvered to nominate for governor Washington Hunt, the state comptroller, who was Fillmore's successor in the post, and the most conservative figure still loyal to Seward. When the convention adopted the pro-Seward resolution, the Silver Grays staged a noisy walkout. Duer, according to Weed, "admitted that he went to Syracuse from Washington with instructions from Mr. Fillmore to bolt in case Mr. Seward's course was approved in the platform." The Democrats, meanwhile, welcomed back the antislavery Barnburners under the leadership of "Prince" John Van Buren with an agreement to share state offices, and for governor nominated Horatio Seymour, a member of the "Softshell Hunker" faction in favor of reconciliation with the prodigal Van Burenites. A gaggle of abolitionists were left isolated outside the Democratic reunion, reducing the Free Soil Party in New York to a remnant. The Silver Grays then held their own convention to endorse the Fugitive Slave Act. A committee of the most notable Silver Grays formed a "Union Safety Committee" under the banner of "Anti-Disunion, Anti-Abolition, Anti-Seward, Anti-Weed,—for Governor, Horatio Seymour." Near Election Day, the group staged a large rally at Castle Garden in Manhattan, where a letter was read from Daniel Webster defending the Fugitive Slave Act that directly attacked Seward as its offender. "No man is at liberty to set up, or affect to set up, his own conscience as above the law," wrote Webster. "It remains to be seen how far the deluded and deluders will go on in this career of faction, folly, and crime." Senator Dickinson of New York, the pro-slavery Cotton Whig instrumental in passing the Compromise, provided another denunciatory communiqué. Under Fillmore's orders, the Whig-controlled customs house served as a chief source of funding for the Democratic ticket. When the ballots were counted, however, Washington Hunt eked out a 262-vote squeaker. The Whigs also captured the legislature—evicting Dickinson from his U.S. Senate seat and replacing him with Seward's protégé, Hamilton Fish. Weed declared it a victory "to restrain the extension of slavery, and to wipe out that black spot, wherever it can be done." But this was simply round one in the battle royal between Fillmore and "the firm."

Daniel Webster, the bold personification of the New England brand of the Whig Party for decades, his expansive idea of nationalism the heart of his identity, had reduced it to a shriveled kernel: the federal authority to enforce the Fugitive Slave Act. He had once opposed the Missouri Compromise, standing literally at Plymouth Rock to vow to "extirpate and destroy" the slave trade. He had denounced slavery in his "Second Reply to Hayne" "as one of the greatest evils, both moral and political." He called the Wilmot Proviso his "thunder" and in 1848 dedicated himself publicly against the extension of slavery "at all times and under all circumstances" and against "all compromises." But then in his March 7 speech in favor of the Compromise, he preached that acceptance of slavery was consistent with the teachings of Jesus Christ: "There was slavery among the Jews. . . . There was slavery among the Greeks. . . . I suppose there is to be found no injunction against that relation between man and man, in the teachings of the Gospel of Jesus Christ, or of any of his Apostles. . . . We must view things as they are. Slavery does exist in the United States."

Restored as secretary of state, contemplating yet another bid for the presidency that he felt was the rightful crown of his career, Webster made himself a hateful figure to the leading moral and literary lights of New England. In their eyes the Godlike Daniel metamorphosed into Black Dan. Used to adoration, loving applause, he lashed out at those excoriating him. His anger went far beyond personal pique or politics. Though he had long represented the large business interests of Boston's State Street, pocketing more than regular fees to finance his luxuries, and the well-heeled leaped to his defense, he was cut to the bone by the harsh condemnations of eminences like Ralph Waldo Emerson. "The word liberty in the mouth of Mr. Webster sounds like the word love in the mouth of a courtesan," Emerson wrote in his journal, adding that Webster's use of the word "Union" was a "ghastly nothing." Later, in a public speech on Webster and the Fugitive Slave Act, Emerson would lament that the man New Englanders rightly saw as "the representative of the American Continent" had fallen to the depths of moral debauchery for slavery. Webster took the reversal of Transcendentalist opinion toward him in response to his own reversal of principles as their betrayal, not his. Despite his obsession with the approval of State Street, he knew that the Sage of Concord carried a moral status that could not be bought. He could feel the ground slipping away beneath him in Massachusetts, his time running out. His age and pride made his struggle existential; his alcoholism undoubtedly intensified his vindictive impulses. When his protégé, Robert C. Winthrop, his interim replacement as senator and a paragon of respectability, the direct descendant of the founder of the Massachusetts Bay Colony, and a stalwart Whig, spoke and voted against the Compromise, Webster was stunned. He labeled him "Judas" for taking what Winthrop considered a principled position that would have accorded with the former Webster. Webster disdained Winthrop's opposition to the Fugitive Slave Act as the result of mere "prejudices" and washed his hands of him. "For my part," he wrote, "I much prefer to see a respectable Democrat elected to Congress, than a professed Whig, tainted with any degree of Free Soil doctrines, or abolitionism."

Of course, it was Webster himself that many in Boston thought bore the mark of Judas. The hellfire of the Puritan jeremiad was unleashed on him as having gone over to the devil. Charles Sumner denounced him as an "archangel ruined," the very definition of Satan. In reply Webster tried to drive his critics into submission with his own rhetorical blasts. The Compromise of 1850 became his alpha and omega. The Fugitive Slave Act was his test of the rule of law, the sign of belief in the Constitution. Webster even began altering his fundamental concept of the Union, which he had wrapped around himself like the flag, to fit his shifting politics. He hoped for a "remodeling of parties," and spoke of creating a new "Union" party, including only those Democrats and Whigs that were loyal to the act's enforcement. There could be "no Whig party in New York, or Massachusetts, which espouses doctrines and utters sentiments hostile to the just and Constitutional rights of the South." He sent letters filled with invective to "Union" rallies, like the one in New York organized to destroy Seward's influence. As the sands of time ran out on his ambition, Webster's rage was untempered.

In Massachusetts, Conscience Whigs and Democrats eyed each other with suspicion, but their mutual contempt for Webster allowed them to act for mutual benefit. Supported by the Conscience Whigs, the Democrats cap-

tured the governorship and other important offices—and a majority in the
state legislature. Webster blamed Winthrop and other defectors "entirely," he
wrote Fillmore, yet his ire had helped foster the political turn of events that
had elevated his nemesis, the Free Soil leader Charles Sumner, into Winthrop's likely replacement. Yet Sumner faced formidable obstacles. A sizable
minority of Democrats, calling themselves the "Indomitables," was hostile to
putting in a "red-hot Abolitionist," while Sumner's chance was also undermined by purist abolitionists within his political circle, such as former congressman John G. Palfrey, the former dean of the Harvard Divinity School,
morally opposed to any coalition with Democrats, and who condescendingly
dismissed the meaning of Sumner's election to the Senate as "overrated." The
legislature seemed hopelessly deadlocked.

Webster's battle with Boston's abolitionists rapidly escalated into a kind of
Bay State civil war. On October 21, 1850, a month after the passage of the Fugitive Slave Act, the Boston Vigilance Committee held a rally of several thousand people at Faneuil Hall, presided over by Charles Francis Adams, son of
the late president John Quincy Adams, and adopted a resolution proclaiming that "we will never let a fugitive slave be carried back from Boston." Its
author was Theodore Parker, the leading Unitarian minister of Boston and
antislavery militant, who was elected the chairman to organize resistance.
Only a few days later, a slave owner in Georgia sent two men to reclaim his
property in Boston. William and Ellen Craft had escaped from a Macon
plantation in 1848, making their way north by the ingenious ruse of Ellen,
a mulatto who could pass as white, disguised as a Southern gentleman with
William posing as "his" servant. In Boston, trained as public speakers, they
became a sensation on the abolitionist circuit. They lived in the free black
community on the slope of Beacon Hill, she working as a seamstress, he as
a carpenter, and were parishioners of Parker's church. When the slave hunters came to Boston, the Vigilance Committee tracked their movements and
issued a poster describing them. Parker hid the Crafts and formally married
them, giving William a gift of a revolver and knife to protect his family. The
slave hunters were slapped with a defamation suit initiated by the Vigilance
Committee and the Boston sheriff arrested them twice, a court setting bail of
$10,000 that was paid by a prominent Cotton Whig with Southern interests.
"It's not the niggers I care about, but the principle of the thing," declared one
of the affronted slave hunters. Upon their release, about sixty members of the
Vigilance Committee confronted them at their hotel, where Parker sternly
informed them "they were not safe another night," and they fled Boston.

Webster was infuriated. He happened to have been in Boston during the fracas and decided that he would personally take charge. "For two days I have been endeavoring to do something to put this business of the attempt to arrest Crafts into a better shape," he wrote Fillmore on November 11. He lamented the incompetence of the district attorney and the state of public opinion. "I am sorry to be obliged to say that the general weight of U.S. officers in this District is against the execution of the Fugitive Slave Law. I hear this when I go into the Streets from every sound Whig, and every Union man I meet." Webster, nonetheless, forced a hesitant federal marshal to seek to capture the Crafts. They would then be turned over to the local commissioner stipulated by the act to enforce it. And in Massachusetts the Fugitive Slave commissioner was George Ticknor Curtis, Webster's lawyer, amanuensis, and biographer, appointed at Webster's behest. Learning of Webster's relentless pursuit, the Vigilance Committee secreted the Crafts on to a ship to England, where they wrote the story of their escape, published in 1860, *Running A Thousand Miles for Freedom*, which became one of the most widely circulated slave narratives, and in which they charged that the Fugitive Slave Act was enacted by "the slave power, with the aid of Daniel Webster and a band of lesser traitors."

In the aftermath of the Crafts' escape, Webster encouraged Curtis to stage a "pro-Union" rally for the Fugitive Slave Act, attended by the "best men," the leading Cotton Whigs, at Faneuil Hall. Benjamin Curtis, George Ticknor Curtis's brother, a prominent Boston attorney, who had offered a brief for the prosecution of the Crafts, said about the fugitives to the cheering multitude of merchants and lawyers: "With the rights of these persons Massachusetts has nothing to do." Webster congratulated George T. Curtis, "The world is filled with the fame of your great meeting." The next year Webster got Fillmore to name Benjamin Curtis to the Supreme Court. (He would, perhaps ironically, be one of the two dissenting votes on the *Dred Scott* decision and quit the court in disgust.)

In February 1851, Commissioner Curtis issued an arrest warrant for a fugitive slave named Frederick Minkins, known as "Shadrach," who had escaped from Virginia a few months earlier, brazenly working as a waiter in a coffeehouse several doors down the block from the office of Garrison's *Liberator*. Chief Justice Lemuel Shaw of the Massachusetts Supreme Judicial Court denied a writ of habeas corpus on the grounds that the Fugitive Slave Act was constitutional. Before the hearing that would have remanded Shadrach to his master, on February 15, members of the Vigilance Committee, whites and free blacks, rushed into the courthouse, freed the prisoner, and carried him away. In four days, he was in Canada. "I think it the noblest deed done in Boston since the destruction of the tea in 1773," said Parker, whose grandfather, Captain John Parker, had fired the first shot in the American Revolution in the Battle of Lexington Green.

Webster was apoplectic. "Was it be conivence [*sic*] or by absolute force? Did the Marshal do his duty. Answer," he telegraphed his close friend Peter Harvey. Then he wrote a "Calling on Citizens to Assist in the Recapture of a Fugitive Slave Arrested in Boston, Massachusetts," signed by Fillmore and himself, describing the episode as "this outrage." He took charge of the prosecution, ordered the U.S. attorney to arrest those involved and to hire certain lawyers to conduct the case. Ten men were promptly indicted, but in the trials of May and June none were convicted, another humiliation.

On Washington's Birthday, Webster issued a message condemning "outrages so abominable" and "a nefarious project," "strictly speaking a case of treason," and, for good measure, "nothing less than treason."

Aroused by the spectacular Shadrach escape, Clay took to the floor of the Senate on February 21 and the 24 to deliver a furious defense of the Fugitive Slave Act. He simply could not believe that free blacks were involved in liberating Shadrach, demanding "condign punishment" for "those who advised, and stimulated, and instigated those unfortunate blacks to these deeds of lawless enormity," and promising that "the really guilty party who lurks behind, putting forward these miserable wretches, will be brought to justice." He pointed his finger at the English abolitionist George Thompson, "a foreign hireling," embarked on "subversion." Clay commended the execution of the Fugitive Slave Act throughout the North, "with the sole exception of the city of Boston," citing the case of a slave caught in New York as "a most beautiful exhibition of the moral power of the law." Then he lavished praise on the Compromise of 1850 for creating "peace." Its measures had "worked wonders," he said, "worked a miracle. They have made thousands of converts among the abolitionists themselves." Finally, he wheeled like a prosecutor on Senator Salmon P. Chase, pressing him to answer whether he was or was not "an abolitionist." Clay drew his own conclusion from his accusation. "All sorts of abolitionists seem to act together. There are some more unblushing and violent than others; there are some who call themselves ministers of God, who from their pulpits denounce the Constitution of the Union, and denounce all the states in which slavery exists. Whether the senator be one of them or not, it is not for me to say." Besides a brief statement a week later, on a River and Harbor bill, which was defeated, Clay's speech, "On Violations of the Fugitive Slave Act," was his last, closing his shining but tragic career.

Webster soon got his chance to rectify the mortifications of the Crafts and Shadrach when, on April 3, a young fugitive slave named Thomas Sims was caught. This time the courthouse doors were secured with iron chains, under which Justice Shaw crawled in order to deny habeas corpus again. Webster arrived in Boston to oversee the rendition. To add insult to his injury, Robert Rantoul stepped forward to represent the fugitive before Commissioner Curtis. Rantoul, one of Boston's leading attorneys, had been a close friend of Webster and a business partner. When the state legislature deadlocked over whom to place in the U.S. Senate seat, Winthrop resigned from it and Rantoul was named as his replacement, but held the position for only a month, leaving in March. Now he argued that the Fugitive Slave Act was unconstitutional, Curtis had no legal authority, and, for good measure, quoted the Declaration of Independence. "There is then," Rantoul said, "a presumption which applies to 'ALL MEN,' black men and white men—to all men created in the image of their Maker, and I have not yet heard that that category includes the idea of any particular color." Curtis, however, ruled that Sims must be returned to slavery. The Vigilance Committee huddled to consider various rescue plans. But early on the morning of April 13 Sims was marched out of the courthouse surrounded by more than one hundred policemen. Parker and the others could only watch as he was hustled on to a waiting ship. He soon arrived back in the hands of his master at Savannah, Georgia, and was publicly whipped. "I congratulate you and the country upon a triumph of law in Boston," Fillmore wrote Webster. "She has done nobly. She has wiped out the stain of the former rescue and freed herself from the reproach of nullification." "Nullification," Calhoun's states' rights doctrine, had become a word that Webster had taken to hurling against Northern opponents of the Fugitive Slave Act. "On this occasion all Boston people are said to have behaved well," Webster wrote Fillmore. "Nothing ever exceeded the malignity with which abolitionists and free-soilers persecute all those who endeavor to see the laws executed. They are insane, but it is an angry and vindictive insanity."

For four months the Massachusetts legislature had been frozen, unable to elect a senator. But within a week of the Sims case the ice broke. Webster had angrily withdrawn his support from Winthrop, who was still standing as the Whig candidate. Thurlow Weed quietly exercised his hidden hand on Massachusetts Whigs to vote for Sumner. The town meeting of Fall River instructed its representatives to vote for him—and one antislavery Whig switched. On April 24, Sumner was elected. If he owed his triumph to one man, it was to Webster. Charles Francis Adams hailed Sumner's victory as "the downfall of Mr. Webster. Nothing in the ordinary course of events will now avail to set him up again before nature shall remove him. . . . Not a fit emblem of puritan Massachusetts. Sumner will come much nearer to it." Webster's allies in the legislature reacted to the shock by signing a document, "To the People of Massachusetts," written by Benjamin Curtis, decrying Sumner's election as the act of "a factious conspiracy to violate a public trust, and as such criminal, not only in morals, but in the law of the land."

Webster embarked on a two-months-long speaking tour to vindicate his course and lay the groundwork for his presidential candidacy. "It is treason, treason, treason, and nothing else," he declaimed in Syracuse, New York, where abolitionists had freed a captured fugitive slave. He traveled to Virginia, where he proclaimed the Blue Ridge Mountains "higher" than Seward's "higher law." But his most memorable phrase-making was at Buffalo, where he spoke about the fractured state of the Union and the Whig Party. He wondered whether the Union could be held together "not by military power, but by the silken cords of mutual, fraternal, patriotic affection." These "cords" were the metaphor introduced by Calhoun that would be "frayed" if Southern demands were unmet. Of his party, Webster said, "If a house be divided against itself, it will fall, and crush everybody in it." Webster's "silken cords . . . of affection," originally Calhoun's, would be transmuted into "the mystic chords of memory" of Lincoln's First Inaugural Address, edited by Seward, and Lincoln would raise the theme of the "house divided" after the Whig Party had shattered, leaving only the stark question of slavery.

For Robert Toombs and Alexander Stephens, Whig congressmen from Georgia, the Fugitive Slave Act, which they had advocated, was hardly a theoretical question. During the debate over the bill, on August 10, 1850, their manservants, Allen and Garland, and one of Toombs's housemaids, were captured fleeing from Washington in a carriage driven by William L. Chaplin, chief conductor of the Underground Railroad in the capital. He was held on $18,000 bond, an extraordinary sum, raised by a committee headed by Chase, Giddings, and Whittier, and mostly paid by the wealthy abolitionist philanthropist Gerrit Smith. Once bailed, Chaplin never returned for his trial. Henry Highland Garnet, the radical free black minister, who would become close to President Lincoln, operated the Underground Railroad station through which he would have transported his passengers in Philadelphia. Chaplin's case effectively severed the link between the Washington and upstate New York abolitionist communities. In the aftermath, Smith and other radicals spent years casting around for other causes, eventually discovering the mesmerizing John Brown.

Toombs's captured slave, Garland H. White, was literate and became an ordained minister. Living in Toombs's Washington residence on Lafayette Park across from the White House, he befriended Seward, who lived two houses away. In 1860, White escaped again, possibly with Seward's help or foreknowledge, and who corresponded with him from Canada. After the Emancipation Proclamation, White joined the 28th U.S. Colored Infantry and through Seward's intervention was appointed its chaplain. He was among the first Union soldiers to liberate Richmond in 1865, where he witnessed Lincoln's visit a few days later, and was reunited with his mother, whom he had not seen since he had been a child.

As soon as the Congress adjourned after enacting the Compromise of 1850, Toombs and Stephens had rushed back to Georgia to quell the Ultras. They had fanned the flames they then tried to stamp out.

Their provocations "had been made with the object of controlling the North by fear of disruption," noted the Southern historian Ulrich B. Phillips. "The people of Georgia, however, had not been shown the underlying intention of their Representatives, and taking their fire-eating speeches and their awful prophesyings in dead earnest had grown so much excited as to be almost ready for immediate secession." Georgia was the epicenter of the movement, the pivot of secession. Months before the Compromise, Governor George W. Towns, objecting to California's admission as a free state, approved an election for delegates to a Sovereign Convention to withdraw from the Union. Governors John A. Quitman of Mississippi and Whitemarsh B. Seabrook of South Carolina scheduled special sessions of their legislatures expecting to ride the wave from Georgia. On August 22, Rhett and Yancey, the supreme orators of disunion, whipped up the crowd at the Southern Rights Mass Meeting at Macon, Georgia, attended by delegates from nearly every county in the state as well as representatives from Alabama and South Carolina. Rhett, who had succeeded Calhoun in the Senate, promised Quitman that if Georgia and Mississippi seceded South Carolina would follow suit. Yancey traveled the region like a circuit rider organizing Southern Rights associations. But Toombs and Stephens formed an alliance with their Democratic rival, Speaker of the House Howell Cobb, bound to defend the Compromise together. "The South has compromised no right, surrendered no principle, and lost not an inch of ground in this great contest," Toombs stated. A majority of Democrats favored secession, but Cobb carried a large plurality with him. Joined with the Whigs behind Toombs and Stephens they gained a majority in the special election of delegates to the Georgia convention. On December 12, 1850, they announced the formation of a new political party, the Constitutional Union Party, and issued a manifesto, the Georgia Platform, which the convention ratified. It was the seminal document for Southern Unionists that, Stephens noted, "showed clearly to the two old Parties that their days were numbered, unless they in their Conventions should proclaim their determination to abide by the settlement so made." Cobb was nominated for governor and easily defeated the would-be secessionist; Toombs was elected U.S. senator. The reverberation was felt in South Carolina, where the Unionists gained control of its Sovereign Convention and secession was sidestepped. "I will secede, if I can, from this Union," Rhett proclaimed, and promptly quit the Senate. In Alabama, the Unionists prevailed and Yancey went into hibernation.

In Mississippi, Quitman, a splenetic secessionist, had led the legislature to censure Senator Foote for voting for the Compromise and formed a States Rights Democratic Party. But after Unionists captured the Georgia Sovereign Convention the secessionist momentum swiftly collapsed. Quitman resigned under a cloud of scandal—indicted for violating the Neutrality Law by his entanglement in a freebooting failed invasion of Cuba. Jefferson Davis, who maintained that California's admission was "unconstitutional" and "a fraud," that the Compromise reflected "the ruling, directing power of hostility to the slave institutions of the South," and that Mississippi must "make a manly and determined resistance now," substituted as the candidate for governor of the States Rights Democratic Party to face his nemesis Senator Henry S. Foote. The Unionist Party, under Foote, in the meantime won the election of delegates to the Mississippi Sovereign Convention by two to one by adopting the Georgia Platform as its own. Davis spent his campaign vainly trying to separate himself from the tainted Quitman and secession, and Foote swept into office. The first act of the new legislature was to replace Davis as senator. While Foote judged Quitman as having "a slow and plodding intellect," being "over ambitious," having "selfishness," and "altogether the dullest and most prosy speaker I have ever known who could speak at all," he had "a far truer heart" than Davis, "inferior to him" in "flippancy of expression, and he was certainly far behind him also in impudent effrontery, in low and vulgar cunning, and in a capacity for bringing into advantageous and effective use the multiplied arts of deception." Presiding as squire in the repose of his Greek Revival mansion overlooking his vast Brierfield plantation at Davis Bend on the Mississippi, Davis declared he was "separated from the exciting strife of politicians," but was already fighting for control of the state party and holding sway over the composition of the delegation to the National Democratic Convention of 1852.

The Georgia Platform laid the foundation for Southern Unionists for the coming decade, but it also set the terms for disunion. It was a ticking time bomb. Declaring that the creation of the Union itself had been "impossible with compromise" among the original thirteen states and that the Compromise of 1850 was in "this spirit," the signers of the platform, while they did "not wholly approve" of every aspect, agreed they "will abide by it as a permanent adjustment of this sectional controversy." And then the platform immediately withdrew the very notion of permanence that it claimed as its bedrock. The Union, it stated, had not established the states, after all, but was a conditional relationship whose future the states could and should decide depending on particular grievances. Accordingly, Georgia "will and ought to resist even (as a last resort), to a disruption of every tie which binds her to the Union, any action of Congress"—and here the platform specified the grounds under which Georgia would be compelled to secede—"upon the subject of slavery in the District of Columbia, or in any places subject to the jurisdiction of Congress incompatible with the safety, domestic tranquility, the rights and honor of the slave-holding States, or any refusal to admit as a State any territory hereafter, applying, because of the existence of slavery therein, or any act prohibiting the introduction of slaves into the territories of New Mexico and Utah, or any act repealing or materially modifying the laws now in force for the recovery of fugitive slaves."

So, the Compromise described in the Georgia Platform did not happen to be the same one passed by the Congress; nor was it an interpretation, but instead a novelty. Upholding the Compromise as the cynosure of stability, the writers of the platform distorted its basis. Whereas the Compromise stated that slavery in New Mexico and Utah would be determined by popular sovereignty, the platform asserted that denying slavery there would break the agreement. The platform, moreover, added that any new legislation on slavery would breach it—and it further stipulated that all new territories must permit slavery. In voting for the Compromise, Toombs, Stephens, and the other Southerners claimed that it superseded the Missouri Compromise of

1820 that prohibited slavery north of the Mason-Dixon Line (excepting Missouri) and established instead the principle of noninterference with slavery in any territory, though Jefferson Davis's effort to extend the line of the Missouri Compromise all the way west through California had been defeated. Toombs et al. ignored the rejection of Davis's motion, heralding an even greater victory, though imaginary. They did not pause at the contradiction between the two historic compromises. Defending their vote for the Compromise of 1850 through the Georgia Platform that claimed entirely different provisions from the actual document hurtled them on a collision course around the bend with Douglas, who rightly read the Compromise as legitimating popular sovereignty wherein people might exclude slavery. Paradoxically, when Douglas's Kansas-Nebraska Act was passed with the co-sponsorship of the authors of the Georgia Platform on their premise that it would open the territory to slavery, the repeal of the Missouri Compromise that they fervently hoped for, they were undone as Unionists. The secessionists were held at bay only until the bright red lines of the Georgia Platform were crossed. Written as the credo of the Southern Unionists, it eventually made possible the rise of the Southern Rights men whose front ranks Toombs would join. At the same time that the platform upheld the Union it established the grounds for secession. Toombs the compromiser paved the way for Toombs the secessionist. Stephens the Whig was on his path to becoming the Confederate vice president and Cobb the Unionist to be the founding president of the first Confederate Congress. The Georgia Platform proved to be anything but "permanent." In that respect, it was organically part of the Compromise, which offered the same illusory effect.

The making of the Compromise had been the making of Stephen A. Douglas. Clay's exhaustion ushered him to the well of the Senate. Douglas was not the stand-in playing for the fallen warhorse, but a new actor inventing his own role. His emergence marked the end of an epoch, the passing of the older generation that had dominated politics for decades. During the Compromise debate, after Calhoun, Clay, and Webster had delivered what were in effect their valedictories, Douglas had arisen on March 13, 1850, to deliver his true opening speech as a national figure. His remarks at the time made little impression, but in retrospect provided the insight to his aspiration. On one level it was a typical Douglas production in which he positioned himself in a movable middle, casting Northerners for the Wilmot Proviso and Southerners against the Compromise as Ultras, while trying to vault into his party's leadership as the foremost advocate of popular sovereignty, which was another of his positioning tools. But there was more to this speech than the maneuvering. With it Douglas shunted the venerable Triumvirate into the past and attempted to render the whole debate between North and South into irrelevance. He stood as the Western man arrived to engineer the future. His speech was a floodlight on his grandiose design. "We have heard so much talk about the North and the South," he said,

> as if those two sections were the only ones necessary to be taken into con-
> sideration, when gentlemen begin to mature their arrangements for disso-
> lution all the union, and to mark the dividing lines upon the maps, that I'm
> gratified to find that there are those who appreciate the important truth,
> but there is a power in this nation greater than either the North or the
> South—a growing, increasing, swelling power, that will be able to speak
> the law to this nation, and to execute the law as spoken. That power is the
> country known as the great West—the Valley of the Mississippi, one and
> invisible from the gulf to the great lakes, and stretching, on the one side
> and the other, to the extreme sources of the Ohio and Missouri—from
> the Alleghenies to the Rocky Mountains. There, sir, is the hope of this
> nation—the resting place of the power that is not only to control, but to
> save, the Union.

Proclaiming a power greater than North or South, Douglas unabashedly presented himself as embodiment of the West itself. He was the "towering genius" of unbounded "ambition" that Lincoln warned of in his 1838 Spring-field Lyceum address, even then with Douglas in mind. Douglas himself was the greater power, steam driven. The Little Giant was the new colossus.

"Oh, young Lochinvar is come out of the West," Walter Scott had writ-ten in his ballad of the brave knight who sweeps a bride away. Douglas now rode in as the "Lochinvar of the Young Democracy," the leader of "Young America," the generational movement proclaimed by the *Democratic Review* as the vanguard of Manifest Destiny, and would announce he was voicing "the spirit of the age."

His career was his greatest speculation of all. His political success was also the basis of his economic fortune—and his monetization of his connec-tions crucial to his legislative success across the board. W. W. Corcoran, the Texas bond lobby, and the Illinois bondholders who became the board of the Illinois Central could testify to his finesse. The Compromise elevated him into a power in the Senate, the leading Democrat of his generation and the

West, and touted by the *New York Herald* as a presidential contender. It was all of a piece and one continuous high-wire act.

What hath Douglas wrought? The ultimate deal maker was the most transformational figure.

The Compromise was only the first car in the train of his success. When it pulled into the station, the Illinois Central was close behind. The Compromise would not be the "final settlement," but the Illinois Central was unstoppable. Douglas's feat was more than a signal legislative triumph. He not only realigned politics but also forged an economic revolution. The Illinois Central Railroad Tax Act and the federal land grants began the explosive growth of railroads, the engine for industrial revolution, replacing canals and turnpikes. And railroads spurred a revolution in manufacturing, the sudden emergence of great cities like Chicago, the creation of a national market economy including in agriculture, and the rapid settlement of the West in scope and scale for which Clay's "American System" was a rudimentary model. Over the next decade, total railroad mileage expanded from nine thousand to thirty thousand, crisscrossing the country with tracks. Chicago became the nation's railroad center, where by 1860 fifteen different lines and more than one hundred trains converged daily, transforming the economic and polit-

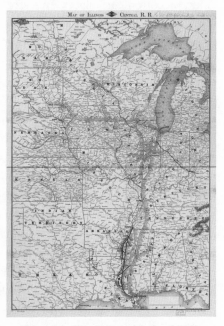

Map of the Illinois Central Railroad, 1860

ical balance of power within Illinois away from the settled and conservative southern counties, and without which Lincoln's emergence would not have been possible.

Some historians have justified the Compromise of 1850 because it "gave the North ten years to build its industrial strength and enable it to overpower the South when the war finally broke out," as Robert V. Remini wrote. His proof was that the South "did not have a railroad system by which to move men and material to the areas where they were most needed." Rationalizing the actions of politicians on the basis of motives and thoughts they did not have, and events that were not and could not be predicted, as though those debating the Compromise of 1850 were preparing for victory in the Civil War, is an illogical omniscience. The facts present yet another difficulty. It was not just the North and the West that rose. While the South was hardly as industrially developed as the North over the coming decade, it was not an isolated pastoral idyll. One third of the growth of the nation's railroads was in the South, largely built by slave labor, linking together the cotton kingdom, and weaving it into the economies of New England and New York—and London. More than three quarters of Southern railroads depended upon slaves for operation. Railroads made possible the exponential increase in the value of cotton and slaves and strengthened the slave system measurably. Through the new technology slavery became more intrinsic than ever to the unprecedented growth of international capitalism in the decade of the 1850s. The South supplied more than three fourths of the cotton for the textile mills of England that employed perhaps a quarter of all English workers and was the basis of half of England's exports. The price of cotton rose continuously over the next decade, making the South the richest section of the country and its aristocracy the wealthiest. "Southern slave-grown cotton was the nation's leading export," wrote historian David Brion Davis. "It powered textile-manufacturing revolutions in both New England and Europe, and paid for American imports of everything from steel to capital. In addition, the demand for slave labor in southwestern states like Mississippi, Louisiana and Texas drove up slave prices and land values throughout the South. In the 19th century, slave values more than tripled. By 1860, a young 'prime field hand' in New Orleans would sell for the equivalent of an expensive car, say a Mercedes-Benz, today. American slaves represented more capital than any other asset in the nation, with the exception of land. In 1860, the value of Southern slaves was about three times the amount invested in manufacturing or railroads nationwide." The spiraling value of slaves, translated financially into an almost limitless source of collateral, mortgages, and derivatives, had a multiplier effect on Southern investments, including in railroads.

Douglas's deeds in Washington did not impress everyone in Illinois. The *Quincy Whig* published an article about his Mississippi plantation, charging him with "owning" slaves. Douglas arranged for the *Illinois Register* to refute the claim by reporting that it was his first wife who was the legal owner. Douglas believed that the antislavery criticism of him had to be countered especially in Chicago, where there was not a reliable Democratic newspaper. Douglas reportedly financed a sheet called the *Argus*, but still sought another outlet.

Northern Illinois remained a hotbed of antislavery sentiment. His return to Chicago was not a triumphal march. Instead, Douglas discovered a full-scale revolt against him. The City Council passed a resolution calling the Fugitive Slave Act "cruel and unjust," refused to "require the city policy to render any assistance for the arrest of fugitive slaves," and called Douglas and all those who voted for it "fit only to be ranked with the traitors, Benedict Arnold and Judas Iscariot, who betrayed his Lord and Master for thirty pieces of silver."

This resolution was to be ratified by a mass meeting of the Chicago Common Council of citizens. Douglas requested permission to address it on October 23, 1850. He entered into a crowd of four thousand, about three quarters of all the eligible voters in Chicago. The City Council members sat at the front and a group of armed blacks, some of them fugitives, stood at the back. Douglas defended the compromise for establishing the doctrine of popular sovereignty, which he explained as the essence of democracy itself. No city, he went on, could void an act of the federal government because that would be "naked, unmitigated nullification." He dismissed the objections to the Fugitive Slave Act, whatever they might be, because, he argued, the Constitution protected slavery in the states. "The real objection," he said, "is not to the new law, nor to the old one, but to the Constitution itself. . . . The whole catalogue of objections would all be moonshine, if the Negro was not required to go back to his master." But he was ready "to maintain and preserve inviolate the Constitution as it is, with all its compromises, to stand or fall by the American Union." He wound up with a patriotic peroration, invoking the "glorious memories of the past and precious hopes for the future," and called for a vote to uphold the Constitution and the law. The crowd, swept away, adopted his resolution, and the next day the City Council ratified it. Then Douglas lobbied the Illinois state legislature to rescind its support for the Wilmot Proviso, now an anachronism, and it passed a resolution praising him for enacting the Compromise.

Douglas was convinced he had subdued the "agitation." In yet another speech he denounced "a systematic organization in many of the free States of this Union, for the purpose of evading the obligations of the Constitution, and to prevent the enforcement of the laws of the United States in relation to fugitive slaves . . . a conspiracy against the government." And he called for swift punishment: "I trust the penalty will fall upon the white abolitionists." After leaving Illinois to return east, he vowed "never to make another speech on the slavery question." Nor did he believe he would ever have to engage the issue again.

About the time that Douglas was subduing the Chicago City Council over the Fugitive Slave Act a letter arrived for a housewife at her home in Brunswick, Maine. It came from Mrs. Edward Beecher, wife of the former president of Illinois College, who had been the close friend of the martyred Elijah Lovejoy. Another alumnus of that college was one William Henry Herndon. The recipient of the letter was Mrs. Beecher's sister-in-law, Harriet Beecher Stowe. It described the travails in Boston of hunted fugitive slaves rescued or captured. "I had been nourishing an Anti-Slavery spirit since Lovejoy was murdered for publishing in his paper articles against slavery and intemperance, when our home was in Illinois," Mrs. Beecher recalled. "These terrible things that were going on in Boston were well calculated to rouse up this spirit. What can I do? I thought. Not much myself, but I know one who can." So she wrote to her sister-in-law, a writer of short stories, religious articles, and the occasional travel piece.

Harriet Beecher Stowe

"Now, Hattie, if I could use a pen as you can, I would write something that would make this whole nation feel what an accursed thing slavery is!" When Stowe read those words, she arose from her chair in the parlor, crumpled the letter, and exclaimed to her family, "God helping me, I will write something. I will if I live."

Harriet Beecher Stowe belonged to the preeminent family in the country of the Puritan theological tradition. The patriarch, Lyman Beecher, a Presbyterian minister, inspired the Second Great Awakening. He preached at the Hanover Street Church in Boston, where his parishioner, William Lloyd Garrison, emulated his fiery style and was catalyzed by his sermons condemning slavery as sinful. But Beecher, who believed in gradual emancipation, education, and colonization, considered Garrison an extremist. "Oh, Garrison, you can't reason that way!" he admonished him. "Great economic and political questions can't be solved so simply. You must take into account what is expedient as well as what is right." Lyman Beecher then founded the Lane Theological Seminary in Cincinnati, where his student Theodore

Weld led a revolt that began his abolitionist career. Harriet's sister, Catherine, was a pioneer of women's education, founding women's colleges. Her brothers, Edward, Charles, and Henry, followed their father to the pulpit, and all became antislavery advocates. Charles served as pastor in Newark, New Jersey. Henry presided at the Plymouth Church in Brooklyn, becoming New York's most renowned preacher. Henry, Catherine, and Harriet all shared their father's criticism of Garrison. "All teeth and claw," Henry said. "A species of moral mono-maniacs," declared Harriet, who also thought "my good brother Theodore," referring to Weld, was lacking in "prudence." Though Lyman Beecher remained critical of Garrison, he considered abolitionism "permitted by Heaven for purposes of national retribution . . . as the fit and fearful ministers of his vengeance upon a people incorrigibly wicked."

Harriet married Calvin Stowe when he taught theology at Lane. He was a biblical scholar, who likely suffered from schizophrenia that took the form of vivid religious hallucinations. The couple shared a fervent Christianity and sharp skepticism about Garrisonian abolitionism. "Ultra Abolitionism here," he wrote Harriet from England, "has the same nasty radicalism, the same dogmatic narrowness, that it has in America." In Cincinnati, she became intimately familiar with the full panoply of antislavery activism.

In January 1850, visiting her brother Edward in Boston she met the Reverend Josiah Henson, an escaped slave, who described the murder of his father at the hands of a cruel overseer. When Webster endorsed the Fugitive Slave Act, Harriet wrote that he had "moved over to the side of evil!" In November, her brother Charles preached a sermon against it, "The Duty of Disobedience to Wicked Laws," calling the act "the monster iniquity of the present age" and "the vilest monument of infamy of the nineteenth century," and extolled "the higher law." Aroused by the dramatic rescue scenes from Boston, she attended church in Brunswick, Maine, and had a vision "as if the crucified, but now risen and glorified Christ, were speaking to her through the poor black man, cut and bleeding under the blows of the slave whip," according to her son and grandson's biography. She raced home and began writing with pencil, partly on brown grocery paper, the chapter called "The Death of Uncle Tom." "It all came before me in visions, one after another, and I put them down in words," she explained. The characters were based on people she had encountered—slaves, slave owners, slave hunters, and slave rescuers. One of those real people was John Van Zandt, the conductor of the Underground Railroad, defended by Chase and Seward, and barely disguised in her writing as John Van Trompe. She also plumbed Weld's documentary exposé, *Slavery as It Is: Testimony of One Thousand Witnesses*. And she would subsequently publish *A Key to Uncle Tom's Cabin* to verify its verisimilitude. But her work was unlike any other antislavery tract.

Uncle Tom's Cabin, or, Life Among the Lowly, was a sentimental passion play of a novel that integrated virtually all the themes of moral regeneration and social reform into its story as well as a Christian allegory of the sin of the Fugitive Slave Act. It began appearing as a serial in the *National Era* on June 1, 1851, and ran for forty weeks. The book was published in March 1852 and sold 300,000 copies in its first year. It became the greatest bestseller of the nineteenth century. Even before it appeared in book form it was turned into a play—and all sorts of versions of "Tom plays" filled the theaters, becoming the most popular drama for decades. The South greeted *Uncle Tom's Cabin* with outrage, partial banning, and a stream of "anti-Tom" novels in which the slave owners were kindly and abolitionists were villains.

Stowe prayed her book would "soften and moderate" the "extreme abolitionists," while converting to "abolitionist views many whom the same bitterness had repelled." But its influence on Northern public opinion was achieved in a political vacuum after the Compromise had scattered the antislavery movement. When the Compromise passed, John P. Hale warned against those who cried: " 'Peace! Peace! But there was no peace.' Let me tell you there is no peace to those who think they have successfully dug the grave in which the hopes, the rights, and the interests of freedom have been buried. No, sir, that peace will be short, and that rejoicing will most assuredly be turned into mourning." But the Wilmot Proviso, the central antislavery organizing principle, had been abandoned. Seward described, even seven years later, how the Compromise "brought on a demoralization over the whole country from which even New England has not yet adequately recovered. Nor has it quite passed away in New York." In the four-years-long slough of despond between the Compromise and the Kansas-Nebraska Act, the rallying event of the antislavery cause was Stowe's novel. But the consequences of *Uncle Tom's Cabin* were not to elicit recognition of Christian love and obedience to the "higher law" as its author hoped. The greater its popularity, the more it contributed to polarization.

Douglas took to the Senate floor to denounce the book. An essential part of his rhetorical repertoire was hatred of England, which represented the twin evils of aristocracy and abolitionism. When, during a debate in 1853, Senator Andrew Butler of South Carolina contested Douglas's belligerent views of England—the cotton trade after all was dependent on the English mills—Douglas launched into an accusation of dark conspiracy. "Does he not know," demanded Douglas, "that abolitionism, which has so seriously threatened the peace and safety of this republic, had its origin in England, and has been incorporated into the policy of that government for the purpose of operating upon the peculiar institutions of some of the States of this confederacy, and thus render the Union itself insecure?" For his proof he cited the popularity of *Uncle Tom's Cabin* in England. English women, he elaborated, served as subversive abolitionist missionaries to American women, and "in the name of philanthropy appeal to them to engage in the treasonable plot against the institutions and government of their own choice in their native land, while millions are being expended to distribute Uncle Tom's Cabin throughout the world, with the view of combining the fanaticism, ignorance, and hatred of all the nations of the earth in a common crusade against the peculiar institutions of the State and section of this Union represented by the senator from South Carolina." Whether Douglas ever actually read *Uncle Tom's Cabin* was never documented.

Lincoln would meet Harriet Beecher Stowe at the White House in late November or early December 1862, about a month before the Emancipation Proclamation was about to be issued on New Year's Day. According to the account given by her son Charles, Seward was seated with Lincoln before a roaring fireplace on a cold winter day. Seward introduced the author to the president. "Why, Mrs. Stowe, right glad to see you!" Lincoln supposedly said. "Then," wrote her son, "with a humorous twinkle in his eye, he said, 'So you're the little woman who wrote the book that made this great war!' " Though the story was almost certainly apocryphal, its poetic license captured the Stowe family's true belief that Lincoln grasped the salient contribution of *Uncle Tom's Cabin*. About that, there can be little doubt. Herndon bought a copy as soon as it was for sale, probably having read the serialization in the *National Era*; he likely shared it with his law partner. At some point Lincoln purchased his own copy. After his nomination for president in 1860, Frank Fuller, a friend of Robert Todd Lincoln, then a student at Philips Academy at Exeter in New Hampshire, visited Lincoln in Springfield. Fuller's father had been a deacon in Lyman Beecher's church. "He knew much about all [the members of] the talented Beecher family," Fuller recalled, "showed me a well worn copy of Harriet Beecher Stowe's Uncle Tom's Cabin, and some clippings of Henry Ward Beecher's sermons and speeches." (Lincoln would appoint Fuller the wartime governor of the Utah Territory to handle difficulties with Brigham Young and the Mormons; afterward, Fuller became an intimate friend of Mark Twain.)

Another book was published in 1851 eight months after *Uncle Tom's Cabin* began its serialization, a novel written through the debates over the Compromise, but by contrast it received paltry and poor reviews, sold few copies, and sank into obscurity. Its author, Herman Melville, had come to live in Pittsfield, Massachusetts, to be near his literary mentor, Nathaniel Hawthorne, a conservative Democrat, who would soon write a campaign biography for his Bowdoin College classmate Franklin Pierce. Melville was married to the daughter of Lemuel Shaw, chief justice of the Massachusetts Supreme Judicial Court, who had issued the decision in favor of the Fugitive Slave Act in the case of Thomas Sims. Yet one of the attorneys appearing on behalf of Sims, Richard Henry Dana, Jr., a member of the Boston Vigilance Committee and author of *Two Years Before the Mast*, was a close friend of Melville. Dana had introduced him to other members of the Vigilance Committee. Melville's brother, Gansevoort Melville, who died in 1846, had been a partisan Democratic enthusiast of Young America, Manifest Destiny, and James K. Polk, for whom he delivered rousing campaign speeches. Melville himself was a nominal Democrat with a mystical belief in Jacksonian democracy, but hardly a regular party man, or regular in any of his ideas.

Moby-Dick, or The Whale was as far from the sentimental tone and stereotypical characters of *Uncle Tom's Cabin*—and mass popularity—as could be. It was at once metaphysical, cosmic, sexual, metaphorical, and Shakespearean—a jeremiad, adventure story, and empirical treatise on the natural world. But it was also symbolic and allegorical, filled with images from the debates over the Compromise—the anchorless ship of state that might break apart on turbulent seas.

The *Pequod*, named for a tribe massacred by Puritans and bound together with hemp from Henry Clay's Kentucky, sets sail with a damned polyglot crew—white, black, brown, and red seamen—and a stowaway, apparently a fugitive slave, the cabin boy Pip. The first mate, a Quaker, Starbuck, is a man of self-control and reason, who warns even to the end that the ship can be steered back to safe harbor. The captain, Ahab, bearing the name of the king of ancient Israel who commanded worship of the false god Baal, bears resemblance to the dark, demonic John C. Calhoun. Ahab's harpoon and wooden leg are made of hickory—"Old Hickory," Jackson's nickname. Ahab is relentless in his hunt of Moby-Dick, heedless of danger, pursuing his Manifest Destiny, seeking whiteness. The harpooned whale breaks the ship to pieces, pulling it to the depths of the ocean. "But as the last whelmings intermixingly poured themselves over the sunken head of the Indian at the mainmast, leaving a few inches of the erect spar yet visible, together with long streaming yards of the flag, which calmly undulated, with ironical co-incidings, over the destroying billows they almost touched;—at that instant, a red arm and a hammer hovered backwardly uplifted in the open air, in the act of nailing the flag faster and yet faster to the subsiding spar." The nail catches a sea hawk's wing, "his imperial beak thrust upwards," as the ship is dragged below. But the Indian sailor Queequeg's coffin, transported on board, suddenly shoots up, buoying on it Ishmael, the narrator and "orphan."

"And what, Mr. President, do you suppose it is?" Henry Clay had declared in his speech before the Senate for the Compromise, flourishing a piece of wood. "It is a fragment of the coffin of Washington . . . a warning voice, coming from the grave to the Congress now in session to beware, to pause, to reflect; before they lend themselves to any purposes which shall destroy that Union which was cemented by his exertions and example."

"I am looking out for no fragment upon which to float away from the wreck," declared Daniel Webster in his Senate oration, "but for the good of the whole."

And Melville wrote: " 'AND I ONLY AM ESCAPED ALONE TO TELL THEE.' Job. *The drama's done. Why then here does any one step forth? — Because one did survive the wreck.*"

CHAPTER FIVE

WHAT IS TO BE DONE?

W illiam Dean Howells, editor of *The Atlantic*, realist novelist, and acclaimed as the "Dean of American Letters" in the late nineteenth century, launched his literary career with the publication in 1860 of his campaign biography of Abraham Lincoln, which the candidate reviewed and approved, earning him the post of U.S. consul to Venice. He described the years after Lincoln's congressional term as a serene interregnum, a period of undisturbed industry and domestic contentment, beyond political anxieties until events pulled the prairie Cincinnatus back into the arena. "After his retirement from Congress," wrote Howells, "he devoted himself, with greater earnestness than ever before, to the duties of his profession, and extended his business and repute. . . . During that lethargy that preceded the dissolution of his party, he had almost relinquished political aspirations. Successful in his profession, happy in his home, secure in the affections of his

Judge David Davis

neighbors, with books, competences, and leisure—ambition could not tempt him." Lincoln was a finished man in repose, awaiting the summons of destiny. So went the authorized fairy tale.

Lincoln sanctioned this bowdlerized version to counter a concerted campaign to demean him. The coruscating assessment of an Illinois Democratic newspaper in 1857, on the eve of Lincoln's Senate race against Douglas, had presented him as an abject failure. "Lincoln is undoubtedly the most unfortunate politician that has ever attempted to rise in Illinois," the *Urbana Constitution* editorialized. "In everything he undertakes, politically, he seems doomed to failure. He has been prostrated often enough in his political schemes to have crushed the life out of any ordinary man." Douglas, in the first debate in 1858, launched his rhetorical attack with the theme of Lincoln as disgraced and discredited, "Ranchero Spotty" turned "Black Republican." "Whilst in Congress he distinguished himself by his opposition to the Mexican War, taking the side of the common enemy against his own country, and when he returned home he found the indignation of the people followed him everywhere, and he was again submerged or obliged to retire into private life, forgotten by his former friends." Douglas's jibe against Lincoln clearly bothered him more than he cared to admit. But it was disappointment, defeat, and depression, not the smug complacency conveyed by his official campaign biography that forged a deeper and more effective Lincoln. When he went underground into a rather ordinary provincial existence, withdrawing from public life not by choice but rejection, he slowly began assimilating the lessons of Washington and Kentucky. He entered his wilderness years a man in pieces and emerged on the other end a coherent steady figure.

By the end of the summer of 1849 Lincoln's hope had withered for a federal appointment to the Land Office he thought suitable to his political standing as an Illinois Whig congressman and original Young Indian. First, he had misplayed his hand; then he overestimated his importance; and finally he was brushed to the side. Lincoln had many friends and acquaintances, influential people he had met in Washington and on his New England campaign tour, but they either did not weigh in on his behalf or lacked gravity. He was left a dangling man, sputtering in a letter that expressed his impotence and exposed his injured pride to Secretary of State Clayton that President Taylor would be judged "a mere man of straw." But there was no backlash against those who had treated him as a negligible character.

By that fall he arrived in Lexington to attempt to recover his wife's family legacy from the grip of her father's mortal enemy. Robert S. Todd had been slurred before his agonizing death and every principle he had upheld was trampled. Lincoln soon discovered he stood no chance to win the lawsuit his father-in-law had initiated and the dream of inheriting a portion of the ancient Todd estate dissolved into thin air.

He reeled from regret to tragedy to trauma. Immediately upon his return to Springfield, his three year-old son, Eddie, fell ill with tuberculosis. Lincoln and Mary hovered helplessly over him for fifty-two days until he died on February 1, 1850. Mary was prostrate with grief, secluded herself and stopped eating. "Eat, Mary, for we must live," Lincoln implored. Within two months she was pregnant. She gave birth to William Wallace Lincoln, Willie, a replacement child named for Mary's brother-in-law, in December. But even a decade later she wept at the mention of Eddie. Lincoln told a friend that if he had "twenty children he would never cease to sorrow for that one." He and Mary had another boy, Thomas, or "Tad," as they called him, three years after Willie, and they became inseparable playmates. During the vigil over Eddie, Mary's grandmother, Elizabeth Parker, to whom she was close, died. In her will she freed her slaves and left an annuity for one of them.

Mary was subject to panic attacks, migraine headaches, and temper tantrums. She was terrified of storms and at the rumble of thunder Lincoln would rush home from his office to comfort her. She feared that her eldest child, Robert, would run away and be killed, and was afraid of being murdered in her home. She was abusive to her household help. Her erratic behavior became a common topic of small-town gossip. Her cousin, Elizabeth Todd Grimsley, said she was "always over-anxious and worried about the boys." Mary was "a very nervous, hysterical woman who was incessantly alarming the neighborhood with her outcries," according to one of her neighbors, Elizabeth A. Capps. Lincoln was described as henpecked, the victim of her lacerating tongue and once her broomstick, and endlessly forbearing. Of her fits, a townsman quoted him as saying, "It does her lots of good and it doesn't hurt me a bit." And yet she conducted her household management up to the new standards of middle-class respectability set by Eliza Leslie's *The House Book* and *Godey's Lady's Book*, the high-end magazine of fashion, culture, and child-rearing, which she closely read. She decorated the house with wallpaper and paintings, practiced birth control, disciplined her children, oversaw their education and religious training, supervised housemaids, sewed, cooked, even chopped wood, and held occasional dinner parties. When a newspaperman appeared to interview the Republican candidate in 1860, he wrote, "An air of quiet refinement pervaded the place. You would have known instantly that she who presided over that modest household was a true type of the American lady. There were flowers upon the table; there were pictures upon the walls. The adornments were few, but chastely appropriate; everything was in its place, and ministered to the general effect. The hand of the domestic artist was everywhere visible. The thought that involuntarily blossomed into speech was—'What a pleasant home Abe Lincoln has.' "

"In fact," wrote one of Mary's biographers, Jean H. Baker, "she offers to history a model example of committed motherhood." She did it all as virtually a single mother, a "circuit-widow" as another of her biographers, Ruth Painter Randall, called her. Lincoln was practicing law on the circuit more than one third of the year, leaving her to manage alone. Always in need of reassurance, spending her youth seeking affection from a distant father married to a unsympathetic stepmother, after the deaths of her father, son, and grandmother, she sought comfort and protection from her husband, but was more or less left to her own devices.

When he was at home, Lincoln was often remote and distracted, indulgent with the boys, allowing them to run riot in his office to the consternation of Herndon, but did not pitch in much to help at home, and was subject to the ups and downs of his legendary depression. Just as he had to cope with Mary's fits, she had to cope with his. "He was a sad-looking man; his melancholy dripped from him as he walked," wrote Herndon. "The perpetual look of sadness," he recalled, was "a matter of frequent discussion among his friends." John Todd Stuart thought the cause was his "abnormal digestion," in other words, constipation. Lincoln's diet on the road was wretched, consisting mainly of greasy meat, gravy, and cabbage—"table greasy—table cloth greasy—floor greasy, and everything else ditto," according to his friend Judge David Davis, describing an inn where they dined together—and the waitress as a "witch." It was no wonder Lincoln's digestion was affected. A decade earlier, when he had suffered his nervous breakdown, Dr. Anson D. Henry had prescribed blue mass pills, a mixture made of mercury, licorice, and honey considered a panacea for nearly every ailment. On Stuart's advice, Lincoln resumed taking them and kept pill popping until five months into his presidency, when, as he told Stuart, he "ceased using them because they made him cross." According to a 2001 scientific study, the supposed medication was highly toxic, exceeding the Environmental Protection Agency's safety standard for mercury by a factor of 9,000. Mercury poisoning, one of the researchers concluded, "certainly could explain Lincoln's known neurological symptoms: insomnia, tremor and the rage attacks," while stopping ended those effects.

"I don't think that Mrs. Lincoln was as bad a woman as she is represented," recalled their next-door neighbor, James Gourley. "She was a good friend of mine. She always said that if her husband had stayed at home as he ought to, that she could love him better." Despite their stresses and arguments, as Mary's half-sister, Emilie Todd Helm, observed, "They understood each other thoroughly, and Mr. Lincoln looked beyond the impulsive words and manner, and knew that his wife was devoted to him and to his interests." Even when he fell into despair, she never gave up her faith in "our Lincoln party."

Just after Mary gave birth to Willie, Lincoln received word from Coles County that his father, Thomas, was dying, the incident a pathetic coda to Lincoln's fraught relationship. He had responded to a similar alarm two years before only to discover his father failing to expire. He declined to make another trip. "My business is such that I could hardly leave home now," he wrote his stepbrother, John D. Johnston. His coldness barely masked his irritation. Three years earlier the ne'er-do-well Johnston had asked Lincoln to lend him $80, for which he chided him for borrowing money from him in the past without repayment. "You are not lazy, and still you are an idler," Lincoln wrote. "I doubt whether since I saw you, you have done a good whole day's work in any one day." He proposed matching every dollar Johnston earned with a dollar lent, but his stepbrother did not take up the offer, proving Lincoln's point. In response to this latest news about his father, he sent an impersonal, cruel, and falsely sentimental note about how the "Maker" remembers "the fall of a sparrow" and "will not forget the dying man." As for putting in a last appearance before his father, "Say to him that if we could meet now, it is doubtful whether it would not be more painful than pleasant," adding that Thomas should prepare for heaven, which Lincoln did not believe existed, where "he will soon have a joyous [meeting] with many loved ones gone before." Lincoln did not attend the funeral or ever provide a gravestone. He bickered with his stepbrother over providing for his stepmother and later learned that Johnston stole the regular money he sent.

Mary never had any use for Lincoln's family, though she once sent his stepmother a kind little note. She never visited, invited them, or arranged for them to see their son's children. Herndon, who was banished from the Lincoln house as a rough and radical character of a lower class and whose proper place was her husband's office, recalled, "You wish to know if Mrs. Lincoln and the Todd aristocratic family did not scorn and detest the Hanks and the Lincoln family; and in answer to which I yell yes. Mrs. Lincoln held the Hanks tribe [Lincoln's mother's relatives] in contempt and the Lincoln family generally, the old folks, Thomas Lincoln and his good old wife. Mrs. Lincoln was terribly aristocratic and as haughty and as imperious as she was aristocratic; she was as cold as a chunk of ice. Thomas Lincoln and his good old wife were never in this city, and I do not suppose that they were ever invited to visit Lincoln's house. Had they appeared, I doubt whether Mrs. Lincoln would have admitted them." Almost certainly, Lincoln's refusal to see his dying father met with Mary's approval.

Lincoln's law practice while he was in Washington had dwindled to the vanishing point. Herndon still hung out their shingle, but mainly had acted as Lincoln's political aide and a sort of town crier. Grant Goodrich, a well-established Chicago lawyer, offered Lincoln a partnership. He had worked on a fraud case with him in 1845 and Goodrich said Lincoln "in closing the case made the best jury argument I ever heard him make." But Lincoln turned him down, though he would appear as a co-counsel with him on a few cases in the future. David Davis recalled that Lincoln told him, "That if he went to Chicago that he would have to sit down and study hard—that it would kill him." But there were other obvious reasons. If he moved to Chicago, while he might open the door to affluence, he would uproot himself and his family, giving up his familiar surroundings and his political base, and have to nurture his reputation and connections in a new place. Even if for the moment he was setting politics aside, he had not put it behind him, limiting his aspiration only to the law.

The office of Lincoln & Herndon was in a red-brick building across from the state capitol and courthouse. One long table and a short one were covered with green baize. Lincoln filled the bookcase with his law books, personal library, and volumes that Herndon collected, all mixed together, among them Blackstone's works, Kent's *Commentaries*, along with Thomas Paine's *Collected Works*, the English historian Thomas Macaulay's *Essays*, the French radical Louis Blanc's *On the Working Classes*, *The American Debater*, and *Elements of Zoology*. Pictures of the Whig giants, Henry Clay and Daniel Webster, were hung on the wall. There was no rug on the wooden floor. As a congressman Lincoln had stockpiled bags of seeds to distribute to farmers as favors and a young clerk sweeping up discovered they had sprouted in the office dirt. The partners kept no ledgers and divided the fees equally, which Mary resented. Lincoln spent many days with his long legs propped on a nearby chair, reading newspapers, journals, and books, and holding forth on "some knotty law point," current event, or "telling a joke or an anecdote." "Billy," he would begin, "I heard a good story while I was up in the country."

Lincoln was what was called a "volume lawyer." His fees generally ranged from $5 to $50 dollars. He argued in Justice of the Peace courts up to the U.S. District Court. He handled virtually every type of case—divorce, slander and libel, and a murder case in 1857 in which he deployed the almanac to gain acquittal of his client, the son of his old Clary's Grove Boys friend Jack Armstrong, who had just died—an incident famously depicted by Henry Fonda in the 1939 film *Young Mr. Lincoln.* But only about 15 percent of Lincoln's cases were criminal, the overwhelming number civil. Nearly two thirds involved debt collection, with Lincoln swooping in as the "repo man," according to the historian Allen Guelzo. He represented banks, insurance companies, and manufacturers. Most of his corporate practice involved railroads, but he represented railroads and those suing railroads almost equally. When he served as an attorney on behalf of railroads it was often for the Illinois Central and the Alton and Sangamon. He began his work for the Illinois Central in 1853, mostly engaged in damage suits. He received these cases as a subcontractor from the IC lawyers given responsibility for sections of the line extending county to county. In 1857 he handled a major case, saving the IC from potential bankruptcy by winning a ruling that counties could not levy taxes on the railroad. When he filed his fee of $5,000, the IC superintendent refused to pay it. "Why, sir," he protested, "this is as much as Daniel Webster himself would have charged. We cannot allow such a claim." Encouraged by his lawyer friends, Lincoln sued and won. Triumphantly counting the dollars into two piles, he remarked to Herndon, "Hold on, Billy; how often have you stretched yourself on that sofa and discoursed of how the corporations are strangling the life out of this nation? This is corporation money!"

The executive who refused to pay Lincoln, regarding him as too lowly to receive a princely sum, was a former West Point officer, George B. McClellan. Wall Street financiers with close ties to Douglas had recommended McClellan for his position with the Illinois Central and he would describe himself as "a strong Democrat of the Stephen A. Douglas school." The son of a Philadelphia doctor, McClellan's first impression of Lincoln remained fixed as "not a man of every strong character, & as he was destitute of refinement—certainly in no sense a gentleman—he was easily wrought upon by the coarse associates whose style of conversation agreed so well with his own." His contempt for Lincoln was consistent with his condescension toward the ordinary people he encountered in Illinois. "The good people of the interior of the state are rather primitive in their appearance and habits," McClellan wrote his wife, ". . . but as they now begin to know that I am one of the 'powers that be' I find things improve—especially at the hotels where a quail or a prairie chicken is always set aside for your humble servant." McClellan's refusal to pay Lincoln his fee was the first of their frictions, the beginning of a chronic history that would encompass his deployment of railroad resources on Douglas's behalf in the Lincoln-Douglas Senate campaign of 1858; disagreement over military strategy that culminated in General McClellan submitting his political agenda against emancipation as an ultimatum to President Lincoln; and his candidacy against Lincoln's reelection in 1864, a race that Lincoln believed he would likely lose resulting in recognition of the Confederacy and the defeat of the United States.

Every spring and fall Lincoln traveled through the prairies on his buckboard wagon pulled by his horse Old Tom across the Eighth Judicial Circuit, covering an expanse of central Illinois larger than Massachusetts, Connecticut, and Rhode Island combined. (Old Tom's successors as Lincoln's main mode of transportation included Old Buck and Old Bob.) When the court convened in each county seat, it would attract the lawyers, politicians, and peddlers from the area in a festive atmosphere. The presiding judge of the Eighth Circuit was David Davis, so massive it was said a surveyor was required to measure his suit. He was well educated, with degrees from Kenyon College and Yale, the leading Whig politician of his town of Bloomington, elected to the state legislature, and was such a shrewd real estate investor that when he died in 1886 he was the largest landholder in Illinois. On the bench, he was efficient, authoritative, and genial. Conducting court by day, he was impresario of the troupe of lawyers at night—"host, entertainer, and head of the social organization of the circuit," recalled Henry Clay Whitney, one of those attorneys who became a close friend of Lincoln and the chronicler of "life on the circuit." "The judge greatly loved attention," he wrote, "to be paid court to; he was extremely fond of prudent and proper conviviality, and was wont to put every newcomer on the circuit on a period of probation, giving him opportunity to prove himself a proper member of our coterie, where, if he succeeded, he was admitted into full membership; from which, if he failed, he was informally excluded, and made to understand thoroughly that he was so."

One of the chief forms of entertainment in the judge's room at the local inn was storytelling, a talent at which Lincoln "was never exceeded." When Davis excused himself from his judicial duty to engage in a real estate trans-action, he would frequently install Lincoln as the judge. "In my opinion," he recalled, "I think Mr. Lincoln was happy—as happy as *he* could be, when on this Circuit—and happy no other place. This was his place of enjoyment. As a general rule when all the lawyers of a Saturday evening would go home and see their families and friends at home Lincoln would refuse to go home. It seemed to me that L was not domestically happy." But the distances often made it difficult for Lincoln to return to Springfield and the wealthy Davis might not have fully appreciated that however "happy" Lincoln might be on the road he was there only because it was how he gained his income.

"In those early days, it should not be forgotten," wrote Whitney, "the law business was not only very meager, but quite informal; cases were not then decided upon *authority*, as I have said, so much as upon logical consideration. Lincoln gained friends at once; politics and law were closely entwined, and political prejudice was quite as intense then as it ever was. Lincoln had been the only Whig from Illinois in the Congress of 1847–48, and partisans of his faith on the circuit were likely to cleave to him both as parties and jurors." Lincoln's manner was informal, sometimes conferring with a client beneath a tree near the courthouse; then he would seclude himself to plan the presen-tation of his case, rarely taking notes, before appearing in court. His method was always to persuade by fact and logic accessible to the common juror. He was, wrote Whitney, "intensely logical, and inclined to make everything ac-cord with undeviating rule, yet he was likewise eminently practical, and was always sedulous to achieve results in the simplest way." "Mr. Lincoln was a slow thinker," remarked one of his most important clients, John W. Bunn. "It seemed as if every proposition submitted to his mind was subjected to the regular process of a syllogism, with its major proposition and its minor proposition and its conclusion. Whatever could not stand the test of sound reasoning, he rejected."

Davis, who saw Lincoln perform more than anyone else, concluded, "He seized the strong points of a cause and presented them with clearness and great compactness. His mind was logical and direct, and he did not indulge in extraneous discussion. Generalities and platitudes had no charm for him. An unfailing vein of humor never deserted him, and he was able to claim the attention of court and jury, when the cause was most uninteresting, by the appropriateness of his anecdotes." But, Davis added, "He had no managing faculty nor organizing power; hence a child could conform to the simple and technical rules, the means and the modes of getting at justice, better than he. The law has its own rules, and a student could get at them and keep with them better than Lincoln. Sometimes he was forced to study these, if he could not get the rubbish of a case removed." Yet Whitney, who tried cases with Lincoln as co-counsel, observed that "many a time have I seen him tear the mask off from a fallacy and shame both the fallacy and its author."

Lincoln's arguments were not built upon citation of precedent or the authority of legal rules but an appeal to reason. Case by case he honed his logical skill, sharpening each point with fact. While he drove the jury to his conclusion through relentless syllogism, it seemed to be simply the unfolding of common sense.

Having only attended a backwoods "blab" school for a session he always felt his education rudimentary. In his first autobiography, submitted in 1858 to a *Dictionary of Congress*, he succinctly wrote: "Education defective. Profession, a lawyer." In another self-description, he confessed, "The little advance I now have upon this store of education, I have picked up from time to time under the pressure of necessity." "I could notice a difference in Lincoln's movement as a lawyer from this time forward," observed Herndon, about Lincoln's return from Congress to the law.

He had begun to realize a certain lack of discipline—a want of mental training and method. Ten years had wrought some change in the law, and more in the lawyers, of Illinois. The conviction had settled in the minds of the people that the pyrotechnics of courtroom and stump oratory did not necessarily imply extensive or profound ability in the lawyer who resorted to it. The courts were becoming graver and more learned, and the lawyer was learning as a preliminary and indispensable condition to success that he must be a close reasoner, besides having at command a broad knowledge of the principles on which the statutory law is constructed. There was of course the same riding on circuit as before, but the courts had improved in tone and morals, and there was less laxity—at least it appeared so to Lincoln.

Perfecting his method, Lincoln devoted himself to the study of Euclid's *Elements* until he had mastered it. He had some knowledge of geometry from his days as a surveyor in the 1830s, even reading books on the subject. Before he had any formal understanding he had an aptitude for engineering and mathematics. He had hailed "reason" in his 1838 Springfield Lyceum speech. He was proud of his patent for lifting boats and thought of himself as an inventor. "Studied Euclid—the Exact Sciences," said Davis. "His mind struggled to arrive at moral and physical—mathematical demonstration." Of the ancients, Euclid was considered an essential source of Enlightenment thought, offering self-evident proof of natural right, studied by Jefferson and highly recommended by Paine. In his *Age of Reason*, the book Lincoln early absorbed, Paine wrote, "I know, however, but of one ancient book that authoritatively challenges universal consent and belief, and that is Euclid's 'Elements of Geometry'; and the reason is, because it is a book of self-evident demonstration, entirely independent of its author, and of everything relating to time, place, and circumstance."

"In the course of my law-reading I constantly came upon the word demonstrate," Lincoln told an interviewer in 1860.

> I thought, at first, that I understood its meaning, but soon became satisfied that I did not. I said to myself, "What do I do when I demonstrate more than when I reason or prove? How does demonstration differ from any other proof?" I consulted Webster's Dictionary. That told of "certain proof," "proof beyond the possibility of doubt"; but I could form no idea what sort of proof that was. I thought a great many things were proved beyond a possibility of doubt, without recourse to any such extraordinary process of reasoning as I understood "demonstration" to be. I consulted all the dictionaries and books of reference I could find, but with no better results. You might as well have defined blue to a blind man. At last I said, "Lincoln, you can never make a lawyer if you do not understand what demonstrate means."

Then he studied "till I could give any propositions in the six books of Euclid at sight. I then found out what 'demonstrate' means, and went back to my law studies." The interviewer, Reverend J. P. Gulliver, an antislavery preacher close to the Beecher family, who had just heard Lincoln speak at Cooper Union, replied that "Euclid would be one of the best books to put on the catalogue of the Tract Society" for churches to distribute. He reported that Lincoln laughed. "I think so," he said. "I vote for Euclid."

Euclid filled a gaping hole in Lincoln's education, part of his endless self-improvement, not only immediately practical to his practice but also shaping the contours of his mind. "He studied and nearly mastered the Six-books of Euclid, since he was a member of Congress," he wrote in his autobiography for Scripps. "He regrets his want of education, and does what he can to supply the want." Lincoln absorbed Euclid's axioms, applying them to more than the law: "things that are equal to the same thing are also equal to one another." The gradual effect of Euclid on his thinking, first apparent in his summations in county courtrooms, at last flourished full-blown in his speech against the Douglas's Kansas-Nebraska Act at Peoria on October 16, 1854, which consisted of a series of ironclad logical proofs on the geometry of slavery and against its extension.

As his thought was developing, so invisibly was his political organization. While he assiduously studied to square his logic, he solidified his inner circle without plan. "Our coterie," moving from courthouse to courthouse, trying cases together, telling stories before fireplaces in the back rooms of taverns, and sharing meals and beds, all under the guidance of maestro Judge Davis, in time rearranged itself into the political central committee managing Lincoln's campaigns for the Senate and the presidency. The lawyers of the Eighth Circuit became the core Lincoln men, his team of loyalists. Henry Clay Whitney, Leonard Swett, and Ward Hill Lamon, among others, knew Lincoln's virtues and flaws as a lawyer, had conducted cases with him, and above all trusted his character. Some of his clients were also part of the "coterie." Jacob Bunn and his brother John W. Bunn, the original Springfield grocers, once the railroads burgeoned built an industrial, financial, and commercial empire, and were among the chief funders of Lincoln's campaigns. Lincoln's years roaming the Eighth Circuit meanwhile acquainted him with literally thousands of ordinary people who felt they knew him. His base widened and deepened on the bonds of personal attachment.

Lincoln preferred in retrospect, when he was again a candidate, to portray himself in this period as virtually retired from politics. According to his autobiography he had served in the Congress for the one term as he had promised. "Upon his return from Congress he went to the practice of the law with greater earnestness than ever before," he told Scripps, emphasizing that after some years "his profession had almost superseded the thought of politics in his mind." Herndon, however, claimed his partner was removed from active politics not by choice but because he had tainted himself. "By Lincoln's course in the Mexican War he politically killed himself here; he offered some resolutions in Congress calling for the 'spot' where the first blood was shed by the Mexicans." He insisted, "When Lincoln returned home from Congress in 1849, he was a politically dead and buried man." While the Democrats had tarred Lincoln with the image of "Ranchero Spotty" and Douglas would never permit him to forget it, Lincoln did not regard himself as interred. The Democratic incumbent who had succeeded him in the Congress,

Thomas Harris, wrote the editor of the *Illinois Register* that he had heard from William Newell, a Whig congressman from New Jersey who was a Lincoln friend, that "Lincoln had told him he [Newell] should be" the Whig candidate for Congress in 1850. "Get him in a quarrel with Yates," the other potential candidate, Harris, urged. Two Whig newspapers endorsed Lincoln's candidacy. But on June 5, Lincoln formally withdrew. "I will add, that in my opinion," he wrote, "the Whigs of the district have several other men, any one of whom they can elect, and that too quite as easily as they could elect me." "He would be willing to run," suggested David Davis, "if the people would send him back without his asking for it, but he don't want to make a contest for the Whig nomination with anybody else." What Lincoln left unmentioned as a factor in declining to run was the death of his son Eddie.

While the great debate over the Compromise of 1850 raged in Washington, supporters in Springfield staged a rally on June 15 organized by a committee of prominent local men from both parties. The Whig endorsers included John Todd Stuart and James Matheny, Lincoln's best man at his wedding. But Lincoln was conspicuously absent. The *Journal*, his newspaper, editorialized in favor of President Taylor, adamantly opposed to the Compromise. After Taylor's death, in October, its supporters held another meeting, a virtual Democratic campaign event, and Lincoln again kept his distance.

The Whig candidate was Richard Yates, a Kentucky native, the first graduate of Edward Beecher's Illinois College, an antislavery academy, protégé in the law office of the fallen war hero John J. Hardin, and who had been the youngest member of the legislature. Lincoln had been "warm personal friends" with Yates since his days in New Salem, when they were introduced by "Slicky Bill" Greene, who had attended Illinois College with him. Herndon, another alumnus, was a delegate at the convention nominating him. When Lincoln dropped from contention, Yates had been challenged within the party by Judge William Brown, who attacked him for being against the Compromise and in the thrall of Lincoln and his supporters—"the Journal Clique." In an article in the *Register* he suggested he would be the stronger candidate because Yates and Lincoln would be vulnerable to having their patriotism contested. "Questions occasionally arise," Brown wrote, "involving the well being of the whole country, which are above party and personal considerations, and in reference to which, every man, for the sake of his country, should boldly express his opinions."

Harris, the Democrat, had defeated Lincoln's old law partner, Stephen T. Logan, on his glittering Mexican War heroism, but now he split his party by supporting Taylor before his death. He delivered a floor speech in the House on March 25 calling for the immediate admission of California as a free state without conditions; for delegates to the Southern Nashville Convention to be greeted with "stale eggs" and "clothed in respectable suits of tar and feathers"; declaring that in the current crisis he believed as a Democrat that "party should become nothing"; and proclaiming, "I shall stand by this" administration. Back in Springfield, cranky Archie Herndon, the father of Lincoln's law partner, denounced Harris as a party heretic and announced his independent candidacy, which he swiftly ditched after Democrats cursed him for throwing the election to the Whig. By this time, Harris had renounced his apostasy and championed the Compromise. He felt confident he could "push the proviso disunion issues on Yates." The *Register* published a false story that Clay had endorsed him as a result, lambasted by the *Journal* as "slanderous." Harris privately wrote the *Register*'s editor, "Money has its uses," and that he would "put $1,000 into the canvass" for a Free Soil candidate to split the Whig vote, but none could be found to take the bribe.

Yates came out against the Fugitive Slave Act and for emancipation in the District of Columbia. Behind the scenes, Lincoln acted as a strategic campaign adviser. He took no public position on the Compromise beyond avoiding any association even with Whigs at the rallies in its favor. Years later, Herndon delivered a lecture under the title "Facts Illustrative of Mr. Lincoln's Patriotism and Statesmanship" in which he stated, "In 1850 he warmly approved the Compromises of that year, with the single exception of the infamous Fugitive Slave bill. That he wanted modified in this—he wanted the fugitive slave to have the sacred right of trial by jury."

Herndon sought even at a late date to defend against the imputation against Lincoln that he was unpatriotic, from the "Spot Resolution" to his failure to embrace the Compromise. But surely Herndon knew that insisting on trial by jury in the Fugitive Slave Act was a demand by antislavery Whigs in the Congress intending to kill it and that opposition to the act was opposition to the Compromise. The Compromise without the act was a dead deal for Southerners.

Lincoln provided Yates with a confidential memo suggesting that he say that "if elected" and "this question shall still be open"—which it would not be—he would follow "the wish of my district"—which had not expressed a wish. He was referring to the "right of instruction" that the Illinois legislature in 1849 had exercised in petitioning the state's U.S. senators, both Democrats, to work for the Wilmot Proviso, which Douglas ignored and finessed without repercussion. The notion that a congressional district possessed the "right of instruction" it might never enforce was a conceit Lincoln was using for purposes of political positioning. After Clay's "Omnibus" crashed in the Senate, Lincoln advised that Yates might say: "Had it passed the Senate"— which it did not—"and I been a member of the lower House I think I should have voted for it, unless my district otherwise directed me"—which it never directed its representative to do. At the same time, Lincoln wrote, "There are, however, some things upon which I feel I am, and shall remain, inflexible. One of them is my opposition to the extension of slavery into territories now free." He noted that Yates was for the Wilmot Proviso, but suggested he say he would "abandon" it if "a dogged adherence to the Proviso by a few, might aid the extension of slavery"—which it would not. None of Lincoln's hypothetical advice, however, was shared with the public.

Yates stunned Harris, winning back the seat for the Whigs. "Beat bad," Harris lamented. "This is virtually a condemnation of the Compromise by the people of this District. Abolitionism henceforth to reign. . . . If this issue continues," he wrote about slavery, "Illinois will give her vote for any Northern Sewardite Whig in 1852."

But Harris's judgment was clouded by his embittered loss. The Compromise had removed the Proviso and the salient question of the extension of slavery from politics. Douglas, who had engineered the Compromise, was victorious in Washington and Illinois. Whigs were hopelessly split. Most Northern Whigs were opposed, but Southern Whigs held on to their party identification only by the thread of the Compromise. Antislavery sentiment was tainted as anti-Unionism. Polarization continued to be driven by the Fugitive Slave Act, but the prospect favored an undisturbed and long period of Democratic control of every branch of the federal government.

Lincoln was cornered in his law practice. His ambition was boxed in. There was no plausible office for him to seek. He had helped a Whig fill his former congressional seat. The next election for the U.S. Senate was not until 1855. The state was overwhelmingly Democratic. There was no chance for a Whig to be elected governor. It was little wonder that he began to withdraw and concentrate on his legal career.

Politics forgot about Lincoln, but he did not forget about politics. His mind did not close it in a separate compartment. His depression, which he treated with poisonous blue mass pills (also supposedly the cure for constipation), was rooted in his demoralization. In the months after he returned from Lexington, his private remarks about slavery and Southern society took on a cutting, harsh, and unyielding tone. Even as events shunted him aside, he spoke about heading toward a resolution. The inner man and the outer man were running on parallel tracks that would not converge until 1854. He did not voice his qualms and anger in public, but remained a stalwart Whig mouthing platitudes through the next national election cycle. He was adrift in an open sea, but did not yet grasp that he was a political orphan clinging to the fragments of a sinking ship.

Beginning in 1849, Lincoln's public and private statements reflected a moderate politician with radical thoughts. On January 10, 1849, the day he planned to introduce his bill to abolish slavery in the District of Columbia, a more acceptable version than that proposed by more radical members, an unsigned article appeared in the *Illinois Journal*. "Washington City has for many years been the headquarters of slave traders," it read. "Their slave pens were almost within hearing of the Capitol. It is not unusual there to see gangs of slaves, designed for distant markets, handcuffed and proceeding on for their destination. All will remember the occurrence a few years since, of a party of handcuffed slaves passing the Capitol, when one of them stopped, shook his chains, and pointing to the gorgeous flag of freedom which flaunted over it, sang—'Hail Columbia! Happy land! Hail ye heroes! Heaven-born land!' "

Lincoln was likely the author of this anonymous article. It provided a detailed first-person account of slavery in Washington and was published on the day Lincoln intended to propose his bill for emancipation in the District. Perhaps the telltale sign that this was his composition was the mockery of the unofficial national anthem, "Hail Columbia." Years later, when Herndon interviewed people on Lincoln's early life, compiling the first oral history of a president, Dennis Hanks told him that as he and Lincoln worked "in the fields," splitting those famous rails, Lincoln would sing a particular song, singing it over and over, to make fun of their condition as laborers. "Hail Columbia! Happy land!" Lincoln sang. "If you ain't broke, I will be damned!"

In the autumn of 1849, Lincoln's sojourn in Lexington representing his wife's family in the *Todd Heirs* case was a turning point in his thinking about the ruthlessness of the pro-slavery forces. The benevolent paternalism of Henry Clay, proponent of gradual emancipation and colonization, which had prevailed as conventional wisdom among upstanding men, was contemptuously crushed as at best antiquated and at worst abolitionism. Kentucky was supposed to have been an example to guide other Southern states to move slowly toward emancipation, becoming like the Northern states that had enacted it before, but instead its politics demonstrated that even there

slavery was on the march. Lincoln feared that slavery was an expansive political and economic power threatening to engulf the free states. The lessons he
learned about the strength of slavery in Kentucky would inform his delicate
handling of emancipation early in the war in order to maintain it within
the Union.

Silent about Kentucky in public, he ruminated aloud in private, dismayed,
outraged and frustrated. "The Kentucky state convention which took place
about 1848, gave Mr. Lincoln his first real, specific alarm about the institution
of slavery," wrote Henry Clay Whitney, "for in that convention, not a single
non-slaveholder appeared, although the issue of slavery was made in the canvass and although the non-slaveholding classes outnumbered the other, ten
to one." Lincoln spoke of a Whig lawyer he knew, Samuel F. Miller, who
ran as an antislavery delegate to the Kentucky constitutional convention and
felt the political atmosphere so menacing that he moved to Iowa—"left the
state immediately after the election by reason of the animus displayed there,
then." (Lincoln would appoint Miller to the Supreme Court in 1862.) "Lincoln would get excited on the question, and believed that the tendency of
the times was to make slavery universal, and that Illinois, which had already
adopted a code of laws about negroes called by its bad pre-eminence 'the
black laws,' would soon legalize slavery there."

Whitney was not the only friend in whom Lincoln confided his fears. Joseph Gillespie, his former colleague from the Illinois state legislature, recalled,
"Mr. Lincoln's sense of justice was intensely strong. It was to this mainly that
his hatred of slavery might be attributed. He abhorred the institution. It was
about the only public question on which he would become excited." He cited
his experience in Kentucky as the illustrative case that could soon prove the
rule. "I recollect meeting with him once at Shelbyville when he remarked
that something must be done or slavery would overrun the whole country.
He said there were about 600,000 non-slave holding whites in Kentucky to
about 33,000 slave holders. That in the convention then recently held it was
expected that the delegates would represent these classes about in proportion
to their respective numbers but when the convention assembled there was
not a single representative of the non-slaveholding class. Every one was in the
interest of the slaveholders and he said this thing is spreading like wild fire
over the country. In a few years we will be ready to accept the institution in
Illinois and the whole country will adopt it."

Experiencing the realities of slavery closely and the political and social
power it bred allowed Lincoln to gain insight into its nature as a class and

caste system based on wealth and status. He obviously had in mind real people, perhaps "Old Duke" Wickliffe and "Young Duke" Wickliffe, by all accounts strutting dandies, when he confided his view to his friend. "I asked
him to what he attributed the change that was going on in public opinion,"
said Gillespie.

> He said he had put that question to a Kentuckian shortly before who an-
> swered by saying—you might have any amount of land, money in your
> pocket or bank stock and while travelling around nobody would be any the
> wiser but if you had a darkey trudging at your heels everybody would see
> him and know that you owned slaves—It is the most glittering ostentatious
> and displaying property in the world and now says he if a young man goes
> courting the only inquiry is how many negroes he or she owns and not what
> other property they may have. The love for slave property was swallowing
> up every other mercenary passion. Its ownership betokened not only the pos-
> session of wealth but indicated the gentleman of leisure who was above and
> scorned labor. These things Mr. Lincoln regarded as highly seductive to the
> thoughtless and giddy headed young men who looked upon work as vulgar
> and ungentlemanly. Mr. Lincoln was really excited and said with great ear-
> nestness that this spirit ought to be met and if possible checked. That slavery
> was a great and crying injustice, an enormous national crime and that we
> could not expect to escape punishment for it. I asked him how he would
> proceed in his efforts to check the spread of slavery. He confessed that he did
> not see his way clearly, but I think he made up his mind from that time that
> he would oppose slavery actively. I know that Mr. Lincoln always contended
> that no man had any right (other than mere brute force gave him) to a slave.
> He used to say that it was singular that the courts would hold that a man
> never lost his right to his property that had been stolen from him but that
> he instantly lost his right to himself if he was stolen. . . . Mr. Lincoln had
> the appearance of being a slow thinker. My impression is that he was not so
> slow as he was careful.

After returning from the Congress, "between the years 1848 and 50," recalled John Todd Stuart, after conducting cases in Tazewell County, he and
Lincoln rode together back home. "The time would soon come in which or
when we must be Democrats or Abolitionists," said Stuart. "When that time
comes my mind is made up," Lincoln replied. "The slavery question can't be
compromised." Stuart added that he spoke "in an emphatic tone."

But that time had not come, not yet. Lincoln would remain a Whig for several more years before finally deciding that its identity had evaporated and he had to become something else or disappear himself along with the Whigs. His own political prospects were dimming while his rival Douglas's were lighting up the sky. But his ambition was not dampened; it simply had no outlet. Despite his self-control, his friends knew that it was eating him alive. "Mr. Douglas's great success in obtaining place and distinction was a standing offence to Mr. Lincoln's self-love and individual ambition," wrote Ward Hill Lamon, who was occasionally Lincoln's co-counsel in the Eighth District. "He was intensely jealous of him, and longed to pull him down, or outstrip him in the race for popular favor, which they united in considering 'the chief end of man.' " Even years later, in 1856, Lincoln constantly measured himself against Douglas, writing in a fragment, "Twenty-two years ago Judge Douglas and I first became acquainted. We were both young then; he a trifle younger than I. Even then, we were both ambitious; I, perhaps, quite as much so as he. With me, the race of ambition has been a failure—a flat failure; with him it has been one of splendid success. His name fills the nation; and is not unknown, even, in foreign lands. I affect no contempt for the high eminence he has reached. So reached, that the oppressed of my species, might have shared with me in the elevation, I would rather stand on that eminence, than wear the richest crown that ever pressed a monarch's brow." Lincoln's self-comparison with his eternal rival was by then entwined with his thinking on slavery. Lincoln's self-identification with slaves in this note was not the first time he linked himself. It was written just months after he had publicly proclaimed to a crowd, referencing the years of his youth when his father contracted him out to work for others and collected the wages himself: "I used to be a slave."

Herndon recalled traveling with Lincoln to Petersburg in 1850 when he unburdened himself of his deepest anxiety that he would leave no mark on the world and simply be forgotten. "The political world was dead: the compromises of 1850 seemed to settle the negro's fate," Herndon said. "Things were stagnant; and all hope for progress in the line of freedom seemed to be crushed out. Lincoln was speculating with me about the deadness of things, and the despair which arose out of it, and deeply regretting that his human strength and power were limited by his nature to rouse and stir up the world. He said gloomily, despairingly, sadly, 'How hard, oh! how hard it is to die and leave one's country no better than if one had never lived for it! The world is dead to hope, deaf to its own death-struggle, made known by a universal cry, What is to be done? Is anything to be done? Who can do anything? and how is it to be done? Did you ever think of these things?' "

But Lincoln's orbit in these years revolved around the Eighth Judicial District, day after day with Judge Davis and "our coterie." "I shall never forget the first time I saw Mr. Lincoln," recalled Leonard Swett, a criminal attorney who became one of Lincoln's closest colleagues and friends, and would be instrumental in his campaigns. Swett came to the town of Danville, where Lincoln was trying cases.

> When I called at the hotel it was after dark, and I was told that he was upstairs in Judge Davis's room. In the region where I had been brought up, the judge of the court was usually a man of more or less gravity so that he could not be approached save with some degree of deference. I was not a little abashed, therefore, after I had climbed the unbanistered stairway, to find myself so near the presence and dignity of Judge Davis in whose room I was told I could find Mr. Lincoln. In response to my timid knock two voices responded almost simultaneously, "Come in." Imagine my surprise when the door opened to find two men undressed, or rather dressed for bed, engaged in a lively battle with pillows, tossing them at each other's heads. One, a low, heavy-set man who leaned against the foot of the bed and puffed like a lizard, answered to the description of Judge Davis. The other was a man of tremendous stature; compared to Davis he looked as if he were eight feet tall. He was encased in a long, indescribable garment, yellow as saffron, which reached to his heels, and from beneath which protruded two of the largest feet I had, up to that time, been in the habit of seeing. This immense shirt, for shirt it must have been, looked as if it had been literally carved out of the original bolt of flannel of which it was made and the pieces joined together without reference to measurement or capacity. The only thing that kept it from slipping off the tall and angular frame it covered was the single button at the throat; and I confess to a succession of shudders when I thought of what might happen should that button by any mischance lose its hold. I cannot describe my sensations as this apparition, with modest announcement, "My name is Lincoln," strode across the room to shake my trembling hand. I will not say he reminded me of Satan, but he was certainly the ungodliest figure I had ever seen.

But after the storytelling and the pillow fights, and the lawyers went to sleep, Lincoln often stayed awake. There was still another Lincoln, a Lincoln not reconciled, a Lincoln mastering axioms, pondering his problems, in a perpetual state of becoming yet another Lincoln. "Frequently I would go out on the circuit with him," said Herndon.

> We, usually, at the little country inns occupied the same bed. In most cases the beds were too short for him, and his feet would hang over the floorboard, thus exposing a limited expanse of shin bone. Placing a candle on a chair at the head of the bed, he would read and study for hours. I have known him to study in this position till two o'clock in the morning. Meanwhile, I and others who chanced to occupy the same room would be safely and soundly asleep. On the circuit in this way he studied Euclid until he could with ease demonstrate all the propositions in the six books. How he could maintain his mental equilibrium or concentrate his thoughts on an abstract mathematical proposition, while Davis, Logan, Swett, Edwards, and I so industriously and volubly filled the air with our interminable snoring was a problem none of us could ever solve.

"What is to be done?"

CHAPTER SIX

A HERO'S WELCOME

On the morning of the first day of the first session of the 32nd Congress, December 1, 1851, caucuses of both parties, the Whigs and the Democrats, convened for the first time, and before even organizing the House of Representatives and Senate, electing their leaders and the speaker, they approved statements affirming the Compromise of 1850—"the final settlement," as President Millard Fillmore pronounced it. This was not the Gag Rule that suppressed antislavery petitions and wracked the Congress in the late 1830s and early 1840s, but its updated functional equivalent, only more efficient, making controversy over slavery superfluous.

The Compromise had rolled up all of the questions that had divided the country since the Mexican War—California was admitted as a free state while New Mexico's antislavery constitution was overthrown and its status

Louis Kossuth

as free or slave left to the future; emancipation in the District of Columbia was taken off the table after notorious slave trading was moved discreetly across the Potomac to Alexandria; and the Fugitive Slave Act, the cornerstone of the deal, the sine qua non for the South, enacted. The "final settlement" was the elemental reality of policy and politics, its center of gravity. To stand against the Compromise was to stand against the Union itself, which Henry Clay, Daniel Webster, Stephen A. Douglas, and Fillmore proclaimed they had saved at last. Slavery was officially a question of the past.

The day after the party caucuses formally ruled discussion of slavery out of order Fillmore's annual message was read to the Congress, declaring that the country had now entered a new era of "peace" and "conciliation." "The agitation which for a time threatened to disturb the fraternal relations which make us one people is fast subsiding, and a year of general prosperity and health has crowned the nation with unusual blessings," he stated. "None can look back to the dangers which are passed or forward to the bright prospect before us without feeling a thrill of gratification."

"Agitation," of course, was the common euphemism for denigrating antislavery opinion. While decrying acts of resistance to the Fugitive Slave Act as "deeply to be regretted" and "aimed against the Constitution itself," Fillmore reassured the country that these were isolated and passing disturbances. With sublime assurance, he described "the general acquiescence in these measures of peace" that had "removed doubts and uncertainties," laying a foundation that would endure, not for the year or even the decade ahead, but for "all succeeding generations."

Slavery as a public matter, national conundrum, and moral outrage was henceforth and forever abolished. The Compromise had turned the Wilmot Proviso, the bill that would have prohibited the expansion of slavery to the territories acquired from Mexico, into a fading artifact. Opposition to slavery was widely considered disruptive, divisive, and disadvantageous. It was a cause that belonged to the impolitic, the unwise, and the intransigent. Those in favor of the Compromise owned the language of the Union. Any critic of the Compromise was an outcast against law and order, patriotism, and common sense. Dissent was relegated to the militants of the Boston Vigilance Committee sheltering escaped slaves and the serialized novel, *Uncle Tom's Cabin* by Harriet Beecher Stowe, then running weekly in the abolitionist newspaper in the capital, the *National Era*. Slavery gripped her readers, but for politics it was a closed book.

"Thus you will see that all causes of dissension had been removed; old sores were fast healing up; the occasional resistance to the Fugitive Slave Law alone furnishing ground of complaint," remarked John Minor Botts, a former Whig congressman from Virginia, a moderate voice, the most loyal Southern adherent of the national Whig Party that was rapidly disintegrating in the South. "The constitutionality of that law was tested before the proper tribunals in several of the states, and in every instance judgment was pronounced in favor of the law; the people of the North were fast becoming reconciled to it, or at least opposition to its execution was on the decline . . . except with a handful of the most violent and mischievous of the Abolitionists, who could of themselves have offered no serious obstacle to its faithful execution."

"The North (or free States) comprises almost two-thirds of all our population; the South (or slave States) but about a third," observed Congressman Horace Mann of Massachusetts, who had filled the seat of John Quincy Adams and advised Abraham Lincoln on his aborted bill on emancipation in the District of Columbia. "The North is really divided into two great parties, Whigs and Democrats. These are arrayed against each other in hostile attitude; and, being nearly equal, they cancel each other. The South is Whig or Democratic only nominally. It is for slavery exclusively and intensely. Hence we now present the astonishing and revolting spectacle of a free people in the nineteenth century, of almost twofold power, not merely surrendering to a pro-slavery people one-half the power, but entering into the most vehement competition to join with them in trampling upon all the great principles of freedom."

More than two thirds of the Democrats voted to affirm the Compromise when the 32nd Congress convened, but less than half of the dispirited Whigs bothered to turn up at their own caucus. Southern Whigs were only "nominally" attached to their national party and had adopted other labels in their states. In Georgia, the leading Whigs, Alexander Stephens and Robert Toombs, allied with the leading Democrat, Howell Cobb, had issued the Georgia Platform threatening that any change in the Compromise would be grounds for secession. The Compromise, stabilizing the balance of power between North and South, conceding advantages to the South, and lending decisive political momentum to the Democrats, was hailed as similar to the compromise that had made the Constitution, the alpha and omega of harmony.

Northern Whigs were in headlong retreat, assailed as unpatriotic for having upheld the Proviso, opposed the Compromise, and disdained the Fugitive Slave Act. Only three of seventy-six of them in the 31st Congress had voted for the hated law. When the rump Whig caucus of the new Congress rubber-stamped the Compromise, pretending as though Whigs had been for it all along, there was no reason to see any difference between them and the Democrats. The Democrats issued a statement howling that it was a trick, censured the Whigs as a "rotten party," and castigated the Northern Whigs that boycotted the caucus vote as abolitionists—the meanest and lowest epithet that could be hurled. Adding insult to injury abolitionists on the sidelines amplified the Democratic contempt for the Whig caucus vote as a fatal fraud. "The debate at once elicited and exhibited the party tactics that controlled the nation, showing not only the disposition of the slave-masters to dictate terms to the rival parties, but the anxiety of party leaders to conciliate and control the political strength of the slave-masters," wrote Henry Wilson, an antislavery member of the Massachusetts legislature, who would be elected to the U.S. Senate in 1855. Democratic triumphalism and Whig defensiveness set the parameters for the election year of 1852.

The overwhelming sensation that the nation was entering a brave new world was celebrated with the sudden entrance of the hero of the hour, incarnation of the inevitable unfolding of liberty, come to pay tribute to the United States as the exceptional nation and shining example to the struggling downtrodden masses of Europe, and to seek its aid. On December 5, Louis Kossuth, leader of the failed Hungarian revolution, symbol of all the suppressed uprisings of 1848, the short-lived Springtime of Nations, sailed into New York harbor after midnight to a twenty-one-gun salute. The next day a crowd of 100,000, a quarter of the city's population, turned out to hail him. Handsome and elegant, with a trim beard and feathered hat, Kossuth's surprisingly fluent and formal English, learned from studying Shakespeare, was a grace note that inspired elaborate and widespread praise. He mounted Black Warrior, the most famous army horse from the Mexican War, and pranced down Broadway, which was festooned with Hungarian flags, the streets echoing with "a continuous roar of cheers likes waves on the shore," according to a reporter. He was the toast of the town, honored at banquets of New York's elite and a special concert at the Metropolitan Opera.

The Hungarian celebrity brought along a ragtag entourage and his own Mitteleuropa agenda. He imagined his electric presence would spark U.S. intervention against the Hapsburg Empire and raise one million dollars for a war chest that he promised would be handsomely redeemed in bonds after liberation. Riding on the magnificent steed down Broadway, thundering with the cheers of the largest crowd in the city's history, he did not grasp that he was a fantasy figure for Americans to project an image about themselves. He mistook the scale of his tumultuous greeting to be about his own glorious cause. Fleeing the brutal oppression of the Old World, Kossuth discovered the confusing cacophony of the New. Extolling the high-flown ideals of democracy, he would flounder amid its mysterious realities. Nothing was what it seemed at first. His initial ecstatic reception that appeared to crystalize newfound national unity almost at once broke into a spectacle of splintering politics. Carrying himself with the bearing of a European head of state, he became an early factor in the presidential campaign. "Each party, each clique of each party," reported the *Philadelphia Public Ledger*, "would appropriate the great Magyar as an electioneering machine for the next Presidency." Each of Kossuth's encounters illustrated aspects of the baffling American scene, turbulent beneath the surface despite Fillmore's promise of permanent placidity.

Kossuth was brought by an act of the Congress to the American shore from Turkey onboard a navy frigate, the USS *Mississippi*. The bill's sponsor was Senator Henry S. Foote of Mississippi, who had proclaimed that the 1848 revolutions proved the end of "the age of tyrants and of slavery." An unabashed slaveholder and histrionic menace, the irony escaped him. Foote's own positions were as changeable as the weather and his attachment to the Democratic Party always tenuous. He expressed unshakable views with utter certitude that shifted on a moment's notice to another equally adamantine position, always depicting himself as defending matters of honor worthy of a duel at ten paces. His demagogy inevitably veered into personal attacks. Once vehemently against the Compromise, he became its resolute promoter. During the debate on the Senate floor he had pulled a revolver on Senator Thomas Hart Benton of Missouri.

Foote opened the congressional session proposing a resolution reaffirming the Compromise: "a final settlement, in principle and substance, of all the distracting questions growing out of African slavery." From the point of view of nearly everybody but himself, this was a redundant and self-defeating exercise, forcing the already decided issue of slavery into the open again. But Foote had disdain for his own party, "even then degenerated into a selfish and spoils-adoring faction," and kept reintroducing the bill to general irritation until there was a vote on April 5, 1852, resulting in predictable anticlimactic approval. He had the same reason for creating this particular friction as he did in championing Kossuth, which was to antagonize his Southern Ultra enemies in his home state who hated the Compromise—Mississippi governor

John Quitman, a secessionist who had embarked on a madcap expedition to seize Cuba from Spain to annex it a slave state, and his ally, Senator Jefferson Davis. Foote postured against the Hapsburg Empire partly to trump Quitman's attack on the Spanish crown. His audience was less Europe than the Magnolia State, his target less Emperor Franz Joseph than Jefferson Davis.

Foote and Davis, both with hair-trigger tempers, had once traded blows at their Washington boardinghouse, and after Quitman was indicted for his Cuban adventure and resigned would battle in 1852 for the governorship. Before he was forced out, Quitman got the legislature to censure Foote for supporting the admission of California as a free state, and he and Foote brawled on a platform during a debate. Quitman had established the Resistance Party, for which Davis wrote the platform, affirming "the right of secession," though declaring it should be reserved "under existing circumstances." Foote, running on his own Union Democratic Party incorporating the Whigs, was opposed by every congressman from the state, but would defeat Davis, who ran as Quitman's stand-in as the candidate of the Southern States Rights Democratic Party, the new name for the Resistance Party. Foote's victory by 999 votes would be the last hurrah of the Whigs in Mississippi, where they would never again win an office.

Before Kossuth arrived in Washington, Senator William Henry Seward of New York offered an official resolution of welcome—a kiss of death. Seward had been a leader against the Compromise, despised the Fugitive Slave Act, and was engaged in a blood feud with President Fillmore.

Fillmore's desire for revenge against Seward was the consequence of the strange train of circumstances that had carried him to the White House.

To near universal shock, Zachary Taylor, installed in the White House to serve as an iconic figurehead—"Old Rough and Ready," a semiliterate Louisiana slaveholder and military hero with no known political opinions other than his affiliation as a Whig—had revealed himself to be firmly opposed to the extension of slavery, determined to crush the Compromise and its Southern supporters, and had no use whatsoever for his vice president. Taylor took Seward as his counselor, who mercilessly cut out Fillmore from patronage in New York. Even before Taylor's demise, Fillmore had jettisoned his previously held antislavery principles, perhaps maintained all along to have curried favor with Seward. After Taylor's sudden death from cholera, Fillmore cast Seward into outer darkness and embraced the Compromise. The Compromise—and the Fugitive Slave Act—clothed him with presidential stature. The hack transformed into the statesman.

Fillmore usually displayed a first-class presentation, though under pressure flashed a second-class temperament. For those gathered around him he was the deliverance from Taylor, but he remained haunted by Taylor's ghost. Fillmore's repeated declarations about the "final settlement" were efforts to banish the specter. Among the living, above all, Fillmore despised his original creators Seward and Weed.

Seward viewed Kossuth's arrival as an opportunity for an opening move in the campaign of 1852, a means to launch an oblique attack on slavery, the Compromise and appeal to German immigrant voters, most refugees from the failed 1848 revolts. He aimed to defeat the conservative Whig faction in New York known as the Silver Grays allied with Fillmore, to deny Fillmore the Whig nomination for president, and to recapture the presidency for his next chosen nominee, for whom he would play the Warwick role as the adviser behind the throne. When Kossuth landed on the dock of Manhattan, Seward's closest political allies magically appeared to take him in hand, Henry J. Raymond, the speaker of the State Assembly who had recently raised funds with Seward's and Weed's help for a Whig newspaper called the *New York Times*, and Simeon Draper, a real estate mogul, banker, and head of the state's canal authority. During Kossuth's six months' peregrinations through the United States, the *Times*, acting as his self-designated house organ, would publish about six hundred articles chronicling his appearances and reproducing many of the full texts of his speeches. Hail the conquering hero!

But even before Kossuth arrived in Washington his approach provoked disarray. When Foote proposed that the Senate offer Kossuth its "great respect," John P. Hale, the antislavery senator of the Free Soil Party from New Hampshire, suggested that the resolution be amended to express support for "victims of oppression everywhere," an obvious attempt to criticize slavery. During the debate over the Compromise, Foote had threatened to hang Hale; now Hale's motion was killed. Seward's welcoming address to Kossuth in the Senate on December 9 was artfully crafted like an antislavery speech, a precursor of his "irrepressible conflict" speech of 1858, but with the word "slavery" absent. "It is clear that the days of despotism are numbered," he said. "We do not know whether its end is to come this year, or next year, or the year after; in this quarter of a century or in this half of a century. But there is to come, sooner or later, a struggle between the representative and the arbitrary systems of government." Then he winked that he was speaking only of Europe. Seward promptly printed a million copies of his speech praising Kossuth, a pamphlet distributed especially to German immigrants he hoped to win for the Whigs in the coming campaign.

Kossuth's visit aroused comparisons to the Marquis de Lafayette's triumphant tour in 1824 and his appearance in Washington followed its protocols—dinner with the president, presentation to the Senate, and a congressional banquet. Though it was similar, nothing was the same. Lafayette was a hero of the American Revolution before the French one, Kossuth only of his own. Washington's comrade-in-arms and Jefferson's kindred spirit was a living testament to the founding generation. Despite his noble bearing and perfect English, Kossuth was a greenhorn seeking new friends. In Washington there was a comic opera appearance to his comings and goings. He wore a military uniform and a long sword that rattled on the ground as he walked. At Brown's Hotel, where he and his retinue stayed, running up an extravagant liquor tab that the Congress paid, armed Hungarians guarded his door. His eloquent orations seeking assistance and his association with Seward's men in New York rankled Fillmore. "You ought to have seen Fillmore when he was received, as rigid as a midshipman on a quarter-deck," Senator James Shields, Democrat of Illinois, wrote in a letter to his law partner. (Shields, a co-sponsor of the welcoming resolution, accompanied Kossuth to the White House.) "He got himself into position and tried to look dignified, but the dignity of intellect and refinement was not there. You have read his reply, it was worse spoken than it read." Stilted and severe, Fillmore insultingly lectured Kossuth on the unbending American policy of neutrality and nonintervention. His rudeness was widely popular, as though it was the foreigner who had affronted the president.

Rebuked by Fillmore, Kossuth next paid a respectful call on Henry Clay in his room at the National Hotel, hopeful that the statesman could rescue his mission to secure aid. The journal closest to Clay, the *American Whig Review*, had hailed Kossuth as "the most remarkable man of the age, the man destined to leave the most enduring mark on it." But Clay's position was no different from Fillmore's, though his sense of moment and sinuous political instinct had not left him even as his health failed. "He began by saying with great solemnity, that he addressed him as a DYING MAN," according to the report in the *New York Times*. Clay indeed was suffering the final phases of tuberculosis. He told Kossuth that he had "worshipped all his life at the shrine of Liberty" and "trusted that Kossuth was as sincere a lover of Liberty, as himself." Then, as a former secretary of state, he expounded on the history of nonintervention back to Washington's Farewell Address that warned against "entangling alliances." When Kossuth left him, the en-feebled Clay rose from his armchair, grasped his hand, and as "tears rolled down the cheeks of the great Kentuckian" asked for God's protection of his visitor and "restoration to his native country." The blessing from Clay would be the most aid Kossuth would receive, except for the Congress picking up the exorbitant hotel bill for his entourage in Washington. Clay's benediction was also his dismissal. Kossuth's dream of securing U.S. intervention in far-away central Europe was chimerical. Clay would soon endorse Fillmore for the Whig nomination, eternally grateful to him for passing the Compromise for which Clay claimed credit as a second Washington, crowning his legacy.

After the Senate passed a resolution greeting Kossuth, almost every Southerner and Fillmore supporter voted against a similar motion in the House. With the exception of Foote, who had his own purposes, nearly all the Southerners were intensely suspicious of Kossuth's capacious rhetoric about freedom and revolution, registering every phrase as a not-so-veiled attack on slavery. They had little interest in being briefed on the struggles of the far-away Hungarians against the combined might of the Austrians and Russians. Whenever he spoke of tyranny, they sullenly took it as insult-ing commentary about themselves. "Kossuth is not a welcome guest to the conservative Americans. They fear him," wrote Shields. "He alarms their conservatism." Southerners raised the portrait of Washington against the Hungarian like a sign of the cross held before a vampire. Congressman Fay-ette McMullen, a Democrat from Virginia, among a host of others, blamed Kossuth for his "impudence" in challenging Washington's sacred neutrality policy.

Kossuth responded to the criticism in his speech after champagne toasts at the overflowing congressional dinner of January 7, 1852, given in his honor at the National Hotel. While flattering Southern sensibilities by praising "states' rights," he passionately urged a declaration in favor of his country's "freedom and independence." A cavalcade of notables mounted the podium to offer tribute, but Senator Sam Houston of Texas sneaked out just before it was his turn to speak and General Winfield Scott, a leading candidate for the Whig presidential nomination, who privately harrumphed that the honoree was "a gigantic humbug," arranged to be in Richmond. That even-ing Alexander Stephens organized an anti-Kossuth counter-dinner and the following month, with Fillmore's encouragement, sponsored a Washington Birthday commemoration marked by hostile remarks directed at the Hun-garian for daring "to influence us to depart from the wise policy" of Washington, according to the main address delivered by Attorney General John J. Crittenden, as clear an official rejection as possible. "We are Americans," Crittenden declared. "We are the teachers." And he drew a straight line of statesmanship extending "from Washington to Fillmore."

After Kossuth left the capital, Seward introduced a resolution condemning Russia's military support of Austria's suppression of Hungary as "wanton and tyrannical" and pledging that the U.S. would not be "indifferent" in the future. But the measure had so little support that it was never even brought to a vote. A similar motion in the House gained only seven votes.

When Kossuth went in search of funds among the wealthy plantation owners of the South he rattled his tin cup to no avail. It was as if he had decided to travel to the Sahara in search of water. He was treated in Charleston as a pox. All doors were shut; nobody greeted him or invited him to speak. He was quarantined. In Louisiana, members of the legislature protested his presence in the state. The *New Orleans Bulletin* editorialized, "If we sanction interference, we will be the first who will be interfered with . . . our own institutions will be the first crushed." In Mississippi, Foote held an event in Natchez that drew an embarrassingly small audience of the curious. The *Mississippi Free Trader*, the leading Democratic newspaper in Natchez, published a fugitive slave notice for "a likely Magyar fellow, named Louis Kossuth." "The whole opposition comes from the South," wrote Horace Mann. "The avowed opposition is based on the question of 'intervention'; but the real motive is slavery."

Kossuth quickly grasped that he should avoid mention of slavery, but his lofty rhetoric about "freedom" and "universal humanity" was an inadvertent dog whistle to slaveholders that signaled he was a covert abolitionist. "Kossuthism is a weight no one can carry south of Pennsylvania and Ohio," remarked J. G. M. Ramsey, an influential pro-slavery Democrat and historian of early Tennessee, warning that he was a negative factor in the upcoming election. Some antislavery people interpreted Kossuth's elusive language as antislavery, at least partly because of the Southern reaction. "Every speech he makes is the best kind of Abolition lecture," exulted the newly elected antislavery senator from Ohio, Benjamin Wade. "This is felt keenly by our Southern brethren." (Wade was the former law partner of Congressman Joshua Giddings, the antislavery leader in the House and the former boardinghouse mate of the departed member from Illinois, Abraham Lincoln.) But the abolitionists themselves fiercely turned on Kossuth when he would not subordinate his cause to theirs.

In New York, Kossuth privately met with the expectant representatives of the American and Foreign Anti-Slavery Society, explaining to them why he could not publicly embrace abolitionism. "I know you are just and generous, and will not endeavor to entangle me with questions of a party character while I am with you," he pleaded. But just as Southerners rejected him for what they inferred, abolitionists rejected him for what he would not say. William Lloyd Garrison condemned his rousing reception in New York as a scene of "national hypocrisy" and called him "as demented as the renowned Don Quixote," "criminal," "cowardly," "slippery," "selfish," and "deaf, dumb and blind." Theodore Parker, head of the Boston Vigilance Committee, delivered a thunderous sermon to his congregation of eminent Transcendentalists. "What greater wrong can he do the slave, than thus to strengthen his foes in their own good opinion of themselves, and weaken, by his example, that public rebuke to which the negro can alone trust for ultimate redemption? He whom tyrants hated on the other side of the ocean is the favored guest of tyrants on this side." Wendell Phillips, Garrison's disciple, the golden voice of Boston abolitionism, eviscerated Kossuth. "The very Congress that invited this man to our shores, and passed a resolution placing a national vessel at his service, is the very Congress that passed the Fugitive Slave Bill," he said. "Men say, 'Why criticize Kossuth, when you have every reason to believe that, in his heart, he sympathizes with you?' Just for that reason we criticize him. Because he endorses the great American lie, that to save or benefit one class, a man may righteously sacrifice the rights of another. Because, while the American world knows him to be a hater of slavery, they see him silent on that question—hear him eulogize a nation of slaveholders."

Defeated at Washington, repelled in the South, and scourged by abolitionists, Kossuth was still greeted like a prophet of human rights throughout the North and West, invited to address many state legislatures. "The spirit of our age is Democracy," he proclaimed before the Ohio legislature. "All for the people and all by the people. Nothing about the people, without the people. That is Democracy, and that is the ruling tendency of the spirit of our age." His words—"for the people . . . by the people"—echoed Italian revolutionary Giuseppe Mazzini's 1833 call for revolution "in the name of the people, for the people, and by the people"—a speech that would have been engraved on his mind—and that also echoed Daniel Webster's ringing peroration of his "Second Reply to Hayne" of 1830, his renowned argument for Unionism against states' rights, a speech that Abraham Lincoln had long ago committed to memory.

Near the end of Kossuth's tour, in May 1852, he attended ceremonies at Lexington and Concord, where ninety-year-old Revolutionary War soldiers marched and Ralph Waldo Emerson addressed him as "the foremost soldier of freedom, in this age." But with that apotheosis he was nearing the end of his line. He had become an unwitting metaphor for a discussion about slavery that could not take place in the Congress. Every word raised in the debate over Kossuth, especially "intervention," was taken as an unacknowledged analogy. Seward had understood the symbolic politics before Kossuth even came to Washington. " 'Hunkerism,' 'Silver Grayism,' 'Slavery,' all took alarm," he wrote Weed on December 26, 1851, "and now, even before he has reached here, he is repudiated by all the interests except odious 'Sewardism.' . . . He comes next week to feast on disappointment."

Throughout the months of Kossuth's presence in the country, towns across the North held public meetings to adopt resolutions of sympathy. One of these was held the day after the Washington congressional banquet, on January 8 at Springfield, Illinois. Fillmore's hostility to Kossuth had stirred up opposition to him in southern Illinois, where local county Whig organizations, expressing fidelity to the president, passed resolutions, one in Franklin County calling Kossuth "wrong in principle and dangerous in its consequences," and another in Hamilton County upholding "the wise, judicious, and law abiding policy of the President of the U. States, in his conduct toward unfortunate Hungary, in his unwillingness . . . to trample the law of nations under the heel of power." But the pro-Kossuth gathering at Springfield was a rare bipartisan occasion drawing together most of the usually contentious political leaders of central Illinois. On one side were the Democrats, the congressman from the district, Thomas Harris, and Lyman Trumbull, an Illinois Supreme Court judge. And on the other, the Whigs, the friends of Abraham Lincoln: the perennial Whig officeholder Dr. Anson D. Henry, Lincoln's physician and confidant, who had nursed him through his nervous breakdown; Edward D. Baker, a former congressman from the district now representing one in the northern corner of the state, so close to Lincoln that Lincoln named his second son after him; and David Davis, the presiding judge of the Eighth Judicial District, the Whig power broker and wealthy landowner who inducted Lincoln into his inner circle. There was also, of course, William Henry Herndon, Lincoln's law partner, political handyman, and the town radical. Milton Hay, the youthful law student working in Lincoln's law office as his assistant, was appointed vice president of the meeting. John Calhoun, the town's mayor, a pro-slavery Democrat, who had been Lincoln's supervisor as surveyor of Sangamon County, was named president of the meeting, and Lincoln put in charge of composing the resolutions—all in all a balanced ticket.

The declaration's first point supported the principle of democratic revolution: "That it is the right of any people, sufficiently numerous for national independence, to throw off, to revolutionize, their existing form of government, and to establish such other in its stead as they may choose." This was nothing more or less than the application of the Declaration of Independence to Europe—"the cause of civil and religious liberty on the continent of Europe," as another of the resolutions stated. None of the participants, including Lincoln, suspected this revolutionary sentiment had any connotation remotely suggesting domestic secession, a subject that had been raised throughout the debate over the Compromise by the Southern Ultras. The case for nonintervention was made in a lawyerly argument. While the United States should adhere to that policy, "no other government may interfere abroad, *to suppress such revolutions*," and that if "mutuality of non-intervention" was not observed then the United States had the right to interfere as "purely a question of policy, to be decided when the exigency arrives." Lincoln's resolutions were unanimously adopted. Though the issue of intervention was entirely theoretical, as a political matter these resolutions were far removed from Fillmore's tightly folded arms policy and the antithesis of the Southern horror at Kossuth's flowing talk about freedom. One of the Springfield resolutions read: "That the sympathies of this country, and the benefits of its position, should be exerted in favor of the people of every nation struggling to be free." It then mentioned the Germans, Irish, and French, a sop to the immigrant vote. But the language begged the question of slavery.

The Kossuth episode was undoubtedly central in broadening Lincoln's international outlook, which was organically connected to his developing politics. He neither spoke nor read any language other than English and would never travel abroad, but he followed the rise and fall of the revolutions of 1848. He saw them as democratic movements based on principles similar to those of the Declaration of Independence and suppressed by a constellation of despotic monarchial powers. He was eager for these movements' success and disappointed at their failure. In 1852, when he wrote the Springfield "Resolutions in Behalf of Hungarian Freedom," he did not link the European and antislavery struggles. Only radical abolitionists were willing to make that logical leap. But just two years later, in his speech at Peoria, on October 16, 1854, he did not hesitate to speak what had shortly before been politically unspeakable. On slavery, he said, "I hate it because it deprives our republican example of its just influence in the world—enables the enemies of free institutions, with plausibility, to taunt us as hypocrites." And he said that compromise on slavery tainted the United States as the leader of "the liberal party throughout the world." He would repeat his exact phrase—"I hate it because it deprives our republican example of its just influence in the world"—in his first debate with Douglas at Ottawa, Illinois, on August 21, 1858. During the decade of the 1850s, Lincoln would befriend many German exiled revolutionaries, who would become instrumental in the formation of the new Republican Party and his indispensable allies. But in early 1852 most Germans favored the Democratic Party, partly drawn to its name, suggestive it was the more liberal party, and partly disgusted with strong veins of nativism among the Whigs. As president, Lincoln understood the Civil War as an international event of the greatest magnitude, the cause of the United States as a liberal republic opposed by the same oppressive forces that had crushed the 1848 revolutions. It was this idea that led him in 1862 to call the United States "the last best hope of Earth."

After his American tour, Kossuth settled into exile in London, where he was embroiled in its claustrophobic factional infighting and descended into threadbare poverty. One of the pilgrims who sought him out was Carl Schurz, a German '48er, shortly before his own departure for America, where he would become an influential journalist and politician—befriending Lincoln and becoming a general in the Civil War. Schurz observed that Kossuth in the United States "was received almost like a superior being, all classes of society surging around him with measureless outbursts of enthusiastic admiration. But he could not move the government of this Republic to active interference in favor of the independence of Hungary, nor did he obtain from his American admirers that 'substantial aid' for his cause which he had looked and worked for, and thus he returned from America a profoundly disappointed man." "Now as to Kossuth," wrote Shields, "he is great because he has a powerful head and the heart of a child. That man will do wonders, not on the Democracy, (he is too delicate, too refined, and too scrupulous for that,) but upon the enlightened liberal mind of the world."

Kossuth's Hungarian rhapsody was the campaign's overture. Once the cynosure of all eyes, his name would be carefully avoided even as he was still wandering around the country acclaimed a hero in the northern hinterlands. But at their conventions the parties would pointedly distance themselves from his cause, the Democrats pressing their advantage and the Whigs reacting defensively. The Democratic platform, noting "the condition of popular institutions in the Old World," declared "a high and sacred duty is devolved, with increased responsibility upon the Democratic Party of this country, as the party of the people, to uphold and maintain the rights of every State"— not nation-states, but states' rights. Thus Kossuth became the trigger for the non sequitur. Another plank clarified: "That the Democratic Party will resist all attempts at renewing, in Congress or out of it, the agitation of the slavery question, under whatever shape or color the attempt may be made." The Whig platform, composed in self-protective panic, waved Washington to ward off Kossuth: "That while struggling freedom everywhere enlists the warmest sympathy of the Whig party, we still adhere to the doctrines of the Father of his Country, as announced in his Farewell Address, of keeping ourselves free from all entangling alliances with foreign countries." The cheers had faded into condescension; the idol of January had become the pariah of June.

CHAPTER SEVEN

THE MAKING OF THE DARK HORSE

During his American sojourn one political figure towered over all the others as Kossuth's greatest enthusiast, who promised him the world. Senator Stephen A. Douglas of Illinois strutted as the new master of the Capitol, the floor leader who passed the Compromise after it had appeared hopelessly lost, subduing both the shrill antislavery and Southern Ultra voices, and then by sheer force of will and concentrating financial interests rammed through the Illinois Central Act, forging the modern railroad corporation and revolutionizing the industrial economy. He advertised himself as the herald of the future, the maker of the new age and front-runner of his generation—the political

Franklin Pierce, engraving published during the campaign of 1852

engine of the piston-driven forces of modernization. He sought to triumph under the banner of Young America and the watchword of Manifest Destiny, the magic jingo words coined for the evangelical nationalism of boundless westward expansion by the editors of the influential *Democratic Review* before the Mexican War. Douglas seized that flag like a crusader, stridently marching in its front rank. Young America took its name from the revolutionary European movements—Young Italy and Young Germany—but was inimitably American in its swirling mélange of democratic preachment, imperialist bravado, and white supremacy. Douglas scorned alike the Old World autocrats and old party spokesmen. He would sweep away both the European monarchies and the Democratic fogies in a blast of bluster. The Little Giant was the spread-eagle American.

As soon as he arrived in the august Senate in 1847 as one of its youngest members Douglas advanced himself as a presidential candidate, more a boast than a bid, too young to be eligible for the executive office. His ambition burned in advance of his age, and its flame grew over the four years that made him eligible. Kossuth had materialized at just the right moment as a bandwagon to ride. Shaking his fist at the monarchs across the sea, Douglas brought it down on his tired rivals for the Democratic nomination, all of them more than a generation older. In his defense of Kossuth, no one exceeded the rage of his chauvinism. When the Senate passed its welcoming resolution, but without unanimity, Douglas seized on the "divided vote," chastising those failing to support it as bent on craven knee. "I do not deem it material whether the reception of Governor Kossuth give offence to the crowned heads of Europe," he declared defiantly, "provided it does not violate the law of nations, and give just *cause* of offense." Implying the patriotism of his rivals was halfhearted he forwarded himself as the avatar of Young America. "The peculiar position of our country requires that we should have an *American policy* in our foreign relations," he said, "based upon the principles of our own government, and adapted to the spirit of the age." Borrowing Kossuth's "spirit of the age" flourish, Douglas presented himself as the zeitgeist itself.

The Little Giant stood atop Kossuth like a pedestal. "I hold," he said, "that the principle laid down by Governor Kossuth as the basis of his action—that each State has a right to dispose of her own destiny, and regulate her internal affairs in her own way, without the intervention of any foreign power—is an axiom in the laws of nations which every State ought to recognize and respect." Kossuth's call for national independence became, *mutatis mutandis*, Douglas's own doctrine of popular sovereignty as Manifest Destiny. Hungary's quest for freedom turned into nothing more or less than his idea of allowing a territory to decide itself whether it would be free or slave, precisely his solution for New Mexico in the Compromise. Popular sovereignty was Douglas's amorphous middle ground between the Wilmot Proviso men who would ban slavery from the territories and the Southern Ultras who would extend it. Just as Southerners chose to hear Kossuth's words about "despotism" and "liberty" as a thinly veiled attack on slavery, Douglas decided to stamp the Hungarian's talk of his country's freedom as his own calling card.

Douglas's rhetorical thrusts lent Kossuth moral support. He provided Senator James Shields, his ally, to serve as his political guide. And Douglas's men promised material aid, too, including a steamship outfitted with guns, an offer Kossuth eagerly accepted as "the greatest made to me since I came to the U.S." But the promise of the gunboat remained unfulfilled as Douglas embarked on his presidential campaign. Kossuth had no Southern appeal, but another issue did. Without missing a beat Douglas's pugnacious demand for Hungarian independence shifted into his siren call for annexation of Cuba, which he had been demanding since 1844 as essential to American destiny as the annexation of Texas—his "bellicose and annexing propensities," as Edward Everett, the former governor of Massachusetts, described them.

"The South does not put forward as yet a single man," remarked Congressman Horace Mann on the developing presidential contest. Southern leaders believed " 'a Northern man with Southern principles' can do more for them than any one of their own. All of them are virtually saying to Northern aspirants, 'Proceed, gentlemen; give us your best terms: and, when you have submitted your proposals, we will make our election between you.' " Mann observed: "And Mr. Douglas, a young senator from Illinois, who aspires to the White House, offers Cuba to the South in addition to all the rest."

Douglas's chief campaign supporter had been the one to dangle the alluring gift of the gunboat before Kossuth. George Nicholas Sanders, indefatigable, infinitely connected, mysterious, and seductive, was the scion of one of the First Families of Kentucky, descended from a promoter of Jefferson's Kentucky Resolutions, the namesake of Kentucky's first attorney general, and one of the most cosmopolitan Americans of his generation. Sanders was a diplomat linked to the higher social and business circles of New York and well married to the daughter of a wealthy New Yorker. He served as political adviser to a host of the most influential politicians of the Democratic Party; a venturesome entrepreneur and partner of big businessmen; owner and publisher of the foremost Democratic journal of political opinion; and comrade to European revolutionaries against monarchial regimes, having stood with them on the barricades. Sanders also happened to be a sleazy lobbyist, arms merchant, and confidence man manipulating a succession of political leaders into one disaster after another. His natural instinct was vindictive retribution. He became the principal American exponent of the theory and practice of political assassination, embroiled with European radicals in murder plots against Emperor Louis Napoleon, and as a Confederate commissioner in Canada mentored John Wilkes Booth. Known to virtually every prominent politician, his natural method was insinuation, creating the aura of a magician, surrounded by the fumes of cigars and the aroma of bourbon. His favorite venue was the smoke-filled room, his ideal forum the sociable dinner party, his preferred organization the cabal, and his wild enterprises dependent on backstage political wire-pulling and bribery. Untrustworthy, unreliable, and uncontrollable, he magnetically attached himself to ambitious men who convinced themselves to trust in his sagacity, and compelled by his grandiosity would pay the price for their cupidity. They all thought they could use him, from Douglas to Jefferson Davis, and all were used. "I have great confidence in your judgment and discretion," Douglas wrote Sanders. "I profit more by your letters than any I receive." Stephen A. Douglas was the first in a long line that stretched to Jefferson Davis and Horace Greeley.

Kossuth had previous dealings with the slippery Sanders. He was not the completely naive character Senator Shields thought him to be. Sanders had schemed in 1848 to sell old muskets used in the Mexican War to Kossuth and other European revolutionaries. In the bargain, Sanders would have skimmed a windfall profit, but President Polk intervened to halt the gunrunning. Sanders's partner in that deal and any number of others was George Law, a buccaneer who owned the U.S. Mail Steamship Company, which held the contract for carrying mail to California and throughout the Caribbean, the Panama Railroad across the isthmus, and the streetcar line in New York City. Law was also a major benefactor of Douglas, politically and personally. He lobbied heavily for passage of the Illinois Central Act, which would connect to his steamship line. Seizing Cuba would have linked Havana to Chicago, where Douglas made a fortune selling his right-of-way lakefront real estate to the railroad. As Douglas launched his campaign, he was dubbed "the steamboat candidate." But George Law was not his only steamboat connection. Douglas also pushed for monopoly government contracts to the Pacific Mail Steamboat Company, owned by William Aspinwall, another major backer and not coincidentally Law's partner in various ventures. Two of the chief investors in the Illinois Central and big Illinois bondholders, J. W. Alsop and G. W. Ludlow, were directors on Aspinwall's board, as well as cozy Douglas supporters. Douglas's financial and political affairs were entangled and seamless. And Sanders was enmeshed in this ever more convoluted nexus.

The means by which Douglas had passed the Compromise and the Illinois Central Act were deployed for his campaign. It was a whirligig of big money, lobbyists, and public relations—"adventurers, politicians, jobbers, lobby-members, loafers, letter writers, and patriots which call themselves 'Young America,'" as Congressman Andrew Johnson of Tennessee, Lincoln's future vice president, described them. Douglas's campaign directorate included not only Sanders but also J. Knox Walker, nephew and personal secretary of the late President Polk, now known as the "Prince of Lobbyists," and Francis J. Grund, the Austrian-born prolific newspaperman who had been the fount of pro–Illinois Central publicity and was handsomely remunerated by W. W. Corcoran, the leading banker in Washington and major Illinois bondholder, another Douglas patron. "Douglas is going it with a rush," Grund declared.

Douglas bowled through New York from the mansions of Fifth Avenue to the gang clubhouses of the Bowery. "What is in the wind?" wondered the *New York Herald*.

He was toasted at banquets and private dinners, inducted into the Tammany Society, toured the orphanage and the immigration processing station, and christened Aspinwall's latest steamship, named the *Illinois* in his honor. He rounded up the support of the Empire Club, a political powerhouse, bossed by Isaiah Rynders, "king of the Five Points gangsters," who had helped deliver the state for Polk. No stone was left unturned, and everything under them petted.

From the beginning of his career Douglas was a daring political pioneer, constantly devising new techniques to leap over the old-boy networks. In Illinois he had introduced the convention system for nominating candidates, which outflanked the established figures of his own party and made him the power broker. Now he decided to solve his Southern problem by attaching a Southerner. So he became the first presidential candidate to announce his running mate before he had the nomination himself. He chose Senator Robert M. T. Hunter of Virginia. Douglas had been the architect of the Compromise; Hunter had opposed it as a Southern Ultra. Douglas reasoned they would unite the party behind him and remove the underlying issue of slavery, "come together upon the basis of entire silence on the slavery question and support 'the Ticket.' " Sanders acted as the go-between. Hunter flatteringly wrote him that Douglas "speaks in the highest terms, of the skill and judgment with which you manage affairs. He himself I think is one of the coolest observers even when he himself is concerned, that I ever saw."

Robert M. T. Hunter

Heir to a plantation fortune, Hunter also was one of those who represented the legacy of the political estate of John C. Calhoun. As speaker of the Virginia House of Representatives, he had been chairman of Calhoun's stillborn campaign for president in 1844. One of the wealthiest slaveholders in Virginia, Hunter represented the Tidewater aristocracy as their hero of the state Democratic faction known as the "Young Chivalry," bellicose in its defense of slavery and hostile to the Richmond Junto of Thomas Ritchie, the old Jacksonian who despised Calhoun and his nullifiers. But Hunter embodied a paradox of militancy and inertia, prominence and lethargy, given to what the acerbic Foote described as "drowsy, phlegmatic and over-crammed discourses."

Douglas calculated that attracting Hunter would align the South behind him. A Vermonter who had transformed himself into a Western man, he never thought of himself as a sectional figure. His bombastic nationalism encompassed the continent. He flung back the curtain to reveal Manifest Destiny all the way to the Pacific. The Illinois Central once built would run on unbroken track from Lake Michigan to the Gulf of Mexico. Douglas, through his first wife, profited from a large plantation in Mississippi. He himself was North, South, East, and West. Douglas believed, moreover, that the Compromise had reset politics, quarantining slavery, just as the Compromise of 1820 had done. Once enacted, normal politics would be reestablished with the Democrats as the natural majority, just like before the Mexican War. Douglas advanced himself as the modernized version of Jacksonianism, the new age on the old premise but with himself as the new man on the revised majority. He was the agent of radical disruption, thinking he would restore the status quo ante. He quivered with the momentum of money and machines so forcefully that he would not acknowledge the powerful undercurrent of Southern nationalism or that the embers of the fire-eaters had not died with the Compromise, or how the forces he helped unleash might threaten Southern interests. In the fall of 1851, before an audience in Buffalo, he attributed sectional strain to mere bias. "Why is it that you have a prejudice against the South?" he lectured the New Yorkers. "Is it because you do not know them?" Why couldn't North and South get along and support him? He would not truly understand the depth of the internal dynamics until they were fatal to his ultimate chance to become president, when in 1860 Southern Democrats revealed they would rather destroy the Democratic Party than allow him to win.

Hunter accepted Douglas's offer to be his running mate, but not the reasons for his campaign. Hunter was immersed in intense private discussions among Southern leaders about securing Southern dominance of the Democratic Party and the federal government to extend slavery, and never ruled out the option of secession. For Douglas the Compromise ended the debate over slavery and began the new era that would make his ascension inevitable. But for Southerners like Hunter, the Compromise was a limited and flawed stopgap measure in a rolling game. Douglas's strategy always conflated the nation's Manifest Destiny with his own; Hunter's was always a Southern strategy.

"It is rather farcical to be sure to those who know to insist on Douglas as most fit," wrote former congressman James A. Seddon of Virginia, a close ally within the Young Chivalry, to Hunter on February 7, 1852. "The best man for the Presidency and yet I have for more than a year thought it was coming to that absurdity." Seddon, who would become the Confederate secretary of war as Hunter would become the Confederate secretary of state, supported him in taking Douglas's offer. "*We* must be practical as politicians and statesmen to be useful—a high position—good—a position of acknowledged influence and confessed participation in the administration ought not to be lost to the States Rights men from over refined scruples and feelings.

As Vice President, I believe you could and would have great influence in the administration and that influence might prove of immense value to our cause in the South." Knowing that two recent presidents had died in office, he noted, "There is the chance of the Presidency by vacancy, not much perhaps but still to be weighed."

Seddon lamented that the Compromise had temporarily blunted the Southern Ultra cause. "I agree with you readily as to the position and duty of the Southern Rights (or as I prefer the States Rights) party of the South in the coming presidential struggle. Personally I should have preferred a separate organization and action on their part and 18 months ago, when I still hoped their spirit and their strength might prove equal to their zeal and the justice of their cause, I should have advised that course. Now however it is apparent, their *cause as a political one is lost* and thus separate action would be more than preposterous—would be suicidal." But the "lost" opportunity dictated a new course of action within the Democratic Party in order to destroy Southern Ultra opponents in the South and gain control of the levers of the government. "We have and can maintain (within certain limits of considerable latitude) ascendency in the Democratic party of the South and probably controlling influence on the general policy and action of the whole party in the Union. The *Union* party, par excellence, we can proscribe and crush. What miserable gulls the *Union* Democrats of the South find them, and I am inclined to think the *Union* Whigs will not fair much better."

Douglas was unabashed in his ambition. His rivals for the nomination had spent lifetimes in pursuit of the prize. He was thirty-eight years old. He was indebted to few people in his party. His political machine was his own device. He had just passed the Compromise and the Illinois Central Act. He was a triumph. He had never lost anything—neither any race nor any important bill. He bore few scars. His longtime principal rival within his home state, the leader of the Whigs there, had served only one term in the Congress and was now riding a horse on the dusty trails of the Eighth Judicial District of central Illinois; nobody remembered his name. Douglas knew he was envied and resented because he had risen like a rocket. He aroused fear and loathing in proportion to the dimensions of the interests working on his behalf. The prominent supporters of James Buchanan, the former secretary of state, also a candidate for the nomination, were especially vociferous. "Every vulture that would prey upon the public carcass and every creature who expects the reward of office, are moving heaven and earth in his behalf," wrote Senator William R. King of Alabama, Buchanan's intimate friend.

Francis Preston Blair, member of Jackson's Kitchen Cabinet, reported to former president Martin Van Buren that "the Lobby of Jobbers at Washington move Douglas as a puppet and draw around him all their forces." Douglas defended himself from criticism at the party's Jackson Day dinner. "I care not," he said, "if a man says I have been inconsistent upon a measure of expediency, provided he will admit that I have always been faithful to my principles, and regulated all questions of expediency by them." "The speech," wrote his biographer Robert Johannsen, "displayed all the confidence of a man about to taste success."

After making the case before the party for his own course, he instructed his campaigners to "refrain from attack upon any candidates." The nomination depended upon a two-thirds majority; he needed the others in the ring to throw their delegates to him after he had exhausted them. Arousing rancor would be a bad tactic.

The *Democratic Review*, jingo for Manifest Destiny and cradle of Young America, had been close to Douglas since he and its editor, John O'Sullivan, paid a visit on President Polk at the White House in 1848 to urge him that his next step after the Mexican War should be to grab Cuba. Sanders bought the journal, probably with financing from George Law, to have his own mouthpiece to tout Young America and Douglas's candidacy. His first editorial, published in the January 1852 issue, ignited a firestorm. In "Eighteen-Fifty-Two and the Presidency," Sanders minced no words: "Age is to be honored, but senility is pitiable." He called for "a new generation" to sweep away the "old politicians" of the Democratic Party. He wrote that "by lack of statesmanship, lack of temper, lack of discretion, and, most of all, by lack of progress, they brought into our ranks discord and dissension, and the party they received united, strong, and far in advance, they left a wreck, a mutinous wreck." The party needed a new hero: "A second Hercules, he comes to cleanse the Augean stable, to hurl out the guilty, and restore with a flood of democratic power the purity of our institutions." This nominee would "bring young blood, young ideas, and young hearts." His identity was without doubt. Nor were the identities of the other candidates cloaked as Sanders described them: "your mere wire-puller and 'judicious bottle holder,' who claims prominence now, on the sole ground that he once played second fiddle to better men, and who cozens himself in his corner with the idea that he can split votes with the abolition and sectional factions he has intrigued with; and, above all, your beaten horse." As every sensate reader of the *Democratic Review* knew, Sanders was referring to the previous Democratic ticket of Lewis Cass and William O. Butler. Sanders hated Butler, an old general and Democratic warhorse from his own state of Kentucky, presumably for opposing his father for political office. He lampooned Cass as the stereotype of old buffoonish hack.

The publication of Sanders's first issue exploded like shrapnel, but the one it wounded was Douglas. "Our friend Sanders is a noble fellow and a man of remarkable vigor of intellect," Douglas wrote Caleb Cushing, the former Massachusetts congressman, serving as an adviser, "but I fear he lacks the requisite prudence to conduct the Review safely at the present time." He told Cushing that he had asked Sanders to cease and desist from his polemics but "it seems that my wishes in this respect are disregarded by him."

Sanders wrote Cushing directly, but not to calm him: "The more fire the better as we intend to make the times hot." He sent a letter to Douglas promising another explosion. "I shall make an attack on Genl Butler more terrific than was ever made against mortal man before. I'll finish him . . . don't be scared it will not be thunder, but it shall be an earthquake."

In an editorial in the next issue, Sanders wrote, "Still water has little force." A Niagara of abuse fell on Butler. "We declare him made up of feeble negatives." Sanders scored him for indecision on Texas annexation: "The hour would strike while he was trying to find out what other men thought. Texas gone, or Washington sacked, before General Butler could get an idea into his head, or a word out of it." As a military figure, "where he has won his only reputation, he has never shown capacity beyond that of a brave subaltern." Then he ridiculed the friends of Cass for having "done him the injury and injustice" of assuming the phrase in the last issue's editorial denouncing a "beaten horse" referred to him, when Sanders triumphantly announced he meant "in fact" Butler. He concluded that "if the morbid sensitiveness of some gentlemen who may feel themselves aggrieved by the course we have marked out, should lead them to advise us with diplomatic suavity not to hurt them, but somebody else in future, our subsequent course will convince them of the folly of such appeals."

Sanders's assault on Butler brought John C. Breckinridge, the youthful congressman from Kentucky, to his feet on the floor of the House of Representatives to defend his honor. Breckinridge declared that the *Democratic Review* had undergone a "great change," exemplified by publishing "a grossly personal and abusive article against General Butler by name, and against the rest of the candidates covertly," and that it was "intending to promote particular interests by traducing the most honored names in our ranks." Breckinridge took on Young America as out of step with the Democratic Party. "I profess to be a friend of rational progress," he said. "But I want no wild and visionary progress, that would sweep away all the immortal principles of our forefathers—hunt up some imaginary genius, place him on a new policy, give him 'Young America' for a fulcrum, and let him turn the world upside down." Breckinridge called out Douglas, "a particular favorite," as the only Democratic candidate who was not assailed. Douglas's friend in the House, William A. Richardson of Illinois, sprang up instantly to protest that Douglas "has no control" over the *Review*.

Sanders launched his missiles in every direction. In the March issue, he labeled Breckinridge a "young fogy" guilty of "hereditary servility" to "old fogydom." Disputing Breckinridge's imputation that Douglas was behind his attacks on Butler, Sanders reproduced a letter he sent to Douglas: "The fogy atmosphere of Washington makes cowards of you all, and the sooner you understand that you cannot direct the columns of the Review, the better." He took on yet another Democratic candidate, William L. Marcy of New York, the former senator, governor, and secretary of war, "spavined, windblown, strained, ring-boned, and with a huge gray spot still sore on his flank." (Marcy was guilty in the Polk administration of stopping Sanders's scheme of gunrunning to European revolutionaries.) Sanders touted Douglas, abused Butler repeatedly, and demeaned Breckinridge: "It is unnecessary to argue with imbecility further." In the next issue, he proudly devoted an editorial to claiming credit for coining the term "old fogy," "one of such exactitude and truth that it has received a very wide acceptance," and called fogies "the creeping parasite," "a mass of crushed and reeking rottenness," "malefactors," "hucksters," and "confessed that we have done justifiable homicide on two individuals, General Butler and Governor Marcy."

Douglas begged Sanders to desist. "If you cease now and make no more attacks upon anybody, and especially none of Gen'l Cass, possibly I may yet regain my lost position," he wrote him. "If these attacks are repeated, my chances are utterly hopeless and I may be compelled to retire from the field and throw my influence in favor of one of these whom the Review strives to crush."

Sanders fired another blast. In his next issue he proclaimed himself a successful political assassin, already an obsessive self-image before his actual participation in European assassination plots and avuncular relationship with John Wilkes Booth. "We have charged with ball-cartridge, and have done execution loyally," he wrote. "We do not seek to overrate our services, while we certainly think no apology should be expected of us for having discharged our duty." On the eve of the convention, he again whipped Butler, Cass, Marcy, and the "old fogy aspirants," urging that the party select a candidate who bore an uncanny resemblance to Douglas. "With a fast man it will win again. Without that, with an old fogy at its head, we can walk calmly to our fate—but that fate is plain, and is death."

But the corpse laid out was Douglas. "Douglas the candidate of the cormorants of our party is now considered a dead cock in the pit, unless some throe in the agony of political death should enable him to kill off his opponents which is not likely to occur," remarked Andrew Johnson. "Vaulting ambition o'erleaps itself and falls on t'other side. But perhaps the little Judge never read Shakespeare, and don't think of this," wrote James Shepherd Pike, the Washington correspondent of the *New York Tribune*. "Yet today there are signs of wavering in his ranks. The late leading article in the Democratic Review on the Presidency of 1852 having given mortal offence in various quarters unfriendly to the Judge's pretensions, and thus done him essential damage, it is now asserted by his friends that the article was a ruse of the enemy, for the especial purpose of hurting the prospects of the small giant. This is a far-fetched explanation of that elaborate paper, but it is doubtful if it will go down."

Douglas's strategy depended upon his unstoppable steam, but he had run off the tracks. Hunter jumped from Douglas's ticket to instead gain support for his reelection to the Senate in Virginia from those backing other presidential contenders. Caleb Cushing, always a chameleon who was drawn to Douglas because he looked like a winner, simply walked away, and after flirting with Butler and Marcy decided to join the stealth campaign of the dark horse candidate, Franklin Pierce, the former U.S. senator from New Hampshire. Gideon Pillow, Polk's former law partner and campaign manager, who had been brought into Douglas's inner circle by his former junior partner, J. Knox Walker, dumped Douglas to enroll in the Pierce effort aiming to become his vice president. But Douglas still thought he could win.

The Democrats arrived for their convention at Baltimore on June 1 with no front-runner. Each candidate counted on the failure of the others. Resolving the deadlock depended upon them exhausting themselves. The truth about the field of worn and weary candidates was not far distant from Sanders's acid pen portraits.

Nearly seventy years old, Senator Lewis Cass, formidable by fame but rickety in reality, carried his presumptive right to the nomination by virtue of being the previous nominee and based his appeal on renewing his past promises of patronage. He had the momentum of inertia. An observer of the scene,

Josiah B. Grinnell, who would become a congressman from Iowa and found Grinnell College, recalled, "The general wore a wig which did not conceal his age, was obese, wheezy and rapid in speech," but was "distrusted by the party slate-makers for honesty, and not strong with the 'bohoys.' " These were, however, merely his superficial liabilities. He was largely indifferent to campaigning and mistrusted by the South in a Southern-dominated party. He had supported the Compromise, denounced the Ultras, waved the banner of "squatter sovereignty," a black flag to slaveholders who believed they had the right to take their property into any territory, and, last but not least, had warmly greeted Kossuth, expressing a sympathy that was anathema to Southerners. Cass was affable enough, but surprisingly not much of a natural politician for someone who had spent decades in back rooms. Grinnell once watched him order a bottle of wine at a dinner with friends. "I remarked, 'He will never be President,' not on account of his beverage, rather because he did not pass it around. Had it been Douglas, stranger and friend would have touched their glasses until many brands had been tried, regardless of costly corkage, and the clinking had become both feeble and monotonous."

James Buchanan, Cass's perennial rival, was tall, white-haired, always immaculately dressed with a freshly starched high collar, and overflowing with courtesy. "The Sage of Wheatland" looked the part of the distinguished senior statesman, his head invariably tilted to one side as though listening intently, though its curvature was an idiosyncratic tic. He seemed to be thinking deep thoughts, but myopic in one eye and farsighted in the other he was just having trouble focusing. A famous bachelor, he shared quarters with Senator King of Alabama, prompting Andrew Jackson to refer to them as "Miss Nancy" and "Aunt Fancy." The former U.S. senator from Pennsylvania and secretary of state, Buchanan was the most stolidly conservative "Northern man of Southern sympathy" in the race. Opposed to the provisions of the Compromise, except the Fugitive Slave Act, for being unjust to the South, he declared he would accept it as "finality," but praised its Southern Ultra opponents for having acted "patriotically." He drew a line in the sand separating himself from Cass—and Douglas—over popular sovereignty, sharing the Southern suspicion that the doctrine was little more than an insidious method of limiting slavery. Buchanan endorsed Jefferson Davis's proposal to extend the Missouri Compromise line straight to the Pacific, which would have secured New Mexico and southern California for slavery. He was stronger in the South than within his own state party.

William L. Marcy, the leading old Jacksonian of New York, who had achieved immortality for uttering "To the victor belong the spoils," was a masterful politician and administrator, inevitably the victor. His unofficial slogan was: "May the Lord have Marcy upon us." The ruthless leader of the conservative Hunker faction of the state party against the antislavery Barnburners that had defected to join the Free Soil Party in 1848, he operated more out of zeal for party than principle. His most important supporter in this cycle was his most unlikely ally, his former mortal enemy Thurlow Weed.

Weed was convinced the Democrats were certain to win the election. He thought the Whig nominee would be either Fillmore or Daniel Webster, both of whom he loathed for waging war upon him and Seward and for supporting the Compromise. "I desired to see those gentlemen left to reap what they had sown," he said. New York, he figured, would be the key state as it had been before, and by running a New Yorker the Democrats were sure to win. So Weed used his influence to reconcile former Barnburner leaders with Marcy.

Marcy's nomination rested on the premise that he would unite New York behind him. Senator Daniel Dickinson, Marcy's rival, was determined to defeat him. Known as "Scrip Dick" for his penchant for quoting Scripture, and representing the Wall Street interests linked to the cotton trade, Dickinson operated through his son-in-law, former New York congressman Ausburn Birdsall, to set Southern delegations against Marcy for his Barnburner support. Marcy was further undermined when almost all of the New York Democratic members of the Congress voted against Foote's resolution in favor of the Compromise. Marcy felt compelled to issue a hedging statement that while he was for the Compromise he would not affirm it as "final" out of deference to New York sentiment against the Fugitive Slave Act. He entered the convention limping behind a sharply divided state delegation.

Yet another hopeful "old fogy," Levi Woodbury of New Hampshire, had held even more notable posts than Buchanan and Marcy—governor of and U.S. senator from New Hampshire, secretary of the treasury, secretary of the navy, and justice of the Supreme Court. His chief ruling on the high bench was the pro-slavery decision in *Jones v. Van Zandt* of 1847, against the Underground Railroad operator from Ohio shielding a runaway slave, defended by Seward and Chase, a case that was fictionalized in *Uncle Tom's Cabin*. A motley crew of politicos with wildly varying motives endorsed him mostly out of hatred of other politicians. Thomas Hart Benton, for example, backed Woodbury in order to have influence with a president who might batter his host of enemies. The candidate, however, dumbfounded his promoters by suddenly dropping dead in September 1851.

Woodbury's demise left a vacuum that the "Concord Cabal," his New Hampshire clique, desperately sought to fill. They decided to wait patiently for the others to fall by the wayside before letting their dark horse loose. It was a tried-and-true strategy. Just as the Whigs reverted to running generals, the Democrats would leap on the dark horse as they had with Polk in 1844, the last time they had won. Within the party, to the extent that he was known, Franklin Pierce had no enemies, bore no grudges, and his only strong feeling was hostility to abolitionists, which strongly commended him. He was a wellborn heir, handsome and young. He was the epitome of the Young Fogy, but too obscure to attract Sanders's malice. His father, Benjamin Pierce, had been a Revolutionary War soldier and governor of New Hampshire. Franklin was the scion of the state's entrenched agrarian Democratic establishment, the darling of its "Old Guard" faction, studying law under Woodbury, elected to the legislature at twenty-four years old, and promptly made speaker of the house while his father was the sitting governor. He was elected to the House of Representatives at twenty-seven, becoming its youngest member, and promoted to the U.S. Senate, again the youngest. Then he abruptly resigned his seat.

Pierce had married the most proper and elevated woman within his range. Jane Appleton was the daughter of the president of Bowdoin College, also a Congregationalist minister, and the niece by marriage of Amos Lawrence, one of the wealthiest Massachusetts mill owners. Pierce had met the college president's daughter when he was a student at Bowdoin. Jane was frail, nervous, and censorious of politicians and political life. The death of their firstborn infant son, Franklin Jr., made her delicate state of mind even more fragile. Pierce also had another problem. He was an alcoholic, who repeatedly broke his vows of temperance to his unforgiving wife.

Pierce's suave manners and fine education distinguished him as a class above his parents. But just as they had lifted him ever upward they also plagued him. His father was notorious for his rough habits, incessant tobacco chewing and spitting, "extremely profane, and seldom talked to men of any profession, when at home, without swearing." Pierce's mother, Anna, "fond of whiskey," engaged in "fantastic capers," offending proper townspeople, shockingly appearing at church services in a short dress and "displaying her comely ankles encircled by red ribbons." Even as his parents receded into his background, he was torn between gentility and vulgarity, aspiration and alcoholism.

When his wife decamped back to New Hampshire without him, he quit the liquid temptations of the capital for her sake. The Old Guard made him state party chairman, where he proved himself by booting out Congressman John P. Hale for his antislavery convictions. The gesture won him the hearts of the Southern Democrats. It helped that "he had never given a vote or written a sentence that the straightest Southern Democrat could wish to blot," according to the journalist Benjamin Perley Poore. Added to this résumé, Pierce had been a brigadier general in the Mexican War, bearing a wound from his horse falling on him, before returning to his law practice, and serving after Woodbury's death as the perfectly pleasant and passive object behind which the hard-bitten members of the Concord Cabal plotted as they had his whole adult life.

"He was always so amiable, so friendly in his manner, so *affectionate* even in his demonstrations, that I never could continue angry with him forty-eight consecutive hours, although the provocations which he gave me were frequent enough and gross enough to make me break with him forever," wrote his friend Maunsell B. Field, a New York poet, novelist, lawyer, and Democratic Party denizen, who would become a Treasury official in the Lincoln administration. "I presume that my own experience was similar to that of thousands of others. He was so absurdly false to his promises, that, where it did not cut too hard, it was positively ludicrous. And yet I never in my own mind accused him of insincerity. He was a weak, imaginative, almost brilliant, undetermined man, who said in the morning that he would do something, and when he said it meant it, but who changed his mind in the afternoon if the smallest obstacle interfered with his purpose. He was no more to be relied upon than Horace Skimpole or Micawber. He had no fixed will of his own. . . . He exhibited the same vacillation to all."

The Democratic convention opened at Baltimore on June 2 after an evening of fireworks and delegates flocking to the free-flowing hotel bars. The first order of business was to expel the most prominent Democrat from Massachusetts for his opposition to the Fugitive Slave Act. Not only had Congressman Robert Rantoul, representing the sole Democratic district in the Bay State, expressed his contempt for the act and the Compromise, but he had only two months before he defended a fugitive slave, Thomas Sims, challenging the constitutionality of the law before the Massachusetts Supreme Judicial Court, which returned the runaway to his Georgia master, who whipped him. For decades, Rantoul had been a leading Boston lawyer and mainstay of the party, serving in the legislature for four terms and as a U.S. senator. He was the Jacksonian as ardent social reformer. Inside and outside the courtroom he defended the rights of labor, crusaded for temperance and public education, and against capital punishment and slavery.

The auspiciously named Edmund Burke was chairman of the convention credentials committee. He was not to be confused with the conservative Irish-British politician and thinker but was a leading figure of the Concord Cabal from New Hampshire secretly organizing for Pierce's nomination. This Edmund Burke was a former congressman, commissioner of patents, and coeditor with Thomas Ritchie of the pro-Polk Democratic newspaper, the *Washington Union*. He had enlisted Cushing and Pillow in his effort and arranged for them to meet quietly with the demurring but purring candidate in Concord. Burke also hired away from Douglas the indefatigable newspaperman, Francis J. Grund, presumably for a higher price, and Grund began filling the *Baltimore Sun* and *Philadelphia Ledger* with articles suggesting Pierce's bright possibility.

At the credentials committee hearing, Rantoul's defenders argued that he had been rightfully elected at a district convention forced by his pro-slavery opponent, one N. J. Lord, whom Rantoul defeated by a majority of 3,151 to 48. Rantoul himself demanded to testify. But he was gaveled out of order, denied a chance to speak, and stripped of his status as a delegate. In his suppressed statement, which he handed to a reporter, he said, "I cannot look upon this attempt except as another experiment to measure the extent of northern servility; to see how far the North will cower before an insolent demand to make independence of opinion, on questions upon which we always differed, a ground of proscription." Marcy's delegates from New York bridled at Rantoul's treatment and refused to go along, a mark against their favorite son before the balloting, another advantage for the dark horse. Two thirds of the New England contingent, however, was whipped to vote for Rantoul's expulsion. Eliminating Rantoul was the ritual auto-da-fé that signaled to Northern opponents of the Fugitive Slave Act they must fall into line or be burned at the stake. Burke's role in conducting the inquisition was not lost on the Southern delegates. Thus Pierce's standing in their eyes was burnished.

On the morning of June 3, immediately after Rantoul's expulsion, the voting for the presidential nomination began. It was a seemingly endless race of lame horses. After eight ballots Cass held an unstable lead of die-hard regulars, followed by Buchanan with his gaggle of Pennsylvanians and Southerners, then Douglas, with Marcy badly trailing. The next day Cass rapidly eroded, Douglas shot up, provoking a scare and a run to Buchanan, who appealed to Marcy to help him, which he mercilessly refused. Buchanan fell, Douglas spurted again, inspiring a desperate retreat of delegates to the safety of Cass, an option Buchanan was determined to thwart. At the session on the 5th, Virginia's delegation, controlled for Buchanan by former congressman Henry A. Wise, Hunter's factional enemy within the state party, suddenly declared for Marcy's enemy Dickinson, which would destroy Cass to whom Dickinson was pledged. Dickinson declined the honor, loyal to Cass to the last. That night, Pierce's letter endorsing the Fugitive Slave Act was read aloud to a meeting of the Virginia delegation, explaining that he had "fought the battle in New Hampshire upon the fugitive slave law, and upon what we believed to be the ground of constitutional right." On the next ballot, the thirty-fifth, Virginia switched to Pierce. Marcy and Buchanan, knowing they had no chance and contemplating the spoils, threw in for the dark horse. On the forty-ninth ballot, Cass and Douglas dwindled to two delegates apiece and Pierce was acclaimed the nominee to the thunder of a cannon.

It was a happy nomination. All the disappointed contenders were strangely content because their rivals had been defeated. Pierce was each one's instrument for frustrating the others. Unity was achieved through mutual *Schadenfreude*. The vice presidential nomination was given as a consolation for Buchanan to bestow upon his dear friend, Senator King, already terminally ill with tuberculosis, and who would die without ever reaching Washington and after only one month formally in office. Then the platform was unanimously approved, hailing the Compromise and denouncing "all efforts of the abolitionists or others, made to induce Congress to interfere with questions of Slavery, or to take incipient steps in relation thereto, are calculated to lead to the most alarming and dangerous consequences; and that all such efforts have an inevitable tendency to diminish the happiness of the people, and endanger the stability and permanency of the Union, and ought not to be countenanced by any friend of our political institutions." The party rushed out to campaign for the newly dubbed "Young Hickory of the Granite Hills."

An unaware Pierce was visiting Boston with his wife. A racing messenger on horseback located him wandering among the marble tombs of the Mount Auburn Cemetery in Cambridge and breathlessly told him the news of his nomination. "Mrs. Pierce," wrote Maunsell Field, who was present, "fainted upon the receipt of the intelligence, as if a disaster, instead of a triumph, had come to her husband." Pierce's Bowdoin College classmate, Nathaniel Hawthorne, famous for *The Scarlet Letter* published two years earlier, met him at his hotel, the Tremont House. "Frank, I pity you!" he said. "Indeed, I do, from the bottom of my heart!" Hawthorne quickly wrote a campaign biography and described Pierce as "deep, deep, deep." He praised his support of the Compromise as "firm and conscientious," and predicted that slavery would someday "vanish like a dream." Of his *Life of Pierce*, Hawthorne explained, "though the story is true, yet it took a romancer to do it." It was the least of his fiction. He was named the U.S. consul to Liverpool, but could not win an appointment for his protégé, Herman Melville.

The night of Pierce's nomination the Buchanan forces held a last conclave. Henry A. Wise rose to celebrate the defeat of their most odious foe. "Thank God," he declared, "the brandy bottle is smashed, the champagne bazaars are closed, and Douglas has crept out of town like a whipped dog with his tail between his legs." Douglas had entered the contest unblemished, but succeeded in alienating all the powers of the party, displayed strength in no section, and was marked indelibly for the first time by failure. "Douglas' case has been overworked, and thus was spoiled," wrote Congressman William H. Bissell, a Democrat from Illinois. "With one-fourth the effort on the part of his friends, and no more, he would have been the nominee. Henceforth he will have to struggle, like other aspirants to the Presidency, and like them take his chance. The prestige of universal good feeling has gone from him, and forever. But he will come up again."

CHAPTER EIGHT

THE VICTORY MARCH OF OLD FUSS AND FEATHERS

Daniel Webster began his presidential campaign almost the instant the Compromise had passed. He had fallen from his magnificence into near decrepitude with his ambition wholly intact. Once the idol of New England, standing at the sacred sites of Faneuil Hall, the Bunker Hill Monument, and Plymouth Rock, his voice ringing with the golden phrases of American nationalism against Southern states' rights— for a federal government "made for the people, made by the people, and answerable to the people"— he had transformed himself into the enforcer of the Fugitive Slave Act, personally overseeing the capture of runaways. Those who had unconditionally loved him, like Ralph Waldo Emerson, now hexed him as the fallen archangel Lucifer. Webster transcended the Transcendentalists in his contempt

Winfield Scott

for them. "Treason, treason, TREASON, and nothing else!" he bellowed about their opposition to the Fugitive Slave Act. For months he fantasized the creation of a new Unionist pro-Compromise political party drawn from the Whigs and Democrats, but when it failed to materialize, partly because no faction was drawn to him as a future president, he sought to capture the Whig nomination, which had time and again eluded him. He could feel in his bones it was his last hurrah. "His health is very much impaired," observed Horace Mann, "and that glorious physique, which should be in full vigor at the age of eighty, is now nearly broken down. He can do nothing but under the inspiration of brandy; and the tide of excitement also must be taken 'at the flood'; for if a little too early, or a little too late, he is sure to fail."

Webster was authoritative as Fillmore's secretary of state, organizing patronage in support of passage of the Compromise and writing the president's statements denouncing those opposing the Fugitive Slave Act. He did not hate Fillmore—he did not rise to that level—but simply thought him a nonentity. Webster presumed his natural primacy as the first among unequals. George Ticknor Curtis, one of Webster's closest protégés and his biographer, claimed, perfectly reflecting Webster's self-image, that he was "in his personal claims as a public man upon the party with which he had long been connected, the person most entitled to receive its nomination for the presidency. This was the last occasion, in all probability, on which that party could have it in its power to place at the head of the Government the first statesman in the land."

Fillmore was impassive in the face of the effort of his secretary of state to replace him. Webster launched his campaign committee with the idea that Fillmore either would not be a candidate or was an inconsequential figure. Fillmore may have privately endorsed him at some point. His attitude was more than vaguely tolerant. Ordinarily, he was vain and obstinate when challenged, but in the case of Webster he seemed deferential, stepping back before "the Godlike Daniel." He bore Webster no ill will. His animus was reserved for his nemesis. He loathed Seward with a bottomless hatred. He knew that Seward with his easy manner, ironic wit, and cosmopolitan range always saw him as a cog that had risen by chance to the presidency. His war against Seward had become an obsession. He tried to purge him from the New York state party, precipitating a vicious split, and lost. His disdain for Kossuth was a displaced aspect of his anger. Fillmore felt Seward's opposition to the Fugitive Slave Act had inspired the resistance to it and with every incident his rage grew.

On September 11, 1851, a Maryland slave owner, Edward Gorsuch, seeking to capture four of his runaway slaves hiding at a Christiana, Pennsylvania, farm, confronted a group of armed free blacks and Quaker members of the Underground Railroad harboring them. In the melee he was shot dead. William Parker, one of the escaped slaves, fled north to the Rochester home of Frederick Douglass, whom he had known as a slave. Before Douglass personally escorted him onto the steamer that would take him to Canada, Parker handed him the pistol he took from Gorsuch as "a token of gratitude." (The killing traumatized the best friend of Gorsuch's son who regarded Gorsuch as a surrogate father figure: John Wilkes Booth.)

The Fillmore administration indicted thirty-six blacks and five whites for treason in what was called the Christiana Riot, an overreaching charge beyond any violation of the Fugitive Slave Act. Thaddeus Stevens served as defense attorney for the first man tried in November, Castner Hanway, a Quaker, who was acquitted. With that, the cases against the others crumbled and were dropped. The administration responded by filing treason charges against members of the Underground Railroad engaged in freeing a fugitive in Syracuse, New York, but those trials resulted in acquittals and hung juries. The Fugitive Slave Act was widely discredited throughout the North.

A humiliated Fillmore glumly told his doctor he would not run for election. Webster was buoyant, writing to his close friend Franklin Haven, president of Boston's Merchants Bank, "the coast will be clear." But Fillmore's support from the conservative forces within the party was galvanized and never stronger.

Webster staged a speaking tour that shocked audiences, replacing their image of the magnificent pillar of strength with the infirm, increasingly incoherent babbling old man standing before them. After being pitched from a carriage at Annapolis, he never truly recovered his physical and mental equilibrium. A crowd mostly of his loyalists assembled at Faneuil Hall to hear what would turn out to be his last Boston speech. Samuel Gridley Howe, a prominent Conscience Whig, wrote his friend, the newly elected senator Charles Sumner:

I heard old Dan last Saturday and was most painfully impressed by the melancholy spectacle which he presented. I do not say that he was drunk, but he appeared like a man who was nearly drunk—or else half paralyzed. I am told that most of the Methodist clergy got the impression that he was very drunk—and were indignant. One thing is certain—most certain; not a fifth part, perhaps not an eighth part could make out what he said; and yet they sat, patient and open-mouthed, waiting for words of power and beauty. Oh! what an awful reckoning it would be if that man had to answer for the hundred talents which were committed to him! Would be? It *is now* awful—how he suffers and how the world suffers, if we consider that when we do not have what we might and ought to have we suffer positive loss.

In every region, Webster found a paucity of support. In New York, the conservative Silver Gray faction shunned him and closely adhered to Fillmore in his feud with Seward. Without New York, Webster stood no chance and Fillmore seemed suddenly viable. He appeared to awaken to the reality that as an incumbent president he had power, especially patronage, to do more than charge abolitionists with treason. Wiping the cobwebs from his inert brain perhaps he remembered that his career was an example of patronage and party preference. The political elements Webster desperately required, Fillmore retained. Now that Fillmore had become a full-fledged candidate, his existence blocking Webster at every turn, Webster resented the nullity as an interloper. So Webster turned for aid to his ancient rival. But when he requested the endorsement of Clay, he was rejected for a last and final time. "Fillmore, by all means," Clay whispered as his deathbed wish. "Nothing," wrote Peter Harvey, Webster's confidant, "wounded him more."

Winfield Scott had been Seward's reserve presidential candidate for more than a dozen years. Though the native Virginian was the greatest military figure of the early nineteenth century after Jackson and Taylor, earning battle stripes from the War of 1812 to the Mexican War, he was twice bypassed in favor of other generals for the Whig nomination. "Old Fuss and Feathers," towering at six foot five inches tall, and adoring the military's elaborate rituals and ribbons, was as brilliant and bold a commander as he was ponderous, pompous, and politically deaf. Scott met Seward when he was settling the bloodless Aroostook War with Canada in 1839 and Seward was governor of New York. Seward and Weed inflated the balloon of Scott in order to deprive Clay of the nomination in 1840. They thought a military man would run best in New York. But Weed dispatched to western New York a political agent who returned with a report that Scott lacked appeal to draw cross-over Democratic votes. That operative was Millard Fillmore. Seward and Weed gingerly switched to William Henry Harrison. But Scott had become infected with the presidential virus. He continued to defer to Seward. "I certainly cannot have a more able, judicious and disinterested counselor than yourself," he wrote him in 1839. During the Mexican War, Polk never trusted his general-in-chief, regarding him as a potential Whig rival, and constantly harassed him in ways large and small. Scott complained of fighting a "fire in the rear." To Polk's shock and chagrin, Scott smartly captured Mexico City. Once again, Seward raised him as a potential candidate before abandoning him for a more viable military hero in Taylor. In 1852 Scott was determined to march to the White House like he had to Chapultepec.

Seward had run out of military heroes except for Scott. Weed, the talent scout, always considered Scott a suspect political prospect. Greeley wrote Weed on December 20, 1851, that the scenario for nominating Scott was not bright: "If Fillmore and Webster will only use each other up, we may possibly recover. But our chance is slim." Weed believed it was "unwise" in any case to oppose Fillmore's nomination; instead, it would be best to stand aside to let him suffer ignominious defeat. Weed left the country on a grand European tour. In April, he received a letter from Greeley: "We are out at sea in the wildest confusion, and have no compass or port in sight. We shall carry the State for Scott, but lose the legislature, and probably everything at home."

The old Whig gambit of inserting a supra-political general was played out. Scott's position was the opposite of successful Whig nominees. Both Harrison and Taylor had been advanced against unpopular incumbent Democratic administrations. Scott, however, was pushed forward to divide his party and overthrow a Whig president. He could not claim to be in the tradition of Taylor, who had been a contentious president, without alienating the Southern Whigs. His attempt to float above politics while Seward transparently loomed behind him was an obvious pretense, and his abundance of bluster and absence of political common sense hardly transformed him into a credible candidate. Seward decided not to heed Weed's advice to let Fillmore hang himself. His contempt for the president who had been his errand boy was too great. Seward wanted to unlatch the trapdoor beneath him. So Seward tried to play Weed to Scott, his Pygmalion. But with the curtain pulled back the political wizard could be plainly seen pulling the levers.

Seward's Washington home was the beehive of the Scott for president campaign. Scott was virtually living at Seward's. "It is one complete whirl here," Seward wrote his wife a week before the convention. "Delegates are coming here, and debates and wrangles and consultations, dragging me in, are around me." Immediately after the Democratic convention concluded, Southern Whigs issued an ultimatum. "The Southern men all demand a platform of 'finality' of the Compromise, and Northern men are preparing to go for it to avoid a break up of the Convention," Seward wrote. "If I advise against it I am denounced as a Dictator. If I listen and refer the subject to the Convention, lo! I have agreed on a platform." His house was a Whig convention in miniature, thronged with delegates from across the country. "My house is full of them, from morning till night," Seward wrote. "I can do nothing . . . General Scott, of course, is badgered out of patience and almost out of his senses. Everybody has schemes for compromise and harmony, and everybody thinks everybody else wrong. Everybody is jealous of everybody's influence."

The Whig convention opened at Baltimore on June 16 with a backstage intrigue. Seward stayed in Washington receiving dispatches. His man on the scene was Henry J. Raymond, editor of the *New York Times* and former speaker of the New York Assembly. When a New York congressman conveniently fell ill, Raymond replaced him as a delegate and served as de facto state chairman. But once Scott moved out of Seward's immediate physical range, former congressman John Minor Botts of Virginia and a group of border state delegates captured the politically naive great man susceptible to flattery. Raymond was cut out of their deal involving the endorsement of the Fugitive Slave Act, but privy to it. He filed a report to his paper: "The Northern Whigs gave way on the platform, with this understanding. If Scott is not nominated, they will charge breach of faith on the South. The Webster men count on an accession of all the Fillmore votes, and *vice versa*. Both will probably be disappointed." He noted that certain Southern delegates would vote for Scott on a later ballot if he endorsed the platform. Raymond further reported, "The New York delegation are very indignant at the summary ejection of the New York Scott men, and if Scott is defeated by it, they will protest against the action of the convention, and disavow its binding force." Every sensational detail accurately reflected the Scott men's scenario and potential reaction to it.

Raymond's rival in the New York newspaper wars, James Watson Webb, editor of the *Courier and Inquirer*, usually a Weed ally but now part of the Webster operation, put copies in the hands of Southern delegates. (Raymond wrote during Kossuth's visit that Webb's paper was "the Austrian organ in Wall Street.") The convention descended into chaos. "Raymond wrote it!" shouted one voice. "Infamous!" When Raymond rose to speak, another yelled, "Take him out!" Southerners introduced a resolution to expel him: "*Whereas,* Mr. H. J. Raymond, who holds a seat in this convention, by a questionable title; and whereas, he has accused its members of corruption and foul play; and whereas it becomes them to disavow these charges most unequivocally; therefore, be it *Resolved,* That this convention will show to the country and the Whig party of the Union its emphatic denial of his imputation on its honor and sincerity, by depriving said Raymond of his seat, and that the said Raymond be and he is hereby expelled from this body." For an entire day, the convention conducted a trial of Raymond, in effect a surrogate trial of Seward. Allowed to defend himself, Raymond called the platform plank "dictated by the South, repugnant" and declared that if the convention failed to nominate Scott it would be the Northern Whigs who would be betrayed. "If *that* be treason or slander—if *that* deserve expulsion—*make the most of it!*" His defiance faced down the bullying. Rather than tear the convention apart over a newspaper story, the motion to expel Raymond was tabled.

Raymond's purge trial was an exercise in Southern influence. The Southerners, after all, got to write the platform plank proclaiming that the Compromise and the Fugitive Slave Act would be "acquiesced in by the Whig Party of the United States as a settlement in principle and substance, of the dangerous and exciting question which they embrace; and, so far as they are concerned, we will maintain them, and insist upon their strict enforcement . . . and we deprecate all further agitation of the question thus settled, as dangerous to our peace."

Webster's men insisted that the convention break with tradition and adopt the platform before the nomination. They figured an open vote would throw Scott off-kilter. Webster's manager at the convention, Rufus Choate, demanded that the convention should "here, now, and thus declare, that, in its judgment, the further agitation of the subject of slavery be excluded from, and forbidden in, the national politics." Before coming to Baltimore, he had sat with Webster while he wrote the wording for the resolution on the Fugitive Slave Act. Maneuvering for Scott, John Minor Botts moved that the platform be gaveled approved, the idea that "it was best to let the platform go through, rather than hazard Scott's nomination by any resistance, except by a silent vote," reported James S. Pike of the *New York Tribune.* But the attempt excited "hisses and cheers and all sorts of noises, and call to order by the President, and over all the leathern throat of the Secretary bawling at the top of a stentorian voice for the vote of the States, in total disregard of propriety and of the authority of the presiding officer." About half the Northern delegates voted against the platform, less than an accurate gauge of their discontent because many swallowed their disgust to help Scott. Pike's published report noted his own vote against the platform as a delegate from Maine. He was meanwhile sending private dispatches to Seward.

"I spent yesterday in receiving and replying to communications from Baltimore, and in the midst of a throng of anxious friends," Seward wrote. "The North, the free States, are divided as usual, the South united. Intimidation, usual in that quarter, has been met, as usual, by concession, and so the platform adopted is one that deprives Scott of the vantage of position he enjoyed. Even those who gave way, feel, and deplore this, while all our enemies, in and out of the party, proclaim it with exultation. I see now no safe way through, but anticipate defeat and desertion in any event. We must be content to look to a distant future for the reaction."

Webster felt supremely confident of his nomination. "If I am nominated, of which now there seems little doubt, I shall make a tour of the West," Choate heard him say. Choate not only trusted him but worshipped him as well. "Next to his God, he believed in Daniel Webster," wrote Choate's biographer. Choate was a former U.S. senator from Massachusetts, lawyer for State Street clients with Southern interests, and a preeminent Cotton Whig. Fillmore had offered him Woodbury's seat on the Supreme Court when he died, but Choate had declined. He was fairly certain there was a majority at the convention for Webster. If he had any qualms, he kept them to himself. On the first ballot Fillmore had 133, receiving all the Southern votes; Scott had 131, with almost all the Northern votes; and Webster had 29, almost all from New England. Despite his stand for the Fugitive Slave Act, he had not a single Southern delegate. For forty-six ballots the delegates voted without any real shifts. "My friends will stand firm," Webster telegraphed the convention. "Let the South answer for the consequences. Remember the 7th of March"—referring to his dramatic floor speech more than two years earlier for the Compromise.

Sulking in his Washington home, Webster muttered curses about Fillmore. He obstinately refused to relent in his favor. "The small vote of Mr. Webster was mortifying to him," reported the Whig journalist Nathan Sargent (Lincoln's former boardinghouse messmate). "It was believed to be in his power at any time, by withdrawing and requesting his friends to support Mr. Fillmore, to have nominated the latter; yet he persistently refused to do this, or release his friends from their obligation to adhere to him, hopeless as it was that he could be nominated."

Robert Toombs and Alexander Stephens, congressmen from Georgia, who admired Webster for staking his reputation and career on the Compro-

mise and Fugitive Slave Act, negotiated a secret deal that 106 of Fillmore's
Southern votes would defect to Webster if he could promise to make up the
difference needed for nomination from the North. (Stephens would prominently display a bust and a portrait of Webster in his plantation manor house
he called Liberty Hall. He insisted that Webster had finally renounced his
nationalism and embraced the Southern "compact" theory of the Constitution that the states had created the nation. "I was exceedingly anxious to see
him President," Stephens wrote.)

Choate raced by train to the capital to attempt to convince the president
to drop out, but Fillmore "made no sign." The Webster effort to dislodge
Northern delegates crashed on the rock of New York, controlled by Seward.
In despair, Webster sent a message to withdraw his bid. At the same time,
Fillmore, seeing his situation as hopeless, relayed word of his own withdrawal. When the messages arrived both Webster's and Fillmore's handlers
independently decided to ignore them. The convention had become a theater of the absurd. If their withdrawals had been honored, Scott would have
been left standing alone. As it was, these antics exhausted both the Fillmore
and Webster camps. While Choate was conducting his fruitless shuttle diplomacy, Scott's managers secured a letter from him endorsing "the platform of
principles which the convention has laid down." He gave his commitment
without consulting Seward. On the fifty-third ballot, a scattering of Southern delegates and most of Pennsylvania's broke for Scott to put him over the
top. A few days afterward, he issued a statement on the platform hedging
his initial unreserved approval, "I accept the nomination with the resolutions
annexed," simultaneously trying to embrace the platform while keeping it at
arm's length.

Toombs, Stephens, and five other Southern Whig congressmen, however, would not accept Scott. They took the glimmer of his ambivalence on
the platform as grounds for releasing them from his nomination. "Under
these circumstances he can never receive my support," declared Toombs.
"Let the Compromise men everywhere—Union Whigs in the North and
the South—rally once more in support of their principles. Let them make
an open and manly resistance to the election of General Scott." Toombs and
Stephens formed a breakaway party in Georgia that put the name of Daniel
Webster on the ballot for president.

On the night of Scott's nomination, a group of Whigs came to Webster's
house to serenade him. He appeared in his robe, telling the crowd that the
starry night would soon be "extinguished" and "I shall rise, God willing,

with the lark." But the next day Peter Harvey, Webster's amanuensis, and Choate came to console him. He met Harvey at the door wearing "an expression of grief." Webster said "sooner would he lose his right hand than to say a word or do a thing in favor of General Scott." "What pains me," he declared, "is that the South, for which I had done and sacrificed so much, did not give me a single vote!" On another morose evening, he predicted that on Election Day the Whig Party "will cease to exist." He reflected, "It began its downward course when it nominated General Harrison"—who was nominated instead of him in 1840. In a letter to a friend, Webster accused the convention of "infidelity." He cast a malediction on Seward, who he said was "subtle and unscrupulous," and "catering" to "the Abolitionists." Scott "would be a puppet in his hands," but that would not be a worry because Pierce, whom he described as a "well-informed, intelligent, ripe, talented man . . . will be elected overwhelmingly." He said that when he had met Pierce he told him, "I always love a New Hampshire man," and announced he would vote for him and so should all his friends.

It was the worst of all possible worlds for Seward: Scott was maligned as Seward's puppet but Seward had lost control of him. Like Pinocchio without his strings he wandered into misadventures. His endorsement of the party platform, which Southerners and Webster preferred to perceive as a rejection, produced revulsion among many Northern Whigs. "We defy it, execrate it, spit upon it," Horace Greeley editorialized in the *New York Tribune* about the platform. "This wretched platform," Seward wrote Weed, "contrived to defeat General Scott in the nomination, or to sink him in the canvass, comes to him like the order of a superior power, and he is incapable of understanding that it is not obligatory on him to execute it. Honor, he thinks, requires that; and you know that freedom and humanity are sentiments which the soldier subordinates under the demand of what is called honor and duty. I am yet aloof." Trying to help Scott, he issued a letter promising he would not accept "any public station or preferment" if he won. Thus Seward underscored his controversial relationship with the candidate while signaling to Northern antislavery Whigs that he was distancing himself. His would-be puppet marched off to political battle with his guide strings severed.

"The Whigs lacked confidence and fervor," reported Nathan Sargent.

> They might admire General Scott as a general, and take just pride in his military renown, but they had no personal attachment to him; he had never served his country in civil life, and they knew not what kind of a statesman

or President he would make, nor whom he would be likely to call into his cabinet. As a general, they knew him to possess a very large share of *esprit du corps,* and a high sense of what was due to a commander-in-chief, and that his organ of self-esteem was of inordinate dimensions; in short, he might be admired simply as a successful general, but could not be easily approached, freely consulted, or by any means advised. He carried with him a chilly atmosphere, and even when he seemed desirous to make himself agreeable, it was the condescension of the conscious superior rather than the frankness of a confiding friend.

Weed returned from his European travels, sequestered himself in his Albany redoubt, and avoided the campaign. But shortly before Election Day Scott came to Albany and invited himself to dinner. "I begged off on the ground that I could not speak cheeringly about a contest which I considered utterly hopeless," Weed recalled. "But, inasmuch as General Scott had expressed a wish to see me, there was no escape. My apprehension of embarrassment was quite unfounded. General Scott needed no information or opinions. He looked forward buoyantly to an easy and triumphant victory. He was in fine health and spirits, and if I could have overcome my surprise and regret at witnessing the deep delusion of a distinguished military chieftain, the dinner would have passed off pleasantly."

"When will there be a North?" Seward lamented in a letter to his wife.

CHAPTER NINE

THE DEATH OF HENRY CLAY

For almost two months, Henry Clay was so enfeebled he could not leave his room. He died on June 29. Politics was suspended for paeans to his life and career. Clay had never reached the presidency, but more than anyone who did not hold the executive he had remade the federal government. As speaker of the house and U.S. senator he transformed each chamber into a vital center of power. His own vivacity had infused the institutions with life.

He was the quintessential border state politician, balancing the conflicting interests of the country and forging the compromises of 1820 and 1850 that would keep it from flying apart. He had stood against Calhoun and the fusion of states' rights and slavery. His visionary "American System" of internal improvements to be financed by the federal government was never implemented, but it remained a template for a future president. And yet his "American System" that would bind the nation together through roads, canals, and bridges

Henry Clay

was divided between free labor and slave labor, the underlying schism for which he offered his compromises.

Clay had begun in politics believing that his state of Kentucky could lead the South in establishing the gradual emancipation of the slaves. He became president of the American Colonization Society, devoted to a philanthropic solution of sending the blacks back to Africa. He never uttered a word in defense of slavery, but also claimed that emancipation would be ruinous to the slaves, an inferior race incapable of self-sufficiency. In 1849, Southern Ultra forces in Kentucky, his perennial enemies, defeated him and his closest Whig allies, including Robert S. Todd, Lincoln's father-in-law, in rewriting the state constitution as a draconian pro-slavery document opening the floodgates to the slave trade there. But Clay convinced himself that he had achieved a new national equilibrium through the Compromise of 1850, and addressing the Kentucky General Assembly at the end of that year he said: "At all event, the field of excitement and agitation has been greatly circumscribed." But the legislature that heard him was dominated by pro-slavery Ultras and repudiated the policies and politics he had spent a lifetime cultivating. Clay's Whig philosophy was on the wane, his last strenuous effort of will to moderate conflict over slavery already superseded in Kentucky. In his will he emancipated the children of his slaves when they reached adulthood.

Clay's coffin was displayed in the Capitol Rotunda, the first time anyone received the honor. One after another, senators stepped forward to deliver obsequies. Seward paid tribute to the beguiling influence of Clay's charm: "His conversation, his gesture, his very look, was persuasive, seductive, irresistible." "On the slavery question," Horace Mann wrote, "he has always been far in advance of the people among whom he lived. Had he belonged to the North, he would have become an antislavery man, and not a treacherous or perfidious one like Mr. Webster. He has lived to see Webster die a moral death, and Webster sees him die a natural one. I have no doubt, such has been the secret hostility between them, that each is rejoiced at the fortune of the other. Rivals for public favor for so many years, their competition is now at an end. Both have failed in the supreme object of their ambition."

Clay's funeral cortege made a stately passage in a grand circle northward from Washington through the cities of the eastern seaboard, up the Hudson River to Albany, borne on Lake Erie to Cleveland, down Ohio to Cincinnati, and finally to Louisville and resting in Lexington. In many other towns, Whig Party stalwarts hung black crepe and staged solemn memorials. His death gave them the occasion to recall their glory days, even though Clay had never achieved his goal of the presidency. As events spun out of control after the chaotic convention, they sought to regain their composure by extolling the defeated champion from their past. It was a funeral for their party.

In Springfield, on July 6, after a service at the Episcopal Church a crowd filled the legislative chamber of the State House to hear the designated eulogist. Lincoln was making his most public appearance since he had ended his controversial one term in the Congress. He was the Illinois man on the Whig National Committee, but mainly working for the state and local party behind the scenes; otherwise, he was spending most of his energy on his law practice. The Illinois Whig Party, like the national one, was cracking apart from the stress bearing down on it from the Compromise. For Lincoln, this was more than a matter of political management; the party's fault line ran through the center of his own family.

Ninian W. Edwards, Lincoln's brother-in-law, a Whig member of the legislature, had become a turncoat, defecting to the Democrats. Edwards personified the upper crust of Springfield, the son of Illinois' first territorial governor, inhabiting a large house atop Aristocracy Hill, the pinnacle of local society, where Lincoln met Mary Todd, sister of Edwards's wife, Elizabeth. His disdain for the lower orders was ill disguised, and he and his wife resisted Mary's marriage to the "plebe" Lincoln, though they held the wedding and party in their home when Mary refused to heed their advice. Usually, Edwards's sniffing at the riffraff was directed at the Locofocos, the Democratic rabble, though it was the antislavery Whigs who had lately provoked his hauteur. He was ambitious for a seat in the Congress, but his party would not slate him precisely because of the aristocratic airs that would have made him a likely loser. He may have hoped that in joining the Democrats, they would elevate their social better for their own good. He began his conversion ritual in January 1851, filing resolutions commending the Compromise and repealing previous legislative support for the Wilmot Proviso. One of those resolutions advanced the theory that the Constitution enshrined the "institution of slavery" and rejected any congressional restriction as "unnecessary and inexpedient because" it would "endanger the perpetuity of our glorious Union." Three months after his resolutions were approved, he switched parties. "Lincoln is his brother-in-law, you know," wrote Judge David Davis to a friend, "and has talked to me on the subject, and is deeply mortified."

While Lincoln helped local Whigs select candidates for city elections, Edwards backed the Democrats, who won. Springfield Whigs held a large meeting demanding that Edwards resign the seat he had gained as a Whig.

He quit, but announced he was running as an "independent" with Democratic support. His opponent was among Lincoln's intimate associates, James Conkling, part of Mary's original "coterie," the former mayor, and member of the Whig state committee. The *Illinois State Register*, Douglas's mouthpiece, served as Edwards's campaign organ. Once again, Douglas and Lincoln were waging a surrogate political war. The *Register* blasted Conkling as "a Sewardite instrument," covered with the "taint of free-soilism," known for his "abolition proclivities; and his refusal to candidly avow what will be his course upon resolutions of instrument, in regard to the fugitive slave act." When Conkling denied he was an "abolitionist," the *Register* wrote: "Probably he is not one of the Fred Douglass stripe," but his reluctance to uphold the Fugitive Slave Act made him "look a little crooked." A *Register* story on June 4, near Election Day, reported: "Nothing could bring him up to the scratch upon the 'nigger' question. . . . He refuses to define his position upon this important question." Conkling at last declared himself in favor of the Compromise, neutralizing the attack and winning the election. The Whigs had been stricken with fear that Edwards might defeat him in one of the state's safest Whig districts. Conkling's victory was an object lesson that rhetorically adhering to the Compromise insulated a Whig against the barrage of accusations. Yet Conkling's win hardly calmed Whig anxiety with the presidential and congressional races looming. Lincoln stepped onto a tightwire when he mounted the podium to laud Clay.

Lincoln's eulogy was part July 4th oration, conflating Clay's life with the nation itself, and part self-made-man tale, conflating Clay with himself. It was also a positioning statement for the wobbly Whigs. Most important, in summing up Clay he began to come to terms with his complicated relationship with his political model, whom he twice opposed for his party's nomination in the belief that it would mean certain defeat. Defining Clay's political virtues, Lincoln disclosed his own aspirations. Restating Clay's original antislavery sentiments Lincoln made it seem he was only paying homage, but even as he was intent on protecting the Whigs from damage in a treacherous electoral cycle he ventured beyond Clay's safe boundaries.

Chronicling Clay's rise from his humble origins, born to "undistinguished parents, and in an obscure district," Lincoln drew a dual portrait of Clay and himself. Throughout his eulogy, he himself was the subtext. "Mr. Clay's lack of a more perfect early education, however it may be regretted generally, teaches at least one profitable lesson," said the man who spent one semester in a frontier "blab" school—"it teaches that in this country, one can scarcely be so poor, but that, if he *will*, he *can* acquire sufficient education to get through the world respectably." The one-term congressman wandering in the political wilderness spoke directly to the question on his own mind, how to handle political setback. "With other men, to be defeated, was to be forgotten," he said of Clay, "but to him, defeat was but a trifling incident, neither changing him, or the world's estimate of him." Defeat, Lincoln announced, not least for himself to hear, was merely an episode.

The orator, whose earlier speeches were marked by either orotund purple passages or ripping sarcasm, explained Clay's art without the artifice. His "eloquence did not consist, as many fine specimens of eloquence" did, of "elegant arrangement of words and sentences; but rather of that deeply earnest and impassioned tone, and manner, which can proceed only from great sincerity and a thorough conviction, in the speaker of the justice and importance of his cause." Clay's speeches were not made to be admired for metaphorical "types and figures." For Lincoln, following Clay, form followed function. "All his efforts were made for practical effect. He never spoke merely to be heard."

Coming to the heart of his matter, Lincoln located Clay's root motive as identification with "the oppressed." "Mr. Clay's predominant sentiment, from first to last, was a deep devotion to the cause of human liberty—a strong sympathy with the oppressed everywhere, and an ardent wish for their elevation. With him, this was a primary and all controlling passion. Subsidiary to this was the conduct of his whole life. He loved his country partly because it was his own country, but mostly because it was a free country." Interpreting Clay as an exemplary politician, Lincoln also interpreted the United States as a beacon to the world. Curiously, he did not mention Clay's signature "American System" of economic nationalism. Lincoln had campaigned for Clay's program, debated it numerous times, especially with Douglas, hammered it into state party platforms, and yet neglected to raise it, a glaring omission. In his reference to "the oppressed everywhere," Lincoln was obviously influenced by the Kossuth episode and he shifted from it directly to the historical debate on slavery.

Lincoln rehearsed the history of the Northwest Ordinance prohibiting slavery and then how the Louisiana Purchase precipitated a crisis over its limits. He quoted at length Jefferson's prophetic statements of how slavery, "like a fire bell in the night, awakened, and filled me with terror"; that "a geographical line, coinciding with a marked principle, moral and political, once conceived, and held up to the angry passions of men, will never be obliterated; and every irritation will mark it deeper and deeper"; and that without a "general emancipation" or expatriating the slaves back to Africa, "we have the wolf by the ears and we can neither hold him, nor safely let him go. Justice is in one scale, and self-preservation in the other." It was at that moment of "extreme peril" that Clay forged the Missouri Compromise, emerging as "the man for the crisis"—Lincoln's definition of ultimate leadership.

None of the formal eulogies delivered in the Senate dwelled at length on Clay's thinking on slavery. But Lincoln put it at the center of his speech. "Having been led to allude to domestic slavery so frequently already, I am unwilling to close without referring more particularly to Mr. Clay's views and conduct in regard to it. He ever was on principle and in feeling opposed to slavery. The very earliest, and one of the latest, public efforts of his life, separated by a period of more than fifty years, were both made in favor of gradual emancipation. He did not perceive that on a question of human right the Negroes were to be excepted from the human race."

The question of blacks' humanity and "human right" ran to the core of slavery's legitimacy. Lincoln acknowledged that Clay's history on this matter was anything but simple. "And yet Mr. Clay was the owner of slaves. Cast into life when slavery was already widely spread and deeply seated, he did not perceive, as I think no wise man has perceived, how it could be at once eradicated without producing a greater evil even to the cause of human liberty itself." Clay indeed owned and even sold slaves. But he also purchased slaves to unite families and freed slaves. When his slaves ran away he never sought their capture. About one of them, he remarked, "that in a reversal of our conditions I would have done the same thing." Instead of sending the slave catchers and hounds after the fugitive, he offered him money for his transportation home if he wished to return, which he did. Clay branded those in favor of reviving the African slave trade with the "detestation of mankind." "Any yet," as Lincoln said—"and yet . . ." Clay considered blacks an inferior race, incapable of taking care of themselves if freed. As president of the American Colonization Society, which he had helped found, presiding as chairman of its first Washington meeting in 1817, he promoted their return to Africa. "And yet . . ." Clay believed that slavery itself had degraded blacks and that if whites were enslaved they would be degraded, too. The colonization movement intended to achieve gradual emancipation through benevolent philanthropy. It was chimerical as a solution, contemptuously dismissed by those abolitionists who urged immediate abolition. "And yet . . ." Most abolitionists were also advocates of colonization. Only for a few did these notions appear diametrically opposed. Colonization was premised on the idea that only when blacks were freed in their native land would they fully exercise their "human right." While colonization's worthy promoters basked in the glow of their charitable virtue, many free blacks also embraced the back-to-Africa movement. Colonization was hardly without aspects of condescension, hypocrisy, and moral posturing, but it was not only that; it always had an ambiguous and paradoxical nature. "And yet . . ." Discussing colonization was a principal opening for raising the idea of blacks as human beings with human rights. As vehement as some abolitionists were against colonization as a scheme that would strengthen slavery, slaveholders from the Deep South were intensely hostile to it as a ploy to delegitimize slavery and as a wedge for emancipation. The colonization movement was largely a border state phenomenon, an element of the conflict between Clay Whigs and Southern Ultras. Its scope extended beyond the question of African repatriation of slaves to the regulation within Kentucky of the slave trade, the openness of debate over slavery, and acknowledgment of blacks' humanity. Lincoln had witnessed the convulsive conclusion of that political struggle in Kentucky in 1849 with Clay's defeat, the rise of the unabashed pro-slavery forces, and the beginning of the end of the Whig Party.

Lincoln positioned Clay as the political center between the radical abolitionists and Southern Ultras. "His feeling and his judgment, therefore, ever led him to oppose both extremes of opinion on the subject." First, Lincoln described the Garrisonians: "Those who would shiver into fragments the Union of these States; tear to tatters its now venerated constitution; and even burn the last copy of the Bible, rather than slavery should continue a single hour." Then he turned with more specificity to the Ultras: "But I would also, if I could, array his name, opinions, and influence against the opposite extreme—against a few, but an increasing number of men, who, for the sake of perpetuating slavery, are beginning to assail and to ridicule the white-man's charter of freedom—the declaration that 'all men are created free and equal.' " Belatedly, Lincoln now settled a score with John C. Calhoun, two years dead, who had slapped him down as an unnamed contemptible "member from Illinois" for raising emancipation in the District of Columbia. "So far as I have learned, the first American, of any note, to do or attempt this, was the late John C. Calhoun; and if I mistake not, it soon after found its way into some of the messages of the Governors of South Carolina. We, however, look for, and are not much shocked by, political eccentricities and heresies in South Carolina." Lincoln identified Calhoun as the enemy of the Declaration of Independence, and located it as the founding document of the nation, especially its phrase "all men are created free and equal," thereby casting Calhoun's views as American sacrilege.

Without a pause, Lincoln continued eviscerating those false to the Declaration. He summoned before the bar another miscreant, but one who was nameless. "But, only last year, I saw with astonishment," he said, "what purported to be a letter of a very distinguished and influential clergyman of Virginia, copied, with apparent approbation, into a St. Louis newspaper, containing the following, to me, very extraordinary language." Lincoln quoted this divine's preachment against the Declaration: "I am fully aware that there is a text in some Bibles that is not in mine. Professional abolitionists have made more use of it, than of any passage in the Bible. It came, however, as I trace it, from Saint Voltaire, and was baptized by Thomas Jefferson, and since almost universally regarded as canonical authority '*All men are born free and equal*.' This is a genuine coin in the political currency of our generation. I am sorry to say that I have never seen two men of whom it is true. But I must admit I never saw the Siamese twins, and therefore will not dogmatically say that no man ever saw a proof of this sage aphorism."

"This sounds strangely in republican America," commented Lincoln. "The like was not heard in the fresher days of the Republic." Earlier in his oration, he had criticized abolitionists, though without label and in such a specific way that it was understood he was voicing his disapproval of the Garrisonians. But here he was disparaging a prominent figure that had attacked "professional abolitionists" and who Lincoln declared at odds with the founders. As a matter of fact, that man was a friend and supporter of Henry Clay, whom Lincoln had come to praise. So what was it that Lincoln was debating? And who?

Perhaps by not identifying the eminence he criticized Lincoln believed he would not spur the vociferous polemicist to respond, turning the eulogy into a wholly different exercise, a religious argument he sought to avoid. Alexander Campbell was one of the country's best known theologians, founder of the Churches of Christ, a breakaway sect from the Presbyterians, who preached that the Catholic and Protestant churches were not truly "Christian" (and the Catholic "anti-American"); that only adult not infant baptism provided for salvation; that all morality must be derived from the literal verses of the Bible; and that through the "restoration" of primitive Christianity, uniting all Christians as Campbellites, a new millennium and the Second Coming would be ushered in. Slavery, however, remained a conundrum. On a visit to Scotland in 1847, Campbell debated the Reverend James Robertson, secretary of the Scottish Anti-Slavery Society, denying he supported slavery while still refusing to denounce it. He turned the debate into a kind of duel when he falsely claimed Robertson was a fraudulent man of the cloth, inspiring a libel suit and his flight back to the United States. Campbell resolved his position in 1851 with a statement of numbered propositions entitled "Slavery and the Fugitive Slave Law." "Is not what is usually called American Slavery, disallowed by the Christian moral law?" Citing chapter and verse from the Old Testament, he concluded that God indeed sanctioned slavery. "Need we more clear, more striking, more invincible proof, that the holding property for life in man, or the owning of man, or the relation of absolute master and slave, is neither immoral nor irreligious, in itself." Then he concluded that it must follow that the Declaration of Independence was contrary to the Word of God. And his words were those that Lincoln quoted.

Lincoln's engagement with the unnamed Campbell was the most consequential part of his speech on Clay. It marked the beginning of his conflict with Southern Christian theology rooted in the defense of slavery that would lead to his magisterial refutation in the Second Inaugural. If, as he said in 1865, North and South "both read the same Bible, and pray to the same God," he knew at least in 1852 that they interpreted that book differently, and had radically divergent conceptions of God's will and imposition of moral duty. Two years before he appeared publicly in the renewed struggle over the extension of slavery, Lincoln used his Clay eulogy to enter into the schismatic battle between North and South already taking place among the churches over slavery.

The religious wars within the churches, irreconcilable over slavery, were harbingers of civil war. After the rise of abolitionism in the 1830s and the fight over the Gag Rule, the Methodists split in 1844. The Presbyterians broke apart, too. And the Southern Baptist Convention was formed in 1845. Sectarianism mirrored sectionalism. Southern theologians sanctified slavery. In the beginning was the Word, and the Word blessed slavery. The South was sacred, the North profane. Slavery was not just "a positive good," as Calhoun declared, but a divinely inspired and righteous institution. Citing the Bible, they recounted that Abraham had practiced slavery and Jesus never condemned it.

That the Bible blessed slavery became an article of faith among most Southerners. Southerners also held with equal fervor that the abolitionist censure of slavery as sinful was nothing less than a blasphemous heresy.

"If the Scriptures do not justify slavery, I know not what they do justify," preached the Reverend Ferdinand Jacobs of the Second Presbyterian Church of Charleston, in 1850, in a sermon entitled "The Committing Our Cause to God." His remarks echoed the thunderous pronouncements of James Henley Thornwell, the preeminent Old School Southern Presbyterian, president of the College of South Carolina and editor of the *Southern Presbyterian Review*, the most influential religious publication in the South. In his sermon on "The Rights and Duties of Masters," delivered earlier in 1850, Thornwell proclaimed that the conflict over slavery was "rocking the solid pillars of this Union"—an apocalyptic battle between the hosts of the Lord and the armies of Satan. "The parties in this conflict are not merely abolitionists and slaveholders—they are atheists, socialists, communists, red republicans, jacobins, on one side, and the friends of order and regulated freedom on the other. In one word, the world is the battleground—Christianity and Atheism the combatants; and the progress of humanity at stake." Resistance to slavery was an offense against God. "The Providence of God," he said, "marks out for the slave the precise services, in the lawful commands of the master, which it is the Divine will that he should render. . . . The slave is to show his reverence for God—the freedom of his inward man—by a cheerful obedience to the lawful commands of his master." Robert Lewis Dabney, another leading Old School Southern Presbyterian theologian and later chief of staff to General Thomas "Stonewall" Jackson, would write, "If slavery is in itself a sinful thing, then the Bible is a sinful book." (After writing *Uncle Tom's Cabin*, Harriet Beecher Stowe collected copious quotations from Southern preachers and churches citing Scripture to justify slavery to fill a lengthy chapter in her new book, *A Key to Uncle Tom's Cabin*, published in 1853.)

The biblical justification of slavery was the first tenet of the Southern Christian theology, becoming a foundation for the Southern states' rights movement, secession, and ultimately the legitimacy of the Confederacy. It was not the reserve of churchmen alone, but at the heart of Southern politicians' rhetoric. Jefferson Davis, rising on the Senate floor to speak in opposition to the Compromise, declared that the slave trade "so far as the African was concerned, was a blessing" that "sold him into a Christian land." Slavery, he explained, "was established by decree of Almighty God, that it is sanctioned in the Bible, in both Testaments, from Genesis to Revelations."

Lincoln had learned to stop attacking religion and preachers during his 1846 campaign for the Congress against his Democratic opponent, the Reverend Peter Cartwright, who attacked him as an "infidel." In fact, Lincoln had been an "infidel," a scoffer at religion, openly ridiculing preachers both in and out of politics, and writing his own little treatise denying the divinity of Jesus Christ that an older friend, anxious about his political viability, grabbed and burned in a stove. Though he remained influenced by Calvinism's foreboding fatalism, Lincoln rejected the religion he grew up with as cruel and mean-spirited for its censorious attitude toward poor fallen people. As he educated himself and rose in the world, he avidly read Paine, Volney, and other anticlerical Enlightenment freethinkers, and urged them on others as his required texts. He considered himself a freethinker, too. But under the pressure in his congressional campaign he declared his respect for the devout. He read theology. He contemplated it after the death of his child Edward. He contributed to churches on behalf of his wife, who attended, and occasionally accompanied her. But he never enlisted as a member himself. Throughout his life clergymen claimed they had converted Lincoln into a heartfelt believer, born again, but none of them had the intimate relationship that they touted. There was no evidence from Lincoln or anyone close to him that any of these preachers had achieved his leap of faith, which they claimed after his death. Whatever religion he had was his own. Campbell's fire and brimstone against "Saint Voltaire" and Jefferson must have rankled Lincoln. He had abandoned his youthful ridicule of religion, his need to debunk it, but now he started to concentrate his fire on the Southern theology that he rebuked to the end.

In his Clay eulogy, Lincoln did not cite Scripture against Scripture, or the spirit of the Good Book against its literal reading, but a politician against a preacher. He posed Clay's words versus Campbell's interpretation of the Word. For Lincoln, Clay, the lover of wine, women, and song, was a more reliable guide on the most important moral question than the man of God. "Let us contrast with it the language of that truly national man, whose life and death we now commemorate and lament." Lincoln used the strongest statement he could find, from 1827, Clay's defense against Southern critics of the American Colonization Society. (At the time Clay was secretary of state serving in the administration of John Quincy Adams, who was always skeptical of colonization.) "If they would repress all tendencies towards liberty, and ultimate emancipation, they must do more than put down the benevolent efforts of this society," said Clay.

> They must go back to the era of our liberty and independence, and muzzle the cannon which thunders its annual joyous return. They must renew the slave trade with all its train of atrocities. They must suppress the workings

of British philanthropy, seeking to meliorate the condition of the unfortunate West Indian slave. They must arrest the career of South American deliverance from thralldom. They must blow out the moral lights around us, and extinguish that greatest torch of all which America presents to a benighted world—pointing the way to their rights, their liberties, and their happiness. And when they have achieved all those purposes their work will be yet incomplete. They must penetrate the human soul, and eradicate the light of reason, and the love of liberty. Then, and not till then, when universal darkness and despair prevail, can you perpetuate slavery, and repress all sympathy, and all humane, and benevolent efforts among free men, in behalf of the unhappy portion of our race doomed to bondage.

Lincoln committed this passage to memory as much as he had memorized Webster's "Second Reply to Hayne" ("of the people . . ."). In debate after debate with Douglas in 1858, Lincoln would repeat the lines about repressing liberty and blowing out "the moral lights," to denounce the *Dred Scott* decision, the extension of slavery, and the idea "that the negro has nothing in the Declaration of Independence." But that was to come.

CHAPTER TEN

THE WATERLOO OF THE WHIGS

A fter both the Whigs and the Democrats passed platforms affirming the Fugitive Slave Act, the Free Soil Party assembled for its convention on August 11, 1852, at Pittsburgh's Lafayette Hall, its leaders feeling compelled to enter the fray again and hopeful for an opening. "We have nothing left us but to make up the issue with both branches of the slave party," Charles Francis Adams, who had been the Free Soil vice presidential candidate in 1848, wrote to Sumner. What the Free Soilers lacked was nearly everything: its main contingent of former supporters—the Barnburners of New York, adherents of Van Buren, had defected back to the Democrats; most of the prominent antislavery politicians—Democrats Robert Rantoul and David Wilmot, on the one hand, and Whigs Seward, Mann, Greeley, and Benjamin Wade, on the other, had refused to join; and they had no presidential candidate. The Free Soil Party had also dispensed with its name, adopting instead the identity of the "Free Democratic Party," alienating potential Whig voters, who were more likely to be antislavery. Its platform had the anti-Whig tone of a Democratic manifesto, proclaiming for "limited government" and against exercising "doubtful constitutional powers." It combined this strict constructionism with strict moralism, calling slavery "a sin against God and a crime against man" and the Fugitive Slave Act "repugnant to the Constitution." The Compromise's "finality" was also firmly rejected: "That no permanent settlement of the slavery question can be looked for except in the practical recognition of the truth that slavery is sectional and freedom national."

Then Gerrit Smith, the trust fund radical who financed much of the abolitionist movement and had earlier created a breakaway group from the Liberty Party because he felt it was too moderate, proposed that the platform include an endorsement of equal political rights for blacks and women, which had been part of the Liberty Party platforms in the past. He also proposed that slavery be declared "piracy." Frederick Douglass, elected secretary of the convention, the first black to hold a position of responsibility for a political party, delivered a ringing speech urging Smith's platform planks. "I am proud to be one of the disciples of Gerrit Smith and this is one of his doctrines," he said, and then expressed the Garrisonian belief that the Constitution was a pro-slavery document, a view not held by most antislavery people, including Smith. "It has been said that our fathers entered into a covenant for this slave-catching. Who are your daddies?"

Smith's resolutions linking antislavery and women's rights planks, however, provoked intense opposition from prominent figures who had been in the forefront of the struggle for black rights. Congressman Joshua Giddings of Ohio, who had once been expelled from the House of Representatives as a result of his antislavery advocacy, argued that the party should not be "embarrassed by indefensible positions." Reverend Owen Lovejoy, who more than any other individual bore the mantle of the movement's martyr, his brother Reverend Elijah Lovejoy murdered for defending his abolitionist press in 1837 at Alton, Illinois, put the moral weight of his presence in the balance. He was "not willing to make fools of ourselves to gain a few votes." The delegates voted overwhelmingly to table the resolutions, 197 to 14, establishing a borderline of abolitionist opinion. Afterward, Douglass bowed to the convention's political will, trying to persuade his fellow radicals wedded to Garrisonian perfectionism to support the Free Democratic ticket. "The fallacy here," he said, "is in the assumption that what is morally right is, at all times, equally politically possible." But by October he ignored his own pragmatic plea, abandoning the Free Democrats, backing a sliver of a remnant of a rump Liberty Party, and devoting himself solely to Gerrit Smith's election as a congressman from New York's 22nd district.

The presumptive candidate of the Free Democrats, Senator John P. Hale, Pierce's historic antagonist from New Hampshire, startled the delegates on the convention's eve with a demurral, likely according to his biographer Richard H. Sewell because of "the impossibility of success." "Its effect will be to throw us into complete confusion," said Adams. The Free Democrats turned to Senator Salmon P. Chase of Ohio, known as "the attorney general for fugitive slaves," whose zigzags had made him widely mistrusted. Chase's political pattern consisted of awkward maneuvers that embroiled him in hot water but also had led to his sudden rise. He had gotten himself elected to the Senate through a deal with the Ohio Democratic powers-that-be that Horace Greeley (a stalwart Whig) called "a series of outrages." Despite helping found the Free Soil Party in 1848, he remained certain that he could transform the Democratic Party into an antislavery vehicle that would embrace him as its leader. In state and local elections in 1851 he had refused to support the Free Soil Party, again seeking to ingratiate himself with the Democrats. He opposed the election to the U.S. Senate of Benjamin Wade, an antislavery Whig state senator and lawyer, who won and was now Chase's colleague. Despite their mutual antislavery sentiment they were Ohio's odd couple: Chase, raised by his Episcopal bishop uncle, ponderous, refined, and stiff; Wade, who began as a worker on the Erie Canal, foul-mouthed and ill-tempered. Though Chase opposed the Compromise and the Fugitive Slave Act, he began the election year of 1852 thinking he might wind up supporting the Democrats. "I am a Democrat," he wrote a friend in March. "I do not go for abolition of slavery at all events and by all means. I never did." But with the Democrats' utterly inevitable support of the Compromise, he reluctantly agreed to support a Free Soil ticket, which he suggested should be called "Independent Democratic," "thoroughly Democratic in name and fact." He adopted the label for himself, refusing to attend the convention. When he was approached about the nomination, he saw it as a threat to his Senate seat. "I shall not sink my individuality in this organization which it seems to me must be temporary," he wrote. He decided that Hale was a "good enough Democrat—far better certainly" than Pierce. After Hale finally agreed to accept the nomination, and George W. Julian, the former Indiana congressman, was tapped as his running mate, Chase campaigned in Ohio for the ticket. Yet he, Sumner, and Hale hoped the Free Democrats would somehow help elect the Whig candidate Winfield Scott. Hale only campaigned in Democratic areas in an effort to draw antislavery Democrats from Pierce. Sumner, whose sense of strategy was often muddled, explained his belief that the Free Democrats would "draw from Democrats rather than Whigs, and thus, so far as we can, consistently with our principles discriminate in favor of Scott." Adams, however, thought they would simply contribute to a Pierce landslide.

The Barnburners' return to the Democratic fold did more to affect the election than the Free Democratic effort. In 1844, the infinitesimal Liberty

Party captured a razor's edge of the vote, tipping New York and therefore the presidency from Henry Clay to James K. Polk, and helping to unleash the deluge. Martin Van Buren, embittered at being denied the Democratic nomination that year as a result of the imposition of the two-thirds rule, which had empowered the South, and by Polk's punitive treatment toward him and his followers, had run as the Free Soil candidate in 1848, ensuring that the Whig candidate would win New York. But now the Barnburner reunion guaranteed that New York would line up for the Democrat. Even before the party conventions, Seward noted, "the Barn-Burners and Free Soilers of New York have surrendered." On the Fourth of July at Tammany Hall a ceremony was held so that "Prince" John Van Buren, the former president's son, could formally endorse Pierce. On the stage the foremost Van Burenite Barnburners flanked him: John A. Dix, the former U.S. senator; Churchill C. Cambreleng, the former House leader for Jackson and Van Buren as chairman of the Ways and Means Committee; and Congressman Preston King, elected as a Free Soiler. A letter from Van Buren himself was read to express his approval that "the disturbing subject of slavery has, by the action of both the great parties of the country, been withdrawn from the canvass." Another Barnburner, Henry B. Stanton, the former secretary of the American Anti-Slavery Society, attended the Democratic convention as a New York delegate and delivered campaign speeches for Pierce in hope of receiving a patronage plum. (His wife, Elizabeth Cady Stanton, a cousin of Gerrit Smith, had founded the women's rights convention in 1848 at Seneca Falls, New York.) "Poor Stanton! How art thou fallen!" editorialized the *National Era*, the antislavery newspaper in Washington. (Stanton's quest for a high post went unrealized until the Lincoln administration, when he was appointed deputy port collector for New York.) The Barnburner surrender was completed with William Cullen Bryant's endorsement of Pierce. Bryant's *New York Post* had been the antislavery voice of the Free Soilers, but now he offered a host of jumbled reasons to justify this about-face—the Free Soilers in the Congress had "wasted their time" trying to repeal the Fugitive Slave Act, leaving it to a lone and unavailing Sumner oration, his first Senate floor speech, that argued the Compromise was unconstitutional; and, Bryant added, they had ignored "free trade" and were spendthrift. "The Free Soil Party is now doing nothing," he wrote his brother John, a poet, who lived in Princeton, Illinois, and was also the editor of an antislavery newspaper, part of the Underground Railroad, neighbor and associate of Owen Lovejoy, and soon to be a founder of the Illinois Republican Party.

The Whig campaign tried to overcome torpor through nostalgia. Two hundred and twenty veterans of the War of 1812 traveled to Niagara Falls to commemorate Scott's great victory in the Battle of Lundy's Lane. The reunion attempted to recapture the excitement of the first successful Whig presidential campaign for another general in 1840, the "Hurrah and Hallelujah" campaign of William Henry Harrison. But the remembrance of a battle fought thirty-eight years earlier struck no chord. Once the old veterans' camp disbanded, the campaign dissolved into sharpshooting at the candidates' characters.

The Democrats ridiculed Scott as pompous and vain, dredging up his letter from the Mexican War about finishing "a hasty plate of soup" and his complaint about "a fire in my rear." One of the pamphlets they produced claimed his bickering with his officers proved he was a poor executive. "Dangers of Electing an Incompetent Man President" was the title of yet another. He was also accused of being involved in the Galphin Claim scandal that implicated members of the Taylor administration. Democrats attacked him as hostile to immigrants and Catholics. Meanwhile, rumors swept through the campaign that Scott, an Episcopalian, whose daughter was educated at a convent, was a secret Catholic who had forced American soldiers to kneel before a crucifix in Mexico. Whigs tried to take advantage of the smear by winning endorsements from Catholic bishops, but were politely rebuffed. While Pierce stayed at his New Hampshire home, Scott made an unprecedented campaign tour, ostensibly to review old soldiers' homes, satirized in the *New York Herald* as "the Iliad of the Nineteenth Century." At a rally in Cleveland, hearing the voice of an Irishman in the crowd, he burst out, "I love that Irish brogue—I have heard it before on many battle fields, and I wish to hear it many times more." At another rally, detecting a German, he called it a "mellifluous accent." Democrats charged that Scott had executed German soldiers in the U.S. Army out of sheer prejudice. Besides making Scott seem awkward, strained, and gaffe-prone, his ethnic appeals appalled nativist Whigs. "For God's sake, Seward, keep Scott at home," one Whig leader wrote Seward. "One more Cleveland speech and we are ruined." But Seward had no influence to prevent Scott from staggering from one political misadventure to another.

On July 9, 1852, three days after the Henry Clay memorial at Springfield, Stephen A. Douglas bounded onto the stump for Franklin Pierce. He was using the campaign to set himself up for the future. Appearing in Richmond, Virginia, at the African Church before an overflow audience, sponsored by the Central Democratic Association, he delivered the most compact and comprehensive analysis of the Whig candidacy as an un-American provocation. General Scott, he charged, would be the frightening second coming of General Taylor, who, by resisting the Compromise and Fugitive Slave Act, "had already committed himself to steps which would have led inevitably to a civil war between the federal government and several sovereign States in our Union." Scott was not really an American political figure, but a South American one, a would-be caudillo. "In those republics," Douglas explained, "when a civilian is the candidate of one side and the commander-in-chief is set up by the opposite party, the civilian is generally elected by the people; but the soldier invariably takes possession of the office by the sword. Hence their civil wars, resulting in anarchy and despotism, and destroying every vestige of liberty. Now, we are importing this unhappy policy, this Mexican policy, into the United States." He insisted, "This practice of setting up the commanders of the army for the highest civil offices, I repeat, is an innovation on our theory and our practice"—ignoring not only General George Washington and General Andrew Jackson but also the last Democratic campaign, which highlighted the military background of General Lewis Cass in the War of 1812 to counter General Taylor.

Douglas now invoked the Almighty as a partisan divinity. God, Douglas declared, had intervened to save the country from Taylor. "It was the hand of Providence that saved us from our first and only military administration." In Taylor's place God inserted "a man who, previous to that time, had never furnished such proofs of superiority of statesmanship as to cause him to be looked to as a candidate for the first office," but yet turned out to be "a real godsend!" In Douglas's divination of God's mysterious workings, the Almighty had decided to intervene at just the right moment to afflict the president with deathly cholera and had placed in the line of succession the savior of the Republic, Millard Fillmore. But for "the calming of the waters when the ship was sinking in the tempest," Fillmore was "repudiated by his party." Douglas posed a series of rhetorical questions to prove his point: "Is not this so? Was not Mr. Fillmore defeated by the abolition sentiment and abolition party of the North, and by that alone? Did not every southern State stick to him to the death? Could all the Whigs in the Union, except Seward and the abolition Whigs, have defeated him at Baltimore?" In conclusion, Douglas assured his Virginia audience, "We must admit that on the subject of slavery Mr. Fillmore has done tolerably well for a Whig." With this little joke, he disparaged the Whigs and commended himself as a good Democrat for the South.

The Whig newspapers unleashed attacks on Pierce as a drunk and military coward whose combat consisted of "two somersaults and a faint," lacking in any legislative accomplishment, and an agent of aristocratic England to boot. Vying for the prize of New York, the antislavery William Cullen Bryant appealed in the *New York Post* to Barnburner voters with an article falsely claiming that Pierce, during John Quincy Adams's fight over the Gag Rule in 1837, had "voted, when in Congress, to respect the right of petition as exercised by the Abolitionists" and "took the same ground with Mr. Adams, as to the propriety of the abolition of slavery in the District." This whole-sale fiction prompted the *National Era* to publish a lengthy refutation, re-viewing in exacting detail the legislative record, and concluding that while Pierce was a member of the House he was "an earnest, thorough, consistent opponent of Anti-Slavery agitation and Anti-Slavery discussion; that he was constantly arrayed against Mr. Adams, the illustrious champion of the right of petition; that, while recognizing the technical right of petition, he uni-formly voted virtually to abrogate it; that when the Slaveholders attempted to crush Mr. Adams, and with him the hope of free discussion in the House, he would not vote so as to secure that venerable man a fair hearing, in a word, that he was the unwavering ally and supporter of the Slaveholding Interest."

Then two antislavery newspapers in New Hampshire, the *Concord Inde-pendent Democrat* and *Manchester Democrat*, reported that at a town meeting in 1851 at New Boston Pierce had said he "loathed" the Fugitive Slave Act and that it gave him a "revolting feeling." The Whig Central Committee in Washington seized upon these remarks, rounded up corroborating affidavits from local citizens who claimed to have heard Pierce, and published the ar-ticles and statements in a pamphlet entitled *Frank. Pierce and His Abolition Allies*, of which more than fifty thousand copies were mailed from Whig congressional offices. Pierce replied to the newspaper about the pamphlet accounts with a letter calling the accusation "grossly and absurdly false." "I am not surprised to know that the attempt to prove me an abolitionist pro-vokes much merriment among men of all parties here," he wrote, "and this weak and untruthful sketch of what purports to be my speech, is really too ridiculous to be considered in any serious light."

Frank. Pierce was the most widely distributed Whig piece of campaign literature, intended to expose the Democratic candidate's hypocrisy and dis-sembling. It included an appendix defending the Whig candidate, "Another Falsehood Nailed Down," in which Senator Benjamin Wade denied as "fab-ricated with a view to prejudice Southern people" a statement that a North Carolina newspaper alleged Scott had made to him: "I would sooner cut off my right hand than lend it to the support of slavery."

After reading an article in the *Illinois State Register*, "The Great Richmond Speech of Judge Douglas," Lincoln remarked, "Time was when I was in his way some, but he has outgrown me and [be]strides the world; and such small men as I am, can hardly be considered worthy of his notice; and I may have to dodge and get between his legs." Lincoln's self-deprecating humor about their respective heights and statures had an envious edge. He insisted, "at my own special request," to speak to a specially convened meeting of the Springfield Scott Club, a short-lived organization that held few gatherings for a candidate nearly everyone thought was doomed. On August 14, he addressed the local Whigs at the courthouse. The ostensible subject of the speech was his case for Scott for president. But he referred to Douglas eighty-one times, far more than to Scott or Pierce. His real subject was Stephen A. Douglas.

"When I first saw it, and read it," he said of the *Register*'s story on the Richmond speech, "I was reminded of old times—of the times when Judge Douglas was not so much greater man than all the rest of us, as he now is"—again a height joke—"of the Harrison campaign, twelve years ago, when I used to hear, and *try* to answer many of his speeches; and believing that the Richmond speech though marked with the same species of 'shirks and quirks' as the old ones, was not marked with any greater ability, I was seized with a strong inclination to attempt an answer to it; and this inclination it was that prompted me to seek the privilege of addressing you on this occasion." Lincoln took up each one of Douglas's partisan points, not missing a minor beat, including about Pierce's "fainting," Providence striking down Taylor, and the danger of generals as presidents. He denounced Douglas's "insinuations," "wailing pathos," and "querulous scolding." He sarcastically deconstructed his rhetoric down to his use of the words "with" and "notwithstanding." "What wonderful acumen the Judge displays on the construction of language!!!" After two hours, Lincoln was only halfway done. He had to stop, but not before leaving the crowd laughing with a crack about Douglas's criticisms of the Whigs: "The man recovered of the bite, the dog it was that died."

Lincoln resumed the second part of his speech on August 26, picking up with an elaborate dissection of old patronage disputes and ridicule of Pierce's military record, and relating tall tales to draw guffaws about his militia training: "Among the rules and regulations, no man is to wear more than five pounds of cod-fish for epaulets, or more than thirty yards of bologna sausages for a sash; and no two men are to dress alike, and if any two should dress alike the one that dresses most alike is to be fined, (I forget how much)."

Having clownishly entertained the crowd he abruptly arrived at his defense of Seward against the demagogic smears of the Democrats, whom he denigrated with the old Whig label as Locofocos.

"I come now to the key-notes of the Richmond speech—Seward—Abolition—free soil, &c. &c.," he said. "It is amusing to observe what a 'Raw Head and Bloody Bones' Seward is to universal Locofocoism"—referring to the crossbones symbol of piracy. "That they do really hate him there is no mistake; but that they do not choose to tell the true reason of their hatred, is manifest from the vagueness of their attacks upon him. His supposed proc-lamation of a 'higher law' is the only specific charge I have seen for a long time. I never read the speech in which that proclamation is said to have been made; so that I cannot by its connection, judge of its import and purpose; and I therefore have only to say of it now, that in so far as it may attempt to foment a disobedience to the constitution, or to the constitutional laws of the country, it has my unqualified condemnation." Denouncing positions he obviously knew that Seward had not taken enabled him to turn on the Democrats, claiming they had manufactured the controversy for political purposes.

"But this is not the true ground of Democratic hatred to Seward; else they would not so fondly cherish so many 'higher law' men in their own ranks"—a reference to the Barnburners.

> The real secret is this: whoever does not get the State of New York will not be elected president. In 1848, in New York, Taylor had 218,538 votes—Cass 114,319, and free soilism, under Van Buren 120,497, Taylor only lacking 16,278 of beating them both. Now in 1852, the free soil organization is broken up, Van Buren has gone back to Locofocoism, and his 120 thousand votes are the stakes for which the game in New York is being played. If Scott can get nine thousand of them he carries the State, and is elected; while Pierce is beaten unless he can get about one hundred and eleven thousand of them. Pierce has all the leaders, and can carry a majority; but that won't do—he cannot live unless he gets nearly all. Standing in the way of this Seward is thought to be the greatest obstacle. In this division of free soil effects, they greatly fear he may be able to get as many as nine out of each hundred, which is more than they can bear; and hence their insane malice against him.

Lincoln now raised the issue of Pierce's alleged statements on the Fugitive Slave Act, a chief Whig talking point.

> The indispensable necessity with the Democrats of getting these New York free soil votes, to my mind, explains why they nominated a man who

"loathes the Fugitive Slave Law." In December or January last Gen. Pierce made a speech, in which, according to two different newspaper reports, published at the time in his vicinity and never questioned by him or any one else till after the nomination, he publicly declared his loathing of the Slave law. Now we shall allow ourselves to be very green, if we conclude the Democratic convention did not know of this when they nominated him. On the contrary, its supposed efficacy to win free soil votes, was the very thing that secured his nomination. His Southern allies will continue to bluster and pretend to disbelieve the report, but they would not, for any consideration, have him to contradict it. And he will not contradict it—mark me, *he will not contradict it.*

He noted that Pierce had written a letter denying the reports. "I see by the dispatches he has already written a letter on the subject; but I have not seen the letter, or any quotation from it. When we shall see it, we shall also see it does not contradict the report—that is, it will not specifically deny the charge that he declared his loathing for the Fugitive Slave Law. I know it will not, because I know the *necessity* of the party will not permit it to be done. The letter will deal in generalities, and will be framed with a view of having it to pass at the South for a denial; but the specific point will not be made and met." Once again, he aimed his arrow at Douglas. "And this being the necessity of the party, and its action and attitude in relation to it, is it not particularly bright—in Judge Douglas to stand up before a slave-holding audience, and make flings at the Whigs about free soil and abolition!"

For his rousing peroration Lincoln drew upon a literary reference from the writings of Frederick Marryat, an English naval officer turned novelist who produced popular sea stories, to explain the complex Democratic politics of New York and how Pierce could win it only by uniting its warring factions, the conservative Hunkers and antislavery Barnburners. "Why Pierce's only chance for presidency, is to be born into it, as a cross between New York old hunkerism, and free soilism, the latter predominating in the offspring. Marryat, in some one of his books, describes the sailors, weighing anchor, and singing:

'Sally is a bright Mullatter,
Oh Sally Brown—
Pretty gal, but can't get at her,
Oh, Sally Brown.'

"Now, should Pierce ever be President, he will, politically speaking, not only be a mulatto; but he will be a good deal darker one than Sally Brown."

Lincoln's reference to "Sally Brown" as a political trope was unoriginal. It had appeared in an article by George N. Sanders in the April issue of the *Democratic Review*, flourished to ridicule the "old fogies" for pretentious claims to exalted genealogies—"whole shrubberies of parentage done on paper like tambour-work"—or intricate embroidery—"by Sally Brown, and discoursing of his blood and his pedigree, as if the people wanted him to breed Presidents, or as if they kept a sacred paddock for their progeny, and judged their statesmen as they would their horses." It was, of course, very possible that Lincoln had read Sanders's notorious pieces intended to promote Lincoln's rival.

Lincoln's speech was an amusing performance of frontier humor and partisan polemics in the style of "the slasher" that he had been at the beginning of his political career. It was as if twenty years had passed and he was unchanged. He argued for no principles, upheld no cause, and offered no serious discussion of any issue. He permitted not a glimmer to show of his inner turmoil over the problem of slavery, the conflict of North and South, and the country's future. His callow speech reflected the strained attempt of a loyal Whig to defend his divided party post-Compromise, reduced to calling its pro-slavery opponent a secret abolitionist. If Lincoln were simply the happy hack he entertainingly represented himself to be in his Scott Club appearance that would have been the end of the matter. Instead, it was the last speech of its kind he would ever give on behalf of a party that would never again field a presidential candidate.

The Democrats in the end did not nominate for the Congress Lincoln's turncoat brother-in-law Ninian W. Edwards, defeated in June for the legislature, instead slating the always available John Calhoun, the former Sangamon County surveyor whom Lincoln had served as deputy, perennial Democratic candidate, elected mayor of Springfield three times in a row. The Whigs ran the incumbent, Richard Yates, Kentucky born, educated at Illinois College, the antislavery academy, then matriculating at Transylvania University in Lexington, Kentucky (Mary's hometown), and serving in the legislature with Lincoln. Calhoun had been close to Douglas since the beginning of his political career and Yates was allied to Lincoln. Once again, politics looked like a shadow match between Douglas and Lincoln. Calhoun declared that not only did he discourage Free Soilers from voting for him but he would also resign if elected with them providing the winning margin.

The *Register,* Douglas's paper, claimed that if reelected Yates would join a yet to be formed antislavery "agitating party in the Congress. . . . A Northern sectional party has been deliberately determined upon, and there cannot be the slightest doubt that Yates has already fully resolved to make his best figure in it." Yates, a former Wilmot Proviso man, protected himself by declaring, "any attempt now to disturb or repeal the Compromise measures would subject the peace and existence of the Union to serious hazard." The local Whig organization mustered its strength, despite the lack of enthusiasm for the presidential contest. "Calhoun was cowed, his friends alarmed," including "Judge Douglas," recalled Yates, and "lying handbills and malignant falsehoods were brought in requisition; but in vain." Yates would narrowly win by three hundred votes.

Scott had always been victorious on the battlefield and remained supremely confident as Election Day approached. When it came, the result, he wrote, struck him with "surprise and mortification." The general was routed. Scott carried only four states, historically the most solidly Whig ones. In the North, he won Massachusetts and Vermont, where Hale racked up his highest totals and Pierce his lowest, and in the South, Kentucky, Clay's bailiwick, and Tennessee. He lost every other formerly dependable Whig stronghold. Across the South, the Whigs withered. The party in the North was fractured by nativism: both Catholics and anti-Catholics voted Democratic, including many nativist Whigs, alienated by Scott's awkward gestures, contributing to the losses of New York, Pennsylvania, and Ohio. The Electoral College went 254 for Pierce and 42 for Scott. Democrats gained 30 seats in the House, giving them an overwhelming majority for the 33rd Congress of 157 members to 71 Whigs. In New York, the epicenter of the Seward-Fillmore feud, the Whigs lost the governorship to Horatio Seymour and the State Assembly by a nearly two-to-one margin. One anonymous wag remarked that the Whig Party "died of an attempt to swallow the Fugitive Slave Act."

But Hale, running under the banner of the Free Democrats, did not benefit, polling about half the total Van Buren received four years earlier. The Free Soil vote in New York collapsed. Free Democrats held no margin tipping any state. Only three of their congressional candidates won, down from twelve in 1848. Their delegations in Northern state legislatures virtually evaporated.

Gloating about the results, Senator Robert Toombs, the Georgia Whig, wrote Attorney General John J. Crittenden, the Kentucky Whig, on December 15 to denigrate President-Elect Pierce, dismiss the loser Scott, and hail the demise of the Whig Party Toombs had helped to shatter as a judgment against Seward. "The nation, with singular unanimity, has determined to take a man without claims or qualifications, surrounded by as dishonest and dirty a lot of political gamesters as ever Cataline assembled, rather than the canting hypocrites who brought out Genl. Scott. The decision was a wise one," he wrote. "We can never have peace and security with Seward, Greeley and Co. in the ascendant in our national counsels, and we had better purchase them by the destruction of the Whig party than of the Union."

"The play is played out for this time," Seward wrote Weed, "and played out practically for us perhaps forever."

"Was there ever such a deluge since Noah's time!" Raymond lamented to Seward. "I can see no resurrection for the Whig party *as such*." Trying to reassure him, Seward replied, "I trust that you mistake in supposing that the Whig party will not come up as such. The Whig party cannot indeed come up again now, nor could any other come up now, nor at any time until occasion calls for one to rise. Can't we sleep in the meantime with our old flag wrapped around us as well as if we should tear it to pieces?" But Weed cast a funereal judgment over the scene, calling it "a Waterloo defeat."

Ten days after Election Day, in the courthouse in Decatur, Illinois, in the case of *Turpin v. Wilson*, Lincoln's client, the defendant, was ordered to pay $5 and legal costs "for injuries done to one large sow and pigs by dogs."

CHAPTER ELEVEN

THE ACTING PRESIDENT OF THE UNITED STATES

"*Nothing can ruin him,*" predicted Nathaniel Hawthorne, Franklin Pierce's friend and biographer, with great confidence. The new president was the youngest man ever to hold the office, handsome, well-spoken, and charming, who "seemed to fill the public ideal in some respects as to what the President of a young nation should be . . . the personification of Young America," according to Senator Hannibal Hamlin, a Democrat from Maine. Pierce had a boyish, sprightly presence. His popularity was astronomical, his reputation unblemished, and public optimism buoyant. The opposition meanwhile was in thorough disarray. Whigs were wrapped in the rituals of loss and mourning when not sniping at

Jefferson Davis

each other, while antislavery activists fell deeper into sanctimonious wrath. The beginning of Pierce's presidency would be like a cleansing of all that, washing away the rancor. It would be the first elected government after the Compromise, the new birth of the Republic.

Pierce mapped out the formation of his cabinet to reflect the newfound harmony of the country he was certain his election affirmed. He decided he would select men from every faction of the party and every region of the country. Under his beneficent leadership all heresies would be things of the past. Pierce would forgive the Free Soilers and Barnburners who had split in 1848, and he would forget that the Southern Rights advocates had opposed the Compromise of 1850. Once in his cabinet they would shed their old animosities. They had all, after all, supported his candidacy. Now they would revolve around him in perfectly balanced symmetry.

Basking in acclaim, Pierce shuttled by train from his home in Concord, New Hampshire, to the Tremont House in Boston, where he held private meetings to consider appointments. Wishing to please, he promised posts to many men who made plans to assume their new responsibilities only to wait months before discovering the jobs had evaporated. "Pierce had such difficulty in making up his mind that often when he had made it up he sought to unmake it," wrote a biographer. Lacking self-assurance, yet seemingly poised and gracious, friendly and desperately eager to be liked, highly suggestible though uncertain, his plan for a harmonious cabinet was based on the wishful thinking that the Compromise had created an enduring peace that would enable him to preside without friction. With an aversion to making anyone unhappy, his indecision slid into deference to those most forceful around him. Two men loomed behind his presidential chair: Caleb Cushing and Jefferson Davis. And Davis was the more powerful of the two. "Davis was the *deus ex machina* of the ill-fated Pierce administration, and Cushing its tool," recalled Hamlin, who was initially supportive of Pierce, caught up in the early euphoria, but quickly disillusioned. "He was dazzled by the pomp and splendor of his great office, and received the tributes paid to him as due him as an individual. He seems to have had a fatuous idea of his power. . . . He soon learned to listen only to the voice of the sycophant. . . . Mr. Pierce easily fell into the hands of those who wanted to use him."

Pierce appointed Caleb Cushing, one of the most accomplished, erudite, and worldly Americans of the age, his attorney general. "Scholar, author, lawyer, statesman, diplomatist, general, and judge, in at least four of these callings he achieved distinction," wrote the historian James Ford Rhodes. Educated at Harvard, Cushing taught mathematics and philosophy there. He inherited wealth that he multiplied into a small fortune. He became a prominent attorney, was elected a Massachusetts state senator and to the Congress, appointed minister to China, and elevated to justice of the Massachusetts Supreme Judicial Court. He regularly wrote learned reviews and essays for the *North American Review* and commentaries for the *Washington Union* newspaper. He spoke several Romance languages fluently, as well as German, Latin, Greek, and apparently Chinese. In the Mexican War he served as a brigadier general. He was a kingmaker, instrumental in orchestrating the Pierce boom for the nomination. Yet distrust of him was as deep as his experience and wide as his reading.

"Is it luck? Is it adroitness?" wondered the *New York Times*. "Is it the confidence he inspires, which has plucked Caleb up again and set him on high? Parts he has; but who can trust them? Known he is; but who trusts or esteems him?" Cushing had defected from the Whigs to become the leader of the rump caucus in the House for John Tyler, who contravened every Whig program and principle when he acceded to the presidency as His Accidency after William Henry Harrison's sudden death. When Tyler attempted to install Cushing as secretary of the treasury, the Whigs in control of the Senate denied his confirmation. Cushing was the ultimate Cotton Whig, so perfect the Northern man with Southern sympathy that he became a Democrat. For antislavery Whigs he was the image of the pro-slavery "doughface." When Pierce named him, the *Times* dubbed him a "Tylerite auctioneer." "He's ben true to one party—an' thet is himself," wrote James Russell Lowell, the antislavery poet. Whigs considered him an apostate Whig, Democrats a bastard Democrat. He was a serious man that nearly everyone thought a pretender. Excoriated for his betrayals, Cushing simmered with hatred of those who hated him. He mixed ambition with vengeance, his deep knowledge with his dark resentments. "There was something like a cynical sneer in his manner of bringing out his sentences, which made him look like Mephistopheles alive," wrote Carl Schurz, who observed him speak at Faneuil Hall, "and I do not remember ever to have heard a public speaker who stirred in me so decided a disinclination to believe what he said." "Of all these," declared Senator Thomas Hart Benton about the members of the Pierce cabinet, "the attorney general is the master spirit. He is a man of talent, of learning, of industry—unscrupulous, double-sexed, double-gendered, and hermaphroditic in politics—with a hinge in his knee, which he often crooks, 'that thrift may follow fawning.' He governs by subserviency; and to him is deferred the master's place in Mr. Pierce's cabinet. When I heard that he was to come into the cabinet I set down Mr. Pierce for a doomed man, and foresaw the swift and full destruction which was to fall upon him." But even Cushing became frustrated with Pierce's weakness. "General," he urged, "be king!" But Cushing knew there was a power behind the throne greater than himself.

When Jefferson Davis opened an effusive letter from Pierce sent on December 7 it was among the first he could read in weeks. Pierce's "confidential" request that his old friend visit him in Boston was the overture to an offer of a cabinet position, but Davis could not make the trip and struck the pose of a reluctant Cincinnatus. He was "a shadow of his former self, and not able to bear a ray of light upon either eye," recalled his wife, Varina. Davis suffered from a venereal disease that he had contracted years earlier, perhaps on his journey to Cuba after his first wife's death, or perhaps during his military service, perhaps in Mexico. The debilitating symptoms of herpes simplex type 1 struck him periodically four or five times a year. Hundreds of small infections surrounded his left eye, coating it with a cloudlike film, swelling it, preventing it from tearing, subjecting his eye to extreme agonizing dryness and irritating his optic nerve. Heat, sunlight, and stress triggered his illness, and combined with his recurrent malaria left him fevered and wasted. In 1851, during his campaign for governor as the candidate of the States Rights Democratic Party, though stricken, he forced himself to speak to crowds wearing odd green-colored "goggle-glasses," as his wife called them, while a doctor scraped his eye and bathed it in chloroform, dosing Davis with quinine and opium. The drugged patient, however, collapsed two months before the election. "For three weeks he slept all day, arose after sundown, and walked through the house all night," wrote Varina. Withered by sunlight, he became a creature of the night. "I sunk exhausted," Davis wrote, "and but narrowly escaped from the jaws of death." Barely recovered from the ordeal, he was blinded again by a severe case in September 1852 during the presidential campaign, padding through the rooms of his mansion only in the dark.

Davis's venereal disease not only acted on his body but also on his personality. It intensified his rigidity, humorlessness, and remoteness. He remained the perfect Southern gentleman, more austere than ever in his aristocratic bearing and sense of command. His formal courtesy was his sign of natural superiority. He instinctively believed in an unyielding caste and class system. As an officer in the Mexican War he looked down upon ordinary soldiers, "from a lower class of the community . . . willing to be ordered around, driven and kicked about, and . . . unaccustomed to personal refinement." During a congressional debate over funding of civil engineers he declared, "Could you expect a common blacksmith or a tailor to have done the delicate engineering work necessary to reduce the bastioned heights of Matamoras?" It was a remark intended to denigrate one congressman who was a blacksmith and another who was a tailor. That tailor, Andrew Johnson of Tennessee, angrily replied that Davis was "a cheap scrub aristocrat." When Senator Hale proposed police protection for the abolitionist newspaper the *National Era*, attacked by a mob after the runaway slaves on the *Pearl* were captured, Davis considered it an affront that demanded the challenge to a duel. "On this ground," he said, on the floor of the Senate, "we will shed our blood. . . . This question is not debatable, it is final. . . . Let the conflict come, here in this Senate chamber let it come, and the sooner the better. This Senate chamber is the theater, and I, sir, am ready." "If any one differs with Mr. Davis," his wife observed, "he resents it and ascribes the difference to the perversity of his opponent."

Pierce's letter beckoning Davis reached him at Brierfield, his thousand-acre plantation on the Mississippi River at Davis Bend just south of Vicksburg, where his slaves, seventy-two by 1840, labored in the cotton fields, making him one of the wealthiest men in Mississippi. Davis called them "my people." In this self-enclosed world he reigned as a benevolent, absolute, and later absent master. He copied his model of slave management from his much older brother, Joseph, owner of the larger adjacent Hurricane plantation, who had acted as his de facto father, subsidizing his education, and giving him the land and initial slaves for Brierfield. Mississippi was on the frontier of slavery, but Jefferson Davis's brother was the pioneer. Joseph E. Davis adapted his notions from early utopian socialists like Robert Owen. Like his brother, Jefferson Davis had an all-purpose slave and close companion, James Pemberton, who served as his overseer until his death in 1850, after which he was replaced by a succession of white men. Following the example at Hurricane, Davis established a slave court called the Hall of Justice to decide punishments for infractions, apparently tried to keep families together, and even brought in a doctor to minister to the ill. "The truly generous temper of my husband was best exhibited toward his inferiors," wrote Varina. "In sum," concluded William J. Cooper, Jr., Davis's biographer, "judging by both the standards of his time and the findings of modern scholarship on slavery, Jefferson Davis was a reasonably humane master, but no evidence presents

Brierfield as unique or as some idyllic garden for its enslaved inhabitants. Brierfield slaves worked very hard, and they felt the arbitrary and, at times, intemperate authority of ever-changing overseers." Few of them lived to be more than forty years old.

In the aftermath of his resounding defeat for governor in 1851 against his hated rival, Senator Henry S. Foote, and still recovering from the wracking effects of his chronic venereal disease, Jefferson Davis nobly disavowed further ambition for political office. His retirement lasted precisely one month, ending with his election as a county delegate to the States Rights Democratic Party convention. As the keynote speaker at the January 1852 event, his energy and bile restored, he denounced his loss to "Fraud and Falsehood and Free-Soil and Foote and Fillmore," and contemptuously dismissed Foote as a "mere demagogue." His hostility to the Compromise was unabated, and he called for a new unity of Mississippi States Rights and Union Democrats against the federal government to "wrest the administration from the imbecile hands into which it has fallen." For months, Davis and Foote traded insults through the newspapers. In one salvo, Davis charged Foote had secretly sought Whig support, calling him "coarse and libelous," "an habitual defamer," and a "malignant accuser." In his first act as governor, Foote requested that the legislature endorse the Compromise, which was rejected. At once he lost control, a lame duck from the beginning. The loser of the election to Foote was again the rising man. Within months the state Democratic Party newspaper praised Davis as "the favorite of all."

By June, Davis stood on the platform of the state Democratic convention, held the week after Pierce received the presidential nomination, proclaiming, " 'Now is the winter of our discontent made glorious summer,' not by the son of York . . . but by the true, gallant and patriotic son of Hampshire." Davis had shared a boardinghouse with Pierce when they were congressmen in 1838, and Pierce brought his friend for the first time to the White House, where he met President Van Buren, who amid conversation of "general politics" remarked on Davis's elegant shoes, which he explained he had made in New Orleans. Now Davis reviewed for Mississippians Pierce's stalwart record against abolitionism and how he "denied the constitutional power thus to invade the rights of the South," once delivering a speech that "even here," in Mississippi, "would by some have been denounced as Southern ultraism." "He was a man," said Davis, "yea, every inch a man." The country, Davis warned, should not have "blind confidence" while it gathered on a "volcanic mountain" that would erupt if the principles of the South, "older than the Union," were ignored. Pierce's election would be decisive. "Never before" had these principles "so nearly been wrecked." But Pierce's nomination was the basis for uniting Democrats, and Davis said it made him "happy . . . happy . . . happy . . . thrice and four times happy."

Davis identified his physical affliction with his politics, projecting his own ordeal into the ordeal of the South and turning his blindness into an explanatory metaphor for the national crisis—the country "blind" on a "volcanic mountain." During the campaign for Pierce, he wrote a friend, "You ask me if I believe that the man who adds twenty years to his present age will see a Southern Republic. I do not believe it, neither do I like yourself pray for it." He regarded "a Southern confederacy" as "the last resort, and our birth right there be preserved. It was a consolation, though to me a melancholy one, and I only looked out to it when I could see no other light. In the summer and fall of 1851 that light either went out, or I have lost the power to see it." With the South "divided and powerless to the last, State honors will borrow reflected light from the federal govt. and state rights will steadily sink as federal patronage and expenditures rise." But Pierce's election, he believed, offered the ray of hope and light he thought was fading. He once was blind, but now could see.

Speculating about the formation of Pierce's cabinet, Senator Robert M. T. Hunter of Virginia wrote in early December, "I know nothing with certainty as to the future course of the President elect," adding, "I guess that his feelings are all on the side of State rights." Hunter rejected any desire to join the cabinet, but wished to counsel Pierce. "I have no right to suppose that he will consult me but should he do so I would give him my opinion pretty frankly as to the claims of the States rights men of the South." Soon enough, on Christmas Day, he was meeting with the president-elect and Cushing at the Tremont House in Boston. He was offered a cabinet post, but turned it down, instead advocating along with Cushing that Jefferson Davis receive an appointment. On New Year's Day 1853, Congressman Albert G. Brown of Mississippi, the former governor, privy to the deal, breathlessly wrote Davis "that you have been selected by Genl Pierce as a member of his cabinet" and "will be offered Secretaryship of War"—"a well-ascertained fact." Brown noted that Hunter had "fully advised as to what your friends desired" and "made a fair and just representation of our views," if Pierce needed any convincing at all to name his old and trusted friend. "It will satisfy me fully if he so far respects the wishes and feelings of the State rights men of Mississippi as to appoint their recognized leader to a cabinet office—*That will be glory enough.*"

When Davis arrived in Washington the day after the inauguration, President Pierce immediately offered him the post of secretary of war and he was confirmed within days. Foote remarked that "in which retirement it is quite certain he would have permanently remained but for Mr. Pierce's being weak enough to act upon this advice." The plan, according to Foote, was not merely for Davis to serve in the cabinet, but after a successful Pierce tenure to make him the next president. The scenario presented the "flattering prospect that Mr. Pierce would himself be re-elected in 1856, or that at least the privilege would be accorded to him of nominating his own successor; which successor would undoubtedly have been the immortal Jeff. Davis himself."

At the dawn of this glorious new age the White House was cloaked in mourning. When the elderly Amos Lawrence, the merchant and industrialist, the uncle of Jane Appleton Pierce, died, the president-elect traveled to Boston to attend the funeral. On the return of the Pierce family, as the train was nearing home at Concord, it tipped off the track. Pierce managed to hold his wife secure, but when he grabbed for his eight-year-old son, Benny, he slipped away, careening down the aisle, and flying debris cut off the back of his head. The Pierces were inconsolable. Two young sons had already died of illness. Benny was their last child. They were not to have any more. "The grief-stricken mother was brought to Washington, more dead than alive," recalled Varina Davis. Jane Pierce draped the public rooms of the White House with black bunting. Secluding herself on the upper floor, where she wrote long letters to her dead son, she wore a heavy black dress and covered her head with a black veil for two years. She was a fearful Calvinist, who had long believed that God was wreaking punishment for her husband's political life and personal weakness. She had prayed he would not become president and believed her son was killed to fulfill God's plan for her husband to concentrate without distraction on his office. Perplexed by her theology, the new president could not remove the burden of guilt he felt for his son's accidental death. Every morning in the White House he gathered his wife and the servants to read aloud from a book entitled *Family Prayers*, a gift from Amos Lawrence. He began drinking again.

The death of his son heightened Pierce's vacillation, complacency, and passivity to the point of near paralysis. His dependence on his two chief counselors became almost complete. Though Cushing was quarantined with a case of scarlet fever throughout January, Pierce gave him the task of replying for him to the many sympathy notes he received from important people. As a result, Cushing gained influence over these connections. Then Pierce relied on him to draft virtually all his important presidential statements.

Franklin and Jane Pierce turned to Jefferson and Varina Davis, already friends, as their most intimate relationship in Washington. "Of Mr. Pierce I cannot speak as reliably as another who loved him less," wrote Varina. Pierce frequently visited the Davises at their home several blocks from the White House, occasionally with Jane, "and such intimate talks, such unrestrained intercourse and pleasantries exchanged are charming memories." When Commodore Matthew Perry returned from his expedition to Japan, Pierce gave the Davises the present of a tiny Japanese dog brought on the voyage back. After the birth of the Davis's second son, Jefferson Jr., Varina hovered "ill unto death for many weeks." Pierce braved a ferocious winter snowstorm on foot to visit. "He reached our house exhausted, having sunk above his waist several times." Jane doted on the first Davis son, Samuel, treating him as her godchild, a substitute son, taking him on carriage rides with her. His death at the age of two from measles in 1854 created an indissoluble bond of heartbreak between the couples. The tightening of every personal bond drew Pierce closer to Davis. Pierce almost always deferred to Davis, "and whatever Davis really desired, Pierce was apt to grant," wrote Davis's biographer William E. Dodd. "Only once, I believe, was there any serious divergence between him and Mr. Davis," Varina recalled. On that sole occasion, Pierce wrote Davis an apologetic note afterward accepting "responsibility."

On a freezing and sleeting Inauguration Day, Pierce rode in a carriage with Millard Fillmore down Pennsylvania Avenue. His grief-stricken wife was absent, refusing to come to Washington for the occasion. She had also declined to attend her son's funeral, sitting alone in a room holding locks of hair of her three dead boys. Pierce's opening line was a confession of Calvinist self-abnegation and an eerie prophecy of his inadequacy. "It is a relief to feel," he said, "that no heart but my own can know the personal regret and bitter sorrow over which I have been borne to a position so suitable for others rather than desirable for myself." He had memorized his speech, holding its pages in his hand but not referring to them, a bit of theater to demonstrate his intellectual stamina. He made clear that the great objective of his presidency would be to resume Manifest Destiny, that the Mexican War had been only its first phase, interrupted by a false Whig pause, and now the acquisition of Cuba and other territories in the Caribbean would be on the agenda. Domestic policy was settled through the Compromise; there was little more to do except to enforce the Fugitive Slave Act. His thrust would be for a new imperialism. He would be the president of Young America. "The policy of my Administration," he declared, "will not be controlled by any timid forebodings of evil from expansion." He candidly defended slavery and the Fugi-tive Slave Act, though he would not use the word. "I believe that involuntary servitude, as it exists in different States of this Confederacy, is recognized by the Constitution." He insisted that "it stands like any other admitted right," and "the rights of the South" must be "respected and obeyed, not with a re-luctance encouraged by abstract opinions as to their propriety in a different state of society, but cheerfully." Mrs. Abigail Fillmore, who held the Bible for Pierce for his oath taking in the absence of his wife, caught pneumonia in the cold and died three weeks later, further casting a pall over the new administration.

Pierce had still not finished assembling his cabinet. Except for the er-ratic brilliant polymath and politically tone-deaf Cushing, he had appointed colorless secondary figures without national reputations from an array of representative states. After his inauguration he met at once with Jefferson Davis. Then he met with John A. Dix, a formidable man to whom Pierce owed a large favor for being crucial in delivering New York state to him in the election. The former U.S. senator had been a Barnburner who ran on the Free Soil ticket for governor of New York in 1848, but was prominent in returning to his party to back Pierce. According to the elementary laws of politics, Pierce owed him. In December Dix was one of the first people he summoned to Concord, where he offered him the position of secretary of state, which would fulfill his idea of harmony. But the prospect of Dix in the cabinet and especially in that exalted position aroused a ferocious reaction from Southerners and Dix's New York factional rivals who would never for-give his apostasy. They waged a harsh campaign against him as corrupt and, worse, an abolitionist. In assaulting Dix, they were rejecting the mainstream tradition of New York's Democratic Party. Dix's personal history ran deep to its roots. He had married the daughter of one of the wealthiest landowners in upstate New York and a congressman, John J. Morgan, who was a close ally of Martin Van Buren. As the New York secretary of state and member of the Assembly, Dix became part of the central committee of the Albany Regency, the Van Buren clique that controlled the party. After he was elected to the U.S. Senate in 1845 he became the state's leading Democrat, but as a supporter of Van Buren the newly elected President Polk shut him out of all patronage in New York. In 1848, he followed Van Buren into the Free Soil Party. When Pierce was nominated, Dix was instrumental in bringing almost the entire Van Buren Barnburner faction back into the party fold. Having served as a diplomat during the Van Buren administration, he was a natural choice for secretary of state. But Southerners and their Northern allies portrayed the possible appointment as "fatal," and "the screws" were tightened on Pierce. "General Pierce had not the force of character to enable him to resist this pressure," Dix recalled. Summoned to the White House for his second interview, Pierce haltingly, "with embarrassment," tried to explain that he might have been "precipitate." He disliked confrontation and disappointing people. Dix, "aware of the intrigue," rescued the president from unpleasantness, withdrawing his nomination. Pierce "could not withhold his thanks," and to "atone" for the "indignity" promised Dix would be named minister to France.

Dix was infuriated at the attack on his reputation. He defended himself as a moderate, protesting, "I am not and have never been an Abolitionist," and, moreover, that he had been "an open and uniform opponent of abolition movements in this State." But when he had been a senator Dix had not only voted for the Wilmot Proviso but had also issued a stern ultimatum: "I say for the State of New York, and in her name . . . that she can never consent to become a party to the extension of slavery to free territory on this continent." In joining the Free Soil Party he was not unprincipled and though he voted for the Compromise he remained an adamant opponent of slavery extension. For that reason, his tentative nomination was castigated as a dire threat and Pierce flayed for exhibiting dangerous Free Soil tendencies. If Dix had been permitted to become secretary of state, he would have stood as an impenetrable wall against the imperialist Southern strategy. Fantasizing about the peaceable kingdom of his administration, Pierce was incapable of recognizing the contradiction at the heart of his dream.

The parallel careers of John A. Dix and Jefferson Davis revealed a Democratic Party early coming apart in 1844. Before Pierce's election both had led third parties at opposite ends of the spectrum on the extension of slavery, Free Soil and Southern Rights. Davis felt that the Mexican War had been a half-measure and that a Southern empire remained to be seized. He envisioned Cuba, the Mexican province of Yucatán, Panama, and more under the U.S. flag as safe territories for slavery, becoming states with two senators apiece, tipping the scales in the balance for the South. "Cuba must be ours" to "increase the numbers of slave holdings constituencies," he declared. While he was against internal improvements that would mainly benefit the North, he sought to build a transcontinental railroad through a Southern route from the Mississippi River to the Pacific that would bind the West to the South—and to slavery. On every point, Jefferson Davis was the living agent of his mentor and prophet, John C. Calhoun. Never really reconciled to the Compromise of 1850 as the final settlement, Davis was determined to overthrow the Compromise of 1820. In 1848, Senator Davis introduced an amendment that would open the Oregon Territory to slavery by prohibiting the application of the Ordinance of 1787. Calhoun rose to endorse the proposal of his protégé. Then Davis declared that it was "the duty of the United States to protect the property of a slave-owner during the transit from one state to another," that the resolutions for "abolition were adopted entirely with a view to obtaining additional political power, and imposed on the South the strongest obligation to rise in self-defense." He finished with a ringing warning. "If nothing would satisfy the north short of destruction of this institution, then it was time for dissolution to come; but let us separate peacefully." But now that Davis was secretary of war he did not need to threaten secession; instead, he would pursue his objectives from the pinnacle of power as the virtual acting president.

Denied Dix, Pierce still needed someone from New York, and he chose the obvious man for secretary of state, William L. Marcy, the politician's politician, eternal member of the Albany Regency, ancient Jacksonian, the former everything—U.S. senator, governor, and secretary of war. If anyone personified the Democratic Party of the Empire State it was Marcy. But precisely because Marcy had tried to unify the contentious factions after the Free Soil schism, allowing the heretics to return under the old banner, mainly to advance his own presidential ambition, he was anathema to the irreconcilable Hunkers. Led by Senator Daniel Dickinson, allied with the Southern conservatives and only grudgingly accepting the Compromise, they now called themselves the "Hards" and their enemies the "Softs." The Hards considered Marcy the most dangerous of the Softs. Pierce's choice of Marcy was taken as his softness to the Softs, a sign of his hidden Free Soilism. Pierce tried to assuage the Hards, offering the lucrative collectorship of the Port of New York to Dickinson, who rejected the olive branch. Then Pierce appointed another Hard, Greene C. Bronson, and, for good measure, named yet another Hard, Charles O'Conor, as the U.S. attorney from New York.

At the chaotic state Democratic convention on September 23 at Syracuse, the Hards and Softs divided into two hostile groups within the same hall, until it became apparent that the Softs had superior numbers, prompting the Hards to walk out trailing condemnations of the Softs. "We have gotten rid of the mischievous traitors," proclaimed Dickinson. Bronson and O'Conor refused to endorse the party nominees, brought about by "fraud and violence" and "convicts and bullies," according to Bronson, and "contaminated" by "agitators," according to O'Conor. Bronson had been "instructed" to spread federal patronage equally between Hards and Softs, but he defied his orders. On October 22, Secretary of the Treasury James Guthrie felt compelled to remove him because of his flagrant defiance. O'Conor promptly resigned. The Hards and their Southern allies blamed the evil Marcy. On the eve of the state elections, on November 3, five thousand Hards packed New York City's Metropolitan Hall, not to rally for the Democratic ticket but against the Softs and Pierce. Senator Dickinson sent a declaration of factional war that was solemnly read aloud: "The battle has been set in array between principles and spoils." Another message of solidarity was read, too, this one from the Southern Rightist movement and editor of the *Washington Sentinel*, Beverley Tucker, decrying the administration for having "verily opened the casket in which the spirit of Free Soilism has been sealed." After roused by speeches denouncing John Van Buren ("our enemy, the Prince!"), Caleb Cushing ("bastard Democrat" and "apostate Whig"), Marcy ("that wily, cunning, crafty, heartless politician"), and Pierce ("endangering this Constitution"), but praising Jefferson Davis for his early opposition to the Compromise of 1850, the crowd marched behind a brass band playing "Hail, Columbia" to Bronson's house off Fifth Avenue to give him three cheers, and marched away to a polka.

Dix, meanwhile, received further humiliations. He was appointed assistant secretary of the treasury in New York while awaiting confirmation as minister to France. He booked his steamer ticket to France and made living arrangements for the next four years, but suddenly the post was removed from him without explanation. To conclude "this wretched business," Dix resigned his Treasury position in disgust.

When Pierce wrote former secretary of state James Buchanan during the transition to inform him that it was his policy not to name any former cabinet members to his cabinet, it was a transparent ploy to exclude Buchanan. Buchanan took the occasion to offer the president-elect some unsolicited advice. "He who attempts to conciliate opposing factions by placing ardent and embittered representatives of each in his cabinet, will discover that he has only infused into these factions new vigor and power for mischief." Instead, he urged Pierce to rely on the wisdom, "especially in regard to the Southern States," of his vice president, William R. King, Buchanan's dearly intimate friend, fatally ill, and who would die one month after the inauguration. Cuba, Buchanan wrote, "will occupy the most conspicuous place in your administration." Therefore, he advised, "Should you desire to acquire Cuba, the choice of suitable ministers to Spain, Naples, England and France will be very important."

Jefferson Davis prevailed. To the victor belonged the spoils. He seized control of the key diplomatic appointments, putting in place those men who believed in the mission of the new expanded empire. With Dix unceremoniously pushed aside as minister to France, he installed "a true Southern man," John Y. Mason of Virginia, Tyler's secretary of the navy and Polk's attorney general. For minister to Spain, the crucial spot for acquiring Cuba, he inserted Senator Pierre Soule of Louisiana over the objection of Marcy. The appointment was an early signal to Marcy of where power resided in the administration. For minister to England, Pierce sent Buchanan. To Davis, there was no more distinguished and reliable Northern man with Southern sympathy to head the important mission to the Court of St. James. After Pierce offered the post to him, Buchanan, knowing where power resided, went straight to Davis's home for a long conversation and, according to Buchanan, "[Davis] has doubtless been the cause I was nominated and confirmed . . . the next day." Nearly all of the diplomatic appointments consisted of members of the Young America faction close to Douglas, including the volatile George N. Sanders, installed as secretary of the legation at London over the objection of Buchanan, whom Sanders had vilified in his *Democratic Review* as one of the decrepit "old fogies."

From England, Buchanan continued to wage war against his perennial rival Marcy. Both of them had sought the presidential nomination, but the contest was not ended. Despite his insistence on harmony, Pierce privately took pleasure at the bickering between his two former rivals and especially at the slighting of Marcy. Buchanan, reported the journalist Benjamin Perley Poore, "had always been jealous of Governor Marcy, then Secretary of State, and instead of addressing his dispatches to the Department of State, as is customary for foreign Ministers, he used to send them direct to the President. It is said that General Pierce rather enjoyed seeing his chief Cabinet officer thus snubbed, and that he used to aggravate the slight by frequently sending answers to Mr. Buchanan's communications himself." Undoubtedly, Davis was behind Marcy's belittling, and it further enhanced his power.

Buchanan immediately caught the political drift. "I had not been in Washington many days before I clearly discovered that the President and cabinet were intent upon his renomination and re-election. This I concluded from the general tendency of affairs, as well as from special communications to that effect from friends whom I shall not name. It was easy to perceive that the object in appointments was to raise up a Pierce party, wholly distinct from the former Buchanan, Cass, and Douglas parties; and I readily perceived, what I had before conjectured, the reason why my recommendations had proved of so little avail. I thought I also discovered considerable jealousy of Governor Marcy, who will probably cherish until the day of his death the anxious desire to become President." Before his departure for London, at a dinner attended by the president, Davis, Cushing, Marcy, and other notables, Buchanan rose to deliver a toast, addressed to Marcy: "We are both growing old, and it is a melancholy spectacle to see old men struggling in the political arena for the honors and offices of this world, as though it were to be their everlasting abode. Should you perform your duties as Secretary of State to the satisfaction of the country during the present Presidential term, and should I perform my duties in the same manner as minister to England, we ought both to be content to retire and leave the field to younger men. President Pierce is a young man, and should his administration prove to be advantageous to the country and honorable to himself, as I trust it will, there is no good reason why he should not be renominated and re-elected for a second term." Afterward, Jefferson Davis escorted Buchanan to his hotel room, "expressing warm approbation of what I had said to Governor Marcy." Buchanan also heard that "the President once alluded to it with evident satisfaction. It is certain that Governor Marcy is no favorite."

The "autocrat of the cabinet," as the *New York Times* described Jefferson Davis, set an example of working long hours at the Department of War, though he was absent briefly after two months on the job when stricken with a recurrence of his sudden blindness and sensitivity to light. He was efficient and effective, aware of "every detail of his office from 'brass howitzers to brass buttons.' " He increased the size of the standing army about 30 percent to 13,821 men, appointing West Point graduates as officers of the new regiments. He built new facilities at West Point, consulting closely on the curriculum for educating cadets with its superintendent, Colonel Robert E. Lee. He drove innovation by developing modern weaponry, ordering the manufacture of new smoothbore rifles and retiring old-fashioned muskets. Concerned that battlefield tactics adapt to new conditions, he oversaw the publication of a new manual, *Rifle and Light Infantry Tactics*. He handpicked a promising West Point–educated young lieutenant for a mission to assess a Southern Pacific railroad route. George Brinton McClellan proudly considered himself one of Secretary Davis's star protégés. "The Secy expressed himself as being very much pleased with the result of my summer's work, & the manner in which it had been conducted," McClellan wrote his mother-in-law. After promoting him to captain, Davis sent his favorite as the third member of a commission to Europe to study the tactics, organization, and fortifications of the powers fighting the Crimean War.

The punctilious secretary of war in charge of all he surveyed frequently flared with temper tantrums. His hair-trigger rages were undoubtedly quickened by the agonizing episodes of his chronic illness. The death of his beloved son Samuel in 1854 must also have been a factor in exciting his violent rhetoric. But his sensitivity to perceived challenges to his authority or even differences of opinion was the imperious attitude of a Southern aristocrat of inherited wealth who believed that the essence of honor was to protect his superior caste position. In near supreme control, he often lost self-control. His temper was natural to his character; he could not restrain himself. Yet his outbursts of invective rose according to the prescribed levels of the Code Duello.

Pierce's patronage policy strictly excluded Whigs, including Southern Whigs who had endorsed the Compromise and were alienated from their party, unmoored and drifting. His notion of unity only applied to Democrats. Davis himself took control of patronage to Southerners, channeling jobs to Southern Rights partisans and systematically excluding Southern Unionists, Whigs and Democrats. Senator Robert Toombs of Georgia, a Southern Whig who was one of the authors of the Georgia Platform upholding the Compromise, criticized Pierce for appointing Southern Rights men who had been against it. Word reached Jefferson Davis that Toombs had called him "a disunionist sitting in the councils of the nation" and he fired off a letter on September 21, 1853, for publication in the newspapers. "I will answer him in monosyllables," he wrote. "IT IS FALSE." He added that it was "radically false and corrupt." Davis explained that in running for governor of Mississippi in 1851, he had "declared the opinion that a state, as a sovereign and equal member of the Union, had a right to withdraw from the Confederation," but "I also spoke of it as a last remedy—the final resort— one to which, under existing circumstances, Mississippi should not appeal." The rest of the letter, most of it, consisted of justification for a Pacific railroad route. Toombs considered Davis's letter a slap in the face. He replied insisting that his comments had been distorted and Davis belonged to "swaggering braggarts and cunning poltroons." Newspapers were filled with reports of an impending duel. Davis had provoked four near duels over the past six years, as well as his boardinghouse fistfight with Foote. It took three years for Southern senators to draw up a formal peace treaty between the would-be combatants, declaring they "would treat each other as is common among gentlemen."

When the Congress voted in 1855 to bestow the exalted rank of brevet lieutenant general upon Winfield Scott, who was still general-in-chief of the army after his unsuccessful presidential campaign, a rank that had previously been held only by George Washington, and made it retroactive to 1847, Scott filed for his back pay and expenses. He was owed tens of thousands of dollars in expenses, much of which he had personally spent in expectation of reimbursement. If he were denied, he might be financially ruined. It should have been a routine matter. But Davis despised Scott, an antagonist since the Mexican War, seeing him as an underhanded and overbearing rival to his former father-in-law, Zachary Taylor, though at the moment of his death Davis was attempting to have him censured by the Senate. Senator Davis had attempted to scuttle Scott's promotion when it was introduced in 1851. Though a presidential commission approved it and it passed the Senate, the full Congress did not enact it until 1855, whereupon "this deadly enemy" Davis "allowed no intermission in his hostility," according to Scott. Rejecting his claim, Davis issued a lengthy letter accusing Scott of fabricating his expenses and abusing funds during the Mexican War. Davis referred the matter to his ally Attorney General Cushing, who unsurprisingly supported him. Davis, moreover, added insult to injury, insisting that he was Scott's superior officer. Scott shot back that his "orders must come from the President" and that Davis was "posing as a cabinet favorite." Davis questioned the general's manhood. "Why, the only wound you ever received came from a fall off a horse on the streets of New York!" Scott charged that Davis was attempting to provoke a duel. "Why did you not fight General Jackson when he challenged you years ago?" Davis mocked. After Pierce upheld Davis's authority over Scott, the general denounced Davis's accusations as "arrogance and superciliousness . . . examples of chicanery and tergiversation," and called him "an enraged imbecile." "Your petulance, characteristic egotism and recklessness of accusation," Davis replied, "have imposed on me the task of unveiling some of your deformities," a host of "groveling vices" such as "querulousness, insubordination, greed of lucre and want of truth." Finally, Scott was granted part of the sum for which he had applied. But Davis's vendetta against him dragged on for two years of widely reported vituperation, aided and abetted by Cushing and Pierce.

From the moment he took office the secretary of war waged political warfare against Southern Unionists. In Mississippi he conducted a single-minded campaign of revenge against his bitter enemy who had defeated him for governor, Henry S. Foote. By mid-1853, Davis and his Southern Rights faction had gained control of the state Democratic Party, nominating for governor Davis's close ally, John J. McRae. In the fall election he beat Foote, who quit before his term expired and self-exiled himself to California. "Mr. Pierce and his worse than purblind Cabinet assistants," wrote Foote, "openly and unblushingly interfered in all the political elections in all the States, (a favorite expedient with the spoils-loving and degenerate Democracy in these modern days), employing patronage everywhere in order to control votes."

In Georgia, Davis ensured that Howell Cobb, the leading Democrat in the state, personification of the old establishment Democratic Party, the former speaker of the house and a Southern Unionist, coauthor of the Georgia Platform, was starved of patronage. Cobb was one of the largest plantation owners in Georgia, indeed in the whole South, but always had been hostile to Calhoun and his threats of nullification and secession. Elected governor in 1851 through a coalition of Whigs and Democratic Unionists on the Constitutional Unionist Party, Cobb supported Pierce, a champion of the Compromise, on the premise that Pierce would need to include Southern Unionists in his administration in order to sustain the national Democratic Party. Cobb thought that the Southern Whigs would be incorporated into the Southern Unionists, as they had been in Georgia, and Toombs had made it clear he would leave the Whigs and join the Democrats. Cobb even hoped for a cabinet appointment. Instead he was frozen out. All the patronage jobs in Georgia down to the post offices went to Southern Rights men. The conciliatory Cobb, with the object of gaining the U.S. Senate seat, urged a "reunion" with the Southern Rights wing, suggesting that the issue of secession, which was purely "abstract," should not divide them. He dumped his alliance with the Whigs, Toombs, and Stephens, and supported the Southern Rights candidate for governor in 1853. He hoped to be made senator as a consensus candidate, but the Southern Rightists opposed him, and the Whigs and Unionists abandoned him. The legislature elected the fire-eating Calhounite Alfred Iverson. Cobb had believed that through the Compromise he would achieve dominance over Georgia politics. But Jefferson Davis's control of federal patronage tilted in favor of the Southern Rightists. Seeking to maintain his preeminence, Cobb chased after his traditional intraparty enemies for acceptance. He succeeded in lending them legitimacy as well as helping them gain the key offices in the state, but having demeaned his Unionist base he was left with little to stand on and nothing to bargain. Whether the Unionists were numerically the majority in Georgia, they would never again hold power.

A third Southern Democratic senator who had supported the Compromise was also cut down in 1853. Jeremiah Clemens of Alabama had initially opposed the deal, but when he switched he enraged the Southern Rightists. During the Mexican War, he had been an officer serving with Pierce and expected some favor from his old comrade, but found himself shunned. Alabama Democrats excommunicated him as a betrayer, denying him renomination. (Clemens became a popular novelist on historical themes and a Unionist during the war, but was never as popular a writer as his second cousin, Samuel Clemens, who took the name of Mark Twain.)

The party nomination in Alabama instead went to Clement Claiborne Clay, son of the former governor and U.S. senator, third cousin of Henry Clay, and a fervent states' rights advocate. Coming to Pierce's Washington, the young Clay was inducted as a junior member of the president's inner circle. Jefferson Davis became infatuated with his wife, Virginia, and she became his mistress. When they began their liaison was uncertain, but it lasted even after the Civil War. She described how the secretary of war "carried himself with such an air of conscious strength and ease and purpose as often to cause a stranger to turn and look at him." She recalled a "brilliant" excursion to Fort Monroe where Pierce and Davis reviewed the troops. "At night the Fort and the waters beyond were lit up by a pyrotechnic display of great gorgeousness, and enthusiasm rose to its highest when, amid the booming of cannon and the plaudits of happy people, an especially ingenious device blazed across the night sky the names of Franklin Pierce and Jefferson Davis!"

Empowering Southern Rightists in state politics, purging Unionists, constantly embroiling himself in petty feuds, and composing vitriolic letters against his enemies did not distract Jefferson Davis from his overarching strategy of creating a Southern imperium. His glistening eye remained fixed on an immense new realm encompassing Cuba, much of the Caribbean, and large parts of northern Mexico, and constructing a Southern Pacific railroad, making the West dependent on an expansive slave economy. The crucial position for enabling the building of the railroad was minister to Mexico, and Davis's man to fill it was the greatest and original advocate of the project, James Gadsden.

Gadsden was heir to one of the wealthiest and most influential families of South Carolina, whose grandfather, Christopher Gadsden, a Revolutionary War leader, designed the famous "Don't Tread On Me" banner, known as the Gadsden flag. After serving as a military aide to Andrew Jackson on his Florida expedition, and trying his hand there unsuccessfully at planting and politics, Gadsden returned to his native Charleston, where he became one of John C. Calhoun's closest allies. As the president of the South Carolina Railroad, he was the champion of connecting the South and West with Charleston as the terminus. He convinced Calhoun that building a Southern transcontinental railroad with federal support was essential for a Southern empire. In 1850, when a dying Calhoun merely condemned the Compromise but did not call for disunion, Gadsden thought he was too moderate and joined the fire-eaters in favor of secession. He organized a group of planters to import eight hundred slaves to southern California in order to create a breakaway slave colony.

Jefferson Davis preempted Marcy to secure the appointment of Gadsden as minister to Mexico, who was dispatched with the mission of purchasing much of the three northern Mexican states and all of Lower California—and equipped with a map depicting its incorporation into the U.S. Davis informed the Congress that this plan was a military necessity and he commissioned the Army Corps of Engineers to conduct surveys of the territory for the railroad route. Pierce approved Davis's maximum proposal and authorized $50 million to achieve it.

As Gadsden began his diplomatic mission, the adventurer William Walker and about forty-five roughnecks he recruited from San Francisco's Barbary Coast with promises of a new Gold Rush and silver mines, and whom he dubbed his "First Independent Battalion," landed in his schooner on Lower California. From a wealthy Tennessee family, a peripatetic lawyer and newspaper editor in New Orleans and San Francisco, the twenty-nine-year-old Walker sought to establish himself as the most daring soldier of fortune, or "filibuster" as they were called. Before he departed, he had sold bonds in the name of his projected "Republic of Sonora." On November 3, 1853, he seized the town of La Paz, near the tip of Lower California, declared himself "President" and issued a decree that the laws of Louisiana would henceforth prevail, abrogating the Mexican prohibition on slavery on Mexican soil. Marching around, two months later he proclaimed he had annexed the huge northwest Mexican state of Sonora, now part of his "Republic." By April 1854, an alliance of Mexican landowners and bandit chiefs scattered the ragtag band of gringo invaders.

Gadsden laid out his map based on the Davis plan, bluntly telling the Mexican foreign minister that the "spirit of the age," the rhetorical trope for Manifest Destiny, would naturally lead the northern Mexican states to be absorbed into the U.S. and that Lower California should belong to the U.S., too. The timing for his grand gesture, however, coincided with William Walker's invasion. His misbegotten expedition persuaded the autocratic Mexico ruler, General Santa Anna, who had seized power again after losing the Mexican War, that the intentions of the United States were ominous. He appealed to France, England, and Spain to bolster him. But as much as Santa Anna had contempt for the blustering Gadsden his treasury was depleted, he faced revolutionary threats to his power, and did not want to provoke another war. Santa Anna tossed aside Gadsden's fantasy map, instead agreeing only to the sale of the Mesilla Valley, the land between the Rio Grande and Gila Rivers, which would provide for the Southern railroad route to the Pacific. Yet he kept raising his price, excited by reports of the boastful talk of a railroad investor, Robert J. Walker, that the U.S. would pay any cost for the right of way. Walker was not just any businessman, but Polk's former secretary of the treasury, the former U.S. senator from Mississippi, and Jefferson Davis's early political mentor. Marcy chided Walker (and Davis indirectly) through a warning to Mexico not to "permit herself to be misled by the speculative views" of men who did not hold government positions. Gadsden finally concluded his treaty negotiations on December 30, 1853, purchasing a strip of land about the size of Pennsylvania for $15 million. Landing at New Orleans, he announced to the customs house official, "Sir, I am General Gadsden. I have nothing in my trunk but my treaty."

Within weeks of Gadsden's return, the *New York Herald* published an exposé, "The Secret History of the Gadsden Treaty," tracing "its origin in the fertile imagination of Jefferson Davis." "Independently of the commercial and political advantages that were to accrue from the South from the development of this policy," the paper reported, "there were private considerations sufficiently powerful in the future aspirations of Mr. Davis to have made the appointment of General Gadsden a paramount necessity. Passing over the existence of certain extensive landed property laying near the boundaries of Louisiana and Texas which General Davis inherited, and which were to be quadrupled in value by their contiguity to the great Pacific road, we come to the necessity of killing Col. [Thomas Hart] Benton . . . not only a dangerous enemy, but a powerful obstacle, to the Presidential aspirations of Jefferson Davis."

The Gadsden Treaty threatened to become a heated controversy dividing an already unsettled Democratic Party. Davis's defense appeared in the administration's organ, the *Washington Union*, which claimed he inherited no such property and would not personally profit. The paper simply ignored the charge about his "Presidential aspirations." In fact, Davis was a partner in the Vicksburg, Shreveport and Texas Railroad, which planned to construct a southern route to the Pacific, and his partner was the speculator Robert J. Walker.

George N. Sanders once again seized the moment, doing all within his powers of mischief to create friction. Just before he departed for London to assume his post at the embassy, he wrote a broadside in his *Democratic Review* denouncing the Pierce policy of distributing patronage to the Softs. "Conciliation must not be carried so far as to corrupt the principles and spirit of the party by the admission of destructive elements," he wrote. "In the admission of the disaffected, and in the distribution of power among them, we must distinguish between the deceivers and the deceived; we must exorcise the demon before we admit those who have possessed with it. Were it not far better that all the enemies of the Constitution and the Union should be ousted from the Democratic party, and collected together, than that they should be distributed amongst ourselves, with power to leaven and corrupt the entire body of the democracy?"

Caleb Cushing stepped into the breach, trying to calm the criticism of the Southern Rightists and the Hards with a letter on November 3, 1853, reassuring them of Pierce's enduring commitments. "If there be any purpose more fixed than another in the mind of the President and those with whom he is accustomed to consult," he wrote, "it is that that dangerous element of abolitionism, under whatever guise or form it may present itself, shall be crushed out so far as this administration is concerned." Cushing's pledge appeared in the pages of the *New York Tribune*, a Whig newspaper of "that dangerous element," a gesture calculated to insult the Softs. The Southerners, however, tossed Cushing's olive branch like kindling onto the bonfire. With the New York state Democratic Party irrevocably split, the Whigs swept the off-year elections there. The Hards blamed Marcy and Pierce for their conciliatory gestures to the Softs.

The crisis of the Pierce presidency was just beginning.

When the 33rd Congress convened in December 1853, one of its first orders of business in its first week was to award the annual U.S. government printing contract, a plum that regularly went to the president's favored editor in Washington. The *Washington Union* was the administration newspaper in the capital. Pierce had approved the appointment of its editor. Cushing contributed an almost daily editorial. It pages were open to Marcy and his minions, who used the paper to wage a constant war on Dickinson and the Hards. In retaliation Southern Ultras and Hards created a fire-eating opposition newspaper, the *Washington Sentinel*, that mercilessly attacked Pierce as an abolitionist controlled by John Van Buren, the former president's son and leading light of the Free Soilers and Softs. The *Sentinel*'s editor was Beverley Tucker, whose lineage ran to the root of Southern radicalism. His great-uncle was John Randolph, the Virginia aristocratic states' rights purist and opponent of his cousin, Thomas Jefferson. Tucker's uncle, Nathaniel Beverley Tucker, had long believed in Southern secession and though intimate with Calhoun worried about him at times as a sellout politician. Tucker would also befriend Sanders, combining like chemical elements of nitroglycerin. (They would wind up as Confederate commissioners together in Canada.) Instead of granting the printing contract to the Union, the overwhelmingly Democratic Congress gave it to the *Sentinel*. Whigs had joined with Southerners and northern Hards to humiliate Pierce. "He is care-worn and the embarrassments of his Administration are obviously oppressing him and his ministers," observed Seward.

Foote wrote gleefully in his memoir of Pierce's collapse after a year in office. "In less than a twelvemonth after Mr. Pierce's induction into the Presidency every man of solid understanding, both in Congress and elsewhere, who had aided this ill-starred scion of the Granite State in his efforts to reach the Presidency, became satisfied of his utter incompetency for the performance of the duties devolved on him, and honest men everywhere were filled with mingled amazement and disgust at nearly all that was from time to time reported to them as occurring under the sinister auspices which clustered around him."

The spoils spread to all the factions were supposed to bind the party together, but instead ripped it apart at the seams. Old animosities would not be forgotten and forgiven. After Bronson resigned to protest Pierce's patronage policy, the Senate held up confirmation of Marcy's handpicked selection, Herman J. Redfield, as port collector of New York. One of the Hards from the New York delegation, Francis B. Cutting, rose to deliver two scorching floor speeches denouncing Pierce's supposed "amnesty" of Free Soilers, betrayal of the Democratic Party and the principles of states' rights, and his nefarious attempt to create a party of personal power. "Can I call it anything less than a clear and palpable coalition of opposite extremes, and cemented by nothing but the hope of present reward, and the absurd hope that they can form of this coalition an administration party—a Pierce party—to renominate the present executive, and to keep him and his friends in office?"

For the Southern Rights men the "finality of the Compromise," which Pierce considered the terra firma of his politics, had hardly settled the matter, but was a momentary obstacle to be demolished. The traumatized president, a sweet-tempered son of privilege who had been shuttled into place throughout his career by sharp political operators and who only wished to please everybody, burdened with his depressed, ill, and reclusive wife blaming him for having the sins of the universe visited upon them, passively watched his dream of harmony dissolve, and reached for consolation to his brandy bottle. "Everything in that mansion seems cold and cheerless," observed Charles Mason, head of the Patent Office. "I have seen hundreds of log cabins which seemed to contain more happiness." Late at night, Pierce rode his black horse named "Union" alone through the streets of Washington. He dropped in unannounced at the house of Senator Clement Clay and his charming wife, who thought him "a very harassed man." Beleaguered and bereft, Pierce turned more than ever to his true friend, Jefferson Davis.

Within the supposedly unified and well-balanced cabinet, a team of allies, Davis was the premier. He paid proper respect to Pierce, who in turn invariably followed his direction. But Davis was wary of even his closest cabinet colleague, Caleb Cushing, who was given most of the formal presidential message duties. According to Virginia Clay, Davis's intimate confidante, "a conspicuous Senator from Mississippi in ante-bellum days" (almost certainly Davis), described Cushing to her: "I had no confidence in Cushing beyond that of a follower to a quicker intellect and a braver heart. He could appreciate the gallantry and fidelity of Pierce, so he followed him. Like the chameleon, he was green, or blue, or brown, according to what he rested upon." And within the administration he rested upon Davis, who had "a quicker intellect and a braver heart." But the true "follower," more like a retriever, was Pierce.

Davis was a singular power, but hardly isolated within his citadel. He was the inside man in the executive branch for the most powerful senators, who controlled the key committees, the center of gravity in Pierce's Washington. It was these senators at the opening of the 33rd Congress who decided to discipline Pierce by giving the printing contract to the *Sentinel*, not the *Union*. They lived together in a boardinghouse called the F Street Mess near the Senate side of the Capitol—Andrew Pickens Butler of South Carolina, chairman of the Judiciary Committee; John M. Mason of Virginia, chairman of the Foreign Relations Committee; Robert M. T. Hunter of Virginia, chairman of the Finance Committee; and David Rice Atchison of Missouri, president pro tempore of the Senate. Collectively they held the greatest concentration of power in the Congress—and they acted collectively. The inhabitants of the F Street Mess had deep personal ties to the late Calhoun, whom they venerated as a god, adhered to the fundamental states' rights dogma that the states had created the Union and could in principle dissolve it through secession if they wished, opposed the Compromise and acquiesced in it only as a temporary tactical retreat, did not believe that Congress had any constitutional right to restrict slavery, and were devoted to finding avenues for its expansion. Davis was their ex officio member.

Andrew Pickens Butler of South Carolina was the heir to one of the founding families of the deeply conservative upcountry county of Edgefield. "His rubicund face, framed in long silver-white hair, the merry twinkle of his eye, and his mobile mouth marked him as a man of bubbling good nature and a jovial companion," observed Carl Schurz. "He was said to have had a liberal education and to be fond of quoting Horace. On the floor he frequently seemed to be engaged in gay and waggish conversation with his neighbors. But when slavery was attacked, he was apt to flare up fiercely, to assume the haughty air of the representative of a higher class, and, in fluent and high-sounding phrase, to make the Northern man feel the superiority of the Cavalier over the Roundhead." His father, William Butler, a Revolutionary War general, was elected as the first congressman from the district and graciously resigned his seat in 1810 in favor of the rising young John C. Calhoun. One brother was governor, another a congressman. As a state legislator A. P. Butler rallied to Calhoun and nullification. After serving as a circuit court judge, he was elected a U.S. senator in 1846, where he followed the lead of his mentor Calhoun. When the battle over the Compromise of 1850 sparked the movement in South Carolina for a secession convention, led by the fire-eating Senator Robert Barnwell Rhett, editor of the *Charleston Mercury*, Butler joined with other Calhounite leaders to oppose "separate secession." They formed what they called the Cooperation Party, based on the notion that secession should only be staged in "cooperation" with other Southern states and not alone. The Cooperationists defeated the "separate" secessionists in electing delegates to the convention, which, meeting on April 26, 1852, limited its provocation to passing a resolution declaring "the right of this State to secede from the Federal Union." During the height of this internecine struggle, Butler wrote Jefferson Davis, then running as a Southern Rights candidate for governor of Mississippi, for "counsel and suggestions." In his letter of June 16, 1851, he expressed his concerns: "How will such a move affect the party of true men in your State? Will it help you, or will it impair the strength or interfere with the onward movements of the States Rights parties in other States?" Butler made his case for "cooperation," enlisting Davis's "opinion, confidentially": "I believe this State could be induced to make any sacrifice for the common cause of those who contend that the General Government is a confederacy and not a consolidated Government. If it is of the latter character, then the Southern States are doomed to degraded subordination. They can hold their rights by no other tenure than sufferance. Should South Carolina move alone, without the assurance from her neighbors of cooperation, she will, I fear, make a vain sacrifice." Like Davis and other Calhoun men, Butler endorsed Pierce, withheld criticism of the Compromise for the moment, and hoped for ascendant influence within the new administration.

When the ill Calhoun chose Butler to read his speech for him on the floor of the Senate denouncing the Compromise, his portentous valedictory, Butler demurred because his eyesight was blurred, so he recommended that the honor fall to the senator from Virginia and his mate at the F Street Mess, James Murray Mason, author of the Fugitive Slave Act. There was no more aristocratic Southerner in the chamber. He was a direct descendant of George Mason, a Cavalier captain in King Charles I's army and member of the House of Commons, who fled England when Oliver Cromwell's republican forces defeated the royalists and Charles was executed. In Virginia he established one of the largest plantations on the banks of the Potomac, bequeathed to generations of Masons. George Mason IV was the author of Virginia's Declaration of Rights in May 1776,

James Murray Mason

the template for the Declaration of Independence and the Bill of Rights, and though a delegate to the Constitutional Convention he refused to sign because he felt it granted the federal government too much power. His attitude toward slavery was that of the enlightened slaveholder, considering it a "poison," and was against its extension but for its protection where it existed. He did not emancipate slaves in his will, unlike his neighbor, George Washington. His grandson, James, had no ambivalence about slavery. "No Senator had a greater reverence for the peculiar institutions of the South, or a more thorough contempt for the Abolitionists of the North," recalled the contemporary journalist Benjamin Perley Poore. James M. Mason's speech, according to Schurz, came from "a sluggish intellect spurred into activity by an overweening self-conceit" intended to make others "bow to his assumed aristocracy and all its claims."

While Calhoun lay dying Mason sat with him in his room as the old man prophesied the coming apocalypse. According to Mason's notes of one of his conversations, Calhoun predicted the downfall of the United States on a timetable. "The Union is doomed to dissolution, there is no mistaking the signs," he said. "I am satisfied in my judgment, even were the questions which now agitate Congress settled to the satisfaction and with the concurrence of the Southern States, it would not avert, or materially delay, the catastrophe." Calhoun foretold that the election of a Northern president committed against the expansion of slavery would bring about the deluge. "I fix its probable occurrence within twelve years or three Presidential terms. You, and others of your age, will probably live to see it; I shall not. The mode by which it will be done is not so clear; it may be brought about in a manner that none now foresee. But the probability is, it will explode in a Presidential election." Calhoun's vision was precise: in the third presidential contest after 1850 the victory of a Northern candidate would trigger secession.

Robert M. T. Hunter, of the "Virginia Chivalry," the longtime acolyte of Calhoun and opponent of the Compromise, was another central figure at the F Street Mess. He had rejected Stephen A. Douglas's offer of being his running mate after initially accepting it, and declined Pierce's tentative suggestion of a cabinet post. He preferred the power he held in the Senate. He weighed in with the president-elect for the appointment of Jefferson Davis, an endorsement that was undoubtedly the unified opinion of the F Street Mess.

After the death of Vice President William R. King a month into the administration, the next in the line of succession to the presidency was yet another messmate, the president pro tempore of the Senate, David Rice Atchison of Missouri. Coarse, profane, and ruthless, yet also considered by his friends to be generous and convivial, he was the most belligerent pro-slavery man in the Senate, the one most quickly prone to outbursts threatening violence.

Atchison was widely considered and even called "the acting vice president." Though he was not a planter or large slaveholder—it was said he might have owned one slave—he was vehement on the subject. Born in Kentucky, he attended Transylvania University, where he befriended his classmate Jefferson Davis, who described him as "a tall country boy, truehearted and honest, with many virtues, but without grace or tact." Atchison became a lawyer and moved to the frontier of western Missouri, where his most notable clients were the Mormons and their Prophet, Joseph Smith, before their expulsion in 1838 to Illinois. They helped elect him to the state legislature, and though he wound up serving in the state militia in forays against them he continued to argue against mob violence until Smith pronounced him "as contemptible as any of them." Atchison was appointed a circuit court judge and in 1843 a U.S. senator to fill the term left by the death of the incumbent; after that, he was elected time and again. He never married and his ideal evening was spent drinking long into the night with like-minded fellows. "He had a strong liking for the mountain dew of old Bourbon, Kentucky," recalled one of his admirers, and even his friends fondly referred to him as "Bourbon Dave." In the Senate he immediately gravitated into the orbit of Calhoun, becoming the only senator from a border state to sign Calhoun's Southern Manifesto of 1849 threatening secession if the Wilmot Proviso were enacted.

The other members of the F Street Mess occupied safe seats, but Atchison was exposed. His popularity among his Democratic colleagues who had elected him to his exalted position belied his precarious situation. He was one of the most vulnerable senators, facing for reelection the most formidable, experienced, and dangerous adversary in Thomas Hart Benton. There was no one the Calhoun men hated and feared more than Benton. The struggle between Benton and Atchison was more than a political death match between two men of violent temperaments. Their brawl over a Senate seat set in motion a melee over the fate of slavery in the new territories beyond to the west.

CHAPTER TWELVE

I, THOMAS HART BENTON

"I Thomas Hart Benton," Benton thundered in announcing himself on his tours of the state he had represented for thirty years in the Senate, since Missouri was admitted to the Union, the longest tenure of any senator in the country's history. Benton stood for his state, but in embodying it seemed to tower over it. He subsumed his party unto himself as well. His opinions were unvarnished, his hatreds unadulterated, and his loyalties unwavering. He was the dominant Democrat in a state that was so overwhelmingly Democratic that not a single Whig was elected to the Congress until 1850. In most of his elections, he defeated his hapless opponents by margins of more than two to one. "I shall crush my enemies as an elephant crushes piss-ants under his tread," he proclaimed. Fierce, slashing, and menacing, he had wounded Andrew Jackson in a hotel brawl in 1813. "General Jackson," declared Benton, "was a very great man. I shot him, sir." Benton became General Jackson's

Thomas Hart Benton

aide-de-camp and President Jackson's Senate floor leader and member of his Kitchen Cabinet. In 1817, Benton shot dead in a duel the prominent U.S. attorney for the Missouri territory, Charles Lucas, for having challenged his right to vote because he had not paid taxes on three slaves. "I never quarrel, sir," he declared, "but I do fight, sir, and when I fight, sir, a funeral follows, sir." On the floor of the Senate during the debate over the Compromise of 1850, which he opposed as "humbug," he had bared his chest to Senator Foote advancing on him with pistol in hand. He was not just dominant, but domineering. "Nobody opposes Benton but a few blackjack prairie lawyers; these are the only opponents of Benton," he said. "Benton and the people, Benton and Democracy are one and the same, sir; synonymous terms, sir; synonymous terms, sir." Challenging him meant to destroy him or be destroyed. One of his political opponents remarked, "He forced his enemies to conspire to kill him, that they might live."

Westward went the course of his empire and Benton followed the star of his Manifest Destiny. Yet he was not alone on his journey. His roots were deeply entangled with those of another supreme politico of the Jackson Kitchen Cabinet. Francis Preston Blair and Thomas Hart Benton were like blood brothers. They were the two complementary lobes of the Jacksonian political brain. Benton was blustery, raging, and preferred facing his rivals at ten paces. Blair was sinuous, maneuvering, and preferred conducting his business in the drawing room of Blair House across from the White House. Benton had profound analytical skills as a lawyer; Blair wielded the stiletto of a journalist. They both loved to win and never accepted defeat. The Blair and Benton children were virtually raised as one brood. Blair's sons, Francis Blair Jr. and Montgomery Blair, were trained as Benton's protégés, each serving as apprentice lawyers in his St. Louis office. Benton's daughter, Jessie, was like their sister. Raised as though she were his son, Jessie was nurtured from birth on politics, literally sat as a child at Jackson's feet, and inherited her father's stubborn and wild intensity. James Buchanan, in an uncommon display of wit, described her as "the square root of Thomas Hart Benton." At the age of sixteen she willfully eloped with the explorer and adventurer John C. Frémont, who, in 1850, she helped guide as his political handler to become the first U.S. senator from California. Montgomery Blair would represent the slave Dred Scott before the Supreme Court, and Jessie Benton Frémont and the Blairs would manage her husband as the first presidential candidate of the Republican Party. Benton's career would end running in 1856 for a futile last hurrah for governor, refusing to support his son-in-law out of loyalty to a party that had rejected him, and instead voting for Buchanan, whom he considered at best as second-rate, "never a leading man." But his endless political wars were a prelude to Civil War—the repeal of the Missouri Compromise, "Bleeding Kansas," and the *Dred Scott* case. In Benton's case all national politics were not only local but also violently personal.

Thomas Hart Benton passionately hated his enemies and above all in his gallery of villains he hated John C. Calhoun. "Citizens," he declaimed, speaking of himself in the third person to a crowd, "no man since the days of Cicero has been abused as has Benton. What Cicero was to Catiline, the Roman conspirator, Benton has been to John Catiline Calhoun, the South Carolina nullifier. Cicero fulminating his philippics against Catiline in the Roman forum; Benton denouncing Calhoun on the floor of the American Senate. Cicero against Catiline—Benton against Calhoun." From the nullification crisis through the Kansas-Nebraska Act to *Dred Scott*, Benton viewed the whole train of events as incidents in his struggle with Calhoun and his political heirs. "He is not dead, sir—he is not dead," Benton said, turning his back on his coffin. "There may be no vitality in his body, but there is in his doctrines."

Benton opposed the annexation of Texas in 1844 as a Calhoun plot, defeating it in the Senate. In retaliation, Calhoun and his allies organized a movement to depose Benton in his reelection, arousing, said Benton, "every Calhoun man and every Calhoun newspaper in the State and in the Nation." But Texas annexation was wildly popular in Missouri and when the newly installed state legislature chose two U.S. senators that year the vote for Atchison was greater than for Benton. Still the most powerful man in the state, Benton opposed the Mexican War until the moment it was declared and blamed Calhoun. "Inexorable History, with her pen of iron and tablets of brass, will so write him down," said Benton. Calhoun was "wrong in all this business, from beginning to ending," citing thirteen examples of his being "wrong," and "more wrong now than ever . . . so do I see in them many nullifications." He attributed every "wrong" in Calhoun "involving his country in war" to his ambition, "no other object than to govern a presidential election."

Benton spanned the decades as the Missouri colossus by force of will, jealously occupying nearly all the center political ground. But his bedrock strength eroded into the source of his weakness. The cogent logic of his Jacksonianism corroded under the acids of time into illogic. His consistency on behalf of the Union in a slave state required antitheses that eventually cracked his support. He was a forthright slaveholder who never apologized. "I was born to the inheritance of slaves," he said, "and have never been without them." But he was also opposed to slavery, at least in abstract principle. He had opposed it since 1804, but had favored admitting Missouri as a slave state in the Compromise of 1820. Until the rise of Calhoun, he viewed anti-slavery agitation as the hidden hand of the old discredited Northern Federalist Party, which he despised. He joined the St. Louis citizens group that drove the abolitionist editor Elijah Lovejoy across the Mississippi into Illinois, endorsing a resolution that denounced Lovejoy and his friends as "misguided fanatics" and insisting that freedom of speech did not include the right "to freely discuss the question of slavery, either orally or through the medium of the press." But then the immovable Benton shifted to an opposite and equally immovable position. His loathing of Calhoun turned his fixation from Northern to Southern aggression. "My personal sentiments, then, are against the institution of slavery, and against its introduction into places in which it does not now exist," he said. "If there was no slavery in Missouri today, I should oppose its coming in." But after the Mexican War he opposed the Wilmot Proviso as a threat to the Union, arguing it was "unnecessary" to prevent the extension of slavery, which he also opposed. Yet he unequivocally declared, "It is absurd to deny to Congress the power to legislate as it pleases upon the subject of slavery in the territories. . . . Congress has power to prohibit, or to admit slavery, and no one else. . . . Congress has the constitutional power to abolish slavery in [the] territories." His refutation of Calhoun's doctrine that Congress had no such right was absolute anathema to the Southern Rights men, far more than a mere difference of opinion, but a declaration of war, as fundamental a heresy as any that provoked medieval religious crusades. Despite his increasingly eccentric positioning, alienating antislavery and pro-slavery alike, his pole star remained his hatred of Calhoun and those who would be Calhoun, and that kept him on a straight collision course.

Before the Mexican War, it was "political death for any man even to whisper a breath against 'Old Bullion,' the idol of Missouri," according to his archenemy Judge William C. Price. But the war fever whipped up a wind at the back of Benton's opponents and gave them courage. Price fervently believed in the divine blessing of slavery and when the Methodist Church split in 1844 over the question he naturally aligned with the Methodist Church, South. Price originated the movement to repeal the Missouri Compromise that had brought the state into the Union on the basis that slavery would be limited according to the Mason-Dixon Line. "Missouri," he preached, "could not remain slave with Iowa free on the north, Illinois free on the east, and a free State on the west. In short, Missouri had to accomplish that Repeal or become a free State." Once a friend of Benton, Price declared holy war on him when Benton repudiated the idea of repeal. "And from that day the radical slave faction of the Missouri Democracy fought him to the death," stated one of Price's confidants. "Judge Price and other radical Southern leaders saw at that time that a conflict was inevitable; they were secessionists *per se*." From that early campaign in 1844, Price was the point man against Benton for the national Southern leadership, and he was "in close and constant communication with Jefferson Davis, Robert Toombs, John C. Calhoun, John C. Breckenridge, Judah P. Benjamin, and other Southern leaders, for many years prior to the Civil War." In New Orleans, in 1850, during the campaign to oust Benton, he conferred on strategy with Davis and Benjamin. (Price was a moving force within a group of powerful state Democrats known as the "Central Clique," once allied with Benton but turned into his mortal enemies. Price could also call for help from his cousin, Sterling Price, speaker of the Missouri House of Representatives, who would be elected governor in 1852 and later become a Confederate general.)

The epicenter of the anti-Benton movement was the six northwestern counties on the fertile right bank of the Missouri River, settled by Southerners, Southern in culture and politics, and rooted in a slave economy. By 1850, these counties had a white population of 56,726 and a slave population of 17,357, property valued at more than $10 million. They were the northernmost outpost of the slave South, the most intensively devoted to slavery in a state increasingly divided over it, and surrounded on three sides by free states, with the territory to the west unsecured for slavery and open to sanctuary for fugitive slaves. The Missouri slaveholders gazed longingly at virgin soil to the west in order to preserve and extend their realm. Repeal was increasingly felt as the answered prayer to an existential crisis. Their political voice was David Atchison, his adviser was William C. Price, and behind them both loomed Calhoun, Jefferson Davis, and the F Street Mess.

Calhoun had laid down the gauntlet in his resolutions of February 17, 1847, that offered the Congress had no power to prohibit slavery in the territories, could not stop slaveholders from migrating there with their property, and could not bar them from forming new slave states in the territories, even north of the Mason-Dixon Line. He traced the denial of such supposed rights back in history to the evil precedents of the Missouri Compromise, the Northwest Ordinance of 1787, and ultimately the proposition in the Declaration of Independence that "all men are created equal," which he called the "most dangerous of political errors." "This attempt, pushed to the verge of breaking up the government in pursuit of a newly invented slavery dogma, was founded in errors too gross for misapprehension," wrote Benton. "This is the last slavery creed of the Calhoun school, and the one on which his disciples now stand—and not with any barren foot. . . . It is impossible to consider such conduct as any thing else than as one of the devices for 'forcing the issue with the North,' " quoting Calhoun himself.

Rejected in the Congress, a version of Calhoun's resolutions was enacted on March 10, 1849, by the Missouri legislature, in the control of Benton's enemies, to defy, taunt, and defeat him. Claiborne F. Jackson, a state senator, and William B. Napton, a state Supreme Court judge, influential figures of the "Central Clique," proposed that the Congress had no power to legislate on slavery; that the state would uphold the Missouri Compromise limiting the extent of slavery only if "future aggression . . . and the spirit of anti-slavery fanaticism be extinguished"; that Missouri would promise "hearty co-operation with the other slave States in measures for protection against Northern fanaticism," a pledge envisioning secession and civil war; and finally instructed the state's senators to promote the resolutions. To which Benton replied, in what he labeled the latest of his "Calhounic" speeches, that the Calhoun resolutions were "the parent" of the Jackson-Napton Resolutions, "a mere copy," and fingered Calhoun as "the head mover and contriver." He further charged, "The whole conception, concoction and passage of the resolutions was done upon conspiracy, perfected by fraud. It was a plot to get me out of the Senate and out of the way of the disunion plotters." His opposition was nothing but "a concerted wolf-howl of 'obey or resign.' " He dismissed the resolutions out of hand as "false in their facts, incendiary in their temper, disunion in their object, nullification in their essence, high treason in their remedy, and usurpation in their character." Referring to their authors and David Atchison, who eagerly declared he would follow their instructions, Benton warned that if any man in Missouri should act upon them, "he will be subject to be hung under the laws of the United States, and if a judge, will deserve to be hung." When Jackson and his friends sat in the front row at one of his rallies intending to heckle him, he gleefully singled them out. "And here are Claib Jackson [and the others named] as demure as three prostitutes at a christening."

Atchison stumped across the state in the election of 1850 for Benton's overthrow. "I have been and am now making war on him, Free Soilism, Abolitionism, and all similar isms," he proclaimed, "and if he is not driven from the United States Senate, it will be no fault of mine." After forty ballots in the legislature the anti-Benton forces combined with the Whigs to elect the Whig candidate, Henry S. Geyer, who would prove to be a reliable pro-slavery ally. The "Antis" believed they had driven a stake through Benton at last. "He should, according to our calculations, have retired when he was defeated," said Price. "But he immediately espoused the cause of Nebraska Territory. . . . He knew we were opposed to it and he knew that the slave power was not prepared to enter upon a struggle for its very existence. He wished to precipitate things."

Benton began writing his epic memoir, *Thirty Years' View*, but hardly cloistered himself. He girded himself for vengeance, telling Hannibal Hamlin "this does not interfere with other works—the redemption of the State of Missouri from the Whigs and nullifiers, and the presidential election." When the Missouri legislature convened in 1852 the "war of the factions" resumed. The "Antis" and Whigs battled with the "Bentons" ballot after ballot over the speakership and down to the hiring of clerks. Leading the "Bentons" was state assemblyman Francis P. Blair, Jr., Benton's protégé and a Free Soiler. Feelings ran so high that a Whig offered: "*Resolved,* That a veil be hung over the portrait of Colonel Benton, now hanging in the Representative Hall; that Claib Jackson be requested to absent himself from the House, and that the members drink no more grog till a Speaker is elected." The resolution was ruled out of order, and the hostilities and drinking continued until a temporary speaker was chosen. After the state Democratic convention in April 1852, Benton declared his candidacy for the House of Representatives from a St. Louis district. His crusade against his enemies resumed where he had left off. In the legislature, Frank Blair declared war, proposing to expunge the Jackson-Napton Resolutions. His resolution was tabled, saving them, but the Democratic Party was irrevocably split.

In his final speech in the Senate, Benton laid down a marker. He proposed a bill to build a transcontinental railroad from St. Louis to San Francisco. Constructing a railroad that would connect the Mississippi with the Pacific would require organizing the Kansas-Nebraska territories under the provision of the Missouri Compromise. Benton raised the railroad as the engine of future economic prosperity as the means to keep slavery out of the territories. After his election to the Congress in 1852, he immediately launched his campaign to reclaim his Senate seat, attacking Atchison as an opponent of the railroad. Thrown on the defensive, Atchison sputtered that he was for the project, at least in theory, and denounced "The Old Senator" for "his arrogant dogmatism." Atchison was for the repeal of the Missouri

Compromise, but conceded that since it was the law he would have to support organization of Kansas-Nebraska under its terms. Yet he cast that into doubt, suggesting that there were other routes, including a Southern one, and that "the discretion" of deciding which one it would be would rest with President Pierce. "So much for the railroad."

During the campaign to remove him from the Senate, Benton's enemies seized upon an obscure local legal case to deliver a judicial rebuke intended as a fatal political blow.

The case was *Dred Scott v. Irene Emerson*. Dred Scott was a slave owned by John Emerson, an army physician, who took him on his assignments to the free state of Illinois and the free territory of Wisconsin until residing in St. Louis. Dr. Emerson died at the age of forty, leaving his property to his widow, who hired out Scott and his wife, a slave whom he had married in Wisconsin, to a grocery storeowner. In 1846, Scott and his wife sued for their freedom based on residence in free states. Long-standing precedent in Missouri law that "once free, always free" under the Ordinance of 1787 had decided many similar cases. On a confused technicality in a circuit court trial in 1847, the jury ruled against Dred Scott. He appealed and in the second trial in 1850 won. Emerson's attorneys appealed to the Missouri Supreme Court.

Here presided William B. Napton, coauthor of the Jackson-Napton Resolutions, who led the three-man court, which was unanimous behind him on this matter. Napton was "determined," he wrote in his diaries, not only "to override the old decisions of our court," but also to rule "that the Missouri Compromise is unconstitutional." His decision was intended to strike down Benton and the entire edifice of law and legislation thwarting the extension of slavery. Benton, however, was defeated before Napton got around to writing his decision while waiting for a certain legal citation. But before he could issue his thundering ruling, the voters evicted him from his seat. Still infused with Napton's righteousness, the court decided in 1852 to remand Dred Scott back to slavery. Judge William Scott wrote that slavery had been introduced "in the providence of God," and that "Times now are not as they were, when the former decisions on this subject were made. Since then not only individuals but States have been possessed with a dark and fell spirit in relation to slavery, whose gratification is sought in the pursuit of measures whose inevitable consequence must be the overthrow and destruction of our government."

From that moment, the little noticed *Dred Scott* case began to gather political momentum and national significance. Dred Scott appealed to the U.S. Circuit Court, lost, and appealed to the U.S. Supreme Court. In *Dred*

Scott v. John Sandford (Mrs. Emerson's brother, who now held title to him), the attorneys for the defendant were Henry S. Geyer, who had taken Benton's Senate seat, and Reverdy Johnson, the former senator from Maryland and Polk's attorney general; and the lawyer for the complainant was Montgomery Blair, whose fees were paid by Gamaliel Bailey, editor of the abolitionist newspaper, the *National Era*. The Supreme Court ruling in *Dred Scott* on March 6, 1857, upholding that "persons of African descent have no rights that white men are bound to respect," would enshrine Calhoun's doctrine that the Congress could not limit slaves from being carried into free states and territory, setting the stage for Lincoln's "House Divided" speech, his debates with Stephen A. Douglas, and the war to come.

"These decisions upon their face show themselves to be political," wrote Benton about the *Dred Scott* ruling. Afterward he wrote a pamphlet tracing those politics to the party of Calhoun, which controlled the administration of Pierce.

Up to Mr. Pierce's administration the plan had been defensive—that is to say, to make the secession of the South a measure of self-defense against the abolition encroachments, aggressions, and crusades of the North: in the time of Mr. Pierce, the plan became offensive—that is to say, to commence the expansion of slavery, and the acquisition of territory to spread it over, so as to overpower the North with new slave States, and drive them out of the Union. In this change of tactics originated the abrogation of the Missouri Compromise, the attempt to purchase the one half of Mexico, and the actual purchase of a large part; the design to take Cuba. . . . Accidents and events have given this party a strange pre-eminence. Under Jackson's administration, proclaimed for treason; since, at the head of the Government and of the Democratic party. The death of Harrison, and the accession of Tyler, was their first great lift; the election of Mr. Pierce was their culminating point. It not only gave them the government, but power to pass themselves for the Union party, and for Democrats; and to stigmatize all who refused to go with them, as disunionists, and abolitionists.

With Benton in the House poised to reclaim his Senate seat, the *Dred Scott* case invisibly but inexorably wending its way upward to the Supreme Court, the repeal of the Missouri Compromise touted, and transcontinental railroad routes proposed, Stephen A. Douglas bounded off his steamer from Liverpool returning from his grand tour of Europe.

CHAPTER THIRTEEN

THE TRIUMPH OF THE F STREET MESS

D ouglas had campaigned for Pierce in 1852 from Virginia to New York, and from Pennsylvania to Ohio, attempting to erase the taint his attempt to grasp the nomination had engendered. In Washington, he declared that the Caribbean and Gulf of Mexico "are American waters." In Richmond, he denounced Free Soilers. At Tammany Hall, he announced that his tottering enemy Lewis Cass was not, after all, an "old fogy," but "a pure young American." He assailed "proud, haughty, and insolent England" and the Whigs for not understanding "the doctrine of progress." In the meantime, he made peace with John Wentworth, the Chicago Democratic political boss and Free Soiler, and helped deliver Illinois for the national ticket and sweeping Wentworth into the Congress. The Democratic majorities were overwhelming in the legisla-

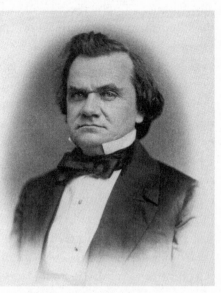

Stephen A. Douglas

ture. His control over the state party was complete. "Shoot the deserters," he proclaimed gleefully. Douglas's reelection to the Senate was virtually unanimous, swamping poor Whig state senator Joe Gillespie, Lincoln's friend, and that night Douglas staged a raucous lubricated party for more than 1,500 at the State House that destroyed the carpeting.

Douglas returned to Washington with the air of the conquering hero, the once and future candidate. Four days after his reelection, on January 8, 1853, on the anniversary of the Battle of New Orleans, he held the honor of delivering the speech dedicating the statue of Andrew Jackson rearing up on his horse in Lafayette Park across from the White House. Old Hickory, said Douglas, "lives in the spirit of the age," his signature phrase, always a self-reference. Less than two weeks later, Douglas was cast into an abyss of anguish. His wife, Martha, died in childbirth; a month afterward, his baby daughter died, too.

After the funeral Douglas did not receive much consolation from the new administration. He had expected to be at the main table distributing the loaves and fishes of patronage. "Show me a man who has no friends to reward and no enemies to punish," he wrote in anticipation, in December 1852, "and I will show you a man whose capacity and qualities as a public man render him incompetent to administer the government." But he was excluded from Pierce's council, never consulted about the selection of any cabinet member or any other important office. He complained to his close ally, Charles Lanphier, editor of the *Illinois State Register* and member of the Illinois party's executive committee, "the offices were awarded to a set of droanes [sic]." While the Democrats of Illinois looked hopefully to Douglas as their provider, he showed only empty hands. So he and Shields, the two Democratic senators, sent Pierce a discreet letter spelling out which offices they believed they were due as "a fair title," adding a touch of diplomacy tinged with subtle threat, "we can assure you before hand that no neglect or injustice of this kind will drive Illinois from the Democratic fold or its senators from the support of your administration." But Douglas was almost completely ignored, though he did manage to wangle the Land Office for his brother-in-law, Julius Granger. Shields told Douglas he got "a general impression that you are to be crushed" and advised that Pierce's policy "is to give your friends nothing."

In May 1853, Douglas set sail for England armed with letters of introduction from August Belmont, the American representative of the House of Rothschild and a major financier of the Democratic Party, and Robert J.

Walker, the railroad lobbyist who was both Jefferson Davis's and Douglas's business partner. Before he landed Douglas had declared Europe "antiquated, decrepit, tottering on the verge of dissolution," but he plunged ahead. At London he met a number of members of Parliament who had invested in the Illinois Central and encountered the exiled Kossuth at a party. After inveigling his new English acquaintances for an invitation to meet Queen Victoria he refused to don "court dress" and snubbed her. His insult won plaudits from the Democratic press at home. On he traveled through Marseilles, Genoa, Florence, Rome, and Athens, then farther east to Constantinople, where he secured a coveted audience with the sultan, but lacked the patience to wait for him, instead pushing on to Russia. Through his connections, he managed to gain a meeting with Czar Nicholas I. He was informed he did not need to wear "court dress," that his black suit would be acceptable. Douglas was brought to a field outside St. Petersburg, where the czar "was reviewing a million of his troops," he recounted to his Illinois friend, Usher Linder. "Linder," he said, "it was the most imposing sight I ever saw." Douglas was mounted on a large steed, its bridle studded with diamonds and covering decorated with gold and silver. The stirrups were a foot too long for him; he could barely peer over the horse's ears. Suddenly, the horse dashed "like the wind" for the czar's cortege as another rider sped toward him. Douglas feared they would crash "like a couple of locomotives," but the approaching rider revealed himself as the czar, who welcomed him to Russia in perfect English. Douglas put aside the denunciations of Russian tyranny he had delivered during Kossuth's visit. According to a report in the *New York Times* headlined "Senator Douglas Abroad, Traveling Adventures of a Small Giant," the czar told him there were "but two proper governments on earth, the one where all the people ruled, and the other where only one ruled—the American and the Russian governments—the other powers were mongrels, and were destined to be absorbed by one or the other of these two 'Governments.' " "Linder," said Douglas, "that was a proud day for my country. . . . It was a stroke of policy on the part of Nicholas. . . . I received every attention that it was possible for mortal man to receive, all of which I knew was intended for my country."

From the moment of Pierce's election Douglas and his advisers had begun plotting his next presidential campaign. One of his few Southern supporters, Senator David Yulee of Florida, wrote him, "The plan which should mark our campaign is plain." If the Northwest states were unified behind him he would be "yielded to at once, and your nomination effected without contest."

The Southerners would control a decisive bloc at the next convention, not enough to award the prize to one of their own, but pivotal in nominating a "doughface" Northerner. Yulee warned Douglas against the ruthless and plundering Indiana political boss, Senator Jesse D. Bright, who had smashed Douglas at the 1852 convention, delivering the Northwest delegates to Cass. Bright had become rich dealing in land and railroads and looting the state bank. He was the closest Northwest ally of the Southerners and especially Jefferson Davis. Few from the region were as pro-slavery, only partly for the crass reason that Bright was a slaveholder, owner of a Kentucky plantation gained through marriage. He viewed Douglas as his greatest competitor for influence, occupying the same political space, a mortal threat. "He is your enemy," Yulee wrote Douglas. "Bright will defeat this desirable 'solidarity' of the N.W. if he can. . . . He does not mean that you shall rise if he can prevent it—and his professed friendship will be more dangerous than his professed enmity." That Douglas had done poorly in winning Northwest delegates at the 1852 convention was not strictly a problem of the Northwest. Bright was the Southerners' linchpin in the region. Douglas's difficulty always resided ultimately with the South. He could not gain dominance as the favorite son of the Northwest without winning the confidence of the Southerners.

Walking down the gangplank in New York from his world travels on October 30, a refreshed Douglas immediately wrote his political confidant Lanphier. Pierce's problems had stirred up a flurry of speculation about Douglas running again for president. "The party is in a distracted condition," he wrote. Douglas wanted to tamp down the talk about himself as a candidate. "I do not wish to occupy that position. . . . I think such a state of things will exist that I shall not desire the nomination. Yet I do not intend to do any act which will deprive me on the control of my own actions. I shall remain entirely non-committal. . . . Let us leave the Presidency out of view at least two years to come." He made clear to Lanphier that he considered Pierce's troubles to be minor and ephemeral—"all is right." But Lanphier replied that Douglas had been out of touch for too long. "Without having heard from us for six months you still express confidence that we are 'all right,' " he wrote. "In these days six months is a long time to be confident that any body is 'right,' without knowing it." He explained that the "everlasting, never-to-be-ended New York quarrel" between the Hards and Softs was a sign of worse to come. "If Mr. Marcy and Mr. Dickinson cannot heal up old sores, I can see no good reason why the Democracy of the other States of the Union should tear themselves to pieces." Between Douglas and Lanphier the question of Douglas's future for the nomination was entirely strategic. It was not a question of whether he would, but when and how—and he would run again and again.

While Douglas calculated his angle on the internal quandaries of the party with Lanphier, he corresponded about certain speculations with his private real estate agent, D. A. Robertson. "Know nothing—say nothing about our affairs to anyone," Robertson wrote him. Douglas's inside trading and investments were inextricable from his grandiose vision of the West as the dynamic center of the country. His interests personal and public, pecuniary and political, were seamless, all of a piece. He had made a windfall profit from real estate holdings on the shore of Lake Michigan sold to the Illinois Central—and built Chicago into the most explosively growing city in the nation. As chairman of the Committee on Territories, he had passed the legislation in 1849 organizing the Territory of Minnesota—and he hurried into speculation in the Lake Superior region to replicate his success in Chicago. He was part of a real estate syndicate to purchase six thousand acres of land, founding a town called Superior City at the head of the lake, just over the border in Wisconsin, that would be the terminus for a transcontinental railroad along a northern route. But he had not abandoned his dream of a transcontinental railroad stemming from Chicago and flowing across a central route. Douglas would be the master builder and the profiteer of not one but two transcontinental railroads, the largest enterprises ever undertaken in American history.

Daniel A. Robertson was a former U.S. marshal, editor and publisher of the *Minnesota Democrat,* and real estate promoter in Douglas's employ. On a trip to New York and Washington in early 1853 he persuaded the banker W. W. Corcoran and all-around operator Robert J. Walker to invest in Superior City as the future hub of the northern railroad route. Corcoran then staked a syndicate of politically influential men with Douglas naturally first in line. Douglas brought in John W. Forney, the Pennsylvania editor and clerk of the House. Douglas's ally, Congressman William Richardson of Illinois, chairman of the House Committee on Territories, got a piece of the action. The others in the syndicate all held key positions, reflecting Douglas's understanding of power. Congressman John L. Dawson of Pennsylvania, a James Buchanan man, was chairman of the Committee on Agriculture. William W. Boyce, a South Carolina congressman, had been in Calhoun's inner circle and was close to Senator Butler. (Boyce would serve in the Confederate Congress.) Another South Carolina congressman, William Aiken, one of the wealthiest planters in the state, hailing from the town named after his family, was also a major stockholder in the South Carolina Railroad Company. Senators Robert M. T. Hunter, Jesse Bright, and John C. Breckinridge, the rising star from Kentucky, were given loans. Walker, of course, was also part of the deal.

The syndicate, however, immediately faced a cutthroat rival in Henry M. Rice, a pioneer fur trader, known to the Chippewa as "White Rice," a founder of St. Paul, and the territorial representative. When Robertson alerted Douglas that Rice "attempted to pirate" Douglas's and the others' land they decided that the scheme could not continue without including Rice as a partner, and so he was dealt in. Rice would become one of the wealthiest men in Minnesota and after he was elected its first U.S. senator he would build three large brick houses near the Capitol called Minnesota Row, occupied by himself, Douglas, and Breckinridge, an association that began with the Superior City deal, whose shares doubled within a year.

Douglas was entangled with his fellow senators and other politicians through more than the business of legislation, but also through business that influenced legislation. His speculations were inseparable from his politics. In both arenas he was a risk-taker, a plunger, going in for the biggest play with the biggest payoff, the greatest return on the dollar, and the greatest office of all. He was constantly scrambling, boom or bust. Douglas's loans from Corcoran for railroad and real estate schemes were part and parcel of his expansive visions. His idea of Manifest Destiny and that of the country were indistinguishable. They must be explained by "a railroad interpretation of American history," according to the historian Frank H. Hodder. "In the development of such an interpretation no fact will prove more striking than the extent to which the repeal of the Missouri Compromise by the Kansas-Nebraska Act was controlled by railroad considerations."

Douglas had been the master craftsman of the Compromise of 1850 and leveraged it to pass the Illinois Central Act. Yet he felt slighted. He nursed a sense of grievance that his spectacular accomplishment had not vaulted him to his destiny. The Illinois Central would run from Lake Michigan to the Gulf of Mexico, but Douglas had not steamed into the White House. He remained rankled for the rest of his life that he had not received full credit and full reward—not just the windfall profit from selling the right-of-way real estate, not just becoming a powerful senator, but the presidency. Both of the campaign biographies he authorized during his 1860 race emphasized "that he is the real author of the Compromise measures of 1850, so generally attributed to Henry Clay," as one put it. It was hardly accidental that these biographies echoed each other nearly word for word on this point. James W. Sheahan, editor of the *Chicago Times*, a newspaper personally financed by Douglas, was among his closest political associates, and Henry Martyn Flint, a Chicago lawyer and contributor to the newspaper, was part of the Douglas operation. Flint's *Life of Stephen A. Douglas* contained a section entitled "Mr. Douglas the Author of the Compromise of 1850," while Sheahan's *Life of Stephen A. Douglas* had Clay telling Douglas as he shook his hand "justice shall nevertheless be done to you as the real author of the measures." (Sheahan's volume was distributed on the chair of every delegate at the 1860 Democratic convention.) Douglas's deference to Clay, who had failed to pass the Compromise but was wreathed with its laurels as he was dying, had in his opinion deprived him of his rightful due. Now Clay and Webster were departed. The titans no longer overshadowed him. He held the stage alone. The vista opened before him, but on an even grander and more momentous scale, a feat spanning the continent with iron rails, reshaping the country so that it would become almost inevitable that its new creator would be delivered the prize he had been denied. He would replay his past and correct it. Now it would have the ending he wanted.

Douglas knew he had not recovered from his abortive campaign of 1852. Sanders's castigation of the "old fogies" left lasting scars. Buchanan had been the Southern favorite, and his "Buchaneers," like the ruthless Senator John Slidell of Louisiana, had stopped Douglas at the convention by throwing their votes to Pierce, and retained their ill will. Their scorn for Douglas had become an intrinsic element of their political identities. Pierce paid no price for excluding Douglas from patronage. The Buchanan men, the Cass men, and the Marcy men were united if on little else than their common object of loathing. No matter how many shots of whiskey he threw back with his fellow senators and how often he patted them on the back hardly any trusted Douglas. Rubbing shoulders with them often rubbed them the wrong way. The greater Douglas's ambition, the greater was the suspicion. Part of their wariness was that he was so obviously out only for himself. They always felt used. Ambition among politicians has never been considered a sin. But the Southerners believed he would never be loyal to a party they controlled. They mistrusted him for who he was. To them, he was a calculating, self-interested Vermont-born Yankee working on his own account. The aristocratic slaveholders among the politicians regarded his vulgarity with distaste. They recoiled from his appeals to Northern voters as a self-made man, a low figure appealing to lowly masses, and a classic rabble-rousing demagogue. His frequent spewing of the word "nigger" and his first wife's ownership of a plantation grated on them. They did not take these as nodding gestures of Southern favor, but emblems of a crowd-pleaser and social climber. They saw through him to the expedient heart of his contrived and plagiarized political philosophy of "popular sovereignty" as the vapid expression of his devious undependability. "Popular sovereignty" was marketing, and the product being sold was Douglas himself. By representing the dynamic potential of his own region, which would forge a unified north from sea to sea, a commercial nation that would inexorably dominate the South, they saw him as more insidiously dangerous than any mere abolitionist. His success on his own terms would advance the Free Soil agenda more effectively than any Free Soiler. But this was not how Douglas saw himself, and he sought to maneuver himself to become the leader of the whole party. But the more he contrived to get ahead, the more they loathed him.

Jefferson Davis developed a particular dislike for Douglas. His animosity curdled over time into a pet hate—"our little grog-drinking, electioneering demagogue," he called him in a letter to Franklin Pierce in 1860. He would denounce his "popular sovereignty" as a "dangerous innovation" and a "siren's song . . . a thing shadowy and fleeting, changing its color as often as a chameleon," and Douglas as "full of heresy." Davis began to despise Douglas after Davis had gleefully demolished Clay's "Omnibus" for the Compromise, driving Clay as a physically and politically wrecked man from the Senate, whereupon Douglas stepped in masterfully to manage passage of the legislation, making Davis the one to leave "weary" and "disgusted." However much Douglas repelled him then, Davis was by 1854 only at the early point in his contempt for the man and his manner.

Douglas believed in the raw power of the forces he arrayed behind himself. Through railroad politics, he would transform everything. He would concentrate the sheer dynamism of money and machine to a fine point. His magnetism would irresistibly sweep through all obstacles. He would deal with the Southerners, cutting them in as partners, his co-investors, just as he had cut in the Southern railroad men on the Illinois Central and Bright and the Southerners in the Superior City scheme. He would lay the track, be the engineer, and arrive triumphantly at the station. The hero of his party, he would rescue it from itself. He explained in 1855 "that his party, in the election of Pierce, had consumed all its powder, and that, therefore, without a deep-reaching agitation, it would have no more ammunition for its artillery."

His true view of his party was the one Sanders expressed about the "fogies." They were used up; only he had the reserve of power.

But there was more than a tinge of anxiety seeping through his confidence. If there was one consistent thread running through Douglas's congressional career it was his advocacy of the Pacific railroad, and if he had one imperative it was to build a northern route, and if there was one issue that united the South against him it was that. He had first proposed a transcontinental railroad in 1844, in his first term in the Congress, the first and only member to advance it. He brought it up again in 1848, and again in 1852. When Southerners defeated his bill that would provide federal protection for settlers in the territory, he assailed them with a "direct, open hostility to that section of the country."

After Pierce's election, in December 1852, Senator Thomas J. Rusk of Texas introduced a bill that would authorize the new president to choose a Pacific route. Rusk was a strenuous proponent of the Southern route that would run the entire length of Texas. He was a native South Carolinian, born in a house his tenant farmer father rented from John C. Calhoun, who apprenticed Rusk as a lawyer and protégé. After going west, he became the secretary of war of the Texas Republic, and was elected along with Sam Houston as the state's first U.S. senators. Rusk championed the building of railroads, and got himself cut in as an investor in railroad corporations and in the purchase of extensive tracts of land along which a Southern route would presumably be laid. Douglas, however, blocked Rusk's bill, guiding Shields to offer an amendment that funds could only be used for "a road within the limits of any existing state of the Union." That effectively killed the Rusk measure and a Southern route.

In early 1853, Douglas tried again through his ally Congressman Richardson in the House, who originated a Pacific railroad bill through the Nebraska Territory. Southerners suddenly announced themselves fervent protectors of the rights of Indians that would be trampled. Douglas's cause was not helped when Joshua Giddings interjected slavery into the debate, defending the sanctity of the Missouri Compromise. "This law stands perpetually," he proclaimed. On the morning of the final day of the 32nd Congress, March 4, Pierce's inaugural day, Southerners in the Senate defeated Douglas's bill. "I have been struck with the zeal which burns in some gentlemen's bosoms in behalf of the poor Indian," he remarked, observing, "it is necessary for them to avail themselves of some argument by which to resist this bill, and sympathy for the poor Indian is the argument that is resorted to."

The dead Douglas bill had one live offspring—funding for the next secretary of war's survey for a Pacific route. And when Jefferson Davis dispatched his surveyors they pointedly did not map a central route. He sent Gadsden for the purpose of purchasing the land from Mexico for the Southern way. In June, about one thousand Southern delegates gathered at the Memphis Commercial Convention that "demanded" a railroad "from the Mississippi Valley to the Pacific Ocean." (Calhoun had been chairman of a similar convention at Memphis in 1845 and Jefferson Davis had attended another in 1849.) On their way to the Crystal Palace Exhibition in New York, Davis and Pierce stopped in Philadelphia, where Davis stepped in to deliver a speech for the president, who had a cold. The July 12 speech was a ringing declaration of the president's intention to build a transcontinental railroad—a speech filled with hostile references clearly aimed at Douglas. Davis stated that the link to the Pacific was "not to be effected by stretching the powers of the federal government beyond their legitimate sphere"—an attack on Douglas's use of the "general welfare" clause as a basis for federal support for a railroad. Everyone knew, Davis said, he "belonged to the strict-construction school, which never turned to the right nor to the left to serve any purpose of expediency"—"expediency" his dismissive shorthand contemptuous word for Douglas. Only "the common defense" could serve as a constitutional basis for building the railroad; it was "a purely military question." And Davis had "always repelled the supposition that this government could build a road outside of the United States"—through the Nebraska Territory—which meant he favored only a Southern route. Shortly after Davis's speech the Texas legislature granted a railroad charter and land grant, for which the accepted bidder was the Atlantic and Pacific Company whose privileged investors included Senator Rusk.

By 1853, only about one thousand white people lived in the vast territory called Nebraska, an expanse larger than the eastern U.S., encompassing what would become the states of Nebraska, Kansas, the Dakotas, Montana, Colorado, and part of Wyoming. The main inhabitants were the Wyandot Indians, originally part of the Iroquois Nation, removed from New York and Ohio, most of them English speaking, as well as literate Methodists and farmers, who in 1853 took the initiative in setting up a provisional government to elect a congressional delegate, a cause championed by Benton. In reaction, Atchison's faction hastily sent its own delegate to Washington. A group of Iowans crossed into the territory and elected yet another delegate. Both men were named Johnson, and the "two Johnsons" demanded recognition, but the Congress rejected them. This miniature comic incident of competing delegates named Johnson was an augury of the blood-soaked revenge tragedy to come. It was also the earliest if unacknowledged applied case of Douglas's notion of popular sovereignty: nobody defined exactly who "the people" were; the presumed legitimacy of those chosen as delegates derived from whoever sent them; and the absence of clear boundaries and rules fostered chaos and conflict, the only true meaning of Douglas's "certain great fundamental principles."

During the debate on Douglas's Nebraska bill in March 1853, Senator David Atchison of Missouri at first opposed it, but reversed himself, "dodging from hedge to hedge like a stoned squirrel," according to the *New York Tribune*'s correspondent. The Indian title to the land "had not been extinguished," Atchison complained. But, most important, "there was no prospect, no hope of a repeal of the Missouri Compromise, excluding slavery from that Territory." He denounced the Ordinance of 1787 and "the next great error," the Missouri Compromise, but resignedly admitted, "There is no remedy for them. We must submit to them." Though he was clear that he supported the Missouri Compromise only under political duress and would repeal it if he could, he broke with every Southern senator to vote for Douglas's bill. At once, Atchison found himself on the defensive. His slaveholding constituents howled and Benton lashed him for his inconsistency. "Atchison vs. Atchison" ran the headline on the pro-Benton *Jefferson Inquirer*, calling him a "dead duck" and "hypocrite and double-dealer." The newspaper also reported Atchison's remark, "I had rather see the whole Territory sunk in hell, than to see it organized as free territory!" Benton traveled to the western Missouri counties that were Atchison's base and declared that the Indian treaties would not prevent immediately opening Nebraska to settlement. The pro-Benton *St. Louis Evening News* derided Atchison for his "ignorance." "Let him resign and hide himself in shame," the paper demanded.

The reeling Atchison tried to locate firm ground. "I will support a bill to organize a government for the Territory upon the condition that such bill contains no restriction upon the subject of slavery, and not otherwise," he pledged in a speech that June at Platte City in western Missouri. "I will vote for a bill that leaves the slaveholder and the non-slaveholder upon terms of equality. I am willing that the people who may settle there and who have the deepest interest in this question should decide it for themselves." At Platte City, the citizens that had gathered to hear him passed a resolution: "Resolved, that if the territory shall be opened to settlement, we pledge ourselves to each other to extend the institutions of Missouri over the territory, at whatever sacrifice of blood or treasure."

At rally after rally around the state Atchison pleaded for his new position. Fighting for his political life, he explained that it was a matter of life or death for Missouri. In August, at Parkville, he said:

> A large portion of my constituents are slaveholders. Could it be expected that I would be very anxious about organizing a Territory from which a large portion of my constituents would be excluded? The State of Missouri is now bounded on two sides by free States; organize this Territory as free territory then we are bounded on three sides by free States or Territories. What would be the effect upon slave property in Missouri and in this neighborhood it requires no prophet to tell. It is a problem not difficult to solve. The free States have a pious and philanthropic class of men who observe the "higher law" and whose duty it is to attend to other people's business and think that they are rendering God good service in stealing their neighbors' negroes. But, fellow citizens, that I may be clearly understood in relation to this point, I now declare to you that I will not vote for a bill to organize a government for the Territory of Nebraska unless that bill leaves the Territory open for settlement to all the people of the United States without restriction or limitation; open to the slaveholder as well as to the non-slaveholder. I will vote for no bill that directly or indirectly makes a discrimination between the citizens of the different States of this Union, North or South, slave or non-slaveholding; no bill that strikes at the equality of the States of this Confederacy.

On behalf of the extension of slavery he declared himself against "discrimination" and for "equality," while those he inspired pledged "blood or treasure." But Atchison did not claim he would demand repeal of the Missouri Compromise and his solution seemed to be popular sovereignty.

After hours Bourbon Dave and

David Rice Atchison

the Little Giant were "boon companions," and they shared fear and loathing of Benton. "He hates everybody and only regrets that every leading Democrat in America cannot be prostrated at once," Douglas wrote Lanphier about Benton. But Atchison mistrusted Douglas as much as any other member of the F Street Mess, perhaps more so because more was at stake for him. Douglas's insistent pursuit of his Pacific railroad, after all, had contributed to Atchison's jeopardy.

While Atchison savored late night drinks with Douglas he was more than willing to sacrifice him on the altar of his anxiety. He boasted that he had informed Douglas he would push him aside as chairman of the Committee on Territories in order to introduce a bill on Nebraska that would remove the prohibition on slavery if Douglas would not do it. The matter was so urgent that Atchison said he would resign as president pro tempore to take charge of the committee. According to Atchison's account, Douglas asked for twenty-four hours to consider the ultimatum. His control of the committee, in fact, was shaky. He only had a one-vote party majority, and that man was the utterly independent and unpredictable Sam Houston. Bright compounded the problem by adding a Democrat to every committee, each one loyal to the Southern Senate leadership. And the existing committee members were not followers of Chairman Douglas but mostly had long-standing ties to the leadership. Later, under intense criticism, Atchison renounced his story, explaining that he was "in liquor at the time." In a Senate debate in 1855, when antislavery senator Henry Wilson of Massachusetts claimed there had been "secret conclaves," Douglas vehemently insisted that was false. "No, sir," he said, "the Nebraska bill was not concocted in any conclave, night or day. It was written by myself, at my own house, with no man present." But, on the narrow question of Atchison, there were contemporary newspaper stories based on eyewitnesses who had heard " 'Dave' himself" at Parkville, Missouri, in September 1854 having "got 'glorious' a little earlier in the day than usual," standing in an "old wagon" to hold forth to the crowd, "with much spitting on his shirt." "Gentlemen," he was quoted, "you make a damned fuss about Douglas, but Douglas don't deserve the credit of this Nebraska bill. I told Douglas to introduce it. I originated it. I got Pierce committed to it, and all the glory belongs to me." In a subsequent speech at Platte City in 1855 at which he did not appear to be under the influence of liquor, even after his denial, Atchison claimed his credit: "Well, it was done. I do not say that I did it, but I was a prominent agent."

Years later, in 1880, in an article entitled "What Led to the War, or the Secret History of the Kansas-Nebraska Act," Colonel John A. Parker unambiguously asserted, "The author of the Kansas-Nebraska bill was not Mr. Douglas, but Mr. Atchison." Parker had been politically and socially well connected in Washington for decades, a longtime figure in the circle of Thomas Ritchie, chief of the Richmond Junto, editor of the *Richmond Enquirer* and in Pierce's time the *Washington Union*. Parker had been an intimate of Andrew Jackson, acted with Ritchie's son-in-law Thomas Green as claims agents in the capital for the Commonwealth of Virginia, was librarian of the House of Representatives, the secretary of the House Judiciary Committee, and would be appointed register of the Land Office of Nebraska. (Green would become a Confederate secret service agent at the center of the spy network in Washington, and after Lincoln's assassination was detained and questioned. Undoubtedly, he covered up his knowledge.) Parker was closely involved with the center of congressional power—the F Street Mess—and their intrigues. His firing as House librarian by John Forney, the House clerk who was installed by Pierce as editor of the administration's organ, the *Washington Union*, was among the precipitating causes of the F Street Mess withdrawing the government printing contract from the Union and giving it to the Southern Ultra–oriented *Sentinel*, an early signal of trouble to come.

According to Parker's account, Atchison's political fate was at the root of the matter. "His term in the Senate was about to expire and Mr. Benton was his most formidable competitor. The result of the contest was considered doubtful, and it was deemed by Mr. Atchison's friends important to strengthen him in Missouri, and to weaken Mr. Benton. How to do this was considered in 'secret session.' It is thought that only three, besides Mr. Atchison, knew in the early stages the programme marked out. Subsequently others were made acquainted with it. The originators of the plan fixed upon were Mr. Atchison and three other able and distinguished Southern Senators, men of great influence in the whole country, and especially influential in the South." Parker's account neglected many other factors surrounding the events, focused solely on Atchison and sketchy, but he was not an uninformed source.

Jefferson Davis offered further testimony in 1886 in a letter to a friend. "So far as I know and believe," he wrote, "they never were in such relation to each other as would have caused Douglas to ask Atchison's help in preparing the bill, and I think the whole discussion shows that Douglas originated the bill, and for a year or two vaunted himself on its paternity." The story, however, was not that Douglas sought Atchison's help or that Atchison assisted in literally "preparing" it, but that Atchison pressured Douglas. So, long after the events had transpired, Davis carefully elided whatever he knew on a note of contempt for the transparent opportunism of the Little Giant, still burning bright twenty-five years after his death.

Butler, the senior statesman of the F Street Mess, simply declared two years later on the floor of the Senate that Atchison "had perhaps more to do with the bill than any other Senator." And another interested party, Atchison's confederate Judge Price, insisted, "the South used Douglas," who was willing to be used in the belief he was also using the Southerners.

In the making of the Kansas-Nebraska Act there were many "secret conclaves." The "influential" Southerners around Atchison that Parker described were, of course, those of the F Street Mess. Frank Blair, then a congressman, spelled out the identities of Parker's three Southern senators in a speech in 1854: "Mr. Douglas has the credit of having originated this scheme of breaking compacts, fraught with such fatal tendencies. He does not deserve this precedence. It will be remembered that at the last session of Congress, Mr. Atchison broached the idea of dissolving the Missouri Compromise, in connection with the then pending Nebraska bill. Mr. Calhoun's Southern unit contrived to get Mr. Atchison made President *pro tem*, of the Senate. From that hour he became the tool of the Nullifiers, and when Mr. Calhoun died, he left his swaggering and sometimes staggering President *pro tem*, to the care of Messrs. Mason, Hunter and Butler, who were his factotums at the close of his life, and may be considered the executors of his estate of Nullification." In a letter to the *Missouri Democrat* on March 1, 1856, Blair wrote that the bill was "dictated by a squad of Nullifiers (*Atchison, Mason, Hunter & Co.*) to the Doughface Presidential aspirants from the North; that when Atchison, as he himself boasted, gave 'Douglas twenty-four hours to bring in the bill,' and the other Doughfaces had been won to the scheme by similar persuasives operating upon their anxiety for Presidential honors, of which being unworthy, they could only hope to gain by truckling and subserviency." Blair's pinpointing of the F Street Mess's influence was not a paranoid conspiracy theory about a cabal akin to the Illuminati, but as general a piece of knowledge among the political class in Washington as the weather. Saying the Mess had power was like saying the sky was blue. For his own purposes Blair's accusation made Douglas into a one-dimensional puppet. Yet if the willful Douglas was hardly likely to meekly accept dictation, he was cornered. His failure to pass his railroad bill at the conclusion of the last Congress had already convinced him he had to satisfy his Southern critics if he wished to accomplish his greater goals.

From everyone's point of view at the time, it was a complex case of mutual interest, advantage, and hatred. The Calhounites used Atchison's convenient predicament as a motive to repeal the Missouri Compromise, but by themselves were insufficient to accomplish the task. Just as the Southerners could control the presidency but only through a Northerner in the White House, they and Atchison needed the deus ex machina of Douglas, even if they thought him obnoxious and dangerous. Douglas, for his part, needed Atchison, the F Street Mess, Jefferson Davis, and President Pierce if he were to realize his railroad and political ambitions. From Douglas's point of view, having the common enemy in Benton proved fortuitous. If by forging the railroad he could save Atchison and finally kill off Benton he would receive the gratitude of the F Street Mess. Douglas would at last find his way through Southern mistrust. He would be recognized for his grand achievement, as he had not been for the Compromise of 1850. He would supersede his rivals, the "old fogies" and their cunning lieutenants Bright and Slidell. He would turn his investments in Superior City and Chicago into gold mines. He would solidify his supremacy over Illinois and the Northwest. He would stand as the most powerful Democrat, inevitable for anointment as the party's nominee and president. His motives were not one thing or another, but all of these, and he had no time whatsoever to contemplate which of his reasons might be foremost. Suspicion, contempt, and misgivings were overcome for a brief moment to get the business done.

Even before Douglas introduced any bill in the new session Atchison's desire to repeal the Missouri Compromise as the price for organizing the Nebraska Territory was an open secret. The *New York Post*, the newspaper of the Softs, observed on November 15, 1853, that Atchison "has declared his determination to oppose the early organization of the Territory of Nebraska and the opening of the country to white colonists . . . he intimated that he was unwilling to consent to the organization of another Territory on the principle of the Ordinance of 1787." The *New York Journal of Commerce* reported on December 14, "Mr. Atchison of Missouri will move to repeal that restriction in regard to Nebraska." The *Richmond Enquirer* was especially well informed, its Washington correspondent, "Fairfax," writing on December 16, "Notice has been given in Congress of the introduction of a bill for the creation of a territorial government for Nebraska." The threat of Benton loomed over the process. "The facts relating to the matter should be understood and the objects of Mr. Benton and those who act with him cannot be mistaken. To prevent the Southerners from carrying their property into Nebraska, to have another free State touching the slave State of Missouri, to influence the next August elections in Missouri, and the presidential campaign of 1856: these are the objects of Mr. Benton and his freesoil allies." Ten days later, "Fairfax" presciently reported, "The President of the Senate, Mr. Atchison, is pledged by his speeches before the people of Missouri to move the repeal of the law prohibiting slavery in the Territory north of the parallel 36° 30'. He will oppose the Nebraska territorial bill and insist upon the admission of slavery into the Territory, if it be established at all, both on the original constitutional ground, and also upon the ground that it would be prejudicial to the interests of Missouri to be surrounded by a cordon of free States. Mr. Douglas will soon report the Nebraska bill and we shall witness a renewal thereupon of slavery agitation." The state of play was already known.

The action began on the first day of the 34th Congress on December 5 when committee assignments were given and chairmen selected. Senator Augustus Caesar Dodge of Iowa, an ally of Douglas on the Pacific railroad, was designated chairman of the Committee on Public Lands, and he promptly gave notice he would file a bill for the organization of Nebraska, which he did on the 14th, a bill identical to the Douglas bill that had been defeated on the last day of the previous Congress. For Dodge, as for Douglas, building the railroad was an urgent priority. He and his fellow Iowa senator, George Wallace Jones, had originally sought to amend the original Illinois Central Act for the road to extend its western terminus to Dubuque, supported by Douglas, but stymied by Congressman Edward D. Baker, Lincoln's friend, who represented the northwest corner of Illinois and insisted that the Illinois Central's western extension end there, in Galena. Dodge, who had been register of the Land Office in Iowa in the 1840s, had accumulated wide real estate interests through western Iowa, as did Senator Jones, from Dubuque. Both were heavily invested in railroads and their potential. Dodge was a director of the Dubuque and Pacific Railroad Company, whose future depended on linking to the transcontinental railroad. Within months of filing his bill, both Dodge and Jones were among the initial investors forming the Sioux City Land Company to found a new city in western Iowa along the projected route.

Dodge and Jones were, along with Bright, the two senators from the Northwest most tightly connected to the Southern leadership, and both had been close to Jefferson Davis since their youth. Dodge was the son of Henry Dodge, the senator from Wisconsin, the only father and son ever to serve simultaneously. Henry Dodge was a slaveholder, who brazenly brought his slaves from Missouri to the free state of Illinois and territory of Wisconsin to work in his lead mines. He became the first governor of the Wisconsin Territory. Jones was Henry Dodge's best friend since they were young men together in the frontier town of Ste. Genevieve, Missouri. When Colonel Dodge Sr. led the Mounted Rangers in the Black Hawk War he naturally named Jones his aide-de-camp. Dodge Sr.'s adjutant was Lieutenant Jefferson Davis. Jones had been a classmate of both Davis and David Atchison at Transylvania University, and with Davis he established "a friendship whose warmth knew no abatement during life," according to Jones's biographer. Jones, he wrote, "was a Democrat in politics and a Southerner in instincts." Young Augustus Dodge accompanied his father and Jones as an aide-de-camp during the Black Hawk War, and "divided his rations" with Jefferson Davis. Just as Dodge Sr. acted as Jones's mentor, Jones was Dodge Jr.'s in his Iowa political career. (Iowa was originally part of the Wisconsin Territory.) When Dodge was elected a senator in 1848, Senator Jefferson Davis performed the honor of presenting his credentials. Both Dodge and Jones remained close friends of Davis, but especially Jones, who also served on Douglas's Committee on Territories, ostensibly part of the Northern balance but always a reliable Southern vote, a constant reminder to Douglas of his tenuous situation. It was almost certain that Dodge and Jones ensured that Jefferson Davis was kept well informed.

Dodge's bill was reported to Douglas and his committee, and he launched on his journey down his slippery slope of popular sovereignty. The *Illinois State Register*, Douglas's mouthpiece, on December 22 signaled that the doctrine would be applied to Nebraska. "The Territories," Lanphier editorialized, "should be admitted to exercise, as nearly as practicable, all the rights claimed by the States and to adopt all such political regulations and institutions as their wisdom may suggest."

On January 4, Douglas presented his report with amendments to the original Dodge bill, adding the exact language from the Utah and New Mexico Territorial Acts that were part of the Compromise of 1850. Meditating on the Missouri Compromise, he paid homage to the Calhounite view but reserved judgment on taking the leap. "In the opinion of those eminent statesmen, who hold that Congress is invested with no rightful authority to legislate upon the subject of slavery in the Territories," he wrote, "the 8th section of the act preparatory to the admission of Missouri is null and void; while the prevailing sentiment in large portions of the Union sustains the doctrine that the Constitution of the United States secures to every citizen an inalienable right to move into any of the Territories with his property, of whatever kind and description, and to hold and enjoy the same under the sanction of law. Your committee do not feel themselves called upon to enter upon the discussion of these controverted questions. They involve the same grave issues which produced the agitation, the sectional strife, and the fearful struggle of 1850."

While giving credence to the Southern Rightist view, Douglas asserted that "the same grave issues" involved in 1850 were at stake with Nebraska. His solution was to impose the same answer used for the Utah and New Mexico territories. But those territories were not the same historically or legally. Nebraska fell under the Missouri Compromise of 1820 while Utah and New Mexico had been gained through the Mexican War, and under Mexican law had prohibited slavery. The Compromise of 1850 dealing with those two territories also ratified within it the Missouri Compromise, which retained Nebraska in the sphere for future free states. While that compromise laid a border that prohibited slavery "forever" in the North, Douglas tried to get around that seeming obstacle through the artful suggestion that he was merely extending part of the Compromise of 1850. He somehow convinced himself that nobody would notice. He hoped that his fog of ambiguity, sophistry, and historical amnesia would obscure the entire question. Cleverness would do the trick.

In 1849 Douglas had called the Missouri Compromise "a sacred thing, which no ruthless hand would ever be reckless enough to disturb." But now he was attempting to alter the status of Nebraska through sleight of hand. "At what precise time Mr. Douglas changed his views on this subject cannot be determined," wondered George Ticknor Curtis, Webster's friend and the biographer of James Buchanan. Curtis was not alone among contemporaries who watched the play but could not see the backstage machinations, though sensing them.

In the three days between the publication of Douglas's bill on December 7 and its publication again on the 10th the text suddenly gained a new section—Section Twenty-one—originally omitted because of a "clerical error," according to the *Washington Sentinel*. Whatever caused the addition it displayed physical evidence of Douglas's panic. A copyist in the employ of the committee had carefully written the first twenty sections on unblemished white paper. Attached to this flawlessly produced document was a single sheet of blue paper, ripped in half, with the twenty-first section written in Douglas's scrawl, pasted to the other pages with sealing wax. At the bottom of the bill appeared words dashed in pencil: "Douglas reports Bill & read 1 & to 2 reading special report Print agreed."

Douglas's original report did not mention slavery. But the bill incorporated explicitly what had only been previously hinted.

> *Section 21. And be it further enacted,* That in order to avoid all misconstruction, it is hereby declared to be the true intent and meaning of this act, so far as the question of slavery is concerned, to carry into practical operation the following propositions and principles established by the compromise measures of 1850, to-wit: *First:* That all questions pertaining to slavery in the Territories and in the new States to be formed therefrom, are to be left to the decision of the people residing therein, through their appropriate representatives. *Second:* That all cases involving "title to slaves," and "questions of personal freedom," are referred to the adjudication of the local tribunals, with the right of appeal to the Supreme Court of the United States.

What Douglas had sought to imply slyly in his committee report he now openly stated in his amended bill. Within seventy-two hours, his measure passed from suggestion to proclamation. Its mysterious transformation spawned endless speculation. Two years later, during a Senate debate, Senator Henry Wilson of Massachusetts said that he had "conversed with gentlemen whose veracity I cannot question" who had heard Atchison brag he was the author of the repeal of the Missouri Compromise and that he had pressured Douglas. Douglas responded calling the claim that Atchison had given him twenty-four hours to accept repeal or he would usurp his chairmanship "a vile Abolition libel." Douglas's defense rested on this sole objection, quibbling over whether Atchison had threatened him on the fine points of overt repeal and the twenty-four-hour ultimatum. Douglas then explained he had shown his bill first to Bright and "another northwestern senator," and after they endorsed it "we consulted our Southern friends." Douglas created the impression he had not spoken to Atchison but instead an unnamed "northwestern senator," though both Atchison and Benton called Missouri a "northwestern" state, a fairly common designation. About the identities of "our Southern friends" Douglas was silent. On the timing of these meetings, Douglas produced no dates. Whatever his dodging, Douglas appeared to be forthright about the substance of the matter in another debate in 1856. Challenged by antislavery Senator Lyman Trumbull of Illinois, in exasperation he blurted, "He [Trumbull] knew, or, if not, ought to know that the bill, in the shape in which it was first reported, as effectually repealed the Missouri restriction as it afterwards did when the repeal was put in express terms." But that was far from obvious at the moment to the interested players, who shared an understanding that Douglas was not to be trusted. Far from clearly stating that point from the beginning, Douglas deliberately fudged it. His original bill, in fact, had not "effectively repealed" the Missouri Compromise but incorporated the Compromise of 1850 that reaffirmed it while his Twenty-first section, his "clerical error," proposed a policy of nonintervention establishing popular sovereignty that could trump it. In short, his bill was more than literally pasted together; it was contradictory and self-canceling. More than an untidy document with its torn page and sealing wax, it was a political oxymoron.

After Douglas submitted his report but before filing his bill, the *New York Times* reported on January 6, "Senator Douglas' Nebraska bill dissatisfies ultra Southerners, who are concocting another one, which makes two territories at once." The newspaper observed that Atchison "has for sometime been understood to favor" repealing the Missouri Compromise, "and without which he proposes to vote against the measure." The *Times*'s story clearly identified the source of the pressure that led Douglas to revise his bill a day later, but that cut-and-pasted job was still unsatisfactory.

The day after the bill was filed Congressman Philip Phillips of Alabama quietly approached Senator Hunter and other members of the F Street Mess. His opinions carried great weight with them. The leading lawyer in Alabama, counsel for the Bank of Mobile, the railroads, and other corporations, he had been chairman of the state Democratic Party, and served in the legislature. But that alone did not signify his unique standing. He was a native South Carolinian, the heir to the most prominent Jewish family in Charleston, the oldest Jewish community and among the most populous in the country. His maternal grandfather had been a Revolutionary War hero. Phillips studied

Philip Phillips

law under John Gadsden, mayor of Charleston and U.S. attorney, who was James Gadsden's brother. During the nullification crisis, Phillips was elected to the South Carolina convention and opposed Calhoun. After his marriage to Eugenia Levy, daughter of a wealthy Charleston and Savannah merchant, they moved to Mobile. He reluctantly agreed to election to the House of Representatives, taking a drastic cut in income, but only for one term. In Washington he and his wife were immediately accepted into the highest social circles. Eugenia was a close friend of Virginia Clay, the wife of Senator Clement Clay, who would become Jefferson Davis's mistress, and also part of the intimate Davis coterie. (In 1861, Eugenia was arrested as a Confederate spy and exiled to the South only through her husband's relationship with Edwin Stanton, the former attorney general, though not yet secretary of war, with whom Phillips often practiced before the Supreme Court. Eugenia had carried a coded message hidden in a ball of yarn to Richmond, which she delivered to Jefferson Davis.) To the denizens of the Mess, Phillips was a trusted figure of prudent judgment, possessing an acute legal mind, a Southern Rightist but not a firebrand.

Phillips explained to Hunter that Douglas's bill was "delusive." Far from overriding the Missouri Compromise, it would reinforce it. "By the operation of the Act of 1820, the door is now closed to the Southern man who might choose to locate in these territories with his slaves. You propose only to open the door when a constitution is made for the state. But when this period arrives there can be in the Territory no slave-holder for the Act of 1820 bars him out. If it is desirable to carry out the declaration of the Bill, they must be thrown open to all alike, and this can only be effected by *a repeal of the inhibition in the Act of 1820*." If Phillips felt that Douglas's bill was deficient, then it must be.

The next day Phillips encountered Atchison, who said, "Hunter tells me you say, Douglas' bill does not repeal the Missouri Compromise Act. This surprises me." Atchison apparently had thought that Douglas's newly revised measure was a de facto repeal. But Phillips explained to him why it was not. Atchison asked Phillips to meet him and Douglas the next day in the vice president's private office in the Capitol. Atchison was obviously in close contact with Douglas. And as president pro tempore of the Senate, after Vice President King's death, he occupied all his physical offices, and senators and members of the administration routinely referred to him as the vice president.

The following morning, January 10, Atchison, Douglas, and Phillips met at the vice president's office. "Mr. Atchison opened the conference by stating my opinion," recalled Phillips. "Mr. Douglas said he thought the Bill did repeal the inhibition of the Act of 1820." Phillips patiently laid out his logic, and concluded by telling Douglas nicely but frankly "that repeal by implication was not allowed, but could only be effected by express words, or by the passage of an act so inconsistent with a former act that the two could not co-exist." According to Phillips, "Mr. Douglas seemed impressed with these remarks, and the conference was soon ended." Douglas now knew that his bill was no longer acceptable to Atchison and the Mess.

While Douglas contemplated his next move, a thunderbolt was thrown onto the Senate floor. Without a hint of prior notice, Senator Archibald Dixon, a Whig from Kentucky, flung out an amendment on January 16 to repeal the Missouri Compromise—"that the citizens of the several States and Territories shall be at liberty to take and hold their slaves within any of the Territories of the United States, or of the States to be formed therefrom, as if the said act, entitled as aforesaid and approved as aforesaid, had never been passed." With the Dixon amendment, Douglas's effort to skirt around repeal "by implication" was rendered moot. Dixon's wife claimed he had "consulted no one in this matter." But he was "a personal friend of Mr. Atchison," according to the well-informed Colonel John A. Parker. It is possible if not likely that he had heard rumors of the backroom dealings and as a member of the endangered Southern Whig Party decided to stage a preemptive strike to outflank the Democrats before he was himself outflanked.

Dixon was an old friend and political ally of Henry Clay—and his betrayer. He rose in Kentucky as one of Clay's followers, a dutiful state legislator and lieutenant governor. But by 1849 Dixon joined with the pro-slavery forces of Robert Wickliffe, the Old Duke, the antagonist of Clay and his remaining band of brothers, notably Robert S. Todd, to overturn the old state constitution in order to open the floodgates of the slave trade in Kentucky. "All of his means he invested in land and negroes, and in 1854, he had become one of the wealthiest planters and largest slave-owners in Southern Kentucky," recalled Dixon's wife. He had been "warmly attached" to Henry Clay, "yet he differed with him in toto as regarded emancipation in Kentucky." The convention rewriting Kentucky's constitution rejected Clay's tempering approach that viewed slavery as an evil that should be gradually extinguished and marked the triumph of the Southern Rightist slaveholder faction determined to break down the historic legal constraints that had set Kentucky apart from the Deep South. It was a counter-revolution. And it was the consequence of this debacle—Clay's political defeat at the hands of the pro-slavery faction in the aftermath of Todd's tragic death—that Lincoln witnessed as the attorney brought in to represent the Todd heirs versus Wickliffe in the suit involving the Todd family fortune.

While Lincoln was failing to secure justice for his wife and her family, Dixon served on the executive committee of the constitutional convention, and it was he who proposed the clause in the new constitution protecting slavery, codified in the state's new bill of rights: "The right of property is before and higher than any constitutional sanction; and the right of the owner of a slave to such slave, and its increase, is the same, and as inviolable as the right of the owner of any property whatever." In 1851, Dixon ran for governor, but narrowly lost when Cassius Clay as the candidate of the Emancipation Party split off a sliver of dissident antislavery Whigs. Nonetheless, Dixon was chosen to replace Henry Clay upon his death in the Senate.

Just as Dixon had undone Clay's careful work in maintaining Kentucky as the most moderate Southern state, he came to Washington on a mission to topple Clay's national monument. His wife recalled his thinking: "It was an absolute necessity to the South to have some place of exodus for the large yearly increase of her slave population, which in time threatened to make of her a second San Domingo"—meaning black revolutionary Haiti—"and it was also a necessity to her to acquire more slave States in order to protect herself from the acquirement by the Northern States of that three fourths majority in legislation, which would enable them, *constitutionally*, to set the slaves of the South free, without deportation, without compensation to their owners, and under whatever laws that majority might choose to enact." The Missouri Compromise stood as the obstacle. Its continuing presence threatened future emancipation.

The moment Dixon introduced his amendment Douglas rushed up to him on the Senate floor. "No one," Dixon wrote, "appeared more startled." He "remonstrated against my amendment," arguing that his bill in effect opened the territory and that Dixon should be "wise and patriotic" in withdrawing his measure, which would undermine the Compromise of 1850. Dixon flatly refused.

The morning after Dixon filed his amendment his house was overflowing with celebrants.

"The Kentucky delegation was a unit in enthusiasm over the repeal," wrote his wife. Congressman William Preston, from Louisville, Wickliffe's son-in-law, who had been a delegate to the state constitutional convention, opened the front door halfway, peeked in, broke into a smile and exclaimed, "Eureka!" Congressman John C. Breckinridge, from Lexington, the distant cousin and childhood friend of Mary Todd, burst in, grabbed Dixon's hand, and "said in the most impressive way, and with the greatest emphasis, 'Governor, why did none of us ever think of this before?' "

Charles Sumner took the opening that Dixon had created to offer a counter-amendment upholding the Missouri Compromise, a symmetrical polarization. On January 20, the *Washington Union*, the administration's newspaper, denounced both Dixon's and Sumner's proposals as equally pernicious, and yet exposed its own divided and paralyzed mind. On the one hand, it stated, "it would be uncandid in us if we did not add, that a clause in the compromise of 1800 and in Mr. Douglas's Nebraska bill, declaring the act of 1820 null and void because it contravenes the principle of congressional non-intervention, would have made both of these measures more in consonance with our opinions and wishes." On the other hand, it confessed, "But we accepted the acts of 1850 as they were passed, and approved their passage as a final compromise."

About two days after Dixon had offered his amendment, Douglas came to his house in his carriage and asked him to join him for a drive "so that they might have the opportunity to talk uninterruptedly," recalled Dixon's wife. As they rode through the streets of Washington Douglas made Dixon repeat his arguments. These were, of course, the same ones he had heard from Phillips. By the end of the ride Douglas conceded that he would agree to the repeal. "By God, sir, you are right," he said, "and I will incorporate it in my bill, though I know it will raise a hell of a storm."

Though he gave Dixon the impression he would support his amendment, Douglas would never embrace it. He did not want to reward a Southern Whig who could do nothing for him instead of Southern Democrats who could. If he were to back a repeal bill Southern Democrats would write it, but without his fingerprints. The day after he made his promise to Dixon he visited Phillips at his home along with Breckinridge, who had praised Dixon but was after all a Democrat. Douglas asked Phillips to compose a repeal amendment on the spot. After reading it, Douglas posed a loaded question. "Is this satisfactory to you?" he said. If it were, Douglas could feel safe that it was acceptable to the Mess. "Of course what I myself propose must be satisfactory to me," Phillips replied, "but I understood your inquiry to have a wider significance, and to refer generally to the Southern representatives— and so understanding I say, I have no right to speak for others until their wishes can be ascertained." He told Douglas he would give him his answer in two days.

Either that evening or the next day, Phillips held a "conference with the Mess." All, he recorded, were in attendance—"Vice President Atchison, Senators Hunter and Mason of Virginia, Butler of South Carolina, Goode, Representative of Virginia." (Messmate William O. Goode, a wealthy plantation owner, was closely aligned with his fellow Virginians, Hunter and Mason, and had been a member of the Calhounite Young Chivalry faction.) "There was a general concurrence in the propriety of the repeal," wrote Phillips.

The following day, January 21, he said he "informed Mr. Douglas of this concurrence." "Very good," replied Douglas, "tomorrow night we will go to the White House and see President Pierce on the subject." But that day would be a Sunday and Phillips knew that Pierce did not conduct business on Sundays. Douglas waved away his concern. He "assured me the visit would not be unacceptable—(this would indicate that Mr. D had already conferred with the President)." Phillips's intuition about Douglas's contacts with the White House proved correct.

As Douglas was telling Phillips to prepare to visit the White House on Sunday, a wavering Pierce was presiding over a tumultuous cabinet meeting. Both Marcy and Senator Cass had warned the president that endorsing repeal would shatter the party in the North, and Pierce pledged to Cass that he would stand against it. "It is understood," the New York Herald reported, "Messrs. Jefferson Davis and Dobbin took strong grounds in favor of the abrogation of the compromise of 1820, whilst the other members of the Cabinet sustained the bill as reported by Judge Douglas." (James C. Dobbin, secretary of the navy, Davis's closest cabinet ally, was a former North Carolina congressman, who had declared slavery and its extension protected by "the sacred guarantees of the Constitution"—"the South will maintain her rights"—"Did Mr. Jefferson suppose, when he said that 'all men are created equal,' that this would ever be tortured to support the doctrine that slaves should not be held?") The cabinet adopted a temporizing amendment that left the entire matter "to be adjusted by a decision of the Supreme Court." Pierce and Cushing, the attorney general, believed the Missouri Compromise was unconstitutional and would easily be overturned, a position relieving the administration of the problem they were certain the pro-slavery majority of the Court would decide. Pierce wanted the repeal without the difficulty of the politics of repeal. But the life of the cabinet's amendment did not even last through the day.

The freshly inked document was handed to Breckinridge, ready to act as messenger. He brought it to Douglas, who eagerly approved it, and the Mess, whose members rejected it out of hand. Nothing less than repeal was acceptable to them—and Jefferson Davis was on their side. Douglas had reached out to him to arrange the meeting with Pierce to break his tradition of rest on the Sabbath, and it was set.

On the day of the cabinet conference, but before the event, the *Washington Union* editorialized for repeal as if in expectation. The *Union*, the *New York Herald* reported derisively, would soon attempt to "reconcile its shuffling course. . . . How many hours it may take to repudiate its article of tomorrow must depend upon the number of friends Judge Douglas' amendment proves to have."

That evening, Douglas had dinner at the home of James Campbell, Pierce's postmaster general, of Pennsylvania. The other guests had Pennsylvania connections in common and were all Democrats—Senator Slidell, of Louisiana, was James Buchanan's political confidant, and Congressman Galusha Grow an antislavery Democrat who was David Wilmot's law partner and successor to his House seat. "Douglas, you ought to make one Territory and repeal the Missouri Compromise," Slidell suggested. Presumably, then, the whole territory would be safe for slavery.

"I mentioned to Benton that I had dined with Douglas the night before," Grow recalled, "and that he seemed undecided as to which position he should take in the Kansas and Nebraska Bill, and was fluctuating in his views about slavery expansion. I added that I believed that Douglas was inclined to lead the Democracy away from its moorings. 'My God, Galusha,' cried Benton, 'have you the faintest idea that Steve Douglas is leading the Democracy anywhere? Why, the Democracy has led him around by the nose for years, and he's got so that he would follow it to hell if the majority went in that direction.' " Benton joked that Douglas should have been a milliner. "Trimming," he said, "was his chief vocation!"

The Sunday White House conference was now urgent. The next day, Monday, the Nebraska bill would top the order of business, Dixon's amendment would be attached, the Mess was adamantly for repeal, and the cabinet hopelessly split. A caravan headed to the White House. Douglas picked up Atchison at F Street in his carriage and the rest followed on foot—Hunter, Mason, Goode, Breckinridge, and Phillips.

According to Jefferson Davis's account, written in a letter to Mrs. Dixon in 1879, the entire entourage first dropped by his house. Davis claimed it was his first glimmer of the controversy, which had dominated Washington for two weeks. "Of the preliminary action, my engrossing duties in the War Office rendered me but little attentive," he wrote disingenuously. In fact, he had strenuously favored repeal during the cabinet meeting the day before. "After considering the terms of the bill," he continued, "and seeing in them nothing which I could not approve, or from which I believed the President would dissent, I told the gentlemen that they were either a day too late or too early, that the President received no visitors on Sunday, but that they could readily consult him tomorrow." But Douglas had already consulted with him to arrange the Sunday meeting, which Douglas had explained to Phillips. Davis, however, insisted in his letter that they had to convince him that time was of the essence and "that they had therefore come to me to secure for them an interview with the President." In Davis's telling he marched with them forthwith to the White House, leaving them to cool their heels while he spoke with Pierce, and "after explaining to him the circumstances of the visit, he returned with me to meet the gentlemen waiting."

Every detail of Jefferson Davis's version was incredible. It would have been inconceivable that the secretary of war would have sprung a surprise on the president forcing him on the spot to decide on the most momentous issue he would ever face. As a senator Davis had seized the banner against the Missouri Compromise from Calhoun, had opposed the Compromise of 1850 not least because it incorporated the older compromise, and argued vehemently for repeal in the cabinet. He knew that Pierce was against the Missouri Compromise but wary of the consequences of repeal. He also knew that the Compromise of 1850 was the linchpin of Pierce's politics. Davis would never have brought the wolfish Douglas and the lords of the Congress into a meeting with the president without the slightest advance warning. The F Street Mess, complicit with Davis, had already crippled Pierce, denied his favored newspaper the government printing contract as a warning of his favor to the Softs, and held up patronage in New York to encourage the Hards. They could bury any presidential appointment, proposal, or treaty. Through these defeats and frustrations for Pierce, Davis was using the Mess to play a backdoor game. His claim to have been previously uninformed and disengaged, and to have been startled at the appearance of Douglas and the Mess on his doorstep, paints the self-portrait of the most powerful man in the administration, the acting president, as a faux naïf, and must be taken as self-exculpatory ex post facto fictionalization.

According to an apparently well-informed report in the *New York Her-*

ald published two days after the White House meeting, when the F Street Mess rejected the cabinet proposal Pierce urged that they work out an agreement with Douglas. "This fact having been communicated to the President, he begged his friends to get the leading members together for consultation yesterday (Sunday)." His reticence about meeting with them on a Sunday because of his "religious scruples" was a ploy to avoid his direct participation. "The gentlemen did not appreciate the difference between the propriety of the President directing them to discuss the matter, Sunday though it was, and his joining in the discussion himself, then stated *through Mr. Atchison,* that if the President declined to discuss the proposition, they would take it for granted that he favored it and would regard the amendment abrogating the Missouri Compromise as an Administration measure. Upon this the President spoke and after sundry gyrations, agreed that the bill should be reported, and said the Administration would then take ground." Davis, of course, would have been privy to this little dance.

According to Phillips's account, Douglas and Atchison reached the White House before the others. "When we arrived, we found the President in the Library. He was standing and so were Douglas and Atchison. I was struck by the cold formality which seemed to prevail. The subject was soon entered upon; but I do not propose to repeat what occurred further than this:—The president said, 'Gentlemen, you are entering on a serious undertaking, and the ground should be well surveyed before the first step is taken.' "

In Davis's version, he counseled Pierce before he met with the group. "When the bill had been fully explained to him, its text, its intent, and its purpose, he, as anticipated, declared his opinion in its favor, and the gentlemen left him with the assurance they came to obtain before testing the question of their bill before the two Houses of Congress." Davis's telltale words were "as anticipated," disclosing that Pierce indeed had been prepared, coached, and ready to give his answer. Ultimately, one man forced the decision on the indecisive Pierce, alone with him, while the F Street Mess waited expectantly on the other side of the door, and that was Jefferson Davis.

When Pierce, Davis, Douglas, Phillips, Breckinridge, and the Mess agreed to the terms of a new bill it was more than a mere deal. It was a pact replacing the peace treaties of 1820 and 1850, a new vision of the relations of the North and South, of the compact governing free and slave states, a new Union. It was the opposite of a compromise; it was the collapse of Pierce's belief in the Compromise in the face of the Calhounites through the counsel of Jefferson Davis. Now the territory would be divided into two, Kansas and Nebraska; the Fugitive Slave Act strengthened; Douglas's Twenty-first section, the "clerical error," eliminated, the strained euphemism extraneous; popular sovereignty enshrined, a bone to Douglas; and, in the pièce de résistance, the Missouri Compromise was repealed.

Douglas did not trust Pierce to keep to the bargain, knowing him to make countless promises that simply evaporated. Pierce meant well, imitated the appearance of a man of conviction, shook hands on it, and often forgot whatever he had pledged. He wanted to make people happy, to have them like him, to do the right thing in the eyes of others. But even with Jefferson Davis acting as Pierce's iron spine Douglas would not leave the room until he had irrevocable proof of Pierce's commitment. He asked Pierce to write out the section of the new bill that repealed the Missouri Compromise in his own hand. "Douglas told me," Galusha Grow recalled, "that he kept the penciled amendment so that there should not be any misunderstanding about it afterwards with the President."

Pierce scrawled out for Douglas the crucial lines of the bill, that the Missouri Compromise "was superseded by the principles of the legislation of 1850, commonly called the compromise measures, and is hereby declared inoperative and void," and that "the people" of a territory or state were "perfectly free to form and regulate their domestic regulations in their own way." The repeal was therefore accomplished without using the word "repeal." It was achieved through the sophistry of asserting the Missouri Compromise had been "superseded" by the Compromise of 1850, though that act had incorporated the earlier one, and investing the consent of the governed in "the people," who were an amorphous, undefined, and then nonexistent body. And then Douglas pocketed the paper on which Pierce had written the bill in his own hand.

CHAPTER FOURTEEN

A SELF-EVIDENT LIE

D ouglas believed his best-laid plans would gain him every prize. He would win the favor of all parts of the Democratic Party, sail his bill safely through its factions, North and South, Scylla and Charybdis. He would be hailed for his legislative genius that once again had saved the Union. He would build the transcontinental railroad. He would multiply his wealth into a fortune. He would be president. "It is within the author's personal knowledge," wrote Samuel S. Cox, an influential Ohio Democrat and later a congressman who was close to Douglas, "that Mr. Douglas was averse to the Dixon proposition. Reluctantly he amended his bill by adopting Dixon's proposition." But the version of the Missouri Compromise repeal that he finally adopted was the one that Phillips and the F Street Mess advised the president to sign under the watchful gaze of Jefferson Davis. "He undertook to defend it on a principle"—popular sovereignty. But, according to Cox, Douglas

John Pettit

had an agenda that he did not make public. "He decided to divide the territory into two governments. He thought to make one slave, and one free state." After obliterating the Missouri Compromise, Douglas now would re-create a new line of demarcation, providing something for each side—Kansas a slave state, Nebraska a free one. Cox's reminiscence, undoubtedly based on his conversations with Douglas, disclosed that rather than establishing the basis for Kansas and Nebraska to be free states Douglas intended one of them to be a slave state. His ulterior design contradicted his frequent claim during the debate over the Compromise of 1850 that slavery would be "effectively excluded" from the new territories "by the laws of nature, of climate." The reality known to all was that slavery flourished in western Missouri on land no different from and contiguous with Kansas. In splitting the territory, the nonintervention principle would be invoked to justify an armed intervention to secure slavery in at least half of it. And there was another underlying motive to the division of the territory into Kansas and Nebraska. With two territories there would be two routes for the Pacific railroad, one northern and one central, one originating in Superior City and one in Chicago. Two territories meant that Douglas could achieve all his aims, including two windfall profits. "He proposed," recalled Cox, "but events disposed of his scheme."

As Douglas was leaving the White House with Phillips and Breckinridge, Pierce stopped them and suggested as an afterthought, "I wish you would go and see Marcy." The secretary of state had strongly opposed repeal in the cabinet meeting, was anxious about the holdup of the appointment of the New York port collector, and trying to prevent an irrevocable schism in the New York party. After excluding him from the decisive conference, Pierce wanted someone other than himself to inform the imposing Marcy. But Douglas did not go to see him. Marcy, in any case, was out to dinner. He learned about the decision reading the next morning's newspapers. The *Union* published an editorial, written by Cushing, declaring that the "policy of the administration" had been "directly involved"—but conspicuously not Marcy. Davis, in effect, had staged a coup against him. Now, according to the *Union*, the question would "be regarded by the Administration as a test of Democratic orthodoxy."

"The administration, it is now reported," according to the *New York Herald*, "consider Senator Douglas' Nebraska bill set as a trap to catch the 'softs' on the slavery question." Upon learning of it, the Softs were whipped into an uproar. They packed into the boardinghouse room of Congressman Reuben Fenton, Democrat of New York, and designated him as their representative to venture up Pennsylvania Avenue to discover firsthand what was happening. Pierce was perplexed at the Softs' discontent; after all, he told Fenton, he had "shown them at least equal consideration in the distribution of patronage," and expected their support. Fenton respectfully replied that he could never vote for "a measure so utterly opposed alike to his yawning abyss convictions and his sense of duty." Pierce urged him not to behave hastily and instead to be a good party man. He seemed to believe that although he had just declared the Compromise of 1850 "inoperative and void" it would still serve as a phantom holding the party together. With childlike denial he refused to accept that he had changed the essential dynamics, turning the centripetal into the centrifugal. Politics began to spin apart.

After seeing the president, Fenton went to call on Marcy. The secretary of state felt that the country and party were on the eve of catastrophe. "This Pandora's box—the Nebraska question," he had written his ally, Governor Horatio Seymour of New York. In a darkened mood, uttering "grave apprehensions," Marcy declined to urge Fenton to support the president and instead told him that every man must follow his own conscience. The once great Marcy, power broker from the days of Jackson, was overcome with a sense of futility. "Marcy is sullen, sour, and swears out of both sides of his mouth," a New York newspaper reported. A few days later Marcy summoned a half dozen of his closest friends and allies to his room to advise him on whether he should resign. Some thought the Missouri Compromise repeal was a plot to destroy a future Marcy presidential campaign. Most agreed that if he quit in protest the Hards would gain control of all the New York patronage. At the next cabinet meeting he grudgingly nodded his approval of the repeal to a relieved Pierce. But Marcy withheld his influence from any lobbying for the bill. He sat glowering, brooding and impassive, Achilles in his tent. If he had broken with the administration he would have emerged as the leader of the northern wing of the Democratic Party. Given his preeminence and history Marcy was the only figure who could have assumed that role, but the enormity of the personal offense against him, excluding him from the president's decision making, combined with his rooted sense of party loyalty and how a cabinet secretary ought to behave left him on the sidelines.

John Van Buren, "Prince John," royalty of the Softs, pledged to Marcy his opposition to the bill, and his fine hand operated behind the scenes. He excoriated Douglas in private correspondence that he made sure was printed in the *New York Post*, the leading newspaper of the Softs. "Could anything but a desire to buy the South at the presidential shambles dictate such an outrage?"

he wrote Senator Clemens, who was on Jefferson Davis's enemies list. Van Buren's letter somehow managed to appear on the *Post*'s front page. In the same edition, the newspaper trained its artillery on Douglas and Pierce. "As for Douglas, he is spoken here by friends of the administration in mingled terms of anger and contempt. They regard his Nebraska scheme as an indication of his determination to go beyond any man in subservience to the South, hoping by this means to get its entire support for the Presidency. . . . Pierce, it seems, is resolved not to be outdone by Douglas, and offers the same prize for southern support as Douglas. Neither of these men will obtain the next nomination for the democratic party. Neither of them could be elected if they were nominated."

At the beginning of the 33rd Congress, before Douglas had made his move, its only Free Soil members were at low ebb. The political careers of both Salmon P. Chase and Charles Sumner, the antislavery champions in Washington, appeared to be flickering into irrelevance. Chase had become a senator through a deal with the Ohio Hunkers who exploited him to defeat their intra-party rivals, "the consummation . . . of a series of outrages," wrote Horace Greeley. Pierce's campaign and election had created a crisis for Chase. Calling himself an "Independent Democrat" he flirted in 1852 with the Free Soilers, but then fended them off from nominating him for president while endorsing their platform, and halfheartedly campaigned for the quixotic candidacy of John P. Hale. (Afterward, as a sign of the dissolving abolitionist cause, Hale left the Senate and opened a law firm in New York.)

Charles Sumner

In the election the Democrats carried the Ohio legislature in a landslide. Chase was stranded without a political base and no longer served anybody's ulterior motive. "The Legislature is more completely old Line than I thought possible: which assures me my walking papers," he wrote, adding that he had "no wish ever again to fill a public office."

Sumner was also scrambling to find political traction. "This Congress is the worst—or rather promises to be the worst—since the Constitution was adopted," he wrote. "It is the 'Devil's Own.'" Within the Senate, he was more isolated than any other member, the representative man of moral Boston as an Untouchable. Edward Everett, the other senator from Massachusetts, who as president of Harvard had denied Sumner a professorship at the law school, objected to counting him as a Whig, and therefore prevented him from being assigned any important committee assignments. Even as he was punished for his antislavery stand, Sumner had also alienated various factions of the antislavery movement. The radical followers of William Lloyd Garrison, the Boston abolitionist, were furious at him for failing their litmus test of purity by upholding the Constitution, which they condemned as an evil pact with slavery. After the coalition of Free Soilers and Democrats that had put Sumner in the Senate lost control of the state legislature in the 1852 election, Sumner suddenly leapt into the arms of the leader of the practical political faction, Henry Wilson, a former cobbler from Natick, against his old Conscience Whig cohort. Wilson favored a new state constitution that would gerrymander districts to the disfavor of the Whigs and introduce the secret ballot, which was opposed by Sumner's compatriots Charles F. Adams and John G. Palfrey, who disdained these tactics as an attempt on Wilson's part to gain control over the Democratic Party for his own interests. Wilson was in league with the Troy and Greenfield Railroad lobby that supported rewriting the constitution as a means to get state loans for a new tunnel. When Sumner threw himself into Wilson's campaign for the new constitution, he earned Adams's enmity for following "the siren song of expediency" and having "bowed his neck to the iron rod of party." When the constitution was defeated in a referendum, Sumner was forgiven his trespass. But politically he seemed to be wandering in the weeds. Still, the antislavery men of Massachusetts looked to him as their only true if stifled voice in the Southern-dominated capital, wondering how he could ever advance the cause. Then, like a bolt, came Douglas's bill.

Two days after the conference at the White House, on January 24, when Douglas appeared on the Senate floor to move for consideration of his bill, Chase jumped up to request that it be postponed so that he had time to study it. "Say today week," interjected Sumner. Douglas agreed to the delay as routine matter. Then Senator Archibald Dixon of Kentucky declared his appreciation for Douglas's effort that "virtually repeals" the Missouri Compromise. "I merely wish to remark that, upon the question of slavery, I know no Whiggery, and I know no Democracy. I am a pro-slavery man. I am from a slaveholding state; I represent a slaveholding constituency; and I am here to maintain the rights of that people whenever they are presented before the Senate." Dixon's statement mocked Henry Clay, whom he had replaced and betrayed, and who had famously proclaimed during the debate on the Compromise of 1850, "I know no North—no South—no East—no West"— words engraved on Clay's tombstone.

That afternoon, the abolitionist newspaper, the *National Era*, filled its pages circulated through the streets of Washington with a manifesto against the repeal of the Missouri Compromise and Stephen A. Douglas entitled "The Appeal of the Independent Democrats in Congress to the People of the United States." The *New York Times* and *New York Tribune* published it simultaneously. It was dated January 22, but had been in preparation ever since Douglas had issued his initial committee report. Joshua Giddings, the ancient mariner of Abolition House, who had helped Lincoln frame his emancipation bill for the District of Columbia, had written the first rough draft. Chase had rewritten it, with Sumner and Gerrit Smith, now a congressman from New York, adding stylistic embellishments. Two congressmen, Edward Wade of Ohio and Alexander De Witt of Massachusetts, also signed the document. Chase called it "the most valuable of my works."

"We arraign the bill," they charged, "as a gross violation of a sacred pledge; as a criminal betrayal of precious rights; as part and parcel of an atrocious plot to convert a vast territory, consecrated to freedom, into a dreary region of despotism, inhabited by masters and slaves." After detailing the history of the "non-extension of slavery" back to Jefferson's proviso of 1784 and the Ordinance of 1787, they excoriated Douglas by name for his claim that he was merely acting on the idea of popular sovereignty in the Compromise of 1850—"a manifest falsification of the truth of history. . . . Not a man in Congress, or out of Congress, in 1850 pretended that the compromise measures would repeal the Missouri prohibition. Mr. Douglas himself never advanced such a pretense until this session. His own Nebraska bill, of last session, rejected it. It is a sheer afterthought." Douglas's motive was traced to his political ambition: "Will the people permit their dearest interests to be thus made the mere hazards of a presidential game, and destroyed by false facts and false inferences?" For good measure, they invoked the ghost of Henry Clay: "Were he living now, no one would be more forward, more eloquent, or more indignant in his denunciation of that bad faith, than Henry Clay, the foremost champion of both compromises."

The "Appeal" ignited an anti-Nebraska movement across the North. Rallies and meetings were held, resolutions passed, heated editorials written, and fiery sermons delivered. "Mr. Douglas was burned and hung in effigy in every portion of the free States, sometimes in a hundred different places in the same night, and nearly every pulpit of the Protestant churches poured forth its denunciations and imprecations upon every man who should vote for the measure," recalled James Madison Cutts, Douglas's brother-in-law. An enraged Douglas felt that Chase and Sumner had played a dirty trick on him. He prided himself on being the new master of the Senate, but they had used an ordinary request for postponement to tarnish him. But perhaps even worse the most marginal members of the Senate had outmaneuvered him. "They had thus *lied*—had got *first* before the country, seeking thus *by fraud* to forestall public opinion."

Douglas's sulfurous fury advertised his speech that would open the debate, packing the galleries on January 30. "Little did I suppose," he said twice, suggesting his wounded pride. He wasted no time ripping into "Abolition confederates," "guilty" of having "grossly misrepresented" and "grossly falsified" his bill, "calumniated" his character, and "assembled in secret conclave, plotting by what means to deceive the people of the United States, and prostrate the characters of brother senators." "Mr. President," protested Chase. "I do not yield the floor," said Douglas. "A senator who has violated all the rules of courtesy and propriety . . . who came to me with a smiling face . . . who could get up in the Senate and appeal to my courtesy in order to get time to give the document a wider circulation before its infamy could be exposed; such a senator has no right to my courtesy on the floor." Again and again Chase interrupted, and each time Douglas refused to yield. "The tornado," he said, "has been raised by Abolitionists, and Abolitionists alone." And he warned of their "hope of getting some tender-footed Democrats into their plot." By repealing the Missouri Compromise, Douglas insisted he was only upholding the Compromise of 1850, which was in fact superseded—and "that fundamental principle of democracy," popular sovereignty, his "great principle."

At last Chase got his chance to speak, denouncing Douglas's "diatribe" and insisting that he "exaggerates his importance," and then submitted the entire "Appeal of the Independent Democrats" into the record. "I crave a single moment," cried out Sumner, who arose to defend "strong language" in condemning Douglas's measure. "It is a soulless, eyeless monster—horrid, unshapely and vast . . . and this monster is now let loose upon the country."

"Senator Douglas seems to have been ashamed of the speech he delivered yesterday, if we may judge by the fact that he has published quite a different one," the *New York Times* mockingly reported. Douglas had carefully expunged from the official record of the *Congressional Globe* "such delectable terms" as "nigger" and "unadulterated, Free Soil, Abolition niggerism," which he had uttered, though he allowed to remain his references to the "base falsehood" of "Abolition confederates."

The vituperative tone set at the first moment of the debate never diminished but only rose in its intensity. From that hostile exchange in the Senate, the politics that had been cemented by the "final settlement" of the Compromise of 1850 cracked apart. In an instant, everything changed. Conservative Whigs who had followed Webster through every ordeal to the end turned overnight against the bill. Old Jacksonians who had long hated Calhoun and his legatees saw the drama now playing out again in a new key. Democrats who had supported the Wilmot Proviso but had been willing to back the Compromise of 1850 now believed the Pierce administration was betraying them. Border state Unionist Whigs felt the solid ground beneath them shaking. Southern Whigs as much as Southern Ultras who disliked the sheer expediency of Douglas's vaunted popular sovereignty felt compelled to rally to the bill in the defense of slavery. Through it all, there was never any clearly and generally accepted definition of Douglas's "great principle." But what was clear was that with every one of his arm-twisting efforts to pass his bill, Douglas was fundamentally realigning politics. In the four years after the Compromise of 1850, the "final settlement," slavery had been removed as a source of division. Each and every one of Douglas's clever maneuvers would bring slavery to the forefront again, but on a basis more contentious than ever, and whose shattering potential consequences were not lost on Lincoln as he vigilantly read the newspaper accounts.

While the Senate took up Douglas's measure, Benton gave a running commentary while offering advice behind the scenes. He dined with Chase before he issued the "Appeal," telling him, "Douglas has committed political suicide." After Douglas delivered his Senate speech, Benton refuted his principal argument. "Whoever says that I intended the repeal of the Missouri compromise when I voted for the compromise measures of 1850, lies, sir; he tells a lie, sir," he told the correspondent for the *New York Tribune*.

Francis P. Blair, Benton's old ally and family friend, equal in the intensity of his hostility to Calhoun and his followers, began to exercise his powers of persuasion through his network of Democrats. "You see what a prodigy

Douglas is becoming under the direction of the Southern Nullifiers," he wrote former senator William Allen of Ohio after Douglas's speech. "The whole work was done by the Southern plotters operating through their automaton whom they pull with a string and move with the ease of a supple-Jack. . . . It is all easy of explanation, to one behind the scenes of the Jugglers." Blair described three calculations "of the managers." The first was that "the whole South would be forced to act as a unit on the question of repeal." The next gambit was that Pierce, Cass, Buchanan "and every other northern candiate for the Presidency" would press for the measure to "shame" Douglas as "he sought to leap over their shoulders in the arms of the South." And, finally, all "jobbers and plunderers" would "carry the Bill to carry out their private schemes."

"Well here we are in the midst of the slavery excitement again, the finality of the Compromise to the contrary notwithstanding," lamented Congressman George Washington Jones of Tennessee, a pure Jacksonian of the old school, to his friend Howell Cobb of Georgia, the former speaker of the house who had just been rejected for a Senate seat in favor of an Ultra. Jones saw in the repeal the end of the Democratic Party and in particular the Southern Democratic Party as he knew it. His letter to Cobb was an extended requiem.

A most impolitic and mad movement for the South, no practical good can come of it because there is none in it. . . . It has been concocted by politicians, for political and personal purposes. . . . Some of the best and most discreet are of opinion, privately, that the movement is madness and must result injuriously to the South. But it is upon them. On the other hand our best and most reliable friends from the North, are shivering, and some who will come square up to the work, when called upon to vote will do so with the conviction upon their minds, that the act will work their political destruction. That it will be a self sacrifice for the sake of the party. . . . Cobb, what is called the Democratic party is this day in a worse condition than either of us ever saw it before. . . . Gen. Pierce is treating the true and the tried of the party as his mere vassals, who as a matter of duty would support him or be read out as renegades—and taking his Counsellors, Cabinet advisers from the two extremes of fire-eaters and freesoilers, and a quite recently proselyted Whig [Cushing], and in addition bestowing his patronage upon persons of the same sort almost exclusively, has cooled the ardor and personal regard for him of a host of the best men who were most cordial and sincere in his support in 1852. I fear we have been mistaken in the man, in his capacity, in his executive administrative talent. I fear he is not equal to the tasks imposed upon him. In farmer phrase that he is over craped and with all that he is rather too much of a Yankee. I fear that we are in for it.

But like many others Jones played the good Southerner who would argue and vote for the bill he believed was ruinous.

In Boston, the Cotton Whigs, the heirs of Webster, gathered at Faneuil Hall on February 23 to pass stern resolutions denouncing the repeal of the Missouri Compromise. The main speaker, former speaker of the house Robert C. Winthrop, lashed out at Douglas's popular sovereignty concept. "What, sir! A constructive repeal of a formal compact of more than thirty years' standing! A solemn covenant overturned by an inference; superseded by what is called a principle; emanating—let me rather say extorted—from a settlement of a wholly different and independent issue! Who ever heard of such a proceeding or of such a proposition as this?" His scorn for Douglas's flimsy intellectual pretension was withering. In a private letter written the next day, the normally cautious Winthrop explained that he had been "reluctant" to speak, and had no use for Sumner's "tinsel and tawdry rhetoric," but felt compelled to counter Douglas's mendacity. "Douglas has done a foolish thing, and it looks to me as if a black squall of the worst kind was coming up, which will, to say the least, throw a cloud over some presidential prospects," he wrote. ". . . I have no belief that slavery will make much headway in Kansas or Nebraska. But antislavery will make a prodigious headway in New England if such unwarrantable glosses are to prevail as to the construction of the Compromises of 1850. If I could have prescribed a recipe for reinflating Free-Soilism and Abolitionism, which had collapsed all over the country, I should have singled out this precise potion from the whole *materia medica* of political quackery."

Douglas's bill summoned a forgotten figure from the distant past to defend a tradition he felt was being hijacked. When Edward Coles published a letter in the *National Intelligencer* contradicting Douglas's brazen claim that the Congress had never forbidden slavery in Illinois he carried the authority of history. Coles, who knew Jefferson intimately and had been Madison's private secretary, was the second governor of Illinois, and had staked his career against pro-slavery forces attempting to overturn the Ordinance of 1787. He expressed "astonishment" at the "inconsistency" of "men professing to be of the Jefferson school of politics" who would repeal the principle of the

Ordinance applied to the territories. Douglas replied with a brutal and base-less accusation of corruption—that Coles had left Illinois after his governor-ship and was living in retirement in Philadelphia because "the inducements which took you there could no longer be made available."

But the "inducements" were all on the side of the bill. Words alone were not left to decide the issue. Just as Douglas did in passing the Compromise of 1850, he marshaled the lobbyists representing the great interests at stake, and the White House ruthlessly dangled patronage. "All the methods of in-fluence and intimidation which organization, numbers, and patronage can supply are used without stint at the seat of government to silence those who disapprove of the bill, and engage the wavering to give it support," reported the *New York Post*. "Those who have visited Washington speak of a leaden tyranny which is felt everywhere, weighing upon men's minds, coercing them into a sad, helpless acquiescence in the measure." Attorney General Cushing called on Senator Hamlin, who was prepared to vote against the bill, and offered him control of all the patronage in New England if he would only change his position. Hamlin refused, so the president sent for him. Pierce ex-plained that he must vote in favor as a matter of party loyalty. "Still," he said, "you could not stand up against your party." But Hamlin told him he could not vote for it out of "self-respect." "It is needless to say more," he concluded, "and I shall bid you good-morning."

Northern Democratic senators supporting Douglas's bill were second to no Southerner in their vehement defense of Southern rights. Senator John B. Weller of California, spokesman for the pro-slavery faction in his state, who had been removed from the Mexican border commission by President Taylor for corruption, and served in the Senate as a whip for Jesse Bright, held forth on February 13. "Sir, if the time shall ever come when the North uses its power for the purpose of oppressing the South . . . the time for dissolution will have arrived, and ought to have arrived." "Yes sir, ought to arrive," piped up Senator Dodge.

Dodge delivered his oration on February 25 in defense of nonintervention and slavery, highlighted with a piquant personal reminiscence. He reserved his thunder for Seward, castigating him for declaring "in favor of the ab-solute equality between the races." Seward, he accused, was "the Napoleon of this grand movement against the domestic institutions of the South, the Constitution, and the Union." Dodge held up his father, seated near him as the senator from Wisconsin, as the sterling example of "squatter sovereignty." "Apropos to this slavery question," he observed that when his father settled in Wisconsin more than a quarter century earlier he took with him, "in violation of the Ordinance of 1787 a family of negroes, rather than sell them," among them "the negro woman whom I was wont to call *Mammy*."

Senator John Pettit of Indiana, Bright's shadow, who regarded himself as both a constitutional and biblical scholar, took the floor on February 29. There could be "no justice" prohibiting slave owners from bringing their property into any territory or state, he explained, and "justice" was "their right to determine." "All history and all experience" proved "equality" between races to be false beginning with the Bible. "No principle was better known to or better understood by Moses," who "commanded to put all the ancient Canaanites to death." Not only biblical Scripture but also American scripture proved his point. "I cannot, in the first place, believe that Mr. Jefferson ever intended to give the meaning or force which is attempted now to be applied to this language when he said: 'We hold these truths to be self-evident, that all men are created equal.' I hold it to be a self-evident lie." During the whole debate, this line spoken by one of the Senate's least important members would be the most consequential. Closely reading the speeches published daily in the newspapers, Lincoln would soon seize upon the "self-evident lie" to explain why he put the self-evident truth at the center of his political philosophy.

The scandal of adhering to the Declaration of Independence was a theme running through the debate. Dixon, on February 6, exultantly challenged Senator Benjamin Wade of Ohio: "The Senator, as I understood him, said he was a believer in the Declaration of Independence, and in the doctrines of God, which declare that all men are equal? Does the Senator mean that the slave is equal to those free laborers that he speaks of in the North?" "Yes. Why not equal?" replied Wade. "I say, in the language of the Declaration of Independence, that they were 'created equal,' and you have trampled them under foot, and made them apparently unequal by your own wrong. . . . It is idle to cry 'Abolition' to me. To me it is an honorable name."

Butler of South Carolina, the white-mane patriarch of the F Street Mess, held forth for two days, on February 24 and 25, to rebut the absurdity that the Declaration of Independence proposed that "black man . . . has a right to claim equality with the white man." He invoked divine authority to clinch his point. "Abolitionists cannot make equal whom God has made unequal." "Equality! Equality!" he shouted. "I should like to see a play written on this matter." Posing a rhetorical question about emancipation—"where would these creatures go?"—he readily provided his own answer: "It would be a mercy to cut their throats sooner than condemn them to your philanthropy." Echoing Calhoun from the grave, he declared, "We, of the South, have lost by compromises." Contrasting "secessionists" to "abolitionists," he said, "The former are defending their rights, the latter are aggressors." He warned, "If, however, they mean to go on with this agitation, I give notice, as far as I can speak for the South, that if they keep it up, they must do so at the peril of this Union." In a final fillip, he gave a little history lesson, labeling Massachusetts, the bastion of opposition to the Nebraska bill, a citadel of hypocrisy, "an anti-nigger state," triumphantly declaring, "For it is a notorious fact, that the slaves of the North were oftener sold to the South than emancipated." (Butler's fractured history ignored that slavery had been prohibited there with a 1783 legal case in which the chief justice of the Massachusetts Supreme Judicial Court ruled, "the idea of slavery is inconsistent with our own conduct and Constitution." That judge, William Cushing, later a justice of the U.S. Supreme Court, was a relative of Caleb Cushing, and the lawyer representing the slaves in the case, Levi Lincoln, later Jefferson's attorney general, was a distant relative of Abraham Lincoln.)

Pettit insisted on resuming his argument about the Declaration of Independence on March 2, repeating his line that it was a "self-evident lie" that "all men are created equal." "But blame the Almighty, not me," he said. Wade wondered, "What principle established the American Revolution?" Butler jumped in, demanding that Wade answer whether he considered "a negro equal to a white man." When Wade replied, "Yes, he is, in his right to life, liberty, and the pursuit of happiness," Butler insisted he had not answered and burst into laughter. Pettit turned lawyerly. "The language does not contain the word free," he argued. "Is that not free?" replied Wade. "No, sir, not free," said Pettit. "There is no human right that is not alienable." Gleefully, he asked a question and answered it himself. "Is your wife your equal in all rights political and civil? Nothing of it." At that, an unidentified senator was recorded shouting, "She ought to be."

When Douglas introduced his amendment to declare the Missouri Compromise "inoperative and void," Chase proposed an amendment intended to clarify Douglas's deliberate ambiguity about popular sovereignty in order to drive a wedge into the supporters of the bill. His measure stated: "Under which the people of the Territory, through their appropriate representatives, may, if they see fit, prohibit the existence of slavery therein." The word "prohibit" was poison, and Douglas defeated every one of Chase's attempts, which continued to near the end of the debate. Ambiguity was essential to preserve the fiction that the bill was neutral on slavery, upholding the illusion that "non-intervention" was only the application of the principle of democracy. (During the 1858 Lincoln-Douglas debates, Lincoln would pose a variation of Chase's question to Douglas, forcing him into a corner, where he admitted that through popular sovereignty slavery could be excluded from a territory, a statement that profoundly alienated Southerners.)

Sustaining Douglas's myth that the bill did not open the territory to slavery when it repealed the Missouri Compromise required a feat of cognitive dissonance. Preserving that pretense also involved careful obliviousness to the heated words over slavery flung back and forth. During Chase's last effort on behalf of his amendment, on March 2, Mason of Virginia and F Street cast a malediction on him and other antislavery foes—"if the bill passes their vocation will be gone, the last plank of their political shipwreck will be taken from them, and they will expire, as they deserve to expire, howling—howling like fiends attempting to destroy the country."

On the last night of the debate, March 4, James Pike, the correspondent from the *New York Tribune* in the Senate chamber, described "the bullying, braggart majority, flushed with anticipated victory, and some of them, I am mortified to say, beastly drunk." When the antislavery senator from Maine, William Pitt Fessenden, delivered a speech against the bill, Butler twice "advanced" on him "with clenched fists and flushed face," though the official record, the *Congressional Globe*, failed to note it.

Douglas took the floor again for a final bravura performance. "The reports of his speech . . . will convey but a faint idea of its violence and vulgarity. . . . Only those who know Douglas, of those who heard him, can be aware of his low 'Short Boy' style of speaking. His sneering tone and vulgar grimaces must be heard and seen rather than described. To Senator Seward he said in return to a courteous explanation, 'Ah, you can't crawl behind that free nigger dodge.' He always uses the word 'nigger' and not 'negro' as it appears in his printed speeches." To which Seward, it was reported, though not in the official record, replied, "Douglas, no one who spells Negro with two 'g's will ever be elected President of the United States."

In his private journal Senator Everett described Douglas's speech as "coarse and ungentlemanlike. There was on the part of many members evident excess in liquor."

From the Senate gallery, Carl Schurz fixed on Douglas as "the most conspicuous figure," of "low stature" but "muscular," tossing his hair "like a lion's mane." The longer he watched him, the more he was disturbed. Douglas was clear and forceful, "keen and crafty," while

> twisting logic or in darkening the subject with extraneous, unessential matter . . . he would, with utter unscrupulousness, malign his opponents' motives, distort their sayings, and attribute to them all sorts of iniquitous deeds or purposes of which he must have known them to be guiltless. Indeed, Douglas's style of attack was sometimes so exasperatingly offensive, that it required, on the part of the anti-slavery men in the Senate, a very high degree of self-control to abstain from retaliating. But so far as I can remember, only Mr. Sumner yielded to the temptation to repay him in kind. While for these reasons I should be very far from calling Douglas an ideal debater, it is certain that I have never seen a more formidable parliamentary pugilist. To call him so must not be thought unbecoming, since there was something in his manners which very strongly smacked of the barroom. He was the idol of the rough element of his party, and his convivial association with that element left its unmistakable imprint upon his habits and his deportment.

Douglas launched his rocket-fueled speech on March 3 near midnight and his words flew almost to dawn. It was a tour de force of misdirection, obfuscation, illogic, falsified history, and ad hominem vilification delivered with such vehemence that it sent his enemies reeling in defensive retreat and exhaustion, even in the sanitized form published in the *Congressional Globe*. He carried his audacity in depicting himself as a martyr to patriotism and his defamers motivated by "unworthy ambition" through his incredible stamina. All those opposed to his bill were guilty of distortion. "Each speaker seems to have followed faithfully in the footsteps of his leader in the path marked out by the Abolition confederates in their manifesto. . . . You have seen them on their winding way, meandering the narrow and crooked path in Indian file, each treading close upon the heels of the other, and neither venturing to take a step to the right or left, or to occupy one inch of ground which did not bear the footprint of the Abolition champion. To answer one, therefore, is to answer the whole." Through their "many misrepresentations," a "deliberate act of forgery," they had raised "the false issue" of the repeal of the Missouri Compromise," the "staple article out of which most of the Abolition orators of the small anti-Nebraska meetings manufacture the greater part of their speeches." But focus on the repeal was nothing but an attempt to "divert public attention" from the "real" issue. "That which is a mere incident they choose to consider the principle"—popular sovereignty.

Repealing the Missouri Compromise, he went on, was not "a sacred and irrevocable compact, binding in honor, in conscience, and morals. . . . And now the Abolition press, suddenly, and, as if by miraculous conversion, teems with eulogies upon Mr. Clay and his Missouri compromise of 1820." But Douglas challenged his opponents with his version of history: "His is misread and misquoted. . . . Does not each of these Senators know that Mr. Clay was not the author of the act of 1820? . . . Do they not know that Mr. Clay never came into the Missouri controversy as a compromiser until after the compromise of 1820 was repudiated, and it became necessary to make another?" Clay was not the author of the act of 1820, but of 1821. "How, then, dare you call upon the spirit of that great and gallant statesman to sanction your charge of bad faith against the South on this question?" Under this furious rhetorical assault, Seward took a step backward, conceding his own "misapprehension." Yet in these details, Douglas was false or distorting. Clay had, in fact, been the maker of the Compromise of 1820, which unraveled until he intervened again in 1821. When Clay began his labors, in February 1820, he confided his fear to John Quincy Adams that "it was a shocking thing to think of, but he had not a doubt that within five years from this time the Union would be divided into three distinct confederacies."

Douglas came to praise Clay in order to bury him. The psychological dimension was bound up with the political. Douglas had felt belittled for not receiving the credit for crafting the Compromise of 1850, which went instead to Clay, and that the misplacement of glory contributed to his loss of the nomination. Lifting from Clay his mantle as the Great Compromiser, Douglas wrapped his pilfered fame around himself. He was the true compromiser, true patriot, and true Unionist. The laurels should rightfully be crowned on his brow. He was that "towering genius" who sees "no distinction in adding story to story, upon the monuments of fame, erected to the memory of others," according to Lincoln's premonition in his 1838 Lyceum address.

The opponents of his bill who claimed it had violated a compact, Douglas charged, had created nothing less than "a great injustice." Now he assumed the pose of prosecutor and judge. "You degrade your own states, and induce the people, under the impression that they have been injured, to get up a violent crusade against those whose fidelity and truthfulness will in the end command their respect and administration. In consequence of arousing passions and prejudices, I am now to be found in effigy, hanging by the neck, in all the towns where you have the influence to produce such a result."

He swiveled to accuse Chase. "In your state, sir, I find that I am burnt in effigy in your Abolition towns. All this is done because I have proposed, as it is said, to violate a compact! Now what will those people think of you when they find out that you have stimulated them to these acts, which are disgraceful to your state, disgraceful to your party, and disgraceful to your cause, under a misrepresentation of the facts, which misrepresentation you ought to have been aware of, and should have been made?"

Douglas turned to denounce Fessenden, "enlisted under the banner of Abolition confederates," for being "profoundly ignorant." "I am willing to excuse him on the ground that he did not know what he was talking about, and it is the only excuse which I can make for him." But Douglas went on, "I will say, however, that I do not think he was required by his loyalty to the Abolitionists, to repeat every disreputable insinuation which they made. Why did he throw into his speech that foul innuendo about 'a northern man with southern principles,' and then quote the Senator from Massachusetts as his authority? Ay, sire, I say that foul insinuation." Sumner, Douglas charged, "availed himself of a cant phrase in the public mind, in violation of the truth of history. I know of but one man in this country who ever made it a boast that he was 'a northern man with southern principles,' "—and Douglas turned dramatically to face Sumner—"and he was your candidate for the presidency in 1848." With that triumphant reference to Martin Van Buren as the Free Soil candidate, the galleries erupted into applause.

Now Douglas indicted Chase and Sumner as not only "unworthy," guilty of "indecency," but illegitimate, present in the Senate through corruption. "Mr. President, the Senators from Ohio and Massachusetts have taken the liberty to impeach my motives in bringing forward this measure. . . . I must be permitted to tell the Senator from Ohio, that I did not obtain my seat in this body either by a corrupt bargain or a dishonorable coalition! I must be permitted to remind the Senator from Massachusetts that I did not enter into any combinations or arrangements by which my character, my principles, and my honor, were set up at public auction or private sale in order to procure a seat in the Senate of the United States!"

As if on cue, Douglas's ally Senator Weller jumped up to point his finger at Chase. "But there are some men whom I know that did," he cried. Chase replied, "Do you say that I came here by a bargain?" Douglas yielded the floor to Weller to serve as witness and prosecutor against Chase, recounting that living in Ohio at the time he had observed how "Abolitionists held the balance" in the legislature, and made a deal resulting not only in Chase's election but also the appointment of Democrats to judgeships, and scandalous "repeal of the 'black laws.'" Chase fervently denied he had been party to any political deal, though it had certainly occurred. When he defended the repeal of the Black Laws as "humane," Weller joked that after Chase's election, "I was very glad to have an opportunity of changing my residence on that remarkable occasion." The *Congressional Globe* recorded: "Laughter." Douglas chimed in, comparing Chase to "a receiver of stolen goods" who denies "responsibility for the larceny, while luxuriating in the proceeds of the crime." Chase again tried to defend himself, but was able to get out only a few words, "I came here . . ." before Douglas cut him short, shifting the target of his insult. "I was not speaking of the Senator from Ohio," Douglas said, "but of his confederate in slander, the Senator from Massachusetts."

Before Sumner could speak a syllable in his defense, Douglas slighted another signer of the "Appeal," "so full of slanders and calumnies." "I have a word now to say to the other Senator from Ohio." To denounce Benjamin Wade he charged, "he said that in Ohio a negro was as good as a white man; with the avowal that he did not consider himself any better than a free negro. I have only to say that I should not have noticed it"—the "Appeal"—"if none but free negroes had signed it!" Douglas's jibe was later amended in the *Congressional Globe* to substitute "negro" for the word he repeatedly used, "nigger."

Douglas explained that he had raised "these personal matters" only "in self-defense." Now he came to his uplifting peroration. "Why, then, can we not withdraw this vexed question from politics? . . . Why can we not deprive these agitators of their vocation, and render it impossible for Senators to come here upon bargains on the slavery question?" Paraphrasing Webster's oration on the Compromise of 1850—"I wish to speak today, not as a Massachusetts man, nor as a Northern man, but as an American, and a member of the Senate of the United States"—Douglas said, "I have not brought his question forward as a northern man or as a southern man . . . I have brought it forward as an American Senator." Usurping the role of Clay, he was now usurping Webster.

Appealing "to the whole Union," Douglas declared, "I have nothing to say about northern rights or southern rights." He urged "our southern friends" to "rally around" his "great principle." And he demanded that Northerners renounce that there was any motive of Southerners to extend slavery: "To our northern friends, on the other hand, I desire to say, that from this day hence-forward, they must rebuke the slander which has been uttered against the South, that they desire to legislate slavery into the Territories." Once again, he denounced how "I was assailed and misrepresented," but declared "these assaults have had no other effect upon me than to give me courage and en-ergy." In the end, he would be vindicated. "I say frankly that, in my opinion, this measure will be as popular at the North as at the Southern, when its provisions and principles shall have been fully developed, and become well understood."

The roll call was taken shortly after five in the morning on "An Act to Organize the Territories of Nebraska and Kansas" with the vote in favor an overwhelming 37 to 14, a result always foretold, the Democrats' prohibitive majority augmented by nine Southern Whigs. Only two Southerners voted in the negative, John Bell, a Whig from Tennessee, and the wholly inde-pendent Sam Houston, Democrat from Texas. When the measure passed cannon boomed at the Navy Yard to signal the victory, the roar carrying to the Capitol as Chase and Sumner walked arm-in-arm down the steps to the sound of its thunder. "They celebrate a present victory," remarked Chase, "but the echoes they awake will never rest till slavery itself shall die."

"The bill was thus manfully fought in the Senate by its opponents, and goes into the House with the stamp and seal of more than midnight darkness upon it," reported the *New York Tribune*, whose correspondent, James Pike, interviewed Benton. "The Senate is emasculated, sir. Yes, sir, it is emascu-lated. A majority do not belong to the masculine gender, sir. No, sir, do not belong to the masculine gender."

The "Appeal" had included a section urging clergymen to protest. Har-riet Beecher Stowe, in communication with Sumner, quietly spent some of her royalties from *Uncle Tom's Cabin* to finance the effort. On March 13, Senator Hamilton Fish presented a petition signed by most of the clergy in New York and led by the Episcopal bishop, but it received little notice. The next day a petition signed by 3,050 clergy from New England was submitted, "in the name of Almighty God," to denounce the Nebraska Act as "a great moral wrong, as a breach of faith eminently unjust," and "exposing us to the righteous judgments of the Almighty." This petition produced an explosion such as had not been heard since John Quincy Adams had presented the early petitions against the Gag Rule.

The clergy carefully chose the most distinguished and moderate figure from New England to offer their protest. Edward Everett, a Whig of Massachusetts, was eminence personified—congressman, governor, and secretary of state. He had been the president of Harvard, where his students included Ralph Waldo Emerson, who adored him, and Robert C. Winthrop, who deferred to him, and had also been editor of the *North American Review*, the leading intellectual journal in the country. The boyhood friend of Daniel Webster, he was intermarried with the Adams family—his wife's sister was the wife of Charles Francis Adams, one of his students. He had once been friendly with the brilliant young Sumner but had helped to thwart him from getting a teaching position at the Harvard Law School and receiving committee assignments in the Senate. Everett was widely considered the most prudent politician and erudite orator of the age. (He would deliver an epic address at Gettysburg filled with classical allusions before Lincoln's brief remarks.) When Douglas had submitted his first report in committee, Everett, as a member, voiced his qualms that "the antislavery agitation of 1850 would be reopened," but he was the only dissenter, and his dissent was private. He was unsure that Douglas would act so rashly. "At the beginning of the session," he wrote in his journal, "Douglas said to me in committee that the provisions of the Nebraska bill as at first reported were well calculated to make Northern men hesitate, and that no man was so wild as to think of repealing the Missouri Compromise." Everett was appalled that Douglas had leaped.

When, a month later, 504 clergymen from the Northwestern states, led by those in Chicago, presented Douglas with another petition, he took to the floor to denounce them as "a denomination of men calling themselves preachers of the gospel, who have come forward with an atrocious falsehood and an atrocious calumny against the Senate, desecrated the pulpit, and prostituted the sacred desk to the miserable and corrupting influence of party politics." Douglas observed that between fifteen hundred and two thousand sermons had been preached against him in New England. He demanded that the clergymen "make an open and public confession of the injustice you have done me." He extended his insistence for an apology as well to Senators Mason and Butler of the F Street Mess, and to Senator Pettit of the "self-evident lie."

The Senate bill now went to the House, along with Douglas himself, who arrived to command his political allies and direct a phalanx of lobbyists from the floor. "He has every man in the House of Representatives marked and numbered, and firmly believes the bill will go through by a decisive majority," reported the *New York Tribune*. "He feels that if it does go, that his fortunes are made; but that if it fails, he sinks never to rise again." Pike again quoted Benton, who "expressed the profoundest contempt." "Sir," he said, "the meanest man in our country is a poor white man who marries a woman with niggers"—referring to Douglas's Mississippi plantation. "He is not allowed to associate with gentlemen, sir. He is hooted off the Court House Green, sir. We have nothing to do with him, sir."

The bill nearly died at birth in the House. Douglas's lieutenant, William A. Richardson of Illinois, chairman of the Committee on Territories, naturally assumed it would fall into his grasp, but Congressman Francis B. Cutting of New York daringly filched it, managing its referral to the Committee of the Whole, where it would certainly be suffocated. Cutting was a Hard, hostile to the administration's granting of any patronage to the Softs, and though he claimed to be in favor of the bill insisted that since the Senate debate "the North would seem to have taken up arms." Cutting was also a tiger of Tammany Hall and cog of the Albany Regency, a political soldier alongside William L. Marcy for decades. Whether Cutting's legislative maneuver calculated to kill the bill had received Marcy's quiet benediction remains unknown. But Marcy, master of spoils, lifted not one heavy finger to assist the beleaguered administration measure.

Douglas settled himself like a squatter for the duration in the House, calling the shots with Richardson and Southern leaders. "No slave-driver was ever half so absolute on his own plantation," reported the *New York Tribune*. Douglas was, according to the *New York Times*, "continually present, coaxing one, persuading another, and perhaps 'arranging the terms' with a third." For two months he struggled to get the bill withdrawn from the Committee of the Whole, move it to the top of the calendar and force a vote. Pierce, meanwhile, showered favors on wavering Northern Democratic members.

Benton took to the floor on April 25 hoping that with "a chance at the bill it would have been smashed into atoms and the public aroused to knowledge of the meditated crimes." He had been elected to the Senate as a result of the Missouri Compromise, participated in every major debate there longer than any man, but was now relegated to the House. He remembered everything and did not need history books or legal papers near at hand. He knew in his bones that the bill represented a fundamental rupture in the entire constitutional order. He argued that the Constitution, the Ordinance of 1787, and the Missouri Compromise were "settlements of existing questions, and intended to be perpetual." All contained fugitive slave clauses, he pointed out, without which they would not have been able to be enacted. "A proposition to destroy the slavery compromises in the Constitution would be an open proposition to break up the Union," he said. The Missouri Compromise was "a continuation" of the Ordinance, and "I consider both, with their fugitive slave recovery clauses, and the similar clause in the Constitution, as part and parcel of the same transaction—different articles in the same general settlement." Without the fugitive slave clauses, there would have been no Constitution, no Ordinance, and no Missouri Compromise. "They are founded in agreement—in consent—in compact—and are as sacred and inviolable as human agreements can be." So much for Douglas's claim that there was no compact.

What was Douglas's bill? It was "a silent, secret, limping, halting, creeping, squinting, impish, motion—conceived in the dark—midwifed in a committee room, and sprung upon Congress and the country in the style in which Guy Fawkes intended to blow up the Parliament house, with his five hundred barrels of gunpowder, hid in the cellar under the wood."

And what was Douglas's principle? "Territorial sovereignty is a monstrosity, born of timidity and ambition, hatched into existence in the hot incubation of a presidential canvas, and revolting to the beholders when first presented. Well do I remember that day when it was first shown in the Senate. Mark Antony did not better remember the day when Caesar first put on that mantle through which he was afterwards pierced with three-and-twenty 'envious stabs.' It was in the Senate in 1848, and was received as nonsense—as the essence of nonsense—as the quintessence of nonsense— as the five-times distilled essence of political nonsensicality."

Douglas's popular sovereignty was merely "the end of a stump speech . . . not accidentally here . . . but only there in relation to slavery, and that for its admission—not rejection. Three dogmas now afflict the land . . . squatter sovereignty, non-intervention, and no power in Congress to legislate upon slavery in Territories. And this bill asserts the whole three . . . by knocking one on the head with the other, and trampling each under foot in its turn. Sir, the bill does deny squatter sovereignty, and it does intervene, and it does legislate upon slavery in Territories . . . a bill of assumptions and contradictions—assuming what is unfounded, and contradicting what it assumes— and balancing every affirmation by a negation. . . . It is an *amphibiological* bill."

"*Amphibiology*," he declared, and as that word rolled from his tongue the speaker's gavel rapped, the signal that Benton's time, his allotted hour, had expired. Those opposed to the bill, avid that his voice be heard, hurriedly demanded that he be granted an extension to conclude his remarks. "Frequently consultations were held among men of all political parties opposed to the repeal as to the best means of obtaining for him a full hearing," recalled Congressman John Wentworth, a Democrat from Chicago, an associate of Douglas, but now against his bill. "And here may be said to have originated the idea of the Republican party, when such life-long Democrats as William H. Bissell of Illinois, Reuben E. Fenton of New York, Galusha A. Grow of Pennsylvania, Hannibal Hamlin of Maine, Nathaniel P. Banks of Massachusetts, and myself met with men whom we had ever before opposed, to consult upon a common object." Their protest succeeded in securing the time for Benton, who resumed precisely where he left off: "*Amphibiology . . .*"

While Benton's advocates pressured the speaker, Douglas had strolled with Congressman John C. Breckinridge "arm and arm in the lobby, manifesting the greatest interest," wrote Wentworth, "and, as Benton was concluding, Douglas came to my seat and said, tauntingly: 'The Abolitionists are quite successful under you as their new leader.'"

Richardson called for a suspension of the rules to close debate and bring the bill for a vote. By May 12 the House had been in almost continuous session for days, eighty endless and heated speeches topping each other, as members wandered in and out returning more lubricated by the hour. Douglas prowled through the seats like a policeman on the beat, ringing his arm around the neck of Mike Walsh, a radical Jacksonian Democrat from the streets of New York, sometime poet in high spirits declaiming on the floor, and chief of his own political machine, the Spartan Association, based on the Bowery B'hoys gang. Douglas held him in a gentle headlock while "begging him to withdraw" a motion against the bill, which he "obstinately refused." Then Wentworth called for the regular business of the day to be brought up that would postpone the bill, provoking Congressman Henry A. Edmundson, a Southern Ultra from Virginia, owner of the Fotheringay plantation at the foot of the Blue Ridge Mountains, who approached him, "raising his cane and shaking it within a few inches of his nose," exclaiming, "You damned scoundrel! You God damned infernal scoundrel!" Near midnight, Edmundson, "armed to the teeth and under the influence of liquor," according to the *Tribune*, unbuttoned his vest to get at his bowie knife while shouting threats against Congressman Lewis D. Campbell, a Whig from Ohio, the opposition floor leader, who grabbed him to prevent the knife from being drawn, and Edmundson was arrested by the sergeant-at-arms, forcing an adjournment amid pandemonium. "Senator Douglas was sitting near Edmundson at the time of the occurrence," the *New York Times* correspondent reported. "Whether he had excited this Virginia fighting-man, and prepared him for the disgraceful part he enacted, of course I have no means of knowing; but that a row was a part of the programme for the day I have little doubt." "There is no doubt that Edmundson was put forward to start a fight, and that Douglas was cognizant of it," reported the *Tribune*. The *Times* noted that "some gentlemen (?)—how many cannot be told—carry deadly weapons with them daily into the House."

Douglas whipped the Northern Democrats in the House, struggling to gain a majority. Relying on Democrats alone, despite their more than two-to-one majority, he still fell short. According to the *New York Times*, the resisting Northern members "feel outraged—deeply wronged. They feel that the effort of Douglas and his men is to drive them like sheep, to record their behests. They refuse to be driven." Southern Whigs would have to make up the difference. Congressman Alexander H. Stephens of Georgia, Lincoln's fellow Young Indian, a master of the rules, stepped into the breach. Contemptuous of Northern antislavery Whigs and Democrats alike, he also had little use for the Pierce administration. Of opposition to the bill, he stated in a speech, "They are but the 'ravings,' and 'howlings,' and 'hissings' of the beaten and routed ranks of the factionists and malcontents. They are the wailings of the politically condemned." He had special scorn for the New York Democratic Softs, "like craven and mercenary captives, they turned to power, to see if anything could be made there by subserviency and sycophancy," and through Pierce's patronage they appeared to be "warmed into life." But Stephens warned, "Hydrophobia can never be cured—it will break out on the changes of the moon. And so with the disease of negro-mania. Sir, the viper will hiss and even sting the bosom that nurtures and fosters it."

To alarm the Southern stragglers, the *Washington Union*, the administration's bugle, sounded reveille to join in "those great events with which the future teems," with an optimism that ought to remove "the hesitancy and doubt of some of our southern friends, if such doubt and hesitancy really exist." The *Union* promised that the "principles of this bill" would not be "ended with Nebraska and Kansas," but "prepare northern sentiment" for when "Cuba is admitted into the Union—as in the course of thick coming events she is bound to be admitted," as a slave state, an event that would "defy the worst combinations of northern fanaticism." Manifest Destiny would spread to the Caribbean, even as Jefferson Davis dreamed of annexing Mexico again, the course of empire creating a Southern imperium, the Pacific railroad running through the Gadsden Purchase, linking the economy of South and West, and the political balance of power righted.

Finally, through a series of stunning tactical maneuvers, Stephens closed the general debate, cut off all amendments, broke the stranglehold of the Committee of the Whole, and moved a clean substitute bill to the floor for a vote. On the third reading, on May 22, it passed by a vote of 113 to 100. "The great struggle is over," Stephens wrote, "Nebraska has passed the House. I took the reins in my hand, applied whip and spur, and brought the 'wagon' out at eleven o'clock p.m. Glory enough for one day."

The final vote was not taken by roll call but by members walking to the well of the chamber to file by the clerk as they voiced "aye" or "nay." Each Southern Whig was scrutinized as he stepped forward. Of the twenty-four Southern Whigs, at least ten disliked the bill, some expressing open contempt. Congressman William Cullom of Tennessee, a protégé of Henry Clay, expressed his disdain for Douglas, stating, "the title of it should be so amended as to read, 'A bill to make great men out of small ones, and to sacrifice the public peace and prosperity upon the altar of political ambition.' . . . I repeat, that the author of this movement was a defeated, or, rather, a rejected presidential aspirant in 1852. . . . How does it happen that out of the whole South, no one has been found who loved the South more than the Senator from Illinois? . . . But we have found another northern man with strong southern feelings. Ah! We have tried such before." In the end, seven Southern Whigs voted against the bill. The seventeen who voted in favor provided the winning margin. If ever the three-fifths clause in the Constitution that provided for counting slaves for representation made a decisive difference it was on the repeal of the Missouri Compromise. The South received nineteen additional seats in the House in the 33rd Congress as a result of the three-fifths clause, enough for the margin of victory.

As the Senate took up the House bill for inevitable final passage on May 25, Seward rose to declare portentously the ending of one era and the beginning of another. "The sun has set for the last time upon the guaranteed and certain liberties of all the unsettled and unorganized portions of the American continent that lie within the jurisdiction of the United States," he said. "Tomorrow's sun will rise in dim eclipse over them." In fact, the next day a total eclipse of the sun would occur. "We are on the eve of the consummation of a great national transaction—a transaction which will close a cycle in the history of our country." Since the creation of the nation "the systems of free labor and slave labor" had been "at war." This "contest" had now become a mortal battle. "This antagonism must end either in a separation of the antagonistic parties—the slaveholding states and the free states—or, secondly, in the complete establishment of the influence of the slave power over the free—or else on the other hand, in the establishment of the superior influence of freedom over the interests of slavery." Four years before Lincoln's "House Divided" speech, Seward proposed the idea that the country would become "all one thing, or all the other." That "war" could no longer be postponed. "Come on, then, gentlemen of the slave states. Since there is no escaping your challenge, I accept it in behalf of the cause of freedom. We will engage in competition for the virgin soil of Kansas, and God give the victory to the side which is stronger in numbers as it is in right."

On the night of May 24, the clerk of a clothing store on Brattle Street in downtown Boston was arrested and the next morning marched in manacles from the jail to the federal courthouse. Anthony Burns was an escaped slave, and his owner, Charles Suttle of Virginia, had come to claim him. Word quickly spread. The Boston Vigilance Committee, which had attempted the rescue of the fugitive slave Thomas Sims in 1850, called for an emergency meeting for May 26 at Faneuil Hall. Wendell Phillips told the overflow crowd, "I am against squatter sovereignty in Nebraska, and against kidnappers' sovereignty in Boston. . . . Nebraska, I call knocking a man down, and this is spitting in his face after he is down." Then Theodore Parker, the minister of the largest Unitarian congregation in Boston, consisting of virtually all the Transcendentalists, mounted the platform. The grandson of Captain Parker of Lexington Green appealed to revolutionary patriotism, not against the king of England but slavery. "Fellow citizens of Virginia!" he began to shouts from the audience of "No, no!" "Fellow citizens of Boston, then," he started again to a chorus of "Yes, yes!" "Fellow citizens, a deed which Virginia commands has just been done in the city of John Hancock, and the

Theodore Parker

'brace of Adamses.' " He went on, "Yes, we are the *vassals* of Virginia. It reaches its arm over the graves of our mothers, and it kidnaps men in the city of the Puritans, over the graves of Samuel Adams and John Hancock." "Shame!" cried voices in the crowd. "Shame! So I say; but who is to blame? 'There is no North,' said Mr. Webster," quoted Parker, ironically reciting a phrase from Webster's speech in favor of the Compromise of 1850. "There is none. The South goes clear up to the Canada line. No, gentlemen, there is no Boston today. There was a Boston once. Now, there is a north suburb to the city of Alexandria; that is what Boston is. And you and I, fellow subjects of the State of Virginia." Parker drew the line. "I say, there are two great laws in this country. One is the slave law: that is the law of the President of the United States; it is Senator Douglas's law. . . . There is another law. . . . It is the law of the people, when they are sure they are right and determined to go ahead." He reminded the audience of the Boston Tea Party. "You know what they did with the tea . . . and that law, it is in your hands and your arms." He called on the crowd to reassemble at the courthouse the next morning to execute that "law."

But a voice shouted that a group of free blacks were already at the court-house and the crowd rushed there led by Thomas Wentworth Higginson, a Unitarian minister who had run unsuccessfully as a Free Soil candidate for the Congress. (He would become a financier of John Brown, serve as a colonel of the 1st South Carolina Colored Infantry Regiment during the war, and develop a close relationship with the reclusive poet Emily Dickinson, becoming her mentor, and after her death her publisher.) But Higginson did not have poetry in mind that evening. Along with about a dozen other men he sought to break down the courthouse door with a battering ram. A policeman slashed his face with a cutlass. Bronson Alcott, the utopian Transcendentalist, scurried away on his cane. In the melee one of the mob stabbed a deputy marshal, who died as the attack was repulsed.

Boston was placed under martial law. On the morning of June 2, to execute the order of rendition of Burns, more than one thousand U.S. troops mustered on Boston Common and more than 125 police joined them. A loaded cannon was stationed at the courthouse door aimed at the crowd. More than fifty thousand people filled the streets and crowded every window of the route from State Street to the wharf. Burns was brought out in hand-cuffs and marched at the center of a phalanx of soldiers and police. From the window of a building opposite the Old State House hung a black coffin with a sign: "The Funeral of Liberty." Many windows were draped in black mourning. American flags were hung upside down in the distress signal. There was no military band, just the sound of the soldiers' boots on the cobblestones. But one detachment posted on State Street to hold the crowd back, "filled with liquor," broke into a chorus of "Carry me back to Old Virginny." After Burns was imprisoned below deck on the ship, the cannon from the courthouse was wheeled onboard, and the steamer left Boston harbor. He would return a year later after his freedom was purchased, enroll in Oberlin College, become a minister, but then die of tuberculosis at only twenty-eight years old.

The failed rescue of Thomas Sims in 1850 had marked the end of a period of struggle after the Mexican War to limit slavery in the new territories. It was a desperate gesture against the "final settlement" of the Compromise of 1850 that incorporated the Fugitive Slave Act. Rather than sparking a movement of resistance, however, it seemed at the time to be a last gasp. The abolitionists of Boston were more isolated and excoriated than ever, and Franklin Pierce's election was overwhelming. But the failed rescue of Anthony Burns, involving the same cast of characters of notable Bostonians inveighing against the same law, marked the beginning of a new phase in political conflict after the repeal of the Missouri Compromise. What had radically changed were neither the high moral rhetoric nor the militant tactics, but the circumstances. The Anthony Burns affair was Lexington Green. "We went to bed one night old-fashioned, conservative, compromise Union Whigs & waked up stark mad Abolitionists," said Amos Adams Lawrence, the wealthy mill owner. At an antislavery meeting at Framingham on July 4th, under banners reading "Kansas," "Nebraska," "Virginia," and "Redeem Massachusetts," William Lloyd Garrison set fire to copies of the Fugitive Slave Act, the court order rendering Burns to Georgia, and the Constitution, damning it as "a covenant with death, and an agreement with hell," and calling for "a dissolution of the Union." Henry David Thoreau, of Concord, delivered a speech he entitled "Slavery in Massachusetts." "The law," he said, "will never make men free; it is men who have got to make the law free."

CHAPTER FIFTEEN

CITIZEN KNOW NOTHING

"The storm will soon spend its fury," Douglas predicted to Howell Cobb in April after the bill passed the Senate. Once emotions cooled, he expected the Democratic position to be invincible. He was certain, he wrote Cobb, "the people of the north will sustain the measure when they come to understand it." According to his political scenario, the bill "will form the test of Parties," as he laid it out to Lanphier of the *Illinois State Register*, and "the only alternative" would be "either to stand with the Democracy or rally under Seward, John Van Buren & co." The endlessly flexible Douglas operated from a set of fixed assumptions: the Democrats would remain dominant and the opposition would be discredited. Party discipline would do the rest.

If all things had remained equal since the Democratic landslide of 1852, it seems likely that without any galvanizing issue the slow pressure of partisan domination would have continued unabated. But the

Uncle Sam's Youngest Son, Citizen Know Nothing, 1854 lithograph

political reality imposed through the Compromise of 1850, closing national debate on slavery, cloaking the Democrats in the mantle of Unionism, and tainting the Whigs as divisive, was legislated away with Douglas's Nebraska Act. That political status quo was "superseded," just as the measure stated about the Missouri Compromise. Rather than raising a new standard around which the Democrats could rally, Douglas had hoisted a signal for a Democratic rout.

Parties and presidents had been repudiated before, but there had never been a collapse like that in the midterm elections of 1854. From a two-to-one majority in the House, the Democrats lost seventy-five seats, the greatest loss in congressional elections then recorded. In the North, 84 percent of the Democrats who supported the Nebraska Act were ousted. The Democrats were able to hold on to only twenty-five of their ninety-one Northern seats while losing merely four of sixty-seven Southern ones. The Northern districts they lost were not regained until after the Civil War. Douglas's bill transformed the Democrats into a Southern party. Northern Democrats, once the majority within the House Democratic caucus, were reduced in numbers to half those from the South. The Northern wing was a rump. As the party became more narrowly sectional, Northern Democrats like Douglas were compelled to cast their Northern opponents as the real sectional partisans and themselves as representatives of a national party.

The first test after the passage of the bill took place in August, in Iowa, a bellwether state that since it had been admitted to the Union in 1846 had elected only Democrats to statewide office and voted for Democratic presidential candidates. A fusion of Whigs, Free Soilers, and anti-Nebraska Democrats, a prefiguring of the Republican Party, swept in a new governor and legislature, which promptly swept a stunned Augustus Caesar Dodge out of his Senate seat and replaced him with an antislavery Whig, James Harlan. (Harlan's daughter would marry Robert Todd Lincoln.) A Democrat would not be elected to the Senate again from Iowa for seventy-two years, until 1926. Elections held through the following year saw newly reconfigured state legislatures electing senators who reflected the party realignments, including in Pierce's bastion of New Hampshire, where he was humiliated by the return of his nemesis John P. Hale to the Senate.

The first meeting for the creation of a new party to be called "Republican" was held in a small Congregationalist church in Ripon, Wisconsin, on February 28, 1854, but it was less a formal founding than a discussion of principles and passage of a resolution to "throw old party organizations to the winds, and organize a new party on the sole issue of the non-extension of slavery." A locally prominent Whig, Alvan E. Bovay, responsible for the meeting, came up with the name "Republican," which he had been urging since 1852 on his friend Horace Greeley, who gyrated back and forth, wearily rejecting the idea before enthusiastically promoting it in the *Tribune*. The morning after the House passed the Nebraska Act, Gamaliel Bailey, editor of the *National Era*, encouraged Israel Washburn of Maine to initiate a meeting of antislavery members, who crowded into the boardinghouse rooms of Thomas D. Eliot and Edward Dickinson of Massachusetts to talk about the necessity of a new party, which they thought should be properly named "Republican." On July 6, in Jackson, Michigan, hundreds of Whigs, Democrats, and Free Soilers adopted a platform denouncing the repeal of the Missouri Compromise, took on the name "Republican," and proposed the slogan: "The North Will Defend You." A week later, on July 13, the anniversary of the passage of the Ordinance of 1787, a fusion convention was held in Vermont "to cooperate and be known as Republicans," followed by conventions in Ohio, Indiana, and Iowa.

But these early efforts did not lead seamlessly to the creation of the Republican Party. They were more symptoms of disintegration than clarifying coherence. Politics had entered into a fugue state, a strange period of disorientating vertigo, when people suddenly lost their bearings and identities as though stricken with dizzying amnesia, and adopted a succession of new ones. In the chaos there was no center to hold. While the Northern wing of the Democratic Party was crumpling, the Southern wing of the Whig Party deserted. "We have no longer any bond to Southern Whigs," Seward had written early in the debate on the Nebraska bill. Both parties had lost their equilibrium. Rather than the Northern Whig Party becoming a pillar of strength, it shattered into pieces under the stress. The social elements of Whiggery, its Protestant evangelical reformism, puritanism, and sense of natural order, broke off into their raw elements. There were assorted anti-Nebraska parties, as they were mostly called, and fusion parties, but there was also an explosion of temperance parties, and, even more significant, the emergence of the nativist Know Nothings. In Hartford, Connecticut, twenty-three separate parties were listed on the ballot. Some Whigs, like Seward and Lincoln, believed that if they remained stalwart they could see their party through the crisis. They would not abandon their lifelong attachment; the party had, after all, gone through difficult cycles before, and they would not align with the Know Nothings. It would take them nearly two years to grasp that they were clinging to splinters. Antislavery Democrats for their part would not become Whigs, not only because they had long fought them and disagreed with basic policies such as the tariff but also because the Whig Party was an obviously sinking ship. Their own party had capsized on them, the Whigs were a wreck, and there was no safe harbor. Along the landscape there were scattered groups that called themselves Republican, but there was no Republican Party.

Even before the Nebraska Act achieved final passage a new ghostlike political party suddenly materialized from seemingly nowhere and began sweeping elections. The Know Nothing Party, or American Party, struck first in Philadelphia, winning the mayoralty in a landslide, with an unlikely candidate, Robert T. Conrad, a poet, playwright, and conservative Whig. The party soon elected mayors in Chicago, New York City, and San Francisco—and nine governors.

The Know Nothings sprang from a small nativist sect in New York City called the Order of the Star Spangled Banner. Within months it had an estimated membership of more than a million. Its paranoid nativism feared a Jesuit conspiracy directed by the pope plotting to take over the federal government. Members were inducted into the secret order through mysterious oaths and pledged when asked about the organization to reply, "I know nothing." Seizing upon this rite, Greeley dubbed them "Know Nothings." Only Protestants married to Protestants could join. The key article of its constitution read: "The object of this organization shall be to resist the insidious policy of the Church, of Rome, and other influence against the institutions of our country, by placing in all offices in the gift of the people, or by appointment, none but native-born Protestant citizens."

The Know Nothing Party was less a stable party than an anti-party. Most antediluvian Whigs rushing to take oaths in its secret lodges did not think of themselves as members of a new regular political party but patriots above party and politics, upholding the purity of a mystical and original Unionism. In the flood they believed they were sweeping the country to the high ground. Their secret password was the question, "Have you seen Sam?" "Sam," good old Uncle Sam, and to some a code for "S-AM," or "Southern American," would save the country. According to the Know Nothing mythology, "Sam" had a younger son, the personification of an ideal innocent Americanism, a clean-shaven earnest youth named "Citizen Know Nothing," and whose lithograph portrait was widely distributed.

Between 1845 and 1854 three million immigrants had arrived in the country, the greatest wave in its history. About 40 percent were poor Irish Catholics fleeing the ravages of the potato famine. About another 40 percent were Germans escaping from the failed revolution of 1848. Nearly all of these immigrants aligned with the Democrats. Conservative Protestants viewed the Irish especially as a source of crime, corruption, and poverty. Both the Irish and Germans were beer drinkers, a habit that aroused temperance crusaders who condemned them as drunken, lazy, and sinful. Schuyler Colfax, one of the three Know Nothings elected to the Congress from Indiana, later speaker of the house and Ulysses Grant's vice president, declared, "If I were a candidate for any office, I would tell these paupers and vagabonds, these vile, dirty, filthy, degraded, idiotic foreigners that I did not want their votes."

Bestselling nativist novels, rivaling the sales of *Uncle Tom's Cabin*, featured lascivious "holy fathers" preying on virginal Protestant daughters, who were frequently kidnapped into nunneries, as in *The Awful Disclosures of Maria Monk*. One of the most widely circulated of these novels, *Stanhope Burleigh: The Jesuits in Our Home*, featured a subplot in which characters recognizable as Seward and Weed, both prominently anti-nativist, were active plotters in a Jesuit takeover of the United States. Virtually all of these novels had the same themes of foreign father figures defiling young American women in the absence of their own fathers and brothers. It was up to the outraged readers to get the message that they must be the rescuers of true American virtue and honor. Ned Buntline, the greatest dime novelist of Westerns, who popularized William "Buffalo Bill" Cody and "Wild Bill" Hickok, began his writing career as a Know Nothing with a bodice ripper entitled *The Jesuit's Daughter*, which he later reissued as *The Beautiful Nun*.

Nativism had a long and doleful history before its upsurge into the political vacuum of 1854, especially in New York City, its epicenter, where it was a constant feature since at least the mayoral candidacies of Samuel F. B. Morse, inventor of the telegraph, in 1836 and 1840. The Whigs in the city continually made deals with the nativists in order to prevent them from splitting the natural Whig vote. After anti-Catholic riots and street fights between gangs, which were invariably part of neighborhood political machines, the Whigs made an alliance with the nativists, calling themselves the American Republican Party, to support Henry Clay's presidential candidacy in 1844. On Election Day, the Whigs dutifully voted for the nativists slated for local offices while the nativists in a double-cross voted for Polk for president, along with the Liberty Party vote contributing to Clay's infinitesimal loss of the state and cataclysmic loss of the presidency.

The politics of New York in 1854 were enormously complex and clouded with four candidates for governor. The Democrats' hatred of each other was only matched by the Whigs' self-loathing. Vengeance was the universal motive. The Hards nominated Greene C. Bronson, removed as port collector for his refusal to submit on patronage to Marcy; yet Bronson was opposed to the repeal of the Missouri Compromise while running on a pro-Nebraska platform. The entire point of Bronson's candidacy was to purge the Softs and their candidate, Horatio Seymour, the incumbent and Marcy's ally. At the Softs' convention a majority was ready to vote for an anti-Nebraska plank, but was whipped into line, though Seymour agreed with Marcy the position was disastrous. At a moment when the temperance movement was at its peak both Democrats, dependent on the Irish vote, opposed prohibition. They were ultimately divided, Greeley wrote, "as to whether the contempt universally felt for President Pierce should be openly expressed, or more decorously cherished in silence."

The Know Nothings on the rise had long despised William Seward, who took a liberal attitude toward Catholics. If the State Assembly fell into unfriendly hands Seward would not be reelected to the Senate. Observing the intensity of Know Nothing organization Weed wrote that he did not "see how we are to get through the convention safely." Meanwhile, anti-Nebraska men held a separate convention that intended to nominate its own candidates. Seward and Weed worked behind the scenes to prevent this fragmentation. Nor did they favor fusion, which would create the perception that the Whig Party was collapsing into the arms of a marginal group.

It was at this fraught moment in which Seward's political fate hung in the balance that Horace Greeley knocked on the door of Weed's famous room number 11 at Astor House on Fifth Avenue to announce that he wished to be the candidate for governor. He had just written of the indisputable reality that "in this state Know-Nothingism is notoriously a conspiracy to overthrow Seward, Weed and Greeley, and particularly to defeat Gov. Seward's reelection to the Senate." But slating Greeley would set up a battle royal at the convention that Weed was likely to lose or if Greeley were nominated would guarantee defeat for Seward in the fall. In any case, Weed opposed trying to make Greeley governor, knowing him to be erratic, opinionated, and uncontrollable. When Greeley told him that the "time and circumstances" were "favorable to his election," Weed slyly explained that, "my friends had lost the control of the convention." At first "perplexed," Greeley finally said he understood, but a few days later he asked Weed, "Is there any objection to my running for lieutenant governor?" Once again, Weed walked him through the reasons he should not be a candidate, "and left me in good spirits."

Maneuvering at the convention, Weed secured the gubernatorial nomination for a hack state senator, Myron H. Clark, who was uniquely both a Know Nothing and Seward loyalist, as well as a liquor prohibitionist fanatic. After that coup, Weed arranged the nomination of his favorite for lieutenant governor, Henry J. Raymond, editor of the *New York Times*, whose more tolerant view on prohibition balanced Clark's puritanism. Greeley, who wanted to wage war on the Know Nothings, was also adamantly for liquor limitation. But a month before the election, the Silver Gray faction of the Whigs, still loyal to Fillmore and eternally hostile to Seward, joined with the main Know Nothing organization, the Order of United Americans, to nominate a candidate for governor, Daniel Ullmann, a New York attorney and friend of Fillmore. Anti-Nebraska and pro-temperance, Ullmann's candidacy blurred differences with Clark. His whole purpose was to overthrow Weed and Seward. The nativist Ullmann's provenance was raised against him, a "birther" issue to blot his appeal. Though he was born in Delaware, attended Yale, and was a founder of what became the Young Men's Christian Association, his parents were Alsatian French and he was accused of birth in Calcutta. Whig newspapers circulated the rumor while labeling the Know Nothings "the Hindoos." The absurd charge did its trick; Clark won by a scant 309 votes. It was a victory from which the Whig Party never recovered.

Greeley was inconsolably enraged at the choice of Raymond, his former assistant and chief rival, whom he referred to as "the little villain." In return, Raymond called him "the big villain." On the eve of the election, Greeley wrote Seward to lick his wounds, "Weed likes me, and always did—I don't think he ever had a dog about his house that he liked better—but he thinks I know nothing about politics. . . . I won't try any more to overcome his fixed prepossessions on this point." But a week after the election, on November 11, Greeley wrote an epic letter of accusation to Weed and Seward that declared, "It seems to me a fitting time to announce to you the dissolution of the political firm of Seward, Weed and Greeley, by the withdrawal of the junior partner." He admitted, "I should have hated to serve as lieutenant-governor, but I should have gloried in running for the post." And he conceded, "I should have been beaten in the canvass." Then he came to the core of his complaint: "No other name could have been put on the ticket so bitterly humbling to me as that which was selected." Addressing Seward directly, he promised, "I trust I shall never be found in opposition to you." Upon receipt of this self-pitying document, Weed and Seward, who had dealt with Greeley's outbursts before, ventured to the *Tribune* office to calm and reassure him, but he was still in the mood for venting. "We were discussing future rewards and punishments," Greeley told a young assistant who had overheard his high-pitched shouting.

Three months later, on February 8, 1855, Greeley wrote a letter to a friend explaining his incredible theory that Raymond had tricked a naive Weed. Now it was Weed who didn't understand politics. "Weed can be swindled by men who are fair to his face, but I think he will be more cautious hereafter. It is hard for him to realize that men 'can smile and smile and be a villain'— and he loves those who never seem to oppose his will; but he is, after all, the greatest man we have left—Seward not excepted. . . . Lieutenant Governor Raymond is quietly and industriously laying pipe for the next step. I hope he has been convinced that he cannot be both the Seward and the Hindoo candidate. If he has not, Sam will enlighten him on that point. Ah well, the struggle is over and I am no longer anybody's partisan. I don't care a button whether Seward stops where he is or goes higher." Greeley's perceived slight, which he nursed for years, would have unforeseen consequences eventually played out at the 1860 Republican convention as he furiously worked day and night against Seward's nomination.

In Massachusetts, the dissolution of the parties reached a refined state of confusion, opportunism, and self-righteousness. In response to the universal revulsion against the Nebraska Act the Whigs adopted an antislavery platform, yet rejected fusion with the Free Soilers because of their previous alliance with the Democrats, from whom they had split. The coalition that had elevated Sumner to the Senate was now in shambles. Conservative Whigs were dismayed at the sharp antislavery turn, "completely demoralized," for following a " 'freesoil' lead," according to Edward Everett, while Free Soilers were alienated. When the leader of the Free Soil Democrats, Henry Wilson, called a convention for a new Republican Party, it drew a sparse attendance, "a drum and fife [corps] without followers," as Charles F. Adams derided it, his animosity aroused because Wilson excluded him and his group of the Conscience Whigs. Sumner, however, appeared at the convention to deliver a stemwinding oration urging "Republicans" to battle "the Oligarchs of Slavery." Both his former and present allies mistrusted him, and Wilson would not let him speak at rallies for his gubernatorial candidacy.

Instead, Wilson joined a Know Nothing lodge, cut a deal with the Know Nothings to support him for the Senate in return for backing their candidate for governor, a former conservative Whig. Wilson soon found himself senator. Neither Wilson nor the new governor, Henry J. Gardner, had ever shown any nativist tendencies before or after for that matter. The Know Nothings swept 63 percent of the vote, electing every single state senator and all but two state representatives. Nathaniel P. Banks, an antislavery Democrat elected as a Know Nothing to the Congress, would become speaker of the house of the 34th Congress. "The people were tired of the old parties and they have made a new channel," Sumner rationalized. Rufus Choate, the old Whig and Webster's friend, wrote, "Any thing more low, obscene, feculent, the manifold heavings of history have not cast up." "Poor old Massachusetts!" lamented Winthrop. "Who could have believed the old Whig party would have been so thoroughly demoralized in so short a space of time?"

The new 34th Congress elected in the 1854 elections, but which did not take office until 1855, was an overlapping compound of Know Nothings and anti-Nebraska men. The Know Nothings claimed 121 new members, while the anti-Nebraska fusion parties had 115, but 92 were a helix of both, linked in fear of internal conspiratorial subversion, whether the Vatican or the slave power. But nearly all of them became Republicans. The professional politicians among them—Henry Wilson, Banks, and Colfax—shifted effortlessly from one tent to another. Their unprincipled sojourn as Know Nothings was at the heart of their virtue.

Sweeping statehouses and congressional elections in the North, the Know Nothing wave rolled south through Virginia, seemingly unstoppable as it captured mayoralties and local offices across the state, from Norfolk to Richmond to Lynchburg. Whereas in the North the movement often linked nativism to antislavery sentiment, in the South it joined xenophobia to pro-slavery feeling. In Virginia the Know Nothings were a gathering place for the politically unmoored, Whigs who felt bereft as the Southern Whig leadership merged with the Democrats after the Nebraska Act. Southern Know Nothings united in fear of invasion from immigrant hordes and abolitionist agitators, usually considered one and the same. The *Penny Post*, the leading Know Nothing newspaper, for example, attacked the German community of Richmond as "open and avowed abolitionists." John Minor Botts, one of the state's most stalwart Whigs, who had been instrumental in Winfield Scott's nomination, announced his candidacy as a Know Nothing for the Congress, blaming both the Democrats and "a few inconsiderate and misguided Whigs" for having "done more in the last six months to pro-mote the cause of Free-Soilism than all the Free-Soilers combined could have done in the next twenty years." The bad faith of both parties had destroyed "the harmony and confidence of the two sections of the country," making it "quite manifest that there is about to be a total revolution in the political affairs. . . . And if the organization of the Whig party is to be broken up, it leaves no alternative for us but to choose between the two other parties. The Know-Nothings on the one hand and the Good-for-Nothings on the other."

The Virginia governor's race of 1855 shaped up as a duel between Know Nothings and Democrats. If the nativists breached the Mason-Dixon Line they could claim they were a national party. The London *Times* correspon-dent wrote that if they won in Virginia they would "sweep the country." Thomas Stanhope Flournoy, a former Whig congressman, nominated as the Know Nothing candidate, assumed the traditional aristocratic posture, refusing to lower himself to the indignity of campaigning, his aloofness re-flecting a noble patriotism above parties and expectation of deference. The Richmond Whig newspaper trumpeted Flournoy as a "true Southern man" of "a true chivalrous Southern nature," who had a "perfect hatred" of aboli-tionists. The Democratic candidate, Henry A. Wise, had no compunctions running as a fierce demagogue, whose speeches were described by one Whig political figure as the "ravings of a bedlamite." He had begun his career as a Jacksonian Democrat, then became a Tylerite states' rights anti-Clay Whig, and flipped again, back to the Democrats. He was as widely mistrusted as he was wildly impassioned. With the death in July 1854 of Thomas Ritchie, chief of the Richmond Junto since Jefferson's administration, Wise raced to occupy the political vacuum, and through ambitious presumption, preter-natural energy, and oratorical blasts compelled Ritchie's factional enemies, the Calhounite Virginia Chivalry, led by the F Street messmates Hunter and Mason, to endorse him as the only alternative against the Know Nothing menace. Wise railed against the Know Nothings as a "dark lantern oligar-chy of Northern abolitionism coming South with the Bible in its hands," secretly controlled by Northern antislavery Methodist ministers. If the Know Nothings projected a Jesuit conspiracy, the Southern Democrats countered with a Wesleyan cabal. Senator Mason pitched in, calling the Know Noth-ings just a "Yankee device" to grab the "functions of government, without the sanction of law." The *Richmond Enquirer*, Ritchie's paper, still the most influential, editorialized against the "wooden horse within our gates, with an "armed enemy . . . concealed in the fatal structure." Wise denounced the Know Nothings as doubly evil, the "pet-child" of English abolitionists and the "legitimate offspring of Federal Massachusetts." If Know Nothings warned against the poisonous foreign influence of Rome, Wise trumped it with England and New England. In the greatest turnout for a governor's race in Virginia history, despite underlying Democratic suspicion of the changeable Wise and the feeble candidacy of Flournoy, the Know Nothing captured 47 percent of the vote, and Wise won by a narrow margin of 10,180 votes. His hammering of the nativists as abolitionists was the decisive stroke. Though Democrats danced in town squares around burning effigies of "Sam," Know Nothings still won many offices, including for the Congress. The consequence of this less than splendid triumph was more significant for the Know Nothings outside Virginia than within it.

Just days after the Virginia election in early June the first national convention of the Know Nothings convened in Philadelphia, where the Know Nothing mayor welcomed the delegates at a grand banquet. Hope burned bright that this event would be the historic founding of the new party to supplant the Whigs. After the Virginia defeat, Southern Know Nothings wanted to use the meeting to erase any stigma of being antislavery. The Fillmore faction of Silver Grays from New York, led by James W. Barker, chief of the Order of United Americans and Order of the Star Spangled Banner, saw the gathering as the first step in the restoration of Fillmore as president. Fillmore was already angling for the nomination of the Know Nothings, who he believed would subsume the Whigs. He had written a private letter to a friend that was carefully circulated to key political leaders, denouncing both parties for "corruption," "mockery" of "the rights of native born citizens," "the shameless chaffering for the foreign vote at every election," and demanding that "our country should be governed by American born citizens."

"Americans Only Shall Govern America," proclaimed the Know Nothing slogan. Barker was installed as convention chairman. And the New York delegation wrote a platform that would pledge the party to "submit" to the Nebraska Act repealing the Missouri Compromise in the interest of "giving peace to the country," declare that the Congress had no right to legislate on slavery in the territories, and that any act of Congress on slavery in the District of Columbia was a "breach of national faith." Northern delegates, however, rose in revolt, countering with their own platform calling for the reinstatement of the Missouri Compromise and prohibition of slavery in the territories. Southerners in league with the New Yorkers voted down this manifesto and passed their own. Fourteen Northern delegations walked out and with them some of the men who would become leaders of the Republican Party. The remaining Know Nothings, deliriously believing they had laid the groundwork for a national party and a Fillmore candidacy, staged a victory rally in Independence Square beneath banners reading: "Sam Is Wide Awake," "Sam, Stand Up," "Sam Is Going to Stand Up," and "Sam Has Stood Up." But the effect of forcing "a Pro-slavery platform," reported the *New York Times*, was that "the Know Nothing Party—heretofore so successful, so powerful, and so much wondered at by all and feared by many— has been destroyed."

Antislavery men like Henry Wilson joined the Know Nothings as an alternative to the crumbling parties in the North, until as soon as the slavery issue was raised that rickety structure collapsed, too. Yet in Massachusetts another movement was launched without subterfuge or bigotry that took up the challenge of popular sovereignty in order to deny Kansas to slavery.

CHAPTER SIXTEEN

THE CONQUEST OF KANSAS

Eli Thayer, a state representative from Worcester and representative man of Yankee ingenuity, descended from the family that founded the Massachusetts town of Braintree, and was educated at Amherst College and Brown University. He was a practical reformer who believed in freeing slaves and rights for women, and founded the Oread Institute, the first four-year women's college. He was also a tinkerer, inventing the hydraulic elevator and an automatic boiler cleaner. He liked designing efficient improvements. Elected to the legislature as a Free Soiler, he had withering contempt for Garrison's posturing and had no time to waste for the hand-wringing Free Soilers. When protest meetings against the Nebraska Act swept through Massachusetts, Thayer's impulse was not to light a match to the Constitution. The Garrisonians, "utterly impractical," he wrote, "had always impaired and crippled every cause they had advocated . . . the harbinger of certain defeat and annihilation. So they were not even thought of as a power to resist either the encroachments of Slavery then threatened, or

Eli Thayer, photography
by Mathew Brady

any future encroachments." They were "of too little account." Free Soil political leaders had "no plan of resistance" and were "hopeless as well as helpless." Wringing emotion from true believers was the opposite of his idea of successful enterprise. "That our work was not to make women and children cry in antislavery conventions, by sentimental appeals, BUT TO GO AND PUT AN END TO SLAVERY."

Thayer unveiled his plan to put popular sovereignty to the test at a meeting in Worcester on March 11, 1854, organized against the repeal of the Missouri Compromise. He proposed to create a joint stock corporation to finance the settlement of free state pioneers and build industries. "It was necessary," he wrote, "that Plymouth Rock should repeat itself in Kansas." The Pilgrims had fled oppression, but the Kansas emigrants would "destroy oppression." His scheme would combine profits with philanthropy, putting a moneymaking motive beneath the crusade. He would prove "the superiority of the free labor civilization," establish "a cordon of free States" around the South that would eventually "exterminate slavery," and pay a dividend. The corporation would be called the Massachusetts Emigrant Aid Company. He enlisted a justice of the state Supreme Judicial Court as chairman and a long list of prominent public figures as directors, from Henry Wilson to Samuel Gridley Howe, the prominent reformer, close friend of Charles Sumner, and member of the Vigilance Committee. After winning endorsement of the company with capital of $5 million from the Massachusetts legislature, the enterprising Thayer raised subscriptions for stock from the wealthiest and socially most distinguished men of New England—Amos A. Lawrence, the textile magnate and cousin of the president's wife; John Murray Forbes, the tycoon of the China trade and railroads; John Carter Brown, banker, philanthropist, scholar, and scion of the family that founded Brown University; and Charles Francis Adams. Thayer recruited Theodore Parker, who became an enthusiast for the project, gathering a group of clergy in his study to hear him. Lyman Beecher and Edward Beecher gave him their benediction. Garrison and his followers, however, showered Thayer with vituperation and openly wished for his failure as a greedy huckster of morally compromised half-measures. Never having been to New York, Thayer traveled there to introduce himself to Horace Greeley, whom he flattered as indispensable in saving the country. "You are the one man now needed," he told the editor. "If we lose Kansas the political control of slavery is assured for an indefinite period." Greeley promptly began a crusade in the *Tribune* for what he dubbed Thayer's "Plan for Freedom."

Lawrence advised Thayer that it would be most effective to recast the company from a speculative venture into a charity, relieving it from demanding investors while still hoping for future dividends. The Massachusetts legislature granted a new charter for the renamed New England Emigrant Aid Society. On that basis and given his personal prestige, Lawrence was able to recruit as backers the top echelon of the younger men of the Boston elite, Cabot and Lowell, Endicott and Lee.

On July 17, 1854, twenty-four pilgrims boarded a train at Boston's depot and headed west to be joined by five others along the route. They pitched their tents on August 1 at the site Thayer had chosen on the south bank of the Kaw River about fifty miles from the Missouri border, where they proclaimed their colony the town of Lawrence. Six weeks later a second contingent of 114 pioneers set off to join them, at the railroad station chanting John Greenleaf Whittier's poem composed in their honor: "We cross the prairies, as of old/ The Pilgrims crossed the sea,/ To make the West, as they the East,/ The homestead of the Free." By the end of the year Thayer estimated that about five hundred had left Boston, but they attracted dozens more as they moved toward their destination. Once in Kansas, they immediately began constructing a town on the New England model, building schools, mills, stores, churches, and publishing a newspaper, the *Herald of Freedom*.

As soon as David Atchison announced from the Senate podium that the Nebraska Act had passed, he left Washington to wage his war against Benton and the looming menace of the Emigrant Aid Society. He confided his strategy in a letter to Jefferson Davis on September 24, promising that the free state men would meet the fate of the Mormons.

We have done two things, Benton has been Killed either for good or for evil he will no longer be in our way. . . . We will have difficulty with the Negro thieves in Kansas, they are resolved they say to keep the slave holders out, and our people are resolved to go in and take their "niggers" with them. . . . I on the 21st of this month advised in a public speech the squatters, in Kansas and the people of Missouri, to give a horse thief, robber, or homicide a fair trial, but to hang a Negro thief or Abolitionist, without Judge or Jury, this sentiment met with almost universal applause. . . . We will before six months rolls around, have the Devil to play in Kansas and this State, we are organizing, to meet their Organization we will be compelled, to shoot, burn and hang, but the thing will be soon over, we intend to "Mormonise" the Abolitionists.

Jesse Bright took Atchison's position as president pro tempore, making it a point of contempt to deny Sumner any committee assignments.

The clamor that Greeley and other Northern papers made about the progress of the small bands of the Emigrant Aid Society trekking westward raised a ferocious reaction even before they stepped foot into the Kansas territory. Missourians on the border thought of Kansas as rightfully their property and greeted enactment of the Nebraska Act almost as a reverse Ordinance of 1787 proclaiming it a slave state. The appearance of the New England migrants was a shock, affront, and mortal threat. War fever gripped the border.

On June 10, the first documented group of pro-slavery men held a squatters' meeting at Salt Creek Valley near Fort Leavenworth, declaring its principles: "That we recognize the institution of slavery *as always existing in this Territory*, and recommend slaveholders to introduce their property as early as possible. That we will afford protection to no Abolitionists as settlers of Kansas Territory." A group in Liberty, Missouri, adopted a platform: "Shall we allow such cut-throats and murderers, as the people of Massachusetts are, to settle in the territory adjoining our own State? No! If popular opinion will not keep them back, we should see what virtue there is in the force of arms. . . . Resolve, That Kansas ought of right to be a slave State." The *Platte Argus*, Atchison's mouthpiece, offered a $200 reward for the capture of Eli Thayer—"and meet with just such a course of treatment as one of his sort deserves—hanging!" "It is now time to sound the alarm," trumpeted the *Argus*, calling for "counter organizations" against the free state invaders. "We must meet them at their very threshold and scourge them back to their caverns of darkness." On July 29, Atchison led more than one thousand men at Weston to form the Platte County Self-Defensive Association, which pledged to "drive out from their midst the abolition traitors" and proclaimed itself judge and jury that would "try and punish all abolitionists." Throughout western Missouri secret armed societies were organized, with signs, handshakes, and passwords, named the Kansas League, Platte County Regulators, Sons of the South, Blue Lodge, and Social Band.

The organizational leaders of the pro-slavery forces, closely working with Atchison, were two brothers, Benjamin Franklin Stringfellow and Dr. John H. Stringfellow. J.H. was a founder of the pro-slavery town aptly named Atchison, where he edited the movement's newspaper, the *Squatter Sovereign*, whose motto was "Death to All Yankees and Traitors in Kansas." He explained to a congressional committee in 1856 investigating violence in

Kansas, "Had it not been for the emigrant aid societies the majority in favor of slave institutions would, by the natural course of emigration, have been so great as to have fixed the institutions of the Territory, without any exciting contest. . . . That was the way we regarded the passage of the Kansas-Nebraska bill, as by reserving a restriction to introduce southern institutions into Kansas." The very name of the *Squatter Sovereign* expressed its motivation in a theory of white supremacy that "color, not money marks the class: black is the badge of slavery; white the color of the free man, and the white man, however poor [and] whatever his occupation, feels himself a sovereign." The free state men were alien intruders, a lesser breed of whites, slaves to their rulers, "the Greeleys and the Sewards," "the scum and filth of the Northern cities; sent here as hired servants," "collected from their prisons, brothels, and sink-holes of iniquity," paid to destroy the equality of a superior race.

B. F. Stringfellow, the former attorney general of Missouri, was secretary of the Platte County Self-Defensive Association, and author of the movement's essential document, a "Report" entitled "Negro-Slavery, No Evil." He began with a description of the outside menace, "we find these miscalled emigrants really negro-thieves, their purpose not to procure a home in Kansas, but to drive slaveholders therefrom; that they are not freemen, but paupers, who have sold themselves to Ely [*sic*] Thayer & Co., to do their masters' bidding." These "negro-thieves" were guilty of crime that "ranks, at least, with that of the midnight assassin," inciting "hatred for their masters," which was "often followed by arson and murder." Guarding against these "fearful evils" was "the immediate cause of our organization." The "negro-thieves" were the vanguard of a strategy to "surround Missouri with non-slaveholding States; force her to abolish slavery; then wheel her into their ranks for an attack upon the States south of her." The cause was that of the entire South. "We would be justified in marching to their camp and drive them back to their dens, without waiting for their attack. We are not bound to wait until they have stolen our negroes, burned our slaveholding towns."

Stringfellow stated he would prove his case that slavery was "a blessing to the white race and to the negro" by "facts and figures, about which there can be no dispute." The first of his facts was that in the Bible "slavery was actually established" by "God's holy law." Moses was a slaveholder, Jesus "recognized and regulated" it, and Paul captured a fugitive slave. The second source of his facts was purportedly from the census of 1850. "We thus see that to blindness, insanity and idiocy, the negro, when free, is far more subject than the white. Such being the natural liability of the negro to these afflictions, we yet find that as a slave the negro is almost exempt from them all—not only is he far less afflicted than the free negro, but even less than his master." The slaves' "real condition" was the product of "the watchful care of the master." His next set of facts showed that the South had more churches than New England, which he claimed was also economically more unequal for whites, a region of "paupers." The equality among Southerners, he argued, was due to "the effects of negro slavery." Finally, he refuted those who "prate" about the Declaration of Independence's phrase "all men are created equal," which was "common with abolitionists," but "has no relation to the question of negro slavery." The future existence of the United States required "the institution of slavery." "In the history of the world, there is no instance of a Republic which endured for a generation without the institution of slavery." He concluded with an appeal to patriotism, "let us protect its only safeguard," and a warning, "if we have failed to satisfy our northern friends": "Forbearance is ceasing to be a virtue."

On October 7 the territorial governor arrived. Andrew H. Reeder, a Pennsylvania lawyer so loyal to the state Democratic Party he was said to belong to its Tenth Legion, after the most loyal Roman legion. He received the appointment with Pierce's eye on winning Pennsylvania for nomination again and reelection. John W. Forney, the Pennsylvania politico who was editor of the *Washington Union*, and Congressman Asa Packer of Pennsylvania, the railroad and coal tycoon, gave their imprimaturs. They knew Reeder as an able lawyer who could reliably handle business and political matters, and, according to Forney, was "an extreme sympathizer with the South at all times" and told his Southern friends "he was going to take a slave with him." Reeder launched an inspection tour of Kansas, buying shares in the newly established towns as he went and laying out a prospective capital called Pawnee, of which he was the principal stock and landholder.

After accumulating his nice portfolio of property, Reeder declared the taking of a census for an election on November 29 for a territorial delegate to the Congress. Atchison traveled through Missouri border towns urging the men to ride into Kansas to take control of the polls on that day. "When you reside in one day's journey of the Territory," he said, "and when your peace, your quiet and your property depend upon your action, you can, without an exertion, send five hundred of your young men who will vote in favor of your institutions." But he warned, "If we cannot do this, it is an omen that the institution of slavery is to fall in this and the other Southern states; but it would fall after much strife, civil war, and bloodshed." For his part, he declared, he was prepared "to hang negro thieves."

Reeder's announcement that those eligible to vote would be "residents" who lived in Kansas and intended to remain there permanently provoked the wrath of the pro-slavery groups, which denounced him as favoring abolitionists. The day before the election more than 1,700 men from Missouri under the direction of their secret societies rode into the territory armed with guns and bowie knives, and carting wagons loaded with barrels of whiskey. They pushed poll judges aside, intimidated and roughed up free state voters, and marked ballots for the pro-slavery candidate, J. W. Whitfield, an Indian agent from Tennessee, before departing in a drunken haze. In 1856, the Special Committee Appointed to Investigate the Troubles in Kansas concluded that the election was "unlawful interference" and "a shameless fraud," the pattern established in the territory for "every election." "They declared that they were bound to make Kansas a slave State. They insisted upon their right to vote in the Territory if they were in it one hour. After the election they again returned to their homes in Missouri, camping over night on the way." Whitfield won overwhelmingly. But when the Kansas census was conducted a few months later it revealed that emigrants from Missouri outnumbered those recently imported from northern states by 1,670 to 1,018. The pro-slavery men had stolen an election they would have won in any case. This "mockery," as the congressional committee called it, was the first example of the theory of popular sovereignty in action, and the model that would be followed. Douglas insisted "there could not have been a system of fraud and violence," and that the entire idea "that the Missourians had invaded the territory" lacked "all proof and probably truth," and was simply "the basis of the most inflammatory appeals to all men opposed to the principles of the Kansas-Nebraska act."

After this fraudulent election B. F. Stringfellow traveled to Washington, where he met with members of the F Street Mess and other Southern congressmen. "Two thousand slaves," Stringfellow told them, "actually lodged in Kansas will make a slave state out of it. Once fairly there, nobody will disturb them." They promised they would encourage Southern emigration from their states, but little was actually forthcoming. The Missourians had to rely on themselves.

Reeder now announced an election for a territorial legislature on March 30. "I tell you," Stringfellow declared at a rally at St. Joseph, Missouri, "to mark every scoundrel among you who is the least tainted with abolitionism or free-soilism, and exterminate him. . . . To those who have qualms of conscience as to violating laws, state or national, the time has come when such impositions must be disregarded, as your rights and property are in danger. I advise you, one and all, to enter every election district in Kansas, in defiance of Reeder and his vile myrmidons, and vote at the point of the bowie knife and revolver. Neither give nor take quarter, as the cause demands it. It is enough that the slave-holding interest wills it, from which there is no appeal." On the eve of the election, Atchison crossed into Kansas with a company of men flashing their guns and bowie knives. "There were eleven hundred coming over from Platte County," he boasted, "and if that wasn't enough they could bring five thousand more; that they came to vote and would vote, or kill every God damned abolitionist in the Territory."

The Special Committee documented 4,968 nonresident voters overwhelming the 1,210 actual settlers. The invasion was part military and part spree. Wearing a dragoon officer's coat, "General" Stringfellow waved his soused troops onward. "Atchison was there with bowie knife and revolver, and by God 'twas true," Atchison later boasted. Discounted round-trip steamboat tickets were provided and ballots conveniently printed. One slaveholder tossed one thousand dollars on the table at a rally. "I've just sold a nigger for that," he announced, "and I reckon it's about my share toward cleaning out the dog-gauned Yankees." The night before the election, Claiborne Jackson held a mass meeting outside Lawrence, giving orders for which companies of men would go to which districts. Election judges were offered the choice of resigning on the spot or being shot, and free state voters driven away. One old Missouri planter voted 144 times.

"KANSAS SLAVE STATE" proclaimed the *Kansas Herald* of Leavenworth, hailing the "brilliant and glorious triumph achieved by the noble and unaided efforts of the gallant and chivalrous sons of the South over the combined forces of the abolitionists, free-soilers and Emigrant Aid societies," and that Kansas' "fate is sealed." The vote was "vox populi," "loudly and decisively in favor of slavery," "infallible" proof of popular sovereignty.

Free state men urged Governor Reeder to order an entirely new election. Pro-slavery Missourians widely believed rumors that he might just do that and their newspapers threatened him with hanging and "cutting his throat from ear to ear." He received delegations from both sides in his office on April 5. The pro-slavery men, armed with knives and revolvers in their belts, told him to certify all the elections. Holding a cocked pistol in his hand, in a gesture at Solomonic judgment he tried to cut the decision down the middle. He threw out seven of the thirty-one results, ordered new elections in those districts but certified the rest. "There were a few devoted friends around him expecting to see him murdered on that occasion," Senator Henry Wilson recalled.

Returned to Missouri, the men of the Platte County Association passed resolutions declaring that the pro-Benton newspaper sympathetic to the free staters published in a nearby town, the *Parkville Industrial Luminary*, was "a nuisance," its editors "traitors" who must leave the state, and that any member of the "Northern Methodist Church" preaching in the county would be tar and feathered "for the first offense" and hung "for the second." Atchison's *Platte Argus* editorialized *"the people having determined that Kansas shall become a slave State,* will probably put a *quietus* upon abolition presses in Kansas Territory. The 'freedom of the press' is not for traitors and incendiaries." On April 14, the mob invaded Parkville, carried the press of the *Luminary* with a white cap atop it labeled "Boston Aid," and dumped it in the Missouri River. The editors fled.

In Leavenworth, a lawyer named William Phillips had filed an affidavit documenting the fraudulence of the election there. The pro-slavery men gave him a deadline to leave. "To the peculiar friends of northern *fanatics*, we say, this is not your country, go home and vent your treason, where you may find your sympathy." Another resolution proclaimed slavery the law of the territory: "That the institution of slavery is known and recognized in this Territory, that we repel the doctrine that it is a moral and political evil, and we hurl back with scorn upon its slanderous authors the charge of inhumanity, and we warn all persons not to come to our own peaceful firesides to slander us and sow the seeds of discord between the master and the servant, for much as we may deprecate the necessity to which we may be driven, we cannot be responsible for the consequences." On May 17, the self-styled "Vigilance Committee" kidnapped Phillips to Weston, Missouri, shaved one side of his head, tarred and feathered him, and staged a parody of a slave auction, with one of their slaves acting as the auctioneer. "How much, gentlemen, for a full-blooded abolitionist, dyed in de wool, tar and feathers and all? How much, gentlemen? He'll go at the first bid." Then the men held an assembly that passed resolutions praising themselves. "That we heartily endorse the action of the committee of citizens, that shaved, tarred and feathered, and rode on a rail and had sold by a negro, William Phillips, the moral perjurer."

The pro-slavery forces boycotted the district elections of May 22 to fill the contested seats, so only free staters were elected. Reeder had been writing private letters to President Pierce about the "recklessness and violence" he encountered, "for I had still the fullest confidence that he would share all my indignation at the gross wrong of this foreign interference." He decided he would present the facts to the president in person at Washington. On his way, Reeder delivered remarks that were widely reported. "It was, indeed, too true," he said, "that Kansas had been invaded, conquered, subjugated by armed forces from beyond her borders, led on by a fanatical spirit, trampling under foot the principles of the Kansas bill and the right of suffrage." At the White House, Reeder met the amiable president who wanted to do the likable and easy thing. Pierce told Reeder that he was "highly pleased and satisfied in my course," but wished he had blamed the Emigrant Aid Society. Reeder replied that he didn't know of anything "illegal" it had done. Kansas, Pierce confessed, had "given him more harassing anxiety than anything that had happened since the loss of his son." He revealed that Atchison had "pressed" him "in the most excited manner" to have Reeder dismissed, using the grounds that he had made real estate investments in Kansas. Pierce quickly assured Reeder he had been "fair and honorable," and that the issue was a "pretext." But he said it was "unsafe" for Reeder to return as governor. Reeder replied that it would be "cowardice" to quit, that he would not "betray" his office and "abandon" those subject to "persecutions and oppressions." Pierce asked him to write a full report and plan, which he would endorse, and then suggested Reeder could resign. Would he like to be minister to China? Reeder wrote him a report, but Pierce did not accept it. He promised he would appoint an "upright northern man" to replace him. Reeder again refused to resign. Pierce said he would explain that he had to remove him not for his "official action," but "if I remove you at all, it will be on account of your speculations," adding that "all these matters might be arranged in such a manner as to promote his private interests if he would voluntarily vacate his office." The comedy was over. Feeling insulted, Reeder silently left the president for Kansas.

"From reports now received of Reeder, he never intends returning to our borders," the *Squatter Sovereign* editorialized. "Should he do so, we, without hesitation, say that our people ought to hang him by the neck, like a traitor's dog, as he is, so soon as he puts his unhallowed feet upon our shores." B. F. Stringfellow traveled to Leavenworth, where he stormed into Reeder's room, yelled at him for his speech about the election fraud, hit him, knocking him out of his chair, and then kicked him. (A few months later, in a debate on Kansas, Senator Butler remarked, "I know General Stringfellow very well. . . . As to his whipping Reeder, everybody knows that.") The *Congressional Globe* recorded: "(Laughter)."

Reeder convened the legislature at the new town of Pawnee, one hundred miles distant from the Missouri border, to attempt to diminish the Missourian influence. On July 2, the pro-slavery members refused to accept the results of the May voting, seated the pro-slavery men elected by fraud, and expelled the one remaining free state representative, who resigned in protest. After electing J. H. Stringfellow as speaker of the house, they adjourned to reconvene at Shawnee Mission, one mile from the Missouri border. Reeder vetoed the move declaring it illegal and the legislature dissolved. The free staters referred to it only as the "Bogus Legislature." From that point, power was split in the territory between hostile centers of government that considered each other illegitimate.

At a meeting at Weston, Missouri, Atchison, Judge William C. Price, the Stringfellow brothers, and other pro-slavery leaders devised the first new laws that the "Bogus Legislature" would pass. "I and my friends," Atchison said, "wish to make Kansas in all respects like Missouri." Any person helping a fugitive slave would be condemned to death. Any person writing or speaking, or offering "opinions" that contributed to "disorderly, dangerous or rebellions disaffection among the slaves," would be sentenced to hard labor for five years. Any who "maintain that persons have not the right to hold slaves in this territory" or brought in any antislavery publication would receive a hard labor sentence of two years. No one opposed to slavery would be allowed to serve as a juror. All the codified laws of Missouri were enacted with the word "territory" substituted for "state." For good measure, the "Bogus Legislature" passed a resolution charging Reeder with subversion, treason, and corruption.

The town of Pawnee, the first capital, was located near Fort Riley. Secretary of War Jefferson Davis sent a military commission to redraw the fort's boundaries to circumscribe Pawnee within the military reserve, but his surveyors returned with a map that excluded it. Davis took a red pen, drew a line extending to Pawnee and wrote, "Accepted within the red lines." Then he issued an order for its destruction and the removal of all the residents. One thousand dragoons from Texas marched in to demolish every building.

Reeder was fired on August 10 for "speculations," the "pretext." His replacement was Wilson Shannon, the Hunker former governor of Ohio, Tyler's minister to Mexico, and a congressman who voted for the Nebraska Act. Before entering Kansas, he appeared at an elaborate reception at Westport in Missouri before a large pro-slavery crowd. He declared the Shawnee Mission legislature "legal," condemned those who would "nullify the laws enacted by your legislature," and announced that he was "for slavery in Kansas."

The free state men countered with a series of seven conventions, in September forming the Free State Party, a fusion of Democrats, Whigs, and Free Soilers, for which Reeder wrote the platform. *"Resolved,* That we owe no allegiance or obedience to the tyrannical enactments of this spurious Legislature—that their laws have no validity or binding force upon the people of Kansas." Then the party nominated Reeder as its delegate to the Congress. The free staters met again a month later in Topeka at a constitutional convention that declared "slavery shall not exist in the state," and created a territorial legislature. Kansas now had dual and dueling powers, one pro-slavery and one antislavery, one recognized by President Pierce and one considered outlaw. But in Kansas the antislavery cause was about more than slavery. After invasions, intimidation, fraudulent elections, and suppression of free speech it became a struggle for democracy. The questions were not separate—slavery and democracy—but one and the same, just as they were in John Quincy Adams's struggle over the Gag Rule. "The conquest of Kansas," as the free staters called pro-slavery rule, revealed the extension of slavery. Once it burst the bounds of the South, it was a rapacious antidemocratic force that, the Free State Party platform declared, "libeled the Declaration of Independence, violated the constitutional bill of rights, and brought contempt and disgrace upon our republican institutions at home and abroad." The issue of Kansas became more than Kansas. The idea of the Union became contingent on who defined it.

One month after the Topeka convention, the pro-slavery men under the leadership of the Stringfellows gathered at Leavenworth to form what they called the Law and Order Party. Governor Shannon, a delegate, was elected president of the convention and delivered a speech promising to enforce the laws of the "Bogus Legislature." "The president is behind you!" he shouted. "The president is behind you!" The next speaker was the newly appointed surveyor general of the Kansas Territory, John Calhoun, from Illinois, Lincoln's old employer and political rival, who denounced "vile abolitionists . . . so vile they would lick the slime off the meanest penitentiary in the land," and "would bow down and worship the devil if he would only help them to steal a nigger."

A week later, a pro-slavery man named Franklin Coleman unloaded his shotgun into the back of an antislavery one named Charles Dow in a land dispute outside Lawrence. The free staters burned down Coleman's house. He fled to a pro-slavery county, seeking aid from Sheriff Samuel J. Jones, one of Atchison's and the Stringfellows' men, also postmaster of Westport. He was a mob leader in the first invasion, who waved pistols at election judges amid cries of "kill the damned nigger thief," forcing them at gunpoint to resign on the spot, and who stole ballot boxes. Jones arrived with a posse to arrest the murdered settler's elderly friend, Jacob Branson, who was supposedly said to have threatened retribution against the killer, but a band of armed free staters rescued Branson from his clutches. Jones appealed to Governor Shannon, who sent a dispatch to the "Major General" of the Kansas militia to "report" to the sheriff. But this militia of the "Bogus Legislature" was a fiction. So Shannon issued a proclamation circulated only to pro-slavery towns in Kansas and Missouri, and his secretary wrote Atchison: "The Governor not having the power, you can call out the Platte County rifle company. . . . Do not implicate the Governor whatever you do." The call went out: "If we are defeated this time, the territory is lost to the South." The *Squatter Sovereign* editorialized, "We anticipate bloodshed" and "expect to wade waist deep in the blood of the abolitionists." Shannon recalled, "It was war—war to the knife."

Once again, the "Border Ruffians" invaded, more than fifteen hundred, "a motley crew . . . all had been drinking, and many were staggering about tipsy," according to the reporter from the *New York Tribune*. In Clay County, Missouri, they took over the federal arsenal, seizing its rifles, swords, and cannon. Atchison personally commanded two hundred men encamped on the Kansas River across from Lawrence. "Every hour added to the excitement, and brought new fuel to the flame," said Shannon. They expected to destroy the town and drive out "all the Dambd Abolitionists." But instead of being able to "Mormonise" the free staters, as Atchison wrote Jefferson Davis, the Missourians encountered a surprise.

Since the first fraudulent election the free staters had been quietly importing hundreds of Sharps rifles, the most advanced breech-loading weapons available, paid for by Amos A. Lawrence and other benefactors, and shipped as "books" or "Bibles," some later from Henry Beecher's Plymouth Church in Brooklyn, and know thereafter as "Beecher's Bibles." The settlers were highly organized, drilled in military formations, and entrenched with their superior firepower. The raucous and shabby pro-slavery men prepared for the assault. Shannon decided to go to Lawrence to persuade the free staters to turn over their Sharps rifles, thinking that the display of his authority would frighten them into submission. He was startled to discover a skillfully trained army under tough and shrewd leadership. Shannon negotiated a peace treaty with the free state leaders, declaring the whole standoff had been a "mis-understanding" and ordered the pro-slavery men to disband. Atchison conceded that the position was "impregnable." "If you attack Lawrence now, you attack it as a mob, and what would be the result? You would cause the election of an abolition president and the ruin of the Democratic Party. Wait a little. You cannot now destroy these people without losing more than you would gain." But "General" Stringfellow denounced the agreement, saying, "Shannon has turned traitor."

At the critical juncture, while Shannon was holding off the Missourians and dealing with the free staters, he telegraphed President Pierce to order the use of federal troops at Fort Leavenworth. But that order was never sent from the Department of War to the commander. Jefferson Davis, "as he probably desired a conflict of the militia or posse with the citizens, and knew that the presence of United States troops would prevent it, he declined to send the order, as authorized by the President," surmised Charles Robinson, the free state leader and soon to be governor.

During the diplomacy, a new settler who had just arrived with his sons, equipped with pikes, and revolvers and knives sticking in their belts, vehemently opposed any gesture at peace. John Brown wanted to launch an attack, and even after the agreement was made he mounted a wooden box and harangued a crowd that the crisis could only be settled with blood. The peace was only an armistice. Atchison, the Stringfellow brothers, and John Brown would return. The fifty-six killings ultimately attributed to the conflict only begin to suggest the lethality of "Bleeding Kansas." Nor does the spoken debate about popular sovereignty illuminate the descent into chaos, fear, and violence. Nor do the gaudy details of the Border Ruffians' "Sack of Lawrence," followed by John Brown's grisly "Pottawatomie Massacre," capture the frenzied atmosphere. By themselves these numbers, words, and events do not explain the whole organic history and political momentum that would soon draw in Lincoln.

The war in Kansas killed more than the peace that seemed to have been achieved through the Compromise of 1850. It wrecked more than Stephen A. Douglas's grandiose visions and ruined more than Franklin Pierce's presidency.

CHAPTER SEVENTEEN

IMPERIALISM, THE HIGHEST STAGE OF SLAVERY

The dream of a Caribbean slave empire died on the plains of Kansas. Jefferson Davis's best-laid plans to take Cuba, much of Mexico, and other Caribbean lands came apart. He had overridden Marcy to staff the key embassies with the ministers who were devoted to the mission of a tropical Manifest Destiny. Former Senator Pierre Soule, the new minister to Spain, had once signed a letter to George N. Sanders, now secretary of the legation at London, with "a sweet kiss to young America." When Marcy issued one of his first orders that American ministers should appear in royal courts wearing plain republican suits in the mode of Benjamin Franklin, Soule showed up before the Spanish king and queen attired in embroidered black velvet. Almost as soon as he made his dramatic entrance he challenged the French ambassador to a duel over a perceived insult from a remark over Madame Soule's low-cut dress

William Walker

and maimed him. Unpopular even before he arrived for his views on Cuban annexation, he was virtually persona non grata from the start. In February 1854, Spanish officials in Cuba seized an American merchant steamer, the *Black Warrior*, for failing to declare its cargo. The incident seemed to be an ideal casus belli for a splendid little war to take Cuba. Pierce sent the Congress a message calling it a "wanton injury" and demanded authority "to vindicate the honor of our flag." Soule delivered an ultimatum that the Spanish must pay an indemnity of $300,000 for the affront. Within a few weeks Spain released the boat, sent troops to reinforce the garrison at Havana, emancipated slaves born or arrived after 1835, and for good measure stopped the slave trade there. Soule argued to the president that this amounted to a declaration of war, he should be recalled, and preparations for full-scale war made. Jefferson Davis and Caleb Cushing fully supported this course, while Marcy opposed it. Through Davis's influence at the *Washington Union*, a war fever was stoked with editorials calling for a blockade and predicting that Cuba was soon "bound to be admitted" to the United States. But given that the pretext was removed, the bluster was just wind. Soule was disconsolate and furious at Marcy.

After the *Black Warrior* fiasco, Marcy instructed Soule to investigate "the next desirable object, which is to detach that island from the Spanish dominion" by peaceful purchase. But Marcy already believed that the chance to gain Cuba was lost. "To tell you an unwelcome truth," he wrote Mason, the minister to France, in July 1854, "the Nebraska question has sadly shattered our party in all the free states and deprived it of that strength which was needed and could have been much more profitably used for the acquisition of Cuba." He suggested that the three relevant U.S. ministers—Soule, John Y. Mason at Paris, and James Buchanan at London—gather privately for "a full and free interchange of views," the usual diplomatic language suggesting that nothing should happen except a dispatch to the State Department where it would be appropriately filed for posterity. With the phlegmatic Buchanan, a former secretary of state, as the senior figure presiding, the meeting would be expected to conclude notably with a fine dinner. Conferring at Ostend in the Netherlands in October 1854, they signed a document, hereafter known as the Ostend Manifesto, remarkable for its bombast, chiefly authored by the excitable Soule but approved by Mason, who in private called Soule "a perfect bird charmer," and Buchanan, who abandoned his caution for an opportunity to sideswipe Marcy and damage his presidential prospects. According to the Manifesto, Cuba was "necessary" to the United States and "belongs naturally to that great family of states." If Spain rejected selling it for $120 million, it "should seriously endanger our internal peace," and "by every law, human and Divine, we shall be justified in wresting it," citing "the very same principle that would justify an individual in tearing down the burning house of his neighbor." Failing to follow this course would be "base treason," which would "permit Cuba to be Africanized and become a second St. Domingo, with all its attendant horrors to the white race." By preserving "our own self-respect . . . we can afford to disregard the censures of the world." Marcy received this document on Election Day as he learned that every one of the nine Democratic congressmen from New York who had voted for the Nebraska Act had been defeated. Within two weeks of the Democratic wipeout, the *New York Herald* disclosed the Manifesto, creating a diplomatic and political row. Marcy wrote his ambassadors that their plan "is past my comprehension." "My amazement is without limit," declared Soule upon reading Marcy's rejection. "I am stunned." He was convinced, he said, "The President can neither have inspired nor sanctioned it." He resigned in protest. Mason had a stroke in "a paroxysm of excitement and indignation," according to the secretary of the Paris legation. And Buchanan set himself up for the nomination.

The debacle of Ostend was only the prelude to the more grandiose folly in pursuit of a Caribbean empire. While two strongmen battled for control of Nicaragua, the weaker one, down to a dwindling band of bedraggled followers, desperately took the advice of an American soldier of fortune, Byron Cole, a former San Francisco newspaper publisher, who, in exchange for loot and land, offered to secure the military aid of his former editor and president of the short-lived Republic of Sonora, William Walker. Acquitted for violating the Neutrality Act in his invasion of Mexico, Walker landed on June 16, 1855, with his fifty-six self-styled "immortals," "La Falange Americana," or American Phalanx. By the time he captured the Nicaraguan capital of Granada, after attracting an army of freebooters, both of the contesting caudillos had died, he signed a peace treaty with the opposing general, and made himself commander-in-chief to a figurehead president. Walker made a written agreement with the son of a wealthy Cuban, Domingo de Goicuria, who had participated in various abortive schemes to invade Cuba, that he would help him seize the island. In the meantime, Walker appointed him minister to England, a post he promptly quit after a quarrel. Soon, Walker had the general with whom he had made the treaty shot by a firing squad for alleged treason and shunted aside his makeshift president, staging his own inauguration as head of state. Pierre Soule instantly arrived to arrange the floating of bonds for Walker's government. A month later, on September 22, 1856, undoubtedly encouraged by Soule, President Walker unilaterally re-pealed all Nicaraguan laws and proclaimed it a slave republic. Slavery had been abolished in Nicaragua thirty-two years earlier, but now he declared himself standing for a "cause" that was "right and just." By extending slavery, he saw himself heroically saving the South. "The policy of the act consisted in pointing out to the Southern States the only means, short of revolution, whereby they can preserve their present social organization," he wrote. "To avert the invasion which threatens the South, it is necessary for her to break through the barriers which now surround her on every side, and carry the war between the two forms of labor beyond her own limits."

Walker named as his minister to the U.S. one of the most notorious con men of the era, the one-armed Parker H. French, who scammed his way across the continent from Wall Street to the Gold Rush, becoming a news-paper publisher, California state legislator, pro-slavery Know Nothing, and Walker's minister of hacienda, or finance, from which position he pocketed the taxes and proceeds from government monopolies. Marcy rejected the cre-dentials of the renowned scoundrel. Undaunted, French joined Soule in New Orleans to raise and almost certainly skim funds. French also happened to be the son-in-law of none other than Duff Green, the journalist, diplomat, speculator, Calhoun diehard, and all-around operator, who accompanied "the Ambassador of the Buccaneers" in high style in New York and Wash-ington. Green escorted him through the Capitol in and out of meetings with members of the Congress. "His firm bearing and brilliant style of conver-sation captivates even the old fogies," reported the *New York Herald*. When the New York district attorney began prosecution of French for violating the neutrality law, almost certainly with the knowledge if not encourage-ment of Marcy, Pierce directly interfered, ordering him to cease and desist. Walker named a new minister to the U.S., Father Agustin Vigil, who had showered the Catholic Church's silver and jewels on Walker, whom Vigil consecrated as "Protective Angel." In recognizing Father Vigil, Pierce finally recognized Walker's military regime over Marcy's objections.

Days after Walker executed the Nicaraguan general with whom he had made peace, Secretary of State Marcy instructed the U.S. minister to Nica-ragua not to recognize Walker's regime and to shun him. But that official, John H. Wheeler, a North Carolinian, had become Walker's chief promoter, his "invited guest and welcome friend," who enthusiastically shared "contempt for the Spaniards and those mongrel races, who occupied with indolence and semi-barbarism one of the finest and most productive regions on the continent." Flouting Marcy's instructions, Wheeler recognized Walker's government as legitimate, and was hailed by Walker's "Falange" as "El Ministro Filibustero." Enraged, Marcy recalled Wheeler. Then Pierce stepped in, not to support his secretary of state but instead to protect the insubordinate ambassador. In this and other gestures toward Walker, Jefferson Davis prodded Pierce and set himself within the cabinet against Marcy.

While Wheeler continued to encourage Walker yet another American expedition invaded Nicaragua. Colonel Henry L. Kinney intended to transform Central America into a new Texas. His life had been a series of hyped promotions, financial bubbles, and lucky enterprises. The Colonel was not a colonel. He claimed to have won his rank fighting in the Black Hawk and Seminole wars, but there were no records or corroborating witnesses of his presence. He began in real estate speculation in the 1830s in Peru, Illinois, where he attracted Daniel Webster, who borrowed $3,000 from Caleb Cushing to invest. (It was on Webster's Illinois tour to inspect his property that Lincoln met him and represented his son Fletcher Webster on a small piece of the business.) Kinney lost almost everything in the Panic of 1837, moving on to Texas, where he established a ranch near the Mexican border and founded the town that became Corpus Christi. He was elected to the Texas Senate and was a member of its constitutional convention. During the Mexican War, Kinney profited enormously from his strategically located trading post serving the U.S. Army, and he became a quartermaster. Among the officers he befriended were Franklin Pierce and Jefferson Davis. Kinney scored his largest deal yet when he finagled control of 22.5 million acres of the Mosquito Coast, a British protectorate on the Atlantic side of Nicaragua, from British investors who had been given the original grant by the native king of the Mosquito realm but whose successor declared it illegal and were delighted to unload it.

To exploit his newly found kingdom, Kinney incorporated the Nicaraguan Land and Mining Company, financed by Wall Street investors and dealing in Pierce's closest advisers. Kinney merged his claims with those of Joseph W. Fabens, the U.S. commercial agent in Nicaragua, who had acquired an attractive piece of real estate. Fabens referred to Kinney as "the Romulus of our new Southern empire," and wrote that Pierce summoned him to Washington and blessed the enterprise. Kinney cut in as investors Sidney Webster, Pierce's private secretary, A. O. P. Nicholson, editor of the *Wash-*

ington Union, and John W. Forney, the House clerk (who was also invested in Stephen A. Douglas's Superior City scheme). In a confidential letter franked with the signature of Franklin Pierce, Sidney Webster wrote on April 24, 1855: "My Dear Fabens: I have received the document, and with my associate here am grateful to you and your partner, and entirely satisfied. . . . Don't try to figure in the newspapers." The "associate" unnamed was possibly Pierce himself, though Cushing later vociferously denied his interest when the letter was revealed in legal proceedings in 1857.

Kinney claimed he was engaged in a strictly business proposition as he recruited a gang of hundreds of soldiers of fortune. "We have . . . from the highest authority, a complete account of the aims and objects of the expedition," reported the *New York Herald*, which had leaked the Ostend Manifesto. "It resembles, in its nature, the expedition which was planned here more than twenty years ago, and which, under General Sam Houston, succeeded in colonizing Texas, then in relieving the territory from the government of Mexico, and finally in annexing it to the Union, as one of the sovereign States in the confederacy. . . . The original expedition to Texas introduced the system of African servitude into that State, and the result has proved beneficial both to the whites and blacks. The object of the Kinney expedition is similar. Its leaders propose to set up the system of African servitude in Central America, probably by the introduction of slaves from the Southern States."

Before Kinney embarked, however, the New York district attorney indicted him and Fabens for violating the Neutrality Act, and Marcy dismissed Fabens as U.S. agent. They were acquitted, but their expedition was whittled down to only eighteen men. Upon landing in July 1855 Kinney proclaimed himself "Civil and Military Governor," ruler of the Mosquito Coast. As the monarch of an imaginary domain he presented Walker with a plan to divide the country into two states—Nicaragua and Mosquitia—but Walker simply banished him. (When the Civil War broke out, Kinney was initially anti-secession, but offered his services as a spy to both Jefferson Davis and Lincoln, who refused him, and was killed in a gunfight in Matamoros, Mexico, in 1862.)

The downfall of Kinney foreshadowed that of Walker. They both committed the same offense of arousing the hostility of a greater power, a power of almost limitless money and might—Cornelius Vanderbilt. The richest man in the United States owned the Accessory Transit Company, a steamship and stagecoach line that was the only passage across the isthmus from the Atlantic to the Pacific. When he perceived a threat to the Transit Company from Kinney, his lawyer, Joseph L. White, also close to Marcy, was the one to whisper in the ear of the New York district attorney, who promptly issued indictments. Once Walker made himself president of Nicaragua he revoked the lucrative charter of the Transit Company and handed it to cronies, a "coup d'etat," according to the *New York Times*. Vanderbilt personally came to Washington to lobby Pierce and Marcy, but the president would do nothing on the presumption that Vanderbilt had early on aided Walker. In fact, the administration tilted to Walker, with Jefferson Davis supporting him. But Walker's megalomania had incited an insurrection against his autocratic rule and a war with Costa Rica. Rebuffed by Pierce, Vanderbilt was freed to act on his own. It would be his fortune against Walker's soldiers of fortune. Vanderbilt sent his agents to provide financing and military leadership for the Costa Rican and Honduran armies, who overwhelmed Walker's Phalanx. Instead of making an Alamo out of Granada, Walker ordered the burning of the capital and fled. The conquistador was no match for the Commodore. (After writing his memoir in the style of Caesar's *Commentaries*, Walker invaded Honduras in 1860 to overthrow its government. He was captured by British naval forces and rendered to the Hondurans, who executed him by firing squad, just as he had dealt with his enemies.)

The allure of a tropical Manifest Destiny magnetically attracted an astonishing cast of freebooters, soldiers of fortune, speculators, bandits, and demagogues, who created extraordinary embarrassments, imbroglios, disasters, and wars. It was in the nature of seizing or invading foreign lands that brought these brigands to the forefront. They were so piratical that it took a truly successful pirate on a monumental scale, Cornelius Vanderbilt, to impose law and order. Even after Vanderbilt deposed Walker, the man who was briefly a tin-pot dictator remained celebrated as a folk hero throughout the South. But behind the filibusters and their legends loomed serious men with serious business, not least Jefferson Davis, who declared he would "rejoice" if Walker were to succeed. The bullet drilled into Walker's brain by a Honduran officer to ensure he was quite dead after the firing squad had done its job hardly ended the cause. In 1859, Senator Jefferson Davis, delivering a speech at the Mississippi Democratic State Convention in favor of reopening the international slave trade, said he "hoped the day was not distant when, by the acquisition of tropical territory, the arch would be completed," and pointedly called for the "acquisition" of Cuba as "especially necessary in the event of the formation of a Southern Confederacy." If a future president were ever elected on Seward's "platform," he declared he would be the signal for "the dissolution of the Union."

CHAPTER EIGHTEEN

ARMED LIBERTY

The Southern route of a Pacific railroad was not built, Kansas was not slave territory, and Cuba was not annexed. But Jefferson Davis did succeed at least in beginning a grand project that would symbolize the Union. As senator, in 1850, he had sponsored a bill for reconstruction of the Capitol, and as secretary of war he was in charge of the massive building. In place of the rotting dome he would crown the Capitol with an iron one at whose pinnacle, the highest point in Washington, would be placed a statue to be the icon of the nation. The commission for the statue was awarded to Thomas Crawford, a New Yorker classically trained in Rome, who was designing statues of George Washington surrounded by a host of famous Virginians for Richmond's Capitol Square. Recommended by Edward Everett, the most intellectually accomplished senator, he was a distinguished choice. In 1855 Crawford submitted a drawing for the statue he called *Freedom Triumphant in War and Peace*, a draped female figure with a sword in one hand and

Original design of the *Statue of Freedom* with Liberty Cap

olive branch in the other, and wearing on her head a cloth Phrygian cap, the sign of an emancipated Roman slave, the fashionable symbol of French revolutionaries. More than the aesthetic ideals of the Italian Baroque sculptor Bernini had influenced Crawford. He was a close friend of Charles Sumner and married to Louisa Ward, sister of Julia Ward Howe, the wife of ardent abolitionist Samuel Gridley Howe, and who would write "The Battle Hymn of the Republic." Davis was displeased with Crawford's vision. The cap, he said, was "inappropriate to a people who were born free and should not be enslaved." He ordered a new headdress, a Roman helmet ringed with stars to represent the states and topped with decorative Indian feathers, an American version of the Roman goddess of war Minerva,

renamed "Armed Liberty." Crawford died of cancer in 1857, but left a plaster model. The contract to cast it into bronze was granted in 1860 to a local foundry, and the craftsman who created the statue was Philip Reid, a self-taught slave, who, under Lincoln's Emancipation Act for the District of Columbia, was a free man when *Armed Liberty* was hoisted to the top of the completed Capitol five months after the Battle of Gettysburg.

Jefferson Davis's decision on the design for *Armed Liberty* was one of the crowning and most enduring legacies of Franklin Pierce's presidency.

Pierce wished for a second term as president, but whatever his virtues—a handsome face, a gracious manner—he never had a will to power. His powerful father and his father's friends had lifted the privileged son upward until Jefferson Davis

The *Statue of Freedom* as approved by Jefferson Davis

captured him. Davis, too, wanted another term for Pierce, but the Democrats decided the incumbent was tarnished. The fresh face of four years earlier needed to be replaced with an old face. James Buchanan had avoided being flecked with "Bleeding Kansas" far away as minister to England. The Ostend fiasco burnished his credentials for statesmanship for the South and the time was right for an old fogy who could carry Pennsylvania. Between the election and the inauguration, Jefferson Davis was elected to the Senate. On Inauguration Day, March 4, 1857, at nine in the morning, he came to bid farewell to Pierce before the other outgoing cabinet members appeared. Pierce grasped his hand. "I can scarcely bear the parting from you," he said, "who have been strength and solace to me for four anxious years and never failed me."

Pierce departed from Washington never to return for a grand tour of Europe with his wife. In Rome, he encountered by chance his old friend, Nathaniel Hawthorne, who was "rejoiced to see him, though a little saddened to see the marks of care and coming age, in many a whitening hair, and many a furrow, and, still more, in something that seemed to have passed away out of him, without leaving any trace."

For weeks after the inauguration, Jefferson Davis was unable to stride onto the floor of the Senate. He was an invalid, stricken with recurrence of the symptoms of his venereal disease, confined to darkness, "tortured by neuralgic pains and nervous tension," according to Virginia Clay, and had lost the sight of one eye.

Campaigning for his comrade in 1852, Davis had spoken about the blindness of the country living under a volcano. "A blind confidence not warranted by the past, or by passing events," he said, "is such fatuity as if the inhabitants of a volcanic mountain, whilst it trembled in token of approaching eruption, should crowd to the crater, and lay themselves down to repose." He cautioned that the stakes for the Union in that election were greater than in any "former time," and that "they had before them" an "organized foe" whose "purpose was the consolidation of the states, and the destruction of the domestic institution of the South."

Two years before that, during the debate over the Compromise of 1850, Clay, Webster, and Calhoun had all warned of civil war. They were not blind. Clay, accused by Davis of betraying the South, replied that "if gentlemen suppose they can exact from me an acknowledgment of allegiance to any ideal or future contemplated confederacy of the South, I here declare that I owe no allegiance to it."

Webster spoke of a galactic explosion. "Secession! Peaceable secession!" he exclaimed. "Sir, your eyes and mine are never destined to see that miracle. The dismemberment of this vast country without convulsion!" He described the consequences as the end of the world. "Sir, he who sees these States, now revolving in harmony around a common center, can expect to see them quit their places and fly off without convulsion, may look the next hour to see the heavenly bodies rush from their spheres and jostle against each other in the realms of space without producing a crash of the universe."

Calhoun understood, too, replying to Webster, "I cannot agree with the Senator from Massachusetts that this Union cannot be dissolved. Am I to understand him that no degree of oppression, no outrage, no broken faith, can produce the destruction of this Union? Why, sir, if that becomes a fixed fact, it will itself become the great instrument of producing oppression, outrage, and broken faith. No, sir, the Union can be broken." He added, among his last words, "Disunion must be the work of time."

Edward Coles, Thomas Jefferson's protégé and James Madison's private secretary, the second governor of Illinois, who had secured it as a free state at the price of his political career, broke his long silence to enter the debate against the repeal of the Missouri Compromise and the de facto repeal of the Ordinance of 1787 in the territories, only to have Douglas question his integrity. In 1856, Coles published his views in a short history of the Ordinance in which he concluded, "Since its principles were repudiated, in 1854, we have had nothing but contention, riots, and threats, if not the awful realities of civil war."

Thomas Hart Benton, after the *Dred Scott* decision of 1857, wrote his *Historical and Legal Examination*, a concise history that traced the "dogma of the unconstitutionality of the Missouri Compromise" to his nemesis Calhoun, "a man of head and system, and though working at a dissolution of the Union since the year 1830, his system was to throw upon the North the blame of the separation—to make the segregation of the slave States an act of necessity—of self-defense—forced upon them by aggressions, encroachments, and crusades against their slave property. To attack the Missouri Compromise was to give up that defensive attitude—to make the South the aggressor—and consequently to make it responsible for disturbing the peace and harmony of the Union." The repeal of the Missouri Compromise to claim Kansas for slavery was, Benton wrote, only one of "the intentions of the prime movers of that measure. . . . Certainly that was one of the objects; but there were others far beyond it, far transcending it in importance; and of which the establishment of Kansas as a slave state was only an introduction, and a means of attainment. To form the slave States into a unit for federal elections and legislation, by the revival of the slavery question, was one object, counting upon the federal patronage to gain as much help from the free States as would give the slave States the majority. Vast acquisitions of free territory to the southward, to be made slave (besides Cuba), was another object; and for this purpose the principles of the Kansas-Nebraska bill were doubly contrived."

In the repeal of the Missouri Compromise, and in the coming of the Civil War, the leading men were not sleepwalkers. They could see what they were doing. They were not stumbling day by day to the precipice. They had their reasons, imperatives, and interests—and their expressions of them filled the *Congressional Globe*. The repeal was a deliberate, conscious, and plotted act.

None of those who promoted it was forced against his will. They were not reluctant. Nor did they act in secret, though there were private conclaves. They did not suffer from failures of imagination. They had heard the alarming warnings that nothing less than the sudden collapse of the universe that would follow. They felt they were "inhabitants of a volcanic mountain." They understood there would be a "convulsion," though they thought they could control it. They projected grandiose possibilities of slavery spread, railroads built, empires rising, and presidencies attained. The authors of the catastrophe entered a dark passage by choice and design, with little regard for the possibility of miscalculation or arrival of the unexpected, including the technological, such as Sharps rifles.

In the early and mid-twentieth century, a school of historians called "revisionists" dominated writing and discussion about the origins of the Civil War. They were imbued with a pacifist temper in reaction against World War I, studiously indifferent to the rise of Fascism and Nazism in their own times, and hostile to U.S. international involvement. Their writings that described the Civil War as "needless" were partly aimed at inspiring American isolationist sentiments as Europe seemed on the verge of war again. These historians, Northern men with Southern roots, also accepted the distorted assumptions of the Lost Cause of Reconstruction as corrupt Northern aggression. They dismissed slavery as a cause of the conflict, accused abolitionists in particular of inciting sectionalism and infecting politics with unwarranted emotionalism, and denigrated politics itself as the ultimate source of conflict. Their work was a re-creation of the original justifications of Stephen A. Douglas, James Buchanan, and Clement Vallandigham, the pro-Confederate Northern Democratic Copperhead, but presented in the tone of academic objectivity as "realism." James G. Randall, considered the leading Lincoln scholar of this period, blamed "a blundering generation" with sweeping moral equivalence while rejecting any analysis of slavery and its political and economic system of power. "If one word or phrase were selected to account for the war," he wrote, "that word would not be slavery, or economic grievance, or state rights, or diverse civilizations. It would have to be such a word as fanaticism (on both sides), misunderstanding, misrepresentation, or perhaps politics." The issues were "forced and unnatural," and the Republican Party "produced quarrels out of things that would have settled themselves were it not for political agitation." Avery Craven in his influential *The Coming of the Civil War* made Sumner and Chase his villains and Douglas his hero. He regretted that slavery became "a sectional issue linked to sectional rivalry and territorial expansion." "As a purely social and moral question to be faced and dealt with as such," he wrote, "slavery might not have proved a national tragedy." Slavery, he explained, "became the symbol between 'civilizations.' " It was the abolitionists who "threatened to produce a race problem which had in large part been solved by the institution of slavery." Completely ignoring the machinations that produced the repeal of the Missouri Compromise, he sermonized, "Men ceased to reason, to tolerate, to accept compromise. Good men then had no choice but to kill and to be killed." He concluded that the Union victory achieved worse than nothing. He did not bother to mention the Emancipation Proclamation or the constitutional abolition of slavery. "When the struggle was over," he wrote, "few problems had been solved, and a whole series of new ones had been created far more vexing than those which led to war. Later historians would talk about 'a blundering generation.' " The historians of the "blundering generation" school would spawn blundering generations of historians who continued to operate within their framework even after being eviscerated in an essay published in 1949 by Arthur M. Schlesinger, Jr.

Understandably, neither Randall nor Craven cited the devastating refutation of their views offered by Abraham Lincoln himself in his last debate with Douglas, on October 15, 1858, in Alton, Illinois. His speech was a compact summary of the events to that point that would lead to the war. Lincoln put slavery at the heart of the matter, described how it had divided the whole society, and defended the necessity of politics. First, he exposed Douglas's hypocritical cant about politics with good humor. "You may say and Judge Douglas has intimated the same thing," Lincoln said, "that all this difficulty in regard to the institution of slavery is the mere agitation of office seekers and ambitious Northern politicians. He thinks we want to get 'his place,' I suppose. [Cheers and laughter.] I agree that there are office seekers amongst us. The Bible says somewhere that we are desperately selfish. I think we would have discovered that fact without the Bible. I do not claim that I am any less so than the average of men, but I do claim that I am not more selfish than Judge Douglas. [Roars of laughter and applause.]"

Having won over the crowd with a light touch, Lincoln approached it like a jury. "But is it true that all the difficulty and agitation we have in regard to this institution of slavery springs from office seeking—from the mere ambition of politicians? Is that the truth? How many times have we had danger from this question?"

He asked the people carefully to review the history, the evidence.

Go back to the day of the Missouri Compromise. Go back to the Nullification question, at the bottom of which lay this same slavery question. Go
back to the time of the Annexation of Texas. Go back to the troubles that
led to the Compromise of 1850. You will find that every time, with the single
exception of the Nullification question, they sprung from an endeavor to
spread this institution. There never was a party in the history of this country, and there probably never will be of sufficient strength to disturb the
general peace of the country. Parties themselves may be divided and quarrel
on minor questions, yet it extends not beyond the parties themselves. But
does *not* this question make a disturbance outside of political circles? Does it
not enter into the churches and rend them asunder? What divided the great
Methodist Church into two parts, North and South? What has raised this
constant disturbance in every Presbyterian General Assembly that meets?
What disturbed the Unitarian Church in this very city two years ago? What
has jarred and shaken the great American Tract Society recently, not yet
splitting it, but sure to divide it in the end. Is it not this same mighty, deep
seated power that somehow operates on the minds of men, exciting and
stirring them up in every avenue of society—in politics, in religion, in literature, in morals, in all the manifold relations of life? [Applause.]

Then he turned his rhetoric so that it was those listening who were the
principal political actors, had been the ones to see through the spurious nature of his opponent's flimsy words and finally moved them to his position.

Is this the work of politicians? Is that irresistible power which for fifty years
has shaken the government and agitated the people to be stilled and subdued by pretending that it is an exceedingly simple thing, and we ought not
to talk about it? [Great cheers and laughter.] If you will get everybody else
to stop talking about it, I assure I will quit before they have half done so.
[Renewed laughter.] But where is the philosophy or statesmanship which
assumes that you can quiet that disturbing element in our society which has
disturbed us for more than half a century, which has been the only serious
danger that has threatened our institutions—I say, where is the philosophy
or the statesmanship based on the assumption that we are to quit talking
about it [applause], and that the public mind is all at once to cease being
agitated by it? Yet this is the policy here in the North that Douglas is advocating—that we are to care nothing about it! I ask you if it is not a false philosophy? Is it not a false statesmanship that undertakes to build up a system

of policy upon the basis of caring nothing about *the very thing that every body does care the most about?* ["Yes, yes," and applause]—a thing which all experience has shown we care a very great deal about? [Laughter and applause.]

Douglas was aware from the beginning of the furor over the Nebraska Act he might arouse. Before introducing it he confided to Everett that "no man was so wild as to think of repealing the Missouri Compromise." But his hesitation was momentary. He gambled on the jackpot. He figured that he could win it all replaying the Compromise of 1850, this time receiving the acclaim, two transcontinental railroads, a personal financial windfall, and the presidency. "I passed the Kansas-Nebraska Act myself," he boasted. "I had the authority and power of a dictator throughout the whole controversy in both houses. The speeches were nothing. It was the marshalling and directing of men, and guarding from attacks, and with a ceaseless vigilance preventing surprise." Benton, who knew a great deal about the backstage manipulation of the political pulleys and chains, observed presciently, "Douglas was driven into the Kansas-Nebraska Bill by Atchison and others, the fire-eaters of the South. They threatened to drop him if he would not yield to all their demands. . . . Douglas is now further from the Presidency than ever. The South will ruin him." When the free state settlers trekked to Kansas to exercise their claims under Douglas's doctrine of popular sovereignty, he was startled, offended, and angry. He would repeatedly cast the entire blame for the fight in Kansas on them, proclaiming to the Senate in 1856, "From these facts it is apparent that the whole responsibility of all the disturbances in Kansas rests upon the Massachusetts Emigrant Aid Company and its affiliated societies."

Shortly after the Nebraska Act's passage, Douglas traveled to a political rally for beleaguered Democrats in New York, where he announced, "This is the issue upon which I intend to stand before the American people, and to meet either their approval or disapproval." On July 4th, he delivered the main address at a celebration in Philadelphia, excoriating the Know Nothings, and lambasting opponents of the Nebraska Act as "pure, unadulterated representatives of Abolitionism, Free-Soilism, Niggerism in the Congress of the United States."

After the adjournment of the Congress in August, Douglas campaigned across the country on his way home to Illinois. "I could travel from Boston to Chicago by the light of my own effigy," he recalled. "All along the Western Reserve of Ohio I could find my effigy upon every tree we passed." In one town a group of antislavery women humiliated him with a gift of thirty pieces of silver and called him a Judas.

Douglas intended to use the Nebraska Act as his whip inside the Illinois Democratic Party to enforce party discipline and loyalty. Instead it provoked a party split. Congressman John A. McClernand, one of Douglas's closest allies, condemned his litmus test as "simply an act of senseless and outrageous proscription." While he submitted under protest, other important Democrats broke away—Congressman John Wentworth from Chicago, former Illinois Supreme Court justice Lyman Trumbull, and Lieutenant Governor Gustave Koerner. A Douglas loyalist since the German revolutionary had arrived in exile in Illinois, Koerner was the leader of the German American community that had previously backed the Democrats but was instantly alienated by the Nebraska Act. A meeting of Germans in Chicago passed resolutions calling it an "attempt to import Southern aristocracy and Southern contempt of free labor, into the North," and labeled Douglas "an ambitious and dangerous demagogue." The *Chicago Democrat* newspaper, close to Wentworth, vented its vituperation at Douglas, who unexpectedly found himself without a defender in the city. He scrambled to organize funding and an editor for his own paper, the *Chicago Times*. The *Illinois State Journal*, Lincoln's paper, meanwhile denounced Douglas's bill as "a piece of wrong and treachery," and Douglas as "the tool of designing, faithless and unprincipled southern men" who wanted "to control the government of this great people."

Douglas decided he would seize command of the situation by marching into the lion's den of Chicago to confront and cow the crowd as he had after the Compromise of 1850. Once again, he wished to relive a heroic incident of his past. "They threaten to mob," he wrote Lanphier of the *Register*, "but I have no fears." Chicago was now his hometown. As much as any man he was its true founding father, as the author of the Illinois Central Act responsible for its explosive growth. He announced he would address a meeting at the North Market on the evening of September 1.

On that day the ships along the dock flew their flags at half-mast. The church bells rang a funeral dirge for an hour, summoning a crowd he estimated at ten thousand. According to his account, "the anti-Nebraska men had organized into Know-Nothing lodges," secretly took an oath "not to allow me to speak," and the night before had received 250 Colt revolvers. Once he began his speech, he wrote that he was drowned out by an "unearthly yell practiced in the Know-Nothing lodges, a howl no man can imitate." The *New York Times*, however, reported that "he began by vindicating the repeal of the Missouri Compromise on the ground that it permitted Slavery South. . . . He asked triumphantly, whether there was 'a man in that crowd, who was in favor of recognizing Slavery South of any line.' The Missouri Compromise did recognize it South of a certain line;—therefore its repeal was justifiable." The crowd heard him in "perfect silence" to begin with, according to the *New York Tribune* report, but greeted his opening statement with "a thunder of deep-toned groans as perhaps never was heard in Chicago before, and before which the speaker prudently quailed with bitter mortification." He accused the crowd of ignorance of his bill and "when he received a tart rejoinder, he became petulant, denounced his enemies," which produced "universal confusion." Douglas "soon lost all self-control, threw aside the dignity of the orator, placing his hat on his head, his arms akimbo, and in a very undignified manner leaning on the rail before him, defied and denounced the meeting, and threatened he would put down the 'mob' or stay there till morning." He "declared he had labored for Illinois before most of hearers had ever heard the name of Chicago," and "began to attack the Chicago Tribune," which had editorialized against the Nebraska Act. The *Tribune* correspondent concluded, "I am fully convinced there was no predetermined plan to prevent his speaking. Every outbreak or disturbance was provoked by himself at the time of its occurrence, whether by design or from the uncurbed impulse of a malignant nature I cannot judge." The *Times* observed that the widespread reports that he had been prevented from speaking were false and that he was "interrupted only by replies to his direct appeals, or still more direct misstatements." In his own version, Douglas ended the "wild confusion and fury" by taking his watch from his pocket and announcing, "It is now Sunday morning—I'll go to church, and you may go to hell!"

The Chicago melee received sensational national coverage. "In Illinois we will make all right. The row at Chicago is doing us immense good," Douglas wrote John C. Breckinridge. He staged a barnstorming campaign across the state to make his case and retain a Democratic state legislature. "We have had glorious meetings at Joliet, Morris and Ottawa," he wrote his editor of the *Chicago Times*, James W. Sheahan. But wherever he went opposition speakers, an assortment of abolitionists, Whigs, and anti-Nebraska Democrats, demanded that he divide his time with them. He rebuffed each and every one, telling them these were his meetings. On September 26, he came to speak at Bloomington. Lincoln had been there for two weeks.

Since the middle of August, Lincoln had gone back onto the political stump, giving anti-Nebraska speeches in town after town. On September 11, he was transparently the author of an unsigned article in the *Journal*. It featured a parable to puncture the sophistry of popular sovereignty, whose two main characters were named "Abraham Lincoln" and "John Calhoun," his former employer, the well-known local Democrat and pro-slavery advocate, who had just been appointed chief surveyor of the Kansas territory. "Abraham Lincoln has a fine meadow," Lincoln began,

> containing beautiful springs of water, and well fenced, which John Calhoun had agreed with Abraham (originally owning the land in common) should be his, and the agreement had been consummated in the most solemn manner, regarded by both as sacred. John Calhoun, however, in the course of time, had become owner of an extensive herd of cattle—the prairie grass had become dried up and there was no convenient water to be had. John Calhoun then looks with a longing eye on Lincoln's meadow, and goes to it and throws down the fences, and exposes it to the ravages of his starving and famishing cattle. "You rascal," says Lincoln, "what have you done? what do you do this for?" "Oh," replies Calhoun, "everything is right. I have taken down your fence; but nothing more. It is my true intent and meaning not to drive my cattle into your meadow, nor to exclude them therefrom, but to leave them perfectly free to form their own notions of the feed, and to direct their movements in their own way!"

Lincoln concluded his Aesopian tale with an appeal to the common sense of his readers, the jury, delivered with humorous but fatal ridicule: "Now would not the man who committed this outrage be deemed both a knave and a fool,—a knave in removing the restrictive fence, which he had solemnly pledged himself to sustain;—and a fool in supposing that there could be one man found in the country to believe that he had not pulled down the fence for the purpose of opening the meadow for his cattle?"

The day after Lincoln's article was printed he was in Bloomington, where he addressed a German anti-Nebraska meeting, urging a vote for legislative candidates who would enact an instruction to Douglas to repeal his bill. Then he handled several railroad cases at the courthouse—and then he waited. Douglas had forgotten about Lincoln, but when he arrived Lincoln was there.

"In 1854," Lincoln wrote of himself in his 1860 autobiography, "his profession had almost superseded the thought of politics in his mind, when the repeal of the Missouri compromise aroused him as he had never been before."

CHAPTER NINETEEN

THE FAILURE OF FREE SOCIETY

S tephen A. Douglas had risen so far that Lincoln disappeared from his view. Five years gone from Washington, Lincoln was left to observe the tail of the comet. Roaming through the Eighth Judicial District of central Illinois he remained fixated as ever on his rival streaking across the sky. Douglas gave him little thought. He was consumed with his deals with the F Street Mess, forging real estate syndicates, and head counting the wily and rough members of the Congress. But after Douglas introduced his Nebraska bill he fell within Lincoln's range. Beginning a thousand miles away Lincoln began shadowing him, first through newspaper columns and as he came closer stalking him on foot. Douglas inadvertently cut the path that allowed Lincoln to emerge from his wilderness. Now pursuing Douglas, Lincoln found him unexpectedly vulnerable, Illinois transformed,

George Fitzhugh

politics tumultuous, and discovered his own voice.

Sumner and Chase hurled denunciations at Douglas, Benton demeaned him, and Seward debated, but only Lincoln could meet Douglas on the political battlefield of Illinois. Douglas contended with all the powers-that-be in Washington, yet inevitably he had to return to earth—to Illinois. While playing for the greatest national stakes, his base of support, his organization, and his right to his office were rooted in his home state. As the Little Giant inflated himself into "the spirit of the age," the man of the future, he defined the high stakes in challenging him. Opening the new territories to popular sovereignty, he threw open the politics of the country—and Illinois. Lincoln alone was there.

"Now, however, a live issue was presented to him," recalled William Herndon. "No one realized this sooner than he." It was, to be sure, the chance Lincoln never anticipated. His recollection in his 1860 campaign autobiography that in 1854 "his profession had almost superseded the thought of politics in his mind" was a finely cut Lincolnian line that suggested he had nearly forgotten about politics, "almost," while conceding it was still foremost "in his mind." Lincoln, in fact, never retired from politics. Even as he represented hundreds of clients in a seemingly endless string of petty cases, he cultivated contacts, read intensely, and honed his forensic skills. There was not a double Lincoln, split between the lawyer and the politician. Whatever he gained in sharpening his method as a lawyer he knew or hoped he would apply in politics. For him the courtroom and the campaign were transferable arenas. His speeches in both were addressed to the jury. He had been active in the disastrous Whig effort of 1852, delivering a ridiculously vacuous speech whose hyped-up low humor reflected the underlying desperation of the cause. In the aftermath of the catastrophic defeat, like almost all other disheartened Whigs, Lincoln went to ground. The year 1853, in any case, was politically fallow, without any notable contests.

Douglas's bill plunged Lincoln into a concentrated period of intellectual introspection and political outreach unlike any other since just after he retired from the Congress when he handled the *Todd Heirs* case in Kentucky. There he witnessed firsthand the unbridled arrogance and grasping of the pro-slavery forces as they rewrote the state constitution to fling open the gates to the slave trade and not coincidentally step over the grave of Lincoln's father-in-law, who had opposed them. Here he saw Douglas, whose hubris he had warned against in his first formal speech, at the Springfield Lyceum in 1838, trample down the barrier to the extension of slavery. Before the repeal of the Missouri Compromise, Lincoln had been a perennial local adversary of the great Douglas, but now he became his nemesis. As Lincoln would recount, "he took us by surprise—astounded us—by this measure. We were thunderstruck and stunned; and we reeled and fell in utter confusion. But we rose each fighting, grasping whatever he could first reach—a scythe—a pitchfork—a chopping axe, or a butcher's cleaver. We struck in the direction of the sound; and we are rapidly closing in upon him."

From the moment Douglas proposed his bill Lincoln had been unleashing his arguments, a river of logic, history, metaphor, allusion, storytelling, and emotion that flowed until he finally ended Douglas's ambition. Lincoln never relented in tracing the crisis to its source in slavery, from when he mounted the platform at the Springfield State Fair to when he stood on the Capitol's Portico to deliver his Second Inaugural. It was not the political crisis that Douglas precipitated that converted him to an antislavery position. He had long held it. It was the political nature of slavery that had changed, and it was to that he responded. Lincoln was shocked at the audacity of pro-slavery aggression. He understood that the balance wheel of politics that had set the terms upon which national politics and the two-party system had turned for nearly two generations was breaking. He did not hesitate to throw himself into its madly spinning gears.

For Lincoln the extension of slavery posed a profound set of questions. His father had escaped across the Ohio River from Kentucky to Indiana, from a slave society into a free one. Lincoln himself had broken every bond of poverty and ignorance holding him back to make himself into the preeminent Whig of Illinois, a prosperous lawyer, and a respectable husband to an educated woman from a notable family. The extension of slavery threatened to unravel the entire basis on which he had lifted himself; the crisis engulfed the whole democracy that had made possible the rise of people like him.

The old Whig would become within two years the new Republican, but Lincoln never anticipated this metamorphosis, instead viewing the Nebraska Act initially as an opportunity to revive the Whigs as the antislavery party. As events quickened, his thought deepened, his strategies shifted, and his political goals changed, too.

At the opening of 1854, Lincoln summoned himself from his dormancy to contend again with Douglas, the domineering figure of his party, which had long dominated Illinois, the most racist state in the North. Within days of Douglas's first report on the Nebraska Territory his newspaper, the *Register*, and Lincoln's, the *Journal*, traded salvos. On January 14, the *Register* editorialized that the *Journal* "opens its batteries upon Senator Douglas'

Nebraska bill, following in the wake of the New York Tribune, and renewing the 'agitation' of the 'nigger' question, by humorously ! charging Douglas with opening that question. . . . Niggerdom is preparing for a new onslaught."

The *Journal* assailed the *Register* in an editorial on March 24, almost certainly written by Lincoln. "If he [George Walker, publisher of the *Register*] can find any 'principle' in the constitution that allows George Walker, white man, to enslave George Walker, black man, then he has some ground for 'conscience sake' to stand upon." The Constitution, Lincoln argued, provided no basis for slavery. "If the principle of free government means anything, the black man must stand on the same footing of 'governing himself' as the white. . . . The Register with one blow would annul the grandest principle of free government and GIVE to ten thousand slaveholders from the south, the privilege of setting up slave pens in Nebraska, thus widening the foulest curse, and fostering the most 'insidious enemy' that holds in the bosom of our Republic."

Lincoln's style blazed through these few sentences. The image of "slave pens" was drawn from the repellent sight of those he had seen in Washington near the Capitol. Calling slavery "the most 'insidious enemy' " was the beginning of Lincoln's repeated use of that phrase, referring directly to Douglas's method and meaning. In 1859, he would write that Douglas was "the most dangerous enemy of liberty, because the most insidious one," and Lincoln would repeatedly condemn "insidious popular sovereignty." In his first message to the Congress, on July 4, 1861, Lincoln would use the phrase to describe secession as "an insidious debauching of the public mind." But what especially revealed the *Journal* article as a trademark Lincoln production was his use of its same argument ten months later to refute Douglas on the humanity and rights of blacks, the immorality of slavery, and its ultimate threat to democracy. Unlike few other politicians in speaking against slavery, Lincoln unsentimentally drew his audience into seeing the situation from the empathetic point of view of the slave. He did this, moreover, in a thoroughly and unforgiving racist environment. Holding up George Walker of the *Register* to ridicule as an unprincipled hypocrite sought to elicit more than a laugh, but also to put forward "George Walker, black man." Through his morphing of Walker from white to black, from Douglas's surrogate into a slave, Lincoln made his point that Douglas's policy would lead to the virtual enslavement of white men. From his initial engagement with Douglas he began consistently to make the argument that protecting the rights of whites required recognizing the humanity of blacks. His strategies shifted, but this idea did not.

In the Senate Seward had answered Douglas on February 17 with a speech arguing that the founders intended to limit slavery wherever and whenever they could, recounted the history of the Ordinance of 1787 and the Compromise of 1820, and lambasted the idea of popular sovereignty as "abnegating national authority on the subject of slavery," and "full of absurdities and contradictions"—themes that Lincoln would take up against Douglas. Seward soon received a letter from Herndon flattering him that he had "a fast and growing popularity out West," and, getting to his point, stated, "Mr. Lincoln, my partner and your friend, and formerly Member of Congress from our district, thinks your speech most excellent." Herndon was acting as Lincoln's agent, reaching out to the leading Whig in the country, and reminding him of their acquaintance, which consisted of a campaign appearance in Boston six years earlier trying to channel the Free Soil vote to the Whigs.

When the news reached Springfield that Douglas's bill passed the House, the next day, on May 23, the local artillery militia wheeled out its guns to fire 113 shots in honor of every member voting in favor—and one more as a national tribute. The *Register* hailed the salute. "The booming cannon announced a moral victory more glorious than can be achieved upon the bloody fields of Europe, should her present wars last a century." The *Journal* replied, "The old 'Nebraska swivel' was pulled out last night, and pounded away one hundred and thirteen times to the number of the 'band of traitors' that have just enacted the great lie of 'popular sovereignty' over the heads of the American people."

Three days later, Seward again arose in the Senate. "This antagonism must end either in a separation of the antagonistic parties—the slaveholding States and the free States—or, secondly, in the complete establishment of the influence of the slave power over the free—or else, on the other hand, in the establishment of the superior influence of Freedom over the interests of Slavery." He added portentously that "the day of compromises has passed forever."

In private Lincoln echoed Seward thought after thought and sometimes word for word. "In the office discussions he grew bolder in his utterances," observed Herndon. "He insisted that the social and political difference between slavery and freedom was becoming more marked; that one must overcome the other; and that postponing the struggle between them would only make it the more deadly in the end. 'The day of compromise,' he still contended, 'has passed. These two great ideas have been kept apart only by the most artful means. They are like two wild beasts in sight of each other, but chained and held apart. Some day these deadly antagonists will one or the other break their bonds, and then the question will be settled.' " There were many more conversations, according to Herndon. "It is useless to add more evidence—for it could be piled mountain high—showing that at the very outset Mr. Lincoln was sound to the core on the injustice and crime of human slavery."

Herndon and Lincoln's "office discussions" were stimulated by the daily arrival of newspapers, magazines, and books. Since he had been a "news-boy" Lincoln had been an obsessive newspaper reader. He and Herndon were probably the most voracious consumers of papers in Springfield, receiving a wider variety than the library. They subscribed to the *Chicago Press and Tribune*, the *Louisville Journal*, Greeley's *New York Tribune* (which published a weekly edition and had fifteen thousand subscribers in Illinois), Gamaliel Bailey's antislavery *National Era*, Garrison's *Liberator*, the *National Anti-Slavery Standard* (the weekly of the Anti-Slavery Society, whose motto was "Without Concealment—Without Compromise"), and from the South the fire-eating *Charleston Mercury* and the *Richmond Enquirer*, which under the editorship of Thomas Ritchie had been an anti-Calhoun voice but had become a claxon horn for the Southern Rightists. Once conflict broke out in Kansas, they received the *Leavenworth Register* to keep up with events there. Herndon corresponded with abolitionists, antislavery politicians, and editors, and collected their speeches, especially prizing the sermons of Theodore Parker, "whom I considered grander than all the others." He bought books on a wide range of subjects, including history, biography, and science. When the journalist George Alfred Townsend visited Herndon in 1867 he wrote that he had "one of the best private libraries in the West." Several years later, in 1873, to raise funds Herndon sold more than a thousand of his books at auction, the list of which catalogued an extraordinary range encompassing history, philosophy, science, and literature—and, as advertised, "writings on Slavery, pro and con, and a few Law Books." "I had an excellent private library," Herndon recalled, "probably the best in the city for admired books. To this library Mr. Lincoln had, as a matter of course, full and free access at all times." He also subscribed to two British publications, the *Westminster Review*, a liberal journal that contained essays by James Mill and his son John Stuart Mill, and promoted the work of Charles Darwin, and the *Edinburgh*

Review, the liberal magazine that exemplified the Scottish Enlightenment. When Herndon brought in a copy of the *Annual of Science*, Lincoln, who was fascinated by science and technology, insisted they "must buy the whole set, started out and got them." "Often at the end of an office day," wrote one of his law clerks, Henry Bascom Rankin, "he would remark: 'Billy, what book have you worth while to take home tonight?' or he would already have one, procured at the State Library during the day, and stowed in or on his hat, so that he would be sure not to forget it when starting for home."

The book that had the greatest impact on Lincoln's thinking in this critical year was an impassioned tract against everything he believed. George Fitzhugh's *Sociology for the South, or The Failure of Free Society*, published in 1854, "defended and justified slavery in every conceivable way," recalled Herndon, and "aroused the ire of Lincoln more than most pro-slavery books."

George Fitzhugh was descended from one of the First Families of Virginia; indeed, his original ancestor was the land agent for Lord Fairfax, but after many generations of primacy his father lost the patrimonial plantation. The declassed aristocratic scion writing in shabby gentility along the banks of the Rappahannock conjured up a perfect patriarchy. Fitzhugh's projection of dutiful masters and grateful slaves bound together in an ideal tyranny for the common good was rooted in a strange nostalgia for a past that never existed and an even stranger sentimental depiction of the Southern present that was a complete fantasy. Like Calhoun he argued that slavery was a positive good, the South a superior society, and disdained the Declaration of Independence's assertions of inalienable rights and equality. Unlike Calhoun, who crusaded against the tariff in the name of free trade, Fitzhugh condemned free trade as part of the nonsense of free society. While Calhoun was grimly legalistic and logical, propounding constitutional schemes to enhance Southern political power, Fitzhugh did not bother to offer even impractical proposals. He insisted that his imaginary South was the only true American society. His make-believe utopia was far more bizarre than Bizarre, the weirdly but aptly named plantation of John Randolph, the founding atavistic Southern reactionary romantic, who nonetheless recognized the stark cruelties of slavery through wafting opium fumes. Fitzhugh lacked even a shred of Randolph's unredeemed recognition of reality. Instead, Fitzhugh drew on the authority of the Bible, bits of fanciful anthropology, and the apologetics of the forgotten monarchist, Sir Robert Filmer, the seventeenth-century defender of the absolutist and divine right of kings in his book *Patriarcha*, to create an impressionistic dream palace of communal paradise that held emotional appeal throughout the South, and which had an afterlife in the antebellum mythology of the Lost Cause down to the frolicsome plantations of *Gone With the Wind.*

While Fitzhugh painted a picture of bucolic bliss under slavery the South was undergoing a rapid development as an intrinsic and dynamic sector of the global economy linked to the banks of Wall Street and London's Bond Street. The slaveholders controlled the most valuable commodities in the country—slaves and cotton—and piled up wealth from their ruthless commercialization. By 1860, the twelve richest counties in the United States were all in the South. Fitzhugh's rhapsody of feudal harmony, however, achieved overwhelming popularity as more than a theoretical argument for slavery. He became the leading editorial writer for the *Richmond Enquirer,* the most important Southern newspaper, and simultaneously editor of *De Bow's Review,* the most influential Southern journal. (After the war, in an unexpected turn, he served as an agent for the Freedmen's Bureau, but was unremorseful about the Confederacy's failed "attempt to roll back the reformation in its political phases.") When he claimed Lincoln's attention he was already writing pieces for those papers as well as the *Richmond Examiner* as a peerless propagandist for slavery.

In *Sociology for the South,* Fitzhugh sought to topple the pillars of "free society." "We deny," he wrote, "that there is a society in free countries." He argued that John Locke's idea of individual rights was "heresy," "mischief," and "must infect with falsehood all theories built on it." To prove his point, Fitzhugh classified men as fundamentally no different from "bees and ants" as members of "the hive." According to this insect analogy, he wrote, "society does not owe its sovereign power to the separate consent, volition or agreement of its members." The "system of free society," he triumphantly concluded, was "a system of antagonism and war," but "slave society" was one of "peace and fraternity."

Dismissive of Locke, he was derisive of Jefferson. "Nothing can be found in all history more unphilosophical, more presumptuous, more characteristic of the infidel philosophy of the 18th century, than the language that follows . . ." Fitzhugh wrote—then quoting the Declaration of Independence. He swiped at the Virginia Declaration of Rights, authored by George Mason, his distant relative. Instead he praised "exclusive hereditary privileges and aristocracy," and urged, "let us not be frightened at the names." Demonstrating the falsity of the Declaration of Independence, he wrote, "If all men had been created equal, all would have been competitors, rivals, and enemies.

Subordination, difference of caste and classes, difference of sex, age and slavery beget peace and good will." He mocked the Declaration and scorned Jefferson's famous remark against aristocratic privilege. "Men are not born entitled to 'equal rights'! It would be far nearer the truth to say, 'that some were born with saddles on their backs, and others booted and spurred to ride them,'—and the riding does them good. They need the reins, the bit and the spur. . . .

" 'Life and liberty' are not 'inalienable'; they have been sold in all countries, and in all ages, and must be sold so long as human nature lasts." He praised the slaveholder as the slave's "only friend."

In fragments that Lincoln wrote, dated by his private presidential secretaries and biographers John Hay and John Nicolay to about April 1, 1854, he appeared inspired by his reading of Fitzhugh and used his analogy to the "ant" to turn his argument against him. "The ant," wrote Lincoln, "who has toiled and dragged a crumb to his nest, will furiously defend the fruit of his labor, against whatever robber assails him. So plain, that the most dumb and stupid slave that ever toiled for a master, does constantly *know* that he is wronged. So plain that no one, high or low, ever does mistake it, except in a plainly *selfish* way; for although volume upon volume is written to prove slavery a very good thing, we never hear of the man who wishes to take the good of it, *by being a slave himself.*" In refuting Fitzhugh he continued his train of thought from his editorial on George Walker, the *Register* editor, whom he had portrayed with blackface as George Walker, the slave. Now he made George Fitzhugh, the slavery theoretician, into the one who should become "a slave himself." Even writing only for himself, Lincoln refined his case with the jury in mind. But he was developing more than a legal brief. Time and again, Lincoln would return to the image of metamorphosis from white into black, from free man into slave. He thought of himself as a free man who had transformed himself from his father's slave. He saw the extension of slavery as Southern imperialism that would reverse the process of freedom for the entire nation. Those seeking to impose slavery, he suggested, should try it for themselves.

Lincoln went on in this fragment to repudiate Fitzhugh's scoffing at "equal rights" and democracy. "*Most governments* have been based, practically, on the denial of equal rights of men, as I have, in part, stated them; *ours* began, by *affirming* those rights. *They* said, some men are too *ignorant*, and *vicious*, to share in government. Possibly so, said we; and, by your system, you would always keep them ignorant, and vicious. We proposed to give *all* a chance; and we expected the weak to grow stronger, the ignorant, wiser; and all better, and happier together." The "free society," to Lincoln, was not a "failure," but a success. The individual he described who had been "ignorant" but was given "a chance" and had risen was none other than himself. His family had been the victim of the remnants of primogeniture, the inheritance of his murdered grandfather, the original Abraham Lincoln, going to his father's half-brother, who became an affluent slaveholder while Tom Lincoln became a migrant dirt farmer fleeing slave society. Tom's patriarchal impulse and ingrained sense of inferiority led him to try stifling his lively boy's intelligence and desperate quest for education. By "vicious" Lincoln did not necessarily mean violence; he meant the cruelty of "your system" that kept "all" in class and caste bondage. Within months, he would explain how slavery threatened to engulf whites, destroy their rights and subjugate them. Soon, after he emerged as a Republican, he would explain his break with his past in the startling words, "I used to be a slave." Hereditary aristocratic privilege and feudal patriarchy represented for him existential oppression. In becoming Lincoln he became the American "affirming those rights," the rights implicit in the Declaration's promise that "all men are created equal." "We made the experiment; and the fruit is before us. Look at it—think of it. Look at it, in its aggregate grandeur, of extent of country, and numbers of population—of ship, and steamboat, and rail—" And here the fragment broke off.

It was also at this time, according to Hay and Nicolay, that Lincoln wrote his fragment against slavery based on Euclidean logic.

> If A. can prove, however conclusively, that he may, of right, enslave B.—why may not B. snatch the same argument, and prove equally, that he may enslave A.?—You say A. is white, and B. is black. It is *color*, then; the lighter, having the right to enslave the darker? Take care. By this rule, you are to be slave to the first man you meet, with a fairer skin than your own. You do not mean *color* exactly?—You mean the whites are *intellectually* the superiors of the blacks, and, therefore have the right to enslave them? Take care again. By this rule, you are to be slave to the first man you meet, with an intellect superior to your own. But, say you, it is a question of *interest*; and, if you can make it your *interest*, you have the right to enslave another. Very well. And if he can make it his interest, he has the right to enslave you.

Once again, Lincoln ended with the pro-slavery advocate facing Lincoln's logic that he should be enslaved.

Lincoln was also influenced in the framing of his antislavery arguments by his reading of another book, this one antislavery, Leonard W. Bacon's *Slavery Discussed in Occasional Essays from 1833 to 1846*. Bacon, the pastor of the First Congregational Church of New Haven, Connecticut, a prominent pulpit serving the Yale community, and an original member of the American Anti-Slavery Society, belonged to the group of abolitionists that encompassed Edward Beecher, founder of Illinois College and former associate of Elijah Lovejoy, and Calvin Stowe, the biblical scholar and husband of Beecher's sister, Harriet Beecher Stowe, who all broke with Garrison over his wrathful tactics they believed undermined the cause. In 1848, in the wake of the Mexican War, Bacon founded a newspaper, *The Independent*, devoted to opposition to the extension of slavery. Lincoln read his book sometime in early 1854 as he studied in the wake of Douglas's Nebraska Act. Bacon's work was part theology, part politics, and wholly antislavery, revealing the inner factional politics of clergymen in the movement. Bacon had an unusual pragmatic temper and political mind that appealed to Lincoln's own.

"It is no part of the object, in any of these essays, to *prove* that the slavery which exists in these American States is wrong," Bacon wrote. "To me it seems that the man who needs argument on that point, cannot be argued with. What elementary idea of right and wrong can that man have? If that form of government, that system of social order is not wrong—if those laws of the southern states, by virtue of which slavery exists there, and is what it is, are not wrong—nothing is wrong." He added: "The wrong of that slavery, however, is one thing, and the way to rectify that wrong, is another thing." Time and again, over the years, beginning with his initial responses to Douglas, Lincoln would echo Bacon in saying, "If slavery is not wrong, nothing is wrong."

Bacon's chief theological argument aligned Christianity with the Declaration of Independence as an antislavery statement. "Slavery," he wrote, "is essentially barbarous," contrary to Christianity that "makes all men equal in God's regard . . . slavery abhors the idea that every man is, in respect to rights, the equal of his fellow-man."

Reflecting a particular New England strain that values practicality above sanctimony, Bacon emphasized results above hellfire Puritan preaching. He argued that the most effective means of achieving "abolition of slavery" was not to "excommunicate" the slaveholder, but instead to insist "that the exercise of a despotic power, in any specific form of injustice or oppression, shall be the subject matter of censure." He drew the distinction between the slaveholder and slavery, between the sinner and the sin. Bacon chastised the Garrisonians for making it "easy" for the slaveholder to claim

> the Bible is on his side; if "the Abolitionists" are wrong, he, of course, is right; slavery is therefore all right, and he has nothing to do in the case but to support himself by the labor of his slaves if he can, or by selling them if their labor proves too unproductive. But our proposal presents another issue, and one which the slaveholder cannot get rid of so easily. It comes to him with the question, What are you doing for those poor neighbors of yours, over whose welfare for time and for eternity the providence of God has given you a power so full of awful responsibility? How are you treating them? Do you pretend that God has given to you the dominion over them, as over the beasts of the field? Do you treat them as if they were your cattle? Or do you treat them as your fellow-men, your equals before God, and according to the law, Thou shalt love thy neighbor as thyself? Is their toil for you, uncompensated toil? Or is the power which you have over them so administered by you, that the relation between you and them exists, in fact, for their benefit, rather than for yours? If you rob those helpless beings of their human rights—if you do not render to them that which is just and equal—your pretense to be a Christian is a foul dishonor to the Christian name.

Lincoln would soon adopt Bacon's distinctions between Southern slaveholders and slavery, and always parse the question that way. During the campaign of 1864, when Lincoln was told that Bacon was "earnestly advocating your re-election," he recalled his book. "Well, I read that book some years ago, and at first did not know exactly what to make of it, but I afterwards read it more carefully, and got hold of Dr. Bacon's distinctions, and it had much to do with shaping my own way of thinking on the subject of slavery. He is quite a man."

Lincoln's quest to counter Douglas was fixed on winning the majority in the Illinois legislature that would oust Douglas's ally James Shields from his Senate seat. In the spring of 1854, as Lincoln traveled from courthouse to courthouse, he recruited candidates for the legislature. Lincoln and Judge David Davis often stayed in the town of Monticello at the home of Dr. Henry Johns, whom they kept up to midnight one evening to persuade him to run as the Whig in the district. "Mr. Lincoln's arguments were startling in their intensity, and his attitude towards slavery was one of extreme repulsion," recalled the doctor's wife, Jane Martin Johns. "Mr. Lincoln wrote many letters of advice and instruction regarding the conduct of that campaign, in which he showed remarkable insight into the impulses and motives that may be used in influencing men. These letters were so personal that he 'advised their destruction as soon as read.' If they could have been preserved, they might have been used as valuable lessons in political tactics." Lincoln's counsel extended from how to speak to the issues and to individuals. "He had traveled the circuit of the courts so many years, when court week was every man's holiday, that he knew the people collectively and individually, and was prepared to diagnose the politics and prejudices of every man of any influence in every precinct, and to prescribe the special treatment for his particular case."

Lincoln acted as campaign manager, often invisibly, trying to piece together the battered Whig Party. "To hold Whigs with southern sympathies to party allegiance, to check the violence of the Abolitionists, to alienate Know-Nothings from the Democratic party, whose senatorial candidate, General Shields, an Irishman, was the difficult task set by Mr. Lincoln for his supporters," Jane Johns recalled. "Throughout the pre-election campaign the task of adapting the issues to the location was directed by Mr. Lincoln's shrewd hand. Every section of the State and, in some instances, even precinct divisions, had to be diplomatically managed, and though he carefully abstained from apparent interference in the election of members of the legislature, his guiding hand directed the minutest details."

"Lincoln was always a party man and was careful to observe and to control, within the sphere of his influence, every detail of party organization," recalled John W. Bunn, Springfield merchant, Whig regular, and financier of Lincoln's campaigns. "Between 1850 and 1861, I saw Mr. Lincoln very often. I am proud to say that I was one of his junior political agents. Like very many others, I was always glad to do for him anything that I could do." Lincoln was more than a man of the party; he was its chief, even in the period after his congressional career when he claimed he had nearly lost interest in politics. "He was always in close touch with the leaders of his party in the State. The primaries in his own ward and city, the county convention, and the State convention were each and all matters of deep personal concern to him. I do not mean that he always engaged, personally, in all the details of local campaigns, but the men who did the work were generally in his confidence, and were men who were glad to act upon his advice and suggestions. All these things were matters which Mr. Lincoln not only took pride in but enjoyed, just as any man enjoys the things that he does well and does with success."

The two parties, the Democrats and Whigs, had fought elections in the past like disciplined armies. By the time President Pierce signed Douglas's bill in May the world was turned upside down. Douglas accelerated the whirlwind by acting as the political boss to coerce the Democrats in the legislature to endorse his measure, which made Illinois the only state to do so. He was intent that the Democratic Party should march into battle as the Douglas party. To stamp his image on it before the fall elections, he compelled the county organizations to hold conventions to approve the Nebraska Act and its author as well. His heavy hand provoked a revolt of a host of younger leaders as well as a couple of old bulls, former governor John Reynolds and former U.S. senator Sidney Breese, who had fought Douglas and lost control of the Illinois Central and now denounced Douglas's litmus test over his Nebraska Act as "a bastard plank." In Chicago and northern Illinois, the party was in full-scale rebellion. The *Galena Jeffersonian* suggested a state convention take up "formally excommunicating the adherents of Douglas' Nebraska scheme, from the great democratic brotherhood." Meanwhile, three conservative Whig assemblymen voted for Douglas's pro-Nebraska resolution, prompting the *Journal* to pronounce them party renegades. A small group calling themselves "national Whigs" severed their ties to proclaim their allegiance to "Douglas, Kansas and the Union." Sentiment for or against Douglas's bill was not the only combustible element. After he detonated the political explosion that broke apart the traditional parties, shards of factions flew around with uncertain trajectories. Know Nothing and temperance movements were as volatile as antislavery groups. Before Douglas had introduced his bill, antislavery activists were more galvanized by temperance than any other issue, filling the First Presbyterian Church at Springfield (where Mary Lincoln worshipped) in February 1854 for a convention of the Maine Law Alliance to pressure the legislature to pass an Illinois version of Maine's liquor restriction. The unexpected year of conflict over slavery had actually begun with the abolitionists seeking to abolish drink.

No one could foresee what a new party realignment would be, nor know if the Whig or Democratic parties would be re-created, or disappear. No one recognized the nascent Republican Party as ascendant. While there were calls for "fusion," nobody knew its shape. Each group asserted itself as the core of a new political coalition. Some prohibitionists were nativists, some nativists were antislavery, and many abolitionists were prohibitionists. Some Whigs were all or none of the above, just as were some Democrats. German immigrants, the largest growing swing group in the state, were overwhelmingly antislavery and disaffected with the Democrats, but feared the nativists and hated the prohibitionists. Even as old partisan lines dissolved old partisan rancor heightened. Old Democrats mistrusted old Whigs while third party Free Soilers still mistrusted men from both of the regular parties. Within the abolitionist ranks, the Free Democrats acted as an internal body hostile to pro-Nebraska Democrats but also to antislavery Whigs. Anti-Douglas Democrats despised pro-Douglas Democrats while still loathing Whigs. Necessity would seem to have brought all those opposed to Douglas together, but the talk of fusion made them warily circle each other with mutual suspicion.

"Try to save the Whig Party," David Davis wrote his brother-in-law, Julius Rockwell, the newly seated Whig senator from Massachusetts named to fill Edward Everett's seat. "I don't fancy it being abolitionized—although no one can be more opposed to [the] admission [of] Nebraska than I am." Within days of the enactment of Douglas's bill, Seward wrote Weed on May 29, "The 'Free Soilers' here are engaged in schemes for nominating Colonel Benton, and dissolving the Whig party. We are to have all manner of absurdities practiced, and there are not less than half a dozen parties coming to negotiate with me, as if I were a vendor of votes." Weed editorialized in the *Albany Evening Journal* that "so far, we have not found freedom practically advanced one step except by the Whig party." Two months later, in July, Weed wrote another editorial declaring, "that it is best, now and ever, 'for the Whig party to stand by its colors.' "

Lincoln was just beginning to navigate the strategic quandaries of "fusion." As the most prominent partisan Whig leader of Illinois, he was dedicated to preserving his party, like Seward and Weed in New York, and those who were not Whigs regarded him as all the more suspect. He had to learn how to work with disillusioned Democrats who had looked at him as the enemy for years. And he had to win over the abolitionists, many of whom had their own party identifications with third parties that he had harshly criticized and who considered him little more than a depleted Whig Party hack. Their skepticism about his antislavery commitment was inextricable from and sometimes just a cover for their antagonism toward him as a Whig. Many were resolute party men of a particularly schismatic and blinkered variety, and not yet actually Republicans even after they initially adopted the label. In Illinois it would not be until August 1, 1854, that a small meeting of antislavery activists would first adopt the name "republican," taking it from a Michigan gathering of July 16, to describe their new, unorganized, and unshaped party. Nor was it obvious that this rump group would become a party at all, much less a successor to the Liberty Party or the Free Soil Party. The Republican Party in Illinois would not properly come into being until Lincoln entered into its founding meetings in 1856. His problems in Illinois as a Whig in maneuvering through the fractions and factions in the weeks and months just after passage of Douglas's Nebraska Act led to his endless work in managing the ramshackle coalition that would become the Republican Party composed of Old Whigs, Jacksonian Democrats, Free Soilers, abolitionists, border state Unionists, former Hunkers Soft and Hard, Barnburners, former Know Nothings, and German immigrants. Defining the common ground around opposition to the extension of slavery above all other issues and on that broadest possible platform was Lincoln's self-appointed and uneasy task.

CHAPTER TWENTY

THE BLOOD OF THE REVOLUTION

T he appearance in Springfield of Cassius Marcellus Clay on July 10 dramatically posed the question of "fusion." Virtually driven into exile from Kentucky after his antislavery newspaper *True American* folded and the Emancipation Party collapsed, he barnstormed through Illinois on a speaking tour in tandem with Ichabod Codding, the evangelical abolitionist and protégé of Theodore Weld. In the aftermath of the Whig defeat in

1852, the abolitionist cause in Illinois had reached its nadir as it did throughout the country. In October 1853 the *Western Citizen* newspaper, the leading antislavery voice in the Northwest states, originally the organ of the Illinois Liberty Party, closed from lapsed subscriptions. Codding abandoned Illinois that December for respite in his native Connecticut. But from the moment Douglas introduced his Nebraska Act the movement spontaneously regenerated. The Free Democratic Party, a remnant of the Free Soil Party, revived and rechristened the

Thomas Jefferson, 1788, portrait by John Trumbull

Western Citizen as the *Free West*. The former editor, Zebina Eastman, secretary of the Free Democratic State Committee and former head of the state Liberty Party, was reinstalled as its publisher. Under the Free Democratic Party's auspices and on its payroll, Codding returned in June 1854 to preach as its missionary. The *Free West* urged party members to raise its banner so that "bewildered people may see that there is a point to rally to."

On July 4th, Clay joined Codding at Chicago, and they took the train from town to town, greeted by thousands. In Ottawa, Owen Lovejoy spoke with them on the platform, and they led the crowd in a unanimous pledge "to each other and to the world, to disregard party ties, to revolutionize the State and Nation, voting for no man who will not earnestly oppose every measure of the slave power." When the traveling circus barreled into Springfield handbills advertised that Clay's speech would take place in the State House rotunda, which the Democrats who held control promptly rejected, allowing Clay to protest his freedom of speech had been infringed. New handbills promoted his talk under the "FREE waving branches of a grove" just outside the city limits. Appealing to local Whigs, Clay recruited two stalwarts, Orville H. Browning, an attorney and friend of Lincoln, and Judge Thomas Moffett to chair the event. "Would you help a runaway slave?" shouted a voice from the audience. "That would depend," Clay replied, "upon which way he was running." The battle for Kansas had barely begun, but Clay warned it would be settled "by force of arms. It was in view of the magnitude of this crime, the measureless evils it would perpetrate upon our country, that he had said that every man who voted for the Nebraska bill deserved death." He concluded with a rousing call for "an organization of freemen which should not be conservative but aggressive in its movements, should strike at the monster aggressor wherever it could be reached under the constitution—an organization of men of whatever politics, of Free Soilers, Whigs and Democrats, who should bury past animosities and [repent] past errors" of which all had committed, and "unite in hurling down the gigantic evil which threatened even their own liberty."

Lincoln attended Clay's speech, lying on the ground and listening for two hours as he whittled sticks. Clay had grown up with Mary Todd almost like a cousin, but Lincoln on his visits to Lexington had never met him. They spoke apparently for the first time after Clay's speech. "He, too, was a native Kentuckian," Clay wrote, "and could bear witness, in his own person, to the depressing influence of slavery upon all the races." He recalled, "At all events, he was ever kind and confidential with me."

The *Journal* hailed Clay's "GREAT HEROIC SPEECH," and praised him for defying hecklers—"he spoke boldly, proudly, his sentiments—in the face and eyes of all the contumely and insults thrown upon him." But he was condemned in the *Register* for "sentiments more atrocious never found a place in the heart of the foulest traitor that ever meditated the destruction of his country." The *Register* tarred the *Journal* that it would "boldly and unblushingly indorse the monstrous and revolting doctrines advocated by this insane fanatic." The *Journal* responded that it was Democrats that had sponsored Clay's tour. And this was true in a way: it was the Free Democrats. The *Journal* carefully distanced the Whigs. "Whatever of Mr. Clay's speech was sound, just and patriotic, they [the Whigs] would approve;—whatever was otherwise, they would condemn." The dance of fusion was delicate. The evening of Clay's speech, Codding staged a Free Democratic meeting on the courthouse steps in an effort to attract Whigs but without Clay present. The *Register*'s attack was calculated to drive a wedge between the Whigs and the Free Democrats, to try to thwart any movement toward fusion. As Clay and Codding wended their way through the state into August they sought out local Whig politicians and editors to join them at their rallies. Only a few joined, most did not.

Lincoln's attitude was affirmed in a *Journal* editorial later that month insisting on the enduring centrality of the Whig Party as the only effective organization to represent antislavery opinion. An editorial published on July 27 in the *Journal* that Lincoln likely wrote or certainly approved, predicted that "there will be, in our opinion, no large third party. There always have been but two large permanent parties in the country; and when the Nebraska matter is disposed of, the members of the free soil party will fall into the ranks of one of the parties." For the Whigs, there was "no necessity of breaking up their organization for the purpose of becoming a new political party, with a single object in view." Lincoln still believed in the eternal stability of the party system that was rapidly eroding. He was not alone. David Davis remained as devotedly a Whig as ever. Seward and Weed also upheld the Whig standard, offering the reason that it was the only viable political party to oppose the extension of slavery, the explanation Seward and Lincoln had given speaking together from the stage of the Tremont Temple in Boston in 1848 against the Free Soil Party. They insisted that what was true in 1848 remained true for 1854. Yet the political conditions were utterly different. Then the Whigs were a rising force about to claim the presidency while now they were out of power and splintering into pieces. Yet Lincoln stubbornly clung to the idea that the Whig Party could be revived, a view confirming the image of him as the old party leader demanding Whig primacy.

Zebina Eastman, the *Free West* editor, accompanied Clay and Codding on their tour. While they delivered the speeches, he was on another mission. Clay was the main attraction, Codding the evangelist and organizer, and Eastman the ideological gatekeeper. He inquired around Springfield about Lincoln. First, he spoke to a local man he knew involved in the Underground Railroad, who told him Lincoln was "all right on the Negro question; he gave money, when necessary, to help the fugitive on the way to freedom." Eastman knew that the Lincoln-Herndon law office was a subscriber to the *Western Citizen* and *Free West*, having addressed the copies he mailed. Asking questions around town, he "learned that Mr. Lincoln's law partner was a thorough abolitionist." So he sought out Herndon. They spoke for a couple of hours. Eastman suggested "if it would not be wise for the anti-slavery men to go into the Know-Nothing lodges and rule them," to which Herndon replied, "No, never." "Herndon," Eastman asked, "I know you as a firm and true anti-slavery man, but we anti-slavery men North don't know Mr. Lincoln so well. What are his ideas on slavery and can we trust him?" "Mr. Lincoln is a natural-born anti-slavery man, and now you go home and use the influence of your paper for Lincoln," Herndon recalled saying years later. Eastman's later recollection was that he was persuaded. "After that visit I told all my Liberty Party friends to stand by Abraham Lincoln." But his version, in fact, was the opposite of what occurred, an account perhaps skewed by his subsequent warm feelings about Lincoln, who appointed him the U.S. consul to Bristol, England. The reality of the visit was caught in Herndon's description of Eastman as "a committee man from Chicago who was appointed to investigate," and Eastman's representation of the abolitionist view of the time: "They were in a party of their own, and from repeated betrayals, had learned to distrust all professions of mere politicians."

For Eastman, Whigs were by definition "mere politicians," although Illinois abolitionists had supported two of them for the Congress. "They gave their confidence to men that were worthy of it,—as they gave it to Washburne and Norton," Eastman explained. But even in the places congenial to the fusionists the effort was ragged. Illinois was the least sympathetic Northwestern state to the "republican" movement, which was restricted to the northern districts of the state, had little traction in the center, and none in the south.

Elihu Washburne represented the First District in the northwest corner of the state. He had managed to eke out a victory to win his congressional seat in 1852 with only a three-hundred-vote margin and 44 percent of the vote, facing not only a Democratic but also a Free Soil opponent. He cooperated with the fusionists, accepting their nomination at a convention, but refused to disclaim his Whig allegiance. On the same day he agreed to the fusionist endorsement his Whig followers, unwilling to merge and lose their separate identity, held their own convention nominating him, which he also accepted, angering the anti-Nebraska Democrats, who ran a candidate of their own. Washburne, moreover, never repudiated the Whig label, despite the insistence of the fusionists, nor endorsed fusionism on a statewide basis. He was a longtime

Elihu B. Washburne

friend of Lincoln, becoming a member of his political circle when he traveled to Springfield to practice before the Illinois Supreme Court and for Whig political meetings. Arguing cases in Washington before the U.S. Supreme Court, Lincoln, Washburne wrote, "was the only member of Congress from the State who was in harmony with my own political sentiments. I saw much of him and passed a good deal of time in his room."

Jesse O. Norton represented the Third District, winning in 1852 with only 46 percent, running against a Democrat and Free Soiler. This time he joined a Know Nothing lodge to broaden his appeal. When the abolitionists adopted a platform considered too radical and exclusive for the Whigs, Norton surprised them by endorsing it. They had no choice but to support him. A rump group of Whigs backing another candidate threatened to bolt, but was convinced to concede. The Democratic newspaper, the *Joliet Signal*, attempted to undercut Norton with these Whigs, claiming he had betrayed his party and was stomping "upon the ashes of the immortal Clay." Lincoln had to come into the district to hold Whig voters for Norton, fending off the attack and defending him as still a good Whig.

Eastman's question to Herndon about a Free Soil–Know Nothing alliance was not an academic exercise. He was from Chicago, the Second District, where the abolitionists had their greatest concentration. The incumbent congressman, John Wentworth, a Democrat, was an outspoken opponent of the Nebraska bill and had broken with Douglas. But the Free Soilers wanted to merge with the Know Nothings, which had suddenly erupted as a powerful presence in the city. Wentworth, allied with the Irish voters, denounced the Know Nothings. Many Whigs opposed the Know Nothings, too—"old fogy Whigs," derided Eastman, who was among those engineering the fusion of abolitionists and Know Nothings. A fusion convention endorsed the Democratic mayor, James Woodworth, also a Know Nothing. Douglas Democrats, hating both the Know Nothings and the abolitionists, and especially the traitor Wentworth, endorsed a pro-Douglas candidate. Wentworth and his followers put up an anti-Nebraska Democratic candidate. Whigs nominated their own man. In the four-cornered melee, Woodworth won. The Chicago scene revealed that fusionism aroused more divisiveness than it did cooperation.

On June 14, the former president of the United States arrived at the Springfield train station to the strains of a band and the firing of a cannon. Lincoln stood there waiting as the town's leading Whig introducing the last Whig president, Millard Fillmore. The Rock Island Railroad paid for Fillmore's visit. He had joined a delegation of more than one hundred influential men to celebrate the first rail line from the Atlantic to the Mississippi—and across the first bridge spanning the river, at Galena, opening a new gateway to the West. (Lincoln would successfully defend the company's right to have built the bridge in the 1857 case of *Hurd v. Rock Island Railroad*.) Among the entourage were Francis P. Blair, Thurlow Weed, John A. Dix, Edward Bates, and the theologian Leonard W. Bacon. Springfield was a side stop on Fillmore's grand tour of the West, the beginning of his political comeback. He was already preparing to run for the Whig nomination in 1856 and would soon align himself with the Know Nothings in his own version of Whig-nativist fusion called the American Party.

A month later, on August 9, Lincoln held a less ceremonial but more important meeting at the Springfield depot. It was with Richard Yates, the incumbent Whig congressman, a Lincoln protégé, whom Lincoln had encouraged to run for reelection against the former congressman, Thomas Harris, a Douglas protégé, as close to a surrogate battle between Lincoln and Douglas as possible. A week later, on August 18, Lincoln wrote Yates an admonishing letter filled with precise political instructions: "I am disappointed at not having seen or heard from you since I met you more than a week ago at the railroad depot here. I wish to have the matter we spoke of settled and working to its consummation. I understand that our friend B. S. Edwards is entirely satisfied now, and when I can assure myself of this perfectly I would like, by your leave, to get an additional paragraph into the Journal, about as follows: 'Today we place the name of Hon. Richard Yates at the head of our columns for reelection as the Whig candidate for this congressional district. We do this without consultation with him and subject to the decision of a Whig convention, should the holding of one be deemed necessary; hoping, however, there may be unanimous acquiescence without a convention.' May I do this? Answer by return mail."

Lincoln was desperately trying to steer Yates through the hazards of his candidacy and was irritated that the candidate himself was so passive. Lincoln had won support for Yates from Benjamin S. Edwards, a member of his extended family, the brother of his brother-in-law, who was a leading Know Nothing, and backer of the state's nativist newspaper, the *Springfield Capital Enterprise*. Edwards was an ardent temperance advocate, yet Yates was neither a Know Nothing nor a teetotaler. Lincoln, who had originated Whig Party conventions in Illinois, wanted Yates's nomination to be made without one, but simply through the fiat of an announcement. Avoiding a convention would prevent the Know Nothings from inserting their views into a platform.

Just as Yates was nominated by virtue of having his name published in the *Journal*, Lincoln's friend, William Jayne, had Lincoln's and Stephen T. Logan's names listed there as the Whig candidates for the state legislature. Lincoln happened to be out of town, riding the law circuit, and when he returned Jayne went to his house, where he found Lincoln "almost crying," "walked up and down the floor," "then the saddest man I ever saw—the gloomiest" and protesting "my persuasions to let his name stand in the papers." "No, I can't," Lincoln said. "You don't know all, I say you don't begin to know one half and that's enough." Members of the legislature were prohibited from being a candidate for that office. "It is scarcely needless to say," recalled Henry C. Whitney, Lincoln's youthful legal colleague, "that it was Mrs. Lincoln's opposition which so much disturbed him. She insisted in her imperious way that he must now go to the United States Senate, and that it was a degradation to run him for the Legislature." Yet Lincoln kept his name listed, withdrawing it only after the election. "I only allowed myself to be elected, because it was supposed by doing so would help Yates," he explained.

Lincoln envisioned himself once again as the Whig floor leader in the state legislature, acting as the chief whip. His wife, however, did not believe the Senate seat should be delivered to someone less deserving than her husband. She was furious that his ambition was not as great as hers.

Shortly after Logan and Lincoln were nominated, a delegation of Know Nothings offered their formal endorsement. Logan "cheerfully accepted," and the Know Nothings ventured to see Lincoln at his law office with "no doubt of a favorable result." Richard H. Ballinger, a local young lawyer, to whom Lincoln was friendly, was one of the three-man committee. He came from a prominent Kentucky family of Whigs close to Henry Clay, and though his father was a slaveholder Ballinger left Kentucky for Illinois at the age of fifteen out of antislavery convictions. Lincoln told the Know Nothings "that he had belonged to the old Whig party and must continue to do so until a better one arose to take its place. He could not become identified with the American party"—as the Know Nothings called it—but he suggested "they might vote for him if they wanted to; so might the Democrats; yet he was not in sentiment with this new party. Then he took the question up more in detail and asked us who the native Americans were. 'Do they not,' he said, 'wear the breech-cloth and carry the tomahawk? We pushed them from their homes and now turn upon others not fortunate enough to come over as early as we or our forefathers. Gentlemen of the committee, your party is wrong in principle.' " Lincoln went on to tell an illustrative story. "When the Know Nothing party first came up," he said, "I had an Irishman, Patrick by name, hoeing in my garden. One morning I was there with him, and he said, 'Mr. Lincoln, what about the Know Nothings?' I explained that they would possibly carry a few elections and disappear, and I asked Pat why he was not born in this country. 'Faith, Mr. Lincoln,' he replied, 'I wanted to be, but my mother wouldn't let me.' " Through his gentle ridicule and humor, and political firmness, Lincoln made Ballinger feel embarrassed about being a Know Nothing. "I wished many times before Mr. Lincoln was through that I had refused to serve on the committee." (Ballinger would soon become a law clerk for Leonard Swett, Lincoln's friend, and travel through the prairies in a little caravan with Swett, Lincoln, and Judge Davis. He served as the secretary of the founding convention of the Republican Party in Sangamon County in 1856, and during the war was the colonel of the 3rd Mississippi Colored Volunteers. His son was President William Howard Taft's controversial secretary of the interior.)

Lincoln never openly voiced his feelings about the Know Nothings, however scathing he was in private. Through the 1854 campaign he worked with his old Whig friends who belonged to the secret order, among them Stephen T. Logan, Joseph Gillespie, William Jayne, James Miller, and Ozias M. Hatch, a well-to-do merchant in Meredosia. (Both Miller and Hatch were strongly antislavery and would be elected state treasurer and secretary of state on the Republican ticket in 1856.) Lincoln's adversaries knew of their involvement with the Know Nothings and used his continued association to tag him as one as well.

By the end of August Lincoln hit the trail as a surrogate campaigner for Yates, challenging his opponent Harris to debate. Lincoln had spent many hours in the state library, and he started to test his phrases and themes. In his first public statement at the Scott County Whig Club on August 26, "he exhibited the great wrong and injustice of the repeal of the Missouri Compromise, and the extension of slavery into free territory," according to the *Journal.* Two days later, at Carrollton, he stepped out of a stagecoach as Harris was speaking and then held forth for two hours. When Lincoln departed Harris told the crowd that the Eastern, aristocratic, and unpatriotic Federalist Party was responsible for the Missouri Compromise, a party that was in fact defunct when it was enacted.

Lincoln encouraged the state senator in Yates's district, John M. Palmer, who was one of the few voting against the affirmation of the Douglas bill in the legislature, to speak out as he ran for reelection. His tone was solicitous, delicate about Palmer's political sensitivity, but firm. "You know how anxious I am that this Nebraska measure shall be rebuked and condemned every where," he wrote on September 7. "Of course I hope something from your position; yet I do not expect you to do any thing which may be wrong in your own judgment; nor would I have you do anything personally injurious to yourself." Lincoln coaxed through flattery. "You have had a severe struggle with yourself, and you have determined *not* to swallow the *wrong.* Is it not just to yourself that you should, in a few public speeches, state your reasons, and thus justify yourself? I wish you would; and yet I say 'don't do it, if you think it will injure you.' " He concluded by observing that if Douglas had not forced the Nebraska issue, "you probably would have been the Democratic candidate for congress in the district." Lincoln noted that as a Whig he would not have voted for him, "but I should have made no speeches, written no letters; and you would have been elected by at least a thousand majority."

On September 9, at the Springfield courthouse, Lincoln held a formal debate with John Calhoun, his old supervisor as Sangamon County surveyor, who assailed him for his alliance with abolitionists and Know Nothings. Lincoln, according to the hostile account in the *Register*, "with his usual ability, made the best of a bad position. We have never heard him when more at fault in covering up the heresies which he habitually takes to." When Calhoun confronted him about his ties to the Know Nothings, he "doubted its existence." "Calhoun," recalled Herndon, "gave him more trouble in his debates than Douglas ever did, because he was more captivating in his manner, a more learned man than Douglas." Trying to win the debate after the fact, Lincoln wrote his editorial about "John Calhoun" stealing the meadow of "Abraham Lincoln" as a parable of the extension of slavery into Kansas.

The day after that editorial was published Lincoln spoke at the Bloomington courthouse to a group of anti-Nebraska German Americans to whom he delivered a history lesson about the limitation and extension of slavery going back to Jefferson's Ordinance of 1787 prohibiting slavery in the Northwest territories. He explained that the Missouri Compromise that brought in Missouri as a slave state and Maine as a free one was supposed to have "settled forever" the question, which was again opened as a result of the Mexican War. But after the Compromise of 1850, "the slaveholding power attempted to snatch" the Nebraska Territory. Douglas, he said, had "so constructed" the bill repealing the Missouri Compromise to "open all of the territory to the introduction of slavery," an act "done without the consent of the people."

Published alongside the truncated report in the *Bloomington Pantagraph* was a column from a participant at the meeting identified as "A Hearer," who noted that in calling for "restoration" of the Missouri Compromise Lincoln also had suggested acceptance of the Fugitive Slave Act. "It was a compromise, and as citizens we were bound to stand up to it, and enforce it. Afterwards he added: 'I own, if I were called upon by a Marshal, to assist in catching a fugitive slave, I should suggest to him that others could run a great deal faster than I could.'" Here Lincoln was borrowing Cassius Clay's joke he had heard a couple of months earlier. "He said," "A Hearer" continued, "he would go in for sustaining any Fugitive Slave Law, that did not expose a free negro to any more danger of being carried into slavery, than our present criminal laws do an innocent person to the danger of being hung. But can this be said of the present Fugitive Slave Law . . . ? The fact is it does not." The writer, of course, was correct. Lincoln was rhetorically for that law he also said should not be supported, and which he did not privately support if it failed to grant certain legal rights to slaves, which it did not for those who could not be given such rights.

When Lincoln spoke, Codding was organizing fusion meetings in various northern districts, some of which called for modifying the Fugitive Slave Act and others that called for its abrogation. Lincoln was partly responding to rapidly shifting and varying positions. He "detested" the Fugitive Slave Act, according to one of his friends, to whom he remarked, "It is ungodly! It is ungodly! No doubt it is ungodly! But it is the law of the land, and we must obey it as we find it." Lincoln well knew that the "ungodly" act was not only encoded in the Compromise, but also in a clause of the Constitution. "I hate to see the poor creatures hunted down, and caught, and carried back to their stripes, and unrewarded toils," he wrote Joshua Speed in 1855. His friend John W. Bunn recalled, "The reason Mr. Lincoln appeared in so few suits in behalf of runaway negroes was because of his unwillingness to be a party to a violation of the Fugitive Slave Law, arguing that the way to overcome the difficulty was to repeal the law. I have heard him make that suggestion, and I remember that in one case at least he advised that a few dollars be paid to buy off those who were holding the negro." Less than two weeks after this Bloomington speech, Lincoln wrote an anonymous editorial for the *Journal*, entitled "Political Power in Negroes," attacking the constitutional clause giving Southern states representation based on slaves counted as three-fifths of a person, which he would soon raise publicly. But his immediate imperative as he understood it was to conduct the politics so that the burden of the repeal of the Missouri Compromise weighted down Douglas without bearing the stigma of the abolitionists himself.

After his tumultuous confrontation with the huge crowd of hecklers at Chicago on September 1, Douglas launched on a vindication campaign. "The party are all right everywhere," he insisted to one of his key men, James W. Sheahan, editor of Douglas's *Chicago Times*. "We have had glorious meetings." He instructed Sheahan to conflate all his opponents as abolitionists. The *Journal*, meanwhile, focused attention on Douglas's Mississippi plantation, demanding that Douglas's Springfield paper, the *Register*, publish the exact number of slaves there, evidence of his "peculiar interest" in "the peculiar institution."

The "glorious meetings" that Douglas described were in fact raucous versions of his Chicago collision. Ichabod Codding and a band of abolitionists tracked him from place to place. At Joliet, on September 11, the audience interrupted Douglas with catcalls and hostile questions. "Ichabod Codding," reported the *Joliet Signal*, "with a few desperate abolitionists and niggers, attempted to hiss Judge Douglas down." At Geneva, on September 21, a crowd of two thousand drowned out Douglas. When one of Codding's associates demanded that Douglas allow Codding to reply to him, Douglas declared that he would not permit him to speak because he had demonstrated he was not a gentleman. Codding arose, threatening to physically throw Douglas off the platform. The local sheriff intervened, demanding order. Only after he half apologized for insulting Codding's character did the crowd allow Douglas to finish his speech. After he left, Codding held forth and then roused the audience to endorse a resolution proclaiming Douglas "unworthy to speak to a free people."

Douglas traveled to Bloomington, where he anticipated a sympathetic crowd without trailing abolitionists. The Democratic committee that had invited him arranged for a decanter of whiskey, water pitcher, and glasses on a sideboard in his room at the National Hotel. As small groups of local Democrats entered to greet him they were offered the "red liquor." While Douglas was entertaining, Lincoln walked in unannounced. They engaged in some small talk, Douglas introduced him around and asked if he wanted a drink. Lincoln declined. "What! Are you a member of the Temperance Society?" "No," Lincoln replied, "I am not a member of any temperance society; but I am temperate, in *this*, that I don't drink anything." The alcoholic Douglas, familiar with Lincoln for decades, knew he was a teetotaler. He also knew that this was more than a matter of personal habit. Lincoln, for his part, knew it, too. Both sides were using the polarizing issue to galvanize their supporters.

Just a few months earlier, on April 4, Springfield voters had elected one of the town's temperance crusaders as mayor—Billy Herndon. Under his wife's influence he belonged to all the temperance groups—the Washingtonians, the Temple of Honor, and was president of the Sangamon County Maine Law Alliance. Mayor Herndon instituted a series of far-reaching reforms, building wooden sidewalks, banning hogs in the streets, creating the public school system, and enacting a prohibition on the sale of liquor within a half mile of the city limits. Lincoln, who had represented liquor dealers (some of whom were his close friends like John Bunn), served in May as the defense attorney for nine women in DeWitt County, one of them Herndon's sister-in-law, charged with destroying whiskey barrels in a saloon and rioting, a case designated the *People v. Shurtliff et al.,* but which Lincoln told the jury should be called "The State against Mr. Whiskey." After they were found guilty, the judge levied the minimum fine of $2 apiece plus court costs.

Mayor Herndon marched from saloon to saloon "and told them they must close their doors." Prohibition aroused equally intense opposition. The Catholic newspaper in Chicago, the *Tablet*, urged "every Catholic to protest against such unwarrantable and unjust usurpations," and the *Register* labeled the temperance activists "mischievous bigots." That fall, undoubtedly enlisted by Herndon, Lincoln filed for an indictment before a grand jury of Archie Herndon, Billy's tavern-owning father, who was a conservative Democrat. Just outside town, new saloons were experiencing a booming business, and the next year in a statewide referendum for prohibition was soundly defeated, including among Springfield voters. Billy was not nominated again for office. The short-lived rise and fall of prohibition would have the effect of further concentrating focus on the extension of slavery in the months leading to the formation of the Illinois Republican Party.

When Lincoln left Douglas's hotel room, leaving the whiskey untouched, Jesse W. Fell entered. He was at the innermost circle of the Lincoln men, and none were more devoted to advancing him. Fell was the most enterprising man in Bloomington, a journalist and publisher of the *Bloomington Pantagraph* newspaper, real estate developer, founder of several Illinois towns, industrialist, railroad entrepreneur, horticulturalist, educator who would found Illinois State Normal University, and Judge Davis's former law partner. (Adlai E. Stevenson, governor of Illinois and twice a presidential candidate, was his great-grandson.) Fell had befriended Lincoln in 1834 when he shared a boardinghouse with the young state legislator in Vandalia, and they remained close friends. He was a stalwart Whig, a Quaker, and used his large house as a station of the Underground Railroad. Fully aware of his outspoken antislavery views, it was likely that Lincoln was also aware of Fell's clandestine activity. Fell's wife, Rebecca, an accomplished and educated woman, was an associate of Lucretia Mott, the Quaker abolitionist and organizer of the women's rights convention at Seneca Falls in 1848. Lincoln had tried to recruit Fell to run for the state legislature in 1854, but he had demurred. He was in constant communication with Lincoln and responsible for him being on the spot when Douglas arrived at Bloomington.

Fell summoned Lincoln to Bloomington to challenge Douglas to debate. Almost certainly Fell discussed the idea with Davis, who had written in July, "I honestly believe if Douglas and Lincoln were at the present time before the people of this state for governor on the Nebraska issue that Lincoln would be elected. I would give something pretty, at any rate, to have a trial." Discussing the plan for confronting Douglas, Fell told Lincoln that Illinois had two giants, "that Douglas was the *little* one, as they all knew, but that you were the *big* one, which they didn't all know." Lincoln, however, thought that Douglas would not divide the time of his own meeting, and if he did would "no doubt consume so much of the time that I'll have no chance till in the evening." Instead, he said he would speak that evening at the courthouse.

Fell was still attached to his idea of a real debate. "Judge Douglas," he told him, "many of Mr. Lincoln's friends would be greatly pleased to hear a joint discussion between you and him on these new and important questions now interesting the people, and I will be glad if such a discussion can be arranged." "Mr. Douglas seemed annoyed," recalled James S. Ewing, the hotel owner's son, who was in the room. "Whom does Mr. Lincoln represent in this campaign—is he an Abolitionist or an Old Line Whig?" Douglas demanded. "An Old Line Whig," Fell replied. "No, I won't do it!" said Douglas. "I come to Chicago, and there I am met by an old line abolitionist; I come down to the center of the State, and I am met by an old line Whig; I go to the south end of the State, and I am met by an anti-administration Democrat. I can't hold the abolitionist responsible for what the Whig says; I can't hold the Whig responsible for what the abolitionist says, and I can't hold either responsible for what the Democrat says. It looks like dogging a man over the State. This is my meeting; the people have come to hear me, and I want to talk to them." "Well, Judge," said Fell, "you may be right; perhaps some other time it can be arranged." (Fell would persist until he got Lincoln to corner Douglas into their debates of 1858.)

Fell had already put out the word that Lincoln would debate Douglas in order to attract a large crowd for the event. When Lincoln decided not to force an incident and Fell could not trap Douglas into volunteering half his time, Fell said "our Anti-Nebraska friends were greatly disappointed at not getting his approval of some pretty active (perhaps I should say aggressive) demonstrations, to secure a division of time in the discussion." But the story of Lincoln refusing Douglas's drink was circulated among temperance activists to help build Lincoln's audience.

That afternoon Douglas spoke to several thousand people gathered in a grove, excoriating his critics. "As we got near to the crowd I saw a man sitting on a log, stooping over with his hat on the ground in front of him," recalled a woman who attended. "I didn't recognize the man, but thought to myself he looked rather careless. Once in a while the man would reach down, pick up some paper, write on it, and throw it in his hat. When I came nearer I saw it was Mr. Lincoln. I realized then that he was sitting back there taking notes of what Mr. Douglas was saying." At the conclusion of Douglas's remarks a man, probably Fell, walked onto the stage to announce that Lincoln would speak that night, and Douglas grimaced with "disgust and rage," according to one of those present. "Lincoln was there. Lincoln is apt to be where he isn't wanted," reported Horace White, a correspondent for the *Chicago Journal*, a Whig newspaper that would become a Republican one.

That night Lincoln spoke in a room on the second floor of the McLean County courthouse to about three hundred people. His speech was the beginning of his efforts that would continue through the next six years to debunk Douglas's insinuations, expose his illogic, deconstruct his distortions, and deny his arguments. Three times Lincoln referred to his "sophistry." He described Douglas's skewed version of history as "all afterthoughts—ALL, ALL." He explained Douglas's sinuous ability to confuse. "It is hard to argue against such nonsense. The Judge puts words in the mouths of his audience with which to call them fools. Because no one interrupts him with a denial of his assertions, he takes them as admitted by the people, and builds upon them his monstrous and ridiculous propositions."

Douglas had attempted to tar his opposition through guilt by association with the Know Nothings. Lincoln claimed he "Knew Nothing in regard to the Know Nothings. . . . But he would say in all seriousness, that if such an organization, secret or public, as Judge Douglas had described, really existed, and had for its object interference with the rights of foreigners, the Judge could not deprecate it more severely than himself. . . . But he [Lincoln] would like to be informed on one point: if such a society existed, and the members were bound by such horrid oaths as Judge Douglas told about, he would really like to know how the Judge found out his secrets?"

Douglas had also just begun to smear his opponents as "Black Republicans," to which Lincoln said, "He might call names, and thereby pander to prejudice, as much as he chose." Lincoln pointed out that Douglas's former allies in the Democratic Party were a major dissenting element in the new politics of "fusion." "What right had Judge Douglas to intimate that none but abolitionists and tender-footed Whigs were embraced in the 'fusion,' and that Whigs were the only ones 'swallowed up'? The abolitionists had swallowed up a great many of the Judge's friends, and more of them, if any thing, than of Whigs."

On the Missouri Compromise, Lincoln quoted "a gentleman, in language much finer and more eloquent than he was capable of constructing, expressed himself in reference to it as follows: All the evidences of public opinion at that day seemed to indicate that this Compromise had become canonized in the hearts of the American people as a sacred thing, which no ruthless hand should attempt to disturb. This was certainly very strong, and it was spoken after the Missouri Compromise had been in existence twenty-nine years? Who was it that uttered this sentiment? What 'Black Republican'?" A voice in the crowd cried out, "Douglas!" "No other than Judge Douglas himself," declared Lincoln triumphantly. "A more beautiful or more forcible expression was not to be found in the English language."

After threading his way through Douglas's twisted explanations Lincoln arrived at the reason that the Nebraska Act was "the grossest violation" of the "sacred right of self-government" and Douglas's popular sovereignty a sham. "If we admit that a negro is not a man," said Lincoln, "then it is right for the Government to own him and trade in the race, and it is right to allow the South to take their peculiar institution with them and plant it upon the virgin soil of Kansas and Nebraska. If the negro is not a man, it is consistent to apply the sacred right of popular sovereignty to the question as to whether the people of the territories shall or shall not have slavery; but if the negro, upon soil where slavery is not legalized by law and sanctioned by custom, *is* a man, then there is not even the shadow of popular sovereignty in allowing the first settlers upon such soil to decide whether it shall be right in all future time to hold men in bondage there." No other political figure of stature in Illinois, where a draconian Black Law prevailed, had made an argument resting on the humanity of slaves, a logic that would stretch to emancipation. Lincoln at Bloomington was warming up for his next confrontation with Douglas on a larger stage.

It was almost impossible to secure a room in the overflowing hotels and boardinghouses of Springfield for the State Fair. Great crowds of passengers rolled out of trains. Twelve young women squeezed into one room were lucky to acquire the space while hundreds slept under the stars. One journalist reported, "I thought over the matter strongly, as a philosopher, and came to the conclusion that a bare floor would be an excellent bed, if the boards were sawed straight with the grain." Thousands clamored to the acres of fairgrounds about a mile outside town, piling into carriages and wagons for rides there for 10 cents if they could afford it, to the spectacle of prize steers, horses, hogs, sheep, goats, chickens, ducks, and turkeys; displays of flowers, pies, jams, apples, and pumpkins; new-fangled farm machines from reapers to mowers to corn-shellers; entertainment from fiddlers, peep shows and freak shows, a circus; and haircuts and shaves offered by local black barbers, all free blacks, the only blacks in sight. Hundreds of politicians wandered around, coming for the voters.

Abolitionists headed to Springfield, too. An advertisement appearing in the *Free West* called for a "State Mass Convention" to coincide with the State Fair, "for the organization of a part which shall put the Government upon a Republican track." The *Free West* trumpeted, "Illinois, the most servile of the free states, is fast moving toward a state organization of this kind." The *Register* reported on the scheduled convention as when "the nuptial rites between Illinois abolitionism and Illinois whiggery are to take place. 'Haste to the wedding.' "

A number of the key characters gathered at a reception on the evening of October 2 at the home of Benjamin S. Edwards, according to a young man who said he was there. Clark Carr was a student at Knox College, an abolitionist stronghold, and would become a delegate to the Republican convention of 1860; after serving as a colonel during the war, as a member of the Gettysburg Cemetery Commission he invited Lincoln to speak at its dedication, was later appointed minister to Denmark by President Benjamin Harrison, and ultimately became president of the Illinois State Historical Society. According to his account, those at the Edwards house were "surprised" when Owen Lovejoy walked in, invited by one of the guests, and were even more surprised at his persuasive conversation so that "at that moment, all would have declared themselves Abolitionists." Mary Lincoln, according to Carr, was outspoken about how "someone" needed to take on Douglas to "beat him at his own game," and when David Davis defended Lincoln as the politician to answer Douglas, she supposedly replied, "Yes, he is a politician in a small way here in Springfield, but I want him to do something great." Though these exact words were likely apocryphal and there were no other versions of this event, Carr, who came to know and understand the principals in Illinois intimately, fairly represented their thoughts at the time.

The Democrats had reserved a field for Douglas to speak at the fair that was large enough to accommodate five thousand people, but the night of the Edwards's party a downpour reduced it to a muddy field. "A change of weather occurred in the night, a severe rain and hail storm ushering in a bleak, raw December morning," wrote a reporter. A brass band greeted him at the train station, the Springfield Artillery Company fired a salute, and Douglas was escorted to the State House. He entered to "loud cheers," accompanied by Governor Joel Matteson and a phalanx of supporters. Douglas began by asking Lincoln to "step forward" to make arrangements for his reply, but met with no response. Lincoln was anxiously pacing in the lobby, according to the eyewitness account of a Douglas partisan. But others insist that Lincoln was prominently seated in the front of the hall.

Douglas was exhausted from constant speaking and his voice reportedly strained, yet he went on for more than two hours. His argument was an elaborate defense of popular sovereignty. "This is a simple matter, and easily settled. Shall the people of the Territories determine their local affairs for themselves? . . . We say that they shall—our opponents, that they shall not." Slavery was not a moral question at all, he insisted, but simply a matter like "horse stealing or anything else" to be decided by popular sovereignty in the territories. "But you say this slavery is a great crime, and different from everything else. Now, why?" He falsely accused the Whig newspapers of not publishing his bill, asserted that "all parties repudiated the Missouri Compromise line, and rendered necessary the new compromise measures of 1850," attempted to confuse in people's mind support for the Wilmot Proviso with repeal of the Missouri Compromise, and then sought to isolate the fusion movement of abolitionists and Whigs with a racist epithet. "How is it with Whiggery now? They have changed their name, and now call themselves Republicans! Honest men rarely have need to change their names. The Whigs and fusionists don't claim the word National Republican. That name, with Henry Clay, covered the whole Union. Now see what they advocate—read their platform! A *negro* appears in every clause! Therefore I call them the Black Republican party." According to Clark Carr, who claimed to be present, Douglas denounced "renegades" from his own party that entered into an "unholy alliance" that would "turn the glorious old Democratic Party to the black Abolitionists. . . . I tell you the time has not yet come when a handful of traitors in our camp can turn the great state of Illinois, with all her glorious history and traditions, into a negro-worshipping, negro-equality community." (Douglas never used the word "negro," and every published version of his speeches in which it appears replaces the word he always uttered.) He attacked his critics as sectional, not national, and concluded with a fierce denunciation of the Know Nothings, citing the Declaration of Independence, Lafayette, Von Steuben, and Shields's Mexican War bravery. The crowd cheered three times for Douglas, three times for the Nebraska Act, and three times for Thomas Harris, the Democratic candidate for Congress. The *Register* reported it was "impossible to do justice" to Douglas's speech and that it was "unanswerable."

"I watched Mr. Lincoln," wrote Clark Carr, "almost expecting him to protest openly against such outrageous sentiments. To my surprise, he appeared greatly amused; in fact, he seemed almost hilarious with mirth." After three cheers for the "Little Giant," Lincoln remarked as he left, according to Carr,

"We'll hang the Judge's hide on the fence tomorrow!" He made his way to the fair, where he toured the livestock exhibition, accompanied by his oldest friends from his New Salem days, "Slicky Bill" Greene, Jack Armstrong, and an entourage of Clary's Grove Boys. One of Lincoln's political friends, Richard Oglesby, who would become a founder of the Illinois Republican Party and governor, appeared in Carr's account speaking to a skeptical young woman who wanted Lincoln to tear down Douglas at that moment, "Lovejoy can never bring the old-line Whigs into the Anti-Nebraska party," Oglesby explained. "Mr. Lincoln can do it, if you just let him alone. He knows how. Trust to him. He was born in Kentucky, as I was, and knows us Southern people. He's almost made an Abolitionist of me."

The next morning, Lincoln encountered John W. Bunn on the street. "Did you hear the speech of Judge Douglas last night?" Lincoln asked, to which Bunn replied, "You will have a good deal of trouble to answer it." "I will answer that speech without any trouble," Lincoln insisted, "because Judge Douglas made two misstatements of fact, and upon these two misstatements he built his whole argument. I can show that his facts are not facts, and that will refute his speech." Another account had Bunn remembering Lincoln saying, "Douglas lied. He lied three times and I'll prove it!"

"He has been nosing for weeks in the State Library," the *Register* reported about Lincoln, "pumping his brain and his imagination for points and arguments with which to demolish the champion of popular sovereignty. It is our duty to record the result of his wonderful labors and exertions. He commenced by a number of jokes and witticisms, the character of which will be understood by all who know him, by simply saying they were Lincolnisms."

At two in the afternoon on October 4 Lincoln, wearing shirtsleeves, mounted the dais of the Hall of Representatives at the State House, beneath a large portrait of George Washington. Douglas solemnly took a seat directly in front of him in a raised row on the platform. Lincoln's last major appearance was a buffoonish and trifling mockery of Franklin Pierce's candidacy in 1852. This speech, almost seventeen thousand words in its published form, was perhaps the longest he ever delivered, laying the foundation for his politics through 1860. Like all his speeches he was focused on achieving immediate objectives, including refuting Douglas point by point. His overriding aim was to establish opposition to the extension of slavery as the centerpiece of the emerging politics. By engaging with Douglas he sought to draw others into the anti-Nebraska movement and diminish their other causes so that they became secondary and faded. He set out to dismiss the impression that the Whig Party was dying, and instead to revive it with the live issue. But Lincoln eclipsed his partisanship with his statesmanship. From the beginning of his career he had been unusual if unheralded in his efforts to square the circle of his antislavery conviction with viable politics. As a state legislator and congressman he had tried to frame formulas that were both principled and practical, but in each case were still too far advanced, and, although as carefully constructed as his patented model ship, were instantly swamped. Now he added to his latest construction something radically new. He defined the morality of slavery, and explained how the moral factor could not be separated from slavery as a form of property and basis of Southern political power, nor from its imperial ambition. To this he included another element, deeply felt, veiled yet revelatory of his family history that traced his repulsion toward slavery to its root, and why, as he later wrote, "I am naturally antislavery. If slavery is not wrong, nothing is wrong"—the words of the moral case he would make in this speech—"I can not remember when I did not so think, and feel."

Lincoln's opening line put the burden of responsibility for the broken peace on Douglas. "The repeal of the Missouri Compromise, and the propriety of its restoration, constitute the subject of what I am about to say," he said. He followed with crowd-pleasing "Lincolnisms," humorous gibes that baited Douglas, turning the serious forum into a raucous county courthouse, but hardly frivolous as Lincoln hit his marks. Douglas was used to shouting down his opponents, meeting threats with greater threats, vehemence with louder vehemence. In the Senate, he had splattered mud on the unpopular abolitionists Chase and Sumner. On the stump, he had locked horns with Codding. Lincoln had debated Douglas since their first encounter in 1838 over Van Buren and the sub-treasury in which Lincoln fended off Douglas's charge that the Whigs were secret abolitionists. But Douglas had not had to face Lincoln for years. He was unused to tangling in a contest of wits with an opponent who had by now spent years cajoling Illinois juries to rule in his favor.

Lincoln began praising Douglas for "honesty of intention and true patriotism—referring whatever of wrong he might happen to find among his actions, entirely to a mistaken sense of duty," before drawing him into bantering. He remarked that Douglas "seemed to be very conversant with the objects and principles of this mysterious order," the Know Nothings, but "he knew nothing about them." According to the account in the *Missouri Republican*, Douglas "interrupted the speaker by saying that all Know Nothings would say the same thing, and that he strongly suspected Lincoln for being one of them on this account. Lincoln rejoined that he never did know much and if he should happen to come out a Know Nothing it would not be much of a descent." Douglas had "inferred in his speech that many of the so called Know-Nothings were Abolitionists," and Lincoln recounted that in a recent election in Virginia the Know Nothing candidate had beaten both the Whig and the Democrat. "These Know-Nothings were certainly not Abolitionists!" Lincoln "saw nothing remarkable in Mr. D[.]'s position on the Know-Nothings," according to the *Chicago Journal* account quoting Lincoln. "It was a notorious fact that nineteen twentieths of our foreign population had always supported Mr. Douglas, and if that gentleman could fetch over the other twentieth, it wouldn't prove such a bad speculation." The correspondent reported that the crowd rocked with laughter and Douglas was as "grim as Mont Blanc."

"Fellow citizens," said Lincoln, "my distinguished friend here has told you that the Whig party is dead. If that be so, you have today the extraordinary privilege of being addressed by a dead man." In the Missouri Republican report, he quoted a line of poetry, "Hark, from the tomb a doleful sound." Lincoln said that Douglas "has got the wrong party in the grave," citing the latest election returns. "From what I have been able to learn, it is the *Democratic* party that has gone into the hands of the undertakers."

Beginning his story of the Missouri Compromise, Lincoln declared, "Gentlemen, to show you how it was regarded by some of the leaders of the Democratic party, I will read you a portion of a speech delivered in 1849 by my distinguished friend. It is powerful and eloquent; its language is choice and rich. I wish I was such a master of language as my friend, the Judge; I do indeed." He recited Douglas's words on how the Missouri Compromise was "canonized in the hearts of the American people." "A first rate speech," Douglas piped up. "Indeed so affectionate was the Judge's regard for the Missouri Compromise that when Texas was admitted, and a little strip of it was found to be north of 36°30', he actually had the prohibitory line extended over that also." "And you voted against extending the line, Mr. Lincoln?" "Yes, sir, because I was in favor of running that line much further south." When the applause for Lincoln died down, he went on. "About this time my friend, the Judge, introduced me to a particular friend of his, one Davy Wilmot, of Pennsylvania." "I thought you would be fit associates," said Douglas. "Well," replied Lincoln, according to the *Missouri Republican* report, "in the end it proved we were, and I hope to convince this audience that we may be so yet. (*Uproarious applause.*) I voted in one way or another about forty times for that gentleman's proviso, but some way or other the House adjourned and the proviso didn't pass."

Lincoln then took on Douglas's pride of authorship of the idea of popular sovereignty. "About this time old General Cass began to be talked of for the Presidency, and in order to make the matter sure in the South, he must write a letter that became somewhat famous under the name of the Nicholson letter. My friend here says that all Democrats who voted for General Cass were in favor of abrogating the Missouri Compromise. Well, according to my notion, this Nicholson letter was the primal origin of the doctrine of popular sovereignty. I think the old General after all is the father of the dogma. If I am not right I will thank my distinguished friend to correct me." Douglas replied "(*Solemnly*), 'God Almighty placed man on earth and told him to choose between good and evil. That was the origin of the Nebraska bill.' (*A dead calm.*)" "Well," said Lincoln, "then I think my distinguished friend is deserving of great honor for being the first to discover it." The newspaper reported: "(*Tremendous laughter.*)"

Then Lincoln's rhetorical gamesmanship completely fell away. Tracing the "short history" of the extension of slavery, his first and ultimate authority was Jefferson. "Mr. Jefferson, the author of the Declaration of Independence, and otherwise a chief actor in the revolution; then a delegate in Congress; afterwards twice President; who was, is, and perhaps will continue to be, the most distinguished politician of our history; a Virginian by birth and continued residence, and withal, a slave-holder; conceived the idea of taking that occasion, to prevent slavery ever going into the north-western territory. . . . Thus, with the author of the declaration of Independence, the policy of prohibiting slavery in new territory originated." For Lincoln the Jefferson reference carried even more weight than the Constitution; it was "away back of the constitution, in the pure fresh, free breath of the revolution."

Lincoln seized upon Jefferson in a wholly new crisis. "But *now* new light breaks upon us. Now congress declares this ought never to have been; and the like of it, must never be again. The sacred right of self government is grossly violated by it!" Lincoln held up Jefferson, the guiding light of Democrats, their political and philosophical ancestor, against those Democrats who opened the territories to slavery. "We even find some men, who drew their first breath, and every other breath of their lives, under this very restriction, now live in dread of absolute suffocation, if they should be restricted in the 'sacred right' of taking slaves to Nebraska. That *perfect* liberty they sigh for—the liberty of making slaves of other people—Jefferson never thought of; their own father never thought of; they never thought of themselves, a year ago. How fortunate for them, they did not sooner become sensible of their great misery! Oh, how difficult it is to treat with respect, such assaults upon all we have ever really held sacred."

Through his entire career as a Whig Lincoln had never quoted a line of Jefferson, much less approvingly. The Whig Party, through Henry Clay, was an offshoot of Jefferson's Democratic Party, but Lincoln had never claimed that tradition. Abolitionists of a certain stripe had long claimed Jefferson as their forebearer—the Liberty Party men, who cited the Declaration and the Ordinance as the basis of their politics, exemplified by Salmon Chase, who after all considered himself a Democrat. Lincoln had spoken of the founders, in his 1838 Lyceum address, for example, but only for establishing the pillars of constitutional order. He had not quoted them on slavery. Nor had he any ideas of Jefferson in his eulogy for Clay. But once he began citing Jefferson he never stopped. His use of Jefferson, his reinvention of political tradition, was a pivot point in his thought. Even as he argued as a Whig, he was ceasing to be one. He had previously been a relentless partisan Whig who lambasted Democrats. "Mr. Lincoln hated Jefferson as a man" and "as a politician," according to Herndon. If Herndon were accurate, this would have been an example of Lincoln's sheer partisanship.

If Lincoln shared certain traits in common with Jefferson they were skepticism, freethinking, and pragmatism. He had early entered into an aspect of Jefferson's worldview through Paine's *Age of Reason* and Volney's *Ruins of Empire*. But Jefferson and Lincoln were in many ways diametrically opposite: the obvious contrasts between Monticello and the frontier, the aristocratic democrat and the professional politician, the aesthete and the diamond in the rough, Jefferson's romance for bucolic paradise against Lincoln's embrace of commerce and industry, Jefferson's theoretical conviction in limited government while acting as a swashbuckling executive as opposed to Lincoln's forthright belief in government's central role in economic development. Lincoln did not receive his idea of Jefferson from Henry Clay, who always paid obeisance as the price of his heresy from Jefferson. Lincoln did not have a miraculous epiphany of reverence. He raised Jefferson in reaction to Douglas. Lincoln lifted Douglas's icon as his antislavery source to smash Douglas. Jefferson had become part of a usable past. Lincoln emancipated Jefferson from the enslavement of the party of which he was the founding father.

For the first time, Lincoln was trying to appeal to Democrats. Soon those Democrats would no longer be Democrats, just as he would no longer be a Whig. They would belong to the same political party. His transformation was not simply a matter of organizational fusion, but intellectual metamorphosis. Lincoln was becoming something new, a Republican. The first stage began in the disintegration of the old parties and shaping of ideas. Lincoln would continue his study of Jefferson and the founders on slavery, an exercise he started in his research for this speech, until he wrote in 1859, "All honor to Jefferson," and produce his speech at Cooper Union in 1860, discussing at length his view that the founders were fundamentally antislavery and the Constitution enshrined no right in the property of slaves. Lincoln was less engaged in a psychological quest for surrogate fathers representing virtues cast in marble than seeking a foundation stone for his evolving politics on which he could set the Democratic Party's father, Thomas Jefferson, against Douglas and the Southern apologists for slavery. He was stealing Jefferson for himself, from the Democrats who had denied his credo.

Citing Jefferson, Lincoln was already operating in a new world far beyond Jefferson's. In his Clay eulogy, though little noticed, Lincoln had begun his warfare against the Southern Christian pro-slavery theology that would culminate in his Second Inaugural. As a young politician Lincoln had offered orotund patriotic homage to the founders little different from politicians of any party, but in his current state of mind he recast the Revolution as an unfulfilled and unfinished legacy, and his opponents as subversive. In his Lyceum address he had wondered how he might ever pay sufficient tribute on an "altar" to the founders' enduring and seemingly completed edifice, but in identifying the fatal flaw of slavery and their saving grace in the Declaration of Independence and the Ordinance of 1787, and forging his relationship to the slaveholder Jefferson's antislavery tenets he finally discovered the connection, deeply rooting his claim to legitimacy.

Lincoln was hardly original in his discovery of the antislavery Jefferson. He prepared for his speech scouring the debate over the Nebraska Act in which Chase, Seward, and Sumner all cited Jefferson. "I invoke Jefferson as a witness," declared Chase, who quoted from his *Summary View of the Rights of British America* of 1774: "The abolition of domestic slavery is the great object of desire in those colonies, where it was unhappily introduced in their infant state." Both Seward and Sumner cited Jefferson for authorship of the Ordinance of 1787. And Sumner quoted from the gallery of founders' statements against slavery—Washington, Madison, Hamilton, Jay, and

Franklin—to prove the point that "the institution of Slavery was regarded by them with aversion, so that, though covertly alluded to, it was not named in the instrument; that, according to the debates in the Convention, they refused to give it any 'sanction,' and looked forward to the certain day when this evil and shame would be obliterated from the land"—a point Lincoln would echo.

Into the middle of his discursive historical summary, Lincoln inserted the shocking image of a sight that he had undoubtedly seen, "a peculiar species of slave trade in the District of Columbia, in connection with which, in view from the windows of the capitol, a sort of negro-livery stable, where droves of negroes were collected, temporarily kept, and finally taken to Southern markets, precisely like droves of horses." He had mentioned the slave pens in his Bloomington speech, but this description was more vivid. It was the beginning of his realistic depiction of slavery.

After describing how Douglas led the repeal of the Missouri Compromise, Lincoln's tone became insistent, his words percussive. Three times he said: "Wrong, wrong . . . and wrong." Then three times he uttered the word "hate." He did not say he disagreed, disapproved, or dissented—the word was "hate." His drumbeat of "wrong" was the overture to his "hate" for the elevation of the amoral hypocrisy used in the defense of slavery. He was, of course, referring to Douglas. "This *declared* indifference, but as I must think, covert *real* zeal for the spread of slavery, I can not but hate. I hate it because of the monstrous injustice of slavery itself. I hate it because it deprives our republican example of its just influence in the world—enables the enemies of free institutions, with plausibility, to taunt us as hypocrites—causes the real friends of freedom to doubt our sincerity, and especially because it forces so many really good men amongst ourselves into an open war with the very fundamental principles of civil liberty—criticizing the Declaration of Independence, and insisting that there is no right principle of action but *self-interest.*"

Lincoln's last use of the word "hate" to describe his feeling about the corrosive destruction of the American ideal as an example—"its just influence in the world"—was the worldview of the chairman of the Springfield committee that had met in the same hall only a year earlier to hail the Hungarian leader of its failed revolution as representative of "principles held dear" by Americans. Lincoln's identification of the "spread of slavery" and "monstrous injustice of slavery" as overriding factors in U.S. foreign policy was not vague. Through inferences easily understood to those listening, he linked American slavery with European tyranny and the antislavery struggle with European revolutions. It was a direct appeal to the large German community in Illinois, composed of refugees from the suppressed revolution of 1848, who had abandoned the Democratic Party in protest against the Nebraska Act.

Defending the American "just influence in the world," Lincoln had in mind specific men and recent incidents as menaces. His oblique reference to these threats appeared near the end of his speech when he continued his theme. "Already the liberal party throughout the world, express the apprehension 'that the one retrograde institution in America, is undermining the principles of progress, and fatally violating the noblest political system the world ever saw.' This is not the taunt of enemies, but the warning of friends. Is it quite safe to disregard it—to despise it? Is there no danger to liberty itself, in discarding the earliest practice, and first precept of our ancient faith? In our greedy chase to make profit of the negro, let us beware, lest we 'cancel and tear to pieces' even the white man's charter of freedom."

Lincoln's line referring to "the liberal party throughout the world" was quoted from the *New York Times* of just the week before, on September 29, reprinting an article from the *London Daily News*, whose conclusion warned against "the one retrograde institution in America." The article fiercely condemned Pierce's foreign policy as conducted by his diplomats appointed from the ranks of Young America as a danger to the American "national reputation." Its headline was, "Mr. Soule's 'Vulgar Turbulence'—George Sanders," and it denounced Soule for the Ostend Manifesto and Sanders for his assorted harebrained plots, "from semi-barbarous parts of the Slave states, men who think it chivalrous to bully their neighbors, and then put them in peril of their lives, in the name of honor," men from where "slavery exists, with all the despotism of principle and temper, all the ignorance, all the selfishness, all the gross tendencies, all the license of passion, all the ignorance and self-importance that it involves." The London newspaper confidently predicted that "the nation will save itself . . . be purged of that anomalous institution. . . . The question is, whether it will have done fatal mischief to the national character, reputation, and destiny, before that emancipation can be achieved."

The *London Daily News* article contained all the elements of Lincoln's critique, even its invocation of the founders against the "barbaric cause" of the extension of slavery, which the editorial claimed would have been met with "Jefferson's sarcasm or Washington's frown." In their absence, the London paper took on the task itself of scolding the viceroys of Young America, the movement Douglas had proclaimed to be "the spirit of the age," for "their ignorance and bad taste" and as a "disgrace to the Republic." Lincoln would have read the editorial as a stinging rebuke of Douglas.

Though he did not single out Douglas by name in this passage, Lincoln intended to shatter his grandiose pretensions and unmask the violence of his deed. His speech was filled with literary quotations and allusions, which he assumed his audience would understand whether or not they knew their origins. At the end of his discussion on the American "just influence in the world," quoting but not citing the *London Daily News*, he cautioned that slavery would "cancel and tear to pieces" the Declaration of Independence, that in enslaving blacks the "charter of freedom" for whites would be destroyed. The phrase "cancel and tear to pieces" was lifted from Shakespeare's *Macbeth*, Lincoln's favorite play, in the scene where Macbeth summons his wife to join him in the act of assassinating Duncan under the darkness of night. "Come, seeling night, Scarf up the tender eye of pitiful day, And with thy bloody and invisible hand, Cancel and tear to pieces that great bond, Which keeps me pale."

Like Lincoln's blood-soaked "Spot Resolution" speech in the Congress in 1848, demanding that President Polk identify the exact spot where the first American blood was shed to justify the Mexican War, this speech was specked four times with "blood," including a "drop," an allusion to his Mexican War "spot," but now throwing the burden of guilt on Douglas for "this Nebraska project"—"Will not the first drop of blood so shed, be the real knell of the Union?" In his revised version of his Springfield speech delivered at Peoria, Lincoln cast Douglas as Macbeth—and Jefferson as the Duncan he was assassinating. Again and again upholding Jefferson's Declaration, Lincoln rebutted Douglas's claim that the Nebraska Act was not intended to extend slavery or have that effect. Once again reaching for *Macbeth*, Lincoln said, "Like the 'bloody hand' you may wash it, and wash it, the red witness of guilt still sticks, and stares horribly at you." Douglas's "damn spot" could not be washed away through his sophistry.

Lincoln's view of Douglas as a dangerous demagogue who would "cancel and tear to pieces that great bond" was unaltered since his first formal oration, his Lyceum speech sixteen years earlier, when he described Douglas, though without naming him, as a modern "Napoleon" who would trample the laws of the founders in his path to achieve his ambition for "distinction." Now Lincoln described Douglas again as Napoleon, flamboyantly strutting on the stage waving his Nebraska Act, a bill that "finds no model in any law from Adam till today. As Phillips says of Napoleon, the Nebraska act is grand, gloomy, and peculiar; wrapped in the solitude of its own originality; without a model, and without a shadow upon the earth." "Phillips" was Charles Phillips, a liberal Irish barrister and writer. The line following the one Lincoln quoted from Phillips's *Historical Character of Napoleon* must have seemed apt to Lincoln as a description of Douglas: "A mind bold, independent, and decisive—a will, despotic in its dictates—an energy that distanced expedition, and a conscience pliable to every touch of interest."

Clearing his throat to discuss his own views on slavery, Lincoln began by absolving Southerners of responsibility, adopting the strategy of Leonard W. Bacon in not casting stones at the sinners in order to persuade others of the sin. "Before proceeding, let me say I think I have no prejudice against the Southern people," Lincoln said. "They are just what we would be in their situation. . . . When southern people tell us they are no more responsible for the origin of slavery, than we; I acknowledge the fact. When it is said that the institution exists; and that it is very difficult to get rid of it, in any satisfactory way, I can understand and appreciate the saying. I surely will not blame them for not doing what I should not know how to do myself."

Lincoln expressed his bewilderment at the complexity of the problem. But his bafflement was informed by his deep understanding of the racist undercurrents of Illinois politics that had to be navigated.

If all earthly power were given me, I should not know what to do, as to the existing institution. My first impulse would be to free all the slaves, and send them to Liberia,—to their own native land. But a moment's reflection would convince me, that whatever of high hope, (as I think there is) there may be in this, in the long run, its sudden execution is impossible. If they were all landed there in a day, they would all perish in the next ten days; and there are not surplus shipping and surplus money enough in the world to carry them there in many times ten days. What then? Free them all, and keep them among us as underlings? Is it quite certain that this betters their condition? I think I would not hold one in slavery, at any rate; yet the point is not clear enough for me to denounce people upon. What next? Free them, and make them politically and socially, our equals? My own feelings will not admit of this; and if mine would, we well know that those of the great mass of white people will not. Whether this feeling accords with justice and sound judgment, is not the sole question, if indeed, it is any part of it. A universal feeling, whether well or ill-founded, can not be safely disregarded.

We cannot, then, make them equals. It does seem to me that systems of gradual emancipation might be adopted; but for their tardiness in this, I will not undertake to judge our brethren of the south.

Though bowing to the overwhelming prejudice of public opinion, he laced his speech with ambivalence and ambiguity through phrases of conditionality that at the same time subtlety distanced him: "My own feelings will not admit of this; and if mine would. . . . Whether this feeling accords with justice and sound judgment, is not the sole question. . . . A universal feeling, whether well or ill-founded."

Having claimed to put aside the question of "justice" in his rhetorical device of removing blame from Southerners, Lincoln now reversed himself and attempted to force others to confront it. To begin with he insisted there was no difference in "moral principle" from "bringing of slaves *from* Africa" and "taking them *to* Nebraska." Explaining how the Wilmot Proviso and the Compromise of 1850 preserved the Missouri Compromise, he quickly made lawyerly work of dismissing Douglas's "main argument" that "slavery will not go to Kansas and Nebraska, *in any event*, as a *palliation*—a *lullaby.*" He pointed out that climate would not inhibit slavery. Five slave states, after all, were above the Mason-Dixon Line. "Now, when the restriction is removed, what is to prevent it from going still further? Climate will not. No peculiarity of the country will—nothing in *nature* will. Will the disposition of the people prevent it? Those nearest the scene, are all in favor of the extension. The yankees, who are opposed to it may be more numerous; but in military phrase, the battle-field is too far from *their* base of operations." He described how slavery was insinuated into a territory without the cover of law and made impossible to dislodge. "Wherever slavery is, it has been first introduced without law. The oldest laws we find concerning it, are not laws introducing it; but *regulating* it, as an already existing thing. A white man takes his slave to Nebraska now; who will inform the negro that he is free? Who will take him before court to test the question of his freedom? In ignorance of his legal emancipation, he is kept chopping, splitting and plowing. Others are brought, and move on in the same track. At last, if ever the time for voting comes, on the question of slavery, the institution already in fact exists in the country, and cannot well be removed. The facts of its presence, and the difficulty of its removal will carry the vote in its favor."

Slavery, he explained, also had an inexorable economic momentum behind its expansion, as "the opening of new countries to the institution, increases the demand for, and augments the price of slaves." Southerners insisted it was simple justice and equality that slavery be extended. "Equal justice to the south, it is said, requires us to consent to the extending of slavery to new countries," said Lincoln. "That is to say, inasmuch as you do not object to my taking my hog to Nebraska, therefore I must not object to you taking your slave. Now, I admit this is perfectly logical, if there is no difference between hogs and negroes. But while you thus require me to deny the humanity of the negro, I wish to ask whether you of the south yourselves, have ever been willing to do as much?"

Lincoln had lifted the burden of guilt from the South for slavery and denied any personal evil involved. But suggesting that Southerners were no more "natural tyrants" than other people he pointedly raised those very questions, appealing to Southerners' "sense of the wrong of slavery, and their consciousness that, after all, there is humanity in the negro." Lincoln had closely observed the hypocrisies of Southern society and he flung its most noxious aspect at Southerners to repudiate in order to prove they were not "natural tyrants."

> Again, you have amongst you, a sneaking individual, of the class of native tyrants, known as the "SLAVE-DEALER." He watches your necessities, and crawls up to buy your slave, at a speculating price. If you cannot help it, you sell to him; but if you can help it, you drive him from your door. You despise him utterly. You do not recognize him as a friend, or even as an honest man. Your children must not play with his; they may rollick freely with the little negroes, but not with the "slave-dealers" children. If you are obliged to deal with him, you try to get through the job without so much as touching him. It is common with you to join hands with the men you meet; but with the slave dealer you avoid the ceremony—instinctively shrinking from the snaky contact. If he grows rich and retires from business, you still remember him, and still keep up the ban of non-intercourse upon him and his family. Now why is this? You do not so treat the man who deals in corn, cattle or tobacco.

The disdainful attitude toward slave dealers Lincoln upheld was more a memory of the passing Henry Clay generation of the middle South than the attitude of the current generation especially in the burgeoning trans-Mississippi South. While calling Southerners back to the Southern Old Whig view once prevalent in the border states, Lincoln surely knew that the accelerating rapaciousness of slavery in the economic boom was driven by slave trading, which he had marked in "the price of slaves." The distaste for the ostentatious pro-slavery men and slave traders, paralleling the rise of the Southern Rights factions in Southern state after state, was becoming an anachronism.

The economics of slavery did not escape Lincoln. There were within the United States 433,643 free blacks, which if enslaved would at "$500 per head" be worth $200 million, he noted. Speaking rhetorically above the heads of his Springfield audience to distant Southerners of the slave states, he asked,

> How comes this vast amount of property to be running about without own-
> ers? We do not see free horses or free cattle running at large. How is this?
> All these free blacks are the descendants of slaves, or have been slaves them-
> selves, and they would be slaves now, but for SOMETHING which has
> operated on their white owners, inducing them, at vast pecuniary sacrifices,
> to liberate them. What is that SOMETHING? Is there any mistaking it? In
> all these cases it is your sense of justice, and human sympathy, continually
> telling you, that the poor negro has some natural right to himself—that
> those who deny it, and make mere merchandise of him, deserve kickings,
> contempt and death. And now, why will you ask us to deny the humanity of
> the slave? and estimate him only as the equal of the hog?

(By 1860, only 36,955 free blacks lived in the lower South, about half of those in New Orleans, which was since its colonial days under the Spanish and French a historically free black center.)

Lincoln cut to the infected heart of Douglas's argument, the assumption of injustice at the core of popular sovereignty. "But one great argument in the support of the repeal of the Missouri Compromise, is still to come. That argument is 'the sacred right of self government.' " Whether the doctrine was true or not rested on whether it had "just application," and that, for Lincoln, "depends upon whether a negro is not or is a man. If he is not a man, why in that case, he who is a man may, as a matter of self-government, do just as he pleases with him. But if the negro *is* a man, is it not to that extent, a total destruction of self-government, to say that he too shall not govern *himself*? When the white man governs himself that is self-government; but when he governs himself, and also governs *another* man, that is *more* than self-government—that is despotism. If the negro is a *man*, why then my an-cient faith teaches me that 'all men are created equal'; and that there can be no moral right in connection with one man's making a slave of another."

Lincoln turned Douglas's sneering and overbearing manner against him, but to expose more than his obnoxious style. "Judge Douglas frequently, with bitter irony and sarcasm, paraphrases our argument by saying 'The white people of Nebraska are good enough to govern themselves, *but they are not good enough to govern a few miserable negroes*!!' Well I doubt not that the people of Nebraska are, and will continue to be as good as the average of people elsewhere. I do not say the contrary. What I do say is, that no man is good enough to govern another man, *without that other's consent*. I say this is the leading principle—the sheet anchor of American republicanism."

With that Lincoln proclaimed the preamble of the Declaration of Independence as if it were an oath: "We hold these truths to be self evident: that all men are created equal . . ." For him the revolutionary promise of the American nation, its inalienable rights, made slavery an insufferable wrong. "I have quoted so much at this time merely to show that according to our ancient faith, the just powers of governments are derived from the consent of the governed. Now the relation of masters and slaves is, PRO TANTO, a total violation of this principle. The master not only governs the slave without his consent; but he governs him by a set of rules altogether different from those which he prescribes for himself. Allow ALL the governed an equal voice in the government, and that, and that only is self government."

Douglas, he said, had sought to "bring to his aid the opinions and examples of our revolutionary fathers." Lincoln was "glad" to submit to this test. He would not permit Douglas to claim the Revolution. Against extending slavery, Lincoln made the classic antislavery argument that the revolutionary generation, "the same individuals of the generation, who declared this principle—who declared independence—who fought the war of the revolution through—who afterwards made the constitution under which we still live—these same men passed the ordinance of '87, declaring that slavery should never go to the north-west territory."

Opening the territories under Douglas's popular sovereignty would do nothing less than "surrender the right of self-government." "What is then left of us? What use for the general government, when there is nothing left for it to govern?" Popular sovereignty was not the exercise of democracy, but instead imperiled it. It was the cynical doctrine of slaveholders against freemen. As a practical matter, the Nebraska Act was a mechanism for installing slavery, which once there could not be uprooted. "It enables the first FEW, to deprive the succeeding MANY, of a free exercise of the right of self-government. The first few may get slavery IN, and the subsequent many cannot easily get it OUT."

Douglas's doctrine was more than a ruse, more than a political ploy, and more than a constitutional travesty. It was a mortal threat. "Whether slavery shall go into Nebraska, or other new territories, is not a matter of exclusive concern to the people who may go there. The whole nation is interested that the best use shall be made of these territories." At last Lincoln merged his sense of the nation with his sense of himself. He encapsulated his own family's story as dirt-poor Kentuckians fleeing from their oppression in a slave society. "We want them for the homes of free white people. This they cannot be, to any considerable extent, if slavery shall be planted within them. Slave States are places for poor white people to remove FROM; not to remove TO. New free States are the places for poor people to go to and better their condition." This was the beginning of the story that enabled Lincoln to become the man standing on the stage speaking at that moment. He was a child of the Ordinance of 1787, his most valuable birthright, and it made him Jefferson's rightful descendant.

The Ordinance, for Lincoln, as it was for other antislavery men, derived in a straight line from the Declaration of Independence and taken as a Magna Carta against the extension of slavery. Antedating the Constitution, drafted in 1784, it was the clearest statement from the Declaration's author of its meaning for the future of the new nation and of slavery. The Ordinance was enacted prior to the Constitution by the Confederation Congress, some of whose members were at the same time participating on the Constitutional Convention at Philadelphia. For Lincoln the Constitution was a more complicated matter, a compromise to secure the Union, for which the Missouri Compromise was a later corollary deal. By repealing it the Constitution, as envisioned by the framers to restrict and eventually extinguish slavery, was subverted. Douglas's Nebraska Act aligned the Constitution with slavery, twisting it into an excuse for putting the country on "the high road to a slave empire," as President-elect Lincoln would write to Seward during the secession crisis of 1861. But it was in this Springfield speech that Lincoln began claiming the Constitution as an antislavery document.

The three-fifths clause, he pointed out, created an inequality based on slavery of Southern whites over Northern ones. "Now all this is manifestly unfair; yet I do not mention it to complain of it, in so far as it is already settled. It is in the constitution; and I do not, for that cause, or any other cause, propose to destroy, or alter, or disregard the constitution. I stand to it, fairly, fully, and firmly." But extending slavery broke the compact and reduced Northerners further. "If I am wrong in this—if it really be a sacred right of self-government, in the man who shall go to Nebraska, to decide whether he will be the EQUAL of me or the DOUBLE of me, then after he shall have exercised that right, and thereby shall have reduced me to a still smaller fraction of a man than I already am, I should like for some gentleman deeply skilled in the mysteries of sacred rights, to provide himself with a microscope, and peep about, and find out, if he can, what has become of my sacred rights! They will surely be too small for detection with the naked eye." As "sacred rights" diminished to the vanishing point, "the question of slavery extension" loomed ever larger as "the great Behemoth of danger," an allusion to a strange beast mentioned in the Book of Job.

"But Nebraska is urged as a great Union-saving measure," said Lincoln. In its structure, rhythm, and tone, he borrowed from Shakespeare, from *Julius Caesar*, mimicking Antony's funeral oration for Caesar that mocked and unmasked the motives of his assassin: "But Brutus says he was ambitious; And Brutus is an honorable man."

"Well I too, go for saving the Union," said Lincoln. "Much as I hate slavery, I would consent to the extension of it rather than see the Union dissolved, just as I would consent to any GREAT evil, to avoid a GREATER one." This was Lincoln's earliest formula claiming he would preserve the Union above ending or limiting slavery if it would serve that higher purpose, the rhetorical device he would pose in 1862 in an open letter to Horace Greeley after he had decided to issue the Emancipation Proclamation but had not yet announced it. Now he observed, "But when I go to Union saving, I must believe, at least, that the means I employ has some adaptation to the end. To my mind, Nebraska has no such adaptation." He quoted a line from *Hamlet* to cinch his argument—"It hath no relish of salvation in it"—a line in which Hamlet contemplates murdering the drunken, incestuous, and raging Claudius, who occupies his father's throne through assassination of Hamlet's father and whose "soul may be as damned and black as hell," lacking "salvation." In the background of all Lincoln's Shakespearean allusions lurked the darkness and blood of treasonous assassination.

Before Douglas's act, "all was peace and quiet"—in its own subtle way a dig at Douglas's central role in enacting the Compromise of 1850 whose politics he had overthrown. But now, said Lincoln, "the genius of Discord himself, could scarcely have invented a way of again getting us by the ears, but by turning back and destroying the peace measures of the past. The councils of that genius seem to have prevailed, the Missouri compromise was repealed; and here we are, in the midst of a new slavery agitation, such, I think, as we have never seen before." Lincoln's reference to "the genius of Discord" was drawn from classical mythology to "the apple of discord" that provoked the ruinous Trojan War. If there were a war, it would be traced to "the genius."

Douglas, in his Senate speech, had blamed the "agitation" on those protesting his bill. Lincoln threw his accusation back at Douglas. "Who is responsible for this?" asked Lincoln. "Is it those who resist the measure; or those who, causelessly, brought it forward, and pressed it through, having reason to know, and, in fact, knowing it must and would be so resisted? It could not but be expected by its author, that it would be looked upon as a measure for the extension of slavery, aggravated by a gross breach of faith. Argue as you will, and long as you will, this is the naked FRONT and ASPECT, of the measure. And in this aspect, it could not but produce agitation." So it was none other than Douglas who was "the genius of Discord."

Douglas had attempted to silence his critics on the Senate floor during the debate over the Nebraska Act through his intimidating vehemence. But Lincoln explained why they could never be silenced. Earlier in his speech he rationalized his hesitating deference to racial prejudice as an acknowledgment of "universal feeling," or public opinion, which he said compelled him to set aside judgments of justice: "Whether this feeling accords with justice and sound judgment, is not the sole question." But, now, in the same speech, he made the moral case for justice against slavery supreme above all other arguments. "Slavery is founded in the selfishness of man's nature—opposition to it, is in his love of justice. These principles are an eternal antagonism; and when brought into collision so fiercely, as slavery extension brings them, shocks, and throes, and convulsions must ceaselessly follow. Repeal the Missouri compromise—repeal all compromises—repeal the Declaration of Independence—repeal all past history, you still cannot repeal human nature. It still will be the abundance of man's heart, that slavery extension is wrong; and out of the abundance of his heart, his mouth will continue to speak."

Lincoln the lawyer proceeded to pick apart Douglas's popular sovereignty as a practical matter, leaving it in broken pieces as an absurdity. "The structure, too, of the Nebraska bill is very peculiar," he said. "The people are to decide the question of slavery for themselves; but WHEN they are to decide; or HOW they are to decide; or whether, when the question is once decided, it is to remain so, or is it to be subject to an indefinite succession of new trials, the law does not say, Is it to be decided by the first dozen settlers who arrive there? or is it to await the arrival of a hundred? Is it to be decided by a vote of the people? or a vote of the legislature? or, indeed by a vote of any sort?

To these questions, the law gives no answer. There is a mystery about this; for when a member proposed to give the legislature express authority to exclude slavery, it was hooted down by the friends of the bill. This fact is worth remembering."

But there was already evidence of the bill's true reality. It was less a demonstration of democracy in action as Douglas promised than an augury of violence. Lincoln observed the New England emigrants trekking to the territory, "yankees, in the east," intending "to exclude slavery," being met by Missourians determined "to protect it" and "that abolitionists shall be hung, or driven away. Through all this, bowie-knives and six-shooters are seen plainly enough; but never a glimpse of the ballot-box."

Lincoln could see in the "contest" in Kansas the makings of a "probable" civil war over slavery. "Could there be a more apt invention to bring about collision and violence, on the slavery question, than this Nebraska project is? I do not charge, or believe, that such was intended by Congress; but if they had literally formed a ring, and placed champions within it to fight out the controversy, the fight could be no more likely to come off, than it is. And if this fight should begin, is it likely to take a very peaceful, Union-saving turn? Will not the first drop of blood so shed, be the real knell of the Union?" Again, "Spotty" Lincoln located the precipitating bloodshed.

Lincoln pleaded for restoration of the Missouri Compromise, though he acknowledged that rescinding its repeal would be politically almost impossible, even if anti-Nebraska candidates were to sweep into the House of Representatives because the Senate would still stand as a bulwark. But the issue went far beyond that.

Those who repealed the Missouri Compromise had a larger design in mind than opening the Nebraska Territory. That was simply the first step in the creation of an empire of slavery. "With them, Nebraska alone is a small matter—to establish a principle, for FUTURE USE, is what they particularly desire. That future use is to be the planting of slavery wherever in the wide world, local and unorganized opposition can not prevent it." Who were "they"? And what was the "wide world"? Lincoln was thinking of Soule and Sanders, who had inspired the *London Daily News* editorial he had already quoted, and the filibusters plotting to seize Cuba and parts of Mexico—and standing behind Southern imperialism the most influential administration official as its prime mover, Jefferson Davis.

Arguing for restoration, Lincoln conceded, was a hypothetical political position, vainly attempting to overturn a fait accompli. Beyond restoring the Missouri Compromise, it was an effort at restoration of the Whig Party. Which was more unlikely? His immediate trouble was within his own ranks. Some Whigs, though opposed to the Nebraska Act, chafed at associating with abolitionists. "In central and southern Illinois, to be called an Abolitionist was quite as bad as to be called a thief," recalled Jane Martin Johns of the Old Whig attitude. Lincoln felt compelled to make a public appeal to his own followers to overcome their disdain. Speaking directly to Whigs, he made his most unvarnished partisan statement trying to unify his party.

"Some men, mostly Whigs," he said,

> who condemn the repeal of the Missouri Compromise, nevertheless hesitate to go for its restoration, lest they be thrown in company with the abolitionist. Will they allow me as an old Whig to tell them good humoredly, that I think this is very silly? Stand with anybody that stands RIGHT. Stand with him while he is right and PART with him when he goes wrong. Stand WITH the abolitionist in restoring the Missouri Compromise; and stand AGAINST him when he attempts to repeal the fugitive slave law. In the latter case you stand with the southern disunionist. What of that? You are still right. In both cases you are right. In both cases you oppose the dangerous extremes. In both you stand on middle ground and hold the ship level and steady. In both you are national and nothing less than national. This is good old Whig ground. To desert such ground, because of any company, is to be less than a Whig—less than a man—less than an American.

Persuading conservative Whigs to "stand with the abolitionist" was an unenviable but essential task. Their loathing for abolitionists had to be overcome for the Whigs to become a functional antislavery party, or else it would sink back into its resentments and irrelevance. Lincoln was addressing some of the men who were among his most confidential friends. His former law partner John Todd Stuart recoiled at "the radicals." Judge David Davis, maestro of Lincoln's merry band of legal troubadours and the reigning Whig power of Bloomington, had a visceral hatred of abolitionists and Owen Lovejoy in particular, despite that his former law partner and friend Jesse Fell held an utterly opposite point of view. Raised in a slaveholding family on a large plantation in southern Maryland, a place that in every respect was part of deepest Virginia, Davis had an instinctive reaction upon hearing a New England–inflected voice speak against slavery. He despised the local abolition-minded Bloomington Congregational Church, which he derisively called the "Abolition Church," led by the Yale-educated pastor Elihu Inger-soll, who would depart in 1857 to join the front lines of "Bleeding Kansas."

Earlier in his speech, Lincoln described the Fugitive Slave Act as a pro-fane duty for the sake of the sacred Union, one of the "constitutional rela-tions between the slave and free States, which are degrading to the latter. We are under legal obligations to catch and return their runaway slaves to them—a sort of dirty, disagreeable job, which I believe, as a general rule the slave-holders will not perform for one another." Yet, in another place in his speech, Lincoln ambivalently expressed his support for the act on the one hand and his reservations on the other. "When they remind us of their con-stitutional rights, I acknowledge them, not grudgingly, but fully, and fairly," he said, then proposed changes in the law that would effectively eviscerate it while appearing merely to be reasonable. "I would give them any legisla-tion for the reclaiming of their fugitives, which should not, in its stringency, be more likely to carry a free man into slavery, than our ordinary criminal laws are to hang an innocent one." Lincoln was here referring to the practice of Southern slave hunters snatching free blacks into slavery, like the story of Solomon Northup, whose bestselling memoir, *Twelve Years a Slave*, was published just a year before in 1853. So while offering support out of fealty to the law, Lincoln exposed its seamy underside. In private, his friend Joseph Gillespie recalled, "He used to say that it was singular that the courts would hold that a man never lost his right to his property that had been stolen from him but that he instantly lost his right to himself."

Lincoln's political purpose in affirming the Fugitive Slave Act was stra-tegic in order to hold together the antislavery cause. The act was a wedge issue dividing those who opposed the extension of slavery that, if allowed to become paramount, fostered dissension within the antislavery ranks, espe-cially precarious in Illinois, not only in 1854 but also after the creation of the Republican Party through 1860. Lincoln made the explicit case for removing the Fugitive Slave Act as a source of controversy among Republicans in a let-ter to Salmon Chase, then governor of Ohio, on June 9, 1859, after the Ohio Republican Party adopted a state convention platform denouncing the act. "This is already damaging us here," Lincoln wrote. "I have no doubt that if that plank be even *introduced* into the next Republican National conven-tion, it will explode it. Once introduced, its supporters and its opponents will quarrel irreconcilably. . . . I enter upon no argument one way or the other; but I assure you the cause of Republicanism is hopeless in Illinois, if it be in any way made responsible for that plank." While Lincoln did not state this political logic in his 1854 speeches, it was the imperative that informed his position.

Seamlessly, without the slightest transition, Lincoln shifted from the moral ambiguities of the Fugitive Slave Act to his absolute moral certainty against slavery. "I particularly object to the NEW position which the avowed principle of this Nebraska law gives to slavery in the body politic. I object to it because it assumes that there CAN be MORAL RIGHT in the enslaving of one man by another. I object to it as a dangerous dalliance for a free people—a sad evidence that, feeling prosperity we forget right—that liberty, as a principle, we have ceased to revere."

He offered yet another reason for his revulsion against slavery. "I object to it because the fathers of the republic eschewed, and rejected it." He reviewed the history of slavery in the Constitution, reiterating the account that Chase, Sumner, and Seward had given, that the framers "BEFORE the Constitution," forbade slavery's introduction in the Northwest Territory, "the only country we owned, then free from it." Though Lincoln had cited the three-fifths clause as "unfair," he observed that the framers "forbore to so much as mention the word 'slave' or 'slavery' in the whole instrument. In the provision for the recovery of fugitives, the slave is spoken of as a 'PERSON HELD TO SERVICE OR LABOR.' . . . Thus, the thing is hid away, in the constitution, just as an afflicted man hides away a wen or a cancer, which he dares not cut out at once, lest he bleed to death; with the promise, nevertheless, that the cutting may begin at the end of a given time." Time and again, from his 1858 debates with Douglas to his remarks as President, Lincoln would refer to slavery as a cancer or "wen."

The founding generation tolerated slavery only by "necessity," because it already existed, he said, "the only argument they ever admitted in favor of slavery," meanwhile legislating to limit it with the aim of its ultimate end. "The earliest Congress, under the constitution, took the same view of slavery. They hedged and hemmed it in to the narrowest limits of necessity." Lincoln listed every prohibition of the slave trade from 1794 through 1820. "While all this was passing in the general government, five or six of the original slave States had adopted systems of gradual emancipation; and by which the institution was rapidly becoming extinct within these limits. Thus we see, the plain unmistakable spirit of that age, towards slavery, was hostility to the PRINCIPLE, and toleration, ONLY BY NECESSITY. But NOW it is to be transformed into a 'sacred right.' "

The transformation of slavery into "the chief jewel of the nation—the very figure-head of the ship of State" was a counter-revolution, "giving up the OLD for the NEW faith." Reading slavery out of the Constitution, registering the founders' disapproval and portraying them as gradual emancipationists, he anointed antislavery belief as their creed and pro-slavery conviction heresy. "Near eighty years ago," Lincoln said—nearly four score—"we began by declaring that all men are created equal; but now from that beginning we have run down to the other declaration, that for SOME men to enslave OTHERS is a 'sacred right of self-government.' These principles can not stand together"—Lincoln's first version of "a house divided."

Lincoln singled out for criticism the only other man by name in his speech other than Douglas, Senator John Pettit of Indiana, for calling the Declaration "a self-evident lie," only doing "what consistency and candor require all other Nebraska men to do." Lincoln censured the Senate's silent assent. "Of the forty odd Nebraska Senators who sat present and heard him, no one rebuked him." None had defended the Declaration. "If it had been said in old Independence Hall, seventy-eight years ago, the very doorkeeper would have throttled the man, and thrust him into the street. Let no one be deceived. The spirit of seventy-six and the spirit of Nebraska, are utter antagonisms; and the former is being rapidly displaced by the latter." Lincoln was calling on his audience to take the role of this imaginary doorkeeper.

Now he shifted the scene from a scuffle in Independence Hall, drawing back the curtain on a passion play of death and redemption.

> Our republican robe is soiled, and trailed in the dust. Let us repurify it. Let us turn and wash it white, in the spirit, if not the blood, of the Revolution. Let us turn slavery from its claims of "moral right," back upon its existing legal rights, and its arguments of "necessity." Let us return it to the position our fathers gave it; and there let it rest in peace. Let us re-adopt the Declaration of Independence, and with it, the practices, and policy, which harmonize with it. Let north and south—let all Americans—let all lovers of liberty everywhere—join in the great and good work. If we do this, we shall not only have saved the Union; but we shall have so saved it, as to make, and to keep it, forever worthy of the saving. We shall have so saved it, that the succeeding millions of free happy people, the world over, shall rise up, and call us blessed, to the latest generations.

Chase and Sumner's "Appeal of the Independent Democrats" against the Nebraska Act did more than denounce the violation of the "sacred pledge" of the Missouri Compromise to limit slavery and condemn the "criminal betrayal of precious rights." It did more than invoke Jefferson, John Quincy Adams, and Clay. It summoned "the All-Seeing" deity to "comprehend" the depth of the Nebraska Act's "evil issues." The "Appeal" called on the faithful and clergy to intervene: "We implore Christians and Christian ministers to interpose." It claimed "their divine religion" as inspiration for it "requires them to behold in every man a brother." It declared themselves in obedience to God's higher law: "We will not despair; for the cause of human freedom is the cause of God."

For his peroration, Lincoln drew upon religious themes but not religion. He did not call on the hosts of the Lord. He began holding up the stain of slavery on our "robe," a heavenly garment, dragged through "the dust," the biblical image for death, and offered the hope of salvation, adapting his metaphor from the Book of Revelation: "These are they which came out of great tribulation, and have washed their robes, and made them white in the blood of the Lamb." Four times he spoke of salvation, of the possibility of being "saved" and "saving," and of the people who "shall rise up," of their resurrection and immortal life, "to the latest generations." But Lincoln substituted the Revolution for Christ and the Declaration of Independence for Scripture.

Then he sat down.

The crowd had come in the festive atmosphere of the State Fair to be entertained by dueling political speeches. When Lincoln mounted the platform many had undoubtedly been spectators before at his amusing, sharp, and clever performances. But it was at this moment that the perception of Lincoln altered. Horace White, the reporter for the *Chicago Journal*, was among those who observed him pass from a familiar mundane state into something they had not recognized. His account captured the sensation of witnessing Lincoln's transfiguration.

"I heard the whole of that speech," recalled White.

I observed that, although awkward, he was not in the least embarrassed. He began in a slow and hesitating manner, but without any mistakes of language, dates, or facts. It was evident that he had mastered his subject, that he knew what he was going to say, and that he knew he was right. He had a thin, high-pitched falsetto voice of much carrying power, that could be heard a long distance in spite of the bustle and tumult of a crowd. He had the accent and pronunciation peculiar to his native state, Kentucky. Gradually he warmed up with his subject, his angularity disappeared, and he passed into that attitude of unconscious majesty that is so conspicuous in Saint-Gauden's statue at the entrance of Lincoln Park in Chicago. . . .

Progressing with his theme, his words began to come faster and his face to light up with the rays of genius and his body to move in unison with his thoughts. His gestures were made with his body and head rather than with his arms. They were the natural expression of the man, and so perfectly adapted to what he was saying that anything different from it would have been quite inconceivable. Sometimes his manner was very impassioned, and he seemed transfigured with his subject. Perspiration would stream from his face, and each particular hair would stand on end. Then the inspiration that possessed him took possession of his hearers also. His speaking went to the heart because it came from the heart. I have heard celebrated orators who could start thunders of applause without changing any man's opinion. Mr. Lincoln's eloquence was of the higher type, which produced conviction in others because of the conviction of the speaker himself. His listeners felt that he believed every word he said, and that, like Martin Luther, he would go to the stake rather than abate one jot or tittle of it. In such transfigured moments as these he was the type of the ancient Hebrew prophet as I learned that character at Sunday-school in my childhood.

Herndon, serving as reporter for the *Journal*, described the speech as "the profoundest in our opinion that he has made in his whole life. . . . He quivered with emotion. The whole house was still as death." Douglas's bill was "torn and rent asunder by the hot bolts of truth," as Lincoln exposed its "humbuggery and falsehood." The crowd burst into "loud and continued huzzas," and women "waved their white handkerchiefs."

Horace White in his report described Lincoln as "a mammoth." Douglas "never in his life received so terrible a back fall." When Douglas took the speaker's stand to reply to Lincoln, White reported he was "actually quivering." In his "invariable way," he insisted, "he has been abused in a manner hitherto unparalleled." The *Register*, however, reported that Lincoln "had been selected as the Goliath of the anti-Nebraska black republican fusionists," and after Douglas had slain his arguments "the thunders of the applauding multitude shook the state house from turret top to foundation stone." Herndon answered with an editorial in the *Journal*, "Douglas, it must be confessed, has power. . . . He is the greatest demagogue in America. The fate of Satan is the fate of Douglas."

Lincoln and Douglas restaged their debate nearly two weeks later on

October 16 at Peoria, where Lincoln replied to Douglas's argument that he "always considered this government was made for the white people and not for the negroes." Here Lincoln disclosed the moral hollowness at the core of Douglas's Nebraska bill, his "great mistake." "It shows," he said,

> that the Judge has no very vivid impression that the negro is a human; and consequently has no idea that there can be any moral question in legislating about him. In his view, the question of whether a new country shall be slave or free, is a matter of as utter indifference, as it is whether his neighbor shall plant his farm with tobacco, or stock it with horned cattle. Now, whether this view is right or wrong, it is very certain that the great mass of mankind take a totally different view. They consider slavery a great moral wrong; and their feelings against it, is not evanescent, but eternal. It lies at the very foundation of their sense of justice; and it cannot be trifled with. It is a great and durable element of popular action, and, I think, no statesman can safely disregard it.

Once again, Lincoln swept aside his own initial argument that justice must be a secondary consideration.

The morning after the Peoria debate, according to a witness, Douglas requested a truce with Lincoln, explaining "that Lincoln had given him more trouble than all the opposition in the Senate and then proposed to Lincoln that if he Lincoln would go home and make no more speeches during the campaign that he Douglas would go to no more of his appointments and remain silent." But they made no armistice. On October 17, they were both in the town of Lacon where another clash was planned. But Douglas was ill, and Lincoln "with his accustomed magnanimity declared that it would be unfair and ungenerous in him to present his views to the people, unless Judge Douglas was able to reply," according to one of Lincoln's friends, Dr. Robert Boal, who was also a Whig candidate for the legislature. Thus the Lincoln-Douglas debates of 1854 concluded, to be resumed four years later in the race for the Senate.

Lincoln had delivered his speech without a text or notes several times in longer versions each time. After Peoria, he wrote it down and published it as a series of pieces in the *Journal*. It became known as his "Peoria speech." It was the basis for virtually all of his politics through his election as president.

Immediately after Lincoln spoke at Springfield and before Douglas replied, Owen Lovejoy and Ichabod Codding leapt to the front of the hall to announce the organizing meeting that evening for what they called "the Republican Party." Herndon claimed to have spent the day with them and was privy to their plan "to induce Mr. Lincoln to speak for them at their meeting." Before Lovejoy could proffer the invitation, Herndon said he hustled Lincoln to leave town at once. "Take Bob"—Lincoln's horse—"and drive somewhere into the country and stay till this thing is over." Though Herndon identified himself as an abolitionist, he did not want Lincoln "identified with all the rancor and extremes of Abolitionism." Yet this tale in which Herndon portrayed himself as having "saved Lincoln" seems unlikely. Lincoln, who was promoting the centrality of the Whig Party, would have had no intention in any case of attending fusion meetings. While he left for the court in Tazewell County his departure was probably less an escape than a recognition that it took a full day to travel there, where the diligent lawyer attended to about a dozen waiting clients.

Twenty-six men met that night, former Free Democrats, Free Soilers, several Whigs, and a Know Nothing, uniformly respectable—pastors, doctors, newspaper editors, teachers, successful businessmen, many elected town officials, a few Quakers, some conductors on the Underground Railroad, not only the brother of the martyred Elijah Lovejoy but also one of his closest associates on his suppressed newspaper, and all of them in time to become Lincoln's fervent Republican allies, friends, and even a client or two. They appointed a smaller resolutions committee that met in the office of Erastus Wright, a leading Springfield citizen, the school commissioner and affluent land speculator, who also rode a pet elk. By the light of two candles they adopted a broad and inclusive platform declaring, "freedom is national and slavery sectional and local," the Congress had "the right" to prohibit the extension of slavery, and, as an appeal to Whigs, advocated "river and harbor improvements." The platform also praised those "postponing or disregarding their minor differences of opinion or preferences . . . in the cause of freedom." "The fact was," wrote one of those present, Paul Selby, editor of the *Morgan Journal* of Jacksonville, "that the platform actually adopted at Springfield contained no sentiment more radical than that of opposition to the further extension of slavery, and made no declaration in favor of repeal of the Fugitive Slave Law or of interference with the institution where it already existed under the Constitution. . . . As a matter of fact, and from personal knowledge, I feel justified in saying that a large proportion of the members—I believe a majority—were as conservative in reference to their policy for checking the spread of slavery as was Mr. Lincoln himself. . . . It is true that many of the members of the convention—probably a majority—had been present at the discussion between Douglas and Lincoln. They understood Lincoln's position; and that they approved it was shown by their action on the second day."

The next day the group, slightly expanded in numbers, chose a central committee. Owen Lovejoy enthusiastically proposed the name of Lincoln. When questions were raised about Lincoln's "sympathy with the views maintained by the convention," Selby recalled, "I have a distinct recollection that Owen Lovejoy, in emphatic terms, vouched for his fidelity to the principles enunciated in our platform." So the others deferred to Lovejoy's judgment and elected Lincoln to their committee. The mystery of Lovejoy's promotion of Lincoln could be traced to the influence of Joshua Giddings, Lincoln's boardinghouse mate at Mrs. Sprigg's, who had helped him on his aborted bill on emancipation in the District of Columbia, and wrote Lovejoy to urge him to support Lincoln. What was unusual about Lovejoy among abolitionists was that he possessed a distinct political sense and would never waver from his commitment to Lincoln through the years regardless of abolitionist criticism. He knew that for the new organization to gain sway in Illinois it must encompass the whole state, not just its northern part, that it must include Whigs, and that the most influential, capable, and articulate politician taking an anti-Nebraska position was Lincoln. Lovejoy was one of the first men to recognize the potential in Lincoln.

"The Black Republican Fizzle," ran the headline on the *Register*'s editorial, claiming Lincoln was the inspiration for the abolitionists' convention and had joined them. "It was impossible for this black republican concern to carry on its proceedings without a decided expression in some way of the feelings of the ismites, resulting from Mr. Lincoln's speech. Ichabod raved, and Lovejoy swelled, and all indorsed the sentiments of that speech. . . . They hoped that all would go home remembering the speech . . . that they might know that one great whig had fallen into their fold." The *Register* described the convention led by Codding, "the notorious hireling of abolitionism, with a dozen or more congenial spirits . . . forming a sectional party, and carrying out its nefarious project of dissolving the Union." Rather than accurately reporting its platform, the *Register* printed the radical agenda from an abolitionist meeting in Kane County—"the fraudulent platform," a "forgery," according to Selby. Four years later, in 1858, Douglas triumphantly whipped out the *Register* article at the first debate with Lincoln to read aloud the false platform resolutions—"I now hold them in my hand"—as proof of Lincoln's

"Black Republicanism," which Lincoln exposed as a deception, so "very gross and palpable, it is apt to amuse."

Several weeks after the convention, Lincoln received a letter from Codding requesting his attendance at the central committee meeting in Chicago. He was baffled. "While I have pen in hand allow me to say," Lincoln wrote on November 27, "I have been perplexed some to understand why my name was placed on that committee. I was not consulted on the subject; nor was I apprised of the appointment, until I discovered it by accident two or three weeks afterwards. I suppose my opposition to the principle of slavery is as strong as that of any member of the Republican party; but I had also supposed that the *extent* to which I feel authorized to carry that opposition, practically; was not at all satisfactory to that party. The leading men who organized that party, were present, on the 4th of October at the discussion between Douglas and myself at Springfield, and had full opportunity to not misunderstand my position. Do I misunderstand theirs?" "If he had read anything purporting to represent the views of the convention," wrote Selby, "it was the fraudulent platform printed in a local Springfield paper, with which Douglas confronted him at Ottawa four years later; and it follows very naturally that he did 'misunderstand' the real position of the convention."

After the Springfield debate, and on the eve of the Peoria encounter, the *Register* railed against Lincoln's "abolition harangues through the country. . . . He now proclaims himself in full brotherhood with Garrison, Fred. Douglass, Lovejoy, Codding, & Co." Douglas's *Chicago Times* claimed to expose the secret sexual agenda of his opponents, who intended to "legalize in this State this identical intercourse between negroes and white women, and to place such intercourse, filthy and repulsive as it is, upon the same equal footing as marriages between our white citizens."

With his debates with Douglas ended, Lincoln continued his whirlwind tour on his own, delivering versions of his speech on behalf of Whig candidates, on October 27 addressing a crowd at Chicago's New Market Hall, where Douglas had faced a chorus of disapproval. "Come One, Come All!!!" blared the notice in the *Chicago Journal*. The paper's report on Lincoln's speech emphasized his ridicule of Senator Pettit for calling the Declaration of Independence "a self-evident lie." Another account, in the *Illinois Staats-Zeitung*, the antislavery German language newspaper, observed, "Abraham Lincoln never trims a speech to suit a latitude—he is always the same man." The *Staats-Zeitung* editor, George Schneider, who had organized the first protest meeting against the Nebraska Act and hated the Know Nothings, had invited Lincoln to speak in Chicago. They had met the year before in Springfield and dined after the speech with Isaac N. Arnold, a lawyer, former Democratic and Free Soil state legislator. Both men would become Lincoln's firmest advocates.

There were no more debates with Douglas, but Lincoln continued his campaigning in Quincy on behalf of the Whig candidate, Archie Williams, to give him, as Lincoln put it, "a little life," against William A. Richardson, Douglas's indispensable floor leader in the House. At the Quincy rally, the Quincy Whig hailed Lincoln's speech: "Mr. Lincoln left a most favorable impression upon those who heard him. He is one of the 'truly great men' of Illinois." Privately Lincoln worried about the floundering Yates, who held Lincoln's old congressional seat. Lincoln had just heard that English and German immigrants in the district believed Yates was a Know Nothing, so he quickly drafted a letter denouncing the Know Nothings that he urged Yates to sign and "get in the proper hands before the election," to put "into the hands of a safe man in each precinct. The day before election will do." Yates was also being hurt by the presence in the district of Ichabod Codding, who kept giving speeches, allowing Democrats to accuse Yates of being an abolitionist. The *Journal* countered by raising the specter of Mormonism, tagging Yates's opponent, Thomas L. Harris, as "Polygamy" Harris, for arguing that under the doctrine of popular sovereignty he would allow Utah into the Union under its own terms, permitting polygamy.

The mid-October elections for the Congress were harbingers of Democratic disaster. In Pennsylvania twenty-one of twenty-five Democrats went down to defeat; in Indiana, all but two; in Ohio, every one. "There is no hope for this District," Shields confided to Lanphier about one in the usually reliable southeastern corner of the state where he had campaigned. "All is perfect chaos. And the feeling is such that no effort can accomplish anything. . . . The Anti-Nebraska feeling is too deep—more than I thought it was." "We are nearly in sight of the end," Richardson wrote Douglas. "I fear all is lost."

The Democrats had been the normal governing party in Illinois since the state had been admitted to the Union. This election was their worst defeat. "Never before have the democracy of Illinois been so completely vanquished," mourned the *Joliet Signal*. They lost a majority of the nine seats in the congressional delegation, their lowest representation ever. Three of the losses were to fusion candidates in northern districts and one in the south, there to an anti-Nebraska Democrat, Lyman Trumbull, a former justice on the state

Supreme Court. Nonetheless, both "Polygamy" Harris and Richardson won their races. The lackadaisical Yates had neglected to follow Lincoln's advice on rebutting the charge he was a Know Nothing, therefore, he wrote, "it so happened that I lost my elec[tion]." The *Register* crowed over the defeat of Yates, who was a surrogate for Lincoln: "It was a great victory over malcontents, secret plotters, midnight cabals, fusionists, abolitionists, and open and hidden foes of every repulsive hue."

Douglas preferred to analyze the returns as a referendum on Know Nothingism, his favored enemy. The "crucible" into which was "poured Abolitionism, Maine liquor law-ism, and what there was left of northern Whigism, and then the Protestant feeling against the Catholic, and the native feeling against the foreigner . . . melted, solved, and united was, in every instance, a Know-Nothing lodge." "Let us be of good cheer," he assured a group of Chicago Democrats. "All is well. Though the heavens are partially overcast, the clouds are passing away." He wrote Lanphier confidently, "The Nebraska fight is over and Know Nothingism has taken its place as the chief issue of the future." But Lanphier was filled with anxiety: "They outnumber us—we must outmanage them."

The harshest blow to the Democrats was not losing control of the congressional delegation, but of the state legislature, which would choose a U.S. senator, who would not be James Shields. Douglas ordered Harris to "take personal charge" holding the fort at the State House for Shields. Momentum, after all, seemed to be slipping away from the anti-Nebraska forces when a resolution to instruct Douglas and Shields as senators to restore the Missouri Compromise, Lincoln's position, failed in the legislature. But Shields remained gloomy. "They don't care two pence about Nebraska," he remarked, "but Douglas they have sworn to destroy."

CHAPTER TWENTY-ONE

SENATOR LINCOLN

"I have got it into my head to try to be U.S. Senator," Lincoln wrote on November 29, 1854, to Hugh Lemaster, editor of the *Fulton County Republican* newspaper, who promptly reported back that he had "conversed with some of our most prominent (working) Whigs and they all say elect Lincoln." Lincoln sent a flurry of letters to his network of Whigs throughout the state. "You used to express a good deal of partiality for me; and if you still do, now is the time," he wrote Charles Hoyt, a Whig activist and merchant in DeWitt County. To Herbert W. Fay, a state representative from DeKalb County, he reminded, "When you were in the legislature you helped to pass some bills of mutual interest, at that time either in jest or earnest you suggested me for Senator. My friends are now asking me to make the race. See the representatives and senator of your district and let me know what indorsement [*sic*] I may expect in that locality." To his old

Lyman Trumbull

friend Gillespie, he copied the same phrase he sent Lemaster, "I have got it into my head to try to be U.S. Senator," but added, "we shall have difficulty to unite our forces."

David Davis enlisted as unofficial campaign manager, dispatching his protégé, the lawyer Leonard Swett, to round up votes. "I met [John] Strunk at Wilmington," Swett reported to Lincoln about the Whig legislator from Kankakee. "Had a talk with him about you. . . . I think you will find him right." Writing to E. B. Washburne, Lincoln observed, "I have not ventured to write all the members in your district, lest some of them should be offended by the indelicacy of the thing—that is, coming from a total stranger. Could you not drop some of them a line?" On seven pages of a notebook, Lincoln wrote out the names of every newly elected member of the state legislature. In another letter to Washburne, he chronicled the leanings of more than a dozen legislators. "Besides the ten or a dozen, on our side, who are willing to be known as candidates, I think there are fifty secretly watching for a chance." While soliciting votes he also drafted two resolutions for the legislature to rescind Douglas's Nebraska Act—"To use their utmost endeavors to prevent the said Territories of Nebraska and Kansas, or either of them, or any part of either of them, ever coming into the Union as a Slave-state, or states"—but these resolutions were never introduced, though their authorship was known to antislavery members.

"That man who thinks Lincoln calmly sat down and gathered his robes about him, waiting for the people to call him, has a very erroneous knowledge of Lincoln," wrote Herndon of Lincoln in this campaign. "He was always calculating, and always planning ahead. His ambition was a little engine that knew no rest."

Lincoln resigned the state legislative seat to which he had been elected, creating a special election to fill it. Norman Broadwell, the Whig candidate, was a former clerk in the office of Lincoln & Herndon, but perversely declared that if elected to the legislature he would vote to fill the Senate seat with Yates, who had publicly announced that he would stand if Lincoln were defeated. Broadwell was appealing to disillusionment with Lincoln among those who felt he was putting his personal ambition above all else and should have remained in the legislature to manage the floor battle for an anti-Douglas senator. Broadwell was a Know Nothing, indifferent at best to the antislavery cause, and would defect to the Democrats during the 1856 campaign. The anti-Nebraska Democrats and abolitionists in the district, unable to muster themselves to nominate their own candidate, were furious with Lincoln, his resignation doing "more than any thing else to damage him with the Abolitionists," according to Charles H. Ray, editor of the *Galena Jeffersonian*, correspondent for Greeley's *New York Tribune*, and just appointed clerk of the State Senate. Meanwhile, Lincoln's studied refusal to assist Broadwell enraged the Know Nothings, who were "down on Lincoln—hated him," according to William Jayne. The Douglas operation swiftly turned out the vote for the Democrat, who won Lincoln's vacated seat. "The election of the Nebraska man will be crowed over," David Davis wrote Lincoln, "and I feel very sorry on account of the mortification to you specially and of course to the party." But he added, "It is better for your chances, that Broadwell was out than that he, being elected, should not go for you. That you can readily see would be a severe dig."

Despite his recent trip to Chicago Lincoln was not well known in the northern part of the state where some abolitionists mistrusted him in any case as a Whig. "Mr. Lincoln is a Know Nothing," reported the *Free West*, "and expects the full vote of the Republicans as well as the influence of the Know Nothings. . . . Our opposition is based upon short comings on the Republican basis. He is reported to be a Compromise Whig, and having a full attachment to that mummy of a party, which has . . . brought upon us all the calamities and defeats of the Republican movement." The paper added, "He dares not oppose the fugitive slave law—and he would not pledge himself not to go against the admission of any more Slave States." The *Free West* followed that broadside against Lincoln with another: "We could not advise the republicans to support . . . Lincoln, or any of the moderate men of his stamp. He is only a Whig, and this people's movement is no whig triumph." The paper proclaimed hopefully, "The Whig Party is dead."

Lincoln recruited his two Whig allies, Norton and Washburne, who had been elected to the Congress as fusion candidates to try to persuade the abolitionists and Free Soilers to support him. Jesse Norton told Lincoln that he had "written a kind but pointed letter" to the *Free West*'s editor, Zebina Eastman. "I hope he will see the impropriety of his course." Norton suggested to Lincoln "some concessions, such as could be made by you without any sacrifice of principle. . . . Are you bound to stand by every thing in the Compromise measures of 1850? Couldn't you concede to them a modification of the Fugitive Slave act?" Lincoln had, in fact, already made that gesture in his Peoria speech, but he followed Norton's advice, filling in more detail to legislators his view that runaway slaves must be tried in northern courts and judged by northern juries on the same basis as citizens, which would in effect render the law useless to slave owners.

Washburne worked on Charles H. Ray, who owed his new plum job as

State Senate clerk to his close relationship with the influential state senator Norman B. Judd, attorney for the Rock Island railroad and an anti-Nebraska Democrat. "I am afraid of 'Abe,' " Ray confided to Washburne. "He is Southern by birth, Southern by his associations and Southern, if I mistake not, in his sympathies. . . . His wife, you know, is a Todd, of a pro-Slavery family, and so are all his kin." But on January 4, 1855, Ray attended a speech Lincoln gave to the Springfield chapter of the American Colonization Society on the history of the slave trade and afterward told Washburne "our best source is to go in strong for Lincoln when the day comes." Washburne wrote Lincoln that Ray "looks for an overthrow of the powers that be"—and "something for him in connection with the census." As it happened, Lincoln arranged for Ray to become a trustee of the Illinois and Michigan Canal. Within a year Ray would become co-owner and editor of the *Chicago Tribune* and one of the most important figures promoting Lincoln's advancement.

In Washington, Washburne conferred with the leading abolitionist in the Congress, Joshua Giddings, who he discovered needed no incentive to help Lincoln. "I have this moment had a long talk with Giddings and he is your strongest possible friend and says he would walk clear to Illinois to elect you," Washburne wrote Lincoln on December 26. "He will do anything in the world to aid you, and he will to-day write his views fully on the whole subject to Owen Lovejoy, in order that he may present them to all the freesoilers in the Legislature. He will advise them most strongly to go for you *en masse*."

Washburne also wrote Zebina Eastman, "Friend Eastman," as he addressed his "Private" letter on December 19, assuring him of Lincoln's convictions and commitments—"a man of splendid talents, of great probity of character, and because he threw himself into the late fight on the *republican platform* and made the greatest speech in reply to Douglas ever heard in the State. *I know he is with us in sentiment*, and in such times as these, when we want big men and true men in the Senate, it seems cruel to strike him down. I thought, also he could combine more strength than any other man in the State." He urged Eastman to show a "liberal spirit" and promised that Lincoln "will not only carry out our views fully in the Senate, but he will be with us in our views and feelings." There was another reason, too. "Douglas would rather have any man in the State than Lincoln, because he knows Lincoln is the strongest man in the State." Washburne suggested that Eastman go to Springfield to meet with "old Abe," and "he can speak for himself."

The same day Washburne sent Eastman his letter he wrote Lincoln that he had Eastman well in hand. "He is easy to manage, and he has some influence among the old free-soilers. I think he could be got to favor your interest. I shall write him again, and I think I can satisfy him that you are right, on the 'Main question.' " He reported soon to Lincoln, "Giddings has written another letter to Lovejoy, which he gave to me to read and send off which I have done."

But Eastman did not make the trip to speak with Lincoln himself or take Washburne's advice. Instead, he chose to follow the line of the man he looked to as leader of the Free Democrats, Salmon P. Chase. "It is time," Chase wrote him, "that the notion that the truest, most fearless talent must be forced for half-and-halfs should be indignantly and emphatically repelled. . . . In no event should our friends agree to put in a man who is not reliably with us in principle and action for the future." Chase cited cautionary examples of recent state elections where Whigs were rewarded "while our folks have been put off with crumbs. We must not convert to this unless we are bent on humiliation and disgrace." Chase did not mention Lincoln by name, but in discussing the contest he clearly had him in mind, classifying him as the *Free West* had done as a Know Nothing. "I would rather see Shields back than a Know Nothing," Chase wrote, signing off by telling Eastman to show the letter also to Charles Ray.

Chase was a lame-duck senator. The deal he had struck between conservative pro-slavery Democrats and antislavery Free Soilers that had elected him against the Whigs had come apart. "I am now without a party," he wrote Sumner in the fall of 1854. Chase was not contemplating a new party, but reinvigorating the Free or Independent Democrats. He disdained the label of "Republican," still thinking of himself and his movement as purifying the Democratic Party. He had long labored in the antislavery vineyards with Liberty Party men and Free Democrats, and resented giving offices to hated Whigs as a betrayal. He was beginning to angle for the Ohio governorship in the election to be held in 1855, already thinking of it as his stepping-stone to the presidency. Chase's letter to Eastman was the beginning of his rivalry with Lincoln, whom he did not yet know but would challenge for the Republican nomination in 1860.

Three principal candidates, each representing a tendency within the Democratic Party, challenged Lincoln for senator. Shields rode into battle holding aloft the banner for Douglas, even after Douglas's men decided he was doomed. "I think that all hope of electing Shields is gone," Sheahan, editor of Douglas's *Chicago Times*, wrote Lanphier. "A new man should be talked of at once." Governor Joel Matteson, wealthy as the contractor of the Illinois and

Michigan Canal, as ingratiating to all sides as he was corrupt, was openly pro-Douglas but also quietly offered criticism of the Nebraska Act to those from whom he could profit by the telling. Lyman Trumbull, a state Supreme Court judge just elected to the Congress, was the former junior law partner of Governor Reynolds, had served early on in the state legislature with Lincoln, and was married to Julia Jayne, one of Mary Todd's closest friends, in a ceremony in which Norman B. Judd served as best man. In 1843, he took up a case on behalf of a black held as a slave, Joseph Jarrot, who sued for his wages. In the Circuit Court, Judge James Shields ruled for the slaveholder, but the next year the state Supreme Court ruled that under the Ordinance of 1787 "the descendants of the slaves of the old French settlers . . . cannot be held in slavery in this State." The decision was the effective end of slavery in Illinois. Trumbull possessed a keen legal mind, was diligent and industrious, but charmless and lacked a common touch. His fellow Democratic politicians across the spectrum viewed him warily as "reserved, not to say cold," "cold-blooded," and "devoured by ambition for office."

Before the balloting set for January 23, 1855, many members of the legislature with their wives and "a host of wire-pullers of all parties" spent the weekend on holiday in Chicago. On the return to Springfield a blizzard literally stopped the train in its tracks far from any town. The shivering passengers burned the wooden seats for warmth and devoured the catered feast onboard of "roast turkeys, hams and tongues, oysters, salads, cakes and ices," ordered for the victory celebration. After a rescue train plowed through the snow drifts the Chicago and Alton Railroad issued free travel passes to the legislators to return to Springfield. A new date of February 8 for the vote was agreed upon. Mary Lincoln planned on a grand reception for the new senator-elect that evening.

The Hall of Representatives where five months earlier Lincoln and Douglas had spoken was packed. "Every inch of space on the floor and lobby was occupied by members and their political friends," reported Horace White, "and the gallery was adorned by well-dressed women, including Mrs. Lincoln and Mrs. Matteson, the governor's wife, and her fair daughters." On the first ballot, Lincoln received forty-five votes, only six short of victory; Shields had forty-one; Trumbull, five; and nine scattered.

Trumbull's five votes consisted of anti-Nebraska Democrats determined to teach Douglas a lesson as Democrats who felt that he had placed them in political jeopardy. "These men kept aloof from the caucuses of both parties during the winter," recalled Samuel C. Parks, an old friend of Lincoln, whom he had recruited for election to the legislature. "They could not act with the Democrats from principle and would not act with the Whigs from policy." "At that time," explained a key member of the Trumbull faction, John M. Palmer, "the prejudice against abolitionists was bitter, and affected the minds of three-fourths of the voters. I was only remotely influenced in my course by hostility to slavery, though I avowed my opposition to the institution. I was chiefly concerned by the fact that the repeal of the Missouri Compromise reopened the slavery question." Palmer, who represented a southern district, later described himself as "a native of Kentucky with all the contempt of my race against Negroes." But he was furious with Douglas and personally confronted him. "You may join the Abolitionists if you choose to do so," Douglas told him, "but if you do, there are enough patriotic Whigs to take your place and elect Shields." Palmer answered, "You will fix the imputation of abolitionism upon me, and by that means beat me down: we have fought the Whigs together, you now promise yourself that they will take my place, and help elect Shields. I will fight you until you are defeated, and have learned to value your friends." Palmer acted as Trumbull's floor leader and placed his name in nomination. (In 1856, Palmer would gavel to order as its president the founding convention of the Illinois Republican Party, become part of Lincoln's entourage, serve during the war as the military governor of Kentucky who ended slavery there, and be elected governor of Illinois.)

On the next two ballots, Lincoln fell to forty-three. Logan moved for an adjournment until the next day to halt the momentum of his erosion, but his motion was rejected.

Lincoln fell to thirty-eight, then thirty-six. His doom was foretold. Lovejoy, who had stood by Lincoln for the first three ballots, now abandoned him. On the seventh ballot, the Douglas Democrats began switching from Shields to Governor Matteson. On the ninth, Lincoln dwindled to fifteen, Trumbull had thirty-five, and Matteson forty-seven. Matteson's election seemed inevitable. "Boys," joked Lovejoy to the glum anti-Nebraska men, "if you want me elected, you have got no time to lose, for it will be too late after another ballot."

As his votes tumbled, Lincoln received reliable reports that Matteson was offering bribes to wavering members. One of these stories came from Jane Martin Johns, whose husband, Dr. Johns, was now a Whig state representative. After overhearing several members plotting for Matteson through the wall of her boardinghouse room she rushed to the State House to inform

Lincoln, whom she described as "almost stunned." She witnessed several men hastily coming and going to confer with Lincoln, including Palmer. "Gentlemen," Lincoln suddenly announced, "Lyman Trumbull must be elected to the Senate on the next ballot!" "So I determined to strike at once; and accordingly advised my remaining friends to go for him," Lincoln recounted to Washburne. Logan begged him not to withdraw, but Lincoln declared that Matteson's election would be "an everlasting disgrace to the State." As the clerk prepared to begin the next roll call Lincoln walked to the front of the hall to announce his withdrawal and then mingled with his supporters in their seats to tell them they must vote for Trumbull. "We reluctantly complied with Lincoln's suggestions," recalled Gillespie. Logan wept. Trumbull was elected on that ballot.

At the crucial moment that Lincoln realized he could not be elected Gillespie recalled him saying "unhesitatingly, 'You ought to drop me and go for Trumbull. That is the only way you can defeat Matteson.' " When Logan protested, he remembered Lincoln saying, "If you do you will lose both Trumbull and myself and I think the cause in this case is to be preferred to men." Lincoln could have followed an alternative logic, pursuing his candidacy to the bitter end, thinking he would deny both the pro-Douglas and anti-Douglas factions satisfaction, but that would have enabled Matteson to grab the prize through corrupt means. Even more, by thwarting the anti-Nebraska and antislavery Trumbull, Lincoln would have forfeited the larger issue. "This I think shows that Mr. Lincoln was capable of sinking himself for the cause in which he was engaged," said Gillespie. "Mr. Lincoln's sense of justice was intensely strong. It was to this mainly that his hatred of slavery may be attributed. He abhorred the institution. It was about the only public question on which he would become excited."

"I could have headed off every combination and been elected, had it not been for Matteson's double game—and his defeat now gives me more pleasure than my own gives me pain," Lincoln wrote Washburne. "On the whole, it is perhaps as well for our general cause that Trumbull is elected."

While the voting went on, Lincoln sent Mrs. Johns a note about her discovery about the attempted bribery. "Please forget it all. No one knows that there were traitors in our camp, and no one must ever know. That is a closed incident." But Lincoln was unaware of all the intrigue. According to William Jayne, Lincoln's old friend, William Butler, had acted as a spy for Trumbull. Butler had fed and housed Lincoln as a young man, helped him pay off his debts from the misbegotten venture of the Berry & Lincoln general store, but was simmering with anger over Lincoln's failure to deliver the patronage job of the Land Office to him after the 1848 election, when the victorious Taylor administration mercilessly shunted Lincoln aside. The unforgiving Butler, serving as the clerk to the state treasurer, "pretended however to be L's friend," Jayne later told Herndon. "He was for Trumbull—got into Lincoln's good graces—in Lincoln's camp—heard all and revealed to Trumbull and his camp. Judd and Palmer in the legislature heard all and stuck to Trumbull, knowing what L's plans were."

But in the end political imperatives overwhelmed any accumulated personal resentments. "If we had voted for him," recalled Judd, "we should simply have been denounced by our own papers as renegades who had deserted the Democrats and gone over to the Whigs." Zebina Eastman explained that for the "Free Soilers and the Independent Democrats" a vote for Lincoln would be a vote for the hated Whig Party. "It was thought," he wrote, "that it was asking a little too much that they should be required also to magnify the old Whig party, by giving their power to the Senate also, as they would have done had Mr. Lincoln been elected by their votes, and it would have been accounted a Whig party triumph instead of a triumph of the people, and the Liberty party would have been held responsible for selling out to the Whigs."

But the abolitionists were hardly the decisive factor in preventing Lincoln from gaining the Senate seat. It was the indissoluble rump group of five adamant anti-Douglas Democrats for Trumbull who would not move into his column. The irony was that the great rival of Douglas was thwarted by the intensity of hatred for Douglas among members of his own party. The feeling against Douglas had enabled Lincoln to rise and then perversely struck him down.

The Whigs mourned their loss as a betrayal. "It grieved us to the heart to give up Mr. Lincoln," lamented Gillespie. "There was a great deal of dissatisfaction throughout the State at the result of the election," said Parks. "The Whigs constituted a vast majority of the Anti Nebraska Party; they thought they were entitled to the Senate and that Mr. Lincoln by his contest with Mr. Douglas had earned it; Mr. Lincoln, however, generously exonerated Mr. Trumbull and his friends from all blame in the matter." Logan took to the floor for an outpouring of grief. "The Whigs have been rode, and rode, and rode to death," he declared. "The Whigs had been permitted to make a race for senator, just fast enough to lose money." Those Lincoln "counted upon and looked to for support had deserted him. . . . A feather was light—but it was the last feather that broke the camel's back. They have laid on us that last feather, and my back is broke." Logan shouted in a voice that reached to the top of the State House dome: "No!"

David Davis believed that Lincoln "ought to have been elected. . . . I had spent a good deal of time at Springfield getting things arranged for Lincoln, and it was supposed that his election was certain." But Davis was absent on Election Day, assuming the deal was done. "But if I had been there, there were ten members of the Legislature, who would have fully appreciated the fact that 46 men should not yield their preference to 5." Davis never trusted Trumbull—"a Democrat all his life—dyed in the wool"—and never forgave Judd, even after he became a Republican and labored for Lincoln, calling him a "contemptible fellow." Davis would never again make the complacent assumption that victory would take care of itself and always made sure in the future about "getting things arranged for Lincoln." The shock of the lost Senate race would steel Davis for the long nights in Chicago of the Republican convention of 1860.

Elizabeth Todd Edwards, Mary Lincoln's sister, and her husband, Ninian W. Edwards, rented the large hall located in the center of Springfield for a party to celebrate the election of their brother-in-law. They held the event despite the disappointing result, acting as the hospitable hosts to Lyman Trumbull and his wife, Julia Jayne, Mary's girlhood friend and her bridesmaid. Lincoln and Mary arrived a bit late. Mrs. Edwards and her daughters tried to soften the blow, "saying that they had wished for his success, and that while he must be disappointed, yet he should bear in mind that his principles had won," according to Horace White. Lincoln approached Trumbull. "Not *too* disappointed to congratulate my friend Trumbull," he said, extending his hand for a shake.

Mary, however, never reconciled herself to Lincoln's defeat. She cut off Julia, calling her "ungainly" and "unpopular," shunning every attempt over the years to bring them back together, even after Lincoln's death, declaring, "She is indeed 'a white Sepulchre.' " Her animus toward Lyman Trumbull never abated, confiding to David Davis that he was "a sordid selfish creature, without a soul, almost, yet indebted to my great and good husband, for all."

Sometime on the night of the election either before or after the Edwards's party, Lincoln "came to our room," recalled John Palmer, "and because of the way he assisted us we promised to stand by him in the next fight, two years later, against Douglas." This account may be slightly apocryphal, suggesting that Trumbull's team pledged to back Lincoln in the Senate race of 1858 that evening. But Trumbull never forgot his obligation to Lincoln. Just before the 1858 campaign, he wrote him, "I shall continue to labor for the success of the Republican cause, and the advancement at the next election to the place now occupied by Douglas of that *Friend*, who was instrumental in promoting my own."

In the immediate aftermath Lincoln veered between buoyancy and despair. "I regret my defeat moderately," he wrote Washburne the day after, "but I am not nervous about it."

To a client, a week later, he wrote, "a less good humored man than I, perhaps would not have consented to it." But Gillespie recalled, "I never saw him so dejected. He said the fates seemed to be against him and he thought he would never strive for office again. He could bear defeat inflicted by his enemies with a pretty good grace; but it was hard to be wounded in the house of his friends." Henry Clay Whitney, who traveled with Lincoln on the circuit that spring, described how "his sad face would assume, at times, deeper phases of grief, but no relief came from dark and despairing melancholy, till he was roused by the breaking up of the court, when he emerged from his cave of gloom and came back, like one awakened from sleep, to the world in which he lives, again."

Lincoln held no grudges toward Trumbull, Palmer, or Judd. (He would later appoint Judd minister to Prussia.) "He manifested however no bitterness towards Mr. Judd or the other Anti Nebraska Democrats by whom practically he was beaten, but evidently thought that their motives were right," recalled Samuel Parks. "He told me several times afterwards that the election of Trumbull was the best thing that could have happened." But while Lincoln refused to harbor resentments, he was still paying close attention. "At another time," wrote Whitney, "Lincoln said to me, *sotto voce,* although no one was by: 'Judd and Ray and those fellows think I don't see anything, but I see all around them; I see better what they want to do with me than they do themselves.' "

Lincoln had been confounded by the centrifugal politics of party disintegration. But his sacrifice made others indebted to him. His self-denial rewarded his rival to thwart a common foe. His principled act rescued those who had dismissed him as an expedient hack. It was the most significant act of fusion laying the groundwork for the new politics that he had just rejected. His defeat was the final breath of the dying Whig Party. It never again mounted a statewide slate of candidates. In his last gasp as a Whig Lincoln made possible his emergence as a Republican, though at first he felt like an extinct species.

Hitching up his old horse Bob, he headed off for the county courthouses. "I was dabbling in politics; and, of course, neglecting business," he wrote a client. "Having since been beaten out, I have gone to work again."

In fact, about two weeks after the election for the Senate, Lincoln and Trumbull were conspiring together on which candidates to run for the Congress. "I shall be happy to hear from you frequently," Trumbull wrote him on February 24, "and particularly to know your views as to the best means of meeting and overwhelming the Slavery expansionists in Illinois."

In March, President Pierce appointed the chief justice of the Illinois Supreme Court, Samuel Treat, to the U.S. District Court. Trumbull had sat on the state court with him. He wrote Lincoln, "Treat is a most excellent man in most respects, but on the subject of slavery it does seem to me he is almost a monomaniac. He is the most intolerant, ultra pro slavery of any man I ever knew." Treat's elevation opened his position, which was to be filled by a special election. The campaign became another surrogate contest between Lincoln and Douglas. The Democrats put up Onias Skinner, a friend of Douglas.

Lincoln organized the effort for Stephen T. Logan. After Lincoln's defeat, the Whigs were demoralized and Logan was a perennially poor campaigner despite his recent election to the legislature. The *Register* flayed him as a Know Nothing and abolitionist—"Know-Nothingism is but the tail of abolitionism"—and scored him for "shuffling and dodging on the Negro question." As the Douglas Democrats mobilized their forces the anti-Nebraska men fell into a state of confusion. For the first test after Trumbull's election, there was no fusion but more fragmentation. "Logan is worse beaten than any other man ever was since elections were invented—beaten more than 1200 in this county," Lincoln wrote Whitney on June 7. The Whig Party had descended to a new nadir.

THE REPUBLICAN

T hrough the collapse of the Whigs Ichabod Codding did not cease evangelizing, touring northern Illinois in early 1855 to lecture on the "Principles of the Republican Party," as if it were an existing organization. In April he arrived for a meeting of the hastily assembled central committee consisting of Eastman, Lovejoy, and a few others at the *Free West* office in Chicago, where blood ran in the streets. In the election of March 6 the Know Nothings allied with the temperance movement had gained control of City Hall in the name of the Law and Order Party. Mayor Levi Boone, the grandnephew of Daniel Boone, a strict prohibitionist and virulent anti-Catholic, forbade sale of liquor on Sundays and raised the cost of liquor licenses by 500 percent. After several tavern keepers were arrested for violating the new prohibition, German American immigrants led by a marching band gathered on April 21 to protest at the courthouse, where they were met by cannon and police, who opened fire, killing one and wounding many.

Owen Lovejoy

Nativism threatened to engulf the antislavery cause. The future of fusionism depended on the fate of Know Nothings. One new central committee member had a strategy. John C. Vaughn had just come to Chicago, hired by the new owners of the *Chicago Tribune*, Charles H. Ray and Joseph Medill, as the deputy editor. "Fight them, we must," Vaughn wrote Salmon Chase. "Kill them we must, or else they will kill us." Vaughn was a fierce antislavery man, a native South Carolinian, raised on a plantation, whose Quaker mother freed the family's slaves upon the death of his father. Beginning as a lawyer in Cincinnati, he became a journeyman newspaperman of the movement. He fought at the ramparts with Cassius Clay as his editor of the *True American*. When it was shuttered, he took the subscription list to launch the *Louisville Examiner* as the voice of the Emancipation Party. When it failed he edited the antislavery *Cincinnati Gazette* and the *Cleveland True Democrat*, the newspaper affiliated with Chase. But he broke with Chase when he concluded that Chase was actually serious about being a Democrat and conciliatory toward the Know Nothings in Ohio in order to gain the governorship. In Chicago, Vaughn devised the tactic of creating a new movement called the Know Something Order to outflank the Know Nothings, explicitly rejecting the exclusionary nativist creed and instead embracing the anti-Nebraska cause. The Know Somethings posed their icon of a youthful all-American "Jonathan" against the Know Nothings' "Sam." With Vaughn as president, while continuing his editorial duties at the *Tribune*, the Know Somethings attracted a membership of perhaps ten to twenty thousand, concentrated in Chicago, Massachusetts, and New York. Codding, who intensively conferred with Vaughn, hoped the Know Somethings would be an "effective antidote for the Know-Nothing bane." Medill believed the group might "keep K. N'ism from doing mischief until the fever for secret societies is past."

Beneath the surface the politics within the Know Nothings were murky, elusive, and tricky. Seemingly a blunt force tightly wrapped together with firmly held dogmatism, the Know Nothing Party was ill defined, incoherent, and chaotic. Just as suddenly as it swept into key offices and attracted prominent men into its secret lodges, it swirled with doubt and uncertainty. At the first Illinois State Council meeting at Chicago in early May, the Know Nothings were a movement divided. "We understand they had a very stormy time yesterday afternoon," reported the *Chicago Democrat*. "The council is divided on the Jonathan and Sam question.—The Jonathans . . . appear to be in the ascendant. The Sams are anti-foreign and anti-Catholic. The

Jonathans are anti-slavery, but not against foreigners." The newspaper observed that Douglas met privately with leaders of the "Sams" faction, which
he publicly opposed, but by encouraging its "pro-slavery tendencies, who are
delegates from the Southern part of the State," he sought to further damage
the already crippled Whigs. "He evinces a great interest in the progress of
Sam. . . . The Jonathans, however, are taking the lead." Douglas's manipulation of the Know Nothings was part of his complicated game, denouncing them to win over Irish votes while surreptitiously working with their
pro-Nebraska elements.

By the summer the Know Nothing movement began presenting itself as
the American Party. Millard Fillmore's supporters, the conservative Whig
remnant, systematically took it over as a lever for winning his nomination as
the Whig presidential candidate in 1856. The assumption of his candidacy
was that he would rally all the conservative forces from both the Whigs and
the Democrats to emerge as the only truly national figure against a field of
divisive sectionalists. His nativism was projected as the purest vision of his
patriotic Unionism. Douglas, for his part, saw the American Party as the
final evidence of the Whigs coming apart at the seams, and he did whatever
he could to rip them.

Within the Illinois Know Nothings the split widened. Efforts to patch
it over revealed the movement's disjointedness. In July, the Know Nothings
endorsed a platform of the "American Party of Illinois" that was half nativist and half Free Soil. While one plank called for "the cultivation and development of a purely American sentiment" and another "Resistance to the
corrupting influences and aggressive policy of the Romish Church," the platform also called repeal of the Missouri Compromise "a gross violation and
disregard of a sacred compact," declared that the Congress had "full power
under the Constitution to legislate upon the subject," and decried "assaults
upon the elective franchise in Kansas."

Douglas Democrats carefully tracked the convoluted and shadowy politics of the Know Nothings. The *Register* reported that "recent developments
have softened the harsh features of their proscriptive platform" on the two-
headed American Party document. "The actual leaders in different parts of
the State had not the courage to appear openly in a State Council, but sent
cat's-paws, who had nothing to lose by exposure. Still, their finger marks are
quite apparent." The men behind the scenes that the *Register* referred to were
Jesse Norton and Joseph Gillespie, both closely connected to Lincoln.

Codding continued his ministry for the new Republican Party, spreading the good word through central Illinois, publishing occasional pieces in the *Chicago Tribune*. He described on June 22 his appearance in Alton, where he "addressed for two hours, a thousand people, within sight of the building where Lovejoy was murdered, vindicating his principles. . . . Did Lovejoy fall? . . . Men may shatter the vase, but only to diffuse its sweet contents through the common air."

At the end of July, Codding spoke to a throng in Quincy for five nights, before the election of a county council to form a fusion party of antislavery Whigs, Free Soilers, and anti-Nebraska Democrats. The chairman of the resolutions committee was Archibald Williams, one of Lincoln's oldest political friends. Like Lincoln, he was born in Kentucky, and had been a boarding-house mate of Lincoln when they had served in 1836 in the state legislature at Vandalia. Lincoln described him as "one of the strongest-minded, clearest-headed men in Illinois." Lincoln had just campaigned for him in his losing race for the Congress, which was won by William A. Richardson, Douglas's ally. The platform bore a close resemblance to the resolutions that Lincoln had written just six months earlier for the legislature that had never been introduced. "This is the inauguration of the Republican movement in Middle and Southern Illinois," Codding wrote in the *Tribune*, "and mark my word, it will be responded to and followed up throughout this region of the country, and, in due time."

Owen Lovejoy immediately followed up with letters to Lincoln and Trumbull inviting them "to consult together and to organize with a view of carrying the State for Freedom in 1856." By virtue of wearing the mantle of his martyred brother, the abolitionist editor Elijah Lovejoy, his own talents as an eloquent orator and capable organizer, and his recent election to the legislature, Lovejoy was the preeminent abolitionist in Illinois. He used his influence within the movement to craft a fusion position little different from Lincoln's. In one of his first speeches to the Illinois House, on February 6, he spoke in favor of restoring the Missouri Compromise. "I have no power to enter the State of South Carolina, and abolish slavery there by an act of Congress than I have to go into Brazil and abolish it there," he said. "But we have the power to do it in territories as they are under the exclusive jurisdiction of the people of the United States." Encouraged by Giddings, he had supported Lincoln for senator until the effort became hopeless. Displaying a sensitive political touch, Lovejoy wrote Archie Williams after he drafted the consensus Quincy fusion platform that the abolitionists "see and acknowledge the necessity of not loading the middle and southern portion of the state with too heavy a load." That letter, written on August 6, was sent the day before Lovejoy wrote Lincoln, and obviously with the intent of having Williams influence him.

"Not even *you* are more anxious to prevent the extension of slavery than I; and yet the political atmosphere is such, just now, that I fear to do any thing, lest I do wrong," Lincoln replied promptly to Lovejoy on August 11. The Know Nothings, he explained, were the main source of his anxiety. For him, this was not only a political dilemma but also a personal one. "Know-nothingism has not yet entirely tumbled to pieces—nay, it is even a little encouraged by the late elections in Tennessee, Kentucky & Alabama. Until we can get the elements of this organization, there is not sufficient materials to successfully combat the Nebraska democracy with. We can not get them so long as they cling to a hope of success under their own organization; and I fear an open push by us now, may offend them, and tend to prevent our ever getting them. About us here, they are mostly my old political and personal friends; and I have hoped their organization would die out without the painful necessity of my taking an open stand against them." Lincoln had contempt for nativist bigotry, but he reserved it to private letters. "Of their principles I think little better than I do of those of the slavery extensionists. Indeed I do not perceive how any one professing to be sensitive to the wrongs of the negroes, can join in a league to degrade a class of white men." Lincoln was not opposed to fusion, but he was waiting for the right political moment. The Know Nothings were the chief obstacle. "I have no objection to 'fuse' with any body provided I can fuse on ground which I think is right; and I believe the opponents of slavery extension could now do this, if it were not for this K. N. ism. In many speeches last summer I advised those who did me the honor of a hearing to 'stand with any body who stands right'—and I am still quite willing to follow my own advice." The resolutions of the Quincy fusion platform, he told Lovejoy, "occupy about the ground I should be willing to 'fuse' upon." But until the politics should change, he would be tending to his legal practice, "quite busy trying to pick up my lost crumbs of last year."

Trumbull's reply to Lovejoy paralleled Lincoln's. The effort at fusion, he explained, was premature, the Democrats hopelessly confused, unable to transcend their party prejudices, and Know Nothingism making it impossible to concentrate focus on the anti-Nebraska cause. It was "very questionable" whether "it would be advisable at this time to call a State Convention of all those opposed to the repeal of the Missouri Compromise, irrespective of party." He reported that in Alton, where Codding had attracted a large crowd, the reading of the place as ready for fusion was misguided. Instead, "there is so much party feeling, so great aversion to what is called *fusion*, that very few democrats would be likely to unite in a Convention composed of all parties. If a convention of the Democracy, opposed equally to the spread of slavery, to abolition and Know Nothingism, could be called, we could, I think, get a respectable representation from this part of the State, and such a movement would probably damage the Nebraska democracy more than anything else which could be done; but I do not presume any considerable portion of the North would unite in a Convention of this kind." For the future, he advised, "we must keep out of the pro-slavery party a large number of those who are democrats." But excluding them would first require settling "old party associations, and side issues, such as Know Nothingism and the Temperance question."

A few days after Lincoln wrote Lovejoy, on August 15, Lincoln wrote a letter to George Robertson, his co-counsel in the *Todd Heirs* case, who had visited Springfield in early July when Lincoln was representing clients in Chicago. Robertson left a book for Lincoln, a collection of his speeches and letters over the course of his storied career from his first days in the Congress in 1817 to speaker of the Kentucky House to chief justice of the Kentucky Supreme Court. His book presented his views over the years of one of Henry Clay's most stalwart and conservative men, and unintentionally chronicled the rise and fall of his Whiggism. "I am really grateful for the honor of your kind remembrance, as well as for the book," Lincoln wrote. "The partial reading I have already given it, has afforded me much of both pleasure and instruction." Of particular interest to Lincoln was Robertson's speech in the congressional debate over the Missouri Compromise in its earliest phase in 1819. "It was new to me that the exact question which led to the Missouri compromise, had arisen before it arose in regard to Missouri; and that you had taken so prominent a part in it. Your short, but able and patriotic speech upon that occasion, has not been improved upon since, by those holding the same views; and, with all the lights you then had, the views you took appear to me as very reasonable. You are not a friend of slavery in the abstract. In that speech you spoke of '*the peaceful extinction* of *slavery*' and used other expressions indicating your belief that the thing was, at some time, to have an end."

Lincoln's interpretation of Robertson's speech, even in a private letter to Robertson himself, distorted his reasoning, turning it on its head to make Lincoln's own point. Robertson had proposed a bill for organization of the

Arkansas Territory that became a basis for the Missouri Compromise, a line running through the country north of which slavery would be prohibited and south protected. But Robertson had strenuously defended the existence of slavery and argued against interference: "Congress should leave, as the patriarchs of the constitution left, the domestic institution to the states, and the people of territories of the United States, to be disposed of as each separate community of freemen may choose for themselves; and in this domestic aspect of slavery, Congress ought never to touch it or countenance any agitation concerning it among the states, or the people of the United States, in any form or for any purpose. *It is a sensitive plant, which the national hand cannot touch without injury* or sense of outrage, or extreme danger of both." Robertson conceded that though Congress had a constitutional right to legislate on slavery, or even emancipate slaves, "I deny that such legislation, by Congress, would ever be NECESSARY to the public welfare, or WOULD, IN ANY CASE, WITHOUT THE HEARTY CONCURRENCE OF THE SLAVE STATES, BE EITHER JUST OR PRUDENT. Congress has no power over slavery in any of the states of the Union. Its continuance, therefore, in the United States, under the guarantees of the federal constitution, depends altogether on the will of the respective states in which it exists. An expansion of its area would not, of itself, augment its evils or prolong its existence, but would certainly tend to meliorate its condition." It was then that Robertson wrote of slavery's "peaceful extinction," but precisely in the opposite way that Lincoln cited. Rather than speaking about its "end," as Lincoln had, Robertson argued that any "legislative interference" was "inconsistent with true benevolence," "inconsistent with the compromising spirit of the constitution," and, contrary to antislavery arguments, would "neither hasten the peaceful extinction of slavery, nor improve the condition of slaves in the United States," and "contribute to the unnatural prolongation of the legal existence of slavery in America, rivet chains for slaves, and, in its ultimate issue, might probably even dissolve the Union." Far from calling for the end of slavery, Robertson was mocking those who did so.

Setting up his logic with his fractured quotation from Robertson about "peaceful extinction," Lincoln concluded that Clay's entire approach on slavery, which had undergirded his whole politics, was bankrupt. In his Peoria speech against Douglas, Lincoln objected to his rival's appropriation of Clay's memory. "Mr. Clay was the leading spirit in making the Missouri compromise; is it very credible that if now alive, he would take the lead in the breaking of it?" Lincoln had said. But now he traced the ruin of Clay's political premise, marked by the Missouri Compromise, to his defeat over the Kentucky state constitution in 1849, which Lincoln witnessed when he was co-counsel in the *Todd Heirs* case. "Since then," Lincoln wrote Robertson, beginning with the date of the Missouri Compromise, "we have had thirty six years of experience; and this experience has demonstrated, I think, that there is no peaceful extinction of slavery in prospect for us. The signal failure of Henry Clay, and other good and great men, in 1849, to effect any thing in favor of gradual emancipation in Kentucky, together with a thousand other signs, extinguishes that hope utterly."

Returning to his theme of the founders, Lincoln transformed the Revolution into a slave revolt and the Declaration of Independence into a kind of Emancipation Proclamation.

"On the question of liberty, as a principle, we are not what we have been. When we were the political slaves of King George, and wanted to be free, we called the maxim that 'all men are created equal' a self evident truth; but now when we have grown fat, and have lost all dread of being slaves ourselves, we have become so greedy to be *masters* that we call the same maxim 'a self-evident lie' The fourth of July has not quite dwindled away; it is still a great day—*for burning fire-crackers!!!*"

The pro-slavery forces, a "greedy" class of "masters," had repudiated the foundation of the nation and the antislavery policy of the founders. Again, Lincoln wrote about "peaceful extinction," but as a political anachronism: "That spirit which desired the peaceful extinction of slavery, has itself become extinct, with the *occasion*, and the *men* of the Revolution. Under the impulse of that occasion, nearly half the states adopted systems of emancipation at once; and it is a significant fact, that not a single state has done the like since. So far as peaceful, voluntary emancipation is concerned, the condition of the negro slave in America, scarcely less terrible to the contemplation of a free mind, is now as fixed, and hopeless of change for the better, as that of the lost souls of the finally impenitent. The Autocrat of all the Russias will resign his crown, and proclaim his subjects free republicans sooner than will our American masters voluntarily give up their slaves."

Lincoln's invocation of the czar placed the struggle against slavery within the transatlantic conflict between democracy and tyranny. He had condemned the czar in a resolution in 1853 for suppressing the Hungarian revolution of his European hero, Louis Kossuth. Now he unfavorably compared "American masters" to the Russian "Autocrat," aristocrats against "free republicans."

Lincoln signed off, for the first time using the phrase that he would make the heart of his "House Divided" speech of 1858, a speech in which he would repeat Robertson's phrase about "extinction" but giving it his own definition, explaining his intent to put slavery on "the course of ultimate extinction." Now, in 1855, he wrote: "Our political problem now is 'Can we, as a nation, continue together *permanently—forever*—half slave, and half free?' The problem is too mighty for me. May God, in his mercy, superintend the solution."

(In 1862, after Lincoln issued his Preliminary Emancipation Proclamation, the 22nd Wisconsin Volunteer Infantry, an abolitionist-inspired unit, camped at Lexington, Kentucky, becoming a safe harbor for runaway slaves. On November 12, a "mulatto" boy named Adam, wearing "a heavy collar of rough iron" and whose back displayed "the scars of brutal beating," sought refuge. Two days later George Robertson appeared in a coach driven by his slave valet demanding that the commanding officer, Colonel William Utley, return "his boy." Utley interviewed Adam, who recounted the story of how Robertson had hired him out since the age of five to a cruel contractor. "You can't believe him; niggers will lie," Robertson told Utley. He further explained that he had voted as a congressman for the Missouri Compromise and was a friend of Lincoln. Utley coolly informed Robertson that if he wanted "that boy" he should "try it"—to the cheers of his soldiers. Robertson wrote Lincoln demanding the arrest of Utley. Lincoln offered personally to purchase the slave from Robertson for $500 and free him himself. Robertson angrily declined, proclaiming, "Our people are already ripe for popular uprising against military usurpation and defiance of our laws." He pursued the case until in 1873 he won a judgment of $908.06, the price attached to the slave, authorized paid through a special bill of the Congress. Thus was the distinguished Kentucky jurist, Robert S. Todd's friend and lawyer, Lincoln's co-counsel, the beneficiary of compensated emancipation and nearly responsible for Lincoln becoming the owner of a slave.)

Nine days after writing his letter to Robertson, on August 24, Lincoln wrote to his most intimate old friend, Joshua Speed, at his Kentucky plantation. Speed had written Lincoln in May, but only now did Lincoln respond. "You know what a poor correspondent I am." It was the most personal of the three seminal letters Lincoln composed that August, explaining his frustrations, motives, and rapidly shifting political evolution. Lincoln felt that he could divulge his deepest feelings confidentially to Speed. The tone was at once self-revelatory about his uncertainty, hard in his judgments, and incorrigibly lawyerly, framing his arguments to win even with this trustworthy friend with whom he was engaged in no contest. In this letter Lincoln began on a note similar to the one he had made in his Peoria speech, carefully not blaming Southerners for slavery and acknowledging the right of slavery within the South. "You suggest that in political action now, you and I would differ. I suppose we would; not quite as much, however, as you may think. You know I dislike slavery; and you fully admit the abstract wrong of it. So far there is no cause of difference. But you say that sooner than yield your legal right to the slave—especially at the bidding of those who are not themselves interested, you would see the Union dissolved. I am not aware that *any one* is bidding you to yield that right; very certainly *I* am not. I leave that matter entirely to yourself. I also acknowledge *your* rights and *my* obligations, under the constitution, in regard to your slaves." Lincoln was not referring to "your slaves" in the "abstract." He knew that Speed owned slaves, eighteen by 1850, and that unlike his brother James, to whom Lincoln was also close, he had not denounced slavery as "the greatest national sin," nor like James emancipated the slaves bequeathed by their father.

Lincoln wrote that while he and Speed had "no cause of difference" against slavery he explained the basic difference between his vital opposition and Speed's mere "abstract" one. Then he unfolded a subtle logic.

Lincoln recalled an incident from their travel fourteen years earlier after a sojourn at Speed's home, a journey down the Ohio River on which they encountered a coffle of slaves onboard their boat. In his letter to Speed's sister Mary about that sight, Lincoln described the slaves "strung together precisely like so many fish upon a trot-line. In this condition they were being separated forever from the scenes of their childhood, their friends, their fathers and mothers, and brothers and sisters, and many of them, from their wives and children, and going into perpetual slavery where the lash of the master is proverbially more ruthless and unrelenting than any other where; and yet amid all these distressing circumstances, as we would think them, they were the most cheerful and apparently happy creatures on board."

Now he described his feelings as less that of a passive observer than an anguished witness undergoing a formative experience.

> I confess I hate to see the poor creatures hunted down, and caught, and carried back to their stripes, and unrewarded toils; but I bite my lip and keep quiet. In 1841 you and I had together a tedious low-water trip, on a Steam Boat from Louisville to St. Louis. You may remember, as I well do,

that from Louisville to the mouth of the Ohio there were, on board, ten or a dozen slaves, shackled together with irons. That sight was a continual torment to me; and I see something like it every time I touch the Ohio, or any other slave-border. It is hardly fair for you to assume, that I have no interest in a thing which has, and continually exercises, the power of making me miserable. You ought rather to appreciate how much the great body of the Northern people do crucify their feelings, in order to maintain their loyalty to the constitution and the Union.

Lincoln had an underlying reason for discussing his "torment." Pro-slavery Southerners were a chorus in proclaiming their victimization by abolitionist agitators trampling on their "rights." The debates in the Congress during the Nebraska Act were a procession of Southern speeches against antislavery injustice. Lincoln put his own emotions on the scale to explain the weight of increasingly intense Northern feeling against slavery. "I do oppose the extension of slavery, because my judgment and feelings so prompt me; and I am under no obligation to the contrary. If for this you and I must differ, differ we must." Again, he underlined his difference with Speed was not only more expressively authentic but also principled.

Speed had written Lincoln of his anger against the Missourians trampling free elections in Kansas. Lincoln took up his point to unravel the full pro-slavery political position that Speed did not grasp. "You say if you were President, you would send an army and hang the leaders of the Missouri outrages upon the Kansas elections; still, if Kansas fairly votes herself a slave state, she must be admitted, or the Union must be dissolved. But how if she votes herself a slave state *unfairly*—that is, by the very means for which you say you would hang men? Must she still be admitted, or the Union be dissolved? That will be the phase of the question when it first becomes a practical one." Once again, Lincoln lectured his friend for taking an abstract position that failed to understand its own practical consequences.

But his logic ran even deeper.

In your assumption that there may be a *fair* decision of the slavery question in Kansas, I plainly see you and I would differ about the Nebraska-law. I look upon that enactment not as a *law*, but as *violence* from the beginning. It was conceived in violence, passed in violence, is maintained in violence, and is being executed in violence. I say it was *conceived* in violence, because the destruction of the Missouri Compromise, under the circumstances, was nothing less than violence. It was *passed* in violence, because it could not have passed at all but for the votes of many members, in violent disregard of the known will of their constituents. It is *maintained* in violence because the elections since, clearly demand it's repeal, and this demand is openly disregarded. *You* say men ought to be hung for the way they are executing that law; and *I* say the way it is being executed is quite as good as any of its antecedents. It is being executed in the precise way which was intended from the first; else why does no Nebraska man express astonishment or condemnation? Poor Reeder is the only public man who has been silly enough to believe that any thing like fairness was ever intended; and he has been bravely undeceived.

Lincoln spun out a dire scenario based on the assumption that Kansas would be overrun for slavery. "That Kansas will form a Slave constitution, and, with it, will ask to be admitted into the Union, I take to be an already settled question; and so settled by the very means you so pointedly condemn. By every principle of law, ever held by any court, North or South, every negro taken to Kansas is free; yet in utter disregard of this—in the spirit of violence merely—that beautiful Legislature gravely passes a law to hang men who shall venture to inform a negro of his legal rights. This is the substance, and real object of the law. If, like Haman, they should hang upon the gallows of their own building, I shall not be among the mourners for their fate." Again, Speed was abstract, railing about hanging men who themselves had passed a law to hang the free staters. For the pro-slavery would-be executioners Lincoln proposed the harshest capital punishment.

Lincoln had no expectation that restoring the Missouri Compromise would ever occur. Instead, he considered the pro-slavery forces' attempt to seize Kansas brazen and conducted under false premises. "In my humble sphere, I shall advocate the restoration of the Missouri Compromise, so long as Kansas remains a territory; and when, by all these foul means, it seeks to come into the Union as a Slave-state, I shall oppose it. I am very loath, in any case, to withhold my assent to the enjoyment of property *acquired*, or *located*, in good faith; but I do not admit that *good faith*, in taking a negro to Kansas, to be held in slavery, is a *possibility* with any man. Any man who has sense enough to be the controller of his own property, has too much sense to misunderstand the outrageous character of this whole Nebraska business. But I digress."

Bad faith, according to Lincoln, was not restricted to the pro-slavery invaders of Kansas, but infected the entire matter from beginning to end, and the beginning was located with Douglas. Far from a principled act, Douglas's bill was the product of bribery and coercion. It came from politics, and it was only through politics that Lincoln believed its corrosive effects could be countered.

In my opposition to the admission of Kansas I shall have some company; but we may be beaten. If we are, I shall not, on that account, attempt to dissolve the Union. On the contrary, if we succeed, there will be enough of us to take care of the Union. I think it probable, however, we shall be beaten. Standing as a unit among yourselves, you can, directly, and indirectly, bribe enough of our men to carry the day—as you could on an open proposition to establish monarchy. Get hold of some man in the North, whose position and ability is such, that he can make the support of your measure—whatever it may be—a *democratic party necessity*, and the thing is done. *Appropos* of this, let me tell you an anecdote. Douglas introduced the Nebraska bill in January. In February afterwards, there was a call session of the Illinois Legislature. Of the one hundred members composing the two branches of that body, about seventy were democrats. These latter held a caucus, in which the Nebraska bill was talked of, if not formally discussed. It was thereby discovered that just three, and no more, were in favor of the measure. In a day or two Douglas' orders came on to have resolutions passed approving the bill; and they were passed by large majorities!!! The truth of this is vouched for by a bolting democratic member. The masses too, democratic as well as whig, were even, nearer unanamous [*sic*] against it; but as soon as the party necessity of supporting it, became apparent, the way the democracy began to see the *wisdom* and *justice* of it, was perfectly astonishing.

Lincoln did not hesitate to accuse his friend Speed of sanctimonious hypocrisy. Expressions of religious devotion offered as political justification always rankled Lincoln. But his frankness was not intended in this instance to expose the pretense of religious dogma or embarrass his friend for moral insincerity, but rather to cut through the superficial terms of the debate, unpeeling the rotten layers of Southern politics beneath it.

You say if Kansas fairly votes herself a free state, as a Christian you will rather rejoice at it. All decent slave-holders *talk* that way; and I do not doubt their candor. But they never *vote* that way. Although in a private letter, or conversation, you will express your preference that Kansas shall be free, you would vote for no man for Congress who would say the same thing publicly. No such man could be elected from any district in any slave-state. You think Stringfellow & Co ought to be hung; and yet, at the next presidential election you will vote for the exact type and representative of Stringfellow. The slave-breeders and slave-traders, are a small, odious and detested class, among you; and yet in politics, they dictate the course of all of you, and are as completely your masters, as you are the masters of your own negroes.

(In 1862, Lincoln refused to commute the death sentence of a slave trader, Nathaniel Gordon, who was hung, "like Haman," as Lincoln had suggested in 1855, the only slave trader ever to be executed in American history for his commerce.)

But amid the chaos, where did Lincoln place himself? In short, who did he think he was? And what was he? That was the central question Speed had asked him six months earlier. "You enquire where I now stand. That is a disputed point. I think I am a Whig; but others say there are no Whigs, and that I am an abolitionist. When I was at Washington I voted for the Wilmot Proviso as good as forty times, and I never heard of any one attempting to unwhig me for that. I now do no more than oppose the *extension* of slavery." Lincoln was not really arguing with Speed, but with the velocity of events. When he was a Proviso man in the Congress opposing the extension of slavery before the great Whig victory of 1848, he was living in another era. Now his party was rapidly disintegrating around him under the pressure of circumstances. How he would align himself with those events consumed his thought, more than "a disputed point" for others but also for himself.

Not least in the forefront of his thinking was the threat of the Know Nothings, attracting many of "my old political and personal friends," as he had told Lovejoy, and absorbing the Whig Party itself. "I am not a Know-Nothing. That is certain. How could I be? How can any one who abhors the oppression of negroes, be in favor of degrading classes of white people? Our progress in degeneracy appears to me to be pretty rapid. As a nation, we began by declaring that '*all men are created equal.*' We now practically read it 'all men are created equal, *except negroes.*' When the Know-Nothings get control, it will read 'all men are created equal, except negroes, *and foreigners, and Catholics.*' When it comes to this I should prefer emigrating to some country where they make no pretense of loving liberty—to Russia, for instance, where despotism can be taken pure, and without the base alloy of hypocrisy." Lincoln had unfurled the Declaration of Independence as a shield against the extension of slavery. Now he arrayed it against the Know Nothings. Again, he invoked Russia, not as a comparative tyranny to slavery but to nativism.

Lincoln's condemnation of the Know Nothings to Speed was anything but "abstract" for either of them. The Whig Party of Kentucky, Henry Clay's flagship, had completely collapsed, taken over by the Know Nothings, who had just days before Lincoln's letter staged an anti-immigrant massacre that left twenty-two people murdered in the streets of Louisville, "Bloody Monday." The violence began with the Know Nothing ouster through control of the City Council of Louisville's Whig mayor, James Stephens Speed, Joshua Speed's cousin, who had converted to Catholicism, his wife's religion. Many of the most influential Whigs saw the coup as the trigger to abandon their party and join the Know Nothings in anticipation of supporting Fillmore's presidential candidacy in 1856. Senator-elect John J. Crittenden, Clay's protégé, who had been Fillmore's attorney general, was among them. George D. Prentice, Clay's biographer and editor of the *Louisville Journal*, the proto-Whig newspaper, declared in an editorial on January 15, 1855, that nativism was triumphant and Fillmore its tribune. "It is evident that his foreign question is to override all others, even the slavery question," he wrote, "as we see men of the most opposite views on slavery, forgetting their differences and acting together." He proclaimed the end of the Whig Party and urged a battle against the "illiterate hordes of Irish papists and German infidels which infest our country." A Know Nothing defeated the former Mayor Speed in a special election in April, while Know Nothings swept the elections in Jefferson County, which Joshua Speed had just represented as a state legislator. On the eve of August elections in Louisville, Prentice wrote, "Let the foreigners keep their elbows to themselves to-day at the polls. Americans are you all ready? We think we hear you shout 'ready,' 'well fire!' and may heaven have mercy on the foe." On August 6, Know Nothing gangs at the polls, supported by the police, demanded proof of membership in their party and naturalization papers, and then rampaged through the city, killing immigrants.

One of the witnesses to "Bloody Monday" was James Speed, Joshua's brother, who watched the mobs "fall upon a single Irish or German and beat him with sticks or short clubs—not walking canes, but short clubs." In a letter to his brother Philip several months before the riot, James Speed wrote, "No one can pretend that Mr. Clay ever was or could be a Know

Nothing. . . . Who or what is safe in the hands of such a party? What principle of government is safe with such a party? I have not ceased to be a Whig—'*Semper eadem*' "—always the same. "My Whiggery makes me anti-Know Nothing." (Lincoln would appoint James Speed his attorney general in 1865.)

A month after Henry Clay's Whig Party was swept away in a tide of blood, the Whig Party of New York, the largest state organization, could no longer sustain its old identity. The year began with an alliance in the state legislature of Know Nothings, conservative Silver Grays, and Fillmore men attempting to prevent Seward's reelection to the Senate. The nativists hated Seward for his long-standing contempt of them and defiant statements in favor of tolerance toward immigrants. The regular Whigs under Seward and Weed had made covert coalitions of convenience with the nativists, particularly the bloc-vote-controlling gangs of New York, going back to the election of 1844, when the gang leaders betrayed their part of the bargain and deprived Clay of the presidency. But now the Know Nothings and Seward were engaged in open warfare. After Seward won reelection against "practically an oath-bound majority of the Legislature," as he wrote Weed, he thanked him for "the sagacity and skill by which you saved us all from so imminent a wreck."

In August, the Hards held a Democratic state convention excluding the Softs and approving the Nebraska Act. A few days later the Softs gathered to denounce the latest outrages in Kansas. Even before this definitive split, Seward and Weed had plotted a fusion with the Softs and Free Soilers— "imperative," Weed wrote Seward. On September 26, the Whigs, purified of their Know Nothing defectors, and a collection of the anti-Nebraska groups calling themselves now "Republicans" deliberately held parallel state conventions at Syracuse. Joint committees agreed upon candidates and a platform against the extension of slavery and the Know Nothings. After ratifying it, the Whigs marched en masse to the door of the Republican convention. The Republican convention president, Reuben E. Fenton, a former Democratic congressman, who would later serve as governor and U.S. senator, "remarked that the marriage ceremonies would take place as soon as the bride should be comfortably seated," according to the report in the *New York Times*. "A delegate from the rural districts moved that the President be requested to kiss the bride"—unanimously "considered carried." The doors were opened. "The Whig Convention now appeared, and was received with three cheers." All acclaimed themselves to be Republicans, and the convention adjourned *sine die* on the motion of Horace Greeley.

But not all antislavery men in New York joined the Republicans. A rump group of the Liberty Party nominated its own ticket including Frederick Douglass for secretary of state, a boon for the sale of his extraordinary auto-biography, *My Bondage and My Freedom*. On the other side, some Old Whigs, including Senator Hamilton Fish, Seward's protégé, withheld themselves, suspicious of affiliating with Democrats and abolitionists. Seward attempted to address concerns across the spectrum with a speech at the State House at Albany on October 12 urging "familiar friends" to leave behind "dissolv-ing parties." He described a struggle renewing the "spirit" of the Ameri-can Revolution against an "aristocracy," a "privileged class" of slaveholders, "one-hundredth part of the entire population"—the one percent—that had seized political control of the federal government. "What then is wanted? Organization. Organization! Nothing but organization."

One by one, Seward assessed the political parties. "Shall we take the Know Nothing party, or the American party, as it now more ambitiously names itself?" With "its clandestine councils and its dark conspiracies, its mobs and its murders," he concluded, "Let it pass by." He then asked, "Shall we unite ourselves to the Democratic party? If so, to which section or fac-tion? The Hards, who are so stern in defending the aggressions of the privi-leged class, and in rebuking the Administration through whose agency they are committed? or the Softs, who protest against these aggressions, while they sustain and invigorate that Administration? . . . Let the Democratic party pass." Finally, he came to the Whig Party, "wounded on all sides," and condemned to "ultimately dwindle and dwarf into a mere faction." Over the once great organization he had created out of the Anti-Mason Party, he de-livered a eulogy. "Let, then, the Whig party pass." Seward proclaimed him-self the stalwart of the new Republican Party. "Its banner is untorn in former battles, and unsullied by past errors. That is the party for us."

In September, Joshua Giddings followed up Lovejoy's letter to Lincoln with his own invitation to join a new party. He suggested that when he vis-ited Springfield Lincoln meet with him. "You my dear sir," wrote Giddings, "may now by your own personal efforts give direction to those movements which are to determine the next Presidential election." Lincoln could not accept Giddings's offer, not because he rejected it out of hand but because he would be trying cases. He and Trumbull were also stalking Douglas on his speaking tour through the state. Sometimes Trumbull answered him after-ward, and sometimes Lincoln. Though there are no accounts of what they said, it seems that it was a road-show performance of their speeches from the previous year.

That September Lincoln focused on what he thought would be the biggest case of his career. Washburne had referred to him a leading business in his district, the Manny Company of Rockford, to defend it in a patent infringement suit brought by Cyrus McCormick, inventor of the reaper. Lincoln prepared diligently for a courtroom match with the plaintiff's distinguished lawyer, Reverdy Johnson, the former attorney general of the United States, conducted in Cincinnati before the august associate justice of the Supreme Court, John McLean. Lincoln devoted hours mastering the details of the case to prepare for his summation. But Peter H. Watson, who had acquired the Manny patents, had also hired another lawyer far more prominent, the well-known corporate attorney Edwin Stanton of Pittsburgh. When the time came for the dramatic conclusion of the defense, the speaking role was given to Stanton. "Mr. Lincoln acquiesced in this, but was deeply grieved and mortified," recalled William W. Dickson, a Cincinnati attorney whose wife was Mary Lincoln's cousin and with whom Lincoln resided while there. "He seemed to be greatly depressed, and gave evidence of that tendency to melancholy which so marked his character. . . . He came with the fond hope of making fame in a forensic contest with Reverdy Johnson. He was pushed aside, humiliated and mortified." Ralph Emerson, a young attorney from Rockford also joined to the Manny defense, recalled that Lincoln confided to him his sense of inadequacy. "The hearing had hardly progressed two days before Mr. Lincoln expressed to me his satisfaction that he was not to take part in the argument. So many and so deep were the questions involved that he realized he had not given the subject sufficient study to have done himself justice." After listening raptly to Stanton's summation, he remarked to his youthful colleague, "Emerson, I am going home. I am going home to study law." "Mr. Lincoln," replied Emerson, "you stand at the head of the bar in Illinois now! What are you talking about?" "I do occupy a good position there, and I think that I can get along with the way things are done there now," he said. "But these college-trained men, who have devoted their whole lives to study, are coming West, don't you see? And they study their cases as we never do. They have got as far as Cincinnati now. They will soon be in Illinois." He paused, and spoke again. "I am as good as any of them, and when they get out to Illinois I will be ready for them." Observing Lincoln's treatment, which he considered "unjust," Emerson became disillusioned with the law as a career. He asked Lincoln, "Is it possible for a man to practice law and always do by others as he would be done by?" "Lincoln's head dropped on his breast, and he walked in silence for a long way; then he heaved a heavy sigh," Emerson wrote. "When he finally spoke, it was of a foreign matter."

Lincoln had envisioned himself through the Manny case catapulted to the top rank of his profession, but instead was flung back as a country lawyer who had overstepped his bounds. He was not even allowed to utter a word before Justice McLean. Nobody in the courtroom paid him the slightest deference. They did not think of him as the figure that had transfixed crowds taking on Douglas. "Mr L. felt that he had been 'tricked' out of the case and the transaction deeply affected him," according to Dickson. "He said McLean was not friendly to him and he felt he had been shabbily treated all round." His fee was paid, the largest he had ever made, but when he departed he told Mrs. Dickson, "I have nothing against the city, but things have so happened here as to make it undesirable for me ever to return here." Of course, Lincoln would return as president-elect on his journey from Springfield to Washington. The lawyer on the Manny defense team who was awarded precedence above him held a low opinion of Lincoln and maintained it through his first year as president. Then Lincoln appointed Stanton secretary of war, and their indispensable partnership developed into a close friendship.

The month after the Manny trial, in October, Lincoln argued a peculiar slander case in the DeWitt County Courthouse. William Dungey, a dark-skinned man of Portuguese extraction, had quarreled with his brother-in-law, Joseph Spencer, who accused "Black Bill" of being "a nigger" and, worse, "a nigger married to a white woman." The racial accusation was not merely a slur. Under Section 10 of Illinois' Black Code, passed in 1853, "Every person who shall have one-fourth negro blood shall be deemed a mulatto." If Dungey was, in fact, "Negro," he was in the state illegally, his marriage a crime, which would be dissolved, and his property expropriated. In the courtroom, Spencer admitted freely calling his brother-in-law "a nigger." "My client," said Lincoln, "is not a Negro, though it is not a crime to be a Negro—no crime to be born with a black skin. But my client is not a Negro. His skin may not be as white as ours, but I say he is not a Negro, though he may be a Moore." "Mr. Lincoln," interjected the judge, who happened to be David Davis, "you mean a Moor, not Moore." "Well, your Honor, Moor, not C. H. Moore," replied Mr. Lincoln, pointing at the table where Spencer's lawyer, C. H. Moore, sat. "I say my client may be a Moor, but he is not a Negro." The jury granted large damages for Dungey and for Lincoln to receive his $25 dollar legal fee.

In the Manny case, Lincoln reached the limit of his legal career. His humiliation brought him to the stark realization that he would likely never emerge within his profession beyond the confines of county courthouses in Illinois. His avenue forward was through politics. In the Dungey case, despite its amusing sidelights, Lincoln confronted the harsh reality of racism in Illinois, which Douglas was exploiting against the "Black Republican Party."

"Illinois is the battle ground for the Slave Power and for the Republicans too. Here is to be the fight," Herndon wrote to his idol, Theodore Parker, on October 30. He reported that after Douglas had appeared in Springfield the speaker countering him was none other than Giddings. The *Joliet Signal*, a pro-Douglas newspaper, took note of his presence, "perambulating the northern sections of the state with the Rev. Ichabod Codding, organizing the Republican party. . . . A nigger-stealing, stinking, putrid, abolition party." To Herndon's disappointment, Giddings "did not speak with eloquence and power." Then, he noted, Henry Ward Beecher came to town, "intense in his passages of sympathy and energetic in his reprobation of conservative cowardice." Parker replied with a prediction, "I expect another violent slavery President with a strong opposition in the House and before long in the Senate. Mexico will fall into our hands even, I think, before 1860. Then in 1860 comes the real struggle between the North and South. Freedom and Slavery! I think not before."

Some months later, Herndon mentioned in passing in a letter to Parker a major political development in Springfield, that "the paper I used to write for—been kicked off, as it became Know-Nothing. I have nothing to do with it now, nor for months." The *Journal* had been Lincoln's vital organ, his mouthpiece, for which he and Herndon had written probably hundreds of articles anonymously and encouraged countless others. Simeon Francis, the publisher and editor since 1831, had been Lincoln's steadfast supporter through every oscillation of his career. Eliza Francis had been instrumental as a matchmaker bringing Mary and Lincoln together after their early estrangement. But in June Francis sold the paper to two ambitious young men, William H. Bailhache, former editor of the *Alton Telegraph*, and Edward L. Baker, a lawyer who married one of Mary Lincoln's nieces, promptly taking the editorial line of Old Whigs in favor of the Know Nothings. Francis later complained to Lincoln that he had not sufficiently backed him against the Know Nothing publishers. "I was against it from policy and principle," he wrote Lincoln.

I kept the Journal against it. The party still increased, mainly out of the Whig party. . . . Bailhache and Baker stopped their paper in Alton to come to Springfield. They published about that they were coming to publish a paper. The project suited the Know Nothings. I knew that I could not sustain the paper with a diminished patronage. I was anxious, but no friends came to me to say they would stand by me in a struggle for keeping up under a rivalship with those young men. I never had cheering word from you or Judge Logan, or any of those for whom I had worked with all the little ability I possessed. I saw nothing but ruin before me; and thus unsustained, abandoned as I thought by friends for whom I had labored without regard to myself consequences—I sold out. You say this was in error. It may be so—it probably was so. What could I then do?

(Francis moved to Oregon in 1859, became editor of the *Oregonian* newspaper, and Lincoln appointed him an army major and paymaster.)

Lincoln, however, maintained a relationship with the new *Journal* editors, unlike Herndon, who was banished; but Lincoln could not have been pleased with the drumbeat in its pages for the candidacy of Millard Fillmore and the American Party and hostility to the Republicans. On November 23, the *Journal* published an article declaring, "The Republican movement has proved a failure. . . . Hereafter it will be a mere faction." It accused the Republicans of plotting to "build up a great Northern party, based upon the anti-slavery sentiment alone, and, relying upon the superior numerical force of the populace over the slave States, strike for a supremacy in the Union through the power of sectional prejudices." There was no justification for "an organization so full of evil, so pregnant with discord and angry contention, so imminently dangerous to the integrity and perpetuity of the Union." "The Whig party has always been in its broadest sense an American Party," the *Journal* editorialized on December 19. "To make a successful opposition to the Democracy the Know Nothings must move forward to this old Whig ground." Conjecturing that there would be no decisive winner for president in 1856, the *Journal* editorialized hopefully on December 21, "Should the next Presidential election go into the House of Representatives, the balance of power will also rest with the Americans and Whigs."

At last the *Journal* revealed itself wholeheartedly for Fillmore. "Mr. Fillmore for President" ran the headline on its front page on December 26, endorsing the "distinguished patriot," who had announced himself as a Know Nothing. The newspaper began filling its pages with articles favorable to Fillmore, promoting him as the best president in memory, and that "nothing would give us greater satisfaction than to see him elevated to the chief magistracy of the country."

Despite the internal splits within the American Party, especially between anti-Nebraska men and those who saw raising the issue as dangerously offensive to the South, it continued to subsume Whigs in state after state. Without New York the Whig Party, broken between the Know Nothings and the Republicans, was no longer a viable national party. It had already evaporated throughout the South. Without Kentucky it lost its bearings. In Illinois the movement of Old Whigs accelerated into the American Party as the presidential politics of 1856 became a driving factor. If there were no alternative, the Whigs through inertia would mostly become Know Nothings, leaving perhaps only a nub behind, the anti-Nebraska groups would remain scattered, and Douglas's Democrats would reign supreme over the political disorder.

In the light of the Know Nothing capture of the governorships in New York and Massachusetts in the fall elections of 1855, David Davis gloomily observed that their victories provided "such an impetus and weakened the opposition to the democracy, that the next Presidential race will certainly be spoiled."

"The man who is of neither party is not—cannot be, of any consequence," Lincoln had said in his Clay eulogy. But what if his party could not be of any consequence? After losing to Trumbull, Lincoln went through his usual stages of political grief, but this time, however, there was another stage after acceptance. "Finding himself drafting about with the disorganized elements that floated together after the angry political waters had subsided," recalled Herndon, "it became apparent to Lincoln that if he expected to figure as a leader he must take a stand himself. Mere hatred of slavery and opposition to the injustice of the Kansas-Nebraska legislation were not all that were required of him. He must be a Democrat, Know-Nothing, Abolitionist, or Republican, or forever float about in the great political sea without compass, rudder, or sail."

In January 1856, Paul Selby, editor of the *Morgan Journal*, who had been part of the original Republican group that met in Springfield during the Lincoln-Douglas confrontation, posted a notice in his newspaper and circulated it to other editors: "All editors in Illinois opposed to the Nebraska bill are requested to meet in convention at Decatur, Illinois, on the 22d of February next, for the purpose of making arrangements for the organization of the Anti-Nebraska forces in this state for the coming contest." The twenty-three-year-old German editor of the *Pike County Free Press,* John Nicolay, who saw the meeting as a way to exercise "the power and influence of the Political Press," was among the first of more than twenty-five pledging they would participate. (Nicolay would become one of Lincoln's private secretaries, with John Hay the other half of what Lincoln called "the boys.")

A week before the meeting, Selby wrote Yates, "I have had an interview with Mr. Lincoln today, and some conversation in reference to matters we were talking about last evening. I wish you would endeavor to see him soon, at least before the Editorial Convention. He tells me he thinks he will try and have some business at Decatur at the time of the Convention. Can't you do the same? I think we all agree as to what is to be done at the Convention." Selby mentioned that Edward L. Baker, the new coeditor of the *Illinois State Journal*, "tells me he thinks he will be present but he is afraid of too much ultraism." Clearly, Lincoln's invisible hand played a role in transporting the Know Nothing to the Republican gathering.

Selby also noted that he had received a letter from William H. Bissell, "which contains the assurances you have been seeking for." Bissell, an anti-Nebraska former Democratic congressman, a Mexican War hero, who had once challenged Jefferson Davis to a duel, was emerging as the secret consensus candidate for governor. Through January 1856 Lincoln had held a series of private conversations with a wide range of men, Democrats and Whigs, old rivals and old friends, all now within his circle of trust, on how to deal with the Republican editors convention and the Know Nothing menace. They agreed that slating the former Democrat Bissell would give them the best chance to win the governorship. Among those Lincoln consulted was Trumbull, still wary of fusion but concurring on Bissell. Agreement on the candidate amounted to fusion in fact while resisted in theory.

The day before the convention in Decatur on Washington's Birthday a fierce blizzard descended on central Illinois, freezing all movement. The editor of the *Decatur Chronicle*, William J. Usrey, had expected a turnout exceeding fifty, but only a dozen managed to trek through the snowdrifts. Lincoln was already comfortably ensconced in Decatur, having arranged to have business there. Throughout the day Lincoln cowrote the platform with Charles Ray of the *Chicago Tribune*. The resolutions against the extension of slavery and even respecting the Fugitive Slave Act and slavery where it existed were easily agreed upon. Lincoln wrote a "States Rights Plank" puncturing the hypocrisy of the greatest Southern principle: "Resolved, That the conditions which are demanded under pleas of 'rights' as being essential to the security of Slavery throughout its expanded and expanding area, are inconsistent with freedom, an invasion of our rights, oppressive and unjust,

and must be resisted." But when George Schneider of the *Staats-Zeitung* proposed a plank denouncing Know Nothingism he threw the meeting into
an uproar. Schneider announced
he would submit his resolution to
Lincoln and "abide by his decision." "Gentlemen," declared Lincoln, "The resolution introduced
by Mr. Schneider is nothing new.
It is already contained in the Declaration of Independence and you
cannot form a new party on pre-
scriptive principles." "This declaration of Mr. Lincoln's," Schneider
recalled, "saved the resolution and
in fact, helped to establish the new
party on the most liberal democratic basis."

George Schneider

That evening the delegates
convened in the dining room of
the Cassell House, where they
heard Ray hold forth on the outrages of Kansas. Afterward, Richard J.
Oglesby, a prominent Decatur politician and one of Lincoln's old friends, a
Kentuckian by birth, a Springfield lawyer and stalwart Whig, toasted Lincoln as "the warm and consistent friend of Illinois, and our next candidate
for the U.S. Senate," to "prolonged applause," according to Usrey's account.
Lincoln arose to respond, declaring, "The latter part of that sentiment I am
in favor of. Mr. L. said, that he was very much in the position of the man
who was attacked by a robber, demanding his money, when he answered,
'My dear fellow, I have no money, but if you will go with me to the light,
I will give you my note,' and, resumed Mr. L., if you will let me off I will
give you my note." Lincoln spoke for a half hour, disclaiming any ambition
to run for governor, which several of the editors encouraged. "I wish to say
why I should not be a candidate. If I should be chosen, the Democrats would
say it was nothing more than an attempt to resurrect the dead body of the
old Whig party. I would secure the vote of that party and no more, and our
defeat will follow as a matter of course. But I can suggest a name that will
secure not only the old Whig vote, but enough Anti-Nebraska Democrats to
give us the victory. The man is Colonel William H. Bissell." In effect, Lin-

coln nominated Bissell, achieving the plan he, Trumbull, Selby, and others had discussed. There was more self-deprecating humor. Lincoln said "he felt like the ugly man riding through a wood who met a woman, also on horseback, who stopped and said: 'Well, for land sake, you are the homeliest man I ever saw.' 'Yes, madam, but I can't help it,' he replied. 'No, I suppose not,' she observed, 'but you might stay at home.' " To top the night, E. L. Baker of the *Journal* was asked to deliver a toast, which he did: "Dick Oglesby, the next Secretary of State." Baker and the *Journal* were onboard.

The most important business of the meeting was to establish a committee to organize a state convention of the new party in Bloomington on May 29. Of its eleven members, some, according to Selby, "were suggested by Mr. Lincoln, while the others received his approval"—including Herndon and Gillespie, still formally a Know Nothing.

On the same day as the editors' convention at Decatur, two other conventions were gaveled to order. At Philadelphia, the American Party gathered to nominate Millard Fillmore for president and Andrew Donelson, Andrew Jackson's stepson, for vice president. Meanwhile, at Pittsburgh, about three hundred delegates met for an informal convention to create a national Republican Party. Lincoln had been invited but chose instead to go to Decatur.

The night before the Republican convention began, the *New York Times* reported, the New York and Pennsylvania men clambered into a hotel parlor to listen to the riveting stories from the sole delegate from Kansas, named Samuel N. Wood, "apparently thirty years of age; lean, sallow, and full of humor; greatly given to Free Soil." The next morning, Horace Greeley uncharacteristically assumed the pose of the conservative elder, relaying advice from "friends of the cause at Washington," urging "extreme caution," and, though he had been militantly against the Know Nothings, "recommended that the American party be conciliated rather than abused." Joshua Giddings followed him to the podium to ridicule Washington as "the last place to look for advice," and to declare, "he was a good deal opposed to extreme caution." Owen Lovejoy, speaking of the assaults in Kansas on free staters, announced, "Parson as he was . . . he would have a notion to be captain of a troop, or if they wouldn't accept him as a captain he would go as a private. . . . He was in favor of carrying on war to the knife, and the knife to the hilt." "Great sensation," the *Times* reported about the reaction in the hall.

Then Francis P. Blair, at whose Silver Spring, Maryland, home on Christmas Day 1855 Sumner, Chase, and Gamaliel Bailey, among other eminences, had gathered to plan this event, was unanimously elected convention president. The presence of the Jacksonian icon marked the definitive end of that era. Before he came to the convention, Blair wrote Martin Van Buren that the Democratic Party had turned into "a rotten organization composed and managed altogether by rotten men." He accepted the honor declaring that the South would "astonish the North" by accepting the Republican platform, understanding "its object is to prevent a nullification of the rights of the North." It was not completely lost on many of the delegates that the president of the first Republican convention was a slaveholder.

The afternoon session ended with "great excitement" when a telegram was received and read from a dissident at the American party convention, Thomas Spooner, leader of the Ohio Know Nothings, but also an ally of Chase. After the American Party convention rejected a resolution opposing the extension of slavery, Spooner sent a dispatch: "American Party no longer unite. Raise Republican banner. No further extension of Slavery. Americans are with you."

That evening, after John Vaughn of the *Chicago Tribune* spoke, Giddings again came forward to announce, "he had for twenty years been termed a fanatic, and had heard it so often that he had begun to believe it." The next day, a letter from Cassius Clay was read: "It is no longer a question of whether blacks shall be slaves, but whether whites shall be free." The platform written by Henry J. Raymond, the lieutenant governor of New York and editor of the *New York Times*, opposing the extension of slavery but leaving the Fugitive Slave Act unmentioned, was adopted without objection. And a resolution to reconvene in June to nominate a presidential candidate was approved.

The action moved to the roughhouse politics of Chicago. In its mayoral contest on March 4, Francis Sherman, a Democrat who had been elected mayor in 1841, stood to represent the antislavery coalition against Thomas Dyer, a close ally of Douglas and outspoken supporter of the Nebraska Act. Sherman was undermined when the Know Nothings endorsed him and slated the rest of the citywide candidates with their own people, alienating the Germans. Douglas's men almost certainly were involved in arranging the mischievous and discrediting Know Nothing endorsement of Sherman. "I was accused of being a Douglas man, and a Democrat approving the Nebraska act," the triumphant Dyer declared in his inaugural address on March 11, "and as this was almost the only accusation made against me that was true, it was the only one that I never denied." Douglas had regained control in Chicago.

Bissell suddenly got cold feet. He had been quietly promoting his candidacy for governor through Trumbull, Ebenezer Peck, an antislavery Democrat, and Joe Gillespie, Lincoln's staunch friend who had become a prominent Know Nothing. But after Douglas's victory in Chicago, Democrats throughout the state wavered about leaving the party for an uncertain organization aligned with abolitionists. Bissell explained to Trumbull his mistrust about the upcoming Republican convention: "The Convention at Bloomington is too likely to be composed of the same persons, and very few others, that composed the Decatur Convention. And nominations by such a convention are but the surest modes of killing off nominees." Trumbull also stepped back, writing John M. Palmer that he would join the Republicans only on the condition that they "abandon their altruisms." Gustave Koerner, the lieutenant governor, a Democrat and leader of the German community, also refused to endorse the Bloomington convention. The most influential antislavery Democrats somehow believed that fusion was a mirage that would inevitably fade along with the Kansas issue. They still considered themselves to be contending with Douglas "inside party lines," according to Palmer.

In the wake of Douglas's Chicago victory, the Illinois Democrats held a convention on May 1 that nominated Douglas's right-hand man, William A. Richardson, for governor, and passed a resolution reading Trumbull by name as a heretic out of the party. "You will see by the Tribune that I have been to Springfield attending the Pro-slavery Convention," Charles Ray, the *Tribune*'s editor, wrote Washburne on May 4. Despite that "the attendance was large, that the enthusiasm was unbounded and the determination to beat us," Ray remained confident that the Republicans could still win. "Now then, we can name Bissell and some good Whig from the South on the same ticket, we can beat 'em 'like a sack.'" But that would not be as straightforward as it might seem.

"While in Springfield I opened a pretty plot," Ray wrote. He had uncovered how the Douglas Democrats were manipulating the Know Nothings in a shadow war against the Republicans through a clandestine and corrupt relationship with William W. Danenhower, the Know Nothing leader in Chicago and editor of its daily newspaper, the *Native Citizen*. "The Fillmore KNs have their State Council on Tuesday next. Danenhower of the Native Citizen, who by the way is *undoubtedly in the pay of the Nebraskas*, has been agitating to get Bissell nominated in the State Council anterior to the Bloomington Convention, just as Sherman was nominated first, and by affixing the stain of 'Americanism' upon him, ruin him with the Germans." Ray had discovered the plot "by accident—through the indiscretion" of a Know

Nothing, and he informed Washburne he had already "set at work at once to defeat it."

Ray planned to enlist Gillespie, who was a member of the State Council, in his operation. "I am going down and hope to meet Gillespie, to whom I wrote, and rip the whole thing up, impeach Danenhower and make the Council adjourn *sine die*. It is a big labor for an outsider to undertake but I hope to succeed."

He was also incredulous to learn that Trumbull was being promoted for president in 1856. "I am surprised to hear Trumbull talked up among his friends in Central Illinois as a candidate for the Presidency. Is there any talk of the kind in Washington? Who are our friends now thinking of?" Ray wrote Washburne that he should ensure that Trumbull was aware that the state Democratic convention had censured him.

Gillespie was operating hand-in-glove with Lincoln, who had just named him to the state council of the nascent Republican Party. At the American Party convention at Springfield on May 6, Gillespie acted as the agent of Ray's intrigue. It would have been inconceivable that Lincoln was not informed. Thwarting the plot to nominate Bissell in order to tarnish him, Gillespie substituted for governor the name of William B. Archer, an Old Whig, who happened to be one of Lincoln's friends. Archer had served as a captain in the Black Hawk War, in the legislature with Lincoln, and was in 1854 an anti-Nebraska candidate for the Congress. Two days after the convention nominated Archer, the *Journal* editorialized, "we trust [he] will decline the honor here conferred upon him. And so with the others. They are all opposed to the policy of the Douglas Democracy, and will be careful not to be made by designing men to play into the hands of the slavery propagandists."

Just as the *Journal* suggested, but waiting strategically until shortly after the Republican convention at the end of the month, Archer declined the honor, leaving the Know Nothings scrambling to find a substitute. On the eve of the Republican convention, they were broken and never recovered. "Lincoln and myself," Herndon wrote Trumbull on May 20, "had a long talk in reference to affairs, and I have never seen him so sanguine of success, as in this Election—*he is warm*." The *Journal* published a front page editorial directed at wavering Democrats: "The false Democracy are daily calling upon you to return to their standard; but Judas like, they will one moment kiss and the next betray you." Bissell, just as suddenly, reversed course, declaring that he would be the Republican candidate for governor. And Palmer would serve as the convention president. (Danenhower would endorse Lincoln for the Senate in 1858 and for the presidency in 1860, and Lincoln appointed him a Treasury Department clerk in 1863.)

One of the enduring Lincoln myths was that he was reticent even after the Decatur meeting to embrace the Republican cause. "Lincoln continued to remain aloof from the Republican party," the historian Reinhard H. Luthin wrote in an influential article in 1944, following the view of Albert J. Beveridge in his two-volume biography of 1928, though later historians David Herbert Donald and Don E. Fehrenbacher took issue with this legend. It was earliest debunked by Joseph Wilson Fifer, who was governor of Illinois from 1889 to 1893, in a lecture to the state bar association in 1930. "Beveridge, in his Life of Lincoln, makes an egregious error when he says that Lincoln went into the Republican Party hesitatingly and reluctantly," Fifer stated.

> He did nothing of the kind. I have talked with his old friends at Springfield and Bloomington, and they are one voice in telling me that he, more than any man of his period, saw that a new party must be formed to arrest the further spread of slavery, and he stayed back purposely with his old Whig friends to talk to them as a Whig on the subject of the new party. It appeared on the surface as though his hold-back straps were stronger than his traces. As long as he remained a Whig they would listen to him, he knew that, but when he went over, bag and baggage, into the new party, antagonism would grow up and he would lose his influence. These intimate friends of his told me that he made up his mind to burn the bridges behind him and to go over, bag and baggage, into the new party in the convention that was held here in Bloomington.

The myth of the laconic Lincoln in this period can be traced to Herndon, who wished to take credit as the man behind the scenes. "Mr. Lincoln," he wrote Ward Hill Lamon in 1870, "was then backward—sorter dodgey—*sorter so and not so*. I was determined to make him take a stand, if he would not do it willingly." He was referring to a notice published on the front page of the *Journal* on May 16 calling for a county convention to appoint delegates to the Republican convention at Bloomington. Lincoln's name appeared first right above Herndon's and atop 129 prominent local men. These were more or less the friends of Abraham Lincoln—Whigs; law clients; men he had known for decades, like William Butler, finally reconciled; Trumbull's brother-in-law, Know Nothing, and old friend, William Jayne; Lincoln's former law partner, Stephen T. Logan; surprisingly, a notable defector, the former editor of Douglas's *Register*, George R. Weber; and, most important, the editors of the *Journal*, William H. Bailhache and Edward L. Baker. It is implausible that many if not most of these men signed the appeal without discussing the matter beforehand with Lincoln. Herndon claimed that he was the sole author of the call for the convention, circulating it while Lincoln was trying cases elsewhere. "I signed Mr. Lincoln's name without authority," he told Lamon. And he repeated the story in his biography of Lincoln: "Lincoln was absent at the time and, believing I knew what his 'feelings and judgment' on the vital questions of the hour were, I took the liberty to sign his name to the call." All this seems half right—that Herndon signed Lincoln's name in his absence knowing it was tacitly agreed. But that Lincoln was reluctant was belied by his central part in the Decatur conference, coauthoring the party platform, and not least placing Herndon on the central committee to plan the Bloomington convention. The notion of his hesitance was further belied by the clever and stealthy demolition of the Know Nothings in which his close friends played the key roles.

But what does ring completely authentic in Herndon's account was the reaction of John Todd Stuart, Lincoln's first law partner, his early mentor in state politics. "No sooner had it appeared than John T. Stuart, who, with others was endeavoring to retard Lincoln in his advanced movements, rushed into the office and excitedly asked if 'Lincoln had signed the Abolition call in the Journal?' I answered in the negative, adding that I had signed his name myself. To the question, 'Did Lincoln authorize you to sign it?' I returned an emphatic 'No.' 'Then,' exclaimed the startled and indignant Stuart, 'you have ruined him.' " (The Old Whig Stuart would soon in his disillusionment become a Democrat and endorse Douglas against Lincoln for the Senate in 1858.)

Lincoln's reply as reported by Herndon also seems genuine. "I thought I understood Lincoln thoroughly," Herndon wrote, "but in order to vindicate myself if assailed I immediately sat down, after Stuart had rushed out of the office, and wrote Lincoln, who was then in Tazewell County attending court, a brief account of what I had done and how much stir it was creating in the ranks of his conservative friends. If he approved or disapproved my course I asked him to write or telegraph me at once. In a brief time came his answer: 'All right; go ahead. Will meet you—radicals and all.' "

CHAPTER TWENTY-THREE

DESTINY AND POWER

R alph Waldo Emerson, the Sage of Concord, voice of Transcendentalism,
the leading intellectual of the age, came to Springfield in January 1853 to
deliver lectures in the Hall of the House of Representatives at the invitation
of the Library Association, headed by William H. Herndon, who venerated
him as the "genius of the spiritual and ideal." "Here I am in the deep mud of
the prairie," Emerson wrote in his journal. "It rains, and thaws incessantly,

and, if we step off the short street,
we go up to the shoulders, perhaps,
in mud." He referred to "Illinois, or
the big bog."

After the lectures the ladies of
the First Presbyterian Church of
which Mary Lincoln was a member
hosted a dinner in his honor in the
Senate chamber. Lincoln was likely
present to hear the distinguished
visitor, though there is no record of
his attendance.

"Power" was the subject of one
of Emerson's lectures, after his 1837
essay. Emerson was profoundly
antislavery, had spoken first against

Ralph Waldo Emerson

it aroused by the murder of Elijah Lovejoy, was an admirer of his family's old friend John Quincy Adams, intimate with the circle of the Boston abolitionists, close to Charles Sumner, a mentor to Henry David Thoreau, and had excoriated Daniel Webster for supporting the Fugitive Slave Act. But he had not come to Springfield to speak against slavery, or on any of the issues of the day. Instead, he gave his full-blown version of German Idealist philosophy filtered through the influence of the English Romantic reactionary Thomas Carlyle, whose book *On Heroes, Hero-Worship, and the Heroic in History* was the basic text from which Emerson borrowed his thoughts about the Great Man in history. The Carlylean sweep of Emerson's *Representative Men*, recently published in 1850, was filled with mystical idol worshipping of Napoleon as the "Child of Destiny," who possessed "a directness of action never before combined with so much comprehension."

Emerson's ethereal aesthetics on "Power" enraptured his provincial audience filled with people who were among the most cunning, subtle, and adroit practitioners of American politics and would soon collectively advance one of their own to the presidency. The *Illinois Journal* waxed rhapsodically on Emerson's talk, "extending through the higher and subtle regions of the intellectual and moral and spiritual forces."

"Who shall set a limit to the influence of a human being?" Emerson inquired. "There are men, who, by their sympathetic attractions, carry nations with them, and lead the activity of the human race. . . . All successful men have agreed in one thing—they were *causationists*. They believed that things went not by luck, but by law; that there was not a weak or a cracked link in the chain that joins the first and last of things."

Emerson's great men achieved their destinies riding events as acts of nature, possessing a sixth sense charting the course of history. Mind became matter, and triumphed over it. "The mind that is parallel with the laws of nature will be in the current of events and strong with their strength," said Emerson. "One man is made of the same stuff of which events are made; is in sympathy with the course of things; can predict it. Whatever befalls, befalls him first; so that he is equal to whatever shall happen."

If Lincoln was in that audience listening to Emerson's gusts on men and events he must have felt left behind by galloping history on horseback. He was then at the low ebb of his political career, mired in his own bog, after one frustrating term in the Congress and the sinking of the Whigs in the election fiasco of 1852 only two months earlier, without any visible prospects as far as his horse Bob could take him. Emerson's theory of the Great Man did not fit

Lincoln, but if it fit anyone on the American scene it was Stephen A. Douglas. Like Emerson, the Little Giant was under the influence of Romantic idea, envisioning himself at the world-historical crossroads where Manifest Destiny met the "spirit of the age."

Lincoln had warned against the Napoleonic pretender incarnated in the form of his rival from his address at the Springfield Lyceum onward to his Peoria speech. He disdained theories of great men who were not George Washington. When Herndon gave him a biography of Edmund Burke to read in 1856, Lincoln dabbled in it and threw it aside. "Biographies as generally written are not only misleading, but false," he said. "The author of this life of Burke makes a wonderful hero out of his subject. He magnifies his perfections—if he had any—and suppresses his imperfections. He is so faithful in his zeal and so lavish in praise of his every act that one is almost driven to believe that Burke never made a mistake or a failure in his life."

When Lincoln materialized in New Salem, Illinois, in August 1831, taking a job as a clerk in Denton Offutt's store and assuming his earliest political role as a clerk on the local election board, he hardly presented himself as a "Child of Destiny." "He assured those with whom he came in contact that he was a piece of floating driftwood," according to Herndon, "that after the winter of deep snow, he had come down the river with the freshet; borne along by the swelling waters, and aimlessly floating about, he had accidently [sic] lodged at New Salem." In this Lincoln creation myth, he appeared as a man without a past or family, ferried across the waters as an innocent to a new land, where he would begin his journey of discovery and self-improvement, without any sense of mission or fate, much less bearing a telltale mark of a redeemer. But then he told Jesse Fell, for his first autobiography to be used in the 1860 campaign, he could be identified by "no other marks or brands recollected," the common language of newspaper advertisements for runaway slaves, a very different story, one of identification with the powerless.

Lincoln developed his sense of power and its meaning over decades in politics. Lincoln had dreams that he interpreted as shadows of events to come. He held to numerous superstitions. He had visions, seeing his image double in a mirror, believing it an omen of his death foretold. But his alignment with events was neither mystical divination nor passive adaptation to them.

In retrospect, his closest contemporaries thought him prescient. "Lincoln's whole life was a calculation of the law of forces, and ultimate results. The world to him was a question of cause and effect," reflected Leonard Swett. "He believed the results to which certain causes tended, would surely follow; he did not believe that those results could be materially hastened, or impeded. His whole political history, especially since the agitation of the Slavery question, has been based upon this theory. He believed from the first, I think, that the agitation of Slavery would produce its overthrow, and he acted upon the result as though it was present from the beginning. His tactics were, to get himself in the right place and remain there still, until events would find him in that place."

John W. Bunn, the Springfield merchant and Whig partisan, who funded Lincoln's campaigns and followed his direction, judged Lincoln unique among the politicians. "These things, which I state as facts of my own knowledge," he affirmed, "certainly show that Lincoln was a practical politician, but he was not altogether like many other practical politicians. He had his personal ambitions, but he never told any man his deeper plans, and few, if any, knew his inner thoughts. . . . Lincoln's entire career proves that it is quite possible for a man to be adroit and skillful and effective in politics, without in any degree sacrificing moral principles. Little men try to do the same things he did, and make very bad work of it. They lack the high moral inspiration that animated Lincoln. Lincoln presents the most remarkable case in American history of a man who could be a practical politician and at the same time be a statesman in the highest sense of both terms."

All along the self-made man educated himself in the politics of democracy. He learned peculiar nuances of power that could not be commanded by fiat. He was of the first American generation innovating in party organization, mass media, and public opinion. He apprenticed in logrolling in the wooden legislature at Kaskaskia, the first Illinois capital, which would soon sink into the Mississippi like a frontier Atlantis. Lincoln played at humiliating his elders, learned to whip legislators into line dangling favors, faced scandals and embarrassments, wired party conventions, and won Mary, his most important victory, for it was she who was the founder of "our Lincoln party." As a member of the Young Indian caucus in the Congress he promoted a presidential winner, but gained nothing because he was too slight a figure to matter and was tossed back into obscurity. His floor speech demanding to know the "spot" where the Mexican War began earned him momentary respect from his fellow Young Indians for its partisan sharpness but ridicule in his district as "Spotty Lincoln." His antislavery gestures in the legislature and the Congress came to naught and were largely ignored. When he left his last elected office he was an unbending partisan in an unyielding partisan system. He had learned the arts and letters of politics in the new republic. But even proficiency was insufficient. He was at a dead end. When the events changed he had to change to align himself with them.

Power, for Lincoln, was always a contest, but it became far more than a matter of winning and losing, or even claiming the spoils. In the past, with one party arrayed against another, predictable partisanship prevailed from election to election. But now the gyroscope of politics was smashed, the parties broken. What he and others called "the slave power" suddenly transformed everything. Grounded in the mundane skills of the democracy that had shaped him, he had to raise the powers of democracy to extraordinary heights in its defense.

Lincoln had spent his life in the shadow of Henry Clay, his "beau ideal of a statesman," the originator of the self-descriptive phrase "a self-made man." Lincoln had read his speeches in hand-me-down copies of the *Louisville Journal*, absorbed them for their lessons in history, oratory, and politics. When Lincoln went for the military heroes William Henry Harrison and Zachary Taylor over Clay, it was out of expedience. Even at his earliest political age, Lincoln wanted to win, putting head over heart, though Clay still held his heart. Excitedly meeting Clay at last, in his wife's hometown of Lexington, under the auspices of Robert S. Todd, Lincoln was surprised at the charismatic Clay's coldness and condescension. Unusual among those eulogizing Clay, Lincoln called attention to his denunciations of slavery. In his letter to George Robertson, Lincoln delivered what amounted to a second eulogy, tolling the death of Clay's policy of gradual emancipation in the South. Severing himself from Clay's forlorn hope was not mere coincidence with his abandonment of the Whig Party. He was no longer in anyone's shadow.

Lincoln was locked in mortal combat with Douglas. From then onward, Douglas's pursuit of his own Manifest Destiny blazed the path for Lincoln's. "Lincoln saw his opportunity and Douglas' downfall," said Herndon. "He instantly on the introduction of that bill entered into the political field, and by force of his character, mind, eloquence, he became our abolition leader; he was too conservative for some of us, and I among them, and yet I stuck to Lincoln in the hopes of his sense of justice and eternal right."

Within two years of shedding the husk of the Whig Party and assuming the identity of a Republican, Lincoln sounded his own Emersonian note about destiny, but edged with a resonant biblical tone. "If we could know where we are, and whither we are tending, we could then better judge what to do, and how to do it," he declared in his "House Divided" speech of June 16, 1858. His sense of time and timing had become acute. "The fight must go on," he would write to a friend two weeks after his loss to Douglas in the 1858 Senate race. "The cause of civil liberty must not be surrendered at the end of *one*, or even, one *hundred* defeats. Douglas had the ingenuity to be supported in the late contest both as the best means to *break down*, and to *uphold* the Slave interest. No ingenuity can keep those antagonistic elements in harmony long. Another explosion will soon come."

By then Lincoln had already been carried along by explosion after explosion. When he hurtled on a train to Bloomington for the founding of the Illinois Republican Party on May 29, 1856, it was a familiar trip to a place he had visited many times to practice the law, the home of his friends David Davis and Jesse Fell. But this time the uproar of events heralded his entrance.

On May 21, David Atchison led an army of nearly one thousand pro-slavery Missourians under a red banner inscribed "Southern Rights" into the free state town of Lawrence to ransack it. The next day, in the Senate, while Charles Sumner sat writing at his desk, Congressman Preston Brooks of South Carolina battered him with a cane, nearly killing him, in retribution for Sumner's mocking of Brooks's cousin, Senator Andrew Butler, patriarch of the F Street Mess, in his speech entitled "Crime Against Kansas." Two days later, on May 24, along Pottawatomie Creek in Kansas, John Brown and his band of volunteers hacked five pro-slavery men to death.

When Lincoln proclaimed himself as a Republican five days later before the new party he founded, it was among the most significant events in the coming of the Civil War. Ultimately, Emerson would declare, "His mind mastered the problem of the day; and, as the problem grew, so did his comprehension of it. Rarely was man so fitted to the event." The mystical Emerson invoked "a serene Providence which rules the fate of nations . . . makes its own instruments, creates the man for the time, trains him in poverty, inspires his genius, and arms him for his task."

Lincoln's political education was long, but the moment of Lincoln's awakening from his political slumber was sudden. In early 1855, traveling the county court circuit, staying overnight in a boardinghouse, his discussion with a former judge and fellow lawyer, T. Lyle Dickey, a conservative Old Whig, went on deep into the night. "Judge Dickey contended that slavery was an institution, which the Constitution recognized, and which could not be disturbed. Lincoln argued that ultimately slavery must become extinct," recalled another Illinois lawyer, William Pitt Kellogg. "After a while," said Dickey, "we went upstairs to bed. There were two beds in our room, and I remember that Lincoln sat up in his nightshirt on the edge of the bed arguing the point with me. At last, we went to sleep. Early in the morning I woke up and there was Lincoln half sitting up in bed."

"Dickey," said Lincoln, "I tell you this nation cannot exist half slave and half free."

"Oh, Lincoln," replied Dickey, "go to sleep."

> "If a kingdom is divided against itself, that kingdom
> cannot stand. And if a house is divided against itself, that
> house will not be able to stand."
>
> MARK 3:24–25

> "Every kingdom divided against itself is laid waste, and a
> divided household falls."
>
> LUKE 11:17

ACKNOWLEDGMENTS

———•◦•———

Wrestling with His Angel seamlessly follows *A Self-Made Man* without any pause in historical time. The era's shocks, surprises, and confusions were essential in the making of Abraham Lincoln, who forged himself in a world of uncertainty. The more time I spent with Lincoln the more I began to see that the arc of his story was uneasy, unpredictable, and often unintended. Yet his thoughts and words were the careful result of his intense consciousness. The opacity and silences that his law partner, William Henry Herndon, and others of his friends described as Lincoln's melancholy were also a mask for his concentration, intellectual absorption, and focus. He made his depression as well as every other feeling into instruments of self-discipline in a wilderness of political despair for a destiny he could not foretell. Even when his life seemed to be reduced to simple insignificance he was scanning the horizons and quietly interpreting its signs. His ambition was "a little engine that knew no rest," as Herndon called it, and he was a professional partisan politician, who early in his career in the name of party fidelity purged from the Whig list of candidates for local offices in New Salem, Illinois, his surrogate father, Bowling Green, though he later shed tears over it. He did not arise as recognizably Lincoln until he aligned that fierce ambition and those sharp political skills in the cause of American democracy as a unique experiment that might well be undone from within. Lincoln framed every sentence to anticipate and deflect the most vulgar and the most cunning demagoguery. He crafted every phrase to persuade, his chief means to reach his ends, navigating "point by point," as he would explain his method near the conclusion of the Civil War. *Wrestling with His Angel* describes Lincoln's real dark night of the soul, coming to his revelation of a "House Divided," from which he emerged as the Lincoln of history. He would be that man until his assassination.

I am indebted to those who have made possible my attempt to understand Lincoln. Above all, I am grateful to Alice Mayhew, my editor, who grasps Lincoln and his nature as well as anyone. Her knowledge, subtle intelligence, and broad range have been indispensable. Even more crucial has been her unwavering steadfastness. Stuart Roberts, her assistant editor, has been brilliant, never missing a beat, and a pleasure to work with. Fred Chase, who copy edited this book, has the finest unblinking eye. I am also grateful to Jonathan Karp, president of Simon & Schuster, who has believed in this project from the beginning.

Andrew Edwards, journalist and scholar, admirably performed the intricate job of putting my notes into proper order, a thankless task for which I am eternally thankful. While his area of expertise is the American Revolution, he nimbly knew his way through the pre–Civil War era, too.

Robert Barnett, a rare Washington lawyer with a literary and historical sense, who has a canny understanding of many worlds, has provided invaluable counsel in bringing forth this work.

I produced this work without research assistants and therefore am completely responsible for any errors. I am grateful to librarians at the National Archives and the Library of Congress for locating material I sought.

Sean Wilentz, of Princeton, has been my resolute reader, sounding board, and, most important, unflagging friend, not least in common cause. Our never-ending conversations have been the foundation for many of the ideas in this book.

Scholars in the fields of the Civil War, Lincoln, and the Constitution lent their insight and encouragement, particularly Joan Cashin, of Ohio State University; Terry Alford, of Northern Virginia Community College; Harold Holzer, director of the Roosevelt House Public Policy Institute at Hunter College; and Jeffrey Rosen, president of the National Constitution Center. Dan Weinberg, the owner of the Abraham Lincoln Book Shop, in Chicago, has been a source of fascinating discussions on Lincoln and Lincolniana.

Through the course of writing this book I have been fortunate to have the confidence and closeness of friends who offered their rapport and support, among them John and Christina Ritch, Bill and Renilde Drozdiak, Jim and Deb Fallows, Andrew and Leslie Cockburn, Charles and Bunny Burson, Nick and Louise Wapshott, Walter and Ann Pincus, Jane Mayer, Steve Weisman, Lynn Rothschild, Paul Glastris, Marilyn Melkonian, V. V. Harrison,

Cody Shearer, Richard Parker, Rick Hertzberg, Ben Gerson, Craig Unger, Hillel Schwartz, Shaun Woodward, David Brock, Derek Shearer, Edward Jay Epstein, Steve Bing, Scott Horton, Jonathan Winer, James Carville, Joe Wilson, John Judis, Thomas Edsall, Jeffrey Frank, Joe Conason, and Norman Birnbaum.

My sister Marcia, who is involved as a positive force in the politics of the State of Illinois, has been a constant source of support, not only for me but also for our entire family, especially through the loss of our spirited, devoted, and beloved mother, Claire Stone Blumenthal Miller.

My wife, Jackie, is more than my valued partner, but also a diligent researcher in early American history, an excellent writer, and an observant editor, who managed the feat of winning reelection in 2016 as an Advisory Neighborhood Commissioner with nearly 100 percent of the votes in our neighborhood in Washington, D.C. We enjoy and profit from the endless back-and-forth with our sons, Max and Paul, both journalists engaged in the arena of current affairs. This book is dedicated to Paul and Alison Kim in honor of their marriage with the belief that in good time they will help create a better American future.

Washington, D.C.
November 30, 2016

NOTES

―――――●◦●―――――

ABBREVIATIONS AND SHORT TITLES

HI—Douglas L. Wilson, Rodney O. Davis, Terry Wilson, William Henry Herndon, and Jesse William Weik, eds., *Herndon's Informants: Letters, Interviews, and Statements About Abraham Lincoln* (Urbana: University of Illinois Press, 1998).

CW—Roy P. Basler, ed., *The Collected Works of Abraham Lincoln* (New Brunswick, N.J.: Rutgers University Press, 1953).

Seward, *1831–1846*—Frederick Seward, *William H. Seward, 1831–1846* (New York: Derby & Miller, 1891).

Seward, *1846–1860*—Frederick Seward, *Seward at Washington, 1846–1860* (New York: D. Appleton, 1891).

Seward, *1846–1861*—William Henry Seward and Frederick W. Seward, *Seward at Washington as Senator and Secretary of State, 1846–1861* (New York: Derby & Miller, 1891).

PROLOGUE

1 *"He said gloomily, despairingly, sadly"*: Ivor Debenham Spencer, *The Victor and the Spoils: A Life of William L. Marcy* (Providence: Brown University Press, 1959), 274, 281; *Congressional Globe*, 31st Congress, 1st Session, 391, 115–26; Lydia Lasswell Crist, ed., *The Papers of Jefferson Davis: 1849–1852* (Baton Rouge: Louisiana State University Press, 1983), 268; Virginia Mason, ed., *The Public Life and Diplomatic Correspondence of James M. Mason* (New York: Neale Publishing), 72.

4 *Douglas's newspaper*: Michael Burlingame, *Abraham Lincoln: A Life*, Vol. 1, Chapter 10, Online Edition, 1053, https://www.knox.edu/about-knox/lincoln-studies-center/burlingame-abrahamlincoln-a-life.

4   *In two brief autobiographies:* Ray P. Basler, ed., *The Collected Works of Abraham Lincoln* (New Brunswick, N.J.: Rutgers University Press, 1953), 3:512, 4:67 (hereinafter CW).

5   *It was about this decisive juncture:* William H. Herndon, *Life of Lincoln* (Cleveland: World, 1942), 304.

7   *Sequestering himself:* CW, 5:3, 376.

7   *The growth of Lincoln's politics:* CW, 5:2, 318.

CHAPTER ONE: WHITE NEGROES

9   *The cholera bacteria that invades the intestines:* Dorothy H. Crawford, *Deadly Companions: How Microbes Shaped Our History* (New York: Oxford University Press, 2007), 130–36; William H. Townsend, *Lincoln and the Bluegrass* (Lexington: University of Kentucky Press, 1955), 171–74.

10 *In 1833, after three years of debate:* "Wickliffe, Robert," The Kentucky Encyclopedia, http://kyenc.msudev.com/entry/w/WICKL03.html; "History of the Preston Plantation North Kentucky Views, http://nkyviews.com/trimble/pdf/preston _plantation.pdf; Lowell H. Harrison, "Charles Anderson Wickliffe," in *The Kentucky Encyclopedia*, John E. Kleber, ed. (Lexington: University Press of Kentucky, 1992), 950–51.

11 *One of the chief supporters:* James C. Klotter, *The Breckinridges of Kentucky* (Lexington: University Press of Kentucky, 2006), 21–22, 47.

11 *Wickliffe had been his father's lawyer:* Hambleton Tapp, "The Slavery Controversy Between Robert Wickliffe and Robert J. Breckinridge Prior to the Civil War," Filson Society, filsonhistorical.org/wp-content/uploads/2013/02/19-3-3 _The-Slavery-Controversy-Between-Robert-Wickliffe-and-Robert-J.-Breckinridge -Prior-to-the-Civil-War_Tapp-Hambleton.pdf; Robert J. Breckinridge, *Hints on Slavery*, Vol. 19 (Lexington, Ky.: 1830).

12 *With the passage of the Non-Importation Act:* Asa Earl Martin, *The Anti-Slavery Movement in Kentucky Prior to 1850* (Louisville, Ky.: Standard Publishing, 1918), 102, 108; Klotter, *Breckinridges of Kentucky*, 71; Townsend, *Lincoln and the Bluegrass*, 80.

12 *Breckinridge joined in denouncing abolitionists:* Luke Edward Harlow, "From Border South to Solid South: Religion, Race, and the Making of Confederate Kentucky, 1830–1880" (PhD diss., Rice University, 2009), 52–54, 58; Klotter, *Breckinridges of Kentucky*, 71, 69.

13 *Cash's arguments were as imposing:* Townsend, *Lincoln and the Bluegrass*, 100; Martin, *Anti-Slavery Movement in Kentucky Prior to 1850*, 111; David L. Smiley, *The Lion of White Hall* (Madison: University of Wisconsin Press, 1962), 9.

14 *Sheer acts of violence and duels:* Fiona Young-Brown, *Wicked Lexington, Kentucky* (Charleston, N.C.: The History Press, 2011), 19–21; Jean H. Baker, *Mary Todd Lincoln* (New York: W. W. Norton, 2008), 72.

14 *When Cassius Clay and the Young Duke met:* Cassius Marcellus Clay, *The Life of*

Cassius Marcellus Clay (Cincinnati: J. F. Brennan, 1886), 80, 82; Smiley, *Lion of White Hall*, 52–53, 48.

15 *In the next contest for the congressional seat:* Townsend, *Lincoln and the Bluegrass*, 83–87; Cassius Marcellus Clay, *Life*, 89–90.

15 *But the pro-slavery party was gaining ground:* Lewis Tappan, *Address to the Non-Slaveholders of the South* (New York: American and Foreign Anti-Slavery Society, S. W. Benedict, 1843), 9.

16 *Cash explained his position:* Smiley, *Lion of White Hall*, 57; Cassius Marcellus Clay, *Slavery: The Evil—The Remedy* (New York: Greeley & McElrath, 1844).

16 *On January 1, 1844, Cassius Clay emancipated:* Cassius Marcellus Clay, *Life*, 101–4.

18 *The* True American's *first issue:* George Washington Ranck, *History of Lexington, Kentucky* (Cincinnati: Robert Clarke, 1872), 236; Cassius Marcellus Clay, *Life*, 105–7; Townsend, *Lincoln and the Bluegrass*, 100–3; Smiley, *Lion of White Hall*, 80, 83.

18 *The* Observer *responded to the debut:* Townsend, *Lincoln and the Bluegrass*, 104.

18 *Lexington was rife with rumors:* Stanley Harrold, *Border War: The Long Physical Struggle over Slavery Before the Civil War* (Chapel Hill: University of North Carolina Press, 2010), 126.

18 *The rising temperature over the* True American: Martin, *Anti-Slavery Movement in Kentucky Prior to 1850*, 98; Townsend, *Lincoln and the Bluegrass*, 107–8.

19 *Wickliffe charged that the Whigs:* Townsend, *Lincoln and the Bluegrass*, 108–9; Robert Wickliffe, *To the Freemen of the County of Fayette* (Lexington: Kentucky Gazette Print, 1845).

20 *The voting was spread over three days:* Townsend, *Lincoln and the Bluegrass*, 110.

20 *Cassius Clay was bedridden with typhus:* Lowell Hayes Harrison, *The Antislavery Movement in Kentucky* (Lexington: University Press of Kentucky, 2004), 51.

20 *Four days after the rope factory:* Harrison, 36.

21 *On the morning of August 18:* Smiley, *Lion of White Hall*, 98–99.

21 *One llinois newspaper:* Townsend, *Lincoln and the Bluegrass*, 116–17.

22 *In April 1846:* Frederick Seward, *William H. Seward, 1831–1846* (New York: Derby & Miller, 1891), 799.

22 *When the Mexican War broke out:* Cassius Marcellus Clay, *Life*, 164, 206, 169–70; Smiley, *Lion of White Hall*, 131–32; John Niven, *Salmon P. Chase* (New York: Oxford University Press, 1995), 99–100.

23 *On February 15, 1849, the Democrats of Lexington:* Townsend, *Lincoln and the Bluegrass*, 160; Richard Lawrence Miller, *Lincoln and His World, Volume 3, The Rise to National Prominence, 1843–1853* (Jefferson, N.C.: McFarland, 2011), 3:244.

23 *Repeal had been successfully resisted:* Harrold, *Border War*, 130–31.

24 *Just before the repeal:* Calvin Colton, *The Last Seven Years of the Life of Henry Clay* (New York: A. S. Barnes & Co., 1856), 347–52; Martin, *Anti-Slavery Movement in Kentucky Prior to 1850*, 127.

24   *On April 14, the Fayette County antislavery men:* Townsend, *Lincoln and the Blue-grass*, 161–62.

25   *The first emancipation convention in Kentucky:* Martin, *Anti-Slavery Movement in Kentucky Prior to 1850*, 129–31.

25   *"Thank God!" exclaimed Cassius Clay:* Smiley, *Lion of White Hall*, 133–42; Martin, *Anti-Slavery Movement in Kentucky Prior to 1850*, 133; E. Polk Johnson, *A History of Kentucky and Kentuckians* (Chicago: Lewis Publishing, 1912), 2:877.

26   *Within a month, Todd was dead:* Townsend, *Lincoln and the Bluegrass*, 165–66, 174–75; Charles Clark, "W. Oliver Anderson," Kansas Bogus Legislature, http://kansasboguslegislature.org/mo/anderson_w_o.html.

26   *On Election Day, a gun battle raged:* Harold D. Tallant and Kathleen E. R. Smith, *Evil Necessity: Slavery and Political Culture in Antebellum Kentucky* (Lexington: University Press of Kentucky, 2003), 148–50.

26   *But the fullest case was made:* Richard Sutton, *Report of the Debates and Proceedings of the Convention for the Revision of the Constitution of the State of Kentucky* (Frankfort, Ky.: A. G. Hodges, 1849), 464, 123–26, 856, 139, 140–41.

27   *Finally, Garrett Davis, the Whig congressman:* Ibid., 136, 1106.

28   *The self-styled Emancipation Party:* James Speed, *James Speed: A Personality* (Louisville, Ky.: J. P. Morton, 1914), 28–29.

28   *When the constitutional convention submitted:* Tallant and Smith, *Evil Necessity*, 160.

29   *Cassius Clay was not inclined:* Cassius Marcellus Clay, *Life*, 176, 188–98.

31   *Whigs mostly derided Cash's campaign:* Victor B. Howard, "Robert J. Breckinridge and the Slavery Controversy in Kentucky in 1849," *Filson Club Historical Quarterly* 58, no. 4 (October 1979), 341; Harlow, "From Border South to Solid South," 83–84; Smiley, *Lion of White Hall*, 146–47; Tallant and Smith, *Evil Necessity*, 160, 162; Cassius Marcellus Clay, *Life*, 213.

31   *Cassius Clay gave up on the fate of Kentucky:* Smiley, *Lion of White Hall*, 56; Cassius Marcellus Clay, *Life*, 208–9.

32   *At first glance, the convoluted case:* John J. Breckinridge, *The Third Defense of Robert J. Breckinridge Against the Calumnies of Robert Wickliffe* (Baltimore: R. J. Matchett, 1843), 74; Townsend, *Lincoln and the Bluegrass*, 182.

32   *In his brief Wickliffe pretended:* Townsend, *Lincoln and the Bluegrass*, 178; CW, 1:465.

33   *Breckinridge was Todd's long-standing ally: Journal of the Senate of the Commonwealth of Kentucky* (Frankfort, Ky.: A. G. Hodges, 1838), 378; Breckinridge, *Third Defense*, 89; *The Second Defense of Robert J. Breckinridge Against the Calumnies of Robert Wickliffe* (Baltimore: R. J. Matchett, 1841), 66; *Speech of Robert Wickliffe in Reply to Rev. R. J. Breckinridge* (Lexington, Ky.: Observer & Reporter Print, 1840), 21.

33   *Exactly what Lincoln knew about the sordid background:* Baker, *Mary Todd Lincoln*, 69.

34   *There was, in fact, a living heir:* Townsend, *Lincoln and the Bluegrass*, 180–81.

34 *Breckinridge had exposed the scandal:* Breckinridge, *Third Defense*, 76.

35 *The source of Breckinridge's disclosure inevitably:* Townsend, *Lincoln and the Blue-grass*, 182.

35 *The true father of Alfred Francis Russell:* Harlow, "From Border South to Solid South," 60–61; Klotter, *Breckinridges of Kentucky*, 71–73.

35 *When Todd filed his lawsuit five years:* Townsend, *Lincoln and the Bluegrass*, 184.

36 *Lincoln sat with Judge Robertson:* Mrs. C. Mentelle, *A Short History of the Late Mrs. Mary O. T. Wickliffe* (Lexington: Kentucky Statesman, 1850), 17–20.

36 *Margaret Wickliffe, Mary's best friend:* Randolph Hollingsworth, "She Used Her Power Lightly: A Political History of Margaret Wickliffe Preston of Kentucky" (PhD diss., University of Kentucky, 1999), 53–54.

36 *Their case floundering:* Townsend, *Lincoln and the Bluegrass*, 183.

37 *Lincoln worked with his co-counsel:* Hollingsworth, "She Used Her Power Lightly," 54.

37 *Cassius Clay gave up on transforming Kentucky:* Cassius Marcellus Clay, *Life*, 252.

37 *After his defeat running for delegate:* Smiley, *Lion of White Hall*, 30; Klotter, *Breckinridges of Kentucky*, 76, 86; Adam I. P. Smith, *No Party Now: Politics in the Civil War North* (New York: Oxford University Press, 2006), 102–3.

38 *James Speed had contempt:* Speed, *James Speed*, 37–8, 43.

38 *The true heir:* "A Letter from Liberia Reverend Alfred F. Russell to Robert Wickliffe in Lexington, Kentucky," Kentucky Primary Sources, http://www.uky.edu/~dolph /HIS316/sources/liberia2.html; Adell Patton, Jr., "Kentucky African American Immigrants to Liberia, 1820–43," *Kentucky Ancestors* 39, no. 4 (Summer 2004).

CHAPTER TWO: THE CIVIL WAR OF OLD ROUGH AND READY

42 *"Many causes conspired":* Salmon P. Chase, *Diary and Correspondence* (Washington, D.C.: Government Printing Office, 1903), 142, 140–41.

42 *Chase had begun plotting:* Niven, *Salmon P. Chase*, 113–17.

43 *More than the Senate seat:* Albert Bushnell Hart, *Salmon Portland Chase* (New York: Houghton Mifflin, 1899), 111; William Alexander Taylor and Aubrey Clarence Taylor, *Ohio Statesmen and Annals of Progress: From the Year 1788 to the Year 1900* (Columbia, Ohio: Press of the Westbote Co., 1899), 232.

44 *Stanley Matthews worked out a plan:* Niven, *Salmon P. Chase*, 119–20; Robert S. Harper, *Lincoln and the Press* (New York: McGraw-Hill, 1951), 333–37.

44 *Chase's operatives delivered the two Free Soilers:* Niven, *Salmon P. Chase*, 120; Hart, *Salmon Portland Chase*, 111–12.

44 *The newly elected Senator Chase arrived in Washington:* Niven, *Salmon P. Chase*, 124.

45 *In New York, Seward faced opposition:* Thurlow Weed, *The Life of Thurlow Weed including His Autobiography and Memoir*, Vol. 1 (Boston: Houghton Mifflin, 1884), 586; Walter Stahr, *Seward: Lincoln's Indispensable Man* (New York: Simon & Schuster, 2012), 114–15.

46 *Weed then summoned Seward and Fillmore:* Weed, *The Life of Thurlow Weed,*
586–87; Michael F. Holt, *The Rise and Fall of the Whig Party: Jacksonian Politics
and the Onset of the Civil War* (New York: Oxford University Press, 2003), 386;
William Henry Seward and Frederick W. Seward, *Seward at Washington as Senator and Secretary of State, 1846–1861* (New York: Derby & Miller, 1891), 101, 107;
Robert J. Scarry, *Millard Fillmore* (Jefferson, N.C.: McFarland, 2010), 160–63.

47 *Throughout the summer of 1849:* James Ford Rhodes, *History of the United States
from the Compromise of 1850 to the McKinley-Bryan Campaign of 1896: 1850–1854*
(New York: Macmillan, 1920), 1:105–7.

47 *On December 3, 1849:* Michael F. Holt, "Politics, Patronage, and Public Policy:
The Compromise of 1850," in Paul Finkelman and Donald R. Kennon, eds., *Congress and the Crisis of the 1850s* (Athens: Ohio University Press, 2012), 24.

47 *The new House had 113 Democrats:* Norman D. Brown, *Edward Stanly: Whiggery's
Tarheel "Conqueror"* (Tuscaloosa: University of Alabama Press, 1974), 128–31;
William Kauffman Scarborough, *Masters of the Big House: Elite Slaveholders of the
Mid-Nineteenth-Century South* (Baton Rouge: Louisiana State University Press,
2006), 6.

48 *While they were thwarting Calhoun's attempt:* Ulrich B. Phillips, *The Life of Robert
Toombs* (New York: Macmillan, 1913), 66; Alexander Stephens, "Meredith Poin-
dexter Gentry," in Richard Gentry, *The Gentry Family in America: 1676 to 1909*
(New York: Grafton Press, 1909), 350.

48 *The Free Soilers rejected Winthrop:* Joshua R. Giddings, *History of the Rebellion: Its
Authors and Causes* (New York: Follet, Foster, 1864), 302.

49 *The Southern Whigs, having no trouble sniffing*: *Congressional Globe*, 31st Congress,
1st Session, 28–29.

49 *Horace Mann, who succeeded John Quincy Adams:* Mary Tyler Peabody Mann, *Life
of Horace Mann* (Boston: Walker, Fuller, 1865), 283–84.

50 *The day after the Free Soilers:* Sean Wilentz, *The Rise of American Democracy* (New
York: W. W. Norton, 2005), 635, 633–64; K. Jack Bauer, *Zachary Taylor: Soldier,
Planter, Statesman of the Old Southwest* (Baton Rouge: Louisiana State University
Press, 1993), 109; Rhodes, *History of the United States,* 1:99.

51 *Seward, intent on securing patronage:* Seward, *1846–1861,* 113.

51 *Shortly after Taylor's election:* Henry Clay, *The Works of Henry Clay: Private Correspondence, 1801–1852* (New York: G. P. Putnam's Sons, 1904), 1:584, 586.

52 *At the White House New Year's Day reception*: Benjamin Brown French, ed., Don-
ald B. Cole and John J. McDonough, *Witness to the Young Republic: A Yankee's
Journal, 1828–1870* (Hanover, N.H.: University Press of New England, 1989), 213;
Carl Schurz, *Henry Clay* (New York: Houghton Mifflin, 1899), 2:323–24.

53 *On the evening of January 21:* Merrill D. Peterson, *The Great Triumvirate: Webster,
Clay, and Calhoun* (New York: Oxford University Press, 1987), 451.

53 *Mr. Clay seemed to be very feeble:* Ibid., 480.

54 *When Clay had finished, Webster was persuaded*: George Ticknor Curtis, *Life of Daniel Webster* (New York: D. Appleton, 1889), 2:396–98.

55 *Senator Jefferson Davis of Mississippi turned his contemptuous gaze:* Crist, ed., *Papers of Jefferson Davis*, 4:22.

57 *In 1838, both Clay and Calhoun:* Robert Remini, *Henry Clay: Statesman for the Union* (New York: W. W. Norton, 1991), 508–18.

57 *Jefferson Davis, Calhoun's surrogate: Congressional Globe*, 31st Congress, 1st Session, 246–50.

58 *On February 5, Clay had to be helped up:* Schurz, *Henry Clay*, 2:334.

59 *After making every argument for his resolutions: Congressional Globe*, 31st Congress, 1st Session, 115–26.

60 *Taylor was furious and combative:* Seward, *1846–1861*, 112, 122; Mary Butler Crittenden Coleman, ed., *The Life of John J. Crittenden* (Philadelphia: J. B. Lippincott, 1873), 1:365.

61 *Thurlow Weed followed Hamlin:* Henry Wilson, *History of the Rise and Fall of the Slave Power in America* (Boston: J. R. Osgood, 1875), 2:259; Weed, *The Life of Thurlow Weed*, 2:177–78; Thomas Ford, *A History of Illinois* (Chicago: S. C. Griggs, 1854), 1:134.

61 *On March 1, Horace Mann dined:* Mann, *Life of Horace Mann*, 292–3.

62 *When Clay rose to speak for California's admission:* Stevenson, *Works of Henry Clay*, 398. [full cite TK; short version cited on nn 89 + 144]

62 *John C. Calhoun had been confined with pneumonia:* Charles M. Wiltse, *John C. Calhoun: Sectionalist, 1840–1850* (Indianapolis: Bobbs-Merrill, 1951), 456–61.

64 *The immediate "test question," he stipulated: Congressional Globe*, 31st Congress, 1st Session, 451–55.

66 *Praised in the South, Webster was damned:* Mann, *Life of Horace Mann*, 293.

67 *John Greenleaf Whittier, a founder of the Liberty Party:* John Greenleaf Whittier, *Poems of John Greenleaf Whittier* (New York: T. Y. Crowell, 1902), 185.

67 *At a packed meeting at Faneuil Hall:* Theodore Parker, *Speeches, Addresses, and Occasional Sermons* (Boston: B. Fuller, 1871), 3:213–14, 218–19; William Henry Herndon and Jesse William Weik, *Herndon's Lincoln: The True Story of a Great Life* (New York: Belford, Clarke, 1889), 293.

70 *Seward replied to Weed:* Stahr, *Seward*, 125–27; Wilentz, *Rise of American Democracy*, 921; Seward, *1846–1861*, 129; Stevenson, *Works of Henry Clay*, 446–47.

70 *On the evening of March 30:* Wiltse, *John C. Calhoun: Sectionalist,* 477–79; John Wentworth, *Congressional Reminiscences* (Chicago: Fergus Printing, 1882), 23.

71 *For three weeks, Calhoun's body was transported:* Robert Barnwell Rhett, *The Death and Funeral Ceremonies of John Caldwell Calhoun* (Columbia, S.C.: A. S. Johnston, 1850), 27–28, 77.

71 *The trading of insults went back and forth:* William M. Meigs, *The Life of Thomas Hart Benton* (Philadelphia: J. B. Lippincott, 1904), 392–400; Henry S. Foote,

Casket of Reminiscences (Washington, D.C.: Chronicle Publishing, 1874), 337–9; Holman Hamilton, *Prologue to Conflict: The Crisis and Compromise of 1850* (Lexington: University Press of Kentucky, 1964), 93.

72 *Nine Southern states sent delegates:* Avery Craven, *The Growth of Southern Nationalism* (Baton Rouge: Louisiana State University Press, 1953), 93–98; Eric H. Walther, *The Fire-Eaters* (Baton Rouge: Louisiana State University Press, 1992), 139; Seward, *1846–1861*, 137–38.

73 *President Taylor was in a commanding position:* Foote, *Casket of Reminiscences*, 26.

73 *At a private dinner, the odd couple:* Ibid., 27.

74 *Clay cleverly suggested:* George Fort Milton, *The Eve of Conflict: Stephen A. Douglas and the Needless War* (New York: Octagon, 1969), 69.

74 *Introduced on May 8, Taylor ridiculed the bill: Congressional Globe*, 31st Congress, 1st Session, 612–15.

75 *Despite his rhetorical exertion:* Ford, *History of Illinois*, 172, 175; Remini, *Henry Clay*, 749; Seward, *1846–1861*, 134, 137.

75 *Seward's disgust at Clay:* Seward, *1846–1861*, 139, 141.

76 *"Seward delivered his second major speech": Congressional Globe*, 31st Congress, 1st Session, 1021–24.

76 *While Clay labored:* Helen Haines, *History of New Mexico* (New York: New Mexico Historical Publishing, 1891), 198–200; Le Baron Bradford Prince, *A Concise History of New Mexico* (Cedar Rapids, Iowa: Torch Press, 1912), 189–90; W. W. H. Davis, *El Gringo: New Mexico and Her People* (New York: Harper & Brothers, 1857), 111; Constitution of the State of New Mexico, 1850 (Santa Fe: Stagecoach Press, 1965); Zachary Taylor: "Special Message," The American Presidency Project, http: //www.presidency.ucsb.edu/ws/?pid=68100.

77 *Contemptuous of the president:* Weed, *The Life of Thurlow Weed*, 2:180; Hamilton, *Prologue to Conflict*, 104.

78 *Crawford misled the president:* Rhodes, *History of the United States*, 1:203–4.

78 *Crawford was not only dishonest:* J. F. H. Claiborne, *Life and Correspondence of John A. Quitman: Major-General, U.S.A. and Governor of the State of Mississippi* (New York: Harper & Brothers, 1860), 2:33.

78 *Taylor decided to shake up his cabinet:* Weed, *The Life of Thurlow Weed*, 2:589–91; Phillips, *Life of Robert Toombs*, 79.

79 *Southern Whigs in the Congress:* Phillips, *Life of Robert Toombs*, 83; Claiborne, *Life and Correspondence of John A. Quitman*, 32–33.

79 *Toombs and Stephens visited Taylor:* Alexander Stephens, *Recollections of Alexander H. Stephens* (New York: Doubleday, Page, and Co., 1910), 26.

80 *While Toombs and Stephens delivered: Congressional Globe*, 31st Congress, 1st Session, 1091.

80 *Toombs and Stephens enraged Taylor:* Weed, *The Life of Thurlow Weed*, 2:180.

80 *On July 4th, the* National Intelligencer: Ulrich B. Phillips, ed., *The Correspondence*

of Robert Toombs, Alexander H. Stephens, and Howell Cobb (Washington, D.C.: Government Printing Office, 1913), 193.

81 *As Stephens's inflammatory article was being circulated:* Foote, *Casket of Reminiscences*, 166–68.

81 *On July 6, Congressman Stanly took the House floor:* Edward Stanly, *The Galphin Claim* (Washington, D.C.: Library of Congress, 1850), 8.

81 *In the House, on the morning:* Gerald S. Greenberg, "Ohioans vs. Georgians: The Galphin Claim, Zachary Taylor's Death, and the Congressional Adjournment Vote of 1850," *Georgia Historical Quarterly* 74, no. 4 (Winter 1990), 575–98; Joan F. Cashin, *First Lady of the Confederacy: Varina Davis's Civil War* (Cambridge: Harvard University Press, 2006), 56.

CHAPTER THREE: THE ART OF THE DEAL

83 *Millard Fillmore was now president:* Weed, *The Life of Thurlow Weed*, 2:184, 1:385.

83 *Millard Fillmore's incredible rise:* Rhodes, *History of the United States*, 1:178; Thurlow Weed and Thurlow Weed Barnes, *Memoir of Thurlow Weed* (Boston: Houghton Mifflin, 1884), 2:196; Carl Schurz, *The Reminiscences of Carl Schurz, Volume 2, 1852–1863* (New York: Doubleday, Page, and Co., 1913), 2:7.

85 *As vice president, Fillmore had been surreptitiously:* Michael F. Holt, "Politics, Patronage, and Public Policy," 31; Frank Hayward Severance, ed., *Millard Fillmore Papers* (Buffalo, N.Y.: Buffalo Historical Society, 1907), 11:323.

85 *The day after Taylor's death:* Seward, *1846–1861*, 145–46.

85 *Rumors wafted through Washington:* Ibid., 146; Colton, *The Last Seven Years of the Life of Henry Clay*, 172; Henry Washington Hilliard, *Politics and Pen Pictures at Home and Abroad* (New York: G. P. Putnam's Sons, 1892), 231; Phillips, *Life of Robert Toombs*, 89–90; Calvin Colton, ed., *The Private Correspondence of Henry Clay* (New York: A. S. Barnes & Co., 1855), 201.

89 *Senator William L. Dayton: Congressional Globe*, 31st Congress, 1st Session, July 25, 1850, 1442–47.

90 *The war on Seward and Weed:* Weed, *Life of Thurlow Weed*, 2:184; Seward, *1846–1861*, 148.

91 *By consolidating all the elements:* Seward, *1846–1861*, 150; Remini, *Henry Clay*, 756–58.

91 *Benton, exultant and mocking: Congressional Globe*, 31st Congress, 1st Session, 1484.

92 *At thirty-seven years old:* Thomas J. McCormack, ed., *Memoirs of Gustave Koerner* (Cedar Rapids, Iowa: Torch Press, 1909), 1:449.

92 *The compromise had hit the end of the line:* Henry Parker Willis, *Stephen A. Douglas* (Philadelphia: G. W. Jacobs, 1910), 112; Robert Walter Johannsen, *Stephen A. Douglas* (New York: Oxford University Press, 1973), 309–11; Allen Johnson, *Stephen A. Douglas: A Study in American Politics* (New York: Macmillan, 1908), 169.

93 *Douglas's Illinois Central would not originate:* Jack Harpster, *The Railroad Tycoon*

Who Built Chicago: A Biography of William B. Ogden (Carbondale: Southern Illinois University Press, 2009), 125; Donald L. Miller, *City of the Century: The Epic of Chicago and the Making of America* (New York: Simon & Schuster, 1996), 88, 91.

93 *As Douglas laid the groundwork:* Johannsen, *Stephen A. Douglas*, 335–36.

93 *"He had an inspiration for land":* John W. Forney, *Anecdotes of Public Men* (New York: Harper & Brothers, 1873), 1:18–20.

94 *Douglas's grandiose plan for the Illinois Central:* J. Madison Cutts, *A Brief Treatise on Constitutional and Party Questions* (New York: D. Appleton, 1866), 189–93.

94 *Douglas, however, faced a bigger obstacle:* Ibid., 193; Milton, *Eve of Conflict*, 9–10.

95 *Douglas, once rejected by Mary Todd as louche:* Johannsen, *Stephen A. Douglas*, 207–11.

95 *Douglas never uttered an antislavery sentiment:* Ibid., 236–37.

96 *At the beginning of his brilliant career: Congressional Globe*, 30th Congress, 1st Session, 507.

96 *During the 1848 campaign:* Johannsen, *Stephen A. Douglas*, 253–54.

97 *Facing difficulties in his home state:* Cutts, *Brief Treatise on Constitutional and Party Questions*, 193–95.

98 *Much of the propaganda for the compromise:* Hamilton, *Prologue to Conflict*, 126–28, 131; Holman Hamilton and James L. Crouthamel, "Man for Both Parties: Francis J. Grund as Political Chameleon," *Pennsylvania Magazine of History and Biography* 97, no. 4 (October 1973), 465–84.

98 *When Clay's "Omnibus" failed:* Hamilton, *Prologue to Conflict*, 129.

98 *But there was another persuasive force:* Kermit L. Hall, *The Politics of Justice* (Lincoln: University of Nebraska Press, 1976), 95; Michael F. Holt, "Politics, Patronage, and Public Policy," 27, 29, 31–34; Robert V. Remini, *Daniel Webster: The Man and His Time* (New York: W. W. Norton, 1997), 695.

99 *When the Fugitive Slave Act:* Johannsen, *Stephen A. Douglas*, 296; Milton, *Eve of Conflict*, 77; *Congressional Globe*, 31st Congress, 1st Session, 1664.

99 *In the antic last days of voting:* Hamilton, *Prologue to Conflict*, 157, 160, 128.

100 *"If any man":* Wilentz, *Rise of American Democracy*, 643.

100 *While Douglas was orchestrating passage:* Hamilton, *Prologue to Conflict*, 121; Johannsen, *Stephen A. Douglas*, 313.

100 *The day after the celebration of the compromise:* Johannsen, *Stephen A. Douglas*, 310–14; Wentworth, *Congressional Reminiscences*, 40–42.

101 *"It was the votes of Massachusetts":* William K. Ackerman, *Early Illinois Railroads* (Chicago: Fergus Printing, 1884), 89; Cutts, *Brief Treatise on Constitutional and Party Questions*, 199.

101 *A blue-chip board:* Johannsen, *Stephen A. Douglas,* 316–17.

101 *The legend of the compromise took hold:* Foote, *Casket of Reminiscences*, 30–31.

101 *Clay played the role of the hero:* Remini, *Henry Clay*, 766–68.

102 *In his Annual Message to the Congress:* Millard Fillmore, "First Annual Mes-

sage," The American Presidency Project, http: //www.presidency.ucsb.edu /ws/?pid=29491; *Congressional Globe*, 31st Congress, 1st Session, 1856.

103 *At its core, the "final settlement" contained:* David Morris Potter, *The Impending Crisis, 1848–1861* (New York: Harper & Row, 1976), 156–58.

103 *Fillmore had approved the compromise:* Weed, *The Life of Thurlow Weed*, 2:588; Remini, *Henry Clay*, 762.

104 *In New Mexico, the compromise provided:* Hubert Howe Bancroft, *Arizona and New Mexico, 1530–1888* (San Francisco: A. L. Bancroft, 1888), 681–5; Haines, *History of New Mexico*, 204.

CHAPTER FOUR: THE CONSEQUENCES OF THE PEACE

105 *In the flush of victory, President Fillmore sought:* Seward, *1846–1861*, 155–56.

106 *The first political test of the compromise:* De Alva Stanwood Alexander, *A Political History of the State of New York* (New York: H. Holt, 1906), 2:153–57; Edward Everett, ed., *The Writings and Speeches of Daniel Webster* (Boston: Little, Brown, 1903), 12:252; Weed, *The Life of Thurlow Weed*, 186–89.

108 *Of course, it was Webster himself:* Theodore Parker, *A Discourse Occasioned by the Death of Daniel Webster* (Boston: Benjamin B. Mussey, 1853), 49–53; Joel Porte, ed., *Emerson in His Journals* (Cambridge: Harvard University Press, 1982), 421; Ralph Waldo Emerson, *Complete Works* (Cambridge, Mass.: Riverside Press, 1883), 4:172; Robert C. Winthrop, *Memoir of Robert C. Winthrop* (Boston: Little, Brown, 1897), 198; Everett, ed., *Writings and Speeches of Daniel Webster*, 560, 568–69; David Herbert Donald, *Charles Sumner and the Coming of the Civil War* (Chicago: University of Chicago Press, 1960), 184; Peterson, *Great Triumvirate*, 480.

108 *In Massachusetts, Conscience Whigs and Democrats:* Donald, *Charles Sumner and the Coming of the Civil War*, 192–94; Everett, ed., *Writings and Speeches of Daniel Webster*, 575.

109 *Webster's battle with Boston's abolitionists:* Octavius Brooks Frothingham, *Theodore Parker: A Biography* (Boston: J. R. Osgood, 1874), 401–2; William Still, *Still's Underground Railroad Records* (Philadelphia: William Still, 1886), 368–74; Henry Steele Commager, *Theodore Parker: Yankee Crusader* (Boston: Little, Brown, 1936), 214–15.

110 *Webster was infuriated:* Everett, ed., *Writings and Speeches of Daniel Webster*, 576; Peterson, *Great Triumvirate*, 481; William Craft and Ellen Craft, *Running a Thousand Miles for Freedom: or, The Escape of William and Ellen Craft from Slavery* (London: William Tweedie, 1860), 88.

110 *In the aftermath of the Crafts' escape:* Everett, ed., *Writings and Speeches of Daniel Webster*, 579; Commager, *Theodore Parker*, 219.

110 *In February 1851, Commissioner Curtis issued:* Commager, *Theodore Parker*, 219; Fergus Bordewich, *Bound for Canaan: The Epic Story of the Underground Railroad* (New York: HarperCollins, 2009), 321.

111 *Webster was apoplectic:* Remini, *Daniel Webster,* 696; Millard Fillmore, "Proclamation 56—Calling On Citizens to Assist in the Recapture of a Fugitive Slave Arrested in Boston, Massachusetts," The American Presidency Project, http://www.presidency.ucsb.edu/ws/?pid=68154; Peterson, *Triumvirate,* 481; Holt, *Rise and Fall of the Whig Party,* 605.

111 *On Washington's Birthday:* Everett, ed., *Writings and Speeches of Daniel Webster,* 263.

111 *Aroused by the spectacular Shadrach escape:* Stevenson, *Works of Henry Clay,* 609–28.

112 *Webster soon got his chance: Trial of Thomas Sims* (Boston: W. S. Damrell, 1851), 9; Commager, *Theodore Parker,* 220–23; Remini, *Daniel Webster,* 696; Severance, ed., *Millard Fillmore Papers,* 341; Everett, ed., *Writings and Speeches of Daniel Webster,* 606.

112 *For four months the Massachusetts legislature:* Donald, *Charles Sumner and the Coming of the Civil War,* 200–3; George Ticknor Curtis, *A Memoir of Benjamin Robbins Curtis* (Boston: Little, Brown, 1879), 143.

113 *Webster embarked on a two-months-long:* Daniel Webster, *Mr. Webster's Speeches at Buffalo, Syracuse, and Albany, May, 1851* (New York: Mirror Office, 1851), 8; Peterson, *Great Triumvirate,* 482–83.

114 *Toombs's captured slave:* Stanley Harrold, *Subversives: Antislavery Community in Washington, D.C., 1828–1865* (Baton Rouge: Louisiana University Press, 2002), 146–62; Mark Scroggins, *Robert Toombs: The Civil Wars of a United States Senator and Confederate General* (Jefferson, N.C.: McFarland, 2011), 66–67; Tom Calarco, *The Underground Railroad in the Adirondack Region* (Jefferson, N.C.: McFarland, 2004), 112–13; Ira Berlin, ed., *The Black Military Experience* (New York: Cambridge University Press, 1982), 348–49.

114 *Their provocations "had been made with the object":* Ulrich Bonnell Phillips, "George and State Rights," in *Annual Report of the American Historical Association* (Washington, D.C.: Government Printing Office, 1901), 163–64; John Campbell Butler, *Historical Record of Macon and Central Georgia* (Macon, Ga.: J. W. Burke, 1879), 194–95; William C. Davis, *Rhett: The Turbulent Life and Times of a Fire-Eater* (Columbia: University of South Carolina Press, 2001), 290, 310, 330–31; Phillips, *Life of Robert Toombs,* 96; Alexander Stephens, *A Constitutional View of the War Between the States* (Philadelphia: National Publishing, 1870), 2:235; M. J. White, *The Secession Movement in the United States, 1847–1852* (New Orleans: Tulane University Press, 1910), 86–88.

115 *In Mississippi, Quitman, a splenetic secessionist:* Foote, *Casket of Reminiscences,* 352, 356; William J. Cooper, Jr., *Jefferson Davis, American* (New York: Alfred A. Knopf, 2000), 205–23, 240–41.

116 *So, the Compromise described in the Georgia Platform:* Milton, *Eve of Conflict,* 78; Johnson, *Stephen A. Douglas,* 189–90.

117 *The making of the Compromise: Congressional Globe,* 35th Congress, 1st Session, 365.

118 *"Oh, young Lochinvar":* Edward L. Widmer, *Young America: The Flowering of De-*

mocracy in New York City (New York: Oxford University Press, 1999), 194–95; Roy Franklin Nichols, *The Democratic Machine, 1850–1854* (New York: AMS Press, 1967), 107; Henry M. Flint, *Life of Stephen A. Douglas* (New York: Derby & Jackson, 1860), 51.

118   *His career was his greatest speculation:* Johannsen, *Stephen A. Douglas*, 298.

119   *The Compromise was only the first car:* John E. Clark, *Railroads in the Civil War: The Impact of Management on Victory and Defeat* (Baton Rouge: Louisiana State University Press, 2004), 11–12.

119   *Some historians have justified:* Robert V. Remini, *At the Edge of the Precipice: Henry Clay and the Compromise That Saved the Union* (New York: Basic Books, 2010), xiii, 158. See William G. Thomas, *The Iron Way: Railroads, the Civil War, and the Making of Modern America* (New Haven: Yale University Press, 2011); Aaron Wagner Marrs, *The Iron Horse Turns South: A History of Antebellum Southern Railroads* (Columbia: University of South Carolina, ProQuest, 2006), 113–14; Orville Vernon Burton and Patricia Dora Bonnin, "King Cotton," *The Confederacy*, A Macmillan Information Now Encyclopedia, http://www.civilwarhome.com/kingdom.htm; David Brion Davis, "Free at Last: The Enduring Legacy of the South's Civil War Victory," *New York Times*, August 26, 2001.

121   *This resolution was to be ratified by a mass meeting:* Johannsen, *Stephen A. Douglas*, 301–3; Milton, *Eve of Conflict*, 83.

121   *Douglas was convinced he had subdued:* Flint, *Life of Stephen A. Douglas*, 303, 54–5; Johannsen, *Stephen A. Douglas*, 303.

122   *About the time Douglas was subduing:* Charles Edward Stowe and Harried Beecher Stowe, *Harriet Beecher Stowe: The Story of Her Life* (Boston: Houghton Mifflin, 1911), 138–39;

122   *Harriet Beecher Stowe belonged to the preeminent family:* David S. Reynolds, *Mightier than the Sword: Uncle Tom's Cabin and the Battle for America* (New York: W. W. Norton, 2011), 90–93, 96; Charles Edward Stowe and Lyman Beecher Stowe, *Harriet Beecher Stowe: The Story of Her Life*, Boston: Houghton Mifflin, 1911, 138-9.

123   *Harriet married Calvin Stowe:* Reynolds. *Mightier,* 96.

123   *In January 1850, visiting her brother:* Reynolds, *Mightier,* 105–15, 118–19; Charles Beecher, *The Duty of Disobedience to Wicked Laws: A Sermon on the Fugitive Slave Act* (Newark: J. McIlvaine, 1851), 13; Harriet Beecher Stowe, edited by Annie Fields, *Life and Letters of Harriet Beecher Stowe* (Boston: Houghton Mifflin, 1898), 163.

124   *Stowe prayed her book would:* Reynold, *Mightier than the Sword*, 130; Sewell, *Ballots for Freedom*, 232–33.

124   *Douglas took to the Senate floor to denounce the book: Congressional Globe,* 32nd Congress, 1st Session, 275–76.

125   *Lincoln would meet Harriet Beecher Stowe:* Stowe, *Life and Letters of Harriet Beecher Stowe,* 202–3; Daniel R. Vollaro, "Lincoln, Stowe and the 'Little Woman/*

Great War' Story: The Making, and Breaking, of a Great American Anecdote," *Journal of the Abraham Lincoln Association* 30, no. 1 (Winter 2009); *Lincoln Herald*, Vols. 54–55 (Harrogate, Tenn.: Lincoln Memorial University Press, 1952); Rufus Rockwell Wilson, *Intimate Memories of Lincoln* (Elmira: Primavera Press, 1945), 305.

126 *The* Pequod, *named for a tribe:* Alan Heimert, "Moby-Dick and American Political Symbolism," *American Quarterly* 15, no. 4 (Winter 1963), 498–534; Sidney Kaplan, "The Moby Dick in the Service of the Underground Railroad," *Phylon* 12, no. 2 (November 2, 1951); Wilentz, *The Rise of American Democracy*, 653–54; Herman Melville, *Moby-Dick; or, the Whale* (New York: Scribner, 1902), 491–92.

CHAPTER FIVE: WHAT IS TO BE DONE?

129 *William Dean Howells, editor of* The Atlantic: William Dean Howells, *Life of Abraham Lincoln* (Columbus, Ohio: Follett, Foster, 1860), 69–70; David Herbert Donald, *Lincoln* (New York: Simon & Schuster, 1995), 161.

130 *Lincoln sanctioned this bowdlerized version:* Rodney O. Davis and Douglas L. Wilson, eds., *The Lincoln-Douglas Debates* (Urbana: University of Illinois Press, 2008), 11; Michael Burlingame, *Abraham Lincoln: A Life* (Baltimore: Johns Hopkins University Press, 2008), 1:358.

131 *He reeled from regret to tragedy:* Ruth Painter Randall, *Mary Lincoln: Biography of a Marriage* (New York: Little, Brown, 1959), 140–42, 146; Burlingame, *Abraham Lincoln*, 1:358–59.

131 *Mary was subject to panic attacks:* Randall, *Mary Lincoln*, 118–19, 121; Michael Burlingame, *The Inner World Abraham Lincoln* (Urbana: University of Illinois Press, 1994), 62; Jean H. Baker, "Mary Todd Lincoln: Managing Home, Husband, and Children," *Journal of the Abraham Lincoln Association* 11, no. 1 (1990); "An Evening with Abraham Lincoln," *Sacramento Daily Union*, June 21, 1860.

132 *When he was at home:* Herndon and Weik, *Herndon's Lincoln*, 473; Donald, *Lincoln*, 147; "Lincoln's Little Blue Pills," Science Daily, http://www.sciencedaily.com/releases/2001/07/010719080146.htm; N. Hirschhorn, R. G. Feldman, and I. A. Greaves, "Abraham Lincoln's Blue Pills," *Perspectives in Biology and Medicine* 44 (Summer 2001), 315–32.

133 *"I don't think that Mrs. Lincoln":* Douglas L. Wilson, Rodney O. Davis, Terry Wilson, William Henry Herndon, and Jesse William Weik, eds., *Herndon's Informants: Letters, Interviews, and Statements About Abraham Lincoln* (Urbana: University of Illinois Press, 1998) (hereinafter HI), 453; *Abraham Lincoln Quarterly* 5, no. 7, http://quod.lib.umich.edu/a/alajournals/0599998.0005.007?view =text&seq=14.

133 *Just after Mary gave birth:* CW, 2:15–16, 96–97; Miller, *Lincoln and His World*, 3:288–89.

133 *Mary never had any use:* Emanuel Hertz, *The Hidden Lincoln: From the Letters and Papers of William H. Herndon* (New York: Blue Ribbon Books, 1940), 109.

134 *Lincoln's law practice:* HI, 509, 348.

134 *The office of Lincoln & Herndon was in a red-brick building:* Herndon and Weik, *Herndon's Lincoln*, 255–56; Wayne C. Temple, "Herndon on Lincoln: An Unknown Interview with a List of Books in the Lincoln & Herndon Law Office," *Journal of the Illinois State Historical Society* 98, nos. 1–2 (Spring 2005), 34–50.

135 *Lincoln was what was called:* Burlingame, *Abraham Lincoln*, 1:342–6; Tom Mackaman, "Understanding Lincoln: An Interview with Historian Allen Guelzo," World Socialist Web Site, http://www.wsws.org/en/articles/2013/04/03/guel-a03.html; "The Law Practice of Abraham Lincoln: A Statistical Portrait," The Law Practice of American Lincoln, http://www.lawpracticeofabrahamlincoln.org/Reference.aspx?ref=Reference%20html%20files/StatisticalPortrait.html; Henry Clay Whitney, *Life on the Circuit with Lincoln* (Boston: Estes & Lauriat, 1892), 261–62; Joseph Fort Newton, *Lincoln and Herndon* (Cedar Rapids, Iowa: Torch Press, 1910), 31; Albert A. Woldman, *Lawyer Lincoln* (New York: Houghton Mifflin, 1936), 177–81.

135 *The executive who refused to pay Lincoln:* Stephen W. Sears, *George B. McClellan: The Young Napoleon* (New York: Ticknor & Fields, 1988), 50–51, 59; George Brinton McClellan and William Cowper Prime, *McClellan's Own Story* (New York: C. L. Webster, 1887), 34; William Starr Myers, *A Study in Personality: General George Brinton McClellan* (New York: D. Appleton, 1934), 108.

136 *Every spring and fall:* Whitney, *Life of Lincoln*, 193–94; HI, 348.

137 *"In those early days":* Ibid., 188, 255–56, 258–59.

138 *Having only attended a backwoods:* CW, 2:459, 3:511; Herndon and Weik, *Herndon's Lincoln,* 247–48.

138 *Perfecting his method:* HI, 350; Thomas Paine, *The Age of Reason* (New York: V. Parke, 1908), 110–11; Drew R. McCoy, "An 'Old-Fashioned' Nationalism: Lincoln, Jefferson, and the Classical Tradition," *Journal of the Abraham Lincoln Association* 23, no. 1 (Winter 2002).

139 *"In the course of my law-reading":* "Mr. Lincoln's Early Life.; How He Educated Himself," *New York Times*, September 4, 1864; Francis B. Carpenter, *The Inner Life of Abraham Lincoln: Six Months at the White House* (New York: Hurd & Houghton, 1872), 313–14.

139 *Euclid filled a gaping hole:* CW, 3:62.

140 *As his thought was developing: Transactions of the Illinois State Historical Society for the Year 1919* (Springfield, Ill.: The Society, 1920), 91.

140 *Lincoln preferred in retrospect:* Hertz, *Hidden Lincoln*, 96, 172; CW, 3:67; Paul Findley, *A. Lincoln: The Crucible of Congress* (New York: Crown, 1979), 218; CW, 2:79; Miller, *Lincoln and His World*, 3:280.

141 *While the great debate:* Paul M. Angle, *"Here I Have Lived": A History of Lincoln's Springfield* (New Brunswick, N.J.: Rutgers University Press, 1935), 205–6.

141 *The Whig candidate was Richard Yates:* Usher M. Linder, *Reminiscences of the Early Bench and Bar of Illinois* (Chicago: Chicago Legal News Company, 1879), 229; Lorelei Steuer, "A Logical Alma Mater: Lincoln and Illinois College," *Illinois Heritage* (June 2006); Miller, *Lincoln and His World*, 3:280, 385 fn. 214.

141 *Harris, the Democrat, had defeated: Congressional Globe*, 31st Congress, 1st Session, 413; Miller, *Lincoln and His World*, 3:282–83.

142 *Herndon sought even at a late date:* "Facts Illustrative of Mr. Lincoln's Patriotism and Statesmanship: A Lecture by William H. Herndon," *Abraham Lincoln Quarterly* 3, no. 4 (December 1944), 189.

142 *Lincoln provided Yates:* Findley, *A. Lincoln*, 163.

143 *Yates stunned Harris:* Holt, *Rise and Fall of the Whig Party*, 566–67; Miller, *Lincoln and His World*, 3:284.

144 *Beginning in 1849, Lincoln's public:* Miller, *Lincoln and His World*, 3:223.

144 *Lincoln was likely the author of this anonymous article:* HI, 146.

145 *"The Kentucky state convention":* Whitney, *Life on the Circuit with Lincoln*, 343.

145 *Experiencing the realities of slavery:* HI, 183–84.

146 *After returning from the Congress:* HI, 64.

147 *But that time had not come:* Ward Hill Lamon, *The Life of Abraham Lincoln* (Boston: James R. Osgood, 1872), 2:341; CW, 3:382–83.

147 *Herndon recalled traveling with Lincoln:* Lamon, *Life of Abraham Lincoln*, 2:335.

148 *But Lincoln's orbit in these years:* HI, 731–32.

148 *But after the storytelling and the pillow fights:* HI, 308–9.

CHAPTER SIX: A HERO'S WELCOME

152 *"Agitation," of course:* Millard Fillmore, "Second Annual Message," The American Presidency Project, http://www.presidency.ucsb.edu/ws/?pid=29492.

152 *Thus you will see that all causes:* John Minor Botts, *The Great Rebellion: Its Secret History, Rise, Progress, and Disastrous Failure* (New York: Harper & Brothers, 1866), 110.

153 *"The North (or free States) comprises":* Mann, *Life of Horace Mann*, 353.

153 *Northern Whigs were in headlong retreat:* Wilson, *History of the Rise and Fall of the Slave Power in America*, 2:353–54.

154 *The Hungarian celebrity brought along a ragtag entourage:* Stahr, *Seward*, 134.

155 *Foote opened the congressional session:* Foote, *Casket of Reminiscences*, 87–88; Rhodes, *History of the United States*, 1:243.

156 *Foote and Davis, both with hair-trigger tempers:* William W. Freehling, *The Road to Disunion: Secessionists Triumphant, 1854–1861* (New York: Oxford University Press, 2007), 1:526–28; Don E. Fehrenbacher, *The Slaveholding Republic* (New York: Oxford University Press, 2001), 49.

157 *Seward viewed Kossuth's arrival:* Holt, *Rise and Fall of the Whig Party*, 694; Thomas Bender, *A Nation Among Nations: America's Place in World History* (New York: Hill & Wang, 2006), 127.

157   *But even before Kossuth arrived:* Richard H. Sewell, *Ballots for Freedom: Antislavery Politics in the United States, 1837–1860* (New York: Oxford University Press, 1976), 235; William Henry Seward, *Welcome to Kossuth: Speeches of William H. Seward, on the Joint Resolution in Honor of Louis Kossuth* (Washington D.C.: Congressional Globe Office, 1851).

158   *Kossuth's visit aroused comparisons:* McCormack, *Memoirs of Gustave Koerner,* 578.

158   *Rebuked by Fillmore, Kossuth next paid:* "Kossuth, the Orator and Statesman," *American Whig Review* 15, no. 85 (January 1852); "The Interview Between Kossuth and Henry Clay," *New York Times,* January 13, 1852.

160   *After Kossuth left the capital:* Holt, *Rise and Fall of the Whig Party,* 692–94; Rhodes, *History of the United States,* 1:232–41; Sewell, *Ballots for Freedom,* 235; Benjamin Perley Poore, *Perley's Reminiscences of Sixty Years in the Capital* (Philadelphia: Hubbard Brothers, 1885), 1: 404–6; Robert D. Ilisevich, *Galusha A. Grow: The People's Candidate* (Pittsburgh: University of Pittsburgh Press, 1989), 45; Johannsen, *Stephen A. Douglas,* 331; *The Life of Gov. Louis Kossuth: With His Public Speeches in the United States* (New York: W. Lord, 1852), 151; Richard Malcolm Johnston and William Hand Browne, *Life of Alexander H. Stephens* (Philadelphia: J. B. Lippincott, 1883), 266; Stahr, *Seward,* 134-5.

160   *When Kossuth went in search of funds:* Donald S. Spencer, *Louis Kossuth and Young America: A Study of Sectionalism and Foreign Policy, 1848–1852* (Columbia: University of Missouri Press, 1977), 102–3; Elizabeth Fox-Genovese and Eugene Genovese, *The Mind of the Master Class: History and Faith in the Southern Slaveholders' Worldview* (New York: Cambridge University Press, 2005), 57–61.

160   *Kossuth quickly grasped that he should:* McCormack, *Memoirs of Gustave Koerner,* 1:579.

161   *In New York, Kossuth privately:* Spencer, *Louis Kossuth and Young America,* 67, 78; Rhodes, *History of the United States,* 1:235; Albert Reville, ed., *The Life and Writing of Theodore Parker* (London: British and Foreign Unitarian Association, 1877), 193; Letter to Louis Kossuth, *Concerning Slavery in the United States* (Boston: Wallcut, 1852).

162   *Near the end of Kossuth's tour:* Francis William Newman, *Selected Speeches of Kossuth* (New York: C. S. Francis, 1854), 212; Eugenio F. Biagini, " 'The Principle of Humanity': Lincoln in Germany and Italy, 1859–1865," in *The Global Lincoln,* Richard Carwardine and Jay Sexton, eds. (New York: Oxford University Press, 2011), 81; *Kossuth in New England: A Full Account of the Hungarian Governor's Visit to Massachusetts* (Boston: J.P. Jewett, 1852), 213; Seward, *1846-1860,* 176.

163   *The declaration's first point supported:* Miller, *Lincoln and His World,* 3:305; CW, 2:117; Matthew Norman, "Abraham Lincoln, Stephen A. Douglas, the Model Republic, and the Right of Revolution, 1848–61," in *Politics and Culture of the Civil War Era: Essays in Honor of Robert W. Johannsen,* Daniel J. MacDonough and Kenneth W. Noe, eds. (Selinsgrove, Pa.: Susquehanna University Press, 2006), 160.

163   *The Kossuth episode was undoubtedly central:* CW, 2:255, 276; 3:14.

164   *After his American tour, Kossuth settled into exile:* Schurz, *Reminiscences of Carl Schurz*, 1:51; McCormack, *Memoirs of Gustave Koerner*, 1:579.

164   *Kossuth's Hungarian rhapsody:* "Democratic Party Platform of 1852," The American Presidency Project, http://www.presidency.ucsb.edu/ws/?pid=29575; "Whig Party Platform of 1852," The American Presidency Project, http://www.presidency.ucsb.edu/ws/?pid=25856.

CHAPTER SEVEN: THE MAKING OF THE DARK HORSE

168   *The Little Giant stood atop:* Johnson, *Stephen A. Douglas*, 199–200.

169   *"The South does not put forward":* Edward Widmer, *Young America: The Flowering of Democracy in New York City* (New York: Oxford University Press, 1999), 193; Spencer, *Louis Kossuth and Young America*, 115–16; Johannsen, *Stephen A. Douglas*, 327; Mann, *Life of Horace Mann*, 253.

169   *Douglas's chief campaign supporter:* Johannsen, *Stephen A. Douglas*, 347.

170   *Kossuth had previous dealings:* Tom Chaffin, *Fatal Glory: Narciso López and the First Clandestine U.S. War Against Cuba* (Baton Rouge: Louisiana State University Press, 2003), 25; Yonatan Eyal, *The Young America Movement and the Transformation of the Democratic Party* (New York: Cambridge University Press, 2007), 98–99; Johannsen, *Stephen A. Douglas*, 316.

171   *The means by which Douglas:* Johannsen, *Stephen A. Douglas*, 347; Roy F. Nichols, *The Democratic Machine, 1850–1854* (New York: AMS Press, 1967), 113; Hattie S. Goodman, *The Knox Family* (Richmond, Va.: Whittet & Shepperson, 1905), 129

171   *He was toasted at banquets and private dinners:* Herbert Asbury, *The Gangs of New York* (New York: Random House, 2008), 39; Johannsen, *Stephen A. Douglas*, 349; Nichols, *Democratic Machine*, 111.

171   *From the beginning of his career Douglas:* Johannsen, *Stephen A. Douglas*, 347; Robert Mercer Taliaferro Hunter, *Correspondence of Robert M. T. Hunter, 1826–1876* (Washington, D.C.: Government Printing Office, 1918), 127.

172   *Heir to a plantation fortune:* Wiltse, *John C. Calhoun*, 3:97; Craig M. Simpson, *A Good Southerner: The Life of Henry A. Wise of Virginia* (Chapel Hill: University of North Carolina Press, 2001), 92–93.

172   *Douglas calculated that attracting:* Johannsen, *Stephen A. Douglas*, 355.

174   *Seddon lamented that the Compromise:* Hunter, *Correspondence of Robert M. T. Hunter*, 136–37.

174   *Douglas was unabashed:* Milton, *Eve of Conflict*, 87; Johannsen, *Stephen A. Douglas*, 356–57.

175   *The* Democratic Review: "Eighteen-Fifty-Two and the Presidency," *United States Democratic Review* 31 (January 1852); Johannsen, *Stephen A. Douglas*, 361.

176   *The publication of Sanders's first issue:* Johannsen, *Stephen A. Douglas*, 361.

176 *Sanders wrote Cushing directly:* Ibid.

176 *In an editorial in the next issue:* "The Presidency and the Review," *United States Democratic Review* 31 (February 1852).

176 *Sanders's assault on Butler brought: Congressional Globe,* 32nd Congress, 1st Session, 302.

177 *Sanders launched his missiles in every direction:* "Congress, the Presidency and the Review," *United States Democratic Review* 31 (March 1852); "The Nomination—The 'Old Fogies'—And Fogy Conspiracies," *United States Democratic Review* 31 (April 1852); Nichols, *Democratic Machine,* 102.

177 *Sanders fired another blast:* Milton, *Eve of Conflict,* 88; "Daniel, '76, '98, '44,'48, and a Fast Man!" and "Baltimore Convention—The Future," *United States Democratic Review* 31 (May 1852).

178 *But the corpse laid out was Douglas:* Nichols, *Democratic Machine,* 117; James Shepherd Pike, *First Blows of the Civil War* (New York: American News, 1879), 115.

178 *Douglas's strategy depended upon his unstoppable steam:* John M. Belohlavek, *Broken Glass: Caleb Cushing and the Shattering of the Union* (Kent, Ohio: Kent State University Press, 2005), 234–36.

178 *Nearly seventy years old, Senator Lewis Cass:* Josiah Bushnell Grinnell, *Men and Events of Forty Years* (Boston: D. Lothrop, 1901), 64; Nichols, *Democratic Machine,* 42–52.

179 *James Buchanan, Cass's perennial rival:* Nichols, *Democratic Machine,* 53–78; Philip S. Klein, *President James Buchanan, A Biography* (University Park: Pennsylvania State University Press, 1962), 215.

180 *Marcy's nomination rested on the premise:* Poore, *Perley's Reminiscences of Sixty Years in the Capital,* 1:412; Weed, *Life of Thurlow Weed,* 2:197; Nichols, *Democratic Machine,* 95–105.

180 *Yet another hopeful:* Nichols, *Democratic Machine,* 80–82.

181 *Woodbury's demise left a vacuum:* Ibid., 119–28; Michael F. Holt, *Franklin Pierce* (New York: Macmillan, 2010), 16–22; John Robert Irelan, *History of the Life and Times of Franklin Pierce* (Chicago: Fairbanks & Palmer, 1888), 15, 18; Poore, *Perley's Reminiscences of Sixty Years in the National Metropolis* (Philadelphia: Hubbard Brothers, 1885), 1:414.

182 *"He was always so amiable":* Maunsell Bradhurst Field, *Memories of Many Men* (New York: Harper & Brothers, 1875), 162.

183 *The auspiciously named Edmund Burke:* Nichols, *Democratic Machine,* 125–26.

183 *At the credentials committee hearing:* Robert Rantoul, Jr., *Memoirs, Speeches and Writings of Robert Rantoul, Jr.* (Boston: Jewett, 1854), 816–26; Nichols, *Democratic Machine,* 133–34.

183 *On the morning of June 3:* Nichols, *Democratic Machine,* 134–44; David W. Bartlett, *The Life of Gen. Franklin Pierce of New Hampshire* (New York: Miller, Orton & Mulligan, 1855), 247.

184   *It was a happy nomination:* Nichols, *Democratic Machine*, 144; Bartlett, *Life of Gen. Franklin Pierce of New Hampshire*, 252–53.

184   *An unaware Pierce was meanwhile:* Field, *Memories of Many Men*, 159, 189; Nathaniel Hawthorne, *Life of Franklin Pierce* (Boston: Ticknor, Reed & Fields, 1852); Brenda Wineapple, *Hawthorne: A Life* (New York: Random House, 2004), 265; James M. Lundberg, "Nathaniel Hawthorne: Party Hack," Slate, http://www.slate.com/articles/news_and_politics/history/2012/09/nathaniel_hawthorne_s_biography_of_franklin_pierce_why_d_he_write_it_.html.

185   *The night of Pierce's nomination:* Milton, *Eve of Conflict*, 92.

CHAPTER EIGHT: THE VICTORY MARCH OF OLD FUSS AND FEATHERS

187   *Daniel Webster began his presidential campaign:* Remini, *Great Triumvirate*, 482; Mann, *Life of Horace Mann*, 355.

188   *Webster was authoritative:* Curtis, *Memoir of Benjamin Robbins Curtis*, 2:568.

189   *A humiliated Fillmore glumly:* Paul Finkelman, "Millard Fillmore," in *American Presidents: Critical Essays*, Melvin I. Urofsky, ed. (New York: Taylor & Francis, 2000), 172; Frederick Douglass, *The Life and Times of Frederick Douglass* (Hartford, Conn.: Park Publishing, 1882), 350; Paul Finkelman, *Millard Fillmore* (New York: Macmillan, 2011), 127; Everett, *Writings and Speeches of Daniel Webster*, 4:630.

189   *Webster staged a speaking tour:* Samuel Gridley Howe, *The Servant of Humanity* (Boston: D. Estes, 1909), 379.

190   *In every region, Webster found a paucity:* Peter Harvey, *Reminiscences of Daniel Webster* (Boston: Little, Brown, 1878), 216.

190   *Winfield Scott had been Seward's reserve:* John S. D. Eisenhower, *Agent of Destiny: The Life and Times of General Winfield Scott* (Norman: University of Oklahoma Press, 1999), 205; Stahr, *Seward*, 133.

191   *Seward had run out of military heroes:* Weed, *The Life of Thurlow Weed*, 2:197, 216.

191   *Seward's Washington home was the beehive:* Seward, *1846–1861*, 185.

192   *The Whig convention opened:* Holt, *Rise and Fall of the Whig Party*, 719.

192   *Raymond's rival in the New York:* Augustus Maverick, *Henry J. Raymond and the New York Press, for Thirty Years* (Hartford, Conn.: A. S. Hale, 1870), 119–41.

193   *Raymond's purge trial was an exercise:* "Whig Party Platform of 1852," The American Presidency Project, http://www.presidency.ucsb.edu/ws/?pid=25856.

193   *Webster's men insisted that the convention break:* Samuel Gilman Brown, *The Life of Rufus Choate* (Boston: Little, Brown, 1870), 252; Wilson, *History of the Rise and Fall of the Slave Power in America*, 2:368; Pike, *First Blows of the Civil War*, 152; Holt, *Rise and Fall of the Whig Party*, 723.

194   *"I spent yesterday in receiving":* Seward, *1846–1861*, 187.

194   *Webster felt supremely confident:* Edward G. Parker, *Reminiscences of Rufus Choate* (New York: Mason Brothers, 1860), 259, 66; Peterson, *Triumvirate*, 486.

194   *Sulking in his Washington home:* Nathan Sargent, *Public Men and Events from the Commencement of Mr. Monroe's Administration, in 1817, to the Close of Mr. Fillmore's Administration, in 1853* (Philadelphia: J. B. Lippincott, 1875), 2:389.

195   *Choate raced by train to the capital:* Peterson, *Great Triumvirate,* 486–87; Stephens, *Constitutional View of the Late War Between the States,* 1:336; William E. Gienapp, *The Origins of the Republican Party 1852–1856* (New York: Oxford University Press, 1987), 18–19; Poore, *Perley's Reminiscences of Sixty Years in the National Metropolis,* 1:418; Rhodes, *History of the United States,* 1:257–58, 262.

195   *Toombs, Stephens, and five other:* Phillips, *Life of Robert Toombs*

195   *On the night of Scott's nomination:* Everett, ed., *Writings and Speeches of Daniel Webster,* 4:525, 659; Harvey, *Reminiscences of Daniel Webster,* 195–203; Henry B. Stanton, *Random Recollections* (New York: Harper & Brothers, 1887), 180; Henry Cabot Lodge, *Daniel Webster* (New York: Houghton, Mifflin, 1899), 333.

196   *It was the worst of all possible worlds:* Gienapp, *Origins of the Republican Party,* 19; Seward, *1846–1861,* 187; Rhodes, *History of the United States,* 1:262.

196   *The Whigs lacked confidence and fervor:* Sargent, *Public Men and Events from the Commencement of Mr. Monroe's Administration,* 2:393.

197   *Weed returned from his European travels:* Weed, *The Life of Thurlow Weed,* 2:218–19.

197   *"When will there be a North":* Seward, *1846–1861,* 189; Tyler Dennett, ed., *Lincoln and the Civil War in the Diaries and Letters of John Hay* (New York: Dodd, Mead, 1939), 11.

CHAPTER NINE: THE DEATH OF HENRY CLAY

199   *For almost two months, Henry Clay:* Remini, *Henry Clay,* 783, 766.

200   *Clay's coffin was displayed in the Capitol Rotunda:* "Eulogy of Mr. Seward," in *Monument to the Memory of Henry Clay,* A. H. Carrier, ed. (Cincinnati: W. A. Clarke, 1858), 353–54; Mann, *Life of Horace Mann,* 372–73.

201   *Ninian W. Edwards, Lincoln's brother-in-law:* Miller, *Lincoln and His World,* 3:295–97.

201   *While Lincoln helped local Whigs:* Ibid., 3:307–8.

204   *The question of blacks' humanity:* David S. Heidler and Jeanne T. Heidler, *Henry Clay: The Essential American* (New York: Random House, 2010), 446.

206   *"This sounds strangely in republican America":* Robert Richardson, *Memoirs of Alexander Campbell* (Philadelphia: J. B. Lippincott, 1890), 1:548

206   *Perhaps by not identifying the eminence:* Alexander Campbell, "Slavery and the Fugitive Slave Law," *Millennial Harbinger* 22 (1851), 248–52; D. Newell Williams, Douglas Allen Foster, and Paul M. Blowers, *The Stone-Campbell Movement: A Global History* (St. Louis: Chalice Press, 2013), 37.

207   *"If the Scriptures do not justify slavery":* John Henley Thornwell, *The Rights and Duties of Masters* (Charleston, S.C.: Walker & James, 1850), 14, 25, 37; Fox-Genovese

and, 473, 496, 502; Harriet Beecher Stowe, *The Key to Uncle Tom's Cabin* (London: Clarke, Beeton, 1853), 444–71.

208 *The biblical justification of slavery: Congressional Globe*, 31st Congress, 1st Session, 153.

210 *"Lincoln committed this passage":* CW, 2:121–31.

CHAPTER TEN: THE WATERLOO OF THE WHIGS

211 *"After both the Whigs and the Democrats":* Sewell, *Ballots for Freedom*, 243–45.

212 *"Then Gerrit Smith, the trust fund radical":* Frederick Douglass, *Selected Speeches and Writings*, ed., Philip S. Foner (Chicago: Chicago Review Press, 2000), 208.

212 *Smith's resolutions linking antislavery and women's rights planks, however, provoked intense opposition:* Eric Foner, "Politics and Prejudice: The Free Soil Party and the Negro, 1849–1852," *Journal of Negro History* 50, no. 4 (October 1965), 239–56; Edward Magdol, *Owen Lovejoy: Abolitionist in Congress* (New Brunswick, N.J.: Rutgers University Press, 1967), 99; David W. Blight, *Frederick Douglass' Civil War: Keeping Faith in Jubilee* (Baton Rouge: Louisiana State University Press, 1991), 34–36.

212 *The presumptive candidate of the Free Democrats:* Sewell, *Ballots for Freedom*, 243; Niven, *Salmon P. Chase*, 145–6; George Stanton Denison, ed., *Diary and Correspondence of Salmon P. Chase* (Washington, D.C.: Government Printing Office, 1903), 242–44; Gienapp, *Origins of the Republican Party*, 20.

213 *The Barnburners' return to the Democratic fold:* Seward, *1846–1861*, 184; Alexander, *Political History of the State of New York*, 177; Elisabeth Griffith, *In Her Own Right: The Life of Elizabeth Cady Stanton* (New York: Oxford University Press, 1984), 89; Parke Godwin, *A Biography of W. C. Bryant* (New York: D. Appleton, 1883), 2:63.

215 *The Whig campaign:* Rhodes, *History of the United States*, 1:269–70.

215 *The Democrats ridiculed Scott:* Gienapp, *Origins of the Republican Party*, 23–26; Nichols, *Democratic Machine*, 157–58; Holt, *Rise and Fall of the Whig Party*, 745; Stahr, *Seward*, 138.

216 *Douglas now invoked the Almighty:* Stephen Douglas, *Speech of Hon. Stephen A. Douglas, of Illinois, Delivered in Richmond, Virginia, July 9, 1852* (Richmond, Va.: Richmond Examiner, 1852).

216 *The Whig newspapers unleashed attacks:* Nichols, *Democratic Machine*, 154–57; "A Brief Chapter in the Life of General Franklin Pierce," *National Era*, June 17, 1852.

217 *"Frank. Pierce":* *Frank. Pierce and His Abolition Allies*, Pamphlet, Whig Central Committee, 1852; Nichols, *Democratic Machine*, 156.

218 *After reading an article:* Allen C. Guelzo, *Lincoln and Douglas: The Debates That Defined America* (New York: Simon & Schuster, 2008), 30.

221 *"Now, should Pierce ever be President":* CW, 2:135–57.

221 *Lincoln's reference to "Sally Brown":* George N. Sanders, "The Old Fogies, etc.," *Democratic Review* (April 1852), 375–76.

221 *The Democrats in the end did not nominate*: Miller, *Lincoln and His World*, 3:311–12.

222 *Scott had always been victorious:* Gienapp, *Origins of the Republican Party*, 27–31; Alexander, *Political History of the State of New York*, 2:147.

222 *But Hale, running under the banner:* Sewell, *Ballots for Freedom*, 249.

222 *Gloating about the results:* Phillips, ed., *The Correspondence of Robert Toombs*, 322.

223 *"Was there ever such a deluge":* Stahr, *Seward*, 138; Seward, *1846–1861*, 196.

223 *Ten days after Election Day:* Earl Schenck Miers and William E. Barringer, eds., *Lincoln Day by Day: A Chronology, 1809–1865* (Washington, D.C.: Lincoln Sesquicentennial Commission, Northern Illinois University, 1960), 2:88.

CHAPTER ELEVEN: THE ACTING PRESIDENT OF THE UNITED STATES

225 "Nothing can ruin him": Roy Franklin Nichols, *Franklin Pierce: Young Hickory of the Granite Hills* (University Park: University of Pennsylvania Press, 1931), 217; Charles Eugene Hamlin, *The Life and Times of Hannibal Hamlin* (Cambridge, Mass.: Riverside Press, 1899), 261.

226 *Basking in acclaim:* John M. Belohlavek, *Broken Glass: Caleb Cushing and the Shattering of the Union* (Kent, Ohio: Kent State University Press, 2005), 246; Hamlin, *Life and Times of Hannibal Hamlin,* 261.

226 *Pierce appointed Caleb Cushing:* Rhodes, *History of the United States*, 1:391–92; John W. Forney, *Anecdotes of Public Men* (New York: Harper & Brothers, 1873), 1:229.

227 *"Is it luck? Is it adroitness?":* "The Attorney General," *New York Times*, March 21, and March 19, 1853; Peterson, *Great Triumvirate*, 310; James Russell Lowell, *The Poetical Works: The Biglow Papers* (New York: Houghton Mifflin, 1894), 2:66; Schurz, *Reminiscences of Carl Schurz*, 2:162; Hermann von Holst, *The Constitutional and Political History of the United States, 1850–1854* (Chicago: Callaghan, 1885), 267, 261; Belohlavek, *Broken Glass*, 246.

228 *When Jefferson Davis opened an effusive letter:* Crist, ed., *Papers of Jefferson Davis*, 4:308, 294; Varina Davis, *Jefferson Davis Ex-President of the Confederate States of America* (New York: Belford, 1890), 1:469; Bruce Chadwick, *1858: Abraham Lincoln, Jefferson Davis, Robert E. Lee, Ulysses S. Grant and the War They Failed to See* (Napierville, Ill.: Sourcebooks, 2011), 30; Cooper, *Jefferson Davis*, 216-7.

228 *Davis's venereal disease:* Robert W. Winston, *High Stakes and Hair Trigger: The Life of Jefferson Davis* (New York: Henry Holt, 1930), 55–57.

229 *Pierce's letter beckoning Davis:* Cooper, *Jefferson Davis*, 233, 238; Janet Sharp Hermann, *Joseph E. Davis: Pioneer Patriarch* (Oxford: University Press of Mississippi, 2007), 57; Davis, *Jefferson Davis Ex-President of the Confederate States of America*, 1:480.

230 *In the aftermath of his resounding defeat:* William C. Davis, *Jefferson Davis: The Man and His Hour* (New York: HarperCollins, 1991), 217–18, 242; Cooper, *Jefferson Davis*, 239–41; Crist, ed., *Papers of Jefferson Davis*, 4:150.

230 *By June, Davis stood on the platform:* Crist, ed., *Papers of Jefferson Davis*, 4:264–70; Davis, *Jefferson Davis Ex-President of the Confederate States of America*, 1:166, 169.

231 *Davis identified his physical affliction:* Crist, ed., *Papers of Jefferson Davis*, 4:296.

231 *Speculating about the formation:* Hunter, *Correspondence of Robert M. T. Hunter*, 153–4; Nichols, *Democratic Machine*, 176–77; Crist, ed., *Papers of Jefferson Davis*, 5:3.

232 *When Davis arrived in Washington:* Foote, *Casket of Reminiscences*, 90–91.

232 *At the dawn of this glorious new age:* Jane Walter Venzke and Craig Paul Venzke, "The President's Wife: Jane Means Appleton Pierce, A Woman of Her Time," *Historical New Hampshire*, http://www.nhhistory.org/publications/Revealing_Relationships_Presidents_wife.pdf; David Noon, "Train Wreck," *The Chronicle of Higher Education*, http://chronicle.com/blognetwork/edgeofthewest/2009/01/06/train-wreck/; Davis, *Jefferson Davis Ex-President of the Confederate States of America*, 1:540; Nichols, *Franklin Pierce*, 225, 243.

232 *The death of his son:* Belohlavek, *Broken Glass*, 246.

233 *Franklin and Jane Pierce turned to Jefferson:* William Edward Dodd, *Jefferson Davis* (Lincoln: University of Nebraska Press, 1997), 135; Davis, *Jefferson Davis Ex-President of the Confederate States of America*, 559, 541, 571, 544; Larry Gara, *The Presidency of Franklin Pierce* (Lawrence: University Press of Kansas, 1991), 49.

233 *On a freezing and sleeting Inauguration Day:* "Inaugural Address of Franklin Pierce," The Avalon Project, http://avalon.law.yale.edu/19th_century/pierce.asp; Michael J. C. Taylor, " 'All Hell on Earth': The Pierce Marriage During the White House Years, 1853–1857," in *Life in the White House: A Social History of the First Family and the President's House*, Robert P. Watson, ed. (Albany: State University of New York Press, 2004), 179; Poore, *Perley's Reminiscences of Sixty Years in the National Metropolis*, 424; Rhodes, *History of the United States*, 1:384.

234 *Pierce had still not finished assembling:* Morgan Dix, *Memoirs of John Adams Dix* (New York: Harper & Brothers, 1883), 1:271–72.

235 *Dix was infuriated at the attack:* Ibid., 2:328, 1:207.

235 *The parallel careers:* Paul E. Johnson, James M. McPherson, and Gary Gerstle, *Liberty, Equality, Power: A History of the American People* (Boston: Cengage Learning, 2011), 353; *Congressional Globe*, 30th Congress, 927; Dodd, *Jefferson Davis*, 136.

236 *Denied Dix, Pierce still needed someone:* Holst, *Constitutional and Political History of the United States*, 264.

236 *At the chaotic state Democratic convention:* Alexander, *Political History of the State of New York*, 185–86; Nichols, *Democratic Machine*, 207–8, 211–12; "The Campaign. Hard-Shell Demonstration," *New York Times*, November 4, 1853.

237 *Dix, meanwhile, received further humiliations:* Dix, *Memoirs of John Adams Dix*, 1:277.

237 *When Pierce wrote former secretary of state James Buchanan during the transition:*

George Ticknor Curtis, *Life of James Buchanan: Fifteenth President of the United States* (New York: Harper & Brothers, 1883), 2:71–72.

238 *Jefferson Davis prevailed:* Crist, ed., *Papers of Jefferson Davis*, 5:45; Curtis, *Life of James Buchanan*, 2:78–79.

238 *From England, Buchanan continued to wage war:* Poore, *Perley's Reminiscences of Sixty Years in the National Metropolis*, 1:438.

238 *Buchanan immediately caught the political drift:* Curtis, *Life of James Buchanan*, 2:80.

239 *The "autocrat of the cabinet," as the* New York Times: Davis, *Jefferson Davis: The Man and His Hour*, 243; Cooper, *Jefferson Davis*, 249–55; Sears, *George B. McClellan*, 43–47.

240 *Pierce's patronage policy strictly excluded Whigs:* Cooper, *Jefferson Davis*, 264; "Another Cabinet Letter," *New York Times*, October 26, 1853; Davis, *Jefferson Davis: The Man and His Hour,* 242–43.

241 *When the Congress voted in 1855:* Winfield Scott, *Autobiography of Lieut.-Gen. Winfield Scott* (New York: Sheldon & Co., 1864), 2:593; Cooper, *Jefferson Davis*, 252–54; Winston, *High Stakes and Hair Trigger*, 113–14.

242 *From the moment he took office:* Foote, *Casket of Reminiscences*, 91.

242 *In Georgia, Davis ensured that Howell Cobb:* Helen Ione Greene, "Politics in Georgia, 1853–54: The Ordeal of Howell Cobb," *Georgia Historical Quarterly* 30, no. 3 (September 1946), 185–211.

243 *The party nomination in Alabama:* Nichols, *Franklin Pierce*, 277; Virginia Clay-Clopton, *A Belle of the Fifties* (New York: Doubleday, Page, and Co., 1905), 68.

244 *Jefferson Davis preempted Marcy to secure:* Paul Neff Garber, *The Gadsden Treaty* (Philadelphia: University of Pennsylvania Press, 1924), 78–83, 91, 94; Jere W. Roberson, "The South and the Pacific Railroad, 1845–1855," *Western Historical Quarterly* 5, no. 2 (April 1975), 172.

245 *Gadsden laid out his map based:* Robert E. May, *Manifest Destiny's Underworld: Filibustering in Antebellum America* (Chapel Hill: University of North Carolina Press, 2002), 40–42; William O. Scroggs, *Filibusters and Financiers: The Story of William Walker and His Associates* (New York: Macmillan, 1916), 30–51; Garber, *Gadsden Treaty,* 105–7.

245 *Within weeks of Gadsden's return:* "The Secret History of the Gadsden Treaty," *New York Herald*, January 30, 1854.

245 *The Gadsden Treaty threatened to become a heated:* Garber, *Gadsden Treaty*, 113; Roberson, "The South and the Pacific Railroad," 172.

246 *George N. Sanders once again seized the moment: United States Democratic Review* (July 1853), 89.

246 *Caleb Cushing stepped into the breach:* Rhodes, *History of the United States*, 1:420.

246 *When the 33rd Congress convened: Congressional Globe*, 33rd Congress, 1st Session, 28; Gara, *Presidency of Franklin Pierce*, 52–53, 81; Adam L. Tate, *Conservatism and*

Southern Intellectuals, 1789–1861 (Columbia: University of Missouri Press, 2005), 139–46; Seward, *1846–1860*, 212.

247 *Foote wrote gleefully in his memoir:* Foote, *Casket of Reminiscences*, 91.

247 *The spoils spread to all the factions: Congressional Globe*, 33rd Congress, 1st Session, 194.

248 *For the Southern Rights men:* Nichols, *Democratic Machine*, 225–26; Nichols, *Franklin Pierce*, 313; Clay-Clopton, *Belle of the Fifties*, 58.

248 *Within the supposedly unified and well-balanced cabinet:* Clay-Clopton, *Belle of the Fifties*, 64.

249 *Andrew Pickens Butler of South Carolina was the heir:* Schurz, *Reminiscences of Carl Schurz*, 1:35; John A. Chapman, *History of Edgefield County* (Newberry, S.C.: Elbert H. Hull, 1897), 43; Theodore D. Jervey, "The Butlers of South Carolina," *South Carolina Historical and Genealogical Magazine* 4, no. 4 (October 1903), 296–311; Philip May Hamer, *The Secession Movement in South Carolina, 1847–1852* (Allentown, Pa.: H. R. Haas, 1918), 116, 142; "More of the Jeff. Davis Correspondence," *New York Times*, November 15, 1863.

250 *When the ill Calhoun chose Butler:* Poore, *Perley's Reminiscences of Sixty Years in the National Metropolis*, 1:457; Schurz, *Reminiscences of Carl Schurz*, 1:36–37.

251 *While Calhoun lay dying Mason sat:* Wiltse, *John C. Calhoun: Sectionalist*, 460; Virginia Mason, ed., *The Public Life and Diplomatic Correspondence of James M. Mason* (New York: Neale Publishing, 1906), 72–73.

251 *After the death of Vice President William R. King:* John Wilson Townsend, "David Rice Atchison," *Register of the Kentucky Historical Society* 8 (1910), 38; Richard Lloyd Anderson, "Atchison's Letters and the Causes of Mormon Expulsion from Missouri," *BYU Studies* 26, no. 3 (1986); Henry Miles Moore, *Early History of Leavenworth City and County* (Leavenworth, Kan.: Dodsworth Book Company, 1906), 90.

CHAPTER TWELVE: I, THOMAS HART BENTON

253 *"I, Thomas H. Benton":* Meigs, *Life of Thomas Hart Benton*, 404–5, 409, 452.

254 *Westward went the course of his empire:* Ibid., 302.

255 *Thomas Hart Benton passionately hated his enemies:* Ibid., 452, Wilentz, *Rise of American Democracy*, 645.

255 *Benton opposed the annexation of Texas:* Perley Orman Ray, *The Repeal of the Missouri Compromise: Its Origin and Authorship* (Cleveland: Arthur H. Clark, 1908), 31; Meigs, *Life of Thomas Hart Benton*, 408; Thomas Hart Benton, *Thirty Years' View: Or, A History of the Working of the American Government for Thirty Years from 1820 to 1850* (New York: D. Appleton, 1880), 2:647–49.

255 *Benton spanned the decades as the Missouri colossus:* Harrison Anthony Trexler, *Slavery in Missouri 1804–1865* (Baltimore: Johns Hopkins University Press, 1914), 148; Paul Simon, *Freedom's Champion—Elijah Lovejoy* (Carbondale: Southern

Illinois University Press), 38; Fox-Genovese and Genovese, *Mind of the Master Class*, 86.

256 *Before the Mexican War:* Ray, *Repeal of the Missouri Compromise,* 33, 247–49.

257 *The epicenter of the anti-Benton movement:* Holst, *Constitutional and Political History of the United States*, 286.

257 *Calhoun had laid down the gauntlet:* Peterson, *Great Triumvirate*, 426–27, 444; Benton, *Thirty Years' View*, 2:732.

258 *Rejected in the Congress, a version:* Christopher Phillips, *Missouri's Confederate: Claiborne Fox Jackson and the Creation of Southern Identity in the Border West* (Columbia: University of Missouri Press, 2000), 81–82; Ray, *Repeal of the Missouri Compromise*, 39–42; Meigs, *Life of Thomas Hart Benton*, 409–12, 456.

258 *Atchison stumped across the state:* Trexler, *Slavery in Missouri*, 151; Ray, *Repeal of the Missouri Compromise*, 66, 250.

259 *Benton began writing his epic memoir:* Meigs, *Life of Thomas Hart Benton*, 423; William Franklin Switzler, *Switzler's Illustrated History of Missouri, from 1541 to 1877* (St. Louis: C. R. Barns, 1879), 271; Trexler, *Slavery in Missouri*, 161–62.

259 *In his final speech in the Senate:* Ray, *Repeal of the Missouri Compromise*, 78, 80.

260 *Here presided William B. Napton:* Christopher Phillips and Jason L. Pendleton, eds., *The Union on Trial: The Political Journals of Judge William Barclay Napton, 1829–1883* (Columbia: University of Missouri Press, 2005), 44, 182–83; Walter Ehrlich, *They Have No Rights: Dred Scott's Struggle for Freedom* (Bedford, Mass.: Applewood Press, 2007), 58–59, 66–67.

260 *From that moment, the little noticed* Dred Scott *case:* "Missouri's Dred Scott Case, 1846–1857," Missouri Digital Heritage, http://www.sos.mo.gov/archives /resources/africanamerican/scott/scott.asp.

261 *"These decisions upon their face show":* Thomas Hart Benton, *Historical and Legal Examination of That Part of the Decision of the Supreme Court of the United States in the Dred Scott Case* (New York: D. Appleton, 1857), 184–85.

CHAPTER THIRTEEN: THE TRIUMPH OF THE F STREET MESS

263 *Douglas had campaigned for Pierce:* Johannsen, *Stephen A. Douglas*, 370–73; Milton, *Eve of Conflict*, 95.

264 *Douglas returned to Washington:* Johannsen, *Stephen A. Douglas*, 381; Jon Meacham, *American Lion: Andrew Jackson in the White House* (New York: Random House, 2008), 359–60.

264 *After the funeral Douglas did not receive much:* Johannsen, *Stephen A. Douglas*, 375–76, 380.

264 *In May 1853 Douglas set sail for England:* Ibid., 322, 382–84; Linder, *Reminiscences of the Early Bench and Bar of Illinois*, 79–82; "Senator Douglas Abroad," *New York Times*, November 11, 1853.

265 *From the moment of Pierce's election Douglas:* Milton, *Eve of Conflict*, 96; John J.

Wickre, "Indiana's Southern Senator: Jesse Bright and the Hoosier Democracy" (PhD diss., University of Kentucky, 2013), http://uknowledge.uky.edu/cgi/viewcontent.cgi?article=1013&context=history_etds, 4; Matthew Salafia, *Slavery's Borderland: Freedom and Bondage Along the Ohio River* (Philadelphia: University of Pennsylvania Press, 2013), 222; Rhodes, *History of the United States*, 1:425.

266 *Walking down the gangplank in New York:* Milton, *Eve of Conflict*, 98–99; Johannsen, *Stephen A. Douglas*, 386–87.

267 *Daniel A. Robertson was a former U.S. marshal:* Walter Van Brunt, ed., *Duluth and St. Louis County, Minnesota* (New York: American Historical Society, 1921), 1:67–68; Milton, *Eve of Conflict*, 105–6.

268 *The syndicate, however, immediately faced a cutthroat rival:* Charles E. Flandrau, *Encyclopedia of Biography of Minnesota* (Salem, Mass.: Higginson Book, 1900), 1:364–67; Frank Abial Flower, *Report of the City Statistician* (Milwaukee: King, Fowle, 1890), 49–50; Milton, *Eve of Conflict*, 105; Frank Heywood Hodder, "The Railroad Background of the Kansas-Nebraska Act," *Mississippi Valley Historical Review* 12, no. 10 (June 1925).

268 *Douglas had been the master craftsman:* Henry M. Flint, *Life of Stephen A. Douglas, United States Senator from Illinois* (New York: Derby & Jackson, 1860), 10, 53; James W. Sheahan, *The Life of Stephen A. Douglas* (New York: Harper & Brothers, 1860), 134; Johannsen, *Stephen A. Douglas*, 783; Hodder, "The Railroad Background of the Kansas-Nebraska Act."

269 *Douglas knew he had not recovered:* Nichols, *Democratic Machine*, 136.

270 *Jefferson Davis developed a particular dislike:* William J. Cooper, Jr., *Jefferson Davis: The Essential Writings* (New York: Modern Library, 2004), 176; Crist, ed., *Papers of Jefferson Davis,* 6:vii; William J. Cooper, Jr., *Jefferson Davis: American* (New York: Vintage, 2001), 201–3.

270 *Douglas believed in the raw power:* Holst, *Constitutional and Political History of the United States*, 313.

271 *In early 1853, Douglas tried again:* Potter, *Impending Crisis*, 149–52; Johannsen, *Stephen A. Douglas*, 390–97; Priscilla Myers Benham, "Thomas Jefferson Rusk," Handbook of Texas Online, http://www.tshaonline.org/handbook/online/articles/fru16.

272 *The dead Douglas bill:* Potter, *Impending Crisis*, 153; Nichols, *Franklin Pierce*, 281–82; "The Memphis Convention," *DeBow's Review* 15 (1853), 267; Crist, ed., *Papers of Jefferson Davis*, 5:29–32; Dodd, *Jefferson Davis*, 143–45; Virginia H. Taylor, *The Franco-Texan Land Company* (Austin: University of Texas Press, 2011), 4.

272 *By 1853, only about one thousand white people:* William E. Connelley, *The Provisional Government of Nebraska Territory and the Journals of William Walker* (Lincoln, Neb.: State Journal, 1899), 2–3; Johnson, *Stephen A. Douglas*, 223–26; Cutts, *Brief Treatise on Constitutional and Party Questions*, 84.

273 *During the debate on Douglas's Nebraska bill:* Pike, *First Blows of the Civil War*, 185; Ray, *Repeal of the Missouri Compromise*, 103–4, 112–13, 123.

274 *At rally after rally around the state:* Ray, *Repeal of the Missouri Compromise*, 135–37; Holst, *Constitutional and Political History of the United States*, 285.

274 *After hours Bourbon Dave and the Little Giant:* Roy F. Nichols, "The Kansas-Nebraska Act: A Century of Historiography," *Mississippi Valley Historical Review* 43, no. 2 (September 1956), 187–212; Johannsen, *Stephen A. Douglas*, 359.

275 *While Atchison savored late night drinks:* Ray, *Repeal of the Missouri Compromise*, 277–82; Nichols, "The Kansas-Nebraska Act," 203–4; Johannsen, *Stephen A. Douglas*, 402, 407.

275 *Years later, in 1880:* Nichols, "The Kansas-Nebraska Act," 202.

276 *According to Parker's account:* Ray, *Repeal of the Missouri Compromise*, 229–30, 264–72; Waldorf H. Phillips, *The Missing Link: What Led to the War, or the Secret History of the Kansas-Nebraska Act* (Washington, D.C.: Gray & Clarkson, 1886), 13.

276 *Jefferson Davis offered further testimony:* Davis, *Jefferson Davis Ex-President of the Confederate States of America*, 1:671.

277 *Butler, the senior statesman of the F Street Mess: Congressional Globe*, 34th Congress, 1st Session, 103.

277 *In the making of the Kansas-Nebraska Act:* Ray, *Repeal of the Missouri Compromise*, 181–82, 230–32, 274.

278 *The* Richmond Enquirer *was especially well informed:* Ibid., 197–98.

279 *The action began on the first day:* Johnson, *Stephen A. Douglas*, 228; William Silag, "Sioux City: An Iowa Boom Town," in *American Cities: A Collection of Essays*, Neil L. Shumsky, ed. (New York: Taylor & Francis, 1996), 1:253.

279 *Dodge and Jones were, along with Bright:* John Carl Parish, *George Wallace Jones* (Iowa City: State Historical Society of Iowa, 1912), 11, 6, 36; Louis Pelzer, *Henry Dodge* (Iowa City: State Historical Society of Iowa, 1911), 196; Louis Pelzer, "Augustus Caesar Dodge," (PhD diss., State University of Iowa, 1909), 43, 136; Ray, *Repeal of the Missouri Compromise*, 195.

280 *Dodge's bill was reported to Douglas:* Milton, *Eve of Conflict*, 109.

280 *On January 4, Douglas presented his report:* Gerald M. Capers, *Stephen A. Douglas, Defender of the Union* (Boston: Little, Brown, 1959), 93; Johnson, *Stephen A. Douglas*, 230–31.

281 *While giving credence to the Southern Rightist view:* Milton, *Eve of Conflict*, 109; Holst, *Constitutional and Political History of the United States*, 296–97.

281 *In 1849 Douglas had called the Missouri Compromise:* Eyal, *Young America Movement and the Transformation of the Democratic Party,* 36; George Ticknor Curtis, *Constitutional History of the United States* (New York: Harper & Brothers, 1896), 2:260.

281 *In the three days between the publication:* Johnson, *Stephen A. Douglas*, 233.

282   *Douglas's original report did not mention slavery:* Ray, *Repeal of the Missouri Compromise*, 204–5.

282   *What Douglas had sought to imply slyly:* Congressional Globe, 34th Congress, 1st Session, 398; Ray, *Repeal of the Missouri Compromise*, 285–86; Congressional Globe, 34th Congress, 1st Session, 1374.

283   *After Douglas submitted his report:* "Latest Intelligence," *New York Times*, January 6, 1854.

283   *The day after the bill was filed:* Willis Brewer, *Alabama, Her History, Resources, War Record, and Public Men: From 1540 to 1872* (Montgomery, Ala.: Barrett & Brown, 1872), 406; David T. Morgan, "Eugenia Levy Phillips: The Civil War Experiences of a Southern Jewish Woman," in *Jews of the South: Selected Essays from the Southern Jewish Historical Society*, Samuel Proctor, ed. (Macon, Ga.: Louis Schmier and Malcolm H. Stern, Mercer University Press, 1984), 95–99, Clay-Clopton, *Belle of the Fifties*, 151.

284   *Phillips explained to Hunter:* "Notes of Philip Phillips Left for His Children," Philip and William Hallett Phillips Papers, Box 13, Library of Congress, Washington, D.C.

284   *The next day Phillips encountered Atchison:* Ibid.

284   *The following morning, January 10:* Ibid.

285   *While Douglas contemplated his next move:* Susan Bullitt Dixon, *The True History of the Missouri Compromise and Its Repeal* (Cincinnati: Robert Clarke, 1899), 443, 437; Ray, *Repeal of the Missouri Compromise*, 273.

286   *While Lincoln was failing to secure justice:* Dixon, *True History of the Missouri Compromise and Its Repeal*, 174, 219, 389, 442; *Journal and Proceedings of the Convention of the State of Kentucky* (Frankfort, Ky.: A. G. Hodges, 1849), 64; Daniel T. Rodgers, *Contested Truths: Keywords in American Politics Since Independence* (Cambridge: Harvard University Press, 1998), 99; Holt, *Rise and Fall of the Whig Party*, 970.

286   *Just as Dixon had undone Clay's careful work:* Dixon, *True History of the Missouri Compromise and Its Repeal*, 440–41.

286   *The moment Dixon introduced his amendment:* Ibid., 447.

286   *"The Kentucky delegation was a unit":* Ibid., 444.

287   *Charles Sumner took the opening:* Holst, *Constitutional and Political History of the United States*, 311.

287   *About two days after Dixon had offered:* Dixon, *True History of the Missouri Compromise and Its Repeal*, 445.

287   *Though he gave Dixon the impression:* "Notes of Philip Phillips Left for His Children."

288   *Either that evening or the next day:* Ibid.

288   *The following day, January 21:* Ibid.; Johannsen, *Stephen A. Douglas*, 414.

288   *As Douglas was telling Phillips to prepare:* "Cabinet Discussion on the Nebraska

Bill," *New York Herald*, January 23, 1854; John Livingston, *Portraits of Eminent Americans Now Living* (New York: Lamport, 1854), 3:70.

289 *The freshly inked document:* Johannsen, *Stephen A. Douglas*, 414.

289 *On the day of the cabinet conference:* "Highly Interesting from Washington," *New York Herald*, January 24, 1854; Johannsen, *Stephen A. Douglas*, 415.

289 *"I mentioned to Benton that I had dined":* James T. Du Bois and Gertrude S. Mathews, *Galusha A. Grow: Father of the Homestead Law* (New York: Houghton Mifflin, 1917), 43, 138–39.

289 *According to Jefferson Davis's account:* Mrs. Archibald Dixon, *The True History of the Missouri Compromise and Its Repeal,* Cincinnati: Robert Clarke and Company, 1899, 457-60.

290 *According to an apparently well-informed report:* New York Herald, January 24, 1854; Ray, *Repeal of the Missouri Compromise*, 213.

291 *According to Phillips's account:* "Notes of Philip Phillips Left for His Children."

291 *In Davis's version, he counseled Pierce:* Dixon, *True History of the Missouri Compromise and Its Repeal*, 457–58.

292 *Douglas did not trust Pierce:* Du Bois and Mathews, *Galusha A. Grow*, 139–40.

292 *Pierce scrawled out for Douglas the crucial lines:* Nichols, *Franklin Pierce*, 323.

CHAPTER FOURTEEN: A SELF-EVIDENT LIE

293 *Douglas believed his best-laid plans would:* Samuel S. Cox, *Union-Disunion-Reunion: Three Decades of Federal Legislation 1855 to 1885* (Providence, R.I.: J. A. and R. A. Reid, 1885), 49; Johnson, *Stephen A. Douglas*, 179, 239.

294 *As Douglas was leaving the White House:* Du Bois and Mathews, *Galusha A. Grow*, 140; Milton, *Eve of Conflict*, 119.

294 *"The administration, it is now reported":* "Affairs in Washington City," *New York Herald*, January 25, 1854; Wilson, *History of the Rise and Fall of the Slave Power*, 2:382.

295 *After seeing the president, Fenton went to call on Marcy:* Ivor Debenham Spencer, *The Victor and the Spoils: A Life of William L. Marcy* (Providence, R.I.: Brown University Press, 1959), 274, 281; Johannsen, *Stephen A. Douglas*, 422; Gara, *Presidency of Franklin Pierce,* 95.

295 *John Van Buren, "Prince John," royalty of the Softs: New York Evening Post*, February 11, 1854.

296 *At the beginning of the 33rd Congress:* Niven, *Salmon P. Chase*, 146–47.

297 *Sumner was also scrambling to find political:* Donald, *Charles Sumner and the Coming of the Civil War*, 243–50; Edward L. Pierce, *Memoir and Letters of Charles Sumner* (Boston: Roberts Brothers, 1894), 3:345.

297 *Two days after the conference: Congressional Globe*, 33rd Congress, 1st Session, 239–40.

298 *That afternoon, the abolitionist newspaper:* George Washington Julian, *The Life of*

Joshua R. Giddings (New York: A. C. McClurg, 1892), 311; Sewell, *Ballots for Freedom*, 255; Denison, ed., *Diary and Correspondence of Salmon P. Chase*, 263.

298   *"We arraign the bill":* J. W. Schuckers, *The Life and Public Services of Salmon Portland Chase* (New York: D. Appleton, 1874), 141; Rhodes, *History of the United States*, 1:443.

299   *The "Appeal" ignited an anti-Nebraska movement:* Cutts, *Brief Treatise on Constitutional and Party Questions*, 94.

299   *Douglas's sulfurous fury advertised his speech:* Congressional Globe, 33rd Congress, 1st Session, 275–82.

300   *"Senator Douglas seems to have been ashamed":* "Latest Intelligence," *New York Times*, February 2, 1854.

300   *While the Senate took up Douglas's measure:* Denison, ed., *Diary and Correspondence of Salmon P. Chase,* 255; *New York Tribune,* February 6, 1834; Holst, *Constitutional and Political History of the United States*, 372.

300   *Francis P. Blair, Benton's old ally:* Reginald Charles McGrane, *William Allen: A Study in Western Democracy* (Columbus: Ohio State Archaeological and Historical Society, 1925), 136–37.

301   *"Well here we are in the midst":* R. P. Brooks, ed., "Howell Cobb Papers," *Georgia Historical Quarterly* 6 (1922), 149–51.

302   *In Boston, the Cotton Whigs:* Eli Thayer, *A History of the Kansas Crusade* (New York: Harper, 1889), 6; Winthrop, *Memoir of Robert C. Winthrop*, 165.

302   *Douglas's bill summoned a forgotten figure:* Edward Coles, "History of the Ordinance of 1787," *Historical Society of Pennsylvania* (1856), 32; Johannsen, *Stephen A. Douglas*, 443.

303   *But the "inducements" were all on the side:* Hamlin, *Life and Times of Hannibal Hamlin*, 270–71.

303   *Northern Democratic senators:* Hubert Howe Bancroft, *History of California* (San Francisco: History, 1888), 663; *Congressional Globe*, 33rd Congress, 1st Session, 199.

303   *Dodge delivered his oration:* Congressional Globe, 33rd Congress, 1st Session, 381.

304   *Senator John Pettit of Indiana:* Wickre, "Indiana's Southern Senator," 129; *Congressional Globe*, 33rd Congress, 1st Session, 212–14.

304   *The scandal of adhering to the Declaration of Independence:* Congressional Globe, 33rd Congress, 1st Session, 339.

304   *Butler of South Carolina:* Congressional Globe, 33rd Congress, 1st Session, 232–40; A. Leon Higginbotham, *In the Matter of Color: Race and the American Legal Process, The Colonial Period* (New York: Oxford University Press, 1980), 91–97.

305   *Pettit insisted on resuming his argument:* Congressional Globe, 33rd Congress, 1st Session, 310–11.

306   *Sustaining Douglas's myth that the bill:* Johannsen, *Stephen A. Douglas*, 426–27; *Congressional Globe*, 33rd Congress, 1st Session, Appendix, 299.

306   *Douglas took the floor again:* "A Night in the Senate," *New York Tribune*, March 7,

1854; Doris Kearns Goodwin, *Team of Rivals* (New York: Simon & Schuster, 2006), 163.

306 *From the Senate gallery:* Paul Revere Frothingham, *Edward Everett: Orator and Statesman* (New York: Houghton Mifflin, 1925), 352; Schurz, *Reminiscences of Carl Schurz,* 1:30–33.

308 *Repealing the Missouri Compromise:* Remini, *Henry Clay,* 181–92; John Quincy Adams, *Memoirs of John Quincy Adams: Comprising Portions of His Diary from 1795 to 1848* (Philadelphia: J. B. Lippincott, 1875), 4:526.

310 *Appealing "to the whole Union," Douglas declared:* Congressional Globe, 33rd Congress, 1st Session, 327–38.

311 *The roll call was taken shortly:* Rhodes, *History of the United States,* 1:475; Schuckers, *Life and Public Services of Salmon Portland Chase,* 156.

311 *"The bill was thus manfully fought":* Pike, *First Blows of the Civil War,* 220.

311 *The "Appeal" had included a section:* Donald, *Charles Sumner and the Coming of the Civil War,* 259; Rhodes, *History of the United States,* 1:478.

311 *The clergy carefully chose the most distinguished:* Frothingham, *Edward Everett,* 345, 352–53.

312 *When, a month later, 504 clergymen:* Congressional Globe, 33rd Congress, 1st Session, 354–61.

312 *The Senate bill now went to the House:* Pike, *First Blows of the Civil War,* 221.

313 *The bill nearly died at birth in the House:* Milton, *Eve of Conflict,* 141.

313 *Douglas settled himself like a squatter:* Johannsen, *Stephen A. Douglas,* 433; "Latest Intelligence, Special Dispatch," *New York Times,* May 14, 1854; Nichols, *Franklin Pierce,* 337.

314 *Douglas's popular sovereignty was merely:* Congressional Globe, 33rd Congress, 1st Session, 557–61.

315 *While Benton's advocates pressured:* Wentworth, *Congressional Reminiscences,* 51.

315 *Richardson called for a suspension of the rules:* New York Times, March 15, 1854; Sean Wilentz, *Chants Democratic: New York City and the Rise of the American Working Class, 1788–1850* (New York: Oxford University Press, 2004), 329–30; *New York Tribune,* May 15, 1854.

316 *Douglas whipped the Northern Democrats:* New York Times, May 14, 1854; *Congressional Globe,* 33rd Congress, 1st Session, 197.

316 *To alarm the Southern stragglers:* Holst, *Constitutional and Political History of the United States,* 447.

317 *Finally, through a series of stunning tactical maneuvers:* Ibid., 450–2; William Peterfield Trent, *Southern Statesmen of the Old Régime* (Boston: T. Y. Crowell, 1897), 233.

317 *The final vote was not taken by roll call:* Congressional Globe, 33rd Congress, 1st Session, 538–39; Holt, *Rise and Fall of the Whig Party,* 820; Freehling, *Road to Disunion,* 1:559.

317 *As the Senate took up the House bill:* William H. Seward, *The Works of William H. Seward* (New York: Houghton, Mifflin, 1888), 4:464–79.

318 *On the night of May 24, the clerk of a clothing store:* Charles Emery Stevens, *Anthony Burns: A History* (Boston: Jewett, 1856), 38, 289–95.

319 *But a voice shouted that a group:* Ibid., 41–43.

319 *Boston was placed under martial law:* Ibid., 135–36, 146–50.

320 *The failed rescue of Thomas Sims in 1850:* Richard H. Abbott, *Cotton and Capital: Boston Businessmen and Antislavery Reform, 1854–1868* (Amherst: University of Massachusetts Press, 1991), 26; Garrison and Garrison, *William Lloyd Garrison*, 3:412; Henry David Thoreau, *Political Writings* (Cambridge, U.K.: Cambridge University Press, 1996), 123–36.

CHAPTER FIFTEEN: CITIZEN KNOW NOTHING

321 *"The storm will soon spend its fury":* Gienapp, *Origins of the Republican Party*, 79–80.

322 *Parties and presidents had been repudiated before:* Freehling, *Road to Disunion*, 2:62; Potter, *Impending Crisis*, 175–76.

322 *The first test after the passage of the bill:* Gienapp, *Origins of the Republican Party*, 121–22.

322 *The first meeting for the creation:* Wilson, *History of the Rise and Fall of the Slave Power in America*, 2:409; Francis Curtis, *The Republican Party* (New York: G. P. Putnam's Sons, 1904), 176–93.

323 *But these early efforts did not lead:* Seward, *1846–1861*, 219; Sewell, *Ballots for Freedom*, 265.

324 *The Know Nothings sprang from a small nativist sect:* Holst, *Constitutional and Political History of the United States*, 83.

324 *The Know Nothing Party was less a stable party:* Freehling, *Road to Disunion*, 2:87.

325 *Bestselling nativist novels, rivaling the sales:* Wilentz, *Rise of American Democracy*, 679; Charles Granville Hamilton, *Lincoln and the Know Nothing Movement* (Washington, D.C.: Public Affairs Press, 1954), 4; Potter, *Impending Crisis*, 252; Susan B. Griffin, *Anti-Catholicism and Nineteenth-Century Fiction* (New York: Cambridge University Press, 2004), 92–95.

325 *Nativism had a long and doleful history:* Louis Dow Scisco, *Political Nativism in New York State* (New York: Columbia University Press, 1901), 59–60.

326 *The politics of New York in 1854:* William C. Gover, *The Tammany Hall Democracy of the City of New York* (New York: M. B. Brown, 1875), 32; Alexander, *Political History of the State of New York*, 2:202.

326 *The Know Nothings on the rise:* Stahr, *Seward*, 147.

326 *It was at this fraught moment:* Weed, *Life of Thurlow Weed*, 2:225–26.

327 *Maneuvering at the convention:* Alexander, *Political History of the State of New York*, 202–3; Scisco, *Political Nativism in New York State,* 123–26; Gienapp, *Ori-*

gins of the Republican Party, 153–56; "Obituary: Daniel Ullman," *New York Times*, September 21, 1892.

327   *Greeley was inconsolably enraged:* Don C. Seitz, *Horace Greeley* (Indianapolis: Bobbs-Merrill, 1926), 160–67.

328   *Three months later, on February 8, 1855:* George E. Baker, "Seward, Weed, and Greeley," *Republic Monthly Magazine* 1 (1873), 198.

328   *In Massachusetts, the dissolution of the parties:* Donald, *Charles Sumner and the Coming of the Civil War*, 1:266–68; Holt, *Rise and Fall of the Whig Party*, 890; Potter, *Impending* Crisis, 250; Gienapp, *Origins of the Republican Party*, 134–37.

329   *The new 34th Congress elected in the 1854 elections:* Potter, *Impending Crisis*, 251–53.

329   *Sweeping statehouses and congressional elections:* "The Know-Nothings," *New York Times*, November 21, 1854.

330   *The Virginia governor's race of 1855:* William A. Link, *Roots of Secession: Slavery and Politics in Antebellum Virginia* (Chapel Hill: University of North Carolina Press, 2005), 123–38.

331   *Just days after the Virginia election:* Wilson, *History of the Rise and Fall of the Slave Power in America*, 2:423; W. L. Barre, *Life and Public Service of Millard Fillmore* (Buffalo, N.Y.: Wanzer, McKim, 1856), 382.

331   *"Americans Only Shall Govern America":* "The Know Nothing Convention at Philadelphia," *New York Times*, June 16, 1855; "The Know Nothing Meeting in Independence Square," *New York Times*, June 18, 1855; "Detailed Report of the Proceedings of the Convention," *New York Times*, June 15, 1855.

CHAPTER SIXTEEN: THE CONQUEST OF KANSAS

333   *Eli Thayer, a state representative from Worcester:* Thayer, *History of the Kansas Crusade*

334   *Thayer unveiled his plan to put popular sovereignty:* Ibid., 270, 69, 39–40.

335   *Lawrence advised Thayer that it would be most effective:* Abbott, *Cotton and Capital*, 28–34.

335   *On July 17, 1854, twenty-four pilgrims:* Thayer, *History of the Kansas Crusade*, 69–71, 164–65.

335   *As soon as David Atchison announced from the Senate podium:* Crist, ed., *Papers of Jefferson Davis*, 5:83–84; Charles B. Murphy, *The Political Career of Jesse D. Bright* (Indianapolis: Indiana Historical Society, 1931), 124–25.

336   *On June 10, the first documented group of pro-slavery:* William G. Cutler, *History of the State of Kansas*, Kansas Collection Books, http://www.kancoll.org/books/cutler /terrhist/terrhist-p2.html#LAND_CLAIMED_BY_MISSOURI_SQUATTERS; John N. Holloway, *The History of Kansas* (Lafayette, Ind.: James, Emmons, 1868), 120–22; William McClung Paxton, *Annals of Platte County, Missouri* (Kansas City, Mo.: Hudson-Kimberly Publishing, 1897), 184.

336   *The organizational leaders of the pro-slavery forces:* "Report of the Special Commit-

tee Appointed to Investigate the Troubles in Kansas," House of Representatives, 34th Congress, 1st Session (Washington, D.C.: Cornelius Wendell, 1856), 925; Bill Cecil-Fronsman, " 'Death to All Yankees and Traitors in Kansas': The *Squatter Sovereign* and the Defense of Slavery in Kansas," *Kansas History* (Spring 1993), 22–33.

337 *Stringfellow stated he would prove his case:* B. F. Stringfellow, *Negro-Slavery, No Evil, A Report Made to the Platte County Self-Defensive Association* (St. Louis: M. Nieder, 1854).

338 *On October 7 the territorial governor arrived:* Forney, *Anecdotes of Public Men*, 193; Holst, *Constitutional and Political History of the United States*, 71; Nichols, *Franklin Pierce*, 407–8.

338 *After accumulating his nice portfolio of property:* "Senator Atchison's Farewell to His Constituents," *New York Times*, December 1, 1854.

339 *Reeder's announcement that those eligible to vote:* Holloway, *History of Kansas*, 133–34; "Report of the Special Committee Appointed to Investigate the Troubles in Kansas," 3–4; Potter, *Impending Crisis*, 201; Holst, *Constitutional and Political History of the United States*, 75.

339 *After this fraudulent election B. F. Stringfellow:* Leverett Wilson Spring, *Kansas: Prelude to the War for the Union* (New York: Houghton, Mifflin, 1885), 27.

339 *Reeder now announced an election:* William A. Phillips, *Conquest of Kansas by Missouri and Her Allies* (Boston: Phillips, Sampson, 1856), 47; "Report of the Special Committee Appointed to Investigate the Troubles in Kansas," 29.

340 *The Special Committee documented:* Freehling, *Road to Disunion*, 2:74, Spring, *Kansas,* 44–46; "Important from Kansas," *New York Times*, February 4, 1856; Jay Monaghan, *Civil War on the Western Border, 1854–1865* (Boston: Little, Brown, 1955), 19–20; William E. Connelley, *A Standard History of Kansas and Kansans* (Chicago: Lewis Publishing, 1918), 395.

340 *"KANSAS SLAVE STATE":* Charles Robinson, *The Kansas Conflict* (New York: Harper & Brothers, 1892), 113.

340 *Free state men urged Governor Reeder:* Spring, *Kansas,* 50–51; *Congressional Globe*, 34th Congress, 1st Session, Appendix, 92.

341 *Returned to Missouri, the men:* Charles Robinson, *The Kansas Conflict* (New York: Harper & Brothers, 1892), 130–31; Holloway, *History of Kansas*

341 *In Leavenworth, a lawyer named William Phillips:* "Report of the Special Committee Appointed to Investigate the Troubles in Kansas," 467; Spring, *Kansas,* 50; Holloway, *History of Kansas*, 157.

341 *The pro-slavery forces boycotted the district elections:* "Report of the Special Committee Appointed to Investigate the Troubles in Kansas," 93, Holst, *Constitutional and Political History of the United States*, 146; Holloway, *History of Kansas*, 162.

342 *"From reports now received of Reeder":* Robinson, *Kansas Conflict*, 132, Phillips, *Conquest of Kansas*, 99; *Congressional Globe*, 34th Congress, 1st Session, Appendix, 91.

343   *Reeder convened the legislature:* Holst, *Constitutional and Political History of the United States*, 156–57; Monaghan, *Civil War on the Western Border*, 26; Phillips, *Conquest of Kansas*, 100–101.

343   *At a meeting at Weston, Missouri:* Connelley, *Standard History of Kansas and Kansans*, 403; Spring, *Kansas*, 56; Phillips, *Conquest of Kansas*, 104–8; Holst, *Constitutional and Political History of the United States*, 158.

343   *The town of Pawnee, the first capital:* Holloway, *History of Kansas*, 169.

343   *Reeder was fired on August 10:* Phillips, *Conquest of Kansas*, 115–16.

344   *The free state men countered:* Robinson, *Kansas Conflict*, 171; Phillips, *Conquest of Kansas*, 131; Wilentz, *Rise of American Democracy*, 687–88.

344   *One month after the Topeka convention:* Spring, *Kansas*, 84; Phillips, *Conquest of Kansas*, 149–50.

344   *A week later, a pro-slavery man:* "Report of the Special Committee Appointed to Investigate the Troubles in Kansas," 14–16; Phillips, *Conquest of Kansas*, 151–73; Spring, *Kansas*, 86–92; Holloway, *History of Kansas*, 229.

345   *Once again, the "Border Ruffians" invaded:* Phillips, *Conquest of Kansas*, 171; Holloway, *History of Kansas*, 228–29.

345   *Since the first fraudulent election:* Wilentz, *Rise of American Democracy*, 687; Spring, *Kansas*, 98–100; Holloway, *History of Kansas*, 251.

346   *At the critical juncture, while Shannon:* Robinson, *Kansas Conflict*, 204.

346   *During the diplomacy, a new settler:* Spring, *Kansas*, 101; Robinson, *Kansas Conflict*, 207; Dale E. Watts, "How Bloody Was Bleeding Kansas? Political Killings in Kansas Territory, 1854–1861," *Kansas History: A Journal of the Central Plains* 18, no. 2 (Summer 1995), 116–29.

CHAPTER SEVENTEEN: IMPERIALISM, THE HIGHEST STAGE OF SLAVERY

347   *The dream of a Caribbean slave empire died:* Rhodes, *History of the United States*, 2:2, 11, 13, 23–29; Robert E. May, *Slavery, Race, and Conquest in the Tropics: Lincoln, Douglas, and the Future of Latin America* (New York: Cambridge University Press, 2013), 101; Maunsell Field, *Memories of Many Men and Some Women* (New York: Harper, 1874), 96–97.

348   *After the Black Warrior fiasco:* James A. Rawley, *Race and Politics: Bleeding Kansas and the Coming of the Civil War* (Lincoln: University of Nebraska Press, 1979), 135; Potter, *Impending Crisis*, 189–90; Field, *Memories of Many Men and Some Women*, 99, 76, 100; May, *Slavery, Race, and Conquest in the Tropics*, 2:38–42; Nichols, *Franklin Pierce*, 366–71.

349   *The debacle of Ostend was only the prelude:* James Jeffrey Roche, *The Story of the Filibusters* (London: T. Fisher Unwin, 1891), 70–71; Scroggs, *Filibusters and Financiers*, 79.

350   *Walker named as his minister:* Alejandro Bolaños Geyer, *William Walker: Grey-Eye Man of Destiny* (St. Louis: Privately printed, 1990), 251, 254; "News from Wash-

ington," *New York Herald*, January 3, 1856; Manzar Forooha, *The Catholic Church and Social Change in Nicaragua* (Albany: State University of New York Press, 1989), 8.

350   *Days after Walker executed*: Nichols, *Franklin Pierce*, 398–99; Dodd, *Jefferson Davis*, 142.

351   *While Wheeler continued to encourage Walker*: Coleman McCampbell, "H. L. Kinney and Daniel Webster in Illinois in the 1830s," *Journal of the Illinois State Historical Society* 47, no. 1 (Spring 1954); Amelia W. Williams, "Kinney, Henry Lawrence," Handbook of Texas Online, http://www.tshaonline .org/handbook/online/articles/fki29; Spencer Tucker, *The Encyclopedia of the Mexican-American War* (Santa Barbara, Calif.: ABC-CLIO, 2013), 337–38; Robert E. May, *Manifest Destiny's Underworld: Filibustering in Antebellum America* (Chapel Hill: University of North Carolina Press, 2002), 45–47; Eric H. Walther, *The Shattering of the Union: America in the 1850s* (Lanham, Md.: Rowman & Littlefield, 2004), 103.

351   *To exploit his newly found kingdom*: "The Arrested Filibusters," *New York Times*, February 10, 1857.

352   *Kinney claimed he was engaged*: "The Kinney Expedition to Central America—Its Aims and Objects," *New York Herald*, December 30, 1954.

352   *Before Kinney embarked, however*: Bolaños Geyer, *William Walker*, 294–95; Nichols, *Franklin Pierce*, 462–63.

352   *The downfall of Kinney foreshadowed*: T. J. Stile, *The First Tycoon: The Epic Life of Cornelius Vanderbilt* (New York: Alfred A. Knopf, 2009), 281; May, *Manifest Destiny's Underworld*, 47–51.

353   *The allure of a tropical Manifest Destiny*: Crist, ed., *Papers of Jefferson Davis*, 6:140; "Monthly Record of Current Events," *Harper's Monthly* 19 (June–November 1859), 694–95.

CHAPTER EIGHTEEN: ARMED LIBERTY

355   *The Southern route of a Pacific railroad*: Pierce, *Memoir and Letters of Charles Sumner*, 4:205; Catherine Frances Cavanagh, "Stories of Our Government Bureaus: Strange Stories of the United States Capitol," *The Bookman* 34 (September 1911–February 1912), 200; David Hackett Fischer, *Liberty and Freedom: A Visual History of America's Founding* (New York: Oxford University Press, 2005), 298–300; Guy Gugliotta, *Freedom's Cap: The United States Capitol and the Coming of the Civil War* (New York: Macmillan, 2012), 392–93.

356   *Pierce wished for a second term as president*: Davis, *Jefferson Davis Ex-President of the Confederate States of America*, 1:530.

357   *Pierce departed from Washington*: Nathaniel Hawthorne, *Passages from the French and Italian Note-Books* (Boston: J. R. Osgood, 1873), 228.

357   *For weeks after the inauguration*: Clay, *Belle of the Fifties*, 69.

357 *Campaigning for his comrade in 1852:* Crist, ed., *Papers of Jefferson Davis*, 4:268–70.

358 *Edward Coles, Thomas Jefferson's protégé:* Coles, "History of the Ordinance of 1787," 33.

358 *Thomas Hart Benton, after the* Dred Scott *decision:* Benton, *Historical and Legal Examination*, 186.

359 *In the early and mid-twentieth century:* James G. Randall, "A Blundering Generation," in Kenneth M. Stampp, ed., *The Causes of the Civil War* (New York: Simon & Schuster, 1959), 114–17; Avery Craven, *The Coming of the Civil War* (Chicago: University of Chicago Press, 1942), 2–3; Thomas J. Pressly, *Americans Interpret Their Civil War* (Princeton: Princeton University Press, 1954), 274–75, 281; Arthur M. Schlesinger, Jr., "The Causes of the Civil War: A Note on Historical Sentimentalism," *Partisan Review* 16 (1949), 969–81. For contemporary "revisionism" in the "blundering generation" tradition, see Harry S. Stout, *Upon the Altar of the Nation: A Moral History of the American Civil War* (New York: Viking, 2006), and David Goldfield, *America Aflame: How the Civil War Created a Nation* (New York: Bloomsbury Press, 2011).

361 *Then he turned his rhetoric so that it*: CW, 3:310–11.

362 *Douglas was aware from the beginning of the furor:* Cutts, *Brief Treatise on Constitutional and Party Questions*, 122–23; W. C. Todd, "A Reminiscence of Benton," *Atlantic Monthly*, September 1870; *Congressional Globe*, 34th Congress, 1st Session, Appendix, 288.

362 *Shortly after the Nebraska Act's passage:* Johannsen, *Stephen A. Douglas*, 445–46; Capers, *Stephen A. Douglas*, 119–20.

362 *After the adjournment of the Congress in August:* Milton, *Eve of Conflict*, 173.

363 *Douglas intended to use the Nebraska Act as his whip:* Johannsen, *Stephen A. Douglas*, 449–50: Milton, *Eve of Conflict*, 149–50.

363 *Douglas decided he would seize command:* Milton, *Eve of Conflict*, 175.

363 *On that day the ships along the dock:* Cutts, *Brief Treatise on Constitutional and Party Questions*, 98–100; "Senator Douglas at Home," *New York Times*, September 6, 1854; "The Truth of the Douglas Meeting," *New York Tribune*, September 7, 1854.

364 *The Chicago melee received sensational national coverage:* Johannsen, *Stephen A. Douglas*, 455; Milton, *Eve of Conflict*, 177.

364 *Since the middle of August, Lincoln had gone back:* CW, 2:230.

365 *The day after Lincoln's article was printed:* CW, 2:233.

365 *"In 1854":* CW, 4:67.

CHAPTER NINETEEN: THE FAILURE OF FREE SOCIETY

368 *"Now, however, a live issue":* Herndon and Weik, *Herndon's Lincoln*, 295; CW, 4:67.

369 *At the opening of 1854:* Burlingame, *Abraham Lincoln*, 1:370.

370   *Lincoln's style blazed through:* CW, 3:394, 423.

371   *In the Senate Seward had answered: The Nebraska Question: Comprising Speeches in the United States Senate* (New York: Redfield, 1854), 103; Frederic Bancroft, *The Life of William H. Seward* (New York: Harper & Brothers, 1900), 1:362.

371   *When the news reached Springfield:* Angle, "Here I Have Lived," 210.

371   *Three days later, Seward again arose:* William H. Seward, *Freedom and Public Faith: Speeches* (Washington, D.C.: Buell & Blanchard, 1854), 37–39.

371   *In private Lincoln echoed Seward:* Herndon and Weik, *Herndon's Lincoln*, 295.

372   *Herndon and Lincoln's "office discussions" were stimulated:* Charles White, *Lincoln and the Newspapers* (Hancock, N.Y.: Hancock Herald Print, 1924), 8; Peter Marshall and David Manuel, *Sounding Forth the Trumpet: 1837–1860* (Grand Rapids, Mich.: Revell, 2009), 443; George Alfred Townsend, *The Real Life of Abraham Lincoln: A Talk with Mr. Herndon, His Late Law Partner* (New York: Publication Office, Bible House, 1867), 4–5; Herndon and Weik, *Herndon's Lincoln*, 293, 353; Albert Beveridge, *Abraham Lincoln* (New York: Houghton Mifflin. 1928), 1:519; James Lander, "Herndon's 'Auction List' and Lincoln's Interest in Science," *Journal of the Abraham Lincoln Association* 32, no. 2 (Summer 2011), 16–49; Henry Bascom Rankin, *Personal Recollections of Abraham Lincoln* (New York: G. P. Putnam's Sons, 1916), 123.

373   *The book that had the greatest impact:* Hertz, *Hidden Lincoln*, 97.

374   *While Fitzhugh painted a picture of bucolic bliss:* C. Vann Woodward, ed., *George Fitzhugh, Cannibals All! Slaves Without Masters* (Cambridge: Harvard University Press, 1988), vii–xxxix; Paul Boyer, Clifford Clark, Karen Halttunen, et al., *The Enduring Vision: A History of the American People* (Boston: Cengage Learning, 2010), 1:340.

374   *Dismissive of Locke:* George Fitzhugh, *Sociology for the South, or the Failure of Free Society* (Richmond, Va.: A. Morris, 1854), 25–26, 182–83, 190–91, 179.

376   *It was also at this time:* CW, 2:221.

377   *"It is no part of the object":* Leonard Bacon, *Slavery Discussed in Occasional Essays from 1833 to 1846* (New York: Baker & Scribner, 1846), ix–x; Molly Oshatz, *Slavery and Sin: The Fight Against Slavery and the Rise of Liberal Protestantism* (New York: Oxford University Press, 2011), 43–44.

377   *Bacon's chief theological argument:* Bacon, *Slavery Discussed in Occasional Essays*, 215.

377   *Reflecting a particular New England strain:* Ibid., 225–28.

378   *Lincoln would soon adopt Bacon's distinctions:* Charles Carleton Coffin, *Abraham Lincoln* (New York: Harper & Brothers, 1892), 444.

379   *Lincoln acted as campaign manager:* Jane Martin Johns, "A Momentous Incident in the History of Illinois," *Journal of the Illinois State Historical Association* 10, no. 3 (October 1917).

379   *"Lincoln was always a party man":* Isaac N. Phillips, *Abraham Lincoln, by Some*

Men Who Knew Him (Bloomington, Ill.: Pantagraph Printing & Stationery, 1910), 149–50, 155.

380 *The two parties, the Democrats and Whigs:* Howard, "The Illinois Republican Party, Part I"; Cole, *Centennial History of Illinois*, 126.

381 *"Try to save the Whig Party":* Holt, *Rise and Fall of the Whig Party*, 828–30; Seward, *1846–1861*, 231.

381 *Lincoln was just beginning to navigate:* Cole, *Centennial History of Illinois*, 128.

CHAPTER TWENTY: THE BLOOD OF THE REVOLUTION

383 *The appearance in Springfield:* Magdol, *Owen Lovejoy*, 101–6; Howard, "The Illinois Republican Party, Part I."

384 *On July 4th, Clay joined Codding at Chicago:* Howard, "The Illinois Republican Party, Part I"; Miller, *Lincoln and His World*, 4:41.

384 *Lincoln attended Clay's speech:* Cassius Marcellus Clay, *Life*, 232.

385 *The* Journal *hailed Clay's:* Angle, "Here I Have Lived," 211; Howard, "The Illinois Republican Party, Part I."

385 *Lincoln's attitude was affirmed:* Burlingame, *Abraham Lincoln*, 1:364; Cole, *Centennial History of Illinois*, 127.

386 *Zebina Eastman, the* Free West *editor:* Howard, "The Illinois Republican Party, Part I"; Hertz, *Hidden Lincoln*, 253–54; HI, 149–50.

387 *Elihu Washburne represented the First District:* Ralph S. Havener, Jr., "Elihu Benjamin Washburne" (MA thesis, University of Wisconsin, 1950), 14, 20.

387 *Jesse O. Norton represented the Third District:* Holt, *Rise and Fall of the Whig Party*, 869; Gienapp, *Origins of the Republican Party*, 124; Howard, "The Illinois Republican Party, Part I"; C. P. Merriman et al., *The History of McLean County, Illinois* (Chicago: W. Le Baron, 1879), 419.

387 *Eastman's question to Herndon:* Holt, *Rise and Fall of the Whig Party*, 870.

388 *On June 14, the former president:* Scarry, *Millard Fillmore*, 255.

389 *Lincoln was desperately trying to steer:* CW, 2:226; Matthew Pinsker, "Not Always Such a Whig: Abraham Lincoln Partisan Realignment in the 1850s," *Journal of the Abraham Lincoln Association* 29, no. 2 (November 2002), 27–46.

389 *Just as Yates was nominated by virtue:* CW, 2:266; Henry Clay Whitney, *Lincoln the Citizen* (New York: Current Literature, 1907), 150; CW, 2:289.

390 *Shortly after Logan and Lincoln were nominated:* N. Levering, *Recollections of Abraham Lincoln* (Iowa City: State Historical Society, 1896), 496–99; *The United States Biographical Dictionary: Kansas Volume* (Chicago: S. Lewis, 1879), 614–15.

390 *Lincoln never openly voiced his feelings:* CW, 2:316–17; John B. Senning, "The Know Nothing Movement in Illinois," *Journal of the Illinois State Historical Society* 7, no. 1 (April 1914), 19.

391 *By the end of August Lincoln:* CW, 2:227.

391 *Lincoln encouraged the state senator:* CW, 2:229.

391   *On September 9, at the Springfield courthouse:* CW, 2:229; Lewis Lehrman, *Lincoln at Peoria: The Turning Point* (Mechanicsburg, Pa.: Stackpole Books, 2008), 24.

392   *The day after the editorial was published:* CW, 2:233.

393   *When Lincoln spoke, Codding was organizing fusion:* CW, 2:233; Francis F. Browne, *Every-Day Life of Abraham Lincoln* (Chicago: Browne & Howell, 1913), 355; D. Leigh Henson, "Classical Rhetoric as a Lens for Reading the Key Speeches of Lincoln's Political Rise, 1852–1856," *Journal of the Abraham Lincoln Association* 35, no. 1 (Winter 2014), 1–25; CW, 2:320; Jesse W. Weik, *The Real Lincoln* (New York: Houghton Mifflin, 1922), 198.

393   *The "glorious meetings" that Douglas described:* Johannsen, *Stephen A. Douglas,* 456–57; Milton, *Eve of Conflict,* 177–78; Howard, "The Illinois Republican Party, Part I."

394   *Douglas traveled to Bloomington:* Phillips, *Abraham Lincoln, by Some Men Who Knew Him,* 55.

394   *Just a few months earlier, on April 4:* Donald, *Lincoln's Herndon,* 69–71; Paul M. Angle, "Lincoln and Liquor," *Bulletin of the Abraham Lincoln Association* 28, no. 1 (September 1932); Miller, *Lincoln and His World,* 4:64–68; Daniel W. Stowell, "Femes UnCovert, Women's Encounters with the Law," in *In Tender Consideration: Women, Families, and the Law in Abraham Lincoln's Illinois,* Daniel W. Stowell, ed. (Urbana: University of Illinois Press, 2002), 27–28.

394   *Mayor Herndon marched from saloon to saloon:* Angle, "Here I Have Lived," 195.

395   *When Lincoln left Douglas's hotel room:* Frances M. Morehouse, *The Life of Jesse W. Fell* (Urbana: University of Illinois, 1916), 19, 53; Norman Bateman, Paul Selby, Ezra M. Prince, et al., eds., *Historical Encyclopedia of Illinois and History of McLean County* (La Cross, Wis.: Brookhaven Press, 2001), 2:1027–30.

395   *Fell summoned Lincoln to Bloomington:* Miller, *Lincoln and His World,* 4:42; Osborne H. Oldroyd, *The Lincoln Memorial: Album-immortelles* (New York: G. W. Carleton, 1882), 471.

396   *Fell was still attached to his idea:* Phillips, *Abraham Lincoln, by Some Men who Knew Him,* 55–57; Allen Thorndike Rice, *Reminiscences of Abraham Lincoln by Distinguished Men of His Time* (New York: North American Publishing, 1886), 199.

396   *Fell had already put out the word:* Oldroyd, *Lincoln Memorial,* 471; Milton, *Eve of Conflict,* 179.

396   *That afternoon Douglas spoke to several thousand people:* Stevens, *A Reporter's Lincoln,* 60; Miller, *Lincoln and His World,* 4:49; Graham A. Peck, "New Records of the Lincoln-Douglas Debate at the 1854 Illinois State Fair: The Missouri Republican and the Missouri Democrat Report from Springfield," *Journal of the Abraham Lincoln Association* 30, no. 2 (Summer 2009).

397   *Douglas had attempted to tar his opposition:* Miller, *Lincoln and His World,* 4:50.

398   *After threading his way through:* CW, 2:234–40.

398   *It was almost impossible to secure a room:* Peck, "New Records of the Lincoln-Douglas Debate at the 1854 Illinois State Fair."

399   *Abolitionists headed to Springfield:* Magdol, *Owen Lovejoy*, 108; Amedia Ruth King, "The Last Years of the Whig Party in Illinois—1847–1856," *Transactions of the Illinois State Historical Society*, no. 32 (1925), 143.

399   *A number of the key characters gathered at a reception:* Clark E. Carr, *The Illini: A Story of the Prairies* (Chicago: A. C. McClurg, 1905), 182–88.

399   *The Democrats had reserved a field:* Peck, "New Records of the Lincoln-Douglas Debate at the 1854 Illinois State Fair"; Milton, *Eve of Conflict*, 179–80; Beveridge, *Abraham Lincoln*, 2:242; Lehrman, *Lincoln at Peoria*, 39–40; Carr, *Illini*, 193.

400   *Douglas was exhausted from constant speaking:* Johannsen, *Stephen A. Douglas*, 461; Peck, "New Records of the Lincoln-Douglas Debate at the 1854 Illinois State Fair"; Carr, *Illini*, 192–94; Beveridge, *Abraham Lincoln*, 2:243.

400   *"I watched Mr. Lincoln":* Carr, *Illini*, 194, 199–200.

401   *The next morning, Lincoln encountered:* Phillips, *Abraham Lincoln, by Some Men Who Knew Him*, 147–48; Burlingame, *Abraham Lincoln*, 1:377.

401   *"He has been nosing for weeks":* Herbert Mitgang, *Lincoln: A Press Portrait* (New York: Fordham University Press, 2000), 72.

401   *At two in the afternoon:* Douglas L. Wilson, *Lincoln's Sword: The Presidency and the Power of Words* (New York: Alfred A. Knopf, 2006), 37; CW, 7:281.

404   *Lincoln then took on:* Peck, "New Records of the Lincoln-Douglas Debate at the 1854 Illinois State Fair."

406   *Citing Jefferson, Lincoln was already operating:* Sean Wilentz, "Abraham Lincoln and Jacksonian Democracy," in *Our Lincoln: New Perspectives on Lincoln and His World*, Eric Foner, ed. (New York: W. W. Norton, 2008), 71; Guelzo, *Abraham Lincoln*, 4–20; James Oakes, *Freedom National: The Destruction of Slavery in the United States, 1861–1865* (New York: W. W. Norton, 2013), 46.

406   *Lincoln was hardly original in his discovery:* Nebraska Question, 54, 95, 113.

408   *The* London Daily News *article contained:* "Mr. Soule's 'Vulgar Turbulence'— George Sanders," *New York Times*, February 29, 1854; W. Caleb McDaniel, "New Light on a Lincoln Quote," Rice University, http://wcm1.web.rice.edu/new-light -on-lincoln-quote.html.

409   *Lincoln's view of Douglas as a dangerous demagogue:* Charles Phillips, *The Speeches of Charles Phillips* (New York: Kirk & Mercein, 1817), 200.

413   *The economics of slavery did not escape:* Ira Berlin, *Slaves Without Masters* (New York: Oxford University Press, 1981), 136.

415   *The Ordinance, for Lincoln:* CW, 4:183.

418   *Arguing for restoration:* Johns, "A Momentous Incident in the History of Illinois."

419   *Persuading conservative Whigs:* Willard L. King, *Lincoln's Manager, David Davis* (Chicago: University of Chicago Press, 1960), 104; *Obituary Record of Graduates of Yale University* (New Haven: Yale University, 1880), 363.

420   *Earlier in his speech:* HI, 183–84.

420   *Lincoln's political purpose in affirming the Fugitive Slave Act:* CW, 3:384.

421   *He offered yet another reason:* CW, 3:284; 4:2; 5:327.

422   *Chase and Sumner's "Appeal of the Independent Democrats":* Congressional Globe, 33rd Congress, 1st Session, 281–82.

423   *For his peroration, Lincoln drew upon:* CW, 3:247–83.

424   *"Progressing with his theme":* Horace White, "Lincoln in 1854," in *Transactions of the Illinois State Historical Society for the Year 1908* (Springfield: Illinois State Journal, 1909).

424   *Herndon, serving as reporter:* William Henry Herndon and Jesse William Weik, *Herndon's Lincoln: The True Story of a Great Life* (New York: Belford, Clarke, 1889), 296–97.

424   *Horace White in his report described:* Peck, "New Records of the Lincoln-Douglas Debate at the 1854 Illinois State Fair"; Beveridge, *Abraham Lincoln*, 2:263.

424   *Lincoln and Douglas restaged their debate:* CW, 3:282.

425   *The morning after the Peoria debate:* HI, 142, 164.

425   *Lincoln had delivered his speech:* White, "Lincoln in 1854."

425   *Immediately after Lincoln spoke at Springfield:* Herndon and Weik, *Herndon's Lincoln*, 299–300.

426   *Twenty-six men met that night:* Paul Selby, "The Genesis of the Republican Party in Illinois," in *Transactions of the Illinois State Historical Society* (Springfield: Illinois State Journal, 1906), 270–83; Magdol, *Owen Lovejoy*, 112–13.

427   *The next day the group, slightly expanded in numbers:* Paul Selby, "Republican State Convention, October 1854," *Transactions of the McLean County Historical Society* 3 (1900), 46; John G. Nicolay and John Hay, *Abraham Lincoln: A History* (New York: Century Company, 1890), 1:387.

427   *"The Black Republican Fizzle":* Selby, "Genesis of the Republican Party in Illinois," 275; Beveridge, *Abraham Lincoln*, 2:266; CW, 3:1–13.

428   *Several weeks after the convention:* CW, 2:288; Selby, "Genesis of the Republican Party in Illinois," 278.

428   *After the Springfield debate:* Miller, *Lincoln and His World*, 4:56; Burlingame, *Abraham Lincoln*, 1:365.

428   *With his debates with Douglas ended:* Earl W. Wiley, "Discovery of Record of Lincoln's Chicago Speech of October 27, 1854," *Journal of the Illinois State Historical Society* 21, no. 2 (July 1928), 218–23; Paul Selby, "George Schneider," in *Papers in Illinois History and Transactions* (Springfield: Illinois State Journal, 1906), 331–33.

429   *There were no more debates with Douglas:* CW, 2:284–86; Cole, *Centennial History of Illinois*, 131.

429   *The mid-October elections for the Congress:* Johannsen, *Stephen A. Douglas*, 460; Miller, *Lincoln and His World*, 4:43.

429   *The Democrats had been the normal governing party:* Cole, *Centennial History of Illinois,* 133; Johannsen, *Stephen A. Douglas,* 460; CW, 3:284; Miller, *Lincoln and His World,* 4:60.

430   *Douglas preferred to analyze the returns:* Johannsen, *Stephen A. Douglas,* 461–62.

430   *The harshest blow to the Democrats:* Ibid., 463.

CHAPTER TWENTY-ONE: SENATOR LINCOLN

432   *David Davis enlisted as unofficial campaign manager:* CW, 2:289, 286, 292, 290, 293, 296–97, 300–301, 303–4; King, *Lincoln's Manager,* 104–5.

432   *"That man who thinks Lincoln calmly":* Herndon and Weik, *Herndon's Lincoln,* 304.

432   *Lincoln resigned the state legislative seat:* "N. M. Broadwell Turned Up Again," *Illinois State Journal,* October 1, 1856; Donald, *Lincoln,* 180; HI, 266; King, *Lincoln's Manager,* 106.

433   *Despite his recent trip to Chicago Lincoln:* Beveridge, *Abraham Lincoln,* 2:276; Matthew Pinsker, "Senator Abraham Lincoln," *Journal of the Abraham Lincoln Association* 14, no. 2 (Summer 1993); Howard, "The Illinois Republican Party, Part I," 154.

433   *Lincoln recruited his two Whig allies:* Burlingame, *Abraham Lincoln,* 1:396.

433   *Washburne worked on Charles H. Ray:* Ibid., 1:395; Jay Monaghan, *The Man Who Elected Lincoln* (Indianapolis: Bobbs-Merrill, 1956), 42–45.

434   *In Washington, Washburne conferred:* "Elihu B. Washburne to Abraham Lincoln," Tuesday, December 26, 1854, Abraham Lincoln Papers, Library of Congress, Washington, D.C.

434   *Washburne also wrote Zebina Eastman:* "Elihu Washburne to Zebina Eastman," December 19, 1854, Zebina Eastman Papers, Chicago Historical Society, Chicago.

434   *The same day Washburne sent Eastman his letter:* "Washburne to Lincoln," December 19, 1854, Abraham Lincoln Papers, Library of Congress, Washington, D.C.; "Washburne to Lincoln," January 20, 1855, Abraham Lincoln Papers, Library of Congress, Washington, D.C.

435   *But Eastman did not make the trip to speak:* "Salmon P. Chase to Zebina Eastman," December 17, 1854, Zebina Eastman Papers, Chicago Historical Society, Chicago.

435   *Chase was a lame-duck senator:* Blue, *Salmon P. Chase,* 93; Hart, *Salmon Portland Chase,* 151; John Niven, ed., *Salmon P. Chase Papers, Journals, 1829–1872* (Kent, Ohio: Kent State University Press, 1998), 1:xlix.

435   *Three principal candidates, each representing a tendency:* Burlingame, *Abraham Lincoln,* 1:399–400; Harris, *The History of Negro Servitude in Illinois,* 116–17; McCormack, *Memoirs of Gustave Koerner,* 1:425.

436   *Before the balloting set for January 23, 1855:* Johns, "A Momentous Incident in the History of Illinois," 554–56.

436   *The Hall of Representatives where five months:* Horace White, *The Life of Lyman Trumbull* (New York: Houghton Mifflin, 1913), 41.

436   *Trumbull's five votes consisted of anti-Nebraska Democrats:* HI, 537; "John M. Palmer to Lyman Trumbull," December 28, 1861, Abraham Lincoln Papers, Library of Congress, Washington, D.C.; John M. Palmer, *Personal Recollections of John M. Palmer* (Cincinnati: R. Clarke, 1901), 69.

437   *Lincoln fell to thirty-eight:* Magdol, *Owen Lovejoy*, 431; *Chicago Tribune*, February 13, 1855.

437   *As his votes tumbled:* Johns, "A Momentous Incident in the History of Illinois"; White, *Life of Lyman Trumbull*, 44; HI, 434.

438   *At the crucial moment that Lincoln realized:* HI, 183.

438   *"I could have headed off":* CW, 2:306.

438   *While the voting went on:* Johns, "A Momentous Incident in the History of Illinois"; HI, 267.

439   *But in the end political imperatives:* Burlingame, *Abraham Lincoln*, 1:405; Zebina Eastman, "History of the Anti-Slavery Agitation, and the Growth of the Liberty and Republican Parties in the State of Illinois," in Rufus Blanchard, *Discovery and Conquests of the North-west* (Wheaton, Ill.: R. Blanchard, 1881), 669–71.

439   *The Whigs mourned their loss as a betrayal:* HI, 183, 538; Beveridge, *Abraham Lincoln*, 1:292; Burlingame, *Abraham Lincoln*, 1:404.

440   *David Davis believed that Lincoln:* King, *Lincoln's Manager*, 108.

440   *Elizabeth Todd Edwards:* Caroline Owsley Brown, "Springfield Society Before the Civil War," *Journal of the Illinois State Historical Society* 15, no. 2 (1922), 488–89; White, *Life of Lyman Trumbull*, 45.

440   *Mary, however, never reconciled herself:* Burlingame, *Abraham Lincoln*, 1:404; Justin G. Turner and Linda Levitt Turner, eds., *Mary Todd Lincoln: Her Life and Letters* (New York: Alfred A. Knopf, 1972), 264, 274.

440   *Sometime on the night of the election:* Pinsker, "Senator Abraham Lincoln."

441   *To a client, a week later, he wrote:* CW, 2:306–7; Donald, *Lincoln*, 184; Burlingame, *Inner World of Abraham Lincoln*, 92.

441   *Lincoln held no grudges toward Trumbull:* HI, 538; Whitney, *Life on the Circuit with Lincoln*, 147.

442   *Hitching up his old horse Bob:* CW, 2:308.

442   *In fact, about two weeks after the election:* "Lyman Trumbull to Abraham Lincoln," February 24, 1855, Abraham Lincoln Papers, Library of Congress, Washington, D.C.

442   *Lincoln organized the effort for:* CW, 2:313.

CHAPTER TWENTY-TWO: THE REPUBLICAN

443   *Through the collapse of the Whigs:* Robin Einhorn, "The Lager Beer Riot," The Encyclopedia of Chicago, http://www.encyclopedia.chicagohistory.org/pages/703.html.

444   *Nativism threatened to engulf:* Victor B. Howard, "The Illinois Republican Party:

Part II, The Party Becomes Conservative, 1855–1856," *Journal of the Illinois State Historical Society* (Autumn 1971), 288; Gienapp, *Origins of the Republican Party*, 236; Anbinder, *Nativism and Slavery*, 164.

444 *Beneath the surface the politics:* Senning, "Know Nothing Movement in Illinois," 19–20.

445 *Within the Illinois Know Nothings:* "Illinois American Platform," *Illinois State Journal*, July 11, 1855.

445 *Douglas Democrats carefully tracked the convoluted:* Senning, "Know Nothing Movement in Illinois," 20.

445 *Codding continued his ministry:* I. Codding, "Success," *Chicago Tribune*, June 22, 1855.

446 *At the end of July, Codding spoke to a throng:* John M. Palmer, ed., *The Bench and Bar of Illinois: Historical and Reminiscent* (Chicago: Lewis Publishing, 1899), 1:183; Howard, "The Illinois Republican Party: Part II," 291.

446 *Owen Lovejoy immediately followed up:* Gienapp, *Origins of the Republican Party*, 286; Owen Lovejoy, "Restore the Missouri Compromise Line," Lovejoy Society, http://www.lovejoysociety.org/Speeches/feb_1855.htm.

447 *"Not even you are more anxious":* CW, 2:316–17.

447 *Trumbull's reply to Lovejoy paralleled:* Burlingame, *Abraham Lincoln*, 1:409.

448 *Lincoln's interpretation of Robertson's speech:* George Robertson, *Scrap Book on Law and Politics, Men and Times* (Lexington, Ky.: A. W. Elder, 1855), 25.

449 *Setting up his logic with his fractured quotation:* CW, 2:282.

451 *Lincoln signed off, for the first time:* CW, 2:317–18, 461.

451 *In 1862, after Lincoln issued:* Jerrica A. Giles and Allen Guelzo, "Colonel Utley's Emancipation—or, How Lincoln Offered to Buy a Slave," *Marquette Law Review* 93, no. 4 (Summer 2010), 1263–81; Benjamin Quarles, *Lincoln and the Negro* (New York: Oxford University Press, 1962), 197–98; "Paying for a Runaway Slave," *New York Times*, February 10, 1873.

451 *Nine days after writing his letter:* David Herbert Donald, *"We Are Lincoln Men": Abraham Lincoln and His Friends* (New York: Simon & Schuster, 2003), 54.

457 *Lincoln's condemnation of the Know Nothings:* Thomas Speed, *Records and Memorials of the Speed Family* (Louisville, Ky.: Courier-Journal Job Printing, 1892), 155–56; Holt, *Rise and Fall of the Whig Party*, 936–37; Kenneth Stampp, *America in 1857: A Nation on the Brink* (New York: Oxford University Press, 1990), 38; George H. Yater, "Bloody Monday," in *The Encyclopedia of Louisville*, John E. Kleber, ed. (Lexington: University Press of Kentucky, 2001), 97; Bryan S. Bush, "Bloody Monday Riots," Bryan S. Bush Books, http://www.bryansbush.com/hub.php?page=articles&layer=a0709.

457 *One of the witnesses:* Speed, *James Speed*

458 *A month after Henry Clay's Whig Party:* Seward, *1846–1861*, 245.

458 *In August, the Hards held a Democratic:* Alexander, *Political History of the State of*

New York, 2:209–15; Holt, *Rise and Fall of the Whig Party,* 945; "Republican Convention," *New York Times,* September 29, 1855.

459   *One by one, Seward assessed:* Alexander, *Political History of the State of New York,* 2:216; William H. Seward, "The Dangers in Extending Slavery," in *Republican Association of Washington, Republican Campaign Documents of 1856* (Washington, D.C.: Lewis Clephane, 1857), 173–82.

459   *In September, Joshua Giddings:* Burlingame, *Abraham Lincoln,* 1:409; Newton, *Lincoln and Herndon,* 83.

460   *That September Lincoln focused on what he thought:* William W. Dickson, "Abraham Lincoln in Cincinnati," *Harper's New Monthly Magazine,* June 1884, 69, 62–64; Ida Minerva Tarbell, *The Early Life of Abraham Lincoln* (New York: S. S. McClure, 1896), 1:260–66.

461   *Lincoln had envisioned himself:* HI, 655.

461   *The month after the Manny trial:* William Ward Hayes, ed., *Abraham Lincoln: Tributes from His Associates, Reminiscences of Soldiers, Statesmen and Citizens* (New York: T. Y. Crowell, 1895), 242–44.

462   *"Illinois is the battle ground":* Newton, *Lincoln and Herndon,* 83–85; Beveridge, *Abraham Lincoln,* 1:353.

462   *Some months later, Herndon mentioned:* Newton, *Lincoln and Herndon,* 92; "Simeon Francis to Abraham Lincoln," December 26, 1859, Abraham Lincoln Papers, Library of Congress, Washington, D.C.

463   *Lincoln, however, maintained a relationship:* "The Republican Movement," *Illinois State Journal,* November 23, 1855; *Illinois State Journal,* December 19, 1855; "The Republican Exhibit," *Illinois State Journal,* December 21, 1855.

463   *At last the* Journal *revealed itself wholeheartedly:* "Mr. Fillmore for President," *Illinois State Journal,* December 26, 1855.

464   *In the light of the Know Nothing capture:* Burlingame, *Abraham Lincoln,* 1:411.

464   *"The man who is of neither party is not":* CW, 2:126; Herndon and Weik, *Herndon's Lincoln,* 311.

464   *In January 1856, Paul Selby:* Paul Selby, "The Editorial Convention, February 22, 1856," *in McLean County Historical Society,* Ezra Morton Prince, ed. (Bloomington, Ill.: Pantagraph Printing, 1900), 3:35; Otto R. Kyle, *Lincoln in Decatur* (New York: Vantage Press, 1957), 65.

465   *A week before the meeting:* Reinhard H. Luthin, "Lincoln Becomes a Republican," *Political Science Quarterly* 59, no. 3 (September 1944), 429.

465   *Selby also noted that he had received a letter:* Ibid., 429.

465   *The day before the convention:* Burlingame, *Abraham Lincoln,* 1:413; "Address of George Schneider, Meeting of May 29, 1900 Commemorative of the Convention of May 29, 1856 That Organized the Republican Party in the State of Illinois," in *Transactions of the McLean County Historical Society,* Ezra M. Prince, ed. (Bloomington, Ill.: Pantagraph Printing, 1900), 87–92.

466   *That evening the delegates convened:* Kyle, *Lincoln in Decatur,* 75–76; Tarbell, *Early Life of Abraham Lincoln,* 1:291.

467   *The most important business of the meeting:* Selby, "Editorial Convention," 38–39; Tarbell, *Early Life of Abraham Lincoln,* 1:291.

467   *On the same day as the editors' convention:* Green Berry Raum, *History of Illinois Republicanism* (Chicago: Rollins Publishing, 1900), 27.

467   *Then Francis P. Blair, at whose Silver Spring, Maryland, home:* Gienapp, *Origins of the Republican Party,* 255.

468   *That evening, after John Vaughn:* "Republican Convention," *New York Times,* February 26, 1856.

468   *The action moved to the roughhouse politics:* Fremont O. Bennett, *Politics and Politicians of Chicago* (Chicago: Blakely Printing, 1886), 102; John Moses and Joseph Kirkland, *History of Chicago* (Chicago: Munsell, 1895), 1:131; "Mayor Thomas Dyer Inaugural Address, 1856," Chicago Public Library, http://www.chipublib .org/mayor-thomas-dyer-inaugural-address-1856/.

468   *Bissell suddenly got cold feet:* Don E. Fehrenbacher, *Chicago Giant: A Biography of "Long John" Wentworth* (Chicago: University of Illinois Press, 1983), 135; Gienapp, *Origins of the Republican Party,* 290–91; Cole, *Centennial History of Illinois,* 144; Burlingame, *Abraham Lincoln,* 1:415.

470   *He was also incredulous:* "Charles H. Ray to Elihu B. Washburne," May 4, 1856, Washburne Papers, Library of Congress, Washington, D.C.

470   *Gillespie was operating hand-in-glove:* "Know Nothing State Convention," *Illinois State Journal,* May 8, 1856.

470   *Just as the* Journal *suggested:* Donald, *Lincoln's Herndon,* 87; Gienapp, *Origins of the Republican Party,* 294; "Bloomington Convention," *Illinois State Journal,* May 9, 1856; CW, 6:118.

471   *One of the enduring Lincoln myths:* Luthin, "Lincoln Becomes a Republican," 431; Donald, *Lincoln's Herndon,* 86–88; Donald E. Fehrenbacher, *Prelude to Greatness: Lincoln in the 1850's* (Stanford, Calif.: Stanford University Press, 1962), 45; Rufus Rockwell Wilson, *Intimate Memories of Lincoln* (Elmira, N.Y.: Primavera Press, 1945), 153.

471   *The myth of the laconic Lincoln:* Donald, *Lincoln's Herndon,* 86; Weik, *Real Lincoln,* 254.

472   *Lincoln's reply as reported by Herndon:* Herndon and Weik, *Herndon's Lincoln,* 311–12.

CHAPTER TWENTY-THREE: DESTINY AND POWER

473   *After the lectures the ladies:* Donald, *Lincoln's Herndon,* 54; Eleanor Marguerite Tilton, ed., *The Letters of Ralph Waldo Emerson* (New York: Columbia University Press, 1939), 4:342.

473   *"Power" was the subject of one of Emerson's lectures:* Ralph Waldo Emerson, *Representative Men* (London: George Routledge, 1850), 142–43.

474   *Emerson's ethereal aesthetics:* "Lectures," *Illinois Daily Journal,* January 13, 1853.

474   *Emerson's great men achieved their destinies:* Ralph Waldo Emerson, *Works of Ralph Waldo Emerson* (New York: Houghton Mifflin, 1883), 3:50.

475   *Lincoln had warned against the Napoleonic pretender:* Herndon and Weik, *Herndon's Lincoln,* 353.

475   *When Lincoln materialized in New Salem:* Ibid., 66; CW, 3:512.

475   *In retrospect, his closest contemporaries:* HI, 162.

476   *John W. Bunn, the Springfield merchant*: Phillips, *Abraham Lincoln, by Some Men Who Knew Him,* 151–58.

477   *Lincoln was still locked in mortal combat:* Hertz, *Hidden Lincoln,* 96.

477   *Within two years of shedding the husk:* CW, 2:461; 3:339.

478   *When Lincoln proclaimed himself:* Ralph Waldo Emerson, *Works of Ralph Waldo Emerson: Miscellanies* (New York: Houghton, Mifflin, 1883), 312, 314–15.

479   *"Oh, Lincoln":* Paul M. Angle, editor, "The Recollections of William Pitt Kellogg," *Abraham Lincoln Quarterly* 3, no. 7 (September 1945).

BIBLIOGRAPHY

Abbott, Richard H. *Cotton and Capital: Boston Businessmen and Antislavery Reform, 1854–1868.* Amherst, Mass.: University of Massachusetts Press, 1991.

Adams, John Quincy. *Memoirs of John Quincy Adams: Comprising Portions of His Diary from 1795 to 1848.* Philadelphia: J. B. Lippincott, 1875.

Alexander, De Alva Stanwood. *A Political History of the State of New York, 1833–1861.* New York: Henry Holt, 1906.

Angle, Paul M., ed. "The Recollections of William Pitt Kellogg." *Abraham Lincoln Quarterly* 3, no. 7 (September 1945).

Asbury, Herbert. *The Gangs of New York.* New York: Random House, 2008.

Bacon, Leonard. *Slavery Discussed in Occasional Essays from 1833 to 1846.* New York: Baker & Scribner, 1846.

Baker, Jean H. *Mary Todd Lincoln.* New York: W. W. Norton, 2008.

Bancroft, Frederic. *The Life of William H. Seward.* New York: Harper & Brothers, 1900.

Bartlett, David W. *The Life of Gen. Franklin Pierce of New Hampshire.* New York: Miller, Orton & Mulligan, 1855.

Basler, Roy P., ed. *The Collected Works of Abraham Lincoln.* New Brunswick, N.J.: Rutgers University Press, 1953.

Bauer, K. Jack. *Zachary Taylor: Soldier, Planter, Statesman of the Old Southwest.* Baton Rouge: Louisiana State University Press, 1993.

Beecher, Charles. *The Duty of Disobedience to Wicked Laws: A Sermon on the Fugitive Slave Act.* New York: J. A. Gray, 1851.

Belohlavek, John M. *Broken Glass: Caleb Cushing and the Shattering of the Union.* Kent, Ohio: Kent State University Press, 2005.

Bender, Thomas. *A Nation Among Nations: America's Place in World History.* New York: Hill & Wang, 2006.

Benton, Thomas Hart. *Historical and Legal Examination of That Part of the Decision of the Supreme Court of the United States in the Dred Scott Case.* New York: D. Appleton, 1857.

————. *Thirty Years' View: Or, A History of the Working of the American Government for Thirty Years, from 1820 to 1850.* New York: D. Appleton, 1880.

Berlin, Ira. *Slaves Without Masters.* New York: Oxford University Press, 1981.

Berlin, Ira, ed. *The Black Military Experience.* New York: Cambridge University Press, 1982.

Beveridge, Albert J. *Abraham Lincoln.* New York: Houghton Mifflin, 1928.

Biagini, Eugenio F. " 'The Principle of Humanity': Lincoln in Germany and Italy, 1859–1865," in *The Global Lincoln,* Richard Carwardine and Jay Sexton, eds. New York: Oxford University Press, 2011.

Blight, David W. *Frederick Douglass' Civil War: Keeping Faith in Jubilee.* Baton Rouge: Louisiana State University Press, 1991.

Bolaños Geyer, Alejandro. *William Walker: Grey-Eye Man of Destiny.* St. Louis: Privately printed, 1990.

Bordewich, Fergus. *Bound for Canaan: The Epic Story of the Underground Railroad.* New York: HarperCollins, 2009.

Breckinridge, Robert J. *Hints on Slavery,* vol. 19. Lexington, Ky.: 1830.

Brewer, Willis. *Alabama, Her History, Resources, War Record, and Public Men: From 1540 to 1872.* Montgomery, Ala.: Barrett & Brown, 1872.

Brown, Norman D. *Edward Stanly: Whiggery's Tarheel "Conqueror."* Tuscaloosa: University of Alabama Press, 1974.

Brown, Samuel Gilman. *The Life of Rufus Choate.* Boston: Little, Brown, 1870.

Browne, Francis F. *Every-Day Life of Abraham Lincoln.* Chicago: Browne & Howell, 1913.

Burlingame, Michael. *Abraham Lincoln: A Life.* Baltimore: Johns Hopkins University Press, 2008.

————. *The Inner World of Abraham Lincoln.* Urbana: University of Illinois Press, 1994.

Butler, William Allen. *A Retrospect of Forty Years, 1825–1865.* New York: C. Scribner's Sons, 1911.

————. *Martin Van Buren: Lawyer, Statesman and Man.* New York: D. Appleton, 1862.

Calarco, Tom. *The Underground Railroad in the Adirondack Region.* Jefferson, N.C.: McFarland, 2004.

Capers, Gerald M. *Stephen A. Douglas, Defender of the Union.* Boston: Little, Brown: 1959.

Carpenter, Francis B. *The Inner Life of Abraham Lincoln: Six Months at the White House.* New York: Hurd & Houghton, 1872.

Cashin, Joan E. *First Lady of the Confederacy: Varina Davis's Civil War.* Cambridge: Harvard University Press, 2006.

Cecil-Fronsman, Bill. " 'Death to All Yankees and Traitors in Kansas': The *Squatter Sovereign* and the Defense of Slavery in Kansas." *Kansas History* (Spring 1993).

Chadwick, Bruce. *1858: Abraham Lincoln, Jefferson Davis, Robert E. Lee, Ulysses S. Grant and the War They Failed to See* (Napierville, Ill.: Sourcebooks, 2011).

Chaffin, Tom. *Fatal Glory: Narciso López and the First Clandestine U.S. War Against Cuba.* Baton Rouge: Louisiana State University Press, 2003.

Chase, Salmon P. *Diary and Correspondence.* Washington, D.C.: Government Printing Office, 1903.

Clark, John E. *Railroads in the Civil War: The Impact of Management on Victory and Defeat.* Baton Rouge: Louisiana State University Press, 2004.

Clay, Cassius Marcellus. *The Life of Cassius Marcellus Clay.* Cincinnati: J. F. Brennan, 1886.

———. *Slavery: The Evil—The Remedy.* New York: Greeley & McElrath, 1844.

Clay, Henry. *The Works of Henry Clay: Private Correspondence, 1801–1852.* New York: G. P. Putnam's Sons, 1904.

Coffin, Charles Carleton. *Abraham Lincoln.* New York: Harper & Brothers, 1892.

Commager, Henry Steele. *Theodore Parker: Yankee Crusader.* Boston: Little, Brown, 1936.

Connelley, William E. *A Standard History of Kansas and Kansans.* Chicago: Lewis Publishing, 1918.

Cooper, William J. Jr. *Jefferson Davis, American.* New York: Alfred A. Knopf, 2000.

Cox, Lawanda, and John H. Cox. *Politics, Principle, and Prejudice, 1865–1866.* New York: Free Press, 1963.

Craft, William, and Ellen Craft. *Running a Thousand Miles for Freedom: or, The Escape of William and Ellen Craft from Slavery.* London: William Tweedie, 1860.

Craven, Avery. *The Coming of the Civil War.* Chicago: University of Chicago Press, 1942.

———. *The Growth of Southern Nationalism.* Baton Rouge: Louisiana State University Press, 1953.

Crawford, Dorothy H. *Deadly Companions: How Microbes Shaped Our History.* New York: Oxford University Press, 2007.

Crist, Lynda Lasswell, ed. *The Papers of Jefferson Davis: 1849–1852.* Baton Rouge: Louisiana State University Press, 1983.

Curtis, Francis. *The Republican Party.* New York: G. P. Putnam's Sons, 1904.

Curtis, George Ticknor. *Constitutional History of the United States.* New York: Harper & Brothers, 1896.

———. *Life of Daniel Webster.* New York: D. Appleton, 1889.

———. *Life of James Buchanan: Fifteenth President of the United States.* New York: Harper & Brothers, 1883.

Davis, Rodney O., and Douglas L. Wilson, eds. *The Lincoln-Douglas Debates.* Urbana: University of Illinois Press, 2008.

Davis, Varina. *Jefferson Davis Ex-President of the Confederate States of America*. New York: Belford, 1890.

Davis, William C. *Jefferson Davis: The Man and His Hour*. New York: HarperCollins, 1991.

———. *Rhett: The Turbulent Life and Times of a Fire-Eater*. Columbia: University of South Carolina Press, 2001.

Denison, George Stanton, ed. *Diary and Correspondence of Salmon P. Chase*. Washington, D.C.: Government Printing Office, 1903.

Dennett, Tyler, ed. *Lincoln and the Civil War in the Diaries and Letters of John Hay*. New York: Dodd, Mead, 1939.

Dixon, Susan Bullitt. *The True History of the Missouri Compromise and Its Repeal*. Cincinnati: Robert Clarke, 1899.

Dodd, William Edward. *Jefferson Davis*. Lincoln: University of Nebraska Press, 1997.

Donald, David Herbert. *Charles Sumner and the Coming of the Civil War*. Chicago: University of Chicago Press, 1960.

———. *We Are Lincoln Men*. New York: Simon & Schuster, 2003.

Douglass, Frederick. *The Life and Times of Frederick Douglass*. Hartford, Conn.: Park Publishing, 1882.

———. *Selected Speeches and Writings*, Philip S. Foner, ed. Chicago: Chicago Review Press, 2000.

Du Bois, James T., and Gertrude S. Mathews. *Galusha A. Grow: Father of the Homestead Law*. New York: Houghton Mifflin, 1917.

Eastman, Zebina. "History of the Anti-Slavery Agitation, and the Growth of the Liberty and Republican Parties in the State of Illinois," in Rufus Blanchard, *Discovery and Conquests of the North-west*. Wheaton, Ill.: R. Blanchard, 1881.

Ehrlich, Walter. *They Have No Rights: Dred Scott's Struggle for Freedom*. Bedford, Mass.: Applewood Press, 2007.

Eisenhower, John S. D. *Agent of Destiny: The Life and Times of General Winfield Scott*. Norman: University of Oklahoma Press, 1999.

Everett, Edward, ed. *The Writings and Speeches of Daniel Webster*. Boston: Little, Brown, 1903.

Eyal, Yonatan. *The Young America Movement and the Transformation of the Democratic Party*. New York: Cambridge University Press, 2007.

Fehrenbacher, Don E. *Chicago Giant: A Biography of "Long John" Wentworth*. Chicago: University of Illinois Press, 1983.

———. *Prelude to Greatness: Lincoln in the 1850's*. Stanford, Calif.: Stanford University Press, 1962.

———. *The Slaveholding Republic*. New York: Oxford University Press, 2001.

Fields, Annie, ed. *Life and Letters of Harriet Beecher Stowe*. New York: Houghton, Mifflin, 1898.

Findley, Paul. *A. Lincoln: The Crucible of Congress*. New York: Crown, 1979.

Finkelman, Paul. "Millard Fillmore," in *American Presidents: Critical Essays*, Melvin I. Urofsky, ed. New York: Taylor & Francis, 2000.

———. *Millard Fillmore*. New York: Macmillan, 2011.

Fischer, David Hackett. *Liberty and Freedom: A Visual History of America's Founding*. New York: Oxford University Press, 2005.

Fitzhugh, George. *Sociology for the South, or the Failure of Free Society*. Richmond, Va.: A. Morris, 1854.

Flint, Henry M. *Life of Stephen A. Douglas, United States Senator from Illinois*. New York: Derby & Jackson, 1860.

Foner, Eric. *The Fiery Trial: Abraham Lincoln and American Slavery*. New York: W. W. Norton, 2010.

———. "Politics and Prejudice: The Free Soil Party and the Negro, 1849–1852." *Journal of Negro History* 50, no. 4 (October 1965).

Foote, Henry S. *Casket of Reminiscences*. Washington, D.C.: Chronicle Publishing, 1874.

Ford, Thomas. *A History of Illinois*. Chicago: S. C. Griggs, 1854.

Forooha. Manzar. *The Catholic Church and Social Change in Nicaragua*. Albany, N.Y.: State University of New York Press, 1989.

Fox-Genovese, Elizabeth, and Eugene Genovese. *The Mind of the Master Class: History and Faith in the Southern Slaveholders' Worldview*. New York: Cambridge University Press, 2005.

Freehling, William W. *The Road to Disunion: Secessionists Triumphant, 1854–1861*. New York: Oxford University Press, 2007.

Frothingham, Octavius Brooks. *Theodore Parker: A Biography*. Boston: J. R. Osgood, 1874.

Frothingham, Paul Revere. *Edward Everett: Orator and Statesman*. New York: Houghton Mifflin, 1925.

Gara, Larry. *The Presidency of Franklin Pierce*. Lawrence: University Press of Kansas, 1991.

Giddings, Joshua R. *History of the Rebellion: Its Authors and Causes*. New York: Follet, Foster, 1864.

Gienapp, William E. *The Origins of the Republican Party, 1852–1856*. New York: Oxford University Press, 1987.

Giles, Jerrica A., and Allen Guelzo. "Colonel Utley's Emancipation—or, How Lincoln Offered to Buy a Slave." *Marquette Law Review* 93, no. 4 (Summer 2010).

Goldfield, David. *America Aflame: How the Civil War Created a Nation*. New York: Bloomsbury Press, 2011.

Goodwin, Doris Kearns. *Team of Rivals*. New York: Simon & Schuster, 2006.

Griffin, Susan B. *Anti-Catholicism and Nineteenth-Century Fiction*. New York: Cambridge University Press, 2004.

Griffith, Elisabeth. *In Her Own Right: The Life of Elizabeth Cady Stanton*. New York: Oxford University Press, 1984.

Grinnell, Josiah Bushnell. *Men and Events of Forty Years.* Boston: D. Lothrop, 1901.

Guelzo, Allen C. *Lincoln and Douglas: The Debates That Defined America.* New York: Simon & Schuster, 2008.

Gugliotta, Guy. *Freedom's Cap: The United States Capitol and the Coming of the Civil War.* New York: Macmillan, 2012.

Hall, Kermit L. *The Politics of Justice.* Lincoln: University of Nebraska Press, 1976.

Hamer, Philip May. *The Secession Movement in South Carolina, 1847–1852.* Allentown, Pa.: H. R. Haas, 1918.

Hamilton, Charles Granville. *Lincoln and the Know Nothing Movement.* Washington, D.C.: Public Affairs Press, 1954.

Hamilton, Holman. *Prologue to Conflict: The Crisis and Compromise of 1850.* Lexington: University Press of Kentucky, 1964.

Hamlin, Charles Eugene. *The Life and Times of Hannibal Hamlin.* Cambridge, Mass.: Riverside Press, 1899.

Harlow, Luke Edward. "From Border South to Solid South: Religion, Race, and the Making of Confederate Kentucky, 1830–1880." PhD diss., Rice University, 2009.

Harper, Robert S. *Lincoln and the Press.* New York: McGraw Hill, 1951.

Harpster, Jack. *The Railroad Tycoon Who Built Chicago: A Biography of William B. Ogden.* Carbondale: Southern Illinois University Press, 2009.

Harrison, Lowell Hayes. *The Antislavery Movement in Kentucky.* Lexington: University Press of Kentucky, 2004.

Harrold, Stanley. *Border War: The Long Physical Struggle over Slavery Before the Civil War.* Chapel Hill: University of North Carolina Press, 2010.

———. *Subversives: Antislavery Community in Washington, D.C., 1828–1865.* Baton Rouge: Louisiana State University Press, 2002.

Hart, Albert Bushnell. *Salmon Portland Chase.* New York: Houghton Mifflin, 1899.

Harvey, Peter. *Reminiscences of Daniel Webster.* Boston: Little, Brown, 1878.

Hawthorne, Nathaniel. *Life of Franklin Pierce.* Boston: Ticknor, Reed & Fields, 1852.

Heidler, David S., and Jeanne T. Heidler. *Henry Clay: The Essential American.* New York: Random House, 2010.

Heimert, Alan. "Moby-Dick and American Political Symbolism." *American Quarterly* 15, no. 4 (Winter 1963).

Henson, D. Leigh. "Classical Rhetoric as a Lens for Reading the Key Speeches of Lincoln's Political Rise, 1852–1856." *Journal of the Abraham Lincoln Association* 35, no. 1 (Winter 2014).

Hermann, Janet Sharp. *Joseph E. Davis: Pioneer Patriarch.* Oxford: University Press of Mississippi, 2007.

Herndon, William H. *Life of Lincoln.* Cleveland: World, 1942.

Herndon, William Henry, and Jesse William Weik. *Herndon's Lincoln: The True Story of a Great Life.* New York: Belford, Clarke, 1889.

Hertz, Emanuel. *The Hidden Lincoln: From the Letters and Papers of William H. Herndon.* New York: Blue Ribbon Books, 1940.

Higginbotham, A. Leon. *In the Matter of Color: Race and the American Legal Process, The Colonial Period.* New York: Oxford University Press, 1980.

Hirschhorn, N., R. G. Feldman, and I. A. Greaves. "Abraham Lincoln's Blue Pills." *Perspectives in Biology and Medicine* 44 (Summer 2001).

Hodder, Frank Heywood. "The Railroad Background of the Kansas-Nebraska Act." *Mississippi Valley Historical Review* 12, no. 10 (June 1925).

Hollingsworth, Randolph. "She Used Her Power Lightly: A Political History of Margaret Wickliffe Preston of Kentucky." PhD diss., University of Kentucky, 1999.

Holt, Michael F. *Franklin Pierce.* New York: Macmillan, 2010.

―――. "Politics, Patronage, and Public Policy: The Compromise of 1850," in Paul Finkelman and Donald R. Kennon, eds., *Congress and the Crisis of the 1850s.* Athens: Ohio University Press, 2012.

―――. *The Rise and Fall of the Whig Party: Jacksonian Politics and the Onset of the Civil War.* New York: Oxford University Press, 2003.

Howard, Victor B. "The Illinois Republican Party: Part II, The Party Becomes Conservative, 1855–1856." *Journal of the Illinois State Historical Society* (Autumn 1971).

Howe, Samuel Gridley. *The Servant of Humanity.* Boston: D. Estes, 1909.

Howells, William Dean. *Life and Speeches of Abraham Lincoln and Hannibal Hamlin.* Columbus, Ohio: Follett, Foster, 1860.

―――. *Life of Abraham Lincoln.* Columbus, Ohio: Follett, Foster, 1860.

Ilisevich, Robert D. *Galusha A. Grow: The People's Candidate.* Pittsburgh: University of Pittsburgh Press, 1989.

Johannsen, Robert Walter. *Stephen A. Douglas.* New York: Oxford University Press, 1973.

Johnson, Allen. *Stephen A. Douglas: A Study in American Politics.* New York: Macmillan, 1908.

Johnson, E. Polk. *A History of Kentucky and Kentuckians.* Chicago: Lewis Publishing, 1912.

Julian, George Washington. *The Life of Joshua R. Giddings.* New York: A. C. McClurg, 1892.

Kaplan, Sidney. "The Moby Dick in the Service of the Underground Railroad." *Phylon* 12, no. 2 (1951).

King, Willard L. *Lincoln's Manager, David Davis.* Chicago: University of Chicago Press, 1960.

Klein, Philip S. *President James Buchanan, A Biography.* University Park: Pennsylvania State University Press, 1962.

Klotter, James C. *The Breckinridges of Kentucky.* Lexington: University Press of Kentucky, 2006.

Kyle, Otto R. *Lincoln in Decatur.* New York: Vantage Press, 1957.

Lamon, Ward Hill. *The Life of Abraham Lincoln.* Boston: James R. Osgood, 1872.

Lehrman, Lewis. *Lincoln at Peoria: The Turning Point.* Mechanicsburg, Pa.: Stackpole Books, 2008.

Link, William A. *Roots of Secession: Slavery and Politics in Antebellum Virginia.* Chapel Hill: University of North Carolina Press, 2005.

Livingston, John. *Portraits of Eminent Americans Now Living.* New York: Lamport, 1854.

Lodge, Henry Cabot. *Daniel Webster.* New York: Houghton, Mifflin, 1899.

Luthin, Reinhard H. "Lincoln Becomes a Republican." *Political Science Quarterly* 59, no. 3 (September 1944).

Magdol, Edward. *Owen Lovejoy: Abolitionist in Congress.* New Brunswick, N.J.: Rutgers University Press, 1967.

Mann, Mary Tyler Peabody. *Life of Horace Mann.* Boston: Walker, Fuller, 1865.

Marrs, Aaron Wagner. *The Iron Horse Turns South: A History of Antebellum Southern Railroads.* Columbia: University of South Carolina, ProQuest, 2006.

Marshall, Peter, and David Manuel. *Sounding Forth the Trumpet: 1837–1860.* Grand Rapids, Mich.: Revell, 2009.

Martin, Asa Earl. *The Anti-Slavery Movement in Kentucky Prior to 1850.* Louisville, Ky.: Standard Publishing, 1918.

Maverick, Augustus. *Henry J. Raymond and the New York Press, for Thirty Years.* Hartford, Conn.: A. S. Hale, 1870.

May, Robert E. *Manifest Destiny's Underworld: Filibustering in Antebellum America.* Chapel Hill: University of North Carolina Press, 2002.

———. *Slavery, Race, and Conquest in the Tropics: Lincoln, Douglas, and the Future of Latin America.* New York: Cambridge University Press, 2013.

McCormack, Thomas J., ed. *Memoirs of Gustave Koerner.* Cedar Rapids, Iowa: Torch Press, 1909.

McCoy, Drew R. "An 'Old-Fashioned' Nationalism: Lincoln, Jefferson, and the Classical Tradition." *Journal of the Abraham Lincoln Association* 23, no. 1 (Winter 2002).

McGrane, Reginald Charles. *William Allen: A Study in Western Democracy.* Columbus: Ohio State Archaeological and Historical Society, 1925.

Meacham, Jon. *American Lion: Andrew Jackson in the White House.* New York: Random House, 2008.

Meigs, William M. *The Life of Thomas Hart Benton.* Philadelphia: J. B. Lippincott, 1904.

Mentelle, Mrs. C. *A Short History of the Late Mrs. Mary O. T. Wickliffe.* Lexington: Kentucky Statesman, 1850.

Miers, Earl Schenck, and William E. Baringer, eds. *Lincoln Day by Day: A Chronology, 1809–1865.* Washington, D.C.: Lincoln Sesquicentennial Commission, Northern Illinois University, 1960.

Miller, Donald L. *City of the Century: The Epic of Chicago and the Making of America.* New York: Simon & Schuster, 1996.

Miller, Richard Lawrence. *Lincoln and His World: Volume 3, The Rise to National Prominence, 1843–1853.* Jefferson, N.C.: McFarland, 2011.

———. *Lincoln and His World: Volume 4, The Path to the Presidency, 1854–1860.* Jefferson, N.C.: McFarland, 2012.

Milton, George Fort. *The Eve of Conflict: Stephen A. Douglas and the Needless War.* New York: Octagon, 1969.

Mitchell, Thomas G. *Antislavery Politics in Antebellum and Civil War America.* Westport, Conn.: Greenwood, 2007.

Monaghan, Jay. *Civil War on the Western Border, 1854–1865.* Boston: Little, Brown, 1955.

Morgan, David T. "Eugenia Levy Phillips: The Civil War Experiences of a Southern Jewish Woman," in *Jews of the South: Selected Essays from the Southern Jewish Historical Society*, Samuel Proctor, ed. Macon, Ga.: Louis Schmier and Malcolm H. Stern, Mercer University Press, 1984.

Moses, John, and Joseph Kirkland. *History of Chicago.* Chicago: Munsell, 1895.

Myers, William Starr. *A Study in Personality: General George Brinton McClellan.* New York: D. Appleton, 1934.

Newton, Joseph Fort. *Lincoln and Herndon.* Cedar Rapids, Iowa: Torch Press, 1910.

Nichols, Roy Franklin. *The Democratic Machine, 1850–1854.* New York: AMS Press, 1967.

———. *Franklin Pierce: Young Hickory of the Granite Hills.* University Park: University of Pennsylvania Press, 1931.

———. "The Kansas-Nebraska Act: A Century of Historiography." *Mississippi Valley Historical Review* 43, no. 2 (September 1956).

Nicolay, John G., and John Hay. *Abraham Lincoln: A History.* New York: Century Company, 1890.

Niven, John. *Salmon P. Chase.* New York: Oxford University Press, 1995.

Norman, Matthew. "Abraham Lincoln, Stephen A. Douglas, the Model Republic, and the Right of Revolution, 1848–61," in *Politics and Culture of the Civil War Era: Essays in Honor of Robert W. Johannsen*, Daniel J. MacDonough and Kenneth W. Noe, eds. Selinsgrove, Pa.: Susquehanna University Press, 2006.

Oshatz, Molly, *Slavery and Sin: The Fight Against Slavery and the Rise of Liberal Protestantism.* New York: Oxford University Press, 2011.

Parish, John Carl. *George Wallace Jones.* Iowa City: State Historical Society of Iowa, 1912.

Parker, Edward G. *Reminiscences of Rufus Choate.* New York: Mason Brothers, 1860.

Parker, Theodore. *Speeches, Addresses, and Occasional Sermons.* Boston: B. Fuller, 1871.

Pelzer, Louis. *Henry Dodge.* Iowa City: State Historical Society of Iowa, 1911.

Peterson, Merrill D. *The Great Triumvirate: Webster, Clay, and Calhoun.* New York: Oxford University Press, 1987.

Phillips, Christopher. *Missouri's Confederate: Claiborne Fox Jackson and the Creation of Southern Identity in the Border West*. Columbia: University of Missouri Press, 2000.

Phillips, Christopher, and Jason L. Pendleton, eds. *The Union on Trial: The Political Journals of Judge William Barclay Napton, 1829–1883*. Columbia: University of Missouri Press, 2005.

Phillips, Ulrich Bonnell. *The Life of Robert Toombs*. New York: Macmillan, 1913.

Phillips, Waldorf H. *The Missing Link: What Led to the War, or the Secret History of the Kansas-Nebraska Act*. Washington, D.C.: Gray & Clarkson, 1886.

Pierce, Edward L. *Memoir and Letters of Charles Sumner*. Boston: Roberts Brothers, 1894.

Pike, James Shepherd. *First Blows of the Civil War*. New York: American News, 1879.

Pinsker, Matthew. "Not Always Such a Whig: Abraham Lincoln Partisan Realignment in the 1850s." *Journal of the Abraham Lincoln Association* 29, no. 2 (November 2002).

Poore, Benjamin Perley. *Perley's Reminiscences of Sixty Years in the National Metropolis*. Philadelphia: Hubbard Brothers, 1885.

Potter, David Morris. *The Impending Crisis, 1848–1861*. New York: Harper & Row, 1976.

Pressly, Thomas J. *Americans Interpret Their Civil War*. Princeton: Princeton University Press, 1954.

Quarles, Benjamin. *Lincoln and the Negro*. New York: Oxford University Press, 1962.

Randall, James G. "A Blundering Generation," in *The Causes of the Civil War*, Kenneth M. Stampp, ed. New York: Simon & Schuster, 1959.

Randall, Ruth Painter. *Mary Lincoln: Biography of a Marriage*. New York: Little, Brown, 1959.

Rankin, Henry Bascom. *Personal Recollections of Abraham Lincoln*. New York: G. P. Putnam's Sons, 1916.

Rantoul, Robert Jr. *Memoirs, Speeches and Writings of Robert Rantoul, Jr*. Boston: Jewett, 1854.

Raum, Green Berry. *History of Illinois Republicanism*. Chicago: Rollins Publishing, 1900.

Rawley, James A. *Race and Politics: Bleeding Kansas and the Coming of the Civil War*. Lincoln: University of Nebraska Press, 1979.

Ray, Perley Orman. *The Repeal of the Missouri Compromise: Its Origin and Authorship*. Cleveland: Arthur H. Clark, 1908.

Remini, Robert V. *At the Edge of the Precipice: Henry Clay and the Compromise That Saved the Union*. New York: Basic Books, 2010.

———. *Daniel Webster: The Man and His Time*. New York: W. W. Norton, 1997.

———. *Henry Clay: Statesman for the Union*. New York: W. W. Norton, 1991.

Reynolds, David S. *Mightier than the Sword: Uncle Tom's Cabin and the Battle for America*. New York: W. W. Norton, 2011.

Rhodes, James Ford. *History of the United States from the Compromise of 1850 to the McKinley-Bryan Campaign of 1896: 1850–1854*. New York: Macmillan, 1920.

Rice, Allen Thorndike. *Reminiscences of Abraham Lincoln by Distinguished Men of His Time*. New York: North American Publishing, 1886.

Richardson, Robert. *Memoirs of Alexander Campbell*. Philadelphia: J. B. Lippincott, 1890.

Robertson, George. *Scrap Book on Law and Politics, Men and Times*. Lexington, Ky.: A. W. Elder, 1855.

Robinson, Charles. *The Kansas Conflict*. New York: Harper & Brothers, 1892.

Roche, James Jeffrey. *The Story of the Filibusters*. London: T. Fisher Unwin, 1891.

Rodgers, Daniel T. *Contested Truths: Keywords in American Politics Since Independence*. Cambridge: Harvard University Press, 1998.

Roll, Charles. *Colonel Dick Thompson: The Persistent Whig*. Indianapolis: Indiana Historical Bureau, 1948.

Salafia, Matthew. *Slavery's Borderland: Freedom and Bondage Along the Ohio River*. Philadelphia: University of Pennsylvania Press, 2013.

Scarborough, William Kauffman. *Masters of the Big House: Elite Slaveholders of the Mid-Nineteenth-Century South*. Baton Rouge: Louisiana State University Press, 2006.

Scarry, Robert J. *Millard Fillmore*. Jefferson, N.C.: McFarland, 2010.

Schlesinger, Arthur M. Jr. "The Causes of the Civil War: A Note on Historical Sentimentalism." *Partisan Review* 16 (1949).

Schuckers, J. W. *The Life and Public Services of Salmon Portland Chase*. New York: D. Appleton, 1874.

Schurz, Carl. *Henry Clay*. New York: Houghton Mifflin, 1899.

———. *The Reminiscenses of Carl Schurz, Volume 2, 1852–1863*. New York: Doubleday & Page, 1913.

Scisco, Louis Dow. *Political Nativism in New York State*. New York: Columbia University Press, 1901.

Scroggins, Mark. *Robert Toombs: The Civil Wars of a United States Senator and Confederate General*. Jefferson, N.C.: McFarland, 2011.

Scroggs, William O. *Filibusters and Financiers: The Story of William Walker and His Associates*. New York: Macmillan, 1916.

Sears, Stephen W. *George B. McClellan: The Young Napoleon*. New York: Ticknor & Fields, 1988.

Senning, John B. "The Know Nothing Movement in Illinois." *Journal of the Illinois State Historical Society* 7, no. 1 (April 1914).

Seward, Frederick. *Seward at Washington: 1846–1860*. New York: D. Appleton, 1891.

———. *William H. Seward, 1831–1846*. New York: Derby & Miller, 1891.

Seward, William H. *Freedom and Public Faith: Speeches*. Washington, D.C.: Buell & Blanchard, 1854.

———. *The Works of William H. Seward*. New York: Houghton, Mifflin, 1888.

Seward, William Henry, and Frederick W. Seward. *Seward at Washington as Senator and Secretary of State, 1846–1861*. New York: Derby & Miller, 1891.

Sewell, Richard H. *Ballots for Freedom: Antislavery Politics in the United States, 1837–1860*. New York: Oxford University Press, 1976.

Sheahan, James W. *The Life of Stephen A. Douglas*. New York: Harper & Brothers, 1860.

Shepard, Edward M. *Martin Van Buren*. New York: Houghton, Mifflin, 1896.

Silag, William. "Sioux City: An Iowa Boom Town," in *American Cities: A Collection of Essays*, Neil L. Shumsky, ed. New York: Taylor & Francis, 1996.

Simon, Paul. *Freedom's Champion—Elijah Lovejoy*. Carbondale: Southern Illinois University Press.

Simpson, Craig M. *A Good Southerner: The Life of Henry A. Wise of Virginia*. Chapel Hill: University of North Carolina Press, 2001.

Smiley, David L. *The Lion of White Hall*. Madison: University of Wisconsin Press, 1962.

Smith, Adam I. P. *No Party Now: Politics in the Civil War North*. New York: Oxford University Press, 2006.

Speed, James. *James Speed: A Personality*. Louisville, Ky.: J. P. Morton, 1914.

Spencer, Donald S. *Louis Kossuth and Young America: A Study of Sectionalism and Foreign Policy, 1848–1852*. Columbia: University of Missouri Press, 1977.

Spring, Leverett Wilson. *Kansas: Prelude to the War for the Union*. New York: Houghton, Mifflin, 1885.

Stahr, Walter. *Seward: Lincoln's Indispensable Man*. New York: Simon & Schuster, 2012.

Stampp, Kenneth. *America in 1857: A Nation on the Brink*. New York: Oxford University Press, 1990.

Stephens, Alexander. *A Constitutional View of the Late War Between the States*. Philadelphia: National Publishing, 1868.

———. "Meredith Poindexter Gentry," in Richard Gentry, *The Gentry Family in America: 1676 to 1909*. New York: Grafton Press, 1909.

———. *Recollections of Alexander H. Stephens*. New York: Doubleday, Page, 1910.

Stile, T. J. *The First Tycoon: The Epic Life of Cornelius Vanderbilt*. New York: Alfred A. Knopf, 2009.

Stout, Harry S. *Upon the Altar of the Nation: A Moral History of the American Civil War*. New York: Viking, 2006.

Stowe, Charles Edward, and Lyman Beecher Stowe. *Harriet Beecher Stowe: The Story of Her Life*. New York: Houghton Mifflin, 1911.

Stowe, Harriet Beecher. *The Key to Uncle Tom's Cabin*. London: Clarke, Beeton, 1853.

Stringfellow, B. F. *Negro-Slavery, No Evil, A Report Made to the Platte County Self-Defensive Association*. St. Louis: M. Nieder, 1854.

Tallant, Harold D., and Kathleen E. R. Smith. *Evil Necessity: Slavery and Political Culture in Antebellum Kentucky*. Lexington: University Press of Kentucky, 2003.

Tarbell, Ida Minerva. *The Early Life of Abraham Lincoln.* New York: S. S. McClure, 1896.

Tate, Adam L. *Conservatism and Southern Intellectuals, 1789–1861.* Columbia: University of Missouri Press, 2005.

Thayer, Eli. *A History of the Kansas Crusade.* New York: Harper, 1889.

Thomas, William G. *The Iron Way: Railroads, the Civil War, and the Making of Modern America.* New Haven: Yale University Press, 2011.

Thornwell, John Henley. *The Rights and Duties of Masters.* Charleston, S.C.: Walker & James, 1850.

Townsend, William H. *Lincoln and the Bluegrass.* Lexington: University Press of Kentucky, 1955.

Trent, William Peterfield. *Southern Statesmen of the Old Régime.* Boston: T. Y. Crowell, 1897.

Trexler, Harrison Anthony. *Slavery in Missouri, 1804–1865.* Baltimore: Johns Hopkins University Press, 1914.

Turner, Justin, G., and Linda Levitt Turner. *Mary Todd Lincoln: Her Life and Letters.* New York: Alfred A. Knopf, 1972.

von Holst, Hermann. *The Constitutional and Political History of the United States, 1850–1854.* Chicago: Callaghan, 1885.

Walker, William. *War in Nicaragua.* New York: S. H. Goetzel, 1860.

Walther, Eric H. *The Fire-Eaters.* Baton Rouge: Louisiana State University Press, 1992.

———. *The Shattering of the Union: America in the 1850s.* Lanham, Md.: Rowman & Littlefield, 2004.

Watts, Dale E. "How Bloody Was Bleeding Kansas? Political Killings in Kansas Territory, 1854–1861." *Kansas History: A Journal of the Central Plains* 18, no. 2 (Summer 1995).

Weed, Thurlow. *The Life of Thurlow Weed including His Autobiography and Memoir,* Vol. 1. Boston: Houghton Mifflin, 1884.

Weik, Jesse W. *The Real Lincoln.* New York: Houghton Mifflin, 1922.

Wentworth, John. *Congressional Reminiscences.* Chicago: Fergus Printing, 1882.

White, Charles. *Lincoln and the Newspapers.* Hancock, N.Y.: Hancock Herald Print, 1924.

White, M. J. *The Secession Movement in the United States, 1847–1852.* New Orleans: Tulane University Press, 1910.

Whitney, Henry Clay. *Life on the Circuit with Lincoln.* Boston: Estes & Lauriat, 1892.

Whittier, John Greenleaf. *Poems of John Greenleaf Whittier.* New York: T. Y. Crowell, 1902.

Wickliffe, Robert. *To the Freemen of the County of Fayette.* Lexington: Kentucky Gazette Print, 1845.

Wickre, John J. "Indiana's Southern Senator: Jesse Bright and the Hoosier Democracy." PhD diss., University of Kentucky, 2013.

Widmer, Edward L. *Young America: The Flowering of Democracy in New York City*. New York: Oxford University Press, 1999.

Wilentz. Sean. "Abraham Lincoln and Jacksonian Democracy," in *Our Lincoln: New Perspectives on Lincoln and His World*, Eric Foner, ed. New York: W. W. Norton, 2008.

———. *Chants Democratic: New York City and the Rise of the American Working Class, 1788–1850*. New York: Oxford University Press, 2004.

———. *The Rise of American Democracy*. New York: W. W. Norton, 2005.

Williams, D. Newell, Douglas Allen Foster, and Paul M. Blowers. *The Stone-Campbell Movement: A Global History*. St. Louis: Chalice Press, 2013.

Willis, Henry Parker. *Stephen A. Douglas*. Philadelphia: G. W. Jacobs, 1910.

Wilson, Douglas L. *Lincoln's Sword: The Presidency and the Power of Words*. New York: Alfred A. Knopf, 2006.

Wilson, Douglas S., Rodney O. Davis, Terry Wilson, William Henry Herndon, and Jesse William Weik, eds. *Herndon's Informants: Letters, Interviews, and Statements About Abraham Lincoln*. Urbana: University of Illinois Press, 1998.

Wilson, Henry. *History of the Rise and Fall of the Slave Power in America*. Boston: J. R. Osgood, 1875.

Wilson, Rufus Rockwell. *Intimate Memories of Lincoln*. Elmira, N.Y.: Primavera Press, 1945.

Wiltse, Charles M. *John C. Calhoun: Sectionalist, 1840–1850*. Indianapolis: Bobbs-Merrill, 1951.

Wineapple, Brenda. *Hawthorne: A Life*. New York: Random House, 2004.

Winston, Robert W. *High Stakes and Hair Trigger: The Life of Jefferson Davis*. New York: Henry Holt, 1930.

Woldman, Albert A. *Lawyer Lincoln*. New York: Houghton Mifflin, 1936.

Woodward, C. Vann, ed. *George Fitzhugh, Cannibals All! Slaves Without Masters*. Cambridge: Harvard University Press, 1988.

ILLUSTRATION CREDITS

Endpapers:

Front: *Union*, painted by Tompkins H. Matteson; engraved by Henry S. Sadd, 1852

Front row, left to right: General Winfield Scott, Senator Lewis Cass of Michigan, Senator Henry Clay of Kentucky, Senator John C. Calhoun of South Carolina, Senator Daniel Webster of Massachusetts, and President Millard Fillmore. In the left background, left to right: Speaker of the House Howell Cobb of Georgia, Virginia Representative James McDowell, Senator Thomas Hart Benton of Missouri, and former Secretary of State John M. Clayton of Delaware. Second row at right: Senator Thomas Corwin of Ohio, former Secretary of State James Buchanan of Pennsylvania, Senator Stephen A. Douglas of Illinois, Attorney General John J. Crittenden of Kentucky, Senator Sam Houston of Texas, and Senator Henry Foote of Mississippi. Behind: Senator Willie P. Mangum of North Carolina and Senator W. R. King of Alabama. Far right: Senator Daniel S. Dickinson of New York, Supreme Court Justice John McLean of Ohio, Senator John Bell of Tennessee, and Senator John C. Fremont of California.

Back: John Adams Whipple, photograph, 1860. Abraham Lincoln at his home in Springfield, Illinois, with his sons Tad and Willie

Frontispiece: Library of Congress

Facing Prologue: Library of Congress; digital version courtesy of Daniel Weinberg, the Abraham Lincoln Bookshop, Chicago

9   Library of Congress

11   University of Kentucky Libraries

33   Library of Congress

39   Library of Congress

41   Wikimedia Commons

45   Library of Congress

59   Library of Congress

62   Wikimedia Commons

83   Library of Congress

105 Wikimedia Commons

119 Library of Congress

122 Wikimedia Commons

129 Library of Congress

151 Wikimedia Commons

167 Library of Congress

172 Library of Congress

187 Library of Congress

199 Library of Congress

225 Encyclopedia Virginia, Virginia Foundation for the Humanities

250 National Archives

251 Library of Congress

263 Library of Congress

274 Beinecke Rare Book & Manuscript Library, Yale University

283 Library of Congress

293 Wikimedia Commons

318 Boston Public Library

321 Library of Congress

333 Library of Congress

347 Library of Congress

355 Architect of the Capitol

356 Architect of the Capitol

367 Encyclopedia Virginia, Virginia Foundation for the Humanities

381 Thomas Jefferson Foundation

388 Library of Congress

431 Library of Congress

443 Library of Congress

466 Library of Congress

473 George Eastman House Collection

INDEX

Page numbers in *italics* refer to illustrations.

abolitionists, abolitionism, 19–20, 64, 75, 103, 122–23, 153, 154, 204, 207, 246, 251, 256, 296, 304, 305, 320, 334, 377, 380–81, 382, 383, 397
  AL and, 205, 206, 391–92, 401, 426, 433, 439, 456, 477
  Breckinridge's loathing of, 12–13
  Clay's loathing of, 12, 17, 86–87, 111
  Codding as leader of, 383, 384, 393–94, 429
  Douglas's hatred of, 95, 124–25, 216, 309, 400
  English, 13, 111, 124–25
  Garrisonian, 205, 206, 212, 297, 333, 378
  in Illinois, *see* Illinois, abolitionists in
  Know Nothings and, 403, 444
  Kossuth and, 160–61
  revisionist historians' view of, 359–60
  sectarian divisions among, 6
  Webster's hatred of, 65, 108, 109, 112
  Whigs and, 419, 439
Accessory Transit Company, 352–53
Adam (slave), 451
Adams, Charles Francis, 109, 113, 211, 212, 213, 297, 312, 328, 334
Adams, John Quincy, 19, 49, 53, 73, 84, 153, 209, 217, 308, 344, 474

Age of Reason, The (Paine), 139, 405
Aiken, William, 267–68
Ajax, 38
Alabama, 243
Albany Evening Journal, 22, 45, 90, 99, 105, 381
Albany Regency, 313
Albany Register, 99
Alcott, Bronson, 319
Alien and Sedition Acts, 11
Allen, William, 301
Alsop, J. W., 171
Alton, Ill., 212, 446, 447–48
Alton and Sangamon Railroad, 135
Alton Telegraph, 462
American Anti-Slavery Society, 161, 377
American Colonization Society, 32, 38, 200, 204, 209, 434
American Party, *see* Know Nothings
American Republican Party, 325
American Revolution, 111
American system, 103, 199–200, 203
American Tract Society, 361
American Whig Review, 158
Anderson, Oliver, 25–26
Annual of Science, 373
Anti-Masonic Party, 45, 83, 459

anti-Nebraska movement, 299, 322–23,
    326, 328, 329, 333, 334, 429, 436–37,
    439, 441, 442, 444, 447, 458, 464, 470
    AL and, 4, 364–65, 400, 401, 417, 418,
        424, 427, 438, 466
    Douglas excoriated by, 298–301, 302,
        362–64
antislavery movement, 123, 145, 182, 201,
    217, 297, 302, 380–81
    Compromise of 1850's demoralizing
        effect on, 124
    Uncle Tom's Cabin as rallying cry for,
        124
    see also abolitionists, abolitionism
"Appeal of the Independent Democrats in
    Congress to the People of the United
    States, The," 298–99, 300, 310, 311,
    422–23
Archer, William B., 470
Argus, 120
Aristocracy in America (Grund), 98
Arizona, 54
Arkansas Territory, 448–49
Armed Liberty, 355–56, *355, 356*
Armstrong, Jack, 135, 401
Army, U.S., Davis's modernization of, 239
Army Corps of Engineers, U.S., 244
Arnold, Isaac N., 429
Aroostook War, 190
Ashmun, George, 100
Aspinwall, William, 171
Atchison, David Rice, 259, *274,* 288, 291,
    338, 362
    Benton's war with, 252, 255, 257,
        258–60, 272, 273, 275, 276, 335
    Border Ruffians led by, 340, 345, 478
    Douglas and, 274–75
    as F Street Mess member, 248–49
    Kansas "Bogus Legislature" advised by,
        343
    Kansas free-staters opposed by, 335, 336
    Kansas-Nebraska Act and, *see* Kansas-
        Nebraska Act
    Missouri Compromise repeal supported
        by, 257, 259–60, 273, 278–79, 282, 283

pro-slavery belligerence of, 251–52,
    273–74
as Senate president pro-tempore, 251–52,
    284
Atchison, Kans., 336
Atlantic, 129
Atlantic and Pacific Company, 272
Awful Disclosures of Maria Monk, The,
    325

Bacon, Leonard W., 377–78, 378, 388, 410
Bailey, Gamaliel, 261, 323, 467
Bailhache, William H., 462–63, 472
Baker, Edward D., 162, 279
Baker, Edward L., 462–63, 465, 467, 472
Baker, Jean H., 132
Baldwin, Roger, 89
Ballenger, John L., 26
Ballinger, Richard H., 390
Baltimore Sun, 98, 183
Banks, Nathaniel P., 315, 329
Barker, James W., 331
Barnburners, 106, 180, 211, 213–14, 217,
    219, 220, 226, 234, 382
Barnwell, Robert W., 87, 98
Bates, Edward, 388
"Battle Hymn of the Republic, The," 356
Bayly, Thomas H., 100
Beecher, Catherine, 123
Beecher, Charles, 123
Beecher, Edward, 122, 123, 334, 377
Beecher, Henry Ward, 125, 345, 462
Beecher, Lyman, 122–23, 334
Beecher, Mrs. Edward, 122
Bell, John, 311
Bell, Peter Hansborough, 77
Belmont, August, 264
Benedict, Lewis, 90
Benning, Thomas, 14
Benton, Thomas Hart, 71–72, 91, 155, 180,
    227, *253,* 289, 358
    annexation of Texas opposed by, 255
    Atchison's war with, 252, 255, 257,
        258–60, 272, 273, 275, 276, 335
    Blair and, 254

Calhoun hated by, 255, 256, 257–58, 261,
    358
Douglas and, 278, 368
extension of slavery opposed by, 278–79
final Senate speech of, 259
F Street Mess in battles with, 257
in House of Representatives, 313–15
Jackson and, 253–54
Kansas-Nebraska Act opposed by, 300,
    311, 313–15, 358
Lucas killed in duel with, 254
Missouri Compromise repeal opposed
    by, 255, 257–58, 278–79
Missouri opponents of, 257, 258–59, 260
and preservation of Union, 255, 258, 358
slavery issues and, 255–56
Beveridge, Albert J., 471
Bible, slavery and, 207–8, 304, 337, 373
Bill of Rights, 250
Birdsall, Ausburn, 180
Birney, James G., 12
Bissell, William H., 185, 315, 465, 466–67,
    468–69, 470
Black Hawk War, 280, 470
Black Laws, 43, 44, 99, 104, 145, 310, 398,
    461
"Black Republicans," 397–98, 400, 427–28,
    462
blacks:
    AL on, 204–5
    free, 319, 413
    humanity of, 204–5, 370–71, 398, 412,
        413, 425
    rights of, 212, 370, 413
    see also abolitionists, abolitionism; slaves,
        slavery
Black Warrior, 348
Blair, Francis Preston, 175
Blair, Francis Preston, Jr., 254, 388, 467–68
    as Benton's protégé, 254, 259
    Kansas-Nebraska Act opposed by,
        300–301
Blair, Frank, 277
Blair, Montgomery, 254, 261
Bleak House (Dickens), 32

"Bleeding Kansas," 255, 346, 420
Bloomington, Ill., 364, 365, 392, 394–95
    AL's speech in, 397–98
    Douglas's speech in, 396–97
    Republican convention in, 467, 469, 470,
        471, 478
Bloomington Congregational Church,
    419–20
Bloomington Pantagraph, 392, 395
Boal, Robert, 425
"Bogus Legislature," 343, 344
Boone, Levi, 443
Booth, John Wilkes, 170, 177, 189
Border Ruffians, 340, 345, 453, 454–55, 478
Boston, Mass.:
    free blacks in, 319
    fugitive slaves in, 109–12, 182, 318–20
    Kansas-Nebraska Act denounced in,
        302
    martial law in, 319–20
Boston Tea Party, 319
Boston Vigilance Committee, 126, 152, 161,
    318, 334
    Crafts' escape and, 109–10
    Minkins's escape and, 110–11
Botts, John Minor, 153, 192, 329–30
Bovay, Alvan E., 323
Bowdoin College, 181
Boyce, William W., 267
Branson, Jacob, 345
Breckinridge, John C., 11, 38, 176–77, 268,
    287, 289, 291, 315, 364
Breckinridge, Robert Jefferson, 26, 33,
    37–38
    abolitionists loathed by, 12–13
    at 1864 Republican convention, 38
    as leader of Kentucky antislavery
        movement, 30–31
    Wickliffe's battles with, 11–12, 14, 19,
        33, 34–35, 36
Breese, Sidney, 92–93, 94, 101, 380
Bright, Jesse D., 268, 275, 278, 279, 282, 303
    Douglas's rivalry with, 266
    pro-slavery views of, 266
    as Senate president pro tempore, 336

Broadwell, Norman, 432–33
Bronson, Greene C., 236–37, 247, 326
Brooks, Preston, Sumner assaulted by, 478
Brown, Albert G., 231
Brown, John, 319
    in Pottawatomie Massacre, 346, 478
Brown, John Carter, 334
Brown, Samuel M., 15
Brown, William, 141
Brown, William J., 48–49
Browning, Orville H., 384
Brown's Hotel, Washington, D.C., 158
Bryant, John, 214
Bryant, William Cullen, 214, 217
Buchanan, James, 237, 255, 269, 359
    in 1852 presidential race, 174, 179,
        183–84
    Marcy's feud with, 238
    as Pierce's minister to England, 238,
        348–49, 356
    presidential ambition of, 349
Buena Vista, Battle of, 77
Buffalo Express, 47
Bunn, Jacob, 140
Bunn, John W., 137, 140, 379, 393, 394,
        401
    on AL's combination of morality and
        practical policies, 476
Buntline, Ned, 325
Burke, Edmund, 475
Burke, Edmund (New Hampshire
        politician), 183
Burns, Anthony, 318, 319–20
Butler, Andrew Pickens, 47, 124–25, 277,
        288, 304–5, 306, 312, 342, 478
    Calhoun and, 249, 250
    Davis and, 249–50
    as F Street Mess member, 248–49
    secession and, 249
Butler, William O., 175–76, 249, 438–39,
        471
    Sanders's attacks on, 176, 177–78

Cairo, Ill., 92, 94
Cairo City and Canal Company, 92

Calhoun, James S., 104
Calhoun, John C., 4, 11, 29, 47–48, 51, 56,
        62, 66, 77, 80, 113, 172, 199, 205, 242,
        244, 249, 271, 277, 300
    A. P. Butler and, 249, 250
    Benton's hatred of, 255, 256, 257–58, 261,
        358
    Clay's 1838 clash with, 57
    Compromise of 1850 opposed by,
        63–65
    Davis as protégé of, 236
    death of, 70–71
    dual-presidency plan of, 64
    final illness of, 62–63
    J. M. Mason and, 250, 251
    on preservation of Union, 4, 63–64, 66,
        251, 357–58
    presidential ambitions of, 2, 57, 255
    "Southern Address" of, 72
    Southern Manifesto of, 252
Calhoun, John (Illinois politician), 162–63,
        365
    AL's debate with, 391–92
    appointed surveyor general of Kansas,
        344
    in 1852 congressional election, 221–22
California:
    admitted as free state, 99, 151
    anti-slavery constitution of, 60–62
    slavery issue in, 50–51, 53, 56, 58, 64,
        67–68, 90, 102
Calumet, Lake, 93
Cambreleng, Churchill C., 214
Campbell, Alexander, 206–7
Campbell, James, 289
Campbell, Lewis D., 315
Capitol, U.S., Davis and rebuilding of,
        355–56
Capps, Elizabeth A., 131
Caribbean, 347
    planned Southern imperium in, 76, 233,
        243, 263, 316, 347
Carlyle, Thomas, 474
Carr, Clark, 399, 400–401
Cartwright, Peter, 208

Cass, Lewis, 74, 95, 96–97, 102, 216, 266,
    269, 288, 404
  in 1852 presidential race, 175–76, 177–79,
    183–84
Catholics:
  as immigrants, 325
  Know Nothings' hatred of, 325, 326,
    443, 444, 456, 457
  nativist hatred and fear of, 324–25, 326
Chaplin, William L., 113–14
Charleston Mercury, 73, 87, 249, 372
Chase, Salmon P., 17, 23, 30, 44–45, 90–91,
    111, 113, 180, 296, 311, 359, 405, 420,
    421, 435, 444, 467
  AL's rivalry with, 435
  as antislavery leader, 7, 42, 435
  Douglas denounced by, 368
  Douglas's attacks on, 309–10, 402
  1849 Senate campaign of, 42–44
  Free Democrats and, 212–13
  as Free Soil Party founder, 213
  Kansas-Nebraska Act opposed by, 297,
    298–300, 422–23
  proposed Kansas-Nebraska amendment
    of, 305, 306
Chenault, William, 26
Chicago, Ill., 93, 119, 384, 428
  City Council of, 121, 122
  Common Council of, 121
  Douglas's pro-Kansas-Nebraska Act
    speech in, 363–64, 393
  1856 mayoral election in, 468
  growth of, 6, 267
  Know Nothings in, 388
Chicago Democrat, 363, 444
Chicago Journal, 397, 403, 423, 428
Chicago Press and Tribune, 372
Chicago River, 93
Chicago Times, 269, 363, 364, 393, 428,
    435
Chicago Tribune, 5, 364, 434, 444, 446,
    465, 468
Choate, Rufus, 193, 194, 195, 196, 329
cholera epidemic of 1849, 9, 26, 31, 81
Christiana, Pa., riot in, 189

Christianity:
  slavery and, 206–9, 377–78, 406, 423
  see also specific denominations
Churches of Christ, 206
Cincinnati Gazette, 43, 444
Cincinnati Globe, 43
Cincinnatus, 5
"Citizen Know Nothing," 321, 324
Civil War, U.S., 164
  AL on prospect of, 7
  revisionist historians' view of, 359–60
  Uncle Tom's Cabin and, 125
  see also Union, preservation of
Clark, Myron H., 327
Clary's Grove Boys, 175, 401
Clay, Cassius Marcellus, 9, 286, 444, 468
  blacks as viewed by, 31
  Civil War seen as inevitable by, 37
  in 1851 gubernatorial campaign, 30–31
  family slaves emancipated by, 16–17
  in Illinois tour, 383, 384–85, 386
  as leader of Kentucky antislavery
    movement, 13–15, 20–21
  Lincoln and, 384
  in Mexican War, 22
  open letters to Webster from, 29–30
  as Republican Party founder, 37
  Springfield speech of, 384–85
  Taylor supported by, 23
  Todd family and, 13
  True American founded by, 17–18
  Wickliffe's attacks on, 14–16
Clay, Clement Claiborne, 243, 248, 284
Clay, Henry, 3, 7, 10, 11, 13, 14, 15, 20, 23,
    26, 28, 45, 51, 80, 89, 152, 158, 190,
    199, 214, 285, 298, 390, 405, 449–50
  abolitionists loathed by, 12, 111
  as Adams's secretary of state, 209
  AL's eulogy for, 201, 202–9, 405, 406, 477
  AL's idolization of, 5, 202, 477
  American System of, 103, 199–200, 203
  as author of Missouri Compromise, 308
  Calhoun's 1838 clash with, 57
  and Compromise of 1850, see
    Compromise of 1850

Clay, Henry (*cont.*)
  Davis's rivalry with, 52, 55, 56–57, 87
  death of, 199, 200
  Douglas's misrepresentation of, 308
  in 1844 election, 53, 325
  final illness of, 158, 199
  frailty of, 53, 54
  Fugitive Slave Act supported by, 59, 74,
    111–12
  gradual emancipation favored by, 24, 25,
    31, 144, 200, 204, 285
  political institutions as transformed by,
    199
  posthumous reputation of, 101–2, 104
  and preservation of Union, 3, 55, 59, 62,
    357
  presidential ambitions of, 2, 12, 17,
    22–23, 32, 51, 57, 84, 91, 199, 200–201
  racism of, 88, 204
  reelected to Senate, 51–52
  Seward's "higher law" argument
    attacked by, 70
  slavery opposed by, 209–10
  slave trade abhorred by, 209
  and Taylor's death, 85–86
Clay, James B., 22
Clay, Lucretia, 10
Clay, Mary Jane Warfield, 13
Clay, Virginia, 243, 248, 284, 357
Clayton, John M., 99, 130
Clemens, Jeremiah, 94, 243, 295–96
Cleveland True Democrat, 444
Clingman, Thomas Lanier, 61
Cobb, Howell, 47, 48, 114–15, 117, 242–43,
    301, 321
  elected speaker, 49–50
Codding, Ichabod, 385, 386, 393, 444
  as abolitionist leader, 383, 384, 393–94,
    429
  in founding of Republican Party, 425,
    427, 428, 443, 445–46, 447–48, 462
Cody, William "Buffalo Bill," 325
Cole, Byron, 349
Coleman, Franklin, 344–45
Coles, Edward, 302–3, 358

Colfax, Schuyler, 325, 329
Collier, John A., 45, 46, 47
colonization movement, 24, 32, 33–34, 38,
    122, 144, 200, 204–5, 209
  AL and, 410
Coming of the Civil War, The (Craven),
    359–60
Committee of Thirteen, 73, 74, 90
"Committing Our Cause to God, The"
    (Jacobs), 208
Compromise of 1833, 57
Compromise of 1850, 3, 29, 30, 53–70,
    111, 180, 199, 280, 281, 294, 298, 319,
    322, 361, 362, 363, 371, 392, 411, 416,
    433
  AL's silence on, 141, 142
  antislavery movement as demoralized
    by, 124
  Benton's opposition to, 254
  Calhoun's Senate speech on, 63–65, 250
  Clay-Ritchie alliance in, 73–74
  Clay's claiming of credit for, 101–2, 308
  Clay's "Omnibus" bill for, 73, 74, 75,
    90–91, 98, 103, 143, 270
  Clay's racist argument for, 88
  Clay's Senate speeches on, 54–55, 58–60,
    62, 74–75, 86–88, 127
  and collapse of Whig Party, 201
  Corcoran and, 97–98
  Davis's continued opposition to, 230,
    236, 290
  Davis's Senate speeches on, 55–56, 62,
    208
  Democratic Party as winners in, 103
  Democrats' support of, 153, 213
  Douglas's assumption of leadership in,
    91–92, 98–100, 117, 118–19, 143, 167,
    169, 268–69, 270, 303, 308
  Douglas's defense of, 121
  Douglas's pretended support for, 299
  Douglas's Senate speech on, 117–18
  Fillmore's support of, 151–52, 156–57,
    159
  F Street Mess's opposition to, 249
  Georgia Platform's distortion of, 116–17

as issue in 1852 election, 173–74, 179–80, 182, 184–85, 191–94
mythology of, 101, 104
New Mexico and, 76–81, 88–89, 90, 104, 169
Northern Whigs' opposition to, 153–54
passage of, 99–100
Pierce's endorsement of, 185, 248, 290, 291
political landscape as reset by, 172–73
Scott's ambivalent acceptance of, 195
seen as "final settlement" of disunion peril, 102, 103, 105, 151–53, 157, 173, 191–92, 200, 211, 226, 248, 287, 300, 301, 320
Seward on illusion of, 105–6
Seward's speeches on, 67–68, 76, 88–89
Taylor's opposition to, 60–62, 74, 75, 216
Texas and, 90, 97, 99
Webster's speeches on, 65–67, 98, 107
Whigs and, 99
Concord, N.H., 226
Concord Cabal, 181, 182, 183
Concord Independent Democrat, 217
Confederation Congress, 415
Congressional Globe, 65, 99, 300, 306, 307, 310, 358
Conkling, James, 202
Conrad, Robert T., 324
Constitution, U.S., 320, 415
    slavery and, 7, 16, 29–30, 68, 121, 201, 212, 234, 313–14, 370, 393, 406, 415, 421
    three-fifths clause of, 7, 88, 317, 393, 415, 421
Constitutional Union Party, 115, 242
Cooper, James Fenimore, 27
Cooper, William J., Jr., 229
Cooperation Party, 249
Cooper Union, AL's address at, 68, 139, 406
Corcoran, William W., 97–98, 99, 100, 118, 171, 267, 268
Corcoran and Riggs, 97
Corpus Christi, Tex., 351

Costa Rica, 353
cotton economy, 30, 85, 87, 95, 374
    England and, 120
    railroads and, 120
Cox, Samuel S., 293–94
Craft, William and Ellen, 109–10
Craven, Avery, 359–60
Crawford, George W., 78, 81–82, 85
Crawford, Louisa Ward, 356
Crawford, Thomas, 355–56
"Crime Against Kansas" (Sumner speech), 478
Crimean War, 240
Crittenden, John J., 52, 60, 79, 160, 222, 457
Crystal Palace Exhibition, New York, 272
Cuba:
    Black Warrior incident in, 348
    emancipation of slaves in, 348
Cuba, proposed annexation of, 235, 316, 347, 348, 353, 355, 418
    Davis's desire for, 235, 243
    Douglas's desire for, 169, 175
    Ostend Manifesto and, 348–49, 356, 408
    Pierce's desire for, 233, 237–38
Cuba, slave trade banned from, 348
Cullom, William, 317
Curtis, Benjamin, 110, 113
Curtis, George Ticknor, 110, 112, 188, 281
Cushing, Caleb, 176, 178, 183, 231, 237, 241, 246–47, 248, 288, 294, 303, 348, 351
    influence over Pierce of, 232
    as Pierce's attorney general, 226, 234
    as polymath, 226–27
    widespread distrust of, 227–28
Cushing, William, 305
Custis, George Washington Parke, 81
Cutting, Francis B., 247, 313
Cutts, James Madison, 299

Dabney, Robert Lewis, 208
Daily Standard, 43
Dana, Richard Henry, Jr., 126
Danenhower, William W., 469, 470–71
Dan River, 95
Danville, Ill., 148

Darwin, Charles, 372

Davis, David, *129,* 132, 134, 139, 201, 378, 381, 385, 395, 399, 432, 433, 440, 461, 464, 478
    abolitionists despised by, 419–20
    on AL as lawyer, 137–38
    AL in coterie of, 136–37, 140, 148, 162
    as Eighth Circuit chief judge, 136
    storytelling sessions enjoyed by, 136–37

Davis, David Brion, 120

Davis, Garrett, 15, 27

Davis, Jefferson, 3–4, 39, 52, 61, 73, 82, 90, 94, 97, 100, 103, 115–16, 117, 156, 170, 179, 208, *225,* 248, 252, 257, 266, 279, 280, 288, 335, 343, 348, 351
    antipathy toward Douglas of, 270
    A. P. Butler and, 249–50
    blindness episodes of, 228, 231, 239, 357
    Brierfield plantation of, 229–30
    as Calhoun's protégé, 56, 57–58, 235–36
    Clay's rivalry with, 52, 55, 56–57, 87
    Compromise of 1850 and, *see* Compromise of 1850
    Cuban annexation desired by, 235, 243, 353
    and death of Samuel, 240
    in 1851 gubernatorial campaign, 228, 230
    1856 reelection to Senate of, 356
    in feuds with Southern Democrats, 242–43
    Foote's feud with, 71–72, 230, 240, 242
    further annexation of Mexico desired by, 316–17, 347
    Gadsden Treaty and, 245–46
    illness of, 357
    Kansas-Nebraska Act and, *see* Kansas-Nebraska Act
    Marcy's battles with, 351
    Missouri Compromise repeal supported by, 289, 290
    patronage appointments controlled by, 240, 242, 244
    Pierce candidacy supported by, 230–31
    as Pierce's secretary of war, 232, 236, 239–41, 251, 346
    on Pierce's Sunday meeting on Missouri Compromise repeal, 289–90
    as principal power in Pierce administration, 3, 226, 233, 238, 248
    and rebuilding of U.S. Capitol, 355–56
    Scott attacked by, 241
    sense of superiority of, 228–29
    as slave owner, 229–30
    Southern imperium envisioned by, 235, 243, 353, 418
    Southern Unionists attacked by, 242, 243
    temper of, 156, 230, 240
    Toombs's feud with, 240–41
    transcontinental railroad and, 272, 316–17
    venereal disease of, 228, 357
    Virginia Clay as mistress of, 243, 284
    Walker's Nicaraguan regime supported by, 353

Davis, Jefferson, Jr., 233

Davis, Joseph E., 229

Davis, Samuel, 233, 240

Davis, Varina, 82, 228, 232, 233

Dawson, John L., 267

Dayton, William L., 89

De Bow's Review, 374

Decatur, Ill., 464–65

Decatur Chronicle, 465

Declaration of Independence, 7, 112, 163, 250, 344, 373, 377, 405, 406, 407, 422, 466
    AL's veneration of, 4, 205–6, 207, 376, 404, 409, 414, 415, 422, 423, 450, 457
    Calhoun's attack on, 257
    Campbell's attack on, 207
    Fitzhugh's attack on, 374–75
    Kansas-Nebraska debates and, 304, 305
    slavery and, 304

Declaration of Rights, Virginia, 250

democracy, slavery as threat to, 370

Democracy in America (Tocqueville), 98

Democratic Convention of 1852, 116, 164–65, 178–79, 182–85

Democratic Party, Democrats, 3, 11, 30, 42, 96, 103, 108–9, 164, 170
  AL's appeals to, 406
  anti-Nebraska, 322, 388, 432, 434, 446
  antislavery, 6, 324, 387, 388
  Compromise of 1850 supported by, 153
  Congress controlled by, 49–50
  Jacksonian, 3, 42, 71, 94, 126, 172, 173, 179–80, 182–83, 203, 254, 255, 300, 301, 315, 330, 382
  Jeffersonian, 405
  in Kentucky, 23, 29
  in New Hampshire, 181–82
  in New York, 106
  Northern, 48, 75, 316, 322, 323
  in Ohio, 43–44
  pro-Nebraska, 381
  Southern, 38, 47–48, 49, 287, 322
  as transformed by Kansas-Nebraska Act, 322, 348, 349, 363, 364, 380, 403
Democratic Party, Illinois, 97, 143, 162, 201, 388
  anti-Douglas faction in, 436–37, 439, 441, 469
  Douglas's assertion of control over, 264, 380
  effect of Kansas-Nebraska Act on, 363, 364
  in 1850 election, 141–43
  in 1852 election, 221
  in 1854 elections, 380
  Know Nothings and, 469
Democratic Party, New York, 106, 180, 234, 362
  "Hards" vs. "Softs" in, 236–37, 246, 247, 266, 278, 290, 294–95, 313, 316, 326, 458
Democratic Review, 118, 168, 238
  Sanders's editorials in, 175–78, 221, 246
Democrats, Southern, 38, 47–48, 48, 49, 173, 174, 182
  Davis's feud with, 240
  Douglas distrusted by, 269–70
De Witt, Alexander, 298
Dickens, Charles, 32

Dickey, T. Lyle, 478–79
Dickinson, Daniel J., 85, 107, 180, 184, 236, 266
Dickinson, Edward, 323
Dickinson, Emily, 319
Dickson, William W., 460, 461
Dictionary of Congress, 138
Discourse on the Constitution (Calhoun), 63, 64
Disquisition on Government (Calhoun), 63
District of Columbia:
  AL's emancipation bill for, 153, 205, 298, 356
  slavery issue in, 48, 54, 56, 68, 74–75, 76, 86, 142, 144, 152, 205, 298, 331, 356, 407
  slave trade banned from, 99–100, 102, 152
Dix, John A., 214, 234, 237, 388
Dixon, Archibald, 304
  Kansas-Nebraska Act supported by, 297–98
  Missouri Compromise repeal and, 285–87, 293
Dobbin, James C., 288
Dodd, William E., 233
Dodge, Augustus Caesar, 279–80, 322
  Kansas-Nebraska Act supported by, 303–4
  Seward attacked by, 303
Dodge, Henry, 279–80, 303–4
Donald, David Herbert, 471
Donelson, Andrew, 467
Douglas, Martha Martin, 95, 264
Douglas, Stephen A., 23, 74, 75, 140, 152, 261, 263, 346
  abolitionists hated by, 95, 216, 309, 400
  AL's comparison of Napoleon to, 409–10
  AL's rivalry with, 6, 147, 174, 202, 218, 221, 367, 368–69, 378, 388–89, 477
  ambition of, 118
  annexation of Cuba promoted by, 169, 175
  anti-Nebraska movement attacks on, 362–64

Douglas, Stephen A. (*cont.*)
  Atchison and, 274–75
  Benton and, 278, 368
  "Black Republican" epithet used by,
    397–98, 400, 427–28, 462
  Bloomington speech of, 396–97
  Bright's rivalry with, 266
  as champion of American West, 118–19,
    172
  Chase attacked by, 309–10, 402
  Chase's denunciation of, 368
  Compromise of 1850 and, *see*
    Compromise of 1850
  Davis's antipathy toward, 270
  distrust of, 269, 275, 283
  and Dixon's repeal amendment, 286,
    287, 293
  egotism and self-confidence of, 270–71
  in 1852 presidential race, 169–78,
    183–84, 185, 269
  1852 reelection to Senate of, 264
  1853 European trip of, 264–65
  1853 Nebraska bill of, 271–72, 273,
    298
  in 1858 Senate race, 478
  as Emersonian "Great Man," 475
  England hated by, 124–25
  as excluded from Pierce's patronage
    appointments, 264, 269
  as financial and political speculator,
    92–94, 118, 268, 362, 367
  F Street Mess and, 278
  Fugitive Slave Act defended by, 121
  in House of Representatives, 92, 95
  Hunter and, 172, 173–74, 178, 251
  Illinois Central Act pushed by, 100–101
  Illinois Central Railroad founded by,
    92–93, 97, 100
  Illinois Democrats controlled by, 264
  Kansas-Nebraska Act and, *see* Kansas-
    Nebraska Act
  Know Nothings and, 430, 445
  Kossuth and, 167, 168–69
  land speculation by, 93, 101, 170, 267–68,
    278, 352

  "Little Giant" nickname of, 92
  marriage of Martha Martin and, 95
  and Martha's death, 269
  Mississippi plantation of, 94–95, 97, 120,
    270, 393
  on moral neutrality of slavery, 95, 96
  and Pierce's presidential campaign,
    215–16, 218, 263
  Pierce's promises distrusted by, 292
  in planning for 1856 presidential
    campaign, 265–66
  political successes of, 174
  popular sovereignty doctrine of, 95–96,
    117–18, 121, 169, 270, 273, 280–81,
    283, 293, 298, 302, 305–6, 308, 314,
    362, 368, 371, 398, 400, 404, 413–15,
    417–18
  and preservation of Union, 125, 293
  presidential ambitions of, 168, 174, 185,
    263, 266–67, 268–69, 278, 293, 298,
    302, 362
  pro-Kansas-Nebraska Act Chicago
    speech of, 363–64, 393
  pro-Kansas-Nebraska Act tour of,
    393–94
  revised Nebraska bill of, 280–83
  revisionist historians' view of, 359–60
  on sacredness of Missouri Compromise,
    397–98, 403
  Sanders and, 170, 172, 175–76,
    177–78
  Springfield State House speech of,
    399–400
  Sumner attacked by, 309–10, 402
  Sumner's denunciation of, 368
  in Sunday meeting with Pierce on
    Missouri Compromise repeal,
    289–92
  transcontinental railroad and, 267,
    271–72, 279, 294
  Wilmot Proviso opposed by, 96–97
  as Young America champion, 167–68,
    171, 238, 409
Douglass, Frederick, 189, 212, 459
Dow, Charles, 344

Doyle, Edward J., 24
Draper, Simeon, 157
Dred Scott decision, 110, 210, 255, 260–61, 358
Dubuque and Pacific Railroad Company, 279
duels, dueling, 14, 254
Duer, William A., 106
Dungey, William, 461
Dungey case, 461–62
Dunlap, J. R., 26
Dyer, Thomas, 468

Eastman, Zebina, 384, 386, 433, 434–35, 439
    Herndon and, 386, 387–88
Edinburgh Review, 372–73
Editorial Convention (Decatur), 464–65, 466
    AL at, 465–67
Edmundson, Henry A., 315–16
Edwards, Benjamin S., 389, 399
Edwards, Elizabeth Todd, 201, 440
Edwards, Ninian W., 201–2, 221, 440
Eighth Judicial Circuit, Illinois, 6, 136–37, 140, 148, 162, 367
elections, U.S.:
    of 1844, 22, 53, 84, 325–26
    of 1845, 18
    of 1848, 23, 42, 46, 96–97, 309
    of 1850, 141–43
    of 1856, 5, 388, 457, 458, 463–64
    of 1858, 130, 136, 478
    of 1860, 38
    Whigs in, 188, 189–97, 211, 474
elections, U.S., of 1852, 3, 154, 155, 157, 296, 297
    Benton in, 259
    Democratic field in, 169–85
    Democratic platform in, 184, 211
    Douglas and, 169–78, 263–64, 269
    Free Democratic Party in, 211–12
    Weed and, 180
    Whig field in, 188, 189–97
    Whig platform in, 193–94, 196, 211

elections, U.S., of 1854:
    Democratic losses in, 322, 349, 429
    Greeley and, 326–27
    in Illinois, *see* Illinois, 1854 elections in
    Know Nothings in, 329
    in Massachusetts, 328–29
    in New York, 326–28
    Weed and, 326–27
Elements (Euclid), 6, 138–40
Eliot, Thomas D., 323
emancipation, gradual, 12, 28, 32, 122, 285, 411, 421
    Clay's support of, 24, 25, 31, 144, 200, 204
Emancipation Party, 28, 30, 383, 444
Emancipation Proclamation, 38, 114, 125, 360, 416
Emerson, John, 260
Emerson, Ralph (Rockford lawyer), 460–61
Emerson, Ralph Waldo, 187, 312, *473*
    as abolitionist, 473–74
    on AL, 478
    "Great Man" theory of, 474–75
    Springfield lectures of, 473
    Webster denounced by, 107–8
Empire Club, 171
England:
    abolitionism in, 13, 41, 124–25
    cotton trade and, 120
    Douglas's hatred of, 124–25
Environmental Protection Agency, 132
equality, as "self-evident lie," 304, 305
Euclid, 6, 138–40, 149, 376
Everett, Edward, 169, 297, 306, 311–12, 328, 355, 381
Ewing, James S., 396

Fabens, Joseph W., 351–52
Faneuil Hall, Boston, 67, 189, 302, 318
Fascism, 359
Fay, Herbert W., 431
Featherston, Winfield, 81–82
Federalist Party, 256, 391
Fehrenbacher, Don E., 471

Fell, Jesse W., 5, 419, 475, 478
    AL and, 395–96
Fell, Rebecca, 395
Female Colonization Society, 12
Fenton, Reuben E., 294–95, 315, 458
Fessenden, William Pitt, 306, 309
Field, Maunsell B., 182, 184
Fifer, Joseph Wilson, 471
Fillmore, Abigail, 234
Fillmore, Millard, 45, 46, 47, 53, *83,* 91, 104,
    109, 110, 112, 233, 331
  ascension to presidency of, 83, 85–86
  Christiana Riot and, 189
  Compromise of 1850 supported by, 102,
    103–4, 151–52, 156–57, 159
  as 1848 Whig nominee for vice
    president, 84
  in 1852 presidential race, 188, 189, 190,
    194, 195
  in 1856 presidential race, 388, 445, 457,
    463, 467
  Kossuth rebuked by, 158, 162, 188
  patronage appointments of, 98–99
  political career of, 83–85
  in war with Seward and Weed, 84–85,
    90, 105, 107, 156–57, 180, 188, 190, 191
  Webster named secretary of state by, 85
Filmer, Robert, 373
fire-eaters, 72, 114, 242, 244, 249, 362
First Presbyterian Church, Springfield, 473
Fish, Hamilton, 46, 79, 84, 107, 311, 459
Fitzhugh, George, *367,* 373–75
Flint, Henry Martyn, 269
Flournoy, Thomas Stanhope, 330
Fonda, Henry, 135
Foote, Henry S., 55, 62, 73, 74, 81, 89–90,
    91, 94, 96, 101, 115, 155, 157, 160, 172,
    180, 232, 247, 254
  Davis's feud with, 71–72, 230, 240, 242
  elected governor of Mississippi, 230
Forbes, John Murray, 334
Forney, John W., 93–94, 267, 276, 338, 352
Fort Riley, Kans., 343
Francis, Eliza, 462
Francis, Simeon, 462–63

Frankfort, Ky., 25, 28
Frank Pierce and His Abolition Allies, 217
free blacks, 319, 413
Free Democratic Party, 222, 381, 383–84,
    385, 426, 435
  Chase and, 212–13
  in 1852 election, 211–12
  see also Free Soil Party
free labor, slavery and, 13, 16, 24, 26–27, 28
Free Soil Party, 23, 26, 42, 43–44, 47–49,
    67, 97, 109, 157, 180, 226, 234, 235, 236,
    247, 259, 263, 270, 296, 309, 322, 328,
    330, 333, 381, 382, 383, 385, 387, 426,
    445, 446
  Chase in founding of, 213
  Know Nothings and, 386, 387–88
  in New York, 106
  see also Free Democratic Party
Free State Party, 344
free trade, 373
Free West, 383–84, 386, 399, 433, 435, 443
Frémont, Jessie Benton, 254
Frémont, John C., 50–51, 71, 254–55
  as Republican candidate for president, 5
French, Benjamin Brown, 52
French, Parker H., 350
F Street Mess, 248–49, 283, 304, 339, 367
  Benton's battles with, 257
  Compromise of 1850 opposed by, 249
  Douglas and, 278
  extension of slavery as goal of, 249
  government printing contract and, 248,
    276
  Kansas-Nebraska Act and, 277, 293
  Missouri Compromise repeal and,
    287–88, 289, 290–92
  Pierce's support for, 293
  as states' rights advocates, 249
  see also individual senators
Fugitive Slave Act, 55, 102, 113, 124, 126,
    142, 143, 152, 153, 156, 179, 192, 202,
    211, 250, 292, 320, 426, 465, 468
  AL on, 219–20, 392–93, 419, 420–21,
    433
  Clay's support for, 59, 74, 111–12

Douglas's defense of, 121
Northern opposition to, 103, 109, 180, 182, 183, 189, 214
passage of, 99, 100
Pierce and, 184, 217, 219–20, 233–34
Seward's opposition of, 56, 68, 188
Taylor's opposition to, 216
Webster's support for, 29, 106, 107, 108, 110, 111–12, 123, 187–88, 194–95, 474
Fuller, Frank, 125–26
Fulton County Republican, 431
fusion movement, 322, 323, 326, 328, 329, 344, 380–81, 381, 383, 385, 386–87, 389, 397, 400, 406, 426, 429, 433, 441, 446, 469
AL and, 447
Know Nothings and, 444
Seward and, 458
Trumbull and, 447–48

Gadsden, Christopher, 244
Gadsden, James, 243–44, 244, 272, 284
Gadsden, John, 284
Gadsden Treaty, 245–46, 317
Gag Rule, 84, 95, 151, 207, 217, 344
Galena, Ill., 92, 93, 279, 388
Galena Jeffersonian, 380, 433
Galphin, George, 78
Galphin affair, 78, 81–82, 215
Gardner, Henry J., 329
Garnet, Henry Highland, 113–14
Garrison, William Lloyd, 12, 14, 71, 110, 122, 123, 161, 297, 320, 333, 334, 377
Garrisonians, 205, 206, 212, 297, 333, 378
Geneva, Ill., 393–94
Gentry, Meredith Poindexter, 48
Georgia, 242–43
    secessionist movement in, 114–15
    Sovereign Convention in, 114–15
Georgia Platform, 115, 116–17, 153, 240, 242
German immigrants, 6, 157, 158, 164, 325, 363, 380–81, 382, 392, 408, 443, 469
Gettysburg, Battle of, 356
Geyer, Henry S., 259, 261

Giddings, Joshua, 43–44, 48, 113, 160, 212, 271, 298, 427, 434, 435, 446, 459, 462, 467, 468
Gillespie, Joseph, 145–46, 264, 391, 420, 432, 438, 439, 441, 445, 467, 469, 470
Godey's Lady's Book, 131
Goicuria, Domingo de, 349
Goode, William O., 288
Goodrich, Grant, 134
Gordon, Nathaniel, 456
Gorsuch, Edward, 189
Gourley, James, 133
Granger, Francis, 106
Granger, Julius, 264
Greeley, Horace, 16, 45, 69, 170, 191, 196, 211, 213, 296, 323, 324, 326, 416, 458, 467
    and 1854 elections, 326–27
    Raymond's rivalry with, 327–28
    Seward and, 328
    Thayer's Kansas emigration plan promoted by, 334, 336
    Weed and, 326
Green, Duff, 350
Green, Thomas, 276
Greene, "Slicky Bill," 141, 401
Grimsley, Elizabeth Todd, 131
Grinnell, Josiah B., 178–79
Grow, Galusha A., 289, 292, 315
Grund, Francis J., 98, 171, 183
Guadalupe Hidalgo, Treaty of, 88
Guelzo, Allen, 135
Gulliver, J. P., 139
Guthrie, James, 237

Hale, John P., 44, 87, 89–90, 96, 124, 157, 182, 212, 229, 296
    as 1852 Free Democrat candidate, 213
    in 1852 presidential race, 222
    re-election of, 322
Hamilton, Holman, 97
Hamilton, James, 98
Hamilton County, Ohio, 43
Hamlet (Shakespeare), 416
Hamlin, Edward S., 43, 44

Hamlin, Hannibal, 61, 225, 226, 259, 303, 315
Hammond, James, 73
Hanks, Dennis, 144
Hanway, Castner, 189
Hapsburg Empire, 154, 156
Harlan, James, 322
Harris, Thomas, 162, 388, 391, 400, 429, 430
  in 1850 election, 141–43
Harrison, William Henry, 5, 45, 60, 83, 86, 190, 191, 196, 215, 227, 477
Harvey, Peter, 111, 190, 196
Hatch, Ozias M., 391
Havana, 348
Haven, Franklin, 189
Hawthorne, Nathaniel, 126, 184–85, 225, 357
Hay, John, 375, 376, 465
Hay, Milton, 162
Hayes, Rutherford B., 44
Helm, Emilie Todd, 133
Henry, Anson D., 132, 162
Henson, Josiah, 123
Herald of Freedom, 335
Herald Philanthropist, 43
Herndon, Archie, 142, 395
Herndon, William Henry, 4, 67, 122, 125, 132, 138, 140, 141, 147, 149, 162, 368, 371, 392, 405, 424, 432, 439, 462, 464, 467, 470, 473, 475, 477
  as abolitionist, 426
  on AL's ambition, 5
  as AL's law partner, 1, 6, 134–35
  Eastman and, 386, 387–88
  library of, 372–73
  Mary Lincoln disliked by, 133–34
  myth of AL's reluctance to join Republicans fostered by, 471–72
  as temperance activist, 394–95
Hickok, "Wild Bill," 325
Higginson, Thomas Wentworth, 319
"higher law," Seward's invoking of, 69–70, 89
Hilliard, Henry Washington, 86

Hints on Slavery (Breckinridge), 12
Hispanics, 88
Historical and Legal Examination (Benton), 358
Historical Character of Napoleon (Phillips), 410
Hodder, Frank H., 268
Holbrook, Darius B., 92, 94
Honduras, 353
House Book, The (Leslie), 131
House of Representatives, U.S., 43, 78, 81, 92, 176, 181
  AL in, 2, 10, 41, 137, 140, 298
  Benton in, 313–15
  Committee of the Whole of, 313
  Committee on Territories of, 313
  Democratic control of, 49–50
  Douglas in, 92, 95
  1849 speakership fight in, 47–48
  Kansas-Nebraska Act in, 312–13, 313, 315–16, 317, 371
  Ways and Means Committee of, 100
Houston, Sam, 159, 271, 275, 311, 352
Howe, Julia Ward, 356
Howe, Samuel Gridley, 189–90, 334, 356
Howell, William Dean, 129–30
Hoyt, Charles, 431
Hungary, revolutionary movement in, 154, 169, 450
Hunkers, 220, 236, 296, 382
Hunt, Washington, 106, 107
Hunter, Robert M. T., 172, 180, 268, 283, 288, 330
  Davis and, 251
  Douglas and, 172, 173–74, 178
  as F Street Mess member, 248–49
  Pierce and, 231
  political career of, 172
Hurd v. Rock Island Railroad, 388

"Ichabod" (Whittier), 67
Illinois, 92
  antislavery movement in, 97, 121, 380–81
  Black Laws in, 99, 145, 398, 461
  bond lobby in, 100–101, 118

debt of, 100–101
defeat of prohibition referendum in, 395
Douglas's pro-Nebraska Act tour in, 393–94
1856 gubernatorial race in, 468–71
German immigrants in, 6, 363, 380–81, 382, 392, 408, 443, 469
internal improvement programs of, 100
Know Nothings in, 445
racism in, 369, 410, 462
State Fair in, 423
Illinois, abolitionists in, 386, 388, 399–400, 437
    AL and, 6–7
    AL's Senate campaign opposed by, 432–33, 439
    Codding as leader of, 383, 384, 393–94, 429
Illinois, 1854 elections in:
    AL in, 378–79, 389–93, 428–29
    Democrats in, 380, 388, 429–30
    fusion movement and, 380–81
    Know Nothings in, 380, 387–88, 390
    Whigs in, 379, 380, 387–88, 390
Illinois, SS, 171
Illinois Central Railroad, 92–93, 100–101, 118, *119,* 135, 172, 265, 267, 380
    Mobile Railroad merged with, 97
Illinois Central Railroad Tax Act, 100–101, 119, 167, 170, 268, 279, 363
Illinois House of Representatives:
    AL's 1854 speech against Kansas-Nebraska Act in, 4, 5, 7, 401–24
    Douglas's 1854 speech in, 399–400
Illinois and Michigan Canal, 93, 434, 435–36
Illinois Staats-Zeitung, 428
Illinois State Journal, 141, 142, 369–70, 371, 380, 385, 391, 424, 429, 465, 467, 470, 471, 472, 474
    AL as de facto coeditor of, 6
    AL's unsigned articles and editorials in, 144, 365, 370, 385, 392, 393, 462
    Fillmore's 1856 candidacy backed by, 463

Herndon's anonymous editorials for, 4, 6
Kansas-Nebraska Act denounced by, 363
Know Nothing takeover of, 462–63
Illinois State Normal University, 395
Illinois State Register, 4, 120, 141, 142, 202, 218, 222, 264, 280, 321, 363, 369–70, 371, 385, 392, 395, 399, 400, 401, 424, 427, 428, 430, 442, 445, 472
immigrants, as Catholic, 325
Independent, 377
Indians, 88
Ingersoll, Elihu, 420
internal improvements, 94, 199
    AL as advocate of, 100
Iowa, 279, 322
Irish immigrants, 325
Irvine, Jane Hawkins Todd, 34
isolationism, 359
Iverson, Alfred, 242

Jackson, Andrew, 36, 51, 60, 80, 82, 175, 179, 216, 244, 253–54, 264
Jackson, Claiborne F., 258, 340
Jackson, Mich., 323
Jackson-Napton Resolutions, 258, 259, 260
Jacobs, Ferdinand, 207–8
Jarrot, Joseph, 436
Jayne, William, 389, 391, 433, 438, 471
Jefferson, Thomas, 7, 11, 139, 203, 206, 209, 247, 302, 304, 374–75, *383*
    AL contrasted with, 405
    AL's study of, 406
    extension of slavery opposed by, 298, 392, 404–5, 415
    slavery and, 7, 203–4
Jefferson Inquirer, 273
Jesuit's Daughter, The (Buntline), 325
Johannsen, Robert, 175
Johns, Henry, 378, 437
Johns, Jane Martin, 378–79, 437, 438
Johnson, Andrew, 171, 178, 229
Johnson, Reverdy, 78, 79, 261, 460
Johnston, Albert Sidney, 14, 37
Johnston, John D., 133

Joliet, Ill., 393

Joliet Signal, 387, 393, 429, 462

Jones, George Wallace, 279–80

Jones, George Washington, 301–2

Jones, Samuel J., 345

Judd, Norman B., 434, 436, 439, 440

Julian, George W., 213

Julius Caesar (Shakespeare), 416

Kansas Herald, 340

Kansas-Nebraska Act (1854), 3, 4, 117, 124,
    255, 383, 392
    AL's activism as galvanized by, 365,
        367–72, 377
    AL's Illinois House speech against, 4,
        5, 7
    AL's letter to Joshua Speed on, 453–54
    AL's opposition to, 432–34
    AL's Peoria speech on, 140, 163–64, 409,
        424–25, 433, 449–50
    Atchison and, 275–76, 284
    Atchison's claimed authorship of,
        275–77, 282
    Benton's opposition to, 311, 313–15, 358
    Blair's opposition to, 300–301
    Chase's opposition to, 297, 298–300,
        422–23
    Chase's proposed amendment of, 305,
        306
    clergy's denunciation of, 311–12
    Davis and, 276–77
    Declaration of Independence and, 304,
        305
    as deliberate attempt to extend slavery,
        293–94, 358–59
    Democratic opposition to, 300–301, 316
    Democratic Party as transformed by,
        322, 348, 349, 363, 364, 380, 403
    Democratic support for, 303, 311
    Dodge's speech in support of, 303–4
    Douglas's claimed authorship of, 275–77,
        282
    Douglas's gamble on, 362
    Douglas's mistaken view of effect of,
        321–22
    Douglas's original language for, 280–81
    Douglas's Senate speeches in support of,
        299, 306–11, 417
    enactment of, 317–18
    and founding of Republican Party, 315
    F Street Mess and, 293
    House debate on, 312–13, 313, 315–16
    House passage of, 317, 371
    lobbyists and, 303, 312
    Marcy and, 294, 295
    Missouri Compromise as "superseded"
        by, 292
    Pierce's support of, 293, 313
    popular sovereignty doctrine and, 298,
        302, 305, 308, 314
    railroads and, 268
    reaction to, *see* anti-Nebraska movement
    Senate debate on, 299–300, 303–11, 453
    Senate passage of, 311
    Seward's opposition to, 317–18, 371
    split Whig vote on, 317
    Sumner's opposition to, 297, 298–300
    as supposedly neutral on slavery issue, 306
    Whig opposition to, 300
Kansas Territory, 96, 291–92, 355, 372, 384
    antislavery cause seen as struggle for
        democracy in, 344
    armed free-state militias in, 345–46
    "Bogus Legislature" in, 343–44
    Border Ruffians invasions of, 340, 345,
        453, 454–55, 478
    1854 elections in, 338–39
    1855 legislative elections in, 339–40
    free-state emigrants to, 336–37, 418
    Free State Party in, 344
    nonresident voters in, 338–39, 340
    pro-slavery forces in, 336–37, 418
    Shannon's temporary peace in, 345–46
Kaskaskia, Ill., 476
Kaw River, 335
Kellogg, William Pitt, 478
Kentucky:
    antislavery movement in, 12, 145
    1849 constitutional convention in, 25,
        26–28

1849 emancipation convention in, 24–25, 28

1849 state elections in, 25–26

Non-Importation Act in, *see* Non-Importation Act

pro-slavery forces in, 7, 144–45, 200, 205, 285–86, 298, 368

slavery issue in, 10–31

Kentucky Bill of Rights, slavery amendment to, 27–28

Kentucky Gazette, 14

Kentucky General Assembly, 10, 23, 25, 101–2

Kentucky Resolutions of 1798, 11, 169

Key to Uncle Tom's Cabin, A (Stowe), 124, 208

King, Preston, 214

King, William R., 58, 87–88, 94, 97, 174, 179, 184, 237, 251

Kinney, Henry L., 351–52

Know Nothings (American Party), 2, 37–38, 323–24, 362, 363, 380, 382, 387, 389, 390, 397, 400, 402–3, 426, 428–29, 432, 433, 442, 443–44

abolitionists and, 444

AL and, 390–91

AL on, 447, 456–57

Catholics hated by, 324–25, 325, 326, 443, 444, 456, 457

Democrats and, 469

Douglas and, 430, 445

in 1854 elections, 329

in 1855 Virginia gubernatorial race, 330

Fillmore as presidential candidate of, 445, 457, 463, 467

Free Soilers and, 386, 387–88

fusion movement and, 444

internal divisions in, 444–45, 464, 468

Philadelphia convention of, 331, 467, 468

pro-slavery platform of, 331–32

Protestants and, 324

in Virginia, 329–30

Whigs and, 388, 456, 457, 464

see also nativism

Know Something Order, 444

Koch, Robert, 9

Koerner, Gustave, 363, 469

Kosciuszko, Tadeusz, 81

Kossuth, Louis, *151,* 156, 164, 265, 407, 450

Douglas and, 167, 168–69, 170

Fillmore's rebuke of, 158, 162, 188

Springfield meeting in support of, 162–63

U.S. fundraising tour of, 154–65, 167, 179

Lacon, Ill., 425

Lafayette, Marquis de, 158

Lamon, Ward Hill, 140, 147, 471

land grants, railroads and, 92, 94, 97, 101, 119

Land Office, U.S., 130

Land Office of Nebraska, 276

Lane Theological Seminary, 122–23

Lanphier, Charles Henry, 264, 266–67, 275, 280, 321, 363, 429, 430, 435

La Paz, Mexico, 244

Law, George, 170–71

Law and Order Party, 344

Lawrence, Abbott, 53

Lawrence, Amos Adams, 232, 320, 334, 335, 340, 345

Lawrence, Kans., 335, 344

sacking of, 346, 478

Leavenworth, Kans., 340, 341, 344

Leavenworth Register, 372

Lee, Robert E., 81, 239

Lemaster, Hugh, 431, 432

Leslie, Eliza, 131

Lexington, Ky., 31, 130, 477

cholera epidemic in, 9–10

Lexington and Concord, Battles of, 111, 162, 318

Lexington Observer, 17, 21–22, 23

Liberator, 110, 372

Liberia, 34, 38–39, 410

Liberty, Mo., 336

Liberty Party, 7, 12, 17, 22, 67, 212, 213–14, 326, 382, 386, 405, 435, 459

Life of Pierce (Hawthorne), 185

Life of Stephan A. Douglas (Flint), 269
Life of Stephen A. Douglas (Sheahan), 269
Lincoln, Abraham, *xxiv,* 39
    ambition of, 147
    autobiographies of, 4–5, 475
    Bloomington speech of, 397–98
    Cassius Clay and, 384
    Cooper Union address of, 68, 139, 406
    depressions and melancholy of, 130, 132,
        143, 441, 460
    District of Columbia emancipation bill
        of, 153, 205, 298, 356
    Eddie's death and, 131, 141
    1838 Springfield Lyceum address of, 118,
        138, 308, 368, 405, 406, 409, 475
    1854 Illinois House speech of, 401–24
    1858 Alton speech of, 360–61
    in 1858 Senate race, 136, 478; *see also*
        Lincoln-Douglas debates
    in 1860, 38
    Euclid studied by, 138–40, 149
    and father's death, 133
    growing international outlook of,
        163–64
    "House Divided" speech of (1858), 261,
        318, 451, 477–78
    in House of Representatives, 2, 10, 41,
        137, 140, 298
    Howell's campaign biography of,
        129–30
    inner circle of, 140
    Land Office post sought by, 130
    law practice of, 1, 5, 6, 10, 132, 134–35,
        136–37, 140, 143, 149, 223, 367, 368,
        426, 441, 442, 459–62
    library of, 372–73
    logical skill of, 138
    mathematical and engineering aptitude
        of, 138–39
    nervous breakdown of, 132
    as obsessive newspaper reader, 372
    Peoria speech of, 140, 163–64, 409,
        424–25, 433, 449–50
    political education of, 369, 406, 475–79
    power as viewed by, 476, 477

    as religious skeptic, 208–9
    Second Inaugural Address of, 207, 369
    as self-made man, 476
    as teetotaler, 394
Lincoln, Abraham, 1855 senatorial
        campaign of, 431–38, 464
    abolitionist opposition to, 432–34, 439
    AL's switch to Trumbull in, 438
    Chase's opposition to, 435
    David Davis in, 432, 440
    O. Lovejoy and, 446
    Washburne and, 433–35, 438
Lincoln, Edward, death of, 131, 141, 209
Lincoln, Levi, 305
Lincoln, Mary Todd, 10, 13, 32, 36, 39, 95,
        384, 473
    and AL's frequent absences, 132, 133
    AL's political ambition supported by,
        389–90, 399, 436, 476
    AL's relationship with, 132, 133, 201
    anxiety and panic attacks of, 131
    Eddie's death and, 131
    in 1849 trip to Lexington, 31–32
    Herndon's dislike of, 133–34
    Lincoln family disliked by, 133–34
    Trumbull and, 440
Lincoln, Robert, 131
Lincoln, Thomas, 14, 133, 369, 376
Lincoln, Thomas "Tod," 131
Lincoln, William Wallace "Willie," 131,
        133
Lincoln & Herndon, 134–35, 432
Lincoln-Douglas debates, 130, 164, 210,
        306, 360–61, 396, 427–28
Linder, Usher, 265
Locke, John, 374
Locofocos, 201, 219
Logan, Stephen T., 141, 389, 390, 391, 437,
        438, 439–40, 442, 471
London Daily News, 408–9, 418
London *Times,* 330
Lord, N. J., 183
Lost Cause, 374
Louisiana Purchase, 52, 203
Louis Napoleon, Emperor of France, 170

Louisville, Ky., 26, 457
Louisville Courier, 28
Louisville Examiner, 22, 26, 28, 444
Louisville Journal, 18, 372, 457, 477
Lovejoy, Elijah, 122, 212, 256, 377, 426,
    446, 474
Lovejoy, Owen, 212, 214, 384, 399, 419, 434,
    435, 437, *443,* 467
  as abolitionist leader, 446
  in AL's Senate campaign, 446
  in founding of Republican Party, 425,
    427, 443, 446
Lowell, James Russell, 227
Lower California, 244
Lucas, Charles, 254
Ludlow, G. W., 171
Luke 11:17, 479
Luthin, Reinhard H., 471

Macbeth (Shakespeare), 409
McClellan, George Brinton, 135–36,
    239–40
McClernand, John A., 363
McCormick, Cyrus, 460
McCormick v. Manny, 6, 460–62
McLean, John, 460, 461
McMullen, Fayette, 159
McRae, John J., 242
Madison, John, 302
Maine, 52
Manchester Democrat, 217
Manifest Destiny, 118, 126, 168, 169, 172,
    173, 175, 233, 245, 254, 268, 316, 347,
    353, 475, 477
Mann, Horace, 49–50, 61–62, 66, 153, 160,
    169, 188, 200, 211
Manny case, 6, 460–62
Marcy, William L., 3, 237, 244, 245, 246,
    247, 266, 269, 288, 313, 326
  Buchanan's feud with, 238
  Davis's battles with, 351
  in 1852 presidential race, 177, 179–80,
    183
  as excluded from Pierce's inner circle,
    294, 295

  Kansas-Nebraska Act and, 294, 295
  Nicaragua and, 350–51
  as Pierce's secretary of state, 236, 238,
    239, 347
  war with Spain opposed by, 348
Mark 3:24–5, 479
Marryat, Frederick, 220
Marshall, Thomas F., 20, 21
Martin, Robert, 95
Mason
, Charles, 248
Mason, George, 250, 374
Mason, George, IV, 250–51
Mason, James Murray, 55, 63, 250, 248–49,
    250, 251, 288, 306, 312, 330
Mason, John Y., 238, 348–49
Mason-Dixon Line, 256, 257, 330
Massachusetts, 108–9
  anti-Nebraska movement in, 328, 333,
    334
  antislavery movement in, 109, 182, 297,
    320
  1854 elections in, 328–29
  Know Nothings in, 329, 464
  slavery prohibited in, 305
Massachusetts Emigrant Aid Company, *see*
    New England Emigrant Aid Society
Massachusetts Supreme Judicial Court,
    182, 305
Matheny, James, 141
Matteson, Joel, 399, 435–36, 437–38
Matthews, Stanley, 43, 44
Maxwell, Hugh, 106
Mazzini, Giuseppe, 161
Medary, Samuel, 44
Medill, Joseph, 444
Melville, Gansevoort, 126
Melville, Herman, 126–27, 185
Mentelle, Charlotte, 36
Mercury poisoning, 132–33
Meredith, William M., 78, 79
Methodists, 207, 256, 361
Mexican Cession:
  slavery issue in, 2, 41, 47, 48, 63
  see also specific states and territories

Mexican War, 2, 22, 48, 99, 151, 168, 182, 190, 191, 215, 228, 235, 241, 243, 255, 256, 281, 351
  AL's opposition to, 130, 140, 142, 409, 476
Mexico:
  proposed further annexation of, 316–17, 347, 418
  Walker's invasion of, 244–45
Mill, James, 372
Mill, John Stuart, 372
Miller, James, 391
Miller, Samuel F., 145
Milly (slave), 34, 35, 38–39
Minkins, Frederick "Shadrach," 110–11
Minnesota Democrat, 267
Minnesota Territory, 267
miscegenation, 428
Mississippi:
  1851 gubernatorial race in, 229, 230
  secessionist movement in, 114, 115
  Sovereign Convention of, 115
Mississippi, USS, 155
Mississippi Free Trader, 160
Mississippi River, 92
Missouri, 52, 252
  anti-Benson movement in, 257, 258–59, 260
  Benton as senator from, 253
  Democratic dominance in, 253
  Jackson-Napton Resolutions in, 258, 259, 260
  Kansas free-staters opposed in, 336
  pro-slavery forces in, 256–57, 259, 339, 340, 341, 343, 345, 453, 454–55, 478
Missouri Compromise (1820), 3, 5, 52, 58, 59, 63, 72, 73, 101, 103, 107, 116–17, 179, 199, 204, 256, 259, 271, 280, 281, 361, 391, 392, 393, 411, 415, 448, 449, 450
  AL on possible restoration of, 418–19, 454
  Clay as author of, 308
  Douglas's claimed reverance for, 281, 397–98, 403
  slavery issue in, 313–14

Missouri Compromise, repeal of, 255, 261, 283, 358, 400
  A.C. Dodge and, 279, 280
  Atchison as proponent of, 257, 259–60, 273, 278–79, 282
  Benton's opposition to, 255, 257–58, 278–79
  Davis's support of, 236, 289, 290
  Dixon's amendment for, 285–87, 293
  Dodge/Douglas bill for, 280–85, 292
  Douglas's 1853 bill for, 271–72, 273
  F Street Mess and, 287–88, 289, 290–92
  Kansas-Nebraska Act as means of, *see* Kansas-Nebraska Act
  Pierce and, 288, 289–92
  Price and, 256–57
  Supreme Court and, 288
Missouri Democrat, 277
Missouri Republican, 402–3
Missouri River, 257
Missouri Supreme Court, *Dred Sciott* case in, 260
Mitchell, William D., 26–27
Mobile Railroad, 97
Moby-Dick, or The Whale (Melville), 29, 126–27
Moffett, Thomas, 384
Moore, Charles C., 18–19
morality, slavery and, 95, 96, 402, 411, 413, 417, 421–23, 425
Morgan, John J., 234
Morgan Journal, 426, 464
Mormons, 252, 429
Morse, John, 43–44
Morse, Samuel F. B., 325
Morton, Jackson, 75
Mosquito Coast, 351, 352
Mott, Lucretia, 395
My Bondage and My Freedom (Douglass), 459

Napoleon I, emperor of France, 474
  AL's comparison of Douglas to, 409–10
Napton, William B., 258, 260
Nashville Convention, 72–73, 87, 142

National Anti-Slavery Standard, 372

National Era, 29, 67, 73, 124, 125, 152, 214, 217, 229, 261, 298, 323, 372

National Intelligencer, 80, 302

Native Citizen, 469

nativism, 324–25, 380–81, 388, 444, 445, 447

   see also Know Nothings

Nazism, 359

Nebraska Territory, 103, 259, 271, 272, 291–92

"Negro-Slavery, No Evil" (Stringfellow), 337–38

Neutrality Act, 352

Newell, William, 141

New England Emigrant Aid Society, 334, 335, 336, 362

New Hampshire, 217, 322

New Mexico Territory, 280, 54

   Black Codes of, 104

   slavery issue in, 50, 51, 53–54, 58, 61, 67–68, 76–81, 88–89, 90, 99–100, 102, 104, 151–52, 169

   Texas's attempted annexation of, 77–81, 98, 99

New Orleans, Battle of, 264

New Orleans Bulletin, 160

New Salem, Ill., 475

New York:

   antislavery movement in, 217

   1850 elections in, 106–7

   1854 elections in, 326–28

   Free Soil Party in, 106

   Know Nothings and nativists in, 325–26, 464

   see also Democratic Party, New York; Whig Party, New York

New York Courier and Enquirer, 23, 46, 192

New York Herald, 171, 215, 245, 288, 289, 290–91, 294, 349, 350, 352

New York Journal of Commerce, 278

New York Post, 214, 217, 278, 295–96, 303

New York Times, 157, 158, 192, 227, 265, 283, 298, 300, 313, 315–16, 327, 332, 353, 364, 408, 458, 467, 468

New York Tribune, 16, 17, 21, 69, 178, 193–94, 196, 246, 273, 298, 306, 311, 312–13, 316, 323, 334, 345, 364, 372, 433

Nicaragua:

   Kinney's aborted invasion of, 351–52

   Walker's invasion of, 349–50, 352

   Walker's reestablishment of slavery in, 350

Nicaraguan Land and Mining Company, 351

Nicholas, George, 11

Nicholas I, czar of Russia, 265

Nichols, Eli, 42, 43

Nicholson, A. O. P., 351

Nicholson letter, 404

Nicolay, John, 375, 376, 464–65

Non-Importation Act (Kentucky; 1833), 10, 12, 15, 18–19, 23, 26, 28

   repeal of, 25, 27

non-intervention, concept of, 95, 163, 287, 306, 314

North American Review, 312

Northern Pacific Railroad, 94

Northern Whigs, 17, 30, 51, 54, 71, 75, 143, 153–54, 196

Northup, Solomon, 420

Northwest Ordinance (1787), 7, 63, 67, 203, 236, 257, 260, 273, 278, 298, 302–3, 304, 313–14, 323, 358, 371, 392, 404, 405, 406, 414, 415, 421, 436

Northwest Territory, 67

Norton, Jesse O., 387, 433, 445

nullification, 11, 19, 51, 57, 61, 65, 80, 98, 242, 249, 255, 277, 284, 361

O'Conor, Charles, 236–37

Offutt, Denton, 475

Ogden, William B., 93

Oglesby, Richard, 401, 466, 467

Ohio:

   Black Laws in, 43, 44, 310

   Whig Party in, 43–44

Ohio House of Representatives, 43

Ohio Statesman, 44

Ohio Supreme Court, 43
On Heroes, Hero-Worship, and the Heroic in History (Carlyle), 474
"On Violations of the Fugitive Slave Act" (Clay speech), 112
Order of the Star Spangled Banner, 324, 331
Order of United Americans, 327, 331
Oread Institute, 333
Oregon Territory, 236
Ostend Manifesto, 348–49, 356, 408
O'Sullivan, John, 175
Ottawa, Ill., 384
Owen, Robert, 229

Pacific Mail Steamboat Company, 171
Pacific railroad, *see* transcontinental railroad
Packer, Asa, 338
Paine, Thomas, 139, 209, 405
Palfrey, John G., 109, 297
Palmer, John M., 391, 437, 438, 439, 440, 469, 470
Panama Railroad, 170
Panic of 1837, 92, 100, 351
Parker, Elizabeth, 36–37, 131
Parker, John, 111, 318
Parker, John A., 275–76, 285
Parker, Theodore, 67, 109, 111, 161, 318–19, *318,* 334, 372, 462
Parker, William, 189
Parks, Samuel C., 436–37, 439, 441
Parkville Industrial Luminary, 341
Patriarcha (Filmer), 373
Pawnee, Kans., 338, 343
Pearl River, 95
Peck, Ebenezer, 469
Pemberton, James, 229
Penny Post, 329
People v. Shurtliff et al., 394
Peoria, Ill., AL's speech in, 140, 163–64, 409, 424–25, 433, 449–50
Perry, Matthew, 233
Pettit, John, *293,* 304, 305, 312
    AL's attacks on, 422, 428

Philadelphia, Pa., Know Nothing convention in, 331, 467, 468
Philadelphia Ledger, 183
Philadelphia Public Ledger, 98, 155
Phillips, Charles, 410
Phillips, Eugenia Levy, 284
Phillips, Philip, 283–84, *283,* 287–88, 290, 291
Phillips, Ulrich B., 114
Phillips, Wendell, 161, 318
Phillips, William, 341
Piatt, Donn, 43
Pierce, Anna, 181
Pierce, Benjamin, 181
Pierce, Franklin, 3, 126, *167,* 241, 270, 346, 351, 442
    alcoholism of, 181, 216, 248
    AL's Springfield speech against, 218–21
    amiability of, 182
    annexation of Cuba desired by, 233, 237–38
    cabinet of, 226, 228, 231–32, 234, 236, 248, 251, 288, 301
    Cushing's influence over, 232–33
    Davis appointed secretary of war by, 251
    Davis's influence over, 233, 238, 248
    Davis's support for candidacy of, 230–31
    Democratic factionalism and, 247
    as easily manipulated, 226, 232, 235, 248
    in 1852 presidential race, 178, 181, 184–85, 196, 213, 214, 215–17, 222
    foreign policy of, 408
    Fugitive Slave Act and, 184, 219–20, 233–34
    indecisiveness of, 226, 228, 232, 237, 292
    Kansas election fraud and, 341–42
    Kansas-Nebraska Act supported by, 313
    Kansas's "Bogus Legislature" supported by, 344
    Missouri Compromise repeal and, 288, 289–92
    patronage appointments by, 239, 246, 301, 313, 316
    political rise of, 181–82

popularity of, 225
printing contract and, 247, 248
Reeder and, 342–43
reelection as chief goal of, 238–39,
    247–48, 338, 356
second term denied to, 356
and sons' deaths, 232
Southern imperium plan supported by,
    244
Walker's Nicaragua regime supported
    by, 350–51, 353
Pierce, Jane Appleton, 181, 248
    Davises' friendship with, 233
    and sons' deaths, 232, 233
Pike, James Shepherd, 178, 193–94, 306,
    311, 312–13
Pike County Free Press, 464
Pillow, Gideon, 178, 183
Pittsburgh, Pa., Republican Party
    convention in, 467
Platte Argus, 336, 341
Platte County Self-Defensive Association,
    336, 337, 341
Pleasanton, Alfred, 77, 80
Polk, James K., 44, 73, 92, 126, 170, 171,
    175, 181, 191, 214, 234, 409
Poore, Benjamin Perley, 182, 238, 251
popular sovereignty doctrine, 74, 95–96,
    103, 117–18, 121, 169, 179, 270, 273,
    280–81, 283, 293, 298, 302, 305–6,
    308, 314, 334, 339, 362, 368, 371, 398,
    400, 429
    AL's refutation of, 365, 413–15, 417–18
    Cass as originator of, 404
Pottawatomie Massacre, 346, 478
power, AL's view of, 476, 477
"Power" (Emerson), 473
Pratt, Thomas, 89
Prentice, George D., 18, 457
Presbyterians, 207, 208, 361
Preston, Margaret Wickliffe, 32, 36, 37
Preston, William, 36, 37, 286–87
Preston, William Ballard, 79–80
Price, Sterling, 257
Price, William C., 256–57, 277, 343

Proclamation Against Nullification, 80
prohibition, see temperance movement
Protestants, Know Nothings and, 324

Quakers, 426
Quincy, Ill., 429, 446
Quincy Whig, 120
Quitman, John A., 114, 115, 155–56

racism:
    AL's acknowledgment of, 410–11, 417
    in Illinois, 369, 410, 462
railroads:
    land grants and, 92, 94, 97, 101, 119
    slavery and, 120
Ramsey, J. G. M., 160
Randall, James G., 359, 360
Randall, Ruth Painter, 132
Randolph, John, 247, 373
Rankin, Henry Bascom, 373
Rantoul, Robert, 112, 182–83, 211
Ray, Charles H., 432–34, 435, 444, 465, 466,
    469–70
Raymond, Henry J., 157, 223, 327, 468
    at 1852 Whig convention, 192–93
    Greeley's rivalry with, 327–28
Reconstruction, 359
Redfield, Herman J., 247
Reeder, Andrew H., 342, 454
    Kansas elections and, 338–41
    Pierce's firing of, 343
Reid, Philip, 356
Remini, Robert V., 104, 119
Representative Men (Emerson), 474
Republican Party, Illinois, 214, 395, 437
    AL in founding of, 7, 38, 369, 382,
        420–21, 426, 467, 477, 478
    Bloomington convention of, 390, 467,
        469, 470, 471, 478
    central committee of, 427, 428, 443
    Codding as founder of, 425–26, 427, 428,
        443, 445–46, 447–48, 462
    extension of slavery opposed by, 426–27
    O. Lovejoy as founder of, 425–26, 427,
        443, 446

Republican Party, New York:
  merger of Whigs with, 458
  Seward as founder of, 459
  Syracuse convention of, 458
Republican Party, Republicans, 44, 254,
    332, 359
  Cassius Clay as founder of, 37
  early efforts in creation of, 2, 7, 322–23
  in 1856 elections, 5
  1860 convention of, 328, 440
  1864 convention of, 38
  founding of, 380, 381–82, 420
  Kansas-Nebraska Act and founding of,
    315
  myth of AL's reluctance to join, 471–72
  Pittsburgh convention of, 467–68
Republic of Sonora, 349
Revelation, Book of, 423
revolutions of 1848, 154, 157, 163, 164, 407–8
Reynolds, John, 380, 436
Rhett, Robert Barnwell, 72–73, 87, 114,
    115, 249
Rhodes, James Ford, 227
Rice, Henry M., 268
Richardson, William A., 177, 267, 271, 313,
    315, 429, 430, 446, 469
Richmond, Va., 215
Richmond Enquirer, 24, 72, 73, 276, 278–79,
    330, 372, 374
Richmond Examiner, 374
Rifle and Light Infantry Tactics, 239
"Rights and Duties of Masters, The"
    (Thornwell), 208
Rio Grande, 98
Ripon, Wisc., 322–23
Ritchie, Thomas, 24, 73, 100, 172, 183, 276,
    330, 372
Robertson, Daniel A., 267
Robertson, George "Old Buster," 33, 36–37
  AL's letter to, 448–51, 477
  as slave owner, 451
Robertson, James, 206–7
Robinson, Charles, 346
Rock Island Railroad, 388, 434
Rockwell, Julius, 381

Ruins of Empire (Volney), 405
Running A Thousand Miles for Freedom
    (Craft), 110
Rusk, Thomas J., 271, 272
Russell, Alfred Francis, 34–36, 38–39, 39
Russell, James, 32
Russell, John Todd, 34, 36
Rynders, Isaiah, 171

St. Louis Evening News, 273
St. Paul, Minn., 268
Salt Creek Valley, 336
Sanders, George Nicholas, 238, 246, 269,
    408, 418
  as arms merchant, 170, 177, 181
  background of, 169–70
  Butler attacked by, 176, 177–78
  Democratic Review editorials of, 175–78,
    221
  Douglas and, 170, 172, 175–76, 177–78
  Kossuth and, 170
  political assassination advocated by, 170,
    177
Sangamo Journal, 17, 21
Santa Anna, Antonio López, 245
Sargent, Nathan, 194, 196–97
Scarlet Letter, The (Hawthorne), 184–85
Schlesinger, Arthur M., Jr., 360
Schneider, George, 428–29, 466, 466
Schurz, Carl, 164, 227, 249, 251
  on Douglas's debating style, 306–7
Scott, Dred, 254, 260
Scott, Walter, 118
Scott, William, 260
Scott, Winfield, 5, 159, 187
  Davis's vendetta against, 241
  in 1852 presidential race, 190–93, 194,
    213, 215, 222
  military career of, 190, 191
Scottish Anti-Slavery Society, 206–7
Scottish Enlightenment, 373
Scripps, John L., 5, 139, 140
secession, secessionists, 3, 96, 114–15, 156,
    163, 173, 208, 236, 242, 244, 249, 305,
    357

Second Great Awakening, 122
Second Inaugural Address (Lincoln), 207,
    369
"Second Reply to Hayne" (Webster), 65,
    107, 161, 210
Seddon, James A., 173–74
Selby, Paul, 426–27, 428, 464–65, 467
self-government, AL on, 413–14
Senate, U.S., 42, *59*
    Chase in, 44–45
    Clay reelected to, 51–52
    Committee on Public Lands of, 92, 93,
        101, 279
    Committee on Territories of, 92, 267,
        275, 280
    Compromise of 1850 debated in, *see*
        Compromise of 1850
    Democratic control of, 49
    Finance Committee of, 85
    Pierce's resignation from, 181
    Seward in, 46–47, 51
Seward, Frederick, 105–6
Seward, William Henry, 22, 30, *45,* 46–47,
        51, 60, 74, 83, 91, 106, 114, 125, 180,
        197, 211, 247, 306, 323, 326, 368, 381,
        385, 415, 421
    A.C. Dodge's attack on, 303
    AL influenced by, 371–72
    AL's defense of, 219
    as antislavery leader, 45
    and Compromise of 1850, *see*
        Compromise of 1850
    in 1849 senate campaign, 45–46
    and 1852 election, 223
    in 1856 election, 458
    Fillmore's war with, 84–85, 90, 105, 107,
        156–57, 180, 188, 190, 191
    in founding of Republican Party, 459
    Fugitive Slave Act supported by, 68,
        188
    fusion movement and, 458
    Greeley and, 328
    "higher law" argument of, 69–70, 89
    Kansas-Nebraska Act opposed by,
        317–18, 371

Kossuth's U.S. tour and, 156, 157–58,
        160, 162
    as loyal Whig, 323–24
    Scott's candidacy promoted by, 190–92,
        194, 195, 196, 215
    Southern senators' attacks on, 89–90
    Webster's attack on, 106, 108
Sewell, Richard H., 212
Seymour, Horatio, 106, 222, 295, 326
Shakespeare, William, 409, 416
    AL's passion for, 4
Shannon, Wilson, 343, 344
    temporary peace in Kansas negotiated
        by, 345–46
Shaw, Lemuel, 110, 112, 126
Shawnee Mission, 343
Sheahan, James W., 269, 364, 393, 435
Sherman, Francis, 468
Shields, James, 23, 75, 93, 94, 101, 158, 159,
        164, 169, 170, 264, 378, 379, 429, 430,
        436
    in 1855 Senate race, 435, 437
Shiloh, Battle of, 37
Silver Grays, 106, 157, 190, 327, 331, 458
Sims, Thomas, 112, 126, 182, 318, 320
Sioux City Land Company, 279
Skinner, Onias, 442
slavery, extension of, 47–48, 107, 143, 173,
        207, 235, 249, 251, 260, 310–11, 377,
        395, 415, 468
    AL's opposition to, 4, 361, 369, 375, 401,
        407, 411–12, 414–16, 417, 447, 453, 456
    Atchison and, 273–74
    Benton's opposition to, 256, 278–79
    as deliberate goal of Kansas-Nebraska
        Act, 4, 293–94, 358–59
    Illinois Republicans opposition to,
        426–27
    Jefferson's opposition to, 298, 392, 404–5,
        415
    Taylor's opposition to, 2, 42, 50–51,
        60–62, 76–77, 102, 156
    Whig opposition to, 385
    see also Compromise of 1850
Slavery: The Evil—The Remedy (Clay), 16

"Slavery and the Fugitive Slave Law"
    (Campbell), 207
*Slavery as It Is: Testimony of One Thousand
    Witnesses* (Weld), 124
Slavery Discussed in Occasional Essays
    (Bacon), 377–78
"Slavery to Massachusetts" (Thoreau),
    320
slaves, slavery:
    AL's Clay eulogy as examination of,
        203–4
    AL's Euclidean argument against, 376
    AL's evolving views on, 144–49, 164,
        221, 360–61, 369, 375–76, 402, 407,
        410, 421–23
    AL's self-identification with, 147, 369,
        376
    Bible and, 207–8, 304, 337, 373
    breeding of, 87
    as cancer, 421
    Christianity and, 206–9, 256, 377–78,
        406, 423
    Clay's opposition to, 209–10
    Constitution and, 7, 16, 29–30, 68, 121,
        201, 212, 234, 313–14, 370, 393, 406,
        415, 421
    Declaration of Independence and, 304
    economics of, 374, 412–13
    1848 Lexington uprising of, 23–24
    Fitzhugh's defense of, 373–75
    free labor and, 13, 16, 24, 26–27, 28
    as injurious to American ideal of liberty,
        407–8
    Jefferson and, 7, 203–4
    morality and, 94, 96, 402, 411, 413, 417,
        421–23, 425
    Pierce's defense of, 234
    railroads and, 120
    as threat to democracy, 370
    value of, 120
slave trade, 205, 421
    AL's loathing for, 412–13, 456
    Clay's abhorrence of, 209
Slidell, John, 269, 278, 289
Smith, Gerrit, 113, 212, 298

Smith, John Speed, 15
Smith, Joseph, 252
Snow, John, 9
*Sociology for the South, or The Failure of
    Free Society* (Fitzhugh), 373
Soule, Pierre, 91, 238, 408, 418
    as minister to Spain, 347–48
    resignation of, 349
    Walker's Nicaraguan coup and, 350
South Carolina, 19, 205
    secessionists in, 114, 249, 250
    Sovereign Convention in, 115
South Carolina Railroad Company, 268
Southern Baptist Convention, 207
Southern Democratic Party, 38, 47–48, 49,
    287
Southern imperium, 76, 233, 235, 243, 244,
    263, 316–17, 347, 353, 418
Southern Manifesto, 252
Southern Presbyterian Review, 208
Southern Rights movement, 73, 80, 114,
    117, 226, 235, 237, 240, 242–43, 246,
    248, 249–50, 256, 281, 285, 372
    see also Southern Ultras; states rights
        movement
Southern States Rights Democratic Party,
    156
Southern Ultras, 47–48, 74, 75, 78, 87, 91,
    95, 96, 114, 117, 155–56, 163, 172, 174,
    179, 200, 205, 247, 283, 300, 301, 315
Southern Unionists, 80, 115, 116–17, 240,
    242, 243
Spain:
    Black Warrior incident and, 348
    Soule as minister to, 347–48
Special Committee Appointed to
    Investigate the Troubles in Kansas,
    339, 340
Speed, James, 28, 38, 452, 457–58
Speed, James Stephens, 457
Speed, Joshua, 28, 31, 393
    AL's 1841 Ohio River trip with, 452–53
    AL's 1855 letter to, 451–52
Spencer, Joseph, 461
Spooner, Thomas, 468

Springfield, Ill.:
  Cassius Clay in, 383, 384–85
  1854 abolitionist convention in, 399
  1854 State Fair in, 398, 401
  Emerson in, 473
  Know Nothing convention in, 470
  pro-Kossuth meeting in, 162–63
Springfield Capital Enterprise, 389
Springfield Lyceum, AL's 1838 address
    at, 118, 138, 308, 368, 405, 406, 409,
    475
Springfield Scott Club, 218
Squatter Sovereign, 336–37, 342, 345
squatter sovereignty, 95, 179
Staat-Zeitung, 466
Stanhope Burleigh: The Jesuits in Our Home,
    325
Stanly, Edward, 79, 81
Stanton, Edwin, 6, 284, 460, 461
Stanton, Elizabeth Cady, 214
Stanton, Henry B., 214
States Rights Democratic Party, 115, 228,
    230
states rights movement, 68, 95, 161, 173–74,
    208, 231, 243, 247, 249, 330
  see also Southern Rights movement;
    Southern Ultras
Stephens, Alexander H., 48, 50, 52, 61,
    78, 79–81, 113, 114–15, 117, 153, 159,
    194–95, 242, 316, 317
Stevens, Thaddeus, 189
Stevenson, Adlai E., 395
Stowe, Calvin, 377
Stowe, Charles, 125
Stowe, Harriet Beecher, 122, *122,* 152, 208,
    311, 377
  AL's meeting with, 125
  see also Uncle Tom's Cabin
Stringfellow, Benjamin Franklin, 336,
    337–38, 339, 340–41, 342, 343, 344
Stringfellow, John H., 336–37, 343, 344
Strunk, John, 432
Stuart, John, 36–37
Stuart, John Todd, 132, 141, 146, 419,
    472

Sumner, Charles, 108, 189, 211, 213, 296,
    296, 311, 312, 334, 336, 356, 359, 421,
    435, 467, 474
  as abolitionist, 42, 109
  Brooks's assault on, 478
  distrust of, 328
  Douglas denounced by, 368
  Douglas's attacks on, 309–10, 402
  elected to Senate, 112–13
  Kansas-Nebraska Act opposed by, 29,
    298–300, 422–23
  Missouri Compromise amendment of,
    287
  political isolation of, 297
Superior City, Wisc., 267, 352
Supreme Court, U.S., 254
  Dred Scott decision of, 110, 210, 255,
    260–61, 358
  Jones v. Van Zandt decision of, 180
  Missouri Compromise repeal and, 288
Suttle, Charles, 318
Swett, Leonard, 140, 148, 390, 432
  on AL's political acumen, 475–76
Syracuse, N.Y., 106, 113, 189

Tablet, 395
Talbott, Albert Gallatin, 26
Tammany Hall, 171, 313
Taylor, Zachary, 5, 9, 41, *41,* 45, 47, 73, 130,
    141, 142, 191, 241, 303, 439, 477
  annual message to Congress of, 50–51
  cabinet shake-up planned by, 78–79
  Compromise of 1850 opposed by, 60–62,
    74, 75, 216
  death of, 81–82, 85–86, 102, 141, 156
  in election of 1848, 23, 46, 84
  extension of slavery opposed by, 2, 42,
    50–51, 60–62, 76–77, 102, 156
  Fugitive Slave Act opposed by, 216
  Galphin affair and, 78, 81–82, 215
  patronage appointments by, 46, 53
  and preservation of Union, 61, 80
  and Texas's attempted annexation of
    New Mexico, 77–81
Tazewell County, Ill., 146

temperance movement, 323, 325, 326,
        380–81, 394–95, 443
Texas, 54, 90
    annexation of, 53, 255, 361, 403
    attempted New Mexico annexation of,
        77–81, 98, 99
    bond lobby in, 97–98, 99, 118
Texas Republic, 271
Thayer, Eli, 333–34, *333,* 334–35, 336
Thirty Years' View (Benton), 259
Thompson, George, 13, 111
Thompson, Jacob, 78
Thoreau, Henry David, 320, 474
Thornwell, James Henley, 208
three-fifths clause, 393, 415, 421
Tilden, Samuel, 93
Tocqueville, Alexis de, 98
Todd, John, 32, 34
    missing will of, 32, 36–37
Todd, Robert S., 15, 22, 25, 130–31, 200,
        285, 368, 477
    death of, 10, 26, 32, 38, 286
    in 1845 election for Kentucky senate,
        18–19
    in suit against Wickliffe, *see Todd Heirs
        v. Wickliffe*
    Wickliffe's battles with, 18–20, 33, 35
Todd family, 31
    Cassius Clay and, 13
Todd Heirs v. Wickliffe, 32, 35
    AL as co-counsel in, 7, 10, 31, 33–34,
        36–37, 38, 131, 144, 286, 368, 448,
        450
    AL's thinking on slavery affected by,
        143–45
    Wickliffe's claims upheld in, 37
Toombs, Robert, 48, 49, 60, 61, 78, 79–80,
        113, 114–15, 117, 153, 194–95, 222–23,
        240, 242
    Davis's feud with, 240–41
Topeka, Kans., 344
Towns, George W., 114
Townsend, George Alfred, 372
Townshend, Norton S., 43
Transcendentalists, 161, 187–88, 318, 473

transcontinental railroad, 259, 261
    Davis and, 272, 316–17
    Douglas and, 267, 271–72, 279, 294
    proposed southern route of, 239, 243,
        272, 355
Transylvania University, 9–10, 252, 280
Treat, Samuel, 442
Tremont House, Boston, 226, 231
Trotter, James George, 14
Troy and Greenfield Railroad, 297
True American, 17, 20–21, 22, 383, 444
    mob's closing of, 21–23
    in move to Cincinnati, 22
    see also Louisville Examiner
True Democrat, 43
Trumbull, Julia Jayne, 436, 440
Trumbull, Lyman, 162, 282, 363, 429–30,
        431, 447–48, 459, 465, 467, 469, 470
    AL's relationship with, 440–41, 442
    in 1855 Senate race, 436–37, 440
Tucker, Beverly, 237, 247
Tucker, Nathaniel Beverly, 247
Turner, Cyrus, 25
Turner, Squire, 25
Twelve Years a Slave (Northup), 420
Two Years Before the Mast (Dana), 126
Tyler, John, 11, 83, 86, 227

Ullmann, Daniel, 327
*Uncle Sam's Youngest Son, Citizen Know
        Nothing, 321*
Uncle Tom's Cabin (Stowe), 124, 152, 180,
        208, 311
    as rallying cry for antislavery movement,
        124
    Southern denunciation of, 124–25
    success of, 124
    writing of, 123–24
Underground Railroad, 113–14, 123–24,
        189, 214, 386, 395, 426
Union, preservation of:
    AL on, 416, 420, 422
    Benton and, 255, 256, 358
    Calhoun on, 4, 63–64, 66, 251, 357–58
    Clay and, 3, 55, 59, 62

Douglas and, 125, 293
Taylor and, 61, 80
Webster and, 3, 65, 113
see also Compromise of 1850; secession
Union Democratic Party, 156
Unionists, 382
Union Pacific, 93
Unitarians, 361
United States, neutrality policy of, 158–60
Urbana Constitution, 130
U.S. Mail Steamship Company, 170
Usrey, William J., 465, 466
Utah Territory, 90, 91, 98, 280, 429
   slavery issue in, 53–54, 61, 99–100
Utley, William, 451

Vallandigham, Clement, 359
Van Buren, John, 106, 214, 237, 247, 295
Van Buren, Martin, 57, 175, 211, 214, 222,
   230, 234, 309, 468
Vanderbilt, Cornelius, and Walker's
   Nicaraguan invasion, 352–53
Van Zandt, John, 123–24
Vaughn, John C., 43–44, 444, 468
Vicksburg, Shreveport and Texas Railroad,
   246
Vigil, Agustin, 350
Virginia, 215
   Know Nothings in, 329–30
Virginia Chivalry, 330
Virginia Declaration of Rights, 374
Virginia Resolutions, 11
Volney, Constantin, comte de, 209, 405
Voltaire, 206, 209

Wade, Benjamin, 160, 211, 213, 217, 304,
   305, 310
Wade, Edward, 298
Walker, George, 370, 375
Walker, J. Knox, 171, 178
Walker, Robert J., 245, 246, 264–65, 267–68
Walker, William, *347*
   Mexican invasion of, 244–45
   Nicaraguan invasion and coup of,
   349–50, 352

Walsh, Mike, 315
Ward, Henry, 123
War Department, U.S., Davis's
   modernization program at, 239
War of 1812, 57, 190, 215, 216
Washburn, Israel, 323
Washburne, Elihu B., 387, *387,* 432, 433–35,
   438, 441, 460, 469–70
Washington, D.C., *see* District of
   Columbia
Washington, George, 5, 26, 55, 216, 251
   Farewell Address of, 158–60
Washington Republic, 69–70
Washington Sentinel, 237, 247, 248, 281
Washington Union, 73, 94, 183, 245–47, 276,
   287, 289, 294, 316, 338, 348, 351–52
Watson, Peter H., 460
Webb, James Watson, 46, 192
Weber, George R., 472
Webster, Daniel, 3, 74, *105,* 127, 152, 180,
   200, 300, 310, 319, 351
   abolitionists' battles with, 109
   Cassius Clay's open letters to, 29–30
   and collapse of Whig Party, 107–8, 113
   Compromise of 1850 and, 53, 65–67, 98
   Crafts' escape and, 110
   in 1852 presidential race, 188, 189–90,
   193, 194–96
   as Fillmore's secretary of state, 85,
   98–99, 107, 188
   Fugitive Slave Act supported by, 29, 106,
   107, 108, 110, 111–12, 123, 187–88,
   194–95, 474
   as Harrison's secretary of state, 86
   New England intellectuals'
   denunciations of, 107–8, 123, 187–88,
   474
   patronage jobs and, 98–99
   and preservation of Union, 3, 65, 113,
   357
   presidential ambitions of, 2, 107, 113, 187
   "Second Reply to Hayne" of, 65, 107,
   161, 210
   Seward attacked by, 106, 108
   on Taylor's death, 85–86

Webster, Fletcher, 53
Webster, Sidney, 351–52
Weed, Thurlow, 22, 45, 46, 47, 51, 60, 61,
    70, 75, 78–79, 83, 85, 99, 103–4, 106,
    112, 162, 196, 197, 381, 385, 388
  in 1852 election, 180, 191, 223
  Fillmore's war with, 84–85, 90, 105, 107,
    157, 180
  Greeley and, 326–28
Weld, Theodore, 122–23, 124, 383
Weller, John B., 303, 309–10
Wentworth, John, 100, 263, 315, 363, 388
West:
  Douglas as champion of, 118–19
  railroads and, 120
  slavery issue and, 4, 243, 252; see also
    Compromise of 1850; Kansas-
    Nebraska Act
Western Citizen, 383–84, 386
Westminster Review, 372
Weston, Mo., 343
West Point, U.S. Military Academy at, 239
"What Led to the War, or the Secret
    History of the Kansas-Nebraska Act"
    (Parker), 275–76
Wheeler, John H., 350–51
Whig or Abolition: That's the Question, 45
Whig Party, Illinois, 97, 162, 201, 264, 382,
    390
  collapse of, 201, 381
  in 1850 election, 141–43
  in 1852 election, 221
  in 1854 elections, 379, 380, 387–88, 390
Whig Party, New York, 22, 45–46, 157,
    246
  1850 convention of, 106
  Silver Gray faction of, 106, 157, 190, 327,
    331, 458
Whig Party, Whigs, 259, 322, 328, 400,
    403, 405
  abolitionists and, 419, 439
  AL's attempted resuscitation of, 419, 426
  AL's loyalty to, 5, 6, 144, 147, 221,
    323–24, 368, 369, 381, 382, 385–86,
    390, 405, 433

antislavery movement in, 201, 381, 419,
    446
collapse of, 1–2, 3, 5, 6, 7, 31, 47, 49, 103,
    104, 107–8, 113, 147, 153, 205, 222–23,
    323–24, 327, 329, 385, 433, 439–40,
    441–42, 443, 445, 456, 458, 459, 464,
    477
and Compromise of 1850, 99
Conscience, 108–9, 189, 328
Cotton, 67, 107, 109, 110
in 1848 elections, 23
1852 convention of, 164–65, 192–97
in Kentucky, 11, 15, 19–20, 23, 28–29,
    30, 31, 457
Know Nothings and, 388, 456, 457,
    464
Northern, 17, 30, 51, 54, 71, 75, 143,
    153–54, 196
in Ohio, 43–44
Old, 4, 5, 38, 382, 412, 419, 459, 464
proposed merger of Liberty Party and,
    17
Seward's loyalty to, 323–24
Southern, 47–48, 49, 51, 54, 72, 79, 103,
    143, 153, 156, 191, 240, 242, 287, 300,
    311, 316, 317, 323, 329, 330
Taylor administration and, 41
White, Garland H., 113, 114
White, Horace, 397, 423–24, 436, 440
White, Joseph L., 352–53
"white negroes," 15–16, 26–27, 28
white supremacy, 16, 337
Whitfield, J. W., 339
Whitney, Henry Clay, 136, 137, 138, 140,
    145, 389, 441
Whittier, John Greenleaf, 67, 113, 335
Wickliffe, Charles, 11, 14
Wickliffe, Daniel, 17
Wickliffe, Margaret, see Preston, Margaret
    Wickliffe
Wickliffe, Mary Owen Todd Russell
    "Polly," 32, 33–34
  estate of, 35–36, 38
Wickliffe, Robert, Jr. "Young Duke,"
    13–14, 15, 25, 146

Wickliffe, Robert, Sr. "Old Duke," *11,*
    18–19, 31, 146, 285–86
    death of, 37
    as leader of Kentucky pro-slavery
        movement, 10–11, 12, 14, 24
    Polly Russell's marriage to, 32, 33, 34,
        36
    R.J. Breckinridge's battles with, 11–12,
        14, 19, 33, 34–35, 36
    Robert Todd's battles with, 18–20, 33, 35
    Robert Todd's suit against, *see Todd
        Heirs v. Wickliffe*
    "white negro" argument of, 15–16,
        26–27
Wickliffe family:
    Cassius Clay attacked by, 14
    dueling by, 14
Williams, Archibald, 429, 446
Wilmot, David, 48, 49, 211, 289, 403–4
Wilmot Proviso, 2, 47, 48–49, 58, 60, 65, 75,
        86, 96–97, 99, 107, 117, 121, 124, 142,
        143, 152, 222, 235, 256, 300, 400, 404,
        411, 456
Wilson, Henry, 154, 275, 282, 297, 328, 329,
        332, 334, 341

Winthrop, Robert C., 48, 49–50, 108, 109,
        112–13, 302, 312, 329
Wisconsin Territory, 280
Wise, Henry A., 184, 185, 330–31
women's rights, 212, 395
Wood, Samuel N., 467
Woodbury, Levi, 180–81, 194
Woodworth, James, 388
World War I, 359
Wright, Erastus, 426
Wyandot Indians, 272

Yancey, William Lowndes, 72, 114, 115
Yates, Richard, 432, 465
    AL and, 388–89, 391, 429, 430
    in 1850 election, 141–43
    in 1852 congressional election, 221–22
Young America, 126, 171, 175, 176–77, 225,
        233, 238, 408–9
    Douglas and, 167–68
    Douglas as champion of, 409
Young Chivalry, 172, 173, 288
Young Indians, 48, 316, 476
Young Mr. Lincoln (film), 135
Yulee, David, 265–66

ABOUT THE AUTHOR

SIDNEY BLUMENTHAL is the former assistant and senior adviser to President Bill Clinton. He was a journalist at *The Washington Post*, *The New Yorker*, *The New Republic*, and a columnist for *The Guardian* of London. He is the author of eight previous books, including *A Self-Made Man: The Political Life of Abraham Lincoln, 1809–1849*, *The Permanent Campaign*, *The Rise of the Counter-Establishment*, and *The Clinton Wars*. He was executive producer of the Academy Award– and Emmy Award–winning documentary *Taxi to the Dark Side*. He was born and raised in Chicago, Illinois, and lives in Washington, D.C.

Abraham Lincoln at his home in Springfield, Illinois, with his sons Tad and Willie, 1860